JUDICIARIES IN COMPARATIVE PERSPECTIVE

An independent and impartial judiciary is fundamental to the existence and operation of a liberal democracy. Focusing on Australia, Canada, New Zealand, South Africa, the United Kingdom and the United States, this comparative study explores four major issues affecting the judicial institution. These issues relate to the appointment and discipline of judges; judges and freedom of speech; the performance of non-judicial functions by judges; and judicial bias and recusal, and each is set within the context of the importance of maintaining public confidence in the judiciary. The chapters in this book highlight important episodes or controversies affecting members of the judiciary to illustrate relevant principles.

HOONG PHUN ('HP') LEE holds the Sir John Latham Chair of Law at Monash University and was the Vice-Chairman of the Australian Press Council from 1994 to 2010. He was appointed an Adjunct Professor of Law, City University of Hong Kong in 2009. His areas of teaching and research interests include the judiciary, comparative constitutional law, administrative law and the Malaysian and Singaporean constitutional systems.

JUDICIARIES IN COMPARATIVE PERSPECTIVE

Edited by

H. P. LEE

CAMBRIDGE
UNIVERSITY PRESS

CAMBRIDGE UNIVERSITY PRESS
Cambridge, New York, Melbourne, Madrid, Cape Town,
Singapore, São Paulo, Delhi, Mexico City

Cambridge University Press
The Edinburgh Building, Cambridge CB2 8RU, UK

Published in the United States of America by Cambridge University Press, New York

www.cambridge.org
Information on this title: www.cambridge.org/9780521190602

First published 2011

A catalogue record for this publication is available from the British Library

Library of Congress Cataloguing in Publication Data
Judiciaries in comparative perspective / edited by H.P. Lee.
p. cm.
ISBN 978-0-521-19060-2 (hardback)
1. Judges. I. Lee, H. P., 1947–
K2146.J855 2011
347'.014–dc22
2011000635

ISBN 978-0-521-19060-2 Hardback

CONTENTS

CONTRIBUTORS

EDWIN CAMERON was educated at Stellenbosch University and won a Rhodes Scholarship to Oxford, where he was awarded the Vinerian Scholarship. He conducted a human rights practice in Johannesburg and was a professor at the University of the Witwatersrand's Centre for Applied Legal Studies before President Mandela appointed him to the High Court in 1995. From 2001 to 2008 he served as a Judge of Appeal in the Supreme Court of Appeal, and was appointed a Justice of the Constitutional Court in 2009. He is the author of *Witness to AIDS* (2005), which won the Alan Paton Award, South Africa's premier literary award for non-fiction.

COLIN CAMPBELL holds Masters degrees in law from the universities of Melbourne and Cambridge, and a PhD in law from the University of Cambridge. Formerly a solicitor and a judge's associate, Colin's main research interests lie in the areas of administrative law, regulatory law, especially the law relating to the regulation of privatised bodies, and anti-discrimination law. The topic of Colin's doctoral thesis was 'The Conception of Public Power in Judicial Review'. The thesis examined, among other things, the inter-relationship between the law of judicial review and competition law. Colin has published articles in the *Cambridge Law Journal* and the *Law Quarterly Review*.

HUGH CORDER has been Professor of Public Law at the University of Cape Town since 1987 and was formerly the Dean of the Faculty of Law. A graduate of the universities of Cape Town, Cambridge and Oxford, his main teaching and research interests fall within the field of constitutional and administrative law, particularly judicial appointment and accountability and mechanisms to further administrative accountability. He served as a technical adviser in the drafting of the transitional Bill of Rights for South Africa. He is the author of *Judges at Work* (1984) and *Empowerment and Accountability* (1991); co-author of *A Charter for Social Justice: A Contribution to the South African Bill of Rights Debate* (1992); and

Understanding South Africa's Transitional Bill of Rights (1994, with L. du Plessis); editor of *Essays on Law and Social Practice in South Africa* (1988); *Democracy and the Judiciary* (1989); *Controlling Public Power* (1995, with Fiona McLennan); *Administrative Justice in Southern Africa* (1997, with Tiyanjana Maluwa); *Realising Administrative Justice* (2002 with Linda van de Vivjer); and *Global Administrative Law: Development and Innovation* (2009).

IAIN CURRIE is a Professor of Law at the University of the Witwatersrand, Johannesburg. He has published mostly in the fields of constitutional and administrative law, and is a co-author of *The Bill of Rights Handbook* (2005) and of *The New Constitutional and Administrative Law* (2001) and books on access to information and administrative law. His current research interests include constitutional and administrative law, human rights, particularly the rights to freedom of expression and privacy, and law and new technologies.

PATRICK EMERTON was formerly a Research Officer, Federal–State Relations Committee, Parliament of Victoria. He was also a Sessional Lecturer with the University of Melbourne Philosophy Department and the Monash University Philosophy Department. He was appointed an Assistant Lecturer in 2004 and a Lecturer in 2006 in the Faculty of Law, Monash University. His publications are in the fields of Australian constitutional law, legal and moral philosophy and anti-terrorism laws. His research for this volume was supported under the Australian Research Council's Discovery funding scheme.

KEITH D. EWING is Professor of Public Law at King's College London. Formerly, he was Lecturer, Edinburgh, 1978–83, University Assistant Lecturer, University Lecturer, Fellow of Trinity Hall, Cambridge, 1983–9, Visiting Fellow, University of Melbourne and Monash University 1988, Visiting Professor, Osgoode Hall Law School 1982, University of Alberta 1987–8 and the University of Western Australia 1992. His many publications include: *Constitutional and Administrative Law* (2007, with A. W. Bradley); *Party Funding And Campaign Financing in International Perspective* (2006, with Samuel Issacharoff); *Labour Law, Text, Cases and Materials* (2005, with Hugh Collins and Aileen McColgan); *Skeptical Essays in Human Rights* (2002, with Tom Campbell); *The Struggle for Civil Liberties* (2000); *Freedom under Thatcher: Civil Liberties in Modern Britain* (1990, with Conor Gearty); *Britain and the ILO* (1989); *The Funding of Political Parties in Britain* (2010); and *The Bonfire of the Liberties* (2010).

CHRISTOPHER FORSYTH is Professor of Public and Private International Law as well as Director of the Centre for Public Law in the University of Cambridge and Extraordinary Professor of Law in the University of Stellenbosch. He is the author with the late Sir William Wade QC of *Administrative Law* (2004), as well as several other books including *Judicial Review and the Constitution* (2000); *The Golden Metwand and the Crooked Cord; Public Law Essays in Honour of Sir William Wade* (1998, with Ivan Hare); and *Private International Law – the Modern Roman–Dutch Law including the Jurisdiction of the High Courts* (2003), which is an authoritative work on the subject in Roman–Dutch jurisdictions. He is the author of many articles in learned journals on all aspects of public law and private international law. He has advised several governments on thorny issues of administrative and constitutional law. He is a practising barrister, a Bencher of the Inner Temple and sits as a Recorder in the Crown Court in England.

ROBERT FRENCH was sworn in as the Chief Justice of the High Court of Australia, the highest court in Australia, on 1 September 2008. From 1986 to October 2008, he was a judge of the Federal Court of Australia. He has served as part-time Commissioner of the Australian Law Reform Commission (2006–8), Additional Judge of the Supreme Court of the Australian Capital Territory (2004–8), a Judge of the Supreme Court of Fiji (2003–8) and as President of the National Native Title Tribunal (1994–8).

MARTIN L. FRIEDLAND CC, QC, is University Professor and James M. Tory Professor of Law Emeritus at the Faculty of Law, University of Toronto. He holds a BComm, LLB and honorary LLD from the University of Toronto, and a PhD and LLD from Cambridge University. After teaching at Osgoode Hall Law School, he joined the University of Toronto. He was promoted to professor in 1968 and served as dean (1972–9). He was a full-time member of the Law Reform Commission of Canada in Ottawa (1971–2). As well as many other awards, he was appointed a fellow of the Royal Society of Canada in 1983, an Officer of the Order of Canada in 1990 and made a Companion of the Order of Canada in 2003. In 1995 he was awarded the Canada Council Molson Prize in the Humanities and Social Sciences and in 2003 received the Royal Society of Canada's John William Dawson Medal. He is currently a Fellow of Massey College. His extensive publications include *Detention Before Trial, Double Jeopardy, Access to the Law, A Place Apart: Judicial Independence and Accountability in Canada, The Trials of Israel Lipski, The Case of Valentine Shortis* and *The Death of Old Man Rice.*

CHARLES GARDNER GEYH is the Associate Dean of Research and the John F. Kimberling Chair at the Indiana University Maurer School of Law. He received his BA in political science from the University of Wisconsin and graduated from the University of Wisconsin law school, after which he clerked for the Honorable Thomas A. Clark on the US Court of Appeals for the Eleventh Circuit, was an associate at the Washington, DC law firm of Covington & Burling, and served as counsel to the US House of Representatives Committee on the Judiciary before beginning his teaching career in 1991. His extensive publications include *When Courts and Congress Collide: The Struggle for Control of America's Judicial System* (2006) and *Judicial Conduct and Ethics* (2007, with Lubet and Shaman Alfini). He has served as a reporter to American Bar Association commissions on the Separation of Powers and Judicial Independence, Public Financing of Judicial Campaigns, the 21st Century Judiciary and Revising the Model Code of Judicial Conduct. He has likewise served as director of the American Judicature Society's Center for Judicial Independence, and director and consultant to the ABA's Judicial Disqualification Project.

GRANT HAMMOND, a graduate of the University of Auckland and the University of Illinois, was appointed to the High Court of New Zealand in 1992 and was elevated to the Court of Appeal of New Zealand in 2004. He was seconded as President of the New Zealand Law Commission from 1 December 2010. He was for some years a senior partner in the Hamilton law firm Tompkins Wake & Co. He was a Professor of Law in Canada before taking up appointment as the Director of the Alberta Law Reform Commission and as a Uniformity Commissioner on the Uniform Law Conference of Canada. He returned to New Zealand to take up appointment as Professor of Commercial Law in the Faculty of Law at the University of Auckland. He subsequently became Dean of Law at the University of Auckland. He has been a Visiting Professor at Cornell University and the Law Foundation Professor at the University of Saskatchewan. He was recently elected a Robert S. Campbell Fellow in Law at Magdalen College, Oxford University. His extensive publications include *Personal Property: Cases and Materials* (1990) and *Judicial Recusal – Principles, Process and Problems* (2009).

W. WILLIAM HODES graduated with honours from Harvard College in 1966 and from Rutgers Law School in 1969. In 1979, Hodes served as a Bigelow Teaching Fellow at the University of Chicago Law School, and then joined the faculty at the Indiana University School of Law in

Indianapolis. In 1989, he was a Visiting Scholar and Lecturer at the China University of Politics and Law, teaching a course in American Civil Procedure and conducting research into Chinese People's Mediation. During the October 1996 term of the US Supreme Court, while on sabbatical leave from Indiana University, Professor Hodes served as a law clerk to Justice Ruth Bader Ginsburg. In 1999, he became Professor Emeritus of Law at Indiana University, and established the William Hodes Professional Corporation, a solo consulting practice. He is the co-author, with Professor Geoffrey C. Hazard Jr and Peter R. Jarvis, of *The Law of Lawyering*, a nationally recognised treatise on legal ethics that is updated annually. From 2004 to 2007, Professor Hodes was Co-Reporter to the American Bar Association's Joint Commission to Evaluate the Model Code of Judicial Conduct, which developed the most recent iteration of the Model Code of Judicial Conduct.

CORA HOEXTER lectured in law at her alma mater, the University of Natal (Pietermaritzburg), for several years before joining the University of the Witwatersrand, Johannesburg in 1994. She was appointed to a Chair in the School of Law in 2000. Cora has taught subjects including constitutional law and legal philosophy, but her first love and main research interest is administrative law. Her most recent book on the subject is *Administrative Law in South Africa* (2007). A former member of the South African Law Reform Commission, Cora was Editor-in-Chief of the *Annual Survey of South African Law* for four years and served for ten years on the editorial team of the *South African Law Journal*.

PHILIP A. JOSEPH is Professor of Law at the University of Canterbury, New Zealand and a barrister and solicitor of the High Court. He is author of *Essays on the Constitution* (1995) (now in its third edition), *Constitutional and Administrative Law in New Zealand* (2007), the 'Administrative Law' and 'Constitutional Law' titles for *The Laws of New Zealand*, and many articles and book chapters dealing with pubic law issues. In 2004, he was conferred the degree of Doctor of Laws in recognition of his research contributions. He also consults as a barrister advising in public law matters and acts as adviser to sundry government organisations. He is a member of the Editorial Advisory Boards of *Public Law Review* (Sydney) and *New Zealand Journal of Public and International Law* (Wellington), and is a Contributing Editor to *New Zealand Law Review* (Auckland).

HOONG PHUN ('HP') LEE has held the Sir John Latham Chair of Law at Monash University since 1995. He was Vice-Chairman of the Australian Press Council from 1994 to 2010. He was appointed an Adjunct Professor of Law, City University of Hong Kong in 2009. His many publications include *Constitutional Conflicts in Contemporary Malaysia* (1995) and *The Australian Judiciary* (Cambridge University Press, 2001) (co-author). He is the co-editor of *Australian Constitutional Landmarks* (Cambridge University Press, 2003), *The Constitution of Malaysia: Further Perspectives and Developments* (1986), *The Constitution of Malaysia: Its Development 1957–1977* (1978) and *Australian Administrative Law: Fundamentals, Principles and Doctrines* (Cambridge University Press, 2007). He recently co-edited *Constitutional Advancement in a Frozen Continent* (2009).

KATE MALLESON joined the School of Law at Queen Mary in 2005. She had previously taught at the London School of Economics. She acted as a specialist adviser to the House of Commons Constitutional Affairs Select Committee assisting it in its review of the provisions of the Constitutional Reform Bill. In 2006–7 she chaired a JUSTICE committee on 'A Bill of Rights for Britain'. In 2007 she acted as an adviser to the Northern Ireland Judicial Appointment Commission in relation to research it was undertaking on diversity in the judiciary in Northern Ireland. Before that she was a member of the Commission on Women in the Criminal Justice System established by the Fawcett Society which reported in March 2004. She also sat on the Joint Working Party on Equal Opportunities in Judicial Appointment and Silk set up by the Lord Chancellor's Department. Her many publications include *The New Judiciary: The Effects of Expansion and Activism* (1999) and *The Legal System* (2007), co-editor (with Peter Russell) of *Appointing Judges in an Age of Judicial Power: Critical Perspectives from Around the World* (2006).

GERARD MCCOY QC, SC, is a Barrister of the High Court of New Zealand, of the Supreme Court of New South Wales, the Supreme Court of Victoria, the High Court of Australia, the High Court of Hong Kong, the High Court of Fiji, the High Court of the Isle of Man and the English Bar (Middle Temple) practising in constitutional and public law. He is Professor of Law at City University of Hong Kong and Adjunct Professor at the University of Canterbury, New Zealand. He has been a Deputy Judge of the High Court of Hong Kong since 2001, exercising full civil and criminal law jurisdiction. He is a member of the Hong Kong Law Reform Commission and Hearsay in Criminal Law Subcommittee. He is co-author of a number of books, including *The Most Fundamental Right: Habeas Corpus in the Commonwealth* (2000) and was awarded the Silver Bauhinia Star in the 2005 Hong Kong Honours List for services to law.

PATRICK MONAHAN, a member of Osgoode Hall Law School's faculty since 1982, was appointed the Vice-President Academic and Provost of York University, Ontario with effect from 1 July 2009. He was the Dean of York University's Osgoode Hall Law School from 2003 to 2009. Between 1986 and 1990, he was Senior Policy Adviser to the Attorney-General and Premier of Ontario, respectively, where he played a key role in the negotiation of the 1987 Meech Lake Accord. Professor Monahan has acted as adviser to the federal government as well as to a number of provincial governments with respect to economic, constitutional and international trade matters. He was the Director of the York University Centre for Public Law and Public Policy for most of the 1990s through to 2002. He is the author of several books, including *Constitutional Law* (2006) and *Liability of the Crown* (2000, with Peter Hogg). He is the recipient of the 2008 David W. Mundell Medal for Legal Writing awarded by the Attorney-General of Ontario.

ABIMBOLA A. OLOWOFOYEKU is currently a Professor of Law at Brunel Law School. He has previously held positions as Assistant Legal Adviser, Federal Inland Revenue Department, Lagos (1982–3); Barrister and Solicitor, Chief B. Olowofoyeku & Co., Lagos (1983–4); Lecturer, Liverpool Polytechnic (1987–8); Lecturer, Keele University (1988–95); Visiting Fellow, Centre for International and Public Law, Australian National University (March–August 1995); Senior Lecturer, Keele University (1995–9); Reader, Keele University (1999–2000); Visiting Fellow, Faculty of Law, Australian National University (July 1999–January 2000, December 2000–January 2001); Head of Department, Brunel University (2003–4); Head of the School of Social Sciences and Law (2004–6); Head of Brunel Law School (2006–9). He is the author of *Suing Judges* (1993) and *The Law of Judicial Immunities in Nigeria* (1993). He has published a number of articles in *Public Law*, the *Singapore Journal of Legal Studies* and the *Cambridge Law Journal* pertaining to judicial power, automatic disqualification, recusals, judicial accountability and judicial independence.

KATE O'REGAN served as a judge of the South African Constitutional Court from its establishment in 1994 until 2009, when her fifteen-year term ended. Since 2008, she has chaired the Internal Justice Council of the United Nations whose task is to help ensure independence, professionalism and accountability in the new system of internal justice for the United Nations. She is a member of the International Monetary Fund Arbitration Tribunal and has been appointed an acting judge of the Namibian Supreme Court for 2010. She is also currently a Visiting Professor at the University of Cape Town and the University of Oxford.

GEOFFREY PALMER was President of the Law Commission from 2005 to 2010. Sir Geoffrey has had a long career in the law, as an academic lawyer, a politician and a law practitioner. In 1989–90 he was Prime Minister of New Zealand. Both before entering politics and after leaving it, he was a Professor of Law at the Victoria University of Wellington and at the University of Iowa in the United States. Geoffrey Palmer's extensive publications include *Unbridled Power: An Interpretation of New Zealand's Constitution and Government* (1984). Then co-authoring with Dr Matthew Palmer, the book was re-titled as *Bridled Power: New Zealand's Constitution on Government* (1997, 4th edn., 2004). Since 2002, Geoffrey Palmer has been the New Zealand Commissioner on the International Whaling Commission. He is a member of Her Majesty's Privy Council. He was awarded a KCMG in 1991 and made an Honorary Companion of the Order of Australia in the same year. In 1991 he was listed on the United Nations 'Global 500 Roll of Honour' for his work on environmental issues. Geoffrey Palmer has also sat as a Judge ad hoc on International Court of Justice in 1995.

KENT ROACH, a graduate of the universities of Toronto and Yale and a former law clerk to Justice Bertha Wilson of the Supreme Court of Canada, is Prichard-Wilson Chair of Law and Public Policy at the University of Toronto Faculty of Law, and a Fellow of the Royal Society of Canada. His extensive publications include *Constitutional Remedies in Canada* (winner of the 1997 Owen Prize for best law book), *Due Process and Victims' Rights: The New Law and Politics of Criminal Justice* (short-listed for the 1999 Donner Prize for best public policy book), *The Supreme Court on Trial: Judicial Activism or Democratic Dialogue* (short-listed for the 2001 Donner Prize), *September 11: Consequences for Canada* (named one of the five most significant books of 2003 by the *Literary Review of Canada*) and *Brian Dickson: A Judge's Journey* (with Robert J. Sharpe, winner of the 2004

J. W. Dafoe Prize for best contribution to the understanding of Canada). His other books include *Criminal Law* (2009), *The Charter of Rights and Freedoms* (2009, with Robert J. Sharpe) and *Regulatory and Corporate Liability: From Due Diligence to Risk Management* (2005, with Ken Jull and Todd Archibald).

JEFFREY M. SHAMAN has concentrated much of his scholarship in the area of constitutional law and is a nationally recognised authority on judicial ethics. He served as Senior Fellow of the American Judicature Society and as President of the American Civil Liberties Union of Illinois. He is a member of the American Law Institute, the American Society of Legal History and the US Association of Constitutional Law. Professor Shaman has litigated a number of cases concerning constitutional rights and is the principal author of the Illinois Freedom of Information Act. He has won numerous awards for teaching, scholarship and service to the community, culminating in his appointment as Vincent de Paul Professor of Law. His many publications include *Equality and Liberty in the Golden Age of State Constitutional Law* (2008), *Judicial Conduct and Ethics* (2007, with Steven Lubet, James J. Alfini and Charles Gardner Geyh), *Constitutional Interpretation: Illusion and Reality* (2001), *Judicial Disqualification: An Empirical Study of Judicial Practices and Attitudes* (1995, with Jona Goldschmidt) and *Judicial Conduct & Ethics Curriculum* (1993, with Cynthia Gray).

BYRON SHAW is an associate with the firm McCarthy Tetrault LLP in the firm's Toronto office. Mr Shaw clerked for the Court of Appeal for Ontario prior to being called to the Ontario bar in 2009. He received his BA (Hons) in Economics from the University of British Columbia in 2005 and his LLB from the University of British Columbia in 2008. Mr. Shaw is a member of the Law Society of Upper Canada and the Canadian Bar Association.

SHIMON SHETREET holds the Greenblatt Chair of Public and International Law at the Hebrew University of Jerusalem and is the head of the Sacher Institute of Legislative Research and Comparative Law. He was a member of the Chief Justice Landau Commission on the Israeli Court System (1980), and a judge on the Standard Contract Court (1981–8). He has served as the general coordinator of the International Project of Judicial Independence which drafted the Mt Scopus International Standards of Judicial Independence in 2008 and has organised five international conferences (in Jerusalem Vaduz, Krakow and Cambridge). He served as General Coordinator, International Bar Association Project for Minimum Standards of Judicial Independence (1980–2), as a Member of the Knesset, the Israeli Parliament (1988–96) and also as a cabinet minister in the Rabin Government. His extensive publications include *Judges on Trial* (1976), *Judicial Independence: The Contemporary Debate* (1985), *The Role of Courts in Society* (1988), *National Security and Free Speech* (1991), *Pioneers in Tears: Anthology on North African Jewry* (1991), *Justice in Israel* (1994), *Women in Law* (1998), *The Good Land between Power and Religion* (1998), *Law and Social Pluralism* (2002) and *On Adjudication* (2004).

LORNE SOSSIN is the Dean of the Osgoode Hall Law School of York University. He was formerly a Professor and Associate Dean at the Faculty of Law, University of Toronto. He previously taught at Osgoode and Columbia Law School. He was a litigation lawyer with Borden & Elliot (now Borden Ladner Gervais), a law clerk to the Chief Justice of the Supreme Court of Canada and has served as the city of Toronto's Integrity Commissioner. His extensive publications include *Boundaries of Judicial Review: The Law of Justiciability in Canada* (1999), *Public Law* (2002, with Michael J. Bryant), *Access to Care, Access to Justice: The Legal Debate on Private Health Insurance in Canada* (2005, co-editor with Colleen Flood and Kent Roach) and *Dilemmas of Solidarity: Rethinking Redistribution in the Canadian Federation* (2006, co-editor with Sujit Choudhry and Jean-Francois Gaudreault-Desbien). Dean Sossin also serves on the boards of the National Judicial Institute and the Law Commission of Ontario.

MARK TUSHNET, who graduated from Harvard College and Yale Law School and served as a law clerk to Justice Thurgood Marshall, specialises in constitutional law and theory, including comparative constitutional law. His research includes studies examining (sceptically) the practice of judicial review in the United States and around the world. His extensive publications include *Weak Courts, Strong Rights: Judicial Review and Social Welfare Rights in Comparative Constitutional Law* (2008), *The New Constitutional Order* (2003), *Taking the Constitution Away From the Courts* (1999), *Red, White, and Blue: A Critical Analysis of Constitutional Law* (1988), *A Court Divided: The Rehnquist Court and the Future of Constitutional Law* (2005), *The Oxford Handbook of Legal Studies* (2003, co-editor with Peter Cane) and *Defining the Field of Comparative Constitutional Law* (2002, co-editor with Vicki C. Jackson).

JOHN M. WILLIAMS is Dean and Professor of Law at the University of Adelaide. His research is in the areas of constitutional law and Australian legal history. He is the author of *The Australian Constitution: A Documentary History* (2005) and co-editor of *Peace, Order and Good Government: State Constitutional and Parliamentary Reform* (2003) and *Makers of Miracles: The Cast of the Federation Story* (2000). He co-edited *The New Federalist: The Journal of Australian Federation History* for its entire (and pre-ordained) life: 1998–2001.

FOREWORD

THE HONOURABLE CHIEF JUSTICE ROBERT FRENCH

The High Court of Australia

Comparative law and comparative constitutional law in particular challenge the scholar. This is so even when the scholar's enquiry is confined to the search for useful comparative descriptions of aspects of legal systems. Meaningful exposition must be able to cross boundaries of difference in history, culture and political organisation. To do so successfully, the scholar must find descriptors of general application and relevance.

When focusing upon institutional arrangements, and particularly the judiciaries of different countries, that challenge is no less acute. There are many similarities between the judicial systems of liberal democracies. But even among liberal democracies similarity may mask diversity. When considering the constitutional position and function of judiciaries beyond those found in the democracies, the differences can be profound. Yet judges from many different countries and political systems engage with each other increasingly in international fora, conferences and bilateral meetings. There, many matters of genuinely common interest unite such judges and make engagement and dialogue mutually useful. These matters include court organisation and efficiency, information management, judicial education, case management, alternative dispute resolution and judicial specialisation. It is possible for judges from different legal systems to have a common interest in all of these things and yet to sit in courts which have different relationships with the legislature and the executive and different functions in relation to constitutional interpretation, judicial review and even statutory interpretation. At another level, statements of commitment to such 'fundamentals' as judicial independence may not always apply in one society in a way that is comprehensible to another. Comparative law, which offers too wide a focus across areas of great difference, may yield too diffuse a picture to be useful.

The editor of *Judiciaries in Comparative Perspective* has not tried to bridge unbridgeable gaps. He has nevertheless identified themes illustrative of educative pluralism within mutually comprehensible frames of reference. The authors of the various chapters in this work have written about judiciaries in representative democracies with sufficient common elements in their legal heritage and constitutional arrangements to make comparative consideration useful. The countries about which the contributors to this book have written are Australia, Canada, New Zealand, South Africa, the United Kingdom and the United States.

The chapters are arranged thematically. They are framed by a discussion, by Shimon Shetreet, of judicial independence and accountability. There follow contributions from the six selected jurisdictions on the first theme which is the appointment, discipline and removal of judges. The second theme, relating to judges and free speech, deals both with criticism of the judiciary and with extra-curial speech by judges. Those two aspects of that topic raise different issues, but find their place under the one rubric of freedom of expression in a constitutional setting. Then follows consideration of judicial bias and recusal. The final theme relates to the mixing of judicial and non-judicial functions. Professor Lee draws these themes together in the concluding chapter entitled, 'The judiciary: a comparative conspectus'.

In his discussion of judicial independence and accountability Shimon Shetreet acknowledges the 'marked increase in the relative role of the judiciary in society' in recent decades. That general trend, as he observes, is shared by countries with different legal traditions and various systems of government. It points to the need to re-examine conceptual framework and theoretical underpinning of the position of the judiciary in relation to the other branches of government.

Shimon Shetreet identifies what most readers of this book would accept as fundamental, albeit inter-related, values which lie at the foundations of many, if not most, judicial systems. They are procedural fairness, efficiency, accessibility, public confidence in the courts, judicial independence and constitutionality in the sense of the constitutional protection of the judiciary. Importantly, as the reader is reminded, these values are directed to the core function of the courts which is the hearing and determination of disputes.

An issue which attracts the interest and attention of judges, governments and court administrators across a number of national jurisdictions, is the tension between judicial independence and the public accountability of judges in a democracy. That accountability, like judicial independence, attaches to individual judges and to courts as institutions.

The individual judge is made accountable for his or her decisions by the duty to provide reasons for decisions. Scrutiny of those reasons may lead to the detection of error and the grant of appellate remedies. A second aspect of the accountability of individual judges relates to the judge's efficiency and diligence in the hearing and disposition of cases. In some jurisdictions the judge may have case management responsibilities for a docket of cases and general time targets from filing to disposition. Accountability at the institutional level relates to the efficient use of public resources. The development of reliable and relevant measures of such efficiency is an ongoing project in a number of the countries considered in this book.

Judicial independence is an appropriate theme with which to frame the various issues explored in this book. It is asserted as a fundamental norm in many international instruments, declarations of principle and standards. It is reflected in Article 10 of the Universal Declaration of Human Rights and in Article 14 of the International Covenant on Civil and Political Rights. For the legal systems considered in the book, which are the heirs of a common heritage of constitutionalism, the differences in perspective on judicial independence are not as acute as they may be between those systems and some others with very different histories, cultural traditions and constitutional arrangements.

An interesting question which helps to sharpen consideration of the nature of judicial independence, is the phenomenon of the appointment of judges by popular election in many states of the United States. This is described and discussed by Mark Tushnet in his contribution. Appointment by popular election raises the question: how does an elected judge differ from an unelected judge in the discharge of the same judicial functions? The desirability of judicial elections has been the subject of public debate. Former Justice of the US Supreme Court, Sandra Day O'Connor, has written about their problems. The campaign process has given rise to litigation in the Supreme Court in relation to campaign finance donations from prospective litigants.[1] Relevantly to another theme of this book, discussed by Charles Geyh in his chapter on judicial freedom of speech in the United States, a state law restricting campaign speech by candidates for judicial office was held by a majority in the Supreme Court in 2002 to violate the First Amendment guarantee of free speech.[2]

[1] *Caperton* v. *A. T. Massey Coal Co., Inc.* 173 L.Ed. 2d 1208 (2009).
[2] *Republican Party of Minnesota* v. *White*, 536 US 765 (2002).

The appointment, discipline and removal of judges, which is the first specific theme in the book, are matters of ongoing discussion and development. There is today a general public and governmental interest in transparent and merit-based judicial appointment processes. There is also interest in ensuring that the full range of people potentially available for and worthy of appointment is encouraged to consider applying for appointment. Not that many years have passed, in Australia, since the idea of governments calling for applications or expressions of interest in appointment to a superior court would have been widely, although not universally, regarded as a rather tasteless departure from the practice of the Attorney-General quietly sounding out the senior judiciary and legal profession as to the suitability of prospective candidates for appointment.

Processes for the appointment of judges are generally concerned to ensure that the candidate selected is the most qualified and competent person available against criteria related to legal knowledge and skills, integrity, diligence and efficiency, sound judgement and communication. Case management, both before and during the trial of matters, requires its own skills set. A judge working with other judges in a permanent appeal court, for example, will need some level of skill in working within a collegial environment. For heads of jurisdiction, interpersonal skills and administrative competence are also vital.

Transparency in selection to avoid the perception of what Philip Joseph calls in his chapter 'a self-perpetuating oligarchy, that is manifestly unrepresentative of society' is a widely accepted contemporary goal of selection and appointment processes. The desirability of diversity in appointments is also a common theme. Hugh Corder, writes that in South Africa the Judicial Service Commission, chaired by the Chief Justice, has succeeded in a substantial transformation of the demographic profile of the superior court judiciary in relation to race, although it has been less successful in relation to sex. Martin Friedland, writing about Canada, points out that the enactment of the Charter of Rights and Freedoms, as part of the Constitution in 1982, coupled with public realisation that judges would play an increasingly important role in policy decisions, helped to create a positive climate for changing the system of judicial appointments. That may be seen as a particular application of the general observation by Shetreet, about the changing role of the judiciary in society in countries with different legal traditions and various systems of government.

Judicial independence intersects acutely with the protection of judicial tenure and procedures for the removal of judges for misbehaviour or incapacity. The utility of a procedure to enable allegations of circumstances which might warrant removal to be brought to the attention of the relevant authority is not particularly controversial. More contentious is the question of how to deal with complaints about judicial behaviour which would not, on any view, warrant removal. Quite apart from constitutional considerations which might attend the imposition of some statutory sanction, there is the practical question of the effect of such a sanction, publicly imposed, on the authority and standing and therefore on the effectiveness of the judicial officer concerned. The option of some form of 'counselling' by the head of jurisdiction or administration action, such as removal of a judge from involvement in a particular class of case, raises its own difficult issues.

The discussion of freedom of speech in the six jurisdictions evidences a changing relationship between the judiciary and the society of which it is part. A statement made by Lord Chancellor Kilmuir in 1955 in response to a request from the Director-General of the BBC, that members of the judiciary take part in a radio series on 'great judges of the past', became known as 'the Kilmuir rules'. They represented, and still represent, what John Williams, in his chapter, describes as 'the high watermark for judicial reticence'. A much-quoted part of Lord Kilmuir's statement, which can sometimes lend itself to parody, was his observation that, 'So long as a Judge keeps silent his reputation for wisdom and impartiality remains unassailable'. It goes without saying, of course, that judges, required as they are to give reasons for their decisions, cannot remain silent in the discharge of their functions. In that connection there is an ample supply of assailants, sceptical of judicial wisdom and impartiality, who have not been in the least discouraged by extra-curial silences.

The Kilmuir Rules cannot be dismissed as a relic of a bygone age. As Williams writes, they are 'a readily recognised point for those who wish to debate the wisdom of judicial officers exercising their right as a citizen to speak out on matters of public debate'. Ongoing discussion can usefully be guided, as he points out, by constitutional principles and, in particular, the separation of powers and the maintenance of the rule of law. Both principles have been used to justify restraint and greater public involvement by judges.

The degree of public controversy engendered by extra-curial speech by judges is generally in proportion to the political or social sensitivity of the topic which is addressed. Criminal justice and sentencing laws and the utility of imprisonment are generally high on the sensitivity register. The reaction to a speech by the Chief Justice of New Zealand on the last-mentioned topic, illustrates the point. It is described and discussed in Grant Hammond's chapter on 'Judges and free speech in New Zealand'.

There is no doubt that judges are much in demand as speakers, principally, although not only, at academic or professional conferences. The incidence of extra-curial judicial speech on a variety of legal topics has increased in recent decades, again underpinning the general point made by Shimon Shetreet in his opening chapter. Iain Currie makes the same point about South Africa since 1994. South African judges now routinely participate at academic conferences, give speeches to university students and address gatherings of the legal profession. Judges have also spoken out strongly on the administration of justice and law reform. Currie refers to informal 'Guidelines for Judges' which prohibit involvement by judges in 'political controversy or activity'. An example of one judge who spoke at the boundaries of the rule was Justice Edwin Cameron. As an appeal court judge, he criticised what was referred to as AIDS denialism during the Mbeki administration. In a subsequent defence of his own actions, he referred to the conclusions of the South African Truth Commission that judges during the Apartheid era had failed in their duty not to collaborate in injustice 'by omission, silence and inaction'. Like so many questions of comparative law, this question cannot be considered without reference to local conditions, including history, culture and constitutional arrangements.

The discussion of campaign speech in judicial elections in the United States by Charles Geyh is instructive. Notwithstanding the First Amendment, codes of conduct impose constraints on judicial speech and the authority of judges to respond to criticism. Some constraints would not be particularly controversial in any of the six jurisdictions. Model rule 2.10 of the American Bar Association's *Model Code of Judicial Conduct* (2007), specifically constrains speech in relation to pending matters. It provides that:

> A judge shall not make any public statement that might reasonably be expected to affect the outcome or impair the fairness of a matter pending or impending in any court or make any non-public statement that might substantially interfere with a fair trial or hearing.

Readers of Geyh's chapter from other jurisdictions would be unlikely to cavil with the observation made by the Chief Judge of the Supreme Court of New York, that judges:

> do not duel with public officials about the correctness of their decisions; they do not conduct press conferences about cases; and they have no call – in radio and television shows to explain their rulings. They rely on their decisions whether written or oral, to speak for themselves.

A difficult question is whether some forms of unfair criticism of judges and judicial decisions, falling short of contempt, justify a defence of the judge by the Attorney-General or by the head of jurisdiction. If the criticism emanates from government, it may be appropriate for the head of jurisdiction to respond. Sometimes a sufficient defence will be effected by a response from the relevant Judges' Association, Law Society or Bar Association.

The limits of freedom of speech in criticism of judges must also be guided by constitutional principles. As Kent Roach reports in his chapter on 'Judges and free speech in Canada', the Charter has had the most decisive effect with respect to critical speech about the judiciary as it has invalidated the common law contempt offence of scandalising the court. Before the introduction of the Charter, that offence was used more frequently in Canada than other democracies with respect to criticisms of the judiciary.

The theme of judicial bias and recusal in each of the jurisdictions is comprehensively explored. Colin Campbell in his chapter focuses on the reasonable apprehension of bias test and the way in which it operates in Australia. The rules relating to judicial bias are an important aspect of procedural fairness, which as Shimon Shetreet points out, is one of the fundamental values which lie at the foundations of most judicial systems.

The last section of the book deals with the admixture of judicial and non-judicial functions in the various jurisdictions. This is a matter which has been the subject of litigation on more than one occasion in the High Court of Australia and is discussed in the Australian chapter on this topic written by Patrick Emerton and H. P. Lee. The phenomenon is reflective of a changing relationship between the judiciary and society. There is an increasing tendency for governments in some jurisdictions to seek to use judges to do non-judicial jobs. This is not least because of the reputation for independence and impartiality and detachment from partisan politics that attends the judicial function. In a sense, the use of judges to carry out non-judicial functions, such as the conduct of royal commissions or statutory inquiries or to head up administrative tribunals, may be seen as an appropriation to the executive branch of government of the reputation and attributes of the judicial branch. The trend is evident in Canada where, according to Patrick Monahan and

Byron Shaw, Canadian governments at both federal and provincial levels have increasingly looked to judges to carry out non-judicial tasks.

The use of judges in non-judicial roles raises the issue of the compatibility of such roles with the judicial function, both as a matter of constitutional principle and as a matter of practicality. The latter consideration arises where a judge is appointed to a non-judicial office, which renders the judge effectively unavailable for the discharge of judicial duties. Constitutional considerations arise if the performance of the non-judicial function may reflect upon the reality or appearance of independence and impartiality that is central to the judicial office.

The preceding observations are the merest sample skimmed from the text. It is no mere platitude to observe that the book provides a feast of food for thought. Within the framework provided by its selected themes, it focuses on the judiciary and legal systems similar enough to each other to make such discussion meaningful. At the same time it exposes a pluralism of approach that stimulates reflection and does so within the larger discourse about the fundamentals of the judicial role.

PREFACE

My interest in the judicial institution was heightened by a collaborative work with my late colleague, Emeritus Professor Enid Campbell OBE, AC. The project, funded by an Australian Research Council grant, culminated in *The Australian Judiciary*, published by Cambridge University Press in 2001. Later, I was privileged to have been invited by Professor Shimon Shetreet (Hebrew University of Jerusalem) and Professor Christopher Forsyth (Cambridge University) to participate in a series of conferences relating to their international project on judicial independence. That participation further kindled my interest in exploring comparative dimensions of the functioning of the judiciary in contemporary times. It became clear to me that valuable lessons can be learned from the experience of other liberal democracies on how to ensure that the judiciary can continue to play a pivotal role as an independent and impartial entity in a robust democracy.

In this book distinguished scholars and eminent jurists from six countries, Australia, Canada, New Zealand, South Africa, the United Kingdom and the United States of America, have contributed chapters pertaining to four major themes of contemporary relevance to the judiciary. The various analyses by these authors are placed within an overarching analysis of the notions of judicial accountability and judicial independence. The first theme of the book deals with developments concerning the appointment, discipline and dismissal of judges in these countries. For the second theme, the authors evaluate the exercise of freedom of speech of judges and of the freedom to criticise judges. Particular attention is focused on the intrusion by judges into the arena of political debates and the ethical dimensions of that intrusion. The third theme deals with the legal principles and ethical guidelines which have been developed in relation to the enhancement of judicial neutrality and impartiality. The major focus is on rules regarding the disqualification and recusal of judges on the ground of bias. Chapters on the fourth theme critically evaluate the performance by judges of non-judicial functions and, where relevant, the constitutional dimensions of the separation of powers which impact on the admixture of judicial and non-judicial functions. The appointment of judges to head royal commissions or public inquiries is a major area of focus in some of these chapters.

I am immensely indebted to all the contributors who honoured me by accepting the invitation to contribute to the book. In a book which straddles six jurisdictions and involves the participation of twenty-nine contributors from these six jurisdictions, my role as editor was facilitated by their kind cooperation, patience and understanding. I am extremely grateful to the Honourable Robert French, Chief Justice of the High Court of Australia, for writing the Foreword to the book, despite his many pressing commitments. I owe a special debt to Finola O'Sullivan of Cambridge University Press, who provided her unstinting support and encouragement when I first proffered my idea of the book to her. I thank her and her staff, in particular Richard Woodham, Lyn Flight and Christina Sarigiannidou for their patience and efficiency in the production of the book. I also thank Michael Adams for his efficient and meticulous research assistance.

Finally, I wish to pay tribute to Emeritus Professor Enid Campbell, an outstanding public law scholar, who was looking forward so keenly to writing a chapter for this book but who unexpectedly passed away on 20 January 2010.

TABLE OF CASES

TABLE OF STATUTES

New South Wales

South Australia

Victoria

Western Australia

Canada

Ontario

Quebec

Gibraltar

Israel

New Zealand

South Africa

United Kingdom

United States

PART I

1

Judicial independence and accountability: core values in liberal democracies

SHIMON SHETREET

The study of judicial independence is important in national legal systems as it is an essential guarantee for democracy and liberty. Judicial independence is also an essential feature in ensuring a globalised economy. Corporations must have confidence in the impartiality and independence of the tribunals that will adjudicate disputes in the multiple jurisdictions in which they operate around the world.

Recent decades have witnessed a marked increase in the relative role of the judiciary in society. This general trend is shared by countries with different legal traditions and various systems of government. The judiciary is a significant social institution, and like the other branches of government, contributes to shaping the life of the community. The increasing role which the judiciary has assumed warrants some re-examination of the conceptual framework and the theoretical rationales which define its position in relation to the other branches of the government. One of the most significant aspects of the role of the judiciary in society is its independence and impartiality.

The modern conception of judicial independence is not confined to the independence of an individual judge and to his or her personal and substantive independence. It must include the collective independence of the judiciary as an institution. Likewise, judicial independence should not be perceived only in terms of shielding the judge from executive pressures or legislative interferences. It must also encompass internal independence, namely, the independence of the judge from his or her judicial colleagues or superiors.

The law and practice regarding judges and judicial independence in various countries reveal many common ideas and shared principles, but also sometimes sharp differences and even conflicts. These differences sometimes stem from a different conceptual approach, and at times, from a historical coincidence. The purpose of this chapter is to study the contemporary concept of judicial independence in a comparative context.

This chapter will examine the constitutional and practical dimensions of the key concept of 'judicial independence' and its various facets ('institutional' and 'individual' independence). Why is judicial independence so fundamental to a democratic polity? Is the requirement for judicial 'accountability' incompatible with the notion of judicial independence? The chapter will begin by analysing the broader spectrum of the core values of the judicial system: procedural fairness, public confidence in the courts, efficiency, access to justice and judicial independence. Then the chapter will examine in detail the theoretical foundations of the principle of judicial independence, including individual, collective and internal independence. The chapter will examine the necessary constitutional infrastructure required for the protection of judicial independence.

Judicial independence in the broader spectrum of core values: the fundamental values of the judicial system

General

The proper administration of justice is dependent upon the adherence to certain fundamental values which lie at the foundations of most judicial systems. These values include procedural fairness, efficiency, accessibility, public confidence in the courts and judicial independence[1] and the value of constitutionality, in the sense of the constitutional protection of the judiciary. Each of these values allows the courts to fulfil their main function, namely, the resolution of disputes.

These fundamental values are inter-related. Sometimes they strengthen one another, being the result of, or the condition to, the existence or the application of the other, while at other times there may be a tension between them. A proper legal system is one which advances each of these values on its own, and achieves a suitable balance between them whenever they conflict with one another.

[1] For a detailed discussion of the fundamental values of the administration of justice, see S. Shetreet, 'Practical and Value Problems in the Administration of Justice', in S. Shetreet (ed.), *Recent Developments in Israeli Case Law and Legislation, Collection of Lectures Delivered at the Judges' Conference* (Jerusalem: Harry Sacher Institute, 1977), p. 80; S. Shetreet, 'The Administration of Justice: Practical Problems, Value Conflicts and Changing Concepts' (1979) 13 *University of British Columbia Law Review* 52; S. Shetreet, 'The Limits of Expeditious Justice', in Justice Howland (ed.), *Expeditious Justice* (Canadian Institute for Administration of Justice, 1979), p. 1; S. Shetreet, 'Time Standards of Justice' (1979) 5 *Dalhousie Law Journal* 129; S. Shetreet, 'Adjudication: Challenges of the Present and Blueprints for the Future', in *Festschrift in Honour of Professor Walther J. Habscheid* (West Germany, 1989), p. 295.

Procedural fairness

The courts seek to resolve disputes in accordance with fair procedures and to do justice. In order to ensure justice, special procedural rules have been established to govern the method and manner in which such disputes are resolved by the courts. An elaborate and complex body of laws and rules govern court procedures which regulate the method of evaluating and weighing the facts and evidence submitted to the courts. In particular, these rules are concerned with safeguarding the rights of persons charged with violating the law. The purpose of these rules and laws is to attain justice and to ensure a fair trial by subjecting the conflicting claims to a vigorous and thorough investigation in order to ascertain the truth. It must be mentioned, though, that a strict application of the procedural fairness value, however important, may affect the efficiency of trials or the disclosure of the truth, and this may eventually affect public confidence in the courts. As mentioned above, a suitable balance must be achieved between the conflicting values.

Efficiency

Society expects the courts to ensure procedural fairness, but it also expects them to be efficient. The courts are the machinery for enforcing laws and regulations. The legal system might have very good laws which provide for the granting of substantive rights to citizens in relation to their fellow citizens, and to the government, but these laws are of little value if the legal system does not provide an accessible, convenient and efficient method for enforcing laws and obtaining redress for violation of rights; hence, the demand for efficient court procedure, for a judicial process which is not unreasonably slow and for judicial services which can be obtained at a reasonable cost.[2]

Accessibility

The importance of the need for an accessible judicial system should not be underestimated. The significance of accessibility is to be found first and foremost in the opening up of the doors of the courts to the public. The courts have emphasised the great importance of this value.[3]

[2] The demand for efficiency in the administration of justice is equally strong in the criminal and civil spheres.

[3] Miscellaneous Petitions (M.P.) 678/82 *Tayar* v. *State of Israel* 36(3) PD 386.

Accessibility includes the provision of judicial services to the public at reasonable cost, provision of the means to go to court (legal aid) for those unable to pay the cost, as well as increasing the awareness of the community so that citizens within the community appreciate that they are entitled to turn to the courts in order to defend their rights and obtain redress for wrongs.

The greater accessibility of the courts, particularly through legal aid, has contributed to the increasing number of court cases, especially in criminal matters. It has meant that more defendants are pleading not guilty to charges, and trials are taking more time. As Lord Widgery, the Lord Chief Justice of England commented to the Royal Commission on Legal Services in 1977: 'I find it really inescapable that the increasing length of these trials is in some way connected with the greater freedom of the purse.'[4]

Article 6(1) of the European Convention on Human Rights (ECHR), as interpreted by the European Court of Human Rights, also ensures the fundamental values of access to justice. In this context it is significant to mention the reference to this basic right by the United Kingdom higher courts. Lord Bingham in *Brown* v. *Stott*[5] explained that:

> Article 6(1) contains no express right of access to justice, but in *Golder* v. *UK* the European Court of Human Rights said that it was 'inconceivable' that this provision should give detailed procedural guarantees without protecting access to justice.[6]

The court in the *Golder* case conceded that this implied right was not absolute and so admitted limitations.[7]

Public confidence

The courts can perform their function as an institution to resolve disputes in society only if they enjoy public confidence. The courts have recognised the indispensability of this value to the functioning of the legal system. Justice Barak has held, in *Tzaban* v. *Minister of Religious Affairs*, that 'public confidence in the judiciary is the most valuable asset that this branch possesses. This is also one of the most valuable foundations of the nation.'[8] The courts can enjoy such confidence only if they are seen as independent and unbiased, and if the process of

[4] *The Times*, 1 November 1977. [5] [2003] 1 AC 681, 694, PC.
[6] (1975) 1 EHRR 524, 536 at [35]. [7] (1975) 1 EHRR 524, 536 at [38].
[8] HC 732/84 *Tzaban* v. *Minister of Religious Affairs* (1986) 40(4) PD 141 at 148.

resolving the dispute is fair, efficient, expedient and accessible, as described above. Furthermore, public confidence in the courts is enhanced by numerous principles and practices, which aim to ensure that justice will not only be done but also seen to be done.[9] These principles are discussed as follows:

> The 'open court' principle is one of the fundamental principles of the legal system, and it has also found a basis in statutory law. For example, s. 3 of the Israeli Basic Law: Adjudication[10] states that 'a court shall sit in public unless otherwise provided by Law or unless the court otherwise decide under Law'. This principle has also attained a wide recognition in decisions of the Israeli Supreme Court. This court has designated the open court principle as 'one of the pillars of criminal and civil procedure, and are of the most important means of ensuring a fair and impartial trial'.[11]

Restrictions on the principle have, indeed, been enacted in law.[12] These reservations allow for the hearing of a matter *in camera*, or for the removal of a person from the court, both at the discretion of the court and on grounds which are enumerated in the statute. These grounds include the safeguarding of state security and its foreign relations, the protection of morality, the security of witnesses, the protection of the interests of the parties involved in a sex offence, the privacy of the parties involved in a personal status case and the protection of minors.[13]

Another fundamental and basic requirement for maintaining public confidence in the legal system may be found in the court's duty to state reasons for the decisions it has arrived at.[14] This significant obligation also contributes to the development of logical, analytical methods of thought which lie at the foundations of the legal process, and allows for the review of decisions on appeal, and for a reliance upon them as precedents.

[9] For English examples, see S. Shetreet, *Judges on Trial, A Study of the Appointment and Accountability of the English Judiciary* (Amsterdam: North-Holland, 1976), p. 204.

[10] See *Sefer Ha Hukim*, 8 March 1984, p. 78; 38 *Laws of the State of Israel* 101.

[11] Cr A 334/81 *Haginzer* v. *State of Israel* (1982) 36(1) PD 827.

[12] Israel Courts Law (Consolidated version) 1984, *Sefer Ha Hukim*, p. 198; 38 *Laws of the State of Israel* 271, ss. 68–9.

[13] An additional reservation on the open court principle is the *sub judice* rule, found in s. 70 of the Israel Courts Law.

[14] For a general discussion of the duty to provide a reasoned decision see: R. Gavison, 'The Court and the Duty to Reason' (1970) 2 *Mishpatim* 89; M. Gavish, 'The Duty to State Reasons for Decisions' (1989) 17 *Israel Tax Quarterly* 207; I. Zamir, 'On Justice in the High Court of Justice' (1970) 26 *Hapraklit* 212 at 226–9.

At common law, there is no general obligation to give reasons for judicial decisions.[15] The Court of Appeal in *English* v. *Emery Reimbold & Strick Ltd* noted that Article 6(1) of the ECHR requires a court to provide a reasoned judgment.[16] In that case the court ruled that the convention requires that a judgment should contain reasons that are sufficient to demonstrate that the essential issues that have been raised by the parties have been addressed by the domestic court and how those issues have been resolved.

The importance of public confidence in the courts is also reflected in the rather strict tests applied for self-disqualification of judges for bias.[17] The test does not require proof that bias has actually influenced the judge, but rather that there is a real likelihood that it will influence the judge.[18] The traditions of the bench go even further than the strict requirement of the law of bias.[19]

The concern for public confidence in the court even imposes restrictions on the behaviour of judges outside the courtroom. This is due to the fact that public confidence in the legal system is maintained by proper judicial conduct and is adversely affected by judicial misconduct, on and off the bench.[20]

Public confidence in the courts is also enhanced if the judiciary broadly reflect all social strata, ethnic groups and geographical regions in a given country. In England, the narrow social background of the judiciary, being drawn predominantly from the upper middle class, has been the source of heated public debate for some time.[21]

15 See, M. Akehurst, 'Statements of Reasons for Judicial and Administrative Decisions' (1970) 33 *Modern Law Review* 154; for a discussion of the law in the United States, see *Mildner* v. *Gulotta* 405 F.Supp (EDNY 1975), 182 at 215–20, *per* Weinstein J. (dissenting), aff'd, 425 US (1976) 901. In Canada judicial decisions have sometimes been reversed on account of insufficient reasons given. See, *Barrette* v. *R* 68 DLR (3d) (1977) 260 and the cases cited therein, at 264, *per* Pigeon J. See also, A. Hooper, 'Comment' (1970) 48 *Canadian Bar Review* 584. In Quebec, Article 471 of the Code of Civil Procedure RSC c. C-25 imposes a duty to give reasons.

16 [2002] EWCA Civ. 605; [2002] 1 WLR 2409, CA; and see *Flannery* v. *Halifax Estate Agencies Ltd* [2000] 1 WLR 377, CA; J. A. Jolowicz, 'A Duty to Give Reasons' (2000) 59(2) *Cambridge Law Journal* 263.

17 See S. Shetreet, 'The Administration of Justice: Practical Problems, Value Conflicts and Changing Concepts' (1979) 13 *University of British Columbia Law Review* 52.

18 S. Shetreet, *Judges on Trial*, at pp. 303–5.

19 S. Shetreet, *Judges on Trial*, at pp. 305–14.

20 See more in the *Tzaban* v. *Minister of Religious Affairs* 40(4) PD 141.

21 B. Abel-Smith and R. Stevens, *Lawyers and the Courts* (London: Heinemann, 1967), B. Abel-Smith and R. Stevens, *In Search of Justice* (London: Penguin, 1968); R. M. Jackson, *The Machinery of Justice in England*, 7th edn. (New York: Cambridge University Press, 1977), pp. 473–81; L. J. Blom-Cooper and G. Drewry, *Final Appeal: A Study of the House of Lords in its Judicial Capacity* (Oxford: Clarendon Press, 1972), pp. 152–75; R. G. Hood, *Sentencing*

The media plays a significant role in maintaining public confidence in courts and judges by reporting what is going on in the courts. Courts and judges should not be immune to fair criticism, as long as it is done in good faith and in good taste; judges should use very sparingly the extreme measure of contempt of court to suppress criticism of the courts.

While recognising the importance of exercising the power of contempt of court with great caution and restraint, one should be aware of the dangers which lie in undue popular pressures on judges. Excessive popular pressure and irresponsible journalists, hungry for sensational pieces, may put judges in an unbearable position, and may threaten their independence when they very often have to act against popular wishes to protect dissenters and members of minority groups.

Judicial independence

As Lord Hailsham said in his Lionel Cohen Lecture,[22] there is a continuous tension between judicial independence and the public accountability of judges in a democracy. This tension should be reconciled by the exercise of wisdom and good judgement, so that the proper balance between these very important principles is maintained.

Central to the judicial process is the principle of judicial independence. The meaning and content of this principle vary somewhat from one country to another depending upon the system of government, local traditions and the climate of political opinion, and even in the same country it may carry different meanings in different periods.[23]

The theoretical basis for judicial independence is the doctrine of separation of powers, which in its modern form does not mean total separation of the branches of government but, rather, a system of 'checks and balances'.[24] The judicial branch has to be independent in order to

the Motoring Offender (London: Heinemann Educational, 1972), pp. 41–53; J. Baldwin, 'The Composition of the Magistracy' (1979) 16 *British Journal of Criminology*, 171; S. Shetreet, *Judges on Trial*, pp. 297–8. See also S. Shetreet, 'On Assessing the Role of Courts in Society' (1980) 10 *Manitoba Law Journal*, 357–414.

22 Lord Hailsham, 'The Independence of the Judicial Process' (1978) 13 *Israel Law Review*, 1 at 8–9; see also, P. A. Nejelski, 'Judging in a Democracy: The Tension of Popular Participation' (1977) 61 *Judicature* 166.

23 See generally Lord Hailsham, 'The Independence of the Judicial Process', and Nejelski, 'Judging in a Democracy'.

24 This can be illustrated by the experience in the United States regarding executive control over court administration. Prior to 1939, the central responsibility for court administration at the federal level was vested in the Attorney-General, when in that year the responsibility was vested in the judiciary: 28 USCA 605. See E. C. Friesen, E. C. Gallas

carry out its function of controlling and balancing vis-à-vis the other two principal branches of government: the executive and the legislature.[25]

The importance of the principle of an independent judiciary has grown and received increased attention, particularly as a result of the expanding role of the judiciary in society.[26] This increasing judicialisation is in part a result of social developments, such as massive industrialisation or the expansion of the welfare state. Wide-ranging primary and secondary legislation has been enacted and, consequently, there has been a corresponding expansion in litigation against government services, as well as the development of 'social rights', a typical by-product of the welfare state. In addition, collective procedures, such as the American class action or the French *action collective*, have developed, which have brought about a 'massification' of the law, transforming the traditional two-party litigation into a major multi-party complex litigation.[27]

Judicial independence requires that judicial accountability will be shaped in a very careful way. One of the important points is that incompetence will not be a ground for removal of judges.

Article 6 of the ECHR as a statement of the core values

The transnational jurisprudence, Article 6(1) of the ECHR, represents the formulation of the core values of the justice system. It refers both to the position of the judge and the tribunal that adjudicates and also to the rights

and N. M. Gallas, *Managing the Courts* (Indianapolis: Bobbs-Merrill, 1971), pp. 87–8. Similarly, we have witnessed in several other countries some changes in the concept of judicial independence, particularly in the area of control over judicial administration.

25 As Dr Petren wrote, the maintenance of the independence of the judiciary is 'part of the Montesquian theory of division of powers. The tripartition of the public decision-makers into the executive, the legislative, and the judiciary is based on the idea that each of these three acting parts should have a certain independence in relation to each other': G. Pétren, 'The Independence of the Judiciary', in *Helsinki Symposium*, 1980, p. 95.

26 See further, M. Cappelletti, 'Who Watches the Watchmen? A Comparative Study on Judicial Responsibility' (1983) 31 *American Journal of Comparative Law* 1 at 7–9. For further discussion on the increasing judicial role in society, see E. Vescovi, 'La Independencia de la Magistratura en la Evolucion Actual del Derecho', in W. Habscheid (ed.), *Effectiveness of Judicial Protection and Constitutional Order* (Bielefeld: Gieseking, 1983), pp. 169–72 at 161. See also, C. Das and K. Chandra, *Judges and judicial Accountability* (Commonwealth Lawyers Association, 2003). For an in-depth discussion of the cultural influences on judicial dispute resolution see Oscar G. Chase, *Law Culture and Ritual: Disputing Systems in Cross-Cultural Context* (New York: New York University Press, 2005).

27 For an examination of the massification of the judicial system in criminal cases, see D. H. Whitbread (ed.), *Mass Production Justice and Constitutional Idea* (Charlottesville, VA: Michie, 1970), p. 1. Massification occurs in civil cases as well.

accorded to everyone who stands before the tribunal. The United Kingdom Human Rights Act 1998, which took effect in October 2000, rendered the European Convention on Human Rights directly applicable in English courts. Article 6(1) of the Convention provides that: 'In the determination of his civil rights and obligations or of any criminal charge against him, everyone is entitled to a fair and public hearing within a reasonable time by an independent and impartial tribunal established by law.'[28]

Most of the text of Article 6(1) refers to procedural fairness. The phrase 'fair hearing' includes a number of procedural rights, among others: the right to be present at an adversarial hearing; the right to equality of arms; the right to fair presentation of the evidence; the right to cross-examine opponents' witnesses; the right to a reasoned judgment.[29] It also includes 'public hearing', the public announcement of decisions[30] and hearing within a reasonable time. The text of the article also contains a central requirement that everyone is entitled to be tried before an independent[31] and impartial[32] tribunal established by law. In other treaties it is provided that the tribunal has been previously established by law.[33]

It is very important to note the recent statement of the requirement of judicial independence in new legislation in the United Kingdom. Section 3 of the Constitutional Reform Act 2005 provides that: 'The Lord Chancellor, other Ministers of the Crown and all with responsibility for matters relating

[28] Human Rights Act 1998, s. 1(3), Schedule 1 incorporates the European Convention on Human Rights into United Kingdom law; S. Grocz, J. Beatson and P. Duffy, *Human Rights: The 1998 Act and the European Convention*, 2nd edn. (London: Sweet & Maxwell, 2008); M. W. Janies, R. S. Kay and A. Bradley, *European Human Rights Law: Text and Materials*, 3rd edn. (Oxford University Press, 2008); R. Clayton and H. Tomlinson, *The Law of Human Rights*, 2nd edn. (Oxford University Press, 2008).

[29] R. Clayton and H. Tomlinson, *The Law of Human Rights*, ch. 11; N. Andrews, *English Civil Procedure* (Oxford University Press, 2003), pp. 5.39–68.

[30] Andrews, *English Civil Procedure*, p. 4.59 to the end of chapter. For further discussion see generally N. Andrews, *English Civil Justice and Remedies* (Tokyo: Shinzansha, 2007); N. Andrews, *Contracts and English Dispute Resolution* (Jigakusha: Nagoya University Japan, 2010).

[31] *Starrs* v. *Ruxton* 2000 JC 208 at 243; *The Times*, 17 November 1999 (High Court of Justiciary), *per* Lord Reed; *Millar* v. *Dickson* [2002] 1 WLR 1615, PC; Andrews, *English Civil Procedure*, pp. 4.02–27 (judicial independence).

[32] *Porter* v. *Magill* [2002] 2 AC 357, HL.

[33] Note the term 'previously' (emphasis added) in 'Every person has the right to a hearing, with due guarantees and within a reasonable time, by a competent, independent, and impartial tribunal, *previously* established by law, in the substantiation of any accusation of a criminal nature made against him or for the determination of his rights and obligations of a civil, labor, fiscal, or any other nature': Article 8 of the American Convention on Human Rights 1969.

to the judiciary or otherwise to the administration of justice must uphold the continued independence of the judiciary.' It also provides that: 'The Lord Chancellor and other Ministers of the Crown must not seek to influence particular judicial decisions through any special access to the judiciary.' The Act also imposes a duty on the executive government to uphold judicial independence. It provides that: 'The Lord Chancellor must have regard to (a) the need to defend that independence; (b) the need for the judiciary to have the support necessary to enable them to exercise their functions; (c) the need for the public in regard to matters relating to the judiciary or otherwise to the administration of justice to be properly represented in decisions affecting those matters.'

It is interesting to note that neither Neil Andrews' book in 1994 nor Sir Jack Jacob's article in 1987 mentioned judicial independence as a required foundation of the core values of judicial systems, although they did later recognise its importance as a core value of the judicial system. It is noteworthy that Tony Jolowicz already in 1973 had rightly emphasised the principle of judicial independence stating that:

> Without a judiciary which can and will administer law fairly and fearlessly between the parties, no other guarantee given to the litigants by the law is likely to be of value. The judge must be free from interference by the state itself; he must also be free of interference or influence outside the proceedings from the parties or others; he must also himself be unbiased and personally disinterested in the question at issue in the litigation he has to try.[34]

The increasing role of the judiciary in society may be seen as natural and objective, but there are also causes for increased judicialisation that may be viewed as convenience-based processes of judicialisation. This refers to the judicialisation of issues largely for the political convenience of the other branches of government.[35] A similar trend may be observed in Israel, where the relative role of the executive has declined, whereas the judicial role has increased. Two major processes are taking place. First, the realisation by the

[34] J. A. Jolowicz, 'Angleterre', in M. Cappelletti and D. Tallon (eds.), *Fundamental Guarantees of the Parties in Civil Litigation* (Milan: A. Giuffre, 1973), p. 121–73.

[35] As Sir Ninian Stephen wrote, in 'Judicial Independence – A Fragile Bastion', in S. Shetreet and J. Deschenes (eds.), *Judicial Independence: The Contemporary Debate* (Dordrecht: Martinus Nijhoff, 1985), p. 529 at 543: 'Both the legislature and the executive may find it very convenient to shift to the judiciary the task of initiative – taking in [sensitive] areas . . . Elected bodies may have much to fear if they have to decide such issues for themselves; wise politicians may well prefer to avoid the issue for fear of an electoral backlash.'

public that the ordinary bureaucratic and political institutions are failing to solve issues has diverted them to seek judicial redress where these other institutions have failed. Second, the executive has sometimes intentionally shifted questions to the courts in order to secure a judicial resolution of disputes which are economic or political in nature, to avoid having to pay the political price of the decision.

This author prefers to classify the core values of the justice system into five main categories as outlined earlier: procedural fairness; efficiency; accessibility; public confidence; and judicial independence. Other scholars prefer to formulate the core values in a series of principles. Neil Andrews at one stage formulated eleven principles.[36] At a later stage, he developed his approach and formulated the core values in twenty-four principles. This he has done in connection with the UNIDROIT/American Law Institute (ALI) project, and also with a civil procedure project in which he took part. In his book, *English Civil Procedure*, he enumerated twenty-four principles: judicial independence; judicial impartiality; public or open justice; the principle of due notice; judicial duty to give reasons; avoidance of undue delay; litigants are not to be prejudiced by the court's culpable shortcomings;[37] access to justice; right to choose a lawyer; confidential legal consultation; procedural equality; protection against bad or spurious claims and defences; simplicity of procedure; judicial control of the civil process; proportionality; disclosure; oral proceedings; procedural equity; promoting settlement; accuracy; fair play between litigants; protection of non-parties; effectiveness; and finality.[38] In a recent work, Andrews has developed further his concept on the basic principles of adjudication. He has now narrowed the principles of civil justice to four:[39] access to legal advice and dispute resolution systems; equality and fairness between the parties; a focused and speedy process; and adjudicators of integrity. I prefer the more generalised categorisation of the core values which I proposed earlier.

[36] See N. Andrews, 'Identifying Fundamental Principles of Civil Justice', paper delivered at an international conference on judicial independence, Cambridge, 2009, p. 2 and see N. Andrews, *Principles of Civil Procedure* (London: Sweet & Maxwell, 1994) (discussion of pre-CPR system).

[37] See Andrews, *English Civil Procedure*, chs. 4 and 5.

[38] See Andrews, *English Civil Procedure*, ch. 6; N. Andrews, *The Modern Civil Process. Judicial and Alternative Forms of Dispute Resolution in England* (Tubingen: More Siebeck, 2008), ch. 8.

[39] See N. Andrews, 'The Four Principles of Civil Justice', in S. Shetreet and C. Forsyth (eds.), *The Culture of Judicial Independence: Conceptual Foundations and Practical Challenges* (Dordrecht: Martinus Nijhoff, forthcoming).

The approach of formulating the core values of the justice system that has been followed by the UNIDROIT/ALI project (2000–6) also chose to enumerate in separate principles. This was a working group[40] of the UNIDROIT/ALI project[41] – now known as Principles of Transnational Civil Procedure, published in 2006.[42] The principles were formulated by Rolf Stürner, who was appointed as the General Reporter of UNIDROIT.[43] Neil Andrews rightly suggested that the UNIDROIT/ALI principles can be grouped into three categories: quasi-constitutional declarations of fundamental procedural guarantees; (2) major guidelines concerning the style and course of procedure; and (3) points of important detail.[44] These three groups of principles are outlined below.[45]

[40] The members of the drafting group were distinguished scholars from numerous countries, see Andrews, *English Civil Procedure*.

[41] N. Andrews, 'The Modern Procedural Synthesis: the American Law Institute and UNIDROIT's "Principles and Rules of Transnational Civil Procedure"' (2008) 164 *Revista de Processo* 109–20 (Brazil), also published in (2009) *Tijdschrift voor Civiele Rechtspleging* 52–7 (Netherlands).

[42] ALI–UNIDROIT, *Principles of Transnational Civil Procedure* (Cambridge University Press, 2006).

[43] R. Stürner, 'The Principles of Transnational Civil Procedure . . .' (2005) *Rabels Zeitschrift* (Leipzig: Max Planck Institute), 201–54.

[44] N. Andrews 'Embracing the Noble Quest for Transnational Procedural Principles', in M. Andenas, N. Andrews and R. Nazzini (eds.), *The Future of Transnational Commercial Litigation: English Responses to the ALI–UNIDROIT Draft Principles and Rules of Transnational Civil Procedure* (London: British Institute of Comparative Law, 2003; reprinted 2006), pp. 23–25 (a collection of essays and comments by British judges and commentators on the draft UNIDROIT/ALI's project).

[45] Andrews outlined them in 'Identifying Fundamental Principles of Civil Justice' as follows:

> Fundamental procedural guarantees:
> judicial competence; judicial independence; judicial impartiality; procedural equality; due notice or the right to be heard; publicity; reasoned decisions; prompt and accelerated justice; professional independence of counsel; right to assistance of counsel; attorney-client privilege ('legal professional privilege'); the privilege against self-incrimination.
> Leading principles concerning the style and course of procedure:
> jurisdiction over parties; venue rules; party initiation of proceedings; party's definition of scope of proceedings; joinder rules; allocation of burden and nature of standard of proof; pleadings; parties' duty to avoid false pleading and abuse of process; rights of access to information; judicial initiative in evidential matters; experts judicial management of proceedings; sanctions against default and non-compliance; need for proportionality in use of sanctions; parties' duty to act fairly and to promote efficient and speedy proceedings; parties' duty to co-operate; parties' right to discontinue or settle proceedings; judicial encouragement of settlement, right to oral stage of

Another attempt to outline the core values of civil procedure in common law and civil law countries was the work of Tony Jolowitz and Marcel Storme.[46]

Core values of the concept of judicial independence

I now come to a detailed analysis of the core values of judicial independence. In enumerating the theoretical elements of judicial independence a distinction must be made between two aspects of the concept of the independence of the judiciary: the independence of the individual judges and the collective independence of the judiciary as a body.

Personal and substantive independence

It should be noted that there are different conceptions of the principles of judicial independence. Individual judges must enjoy both personal and substantive independence, both of which are necessary to protect judges from threats to their personal or professional security that may influence their official duties.[47] Characteristics of personal independence include security of office, life tenure and adequate remuneration and pensions. Substantive independence refers to the freedom of judges to perform their judicial functions independently.[48] The Mount Scopus

procedure; final hearing before ultimate adjudicators; judicial responsibility for correct application of the law; basic costs shifting rule; finality of decisions; appeal mechanisms; effective enforcement; recognition by foreign courts; international judicial co-operation.

Points of important detail:

protection of parties lacking capacity; security for costs; expedited forms of communication; non-party submissions; making of judicial 'suggestions'.

See also Andrews, 'Embracing the Noble Quest for Transnational Procedural Principles', in Andenas, Andrews and Nazzini (eds.), *The Future of Transnational Commercial Litigation*, pp. 23–5.

[46] M. Storme (ed.), *Approximation of Judiciary Law in the European Union* (Alphen aan den Rijn: Kluwer Law International, 1994).

[47] See S. D. O'Connor, 'The Importance of Judicial Independence, Remarks before the Arab Judicial Forum', 15 September 2003, *Issues of Democracy* 25 (March 2004), available at: http://italy.usembassy.gov/pdf/ej/ijde0304.pdf.

[48] See Shetreet, in Shetreet and Deschenes (eds.), *Judicial Independence*, pp. 594–9; L. Atkins, 'The Shifting Focus of Judicial Reform: From Independence to Capacity' (August 2002) *EUMAP*, available at: www.eumap.org/journal/features/2002/aug02/indeptocapacity.

Standards require that both personal and substantive independence be preserved.[49]

Institutional or collective independence

The development of the judiciary as a significant social institution with an important constitutional role requires that the concept of judicial independence should not be confined to the independence of the individual judge. It must also extend to the independence of the judiciary as a whole under the rubric of collective independence. It is widely recognised that interference with the independence of individual judges is considered a serious infringement of the rule of law.[50] Interference with the collective independence of the judiciary also has an adverse impact on individual judges as they discharge their official duties. This is due to the fact that the traditional sense of social responsibility that the judiciary imparts on individual judges is a strong instrument for ensuring its independence. Interference with the judiciary as a whole is, therefore, likely to have a negative impact on the sense of independence of individual judges. The collective independence is protected by the rules outlined, which deals with the constitutional position of the judiciary. The Mount Scopus Standards refer to these aspects in ss. 2.12 and 2.13.[51]

Internal judicial independence

Internal judicial independence can be considered collective independence but on a micro-level. It demands that individual judges be free from unjustified influences not only from entities external to the judiciary, but

[49] Section 2.2 makes the distinction between personal and substantive independence: 'Each judge shall enjoy both personal independence and substantive independence'; 2.2.1 'Personal independence means that the terms and conditions of judicial service are adequately secured by law so as to ensure that individual judges are not subject to executive control'; 2.2.2 'Substantive independence means that in the discharge of his judicial function, a judge is subject to nothing but the law and the commands of his conscience', Mount Scopus Approved Revised International Standards of Judicial Independence, 19 March 2008, available at: http://law.huji.ac.il/eng/segel.asp?staff_id=15&cat=441.

[50] Shetreet, in Shetreet and Deschenes (eds.), *Judicial Independence*, p. 643.

[51] Section 2.12 states: 'Judicial matters are exclusively within the responsibility of the Judiciary, both in central judicial administration and in court level judicial administration.' Section 2.13 states: 'The central responsibility for judicial administration shall preferably be vested in the Judiciary or jointly in the Judiciary and the Executive.'

also from within. With regard to certain types of adjudicative functions, independence requires that judges be free from directives or pressures from peers or those who have administrative responsibilities in the court, such as the chief judge of the court or the head of the division in the court.[52] Adjudicative functions are those official functions for which judges are responsible in the discharge of their official duties. As with collective independence, they are, as mentioned above, threefold: administrative; procedural; and substantive. It can be argued that internal independence is applicable only to the substantive and procedural aspects of adjudication.[53] This is because, as a general rule, a judge cannot rely on internal independence as a shield against guidance by other judges who are responsible for court administration.

The substantive and procedural aspects of adjudication vary in different legal systems, as do approaches towards recognising the scope of internal judicial independence. Given this context, it is significant to note that there are conflicting views on the definition of the scope of internal judicial independence vis-à-vis the superior courts. These conflicting views are reflected in the doctrinal approach to precedent. Civil law countries, such as Germany, perceive the concept of substantive internal judicial independence as extending to judges' independence vis-à-vis superior court decisions. With some exceptions, judges are free to disregard precedent. In common law countries, judges are bound by previous decisions of superior courts and sometimes by those of the same court. The doctrine of binding precedent exists in different legal systems in varying degrees.

Administrative independence

With regard to administrative judicial independence, it is generally accepted that judges cannot claim independence from required and necessary guidance and supervision in 'administrative' aspects of adjudication. The US Supreme Court accepts the position that judges should be subject to

[52] See S. Shetreet, 'Models of Constitutional Adjudication: A Comparative Analysis', in A. P. Grinovner and P. Calmon (eds.), *Papers Presented at the XII Congress of Procedural Law* (Rio de Janeiro: Forensa, 2007), pp. 769–98. See also S. Shetreet, 'Judicial Independence on the Scope of Internal Independence', in E. Longo (ed.), *Judicial Independence Today, in honor of Justice Giovanni* (Milan: Giuffre, 1999), pp. 345–57.

[53] Consider M. Cappelletti, 'Who Watches the Watchmen?: A Comparative Study on Judicial Responsibility' (1983) 31 *American Journal of Comparative Law*, 1 at 7–9 (accepting the proposition only in part).

administrative supervision, and the Mount Scopus Standards also refer to this issue of scope of internal judicial independence.[54]

Perceptions and realities

The concept of judicial independence must recognise realities as well as perceptions. As Chief Justice Howland of the Ontario Supreme Court put it in *R* v. *Valente*, a leading Canadian constitutional case in which the principle of judicial independence was discussed at length, 'it is most important that the judiciary be independent and be so perceived by the public. The judges must not have cause to fear that they will be prejudiced by their decisions or that the public would reasonably apprehend this to be the case.'[55] The recognition of public perceptions is required by the need to ensure public confidence in the courts, which, as discussed above, is one of the fundamental values of the administration of justice. The importance of public perception was stressed in the Ontario White Paper on court administration,[56] which stated: 'The value of the courts as an important impartial forum for the resolution of disputes depends upon the public perception of the independence of the courts from the parties and particularly their independence from the government.'[57] In the appeal in the *Valente* case, the court confirmed that it is 'important that a tribunal should be perceived as independent, as well as impartial, and that the test for independence should include that perception'. However, the perception had to 'be a perception of whether the tribunal enjoys essential objective conditions of guarantees of judicial independence, and not a perception of how it will in fact act, regardless of whether it enjoys such conditions and guarantees'.[58]

The reasonable man test

It is submitted that the reasonable man test should be employed only in the absence of other, more defined, criteria. The accepted wisdom of human experience coupled with a high commitment to the value of ensuring completely neutral judicial dispute resolution can establish a more definitive test. The executive controls over the judicial terms of service may make the

[54] See *Chandler* v. *Judicial Council* (10th Cir.) 398 US 74 (1970). See also Mount Scopus Standards, above n. 49, s. 9.

[55] *R* v. *Valente* (1983) 2 CCC (3d) 417 at 423.

[56] Ontario Ministry of Attorney-General, White Paper on Courts Administration (1976).

[57] Ontario Ministry of Attorney-General, White Paper on Courts Administration p. 13.

[58] *Valente* v. *R* [1985] 2 SCR 673 at 689.

tribunal dependent. This conclusion can be drawn without recourse to the test of the reasonable man.

The existence of personal controls on judges inevitably casts a shadow of doubt over their independence. For example, courts' martial judges are military officers, who, subject to the ordinary personal controls under military hierarchy and rules, are personally dependent, and cannot, therefore, try ordinary criminal offences, as distinguished from military offences. According to accepted concepts, their tribunal cannot be considered an independent tribunal. Moreover, even if we apply the test of reasonable suspicion of bias, their institutional bias will leave their impartiality seriously in doubt.[59] Indeed, Article 2.06(e) of the Montreal Declaration[60] provides that the jurisdiction of military courts is limited to military personnel and military offences.

It is important to note that there is a trend to strengthen the independence of tribunal judiciary,[61] as they are referred to in the United Kingdom, or administrative judges, as they are referred to in the United States.[62]

Constitutional infrastructure essential for the protection of judicial independence

Constitutional and legislative regulation

In the normative analysis of the regulation of judicial issues, it must be recognised that certain matters should be regulated in the constitution, whereas others may be regulated by ordinary legislation. When a matter is regulated by ordinary legislation, the legislature can effect an amendment by simple majority. In contrast, protection granted by the constitution is modifiable by constitutional amendment only. Therefore, in order to better guard judicial independence, issues such as the terms of

[59] See judgment of Chief Justice Bora Laskin in *McKay* v. *R* (1980) 54 CCC (2d) 129; 114 DLR (3d) 393, 401–2: 'the military judge is not suited because of his close involvement with the prosecution and with the entire military establishment' (dissenting opinion).

[60] Universal Declaration on the Independence of Justice, unanimously adopted at the final plenary session of the First World Conference on the Independence of Justice held at Montreal, 10 June 1983.

[61] Many officers of the state exercise an adjudicative function, i.e., they resolve disputes, and the question arises which of the state organs exercising adjudicative functions come within the term 'judiciary' and so, according to accepted theory, must be 'independent'? For a detailed discussion of this issue, see S. Shetreet, *Justice in Israel: A Study of the Israeli Judiciary* (Dordrecht: Martibnus Nijhoff, 1994), ch. 12.

[62] See Tribunals, Courts and Enforcement Act 2007, c. 15.

office for judges should be protected in constitutional provisions.[63] For example, the composition of the US Supreme Court – how many judges sit in the court – is not constitutionally regulated and therefore the number of sitting judges has been changed by legislation.[64] During the controversy in the United States over New Deal legislation, President F. D. Roosevelt attempted to pack the court – increasing the number of judges – which he could do by ordinary legislation.[65]

In addition to general constitutional protections of judicial independence, a more detailed constitutional protection should include six fundamental substantive principles. Conceptually, these principles are imperative prerequisites to an independent judicial system.[66] They will be discussed in the following section.

Shetreet's six constitutional principles of judicial independence

In my previous writings I have identified six principles which I define as essential constitutional infrastructure for the protection of judicial independence. The first principle of constitutional protection of judicial independence is a rule against *ad hoc* tribunals. The second is a prohibition against intentionally stripping courts of their jurisdiction and diverting cases to other tribunals with a view to having those cases disposed of by tribunals that do not enjoy the same conditions of independence as the original courts. The third is the standard-judge principle, or the ordinary-judge principle, which requires that judges be selected to hear cases by a predetermined internal plan or assignment schedule prior to the commencement of the case. The fourth principle requires post-decisional independence of the judgment and its respect by the other branches of the

[63] See S. Shetreet, 'Judicial Independence: New Conceptual Dimensions and Contemporary Challenges', in Shetreet and Deschenes (eds.), *Judicial Independence*, ch. 52, p. 590. Consider Canada, the Constitution Act 1982, ss. 96–101, which provide for the appointment, terms of office and remuneration of judges.

[64] The Judiciary Act 1789 initially set the number of Supreme Court judges at six. In later years, the number was increased and decreased until it was finally settled at nine.

[65] See, e.g., *United States* v. *Will* 449 US 200 (1980); *Chandler* v. *Judicial Council* (10th Cir.) 398 US 74 (1970); J. L. Carson and B. A. Kleinerman, 'A Switch in Time Saves Nine: Institutions, Strategic Actors, and FDR's Court-Packing Plan' (2002) 113(3–4) *Public Choice* 301–24; M. Nelson, 'The President and the Court: Reinterpreting the Court-Packing Episode of 1937' (1988) 103 *Political Science Quarterly* 267; G. A. Caldeira, 'Public Opinion and the US Supreme Court: FDR's Court-Packing Plan' (1987) 81 *American Political Science Review* 1139.

[66] Shetreet, 'Judicial Independence', in Shetreet and Deschenes (eds.), *Judicial Independence*, pp. 592, 615.

government. The fifth principle is that judges must not be part of the administrative arm of the executive branch; rather, they should be viewed as independent constitutional or statutory officers of the state, and completely separate from the civil service. The sixth principle is that changes in the terms of judicial office should not be applied to present judges unless such changes serve to improve the terms of judicial service.[67]

A recent commitment to the principle of judicial independence is s. 3 of the United Kingdom Constitutional Reform Act 2005, which provides that 'The Lord Chancellor, other Ministers of the Crown and all with responsibility for matters relating to the judiciary or otherwise to the administration of justice must uphold the continued independence of the judiciary.' It also prohibits attempts to influence judicial proceedings: 'The Lord Chancellor and other Ministers of the Crown must not seek to influence particular judicial decisions through any special access to the judiciary.' It also requires that political leaders must respect judicial independence. It provides that:

> The Lord Chancellor must have regard to (a) the need to defend that independence; (b) the need for the judiciary to have the support necessary to enable them to exercise their functions; (c) the need for the public in regard to matters relating to the judiciary or otherwise to the administration of justice to be properly represented in decisions affecting those matters.

In recent times, Lord Chancellors have frequently emphasised the importance of judicial independence.[68]

67 For a detailed analysis of Shetreet's six constitutional principles for protecting judicial independence, see S. Shetreet, 'The Normative Cycle of Shaping Judicial Independence in Domestic and International Law: The Mutual Impact of National and International Jurisprudence and Contemporary Practical and Conceptual Challenges' (2009) 10 *Chicago Journal of International Law* 275–332.

68 During a Parliamentary debate, Lord Mckay LC expressed this position:

> Judicial independence requires that judges can discharge their judicial duties in accordance with the judicial oath and the laws of the land, without interference, improper influence or pressure from any other individual or organisation.

(HL Deb., vol. 576, col. 196 WA, 16 December 1996), and Lord Irvine LC said:

> The independence of the judiciary is a cornerstone of Britain's constitutional arrangements . . . If judges depend on the goodwill of their government for their continuing employment, they may find themselves unable to resist political or other improper influence in individual cases. So, judges must have security of tenure. They must be able to undertake their responsibilities and exercise their discretion without fear or favour Their appointments and careers must be developed on the basis of

Article 6 of the ECHR and other international standards of judicial independence

The most important statement on judicial independence is Article 6(1) of the ECHR,[69] and the accompanying jurisprudence of the European Court of Human Rights.[70] Other international statements of international standards of judicial independence include the International Bar Association (IBA) standards of judicial independence, which I was privileged to take part in drafting and which were adopted and confirmed at the 1982 IBA convention in New Delhi.[71] I am now privileged to serve once again in the leadership of an academic and professional project to develop revised international standards of judicial independence for national judges and international judges.[72] Other internationally significant projects are the

> objective criteria to avoid any suggestion of favouritism or preferment in return for favours rendered.

Lord Irvine's address at the Commonwealth conference of 1998, reproduced in J. Hatchard and P. Slinn (eds.), *Parliamentary Supremacy and Judicial Independence: A Commonwealth Approach* (London: Cavendish, 1999), p. 167.

69 Article 6(1) of the ECHR (since 2000, incorporated into English law by the Human Rights Act 1998) states:

> Right to a Fair Trial
> In the determination of his civil rights and obligations or of any criminal charge against him, everyone is entitled to a fair and public hearing within a reasonable time by an independent and impartial tribunal established by law. (Cmd 8969)

The Human Rights Act 1998, s. 1(3), Sch. 1 incorporates most of the articles of the European Convention on Human Rights into UK law; S. Grocz, J. Beatson and P. Duffy, *Human Rights: The 1998 Act and the European Convention* (London: Sweet & Maxwell, 2000), pp. 240–1; M. Janis, R. Kay and A. Bradley, *European Human Rights Law: Text and Materials*, 2nd edn (Oxford University Press, 2000), ch. 8.

70 The European Court of Human Rights in *Findlay* v. *UK* [1997] 24 EHRR 221 said:

> in order to establish whether a tribunal can be considered as 'independent', regard must be had *inter alia* to the manner of appointment of its members and their term of office, the existence of guarantees against outside pressures and the question whether the body presents an appearance of independence.

See also *Porter* v. *Magill* [2001] UKHL 67, [2002] 2 AC 357; *Millar* case, [2001] UKPC D4; [2002] 1 WLR 1615, PC.

71 Shetreet, 'Judicial Independence', in Shetreet and Deschenes (eds.), *Judicial Independence*, p. 590.

72 S. Shetreet (ed.), *Proceedings of the Jerusalem Conference on Judicial Independence* (Jerusalem: Sacher Institute, March 2008). See the Mount Scopus Standards of Judicial Independence, available at: http://law.huji.ac.il/upload/InternationalStandardsofJudicialInd2008.doc.

declarations on judicial independence that have been issued by a number of institutions, including Judicial Independence and States Acceding to the EU,[73] the UNIDROIT[74] and the Commonwealth Guidelines on Judicial Independence.[75]

Conclusion

In this chapter I have shown the constitutional and practical dimensions of the key concept of 'judicial independence' and its various facets ('institutional' and 'individual' independence). I have explained the importance of judicial independence to the democratic polity as well as to the due operation of a globalised economy. I have outlined the five core values of the judicial system, namely, procedural fairness, public confidence in the courts, efficiency, access to justice and judicial independence, and discussed other scholars' opinions about the basic principles for the judicial system. The chapter has also analysed the necessary constitutional infrastructure required for the protection of judicial independence.

[73] Venice Commission for 'Democracy through Law' (instituted under the auspices of the Council of Europe). J. Jowell (2001) *Public Law* 675; 'Judges should be independent of all forms of external non-judicial influences which might affect their decision-making process.'

[74] UNIDROIT/ALI's 'Principles of Transnational Civil Procedure' provides that:

> The court and the judges should have judicial independence to decide the dispute according to the facts and the law, including freedom from improper internal and external influence.
>
> Judges should have reasonable tenure in office. Nonprofessional members of the court should be designated by a procedure assuring their independence from the parties, the dispute, and other persons interested in the resolution.

UNIDROIT/ALI, *Principles of Transnational Civil Procedure* (Cambridge University Press, 2006), principles 1.1, 1.2; for other international affirmation of the principle of judicial independence, see Lord Steyn, 'The Case for a Supreme Court' (2002) 118 *Law Quarterly Review* 382 at 392–3.

[75] In June 1998, an important formulation of this constitutional requirement was agreed in the 'Latimer House Guidelines for the Commonwealth' (in Hatchard and Slinn (eds.), *Parliamentary Supremacy and Judicial Independence*, pp. 167ff.); see also 'The Judiciary's Extra-Curial Separation from Political Issues'. See D. G. T. Williams, 'Bias: the Judges and the Separation of Powers' [2000] *Public Law* 45. Also significant are the United Nations, 'Basic Principles on the Independence of the Judiciary', UN Doc A/CONF.121/22/Re v 1 (1985) and the Montreal Declaration, see 'The Emerging Transnational Jurisprudence on Judicial Independence: The IBA Standards and Montreal Declaration', in Shetreet and Deschenes (eds.), *Judicial Independence*, p. 401.

PART II

2

Appointment, discipline and removal of judges in Australia

H. P. LEE

The following assessment of the standing of the judiciary in Australia would be regarded as generally accurate: 'Measured in historical and international terms the Australian judiciary is acknowledged to be of outstanding quality and has enjoyed the public's confidence.'[1] Nevertheless, there have been particular judicial appointments which were claimed to be motivated by political considerations or which were based on cronyism. Simon Evans and John Williams wrote:

> It is a notorious fact that judicial officers have been appointed whose character and intellectual and legal capacities have been doubted and whose appointments have been identified as instances of political patronage.[2]

Such claims exist due to the fact that the process of judicial appointment lacks transparency. In noting calls for greater transparency in judicial appointments processes, the current federal Attorney-General (Robert McClelland) acknowledged that the mystery surrounding the current processes and the controversy over past appointments would give rise to two negative consequences: 'First, it can tarnish or detract from the honour of being appointed to judicial office. Second, at a broader level

[1] S. Evans and J. Williams, 'Appointing Australian Judges: A New Model' (2008) 30(2) *Sydney Law Review* 295. See generally, E. Campbell and H. P. Lee, *The Australian Judiciary* (Melbourne: Cambridge University Press, 2001), chs. 4–5.

[2] Evans and Williams, 'Appointing Australian Judges'. See also, B. Debelle, 'Judicial Appointments: The Case for Reform', Samuel Griffith Society Proceedings, *Upholding the Australian Constitution*, 2009, vol. 21, ch. 11, p. 80; R. Sackville, 'The Judicial Appointments Process in Australia: Towards Independence and Accountability' (2007) 16 *Journal of Judicial Administration* 125 at 128; G. Smith, 'Restoring Faith in Justice – Promoting Transparency in Judicial Appointments in NSW', Liberal Party (NSW) and The Nationals, March 2008.

it can diminish public confidence in the courts and the justice system.'[3] The federal Attorney-General's response to the issue was that improvements could be made through the 'touchstones of increased transparency and greater consultation'.[4] Apart from the growing calls for reforms to the appointments process, increasing interest at the federal level and in a number of the states is also focused on the absence of appropriate mechanisms for handling complaints against judicial officers for misconduct which is not of sufficient seriousness to warrant the extreme measure of removal from office.

Judicial appointments

In Australia, most judicial appointments are effected without much publicity. Senior judicial appointments do attract a degree of media interest, especially appointments to the High Court of Australia. When a vacancy arises in the High Court there is the usual speculation about the identity of the person likely to be appointed to fill the vacancy. At both federal and state levels, judicial appointments are in reality made by the government of the day. In formal constitutional terms, the appointment of federal judges is made by the Governor-General in Council, while the appointment of state judges is made by the Governor in Council. A discussion paper issued by the federal Attorney-General's Department in 1993 succinctly describes the appointment process as varying according to the 'personal preferences of individual Attorneys-General'.[5]

Consultation between the executive and the judiciary or the legal profession is not statutorily prescribed except in relation to the appointment of High Court judges. A former Chief Justice of the High Court of Australia in 1987 said that it is not an uncommon practice for an Attorney-General to consult with the Chief Justice or with other members of the profession with regard to prospective appointments, but noted that 'sometimes an appointment may be made without consultation and sometimes advice may be received but ignored'.[6] A consultation

[3] Address by the Hon. Robert McClelland at the Judicial Appointments Forum, Bar Association of Queensland Annual conference, Sheraton Mirage, Gold Coast, 17 February 2008.

[4] Address by the Hon. Robert McClelland.

[5] Attorney-General's Department, *Judicial Appointments – Procedure and Criteria* (Canberra: AGPS, 1993), para. 1.4.

[6] H. Gibbs, 'The Appointment and Removal of Judges' (1987), *Federal Law Review* 141 at 143–4.

requirement is prescribed by s. 6 of the High Court of Australia Act 1979 (Cth) in relation to the appointment of High Court judges. Thus, the federal Attorney-General is required to consult the Attorneys-General of the states on such appointments.

Although no legislation has been enacted pertaining to the process of judicial selection, at federal level the current federal Attorney-General has established a practice of appointing a panel to provide him with advice regarding appointments to the Federal Court (other than the Chief Justice), Family Court and the Federal Magistrates' Court.[7] This panel includes the Chief Justice (or Chief Federal Magistrate) or their nominee, a retired judge or senior member of the federal or state judiciary and a senior member of the Attorney-General's Department.[8] The role of the advisory panel, according to the federal Attorney-General, is to consider the nominations and provide a report to the Attorney-General recommending appropriate candidates for appointment. The advisory panel may conduct interviews of candidates if that would assist in the making of the report.

The federal Attorney-General has also disclosed the wide spectrum of entities which would be consulted in appointments to the Federal Court (other than the Chief Justice), Family Court and Federal Magistrates' Court. They include the Chief Justices of the Federal Court and Family Court, the Chief Federal Magistrate, the Chief Judge of the Family Court of Western Australia, Law Council of Australia, Australian Bar Association, law societies and bar associations of each state and territory, deans of law schools, Australian Women Lawyers, National Association of Community Legal Centres, National Legal aid, Administrative Appeals Tribunal, Council of Australasian Tribunals and the Veterans' Review Board.[9]

[7] In Tasmania, a 'protocol for judicial appointments' provides for an 'assessment panel' to make recommendations regarding the suitability of applicants to the state Attorney-General. The assessment panel for Supreme Court vacancies is constituted slightly differently from the panel for magistrates' court vacancies. In Victoria, the Attorney-General adopts the practice of using advisory panels to provide advice on judicial appointments to the Magistrates' Court and non-judicial appointments to the Victorian Civil and Administrative Tribunal (VCAT). In New South Wales, a panel conducts interviews of candidates for appointment to the District Court and Local Court and provides an assessment report to the Attorney-General regarding their suitability for judicial office.

[8] Senate Legal and Constitutional Affairs References Committee, *Australia's Judicial System and the Role of Judges*, December 2009, para. 3.17.

[9] *Australia's Judicial System and the Role of Judge*, para. 3.12.

While this current approach is a laudable step in the right direction, it is not a process which is fully transparent. The Senate's Legal and Constitutional Affairs References Committee (hereafter referred to as the 'Senate Committee') in its 2009 report proffered the following criticism:

> The reference in this appointment process to the Attorney-General considering the Advisory Panel's report and then identifying 'the person whom he considers most suitable' is unfortunate. If the Attorney-General identifies the most suitable person based on their assessment against the selection criteria then it is desirable for this to be articulated. On the other hand, if the Attorney-General is not willing to state that selection is directly based on selection criteria then this should also be articulated.[10]

The Senate Committee, while recognising that it is appropriate for the Attorney-General to retain the final decision-making authority, also said that if the Attorney-General makes an appointment other than based on an assessment against selection criteria it would go to the integrity of the process and that transparency would be improved if the Attorney-General made public the number of nominations and applications received for each vacancy.[11] It added that if a shortlist is part of the process, the number of people on the shortlist should be made public. As the current practice adopted by the current federal Attorney-General is not embodied in legislation there is no guarantee that a successor Attorney-General would be obligated to continue this practice.

Nowadays, it is not an uncommon practice for a state or federal government to publish notices in newspapers and the website of the Attorney-General's Department seeking expressions of interest and nominations regarding appointments to the judiciary. Many extremely well qualified candidates may be reluctant to put their names forward in response to an advertisement. Hence, the Senate Committee said that it is important to adopt a comprehensive approach which would include privately canvassing people.[12]

Reforming the judicial appointment process

According to Bruce Debelle, the current process of appointing judges in Australia is 'prone to controversy'.[13] He added:

[10] *Australia's Judicial System and the Role of Judges*, para. 3.20.
[11] *Australia's Judicial System and the Role of Judges*, para. 3.21.
[12] *Australia's Judicial System and the Role of Judges*, paras. 3.42–3.46.
[13] Debelle, 'Judicial Appointments', p. 80.

> It is likely to remain controversial because it is not possible to ascertain by what process an appointment has been made. This unnecessary controversy has a real capacity to undermine public confidence in the judiciary.[14]

There have been sporadic calls for changes to the process of judicial selection. The more popular mode which has been suggested is the establishment of a judicial commission. Such a mode was advocated by Sir Garfield Barwick (Chief Justice of the High Court 1964–81). At first, he proffered the view that such a body should have responsibility to advise the executive government of 'the names of persons who, by reason of their training, knowledge, experience, character and disposition' would be suitable for appointment to judicial office.[15] He subsequently proposed that the judicial commission 'should have the final say'.[16]

Currently, no state government or the federal government has shown much interest in the idea of establishing a judicial appointments commission.[17] At the federal level, appointment of judges by a judicial commission, it has been argued, would be inconsistent with s. 72 of the Australian Constitution. Furthermore, as was asserted by Sir Anthony Mason (Chief Justice of the High Court 1987–95), there is a 'powerful democratic argument' against the transferring of the power of appointment from the executive to a judicial commission consisting, most likely, of un-elected persons.[18] He said:

> One justification for the exercise of judicial power by non-elected judges in a democracy is that the judges are indirectly appointed by the people in that it is the duly elected government that makes the appointments.[19]

Michael Kirby, a former justice of the High Court of Australia, opposes a judicial appointments commission as it has 'all the hallmarks of an institutional arrangement that could deprive our judiciary of the light and shade that tend to come from the present system'.

[14] Debelle, 'Judicial Appointments', p. 80.

[15] G. Barwick, 'The State of the Australian Judicature' (1977) 51 *Australian Law Journal* 480 at 494.

[16] G. Barwick, *A Radical Tory* (Sydney: Federation Press, 1995), p. 230.

[17] www.justice.vic.gov.au/wps/wcm/connect/70b20800435f1661be58ff4f50 1887b2/Reviewing_the_Judicial_Appointments_Process_in_Victoria_Discussion_Paper.pdf?MOD=AJPERES.

[18] A. Mason, 'The Appointment and Removal of Judges', in H. Cunningham (ed.), *Fragile Bastions – Judicial Independence in the Nineties and Beyond* (Judicial Commission of New South Wales, 1997), p. 7.

[19] Mason, 'The Appointment and Removal of Judges', p. 17.

In his view, to have judges choosing judges would be quite 'the wrong way to procure a bench more reflective of the diversity of our country'.[20] His stand is reinforced by the fact that three out of the seven High Court justices are women appointed under the current process.

The Senate Committee, after canvassing all the debates about the establishment of a commission to deal with judicial appointments concluded that it 'is not persuaded that the cost of establishing a separate judicial appointments advisory commission is currently warranted'.[21] It did, however, recognise that a judicial appointments commission would render it difficult for the appointment process to be abused and that therefore it was an issue that 'deserves to be monitored'.[22]

Appointment of acting judges

What has generated a fair degree of concern relates to the appointment of acting judges at state level. This is not a problem at federal level as acting appointments are precluded by the federal Constitution. At state level, acting judges are appointed for a fixed term, generally with the possibility of re-appointment for a further fixed term. For example, in Victoria, the Governor in Council is empowered to appoint as many acting judges as 'are necessary for transacting the business of the Court'.[23] Among other things, an acting judge ceases to hold office at the end of five years from the time of his or her appointment. However, once appointed, an acting judge may be removed from office only 'in the same way and on the same grounds as a Judge of the Court is liable to be removed from office'.[24] In New South Wales, the Governor is empowered to appoint any 'qualified person' as a judge of the Supreme Court for a period of not more than twelve months.[25]

Sir Anthony Mason expressed the view that the appointment of acting judges can be justified 'as a measure to overcome a temporary difficulty'.[26] He also added that the use of acting judges rather than permanent judges 'in order to overcome long-term deficiencies in the court system is extremely difficult to support'.[27] Concerns at the increasing use of acting judges in the

20 M. Kirby, *The Judges* (Sydney: Australian Broadcasting Corporation, 1983), pp. 22–3.
21 *Australia's Judicial System and the Role of Judge*, para. 3.89.
22 *Australia's Judicial System and the Role of Judge*, para. 3.90.
23 Constitution Act 1975, s. 80D. 24 Section 80D(6)(d).
25 Supreme Court Act 1970 (NSW), s. 37.
26 Mason, 'The Appointment and Removal of Judges', p. 9.
27 Mason, 'The Appointment and Removal of Judges', p. 9.

State of New South Wales led to a challenge, which ultimately reached the High Court of Australia in *Forge* v. *Australian Securities and Investments Commission*.[28] In that case, the High Court was required to consider the validity of s. 37 of the Supreme Court Act 1970 (NSW) which empowered the Governor of New South Wales to appoint acting judges. The proceedings before the High Court arose out of actions brought by the Australian Securities and Investments Commission (ASIC) against the applicants and was based on the fact the trial judge was an acting judge of the Supreme Court of New South Wales (Foster AJ, a retired judge of the Federal Court). The High Court, by a 6–1 majority, upheld the validity of s. 37 and of the appointment of Foster AJ as an acting judge.

The challenge relied on the principle in the controversial case of *Kable* v. *Director of Public Prosecutions (NSW)*.[29] Chapter III of the federal Constitution provides for the vesting of the federal judicial power in the High Court of Australia, in such other federal courts as are created by the federal Parliament and 'in such other courts as it invests with federal jurisdiction'.[30] As state Supreme Courts and other state courts are repositories of federal judicial power it led to the formulation of the *Kable* principle encapsulated in the following description by Gleeson CJ:

> Since the Constitution established an integrated court system, and contemplates the exercise of federal jurisdiction by State Supreme Courts, State legislation which purports to confer upon such a court a function which substantially impairs its institutional integrity, and which is therefore incompatible with its roles as a repository of federal jurisdiction, is invalid.[31]

From the terms of Chapter III, state Supreme Courts must answer the description of 'courts'. Gleeson CJ said: 'For a body to answer the description of a court it must satisfy minimum requirements of independence and impartiality.' Would the presence of acting judges on a state Supreme Court deprive it of the character of a court?

The majority judges[32] found that s. 37 of the impugned legislation, in empowering the appointment of acting judges, would not deprive the body of the description of a 'court'. Heydon J pointed out that the practice of using acting judges was borne out by the history of acting judges in the colonies prior to federation.[33] Gleeson CJ likewise pointed

[28] (2006) 228 CLR 45. [29] (1996) 189 CLR 51. [30] Section 71.
[31] (1996) 189 CLR 51 at 67 at [40].
[32] Gleeson CJ, Gummow, Hayne, Crennan, Callinan and Heydon JJ; Kirby J dissenting.
[33] (2006) 228 CLR 45 at 141–6.

to the extensive use of part-time judicial officers in England and Wales.[34] However, in a joint judgment, Gummow, Hayne and Crennan JJ warned that there could be circumstances which would render the appointment of acting judges invalid. They said:

> The institutional integrity of State supreme courts is not inevitably compromised by the appointment of an acting judge. But the institutional integrity of the body may be distorted by [appointments of acting judges] if the informed observer may reasonably conclude that the institution no longer is, and no longer appears to be, independent and impartial as, for example, would be the case if a significant element of its membership stood to gain or lose from the way in which the duties of office were executed.[35]

However, it would not be sufficient to consider the proportion of acting judges on a court. They said that regard must be paid to 'who has been appointed, for how long, to do what, and, no less importantly, why it has been thought necessary to make the acting appointments that have been made'.[36]

In a lone dissent, Kirby J said that at a time of increased media and other attacks on judges in Australia, 'an institutional change that shifts a significant cohort of the State judiciary from permanent tenured judges to part-time judges is seriously threatening to the independence and impartiality of that judiciary'. Adding that such threats are not 'theoretical' Kirby J said:

> Governments are excused from appointing adequate numbers of permanent judges (with implications for staff, facilities and pensions). Litigants are subject to the risk of judges of short tenure and with inappropriate distractions. The tenured judiciary is undermined by such an alteration in its basic composition. The part-time and acting judges inevitably ride on the reputation earned by the tenured judiciary. And although during service the acting judge is immune from day-to-day executive interference, their desire for reappointment as an acting judge (or confirmation as a permanent judge) renders the temporary appointee dependent on a decision by the Executive. This is not a feature of the tenure of permanent judges. Such judges, once appointed, are not beholden to the Executive for any wished-for continuation in office. Typically, they serve for a long interval, terminating on a specified birthday known in advance or upon earlier death or upon resignation decided by the judge. In Australia, the changed practice, instanced in these proceedings, endangers the separation of the senior judiciary from the

34 (2006) 228 CLR 45 at 63 at [27]. 35 (2006) 228 CLR 45 at 86 at [93].
36 (2006) 228 CLR 45 at 88 at [101].

> Executive won in the Act of Settlement 1700. It should be nipped in the bud, although by now the bud is in full flower.[37]

Kirby J noted that in more recent years, short-term appointments of practising lawyers to the Supreme Court of New South Wales have given way to the exclusive appointment of retired judges as acting judges of the Supreme Court. In his view, this does not remove the institutional affront; it merely reduces it. He said that the proper course, consistent with judicial independence and impartiality, is to either extend or remove the mandatory retirement age. The current arrangements for extensions of judicial appointments are confronted with the following objections in principle: each extension is dependent on the will of the executive; some retired judges because of their desire for continuation in office are thus beholden to the will of the executive; some acting judges mix intervals of judicial service with private professional activities on their own behalf, leading to a breakdown of the 'judicial culture of an exclusive, dedicated, tenured service';[38] and acting judges lack the staffing, personal benefits and institutional resources of permanent judges and typically appear to play a more limited role when compared with permanent judges.

Kirby J concluded that the point had been reached when the number of acting judges effected such an institutional change as to undermine the integrity and independence of the Supreme Court of New South Wales. He thus found that Foster A-J's purported commission as an acting judge was invalid and that the orders made by him lacked legal validity.

Removal of judges

The general mode for effecting the removal of a judge is by the Governor-General in relation to federal judicial officers and the Governor in relation to state judicial officers following an address in each House of the Parliament (or the Legislative Assembly in the unicameral Queensland Parliament) on the ground of 'proved misbehaviour' or 'incapacity'.[39] At federal level, no member of the High Court

[37] (2006) 228 CLR 45 at 88 at [101]. [38] (2006) 228 CLR 45 at 132 at [222].

[39] The Victorian Constitution provides for an investigating committee to be appointed by the Attorney-General to determine whether facts exist which could amount to proved misbehaviour or incapacity such as to warrant the removal of a judicial officer-holder from office, prior to an address of both Houses of Parliament. The three members comprising the investigating committee are drawn from a panel of seven retired non-Victorian judges. See G. Taylor, *The Constitution of Victoria* (Sydney: Federation Press,

has been removed by this process, although the process was invoked in relation to Justice Lionel Murphy. Since federation, only one state Supreme Court judge has been successfully removed (Justice Angelo Vasta of the Supreme Court of Queensland). In New South Wales, the removal process was invoked in relation to Justice Vince Bruce on the ground of 'incapacity', but the two houses voted against the resolution to remove him from judicial office.

The 'Murphy affair'

The attempts to remove Justice Murphy[40] have highlighted a number of problems with the current removal process embodied in the federal Constitution. The saga began with the publication by a newspaper (*The Age*) of a series of articles based on telephone conversations (taped illegally by the New South Wales police) of a Sydney solicitor, Morgan Ryan, which were claimed to implicate Justice Murphy. Professor Lindell described the contents of these conversations:

> The transcripts of the telephone conversations between Murphy J and Ryan contained discussions of illegal casinos, blackmail, a real estate development in central Sydney, the possibility of Murphy J supporting the reappointment of a person to a State statutory authority, and interference with police investigations in New South Wales.[41]

Murphy, prior to his appointment as a justice of the High Court of Australia, was a senator of the Australian Parliament, and subsequently became the leader of the Australian Labor Party (ALP) opposition in the Senate. When the ALP came to power in 1972, he became the federal

2006), pp. 416–34. In New South Wales, a Conduct Division of the Judicial Commission of New South Wales provides a report to the Attorney-General, who must then table it before both Houses of the New South Wales Parliament if the Conduct Division is of the view that the matter justifies parliamentary consideration of the removal of a judicial officer. In Queensland, a tribunal consisting of three members is appointed by the Legislative Assembly. A judge is removed if a finding of the tribunal proving misbehaviour or incapacity on the balance of probabilities is accepted by the Legislative Assembly. In the ACT, an enactment relating to the removal of a judicial officer must provide for the appointment of an *ad hoc* commission by the Executive prior to a motion for removal being considered by the Assembly.

40 See A. R. Blackshield, 'The Appointment and Removal of Federal Judges', in B. Opeskin and F. Wheeler (eds.), *The Australian Judicial System* (Melbourne: Melbourne University Press, 2000), pp. 410–22.

41 G. Lindell, 'The Murphy Affair in Retrospect', in H. P. Lee and G. Winterton (eds.), *Australian Constitutional Landmarks* (Melbourne: Cambridge University Press, 2003), pp. 282–3.

Attorney-General and Minister for Customs and Excise. He was appointed to the High Court in 1975. The political heat generated by the publication of the series of articles was so great that the federal Attorney-General (Senator Gareth Evans) sought an opinion from the Commonwealth Solicitor-General on the meaning of 'proved misbehaviour' as a first step to determining whether the judge should be removed from office. The opinion of the Solicitor-General provided a narrow scope to the expression 'proved misbehaviour'.[42] The Solicitor-General in his advisory opinion concluded that 'misbehaviour' in s. 72 is limited in meaning to matters pertaining to '(1) judicial office, including non-attendance, neglect or refusal to perform duties; and (2) the commission of an offence against the general law of such a quality as to indicate that the incumbent is unfit to exercise the office.'[43]

The Senate resolved to appoint a committee to inquire into the various allegations against Justice Murphy. A wider meaning of 'misbehaviour' was asserted by C. W. Pincus QC in an opinion given to the Senate Select Committee on the Conduct of a Judge.[44] It was 'for Parliament to decide whether any conduct alleged against a judge constitutes misbehaviour sufficient to justify removal from office'. Pincus said that there was no 'technical' meaning of the word and rejected the need to prove that an offence has been committed. Following its inconclusive findings, a second select committee, the Senate Select Committee on Allegations Concerning a Judge, which included two retired judges to assist the committee, was established.[45] A majority concluded in a report that Justice Murphy had attempted to influence the course of justice in relation to the proceedings against Ryan and that the conduct of the judge fell within the scope of 'proved misbehaviour'. In a criminal prosecution on charges which included a charge of attempting to pervert the course of justice, Justice Murphy was convicted by the Supreme Court of New South Wales. His conviction was quashed by the New South Wales Court of Appeal, which ordered a retrial. The judge was acquitted at the retrial. Nevertheless, further disclosures led to the

[42] G. Griffith, 'In the Matter of Section 72 of the Constitution', Opinion of the Commonwealth Solicitor-General, 24 February 1984, Cth Parl. Deb. (Senate) 28 February 1984, pp. 32–6.

[43] Griffith, 'In the Matter of Section 72 of the Constitution', at para. 23.

[44] *Report of the Senate Select Committee on the Conduct of a Judge*, Cth Parl. Paper No. 168/1984, App. 4.

[45] *Report of the Senate Select Committee on Allegations Concerning a Judge*, Cth Parl. Paper No. 271/1984.

establishment of a Parliamentary Committee of Inquiry comprising three retired judges. Before the committee could hand down its report, Justice Murphy died of cancer. The evidence relating to the saga was controversially sealed under a special Act of Parliament for 30 years (until 2016). However, the report of the committee relating to its understanding of the phrase 'proved misbehaviour' was published. This committee found that the phrase has a broad meaning. According to Sir George Lush, the word 'misbehaviour' in s. 72 is used in its ordinary meaning and is not used in the restricted sense of 'misconduct in office'. It is also not confined to conduct of a criminal nature.[46] Another member of the committee, Sir Richard Blackburn, said that 'proved misbehaviour' refers to such misconduct 'whether criminal or not, and whether or not displayed in the actual exercise of judicial functions, as, being morally wrong, demonstrates the unfitness for office of the judge in question'.[47] Andrew Wells, construed the word 'misbehaviour' as extending to the 'conduct of the judge in or beyond the execution of his judicial office, that represents so serious a departure from standards of proper behaviour by such a judge that it must be found to have destroyed public confidence that he will continue to do his duty under and pursuant to the Constitution'.[48] Given that the maintenance of public confidence in the judiciary is of fundamental importance, the broad reading of 'proved misbehaviour' is clearly the better view.

The process involved in the attempt to remove Justice Murphy is clearly unsatisfactory. It led to the pertinent observation that in a contested case, with political overtones, 'the traditional parliamentary procedures were unable in any satisfactory way to ascertain what had occurred or whether what had occurred could warrant removal'.[49]

The Ian Callinan affair

In 1998, there were calls for a parliamentary inquiry into certain conduct of Justice Callinan of the High Court of Australia arising from an adverse

[46] 'Parliamentary Commission of Inquiry Re The Honourable Mr Justice Murphy' (1986) 2 *Australian Bar Review* 203 at 209.

[47] 'Parliamentary Commission of Inquiry Re The Honourable Mr Justice Murphy' (1986) 2 *Australian Bar Review* 203 at 221.

[48] 'Parliamentary Commission of Inquiry Re The Honourable Mr Justice Murphy' (1986) 2 *Australian Bar Review* 203 at 230.

[49] R. E. McGarvie, 'The Foundations of Judicial Independence in a Modern Democracy', paper delivered at the Australian Bar Association Conference, Darwin, 8 July 1990, p. 12. See also Campbell and Lee, *The Australian Judiciary*, pp. 108–9.

finding made by a Federal Court judge in proceedings in which Callinan was only a witness.[50] The conduct in question occurred some twelve years before his judicial appointment. He was found in his role as a barrister 'to have acquiesced and approved the institution of legal proceedings against a creditor as a delaying tactic to prevent the enforcement of a claim for moneys owing to the creditors when there was an absence of evidence to support the commencement of the same legal proceedings based on allegations of fraud'.[51] The federal Attorney-General, taking into account the information available to him and the divergent views of eminent constitutional lawyers as to the meaning of 'proved misbehaviour', decided that an inquiry was unwarranted.[52]

The removal of Justice Angelo Vasta

In 1989, Justice Angelo Vasta of the Supreme Court of Queensland became the first judge to be removed from office since federation.[53] His removal by the Queensland Legislative Assembly followed the publication of a report by a commission of inquiry which had been established to advise the Legislative Assembly whether any behaviour of the judge 'since his appointment as a Judge of the Supreme Court either of itself or in conjunction with other behaviour' warranted his removal from judicial office. This inquiry arose from an earlier Commission of Inquiry into Alleged Activities and Associated Police Misconduct headed by Mr Fitzgerald QC. The report of the Parliamentary Judges Commission of Inquiry[54] contained a number of adverse findings against the judge. James Thomas explained:

> Four of these adverse findings are of sham transactions to gain income tax advantages; one was of false claims for taxation deductions in respect of the lease of a library; one was of a false statement to an accountant to facilitate tax evasion by a company run by his brother-in-law; one was of the making and maintaining of conspiracy allegations against the Chief Justice, the Attorney-General and Mr Fitzgerald QC; and one was the giving of false evidence at a defamation hearing.[55]

[50] Campbell and Lee, *The Australian Judiciary*, pp. 103–5.
[51] Lindell, 'The Murphy Affair in Retrospect', p. 288.
[52] Campbell and Lee, *The Australian Judiciary*, pp. 104–5.
[53] Campbell and Lee, *The Australian Judiciary*, pp. 105–6.
[54] The Commission comprised three retired judges: Sir Harry Gibbs (presiding), Sir George Lush and Michael Helsham.
[55] J. Thomas, *Judicial Ethics in Australia*, 3rd edn. (Sydney: LexisNexis Butterworths, 2009), p. 155.

Justice Vasta appeared before the Queensland Parliament to respond to the adverse findings. A seven-hour debate ensued and a motion calling for his removal was carried on the voices.[56] The Parliamentary Judges Commission of Inquiry, in a second report, voiced the opinion that the holding of an inquiry into the question of 'whether "any behaviour" of a judge warrants removal is open to grave objection'. It added:

> It is one thing to inquire into specific allegations of impropriety but it is quite another to conduct an inquisition into all aspects of a judge's life. An inquiry of the latter kind exposes the judiciary to unacceptable risks that pressure will be applied to its members and becomes especially dangerous if instigated by pressure groups or as a result of media clamour.[57]

The Justice Vince Bruce affair

The Justice Vince Bruce affair pertains to the 'incapacity' ground of removal. Following a complaint to the Judicial Commission of New South Wales and a report by its Conduct Division, a motion calling for Justice Bruce to address the Legislative Council and show cause why he should not be removed from judicial office was moved by the state Attorney-General. The majority report stated that there had been a great number of instances of delay in the delivery of reserved judgments which were 'unacceptable by any reasonable standard'. The majority added:

> The failure to adhere to assurances of performance which Justice Bruce knew or suspected would be conveyed to litigants has been shown to result in both distress and hardship to litigants. Incapacity to perform judicial duties has been proven to have been present from, at least, early 1995 and continues.

On 16 June 1998, Justice Bruce addressed the Legislative Council and explained that the delay was occasioned by clinical depression. The Legislative Council voted 24–16 not to remove him from office. On 22 February 1999, the judge resigned from the Supreme Court of New South Wales, following a retrial ordered by the New South Wales Court of Appeal necessitated by substantial errors made by the judge in a murder trial and also further complaints of procrastination and 'failure to deliver reserved judgments within a reasonable time'.[58]

[56] Thomas, *Judicial Ethics in Australia*, p. 157.
[57] Thomas, *Judicial Ethics in Australia*, p. 157.
[58] Thomas, *Judicial Ethics in Australia*, p. 58.

Recent controversies

In 2009, the Attorney-General of the Australian Capital Territory (ACT) announced the establishment of a judicial commission comprising three retired Supreme Court judges from other jurisdictions to inquire into a complaint brought by two magistrates against the Chief Magistrate of the ACT (Ron Cahill) alleging that

> on or about 21 October 2009, the Chief Magistrate caused or procured the creation and transmission of written material to Special Magistrate Peter Lauritsen which had or might have had the effect of interfering with the conduct of criminal proceedings to be heard by him relating to a public figure known professionally and socially to the Chief Magistrate before the proceedings commenced.[59]

The commission, which had not commenced its investigation, was abandoned following the resignation of the Chief Magistrate.[60]

Judicial complaints-handling process

Currently at federal level and among the states (except for New South Wales) there are no formal processes 'to address complaints about judicial officers that are serious, but not serious enough to warrant removal from office'.[61] This is a topic which has attracted much debate in recent times. The 'traditional approach' towards complaints of a less serious nature is to leave it in the hands of the appropriate head of court who would approach and have an informal private discussion with the judge concerned. However, it is also acknowledged that such an approach has its limitation:

> Peer pressure, embarrassment, fear of loss of reputation, respect for the authority of the head of court, or dislike of confrontation, normally enables this informal system to work effectively. However, there is ultimately very little to prevent a judge from ignoring the friendly suggestions of the head or his or her court.[62]

[59] www.chiefminister.act.gov.au/media.php?v=8861, accessed 5 February 2010.

[60] www.abc.net.au/news/stories/2009/11/17/2744775.htm, accessed 9 June 2010. For another instance of a judicial resignation before the completion of an inquiry, see L. J. King, 'Removal of Judges' (2003) 6(2) *The Flinders Journal of Law Reform* 169 at 177.

[61] 'Foreword' by R. Hulls to *Investigating Complaints and Concerns regarding Judicial Conduct*, discussion paper, Department of Justice, Victoria, 2009, p. 1.

[62] *Investigating Complaints and Concerns regarding Judicial Conduct*, para. 3.2.1.

Except for the High Court, the Federal Court, the Family Court and the Federal Magistrates' Court have each published a complaints protocol, which is available on each court's website.

Protocols for handling complaints against judicial officers can be found in some states (For example, Victoria and Western Australia) and the Northern Territory. So far New South Wales is the only state which has a standing statutory body which is empowered to examine complaints against judicial officers. The Judicial Commission of New South Wales was established by the Judicial Officers Act 1986 (NSW) and consists of ten members: six *ex officio* members from the judiciary (including the Chief Justice of the Supreme Court of New South Wales) and four members appointed by the Governor on the nomination of the minister. Of the four appointed members, one shall be a representative of the barristers and solicitors (following consultation with the President of the New South Wales Bar Association and the President of the Law Society of New South Wales) and three are persons nominated following consultation with the state Chief Justice and who, in the opinion of the minister, have 'high standing in the community'.[63]

Anyone may complain to the commission about 'a matter that concerns or may concern the ability or behaviour of a judicial officer'.[64] The state Attorney-General may refer a matter to the commission.[65] On receipt of a complaint, the commission is required to conduct a preliminary investigation; it can then summarily dismiss the complaint, classify it as 'minor' or classify it as 'serious'. A 'serious' complaint is one which, if substantiated, could, in the opinion of the commission, justify parliamentary consideration of the removal of the judicial officer. A 'minor' complaint may be referred to the appropriate head of jurisdiction or to the Conduct Division (a panel consisting of two judicial officers and one community representative[66] nominated by Parliament). All serious complaints are referred to the Conduct Division. If the Conduct Division is of the view that the matter may justify parliamentary consideration of the removal of the judicial officer, the Attorney-General must lay the report before both Houses of Parliament. A judicial officer may be removed by the Governor on an address from both Houses of Parliament seeking

[63] Judicial Officers Act 1986 (NSW), s. 5(5). A quorum of members is seven, of whom at least one must be an appointed member: Schedule 2 to the Act.

[64] Judicial Officers Act 1986 (NSW), s. 15.

[65] Judicial Officers Act 1986 (NSW), s. 16.

[66] The inclusion of a community representative was prescribed by the Judicial Officers Amendment Act 2007 (NSW).

removal on the ground of misbehaviour or incapacity. It should also be noted that apart from examining complaints against judicial officers, the commission has two other principal functions: (1) assisting the courts to achieve consistency in sentencing; and (2) organising and supervising continuing education and training for judicial officers.

Such a body was established against vigorous objections by the judges of the state.[67] After more than two decades of operation of the Judicial Commission of New South Wales, the general view seems to be that it 'has worked well, effectively and fairly, without endangering the independence of the judiciary, or the reputation of individual judges'.[68] Judicial wariness towards a judicial commission has diminished. At federal level, the Senate Legal and Constitutional Affairs References Committee has recommended that the federal government should establish a federal judicial commission modelled on the Judicial Commission of New South Wales.[69] It was further recommended that the current functions of the National Judicial College of Australia be incorporated into the new judicial commission.[70] Federal Chief Magistrate Pascoe has expressly supported the establishment of a federal judicial commission.[71]

In 2006, the Chief Justice of Western Australia, the Hon. Wayne Martin, wrote a letter to the then state Attorney-General (Jim McGinty) stating *inter alia*:

> I receive approximately two complaints per week relating to Judges and Magistrates in various Western Australian courts. I lack any facility or capacity to appropriately investigate or respond to those complaints, although obviously if they were of a kind which suggested significant misconduct, I would refer them to the appropriate Head of Jurisdiction for investigation. However, neither I nor any other Head of Jurisdiction has appropriate facilities or mechanisms for the conduct of such investigations, and there may well be situations in which it may be alleged by either the complainant or the judicial officer that the Head of Jurisdiction has a conflict of interest in the conduct of such an investigation. In my own case, there are also potential difficulties in any personal involvement in complaint assessment if the complaint concerns the conduct of a case

67 See 'New Formalised Judicial Accountability System Established in New South Wales' (1987) 61 *Australian Law Journal* 157 at 158.

68 A. Mason, 'Judicial Accountability, Judicial Conduct and Ethics', Conference Papers, Dublin, Ireland, 6 May 2000, at p. 111, citing, *inter alia*, the views of two former chief justices (Murray Gleeson and Sir Gerard Brennan CJJ).

69 *Australia's Judicial System and the Role of Judges*, para. 7.82.

70 *Australia's Judicial System and the Role of Judges*, para. 7.84.

71 *Australia's Judicial System and the Role of Judges*, para. 7.35.

> which is proceeding and in respect of which an appeal to the Supreme Court is a possibility, because of potential prejudice to my capacity to sit on that appeal, or the possibility of action on my part that might be said to prejudge the outcome of such an appeal.[72]

Chief Justice Wayne Martin proposed the adoption by Western Australia of a judicial commission modelled on the Judicial Commission of New South Wales.[73]

On 2 June 2010, the then Premier of the State of Victoria (John Brumby) announced that his government would introduce a judicial commission to investigate allegations of misconduct against magistrates, judges and members of the Victorian Civil and Administrative Tribunal (VCAT).[74] The then state Attorney-General (Rob Hulls) elaborated on this proposed mechanism. It would consist of the heads of the five Victorian courts and VCAT and four non-judicial, non-lawyer community members.[75] The new coalition government in Victoria is also committed to legislating for the establishment of a judicial complaints commission to investigate complaints about poor or inappropriate performance by judges, magistrates or VCAT officers.

The feasibility of 'a national judicial complaints-handling mechanism to facilitate consistent handling of complaints across jurisdictions' is currently being considered by a Standing Committee of Attorneys-General working group.[76] However, the idea of a national judicial commission has recently been rejected by the Council of Chief Justices.[77]

Suspension of judges

To protect the integrity and reputation of a court when a member is subject to removal proceedings it may be necessary to suspend the judge from office. The view is that in the absence of a statutory provision,

[72] www.aph.govau/senate/committee/legcon_ctte/judicial_system/add_info/ 10_chiefjustice-wa_letter.pdf, accessed 9 June 2010.

[73] *Australia's Judicial System and the Role of Judges*, paras. 7.28–7.29.

[74] The manner in which it was developed was criticised as 'high-handed' and that consultation with the Victorian judges was 'desultory and misleading'. See C. Merritt. 'Getting Judges Offside Hardly the Right Way to Start Reform', *The Australian*, 11 June 2010, p. 38. See also M. Warren, 'Scrutiny, Study: A Marriage Set to Fail', *The Australian*, 11 June 2010, p. 38.

[75] Judicial Commission of Victoria Bill 2010. Second reading on 2 September 2010.

[76] *Australia's Judicial System and the Role of Judges*, para. 7.42.

[77] *Investigating Complaints and Concerns Regarding Judicial Conduct*, para. 3.5.

attempts to suspend the judge 'may be highly questionable'.[78] General statutory provision for the suspension of judicial officers exist in New South Wales and the ACT, while a variety of statutory provisions pertaining to the suspension of magistrates are found in the other states.[79] The federal Constitution does not expressly invest any person or body with a power to suspend a federal judge from office. However, recent amendments effected by the Access to Justice (Civil Litigation Reforms) Amendment Act 2009 (No. 117, 2009), Schedule 3 to the Family Law Act 1975,[80] the Federal Court of Australia Act 1976[81] and the Federal Magistrates' Act 1999[82] have empowered the Chief Judge of the Family Court, the Chief Justice of the Federal Court and the Chief Federal Magistrate to 'temporarily restrict a judge to non-sitting duties' in relation to their respective court.

Conclusion

Insofar as judicial appointments are concerned, there has been no great interest on the part of governments at both federal and state level to alter the current process by transferring the power of appointing judges from the executive to another entity, such as a judicial appointments commission. Neither has there been established a standing judicial commission with the power to make recommendations regarding appointments to the federal and state courts. At federal level there has been some streamlining of the process whereby standing advisory panels are established by the federal Attorney-General to provide him with advice on judicial appointments. There has been some shift in judicial thinking regarding the establishment of a body to deal with complaints concerning judicial conduct which is not sufficiently serious to warrant removal from judicial office.

[78] Campbell and Lee, *The Australian Judiciary*, p. 111.
[79] Campbell and Lee, *The Australian Judiciary*, p. 111. [80] Section 21B.
[81] Section 15(1AA). [82] Section 12(3).

3

Appointment, discipline and removal of judges in Canada

MARTIN L. FRIEDLAND

I had not given much thought to judicial independence until I did a study for the Canadian Judicial Council in the mid-1990s on the subject. My report, A *Place Apart: Judicial Independence and Accountability in Canada*,[1] examined a wide range of issues relating to judicial independence and accountability, including security of tenure, financial security, discipline, codes of conduct, administering the court system and appointments. Those topics were approached from a historical and comparative perspective. I will, of course, be drawing on that study, as well as several later articles, for this chapter on two important aspects of judicial independence: judicial selection and judicial conduct in Canada. First, some background.

What is the Canadian Judicial Council? The Council is composed of all the federally appointed chief justices and associate chief justices in Canada – at present thirty-nine in total – and was chaired at the time of my study by Chief Justice Antonio Lamer. The Council, which had been established by legislation in 1971 by the then Minister of Justice, John Turner, grew out of the annual conference of federal chief justices that John Edwards of the University of Toronto's Centre of Criminology had established in 1964. The Council would, as was stated on second reading of the legislation, 'provide a national forum for the judiciary in Canada, and . . . strive to bring about greater efficiency and uniformity in judicial services and to improve their quality'. It would also provide a new and better forum to investigate complaints against the federal judiciary, at

[1] M. L. Friedland, *A Place Apart: Judicial Independence and Accountability in Canada* (Ottawa, 1995). The phrase 'a place apart' comes from a speech given by Senator Arthur Meighen in the Canadian Senate in 1932, where he stated that 'a judge is in no sense under the direction of the Government . . . The judge is in a place apart'.

the time handled by the Department of Justice, which could be followed by an *ad hoc* commission, such as the much criticized single-judge inquiry several years earlier into the conduct of Justice Leo Landreville.[2]

A wide-ranging study was thought necessary in the early 1990s because many matters involving the independence of the judiciary were then the subject of debate. One important question was what role the judiciary should play in the running of the courts. In 1981, Jules Deschênes, the Chief Justice of Quebec, had written a report in collaboration with Professor Carl Baar on the issue. The Deschênes report, *Masters in Their Own House* (*Maîtres chez eux*),[3] which had been commissioned by the Council, advocated greater administrative and budgetary independence for the judiciary along the lines of federal courts in the United States. Since the report's publication relatively little progress had been made, and some members of the Council wanted action.

Another issue then being debated was the disciplining of judges. The then Minister of Justice in the Mulroney Government, Kim Campbell, had met with the full Council in March 1992 and had expressed concern about the discipline process. 'Some of my provincial and territorial colleagues,' she told Council, 'had serious concerns that judicial independence was being used as a shield from public scrutiny.' Some former judges, her colleagues were suggesting, had avoided disciplinary hearings by claiming a medical disability, and in some of these cases the former judge had returned to gainful employment while continuing to receive a full pension.[4]

The judiciary had other concerns, such as the possibility that some form of judicial evaluation would be brought in and that sensitivity training through judicial education would be imposed. Nova Scotia was considering introducing judicial evaluation, and former Supreme Court of Canada justice Bertha Wilson was at the time chairing a committee that was about to bring in a report for the Canadian Bar Association that might recommend compulsory sensitivity training.[5]

[2] Friedland, *A Place Apart*, pp. 87–90.

[3] J. Deschênes, *Masters in their Own House: A Study on the Independent Judicial Administration of the Courts* (Ottawa: Canadian Judicial Council, 1981).

[4] M. L. Friedland, *My Life in Crime and Other Academic Adventures* (Osgoode Society and University of Toronto Press, 2007), p. 383.

[5] Canadian Bar Association Task Force on Gender Equality in the Legal Profession, *Touchstones for Change: Equality, Diversity and Accountability* (Ottawa: CBA, 1993) (Chair: Bertha Wilson).

I had not taken public positions on any of the topics, and so it was probably thought that I could examine the issues reasonably objectively; hence, my selection for that interesting project.

In the spring of 1994, after I had done considerable research with the assistance of a number of excellent research assistants and had formed some tentative ideas, I travelled to every province and territory in Canada, meeting with chief justices, other members of the judiciary, government officials, lawyers and academics. The process of consultation was often tricky. Federally appointed judges have a lobby group, called at the time the Canadian Judges Conference, that does not always agree with the positions taken by the Canadian Judicial Council. In setting up meetings with regular judges, I made sure that members of the conference were well represented. I usually met separately with Court of Appeal judges. I also met separately with provincially appointed judges, sometimes with and sometimes without their chief judge being present. Although the study was done for the Council responsible for federally appointed judges, I took the position that the independence of the provincially appointed judges should be studied as well. For the most part, the public does not distinguish between federally and provincially appointed judges.

These meetings were very helpful in sorting out my thoughts. Moreover, I was able to see parts of the country that I might not otherwise have seen, such as Yellowknife in the Northwest Territories and Whitehorse in the Yukon. In Whitehorse, the courthouse and the Attorney-General's department were in the same building, constructed in the mid-1980s, but separated by an atrium with an upper walkway between the two sides. The judges objected to the walkway because it gave the appearance of too close a connection between the courts and the executive. The solution was to place several large potted trees on the walkway, which prevented passage between the two sides. I took a number of pictures of the walkway, which at one point I thought might appear on the cover of my report. I do not know if the trees are still there.[6]

I also spent a productive week in England, meeting with a number of knowledgeable academics, such as Robert Stevens, who had recently written a book on judicial independence, with some key people in the Lord Chancellor's office, with the chair of the Law Commission, Sir Henry Brooke, and with the Lord Chief Justice of England, Peter Taylor. I also met with a number of barristers, including David Pannick, who subsequently

[6] Friedland, *My Life in Crime*, p. 387.

wrote a favourable article in the London *Times* ('Wanted: judges to judge the judges') on my report. The visit to England was particularly valuable because change was in the air in the United Kingdom, but was not yet publicly documented, such as changes in the appointment process and the administration of the courts.[7]

Let me give a brief summary of the structure of the Canadian judiciary and some of the relevant constitutional provisions. There are a little over 1,000 federally appointed judges in Canada, including appellate courts and supernumerary judges, and about 1,500 provincially appointed judges.[8] In s. 96 of the 1867 British North America Act, now the Constitution Act, the federal government was given the power to appoint judges to the superior courts, even though the power over the administration of justice in each province was given to the provinces. In almost all federations the provinces or states have the appointing power over their own courts. The exceptions, according to one writer, are India, Austria and Venezuela.[9] I speculate in my study that the main reason that the federal government was given the appointing power was that 'the key players in Confederation who were moving on to the federal stage wanted to keep patronage over appointments in their own hands'.[10]

The key provision in the Constitution Act[11] relating to judicial independence is s. 99 which provides: 'The Judges of the Superior Courts shall hold office during good behaviour, but shall be removable by the Governor-General on Address of the Senate and House of Commons.' I will, of course, say more about this section when I deal with the removal of judges.

A third provision relating to pay and pensions, which I will not deal with in this chapter, is s. 100 which provides: 'The Salaries, Allowances, and Pensions of the Judges of the Superior, District, and County Courts ... shall be fixed and provided by the Parliament of Canada.' The only constitutional amendment to the above provisions was in 1960, when a further clause was added to s. 99, making retirement at age 75 compulsory for all superior court judges.

[7] Friedland, *My Life in Crime*, p. 389.

[8] See F. L. Morton, 'Judicial Appointments in Post-Charter Canada: A System in Transition', in K. Malleson and P. H Russell (eds.), *Appointing Judges in an Age of Judicial Power: Critical Perspectives from around the World* (University of Toronto Press, 2006), pp. 56–7.

[9] Morton, 'Judicial Appointments in Post-Charter Canada', p. 73.

[10] Friedland, *A Place Apart*, p. 234.

[11] The Constitution Act 1982, being Schedule B to the Canada Act 1982 (UK), 1982, c. 11.

The preamble to the Act, which states that Canada is to have a Constitution 'similar in Principle to that of the United Kingdom', has also played a role in enhancing judicial independence. Chief Justice Brian Dickson, for example, stated in a 1985 Supreme Court of Canada case that: 'Since judicial independence has been for centuries an important principle of the Constitution of the United Kingdom, it is fair to infer that it was transferred to Canada by the constitutional language of the preamble.'[12] The preamble was also relied on by Chief Justice Lamer for the court in the 1997 *Remuneration of Judges of the Provincial Court* case,[13] who referred to the preamble as 'the grand entrance hall to the castle of the Constitution'. In that important case the Supreme Court held that judicial independence requires that all governments in Canada set up an 'independent, objective, and effective' commission to determine salaries and benefits.[14] That case was the subject of a recent conference[15] held at the University of Toronto Law School and a book that grew out of the conference.[16]

The three key sections of the Constitution Act – s. 96 (the appointing power), s. 99 (hold office during 'good behaviour') and s. 100 (salaries 'fixed and provided') – were referred to by Lord Atkin in a 1938 Privy Council case as 'three principal pillars in the temple of justice' and, he went on to say, 'they are not to be undermined'.[17]

In addition to the above provisions, Canada now has a Charter of Rights and Freedoms, enacted as part of the Constitution in 1982. Section 11(d) of the Charter states that a person 'charged with an offence has the right . . . to be presumed innocent until proven guilty according to law in a fair and public hearing by an independent and impartial tribunal'.[18] The section applies to those 'charged with an offence', and this encompasses criminal and quasi-criminal charges. Section 7 of the Charter could also be used to enhance judicial independence: 'Everyone has the right to life, liberty and security of the person and the right not to be deprived thereof except in accordance with the principles of

[12] Friedland, *A Place Apart*, p. 234; *R* v. *Beauregard* [1986] 2 SCR 56 at 72.

[13] *Ref. re Remuneration of Judges of the Provincial Court of P.E.I.* [1997] 3 SCR 3.

[14] *Ref. re Remuneration of Judges of the Provincial Court of PARTEE.I.* [1997] 3 SCR 3 at 103.

[15] See www.law-lib.utoronto.ca/conferences/judicial_independence/index.htm.

[16] A. Dodek and L. Sossin (eds.), *Judicial Independence in Context* (Toronto: Irwin Law, 2010).

[17] *Toronto* v. *York* [1938] AC 415 at 426; Friedland, *A Place Apart*, p. 7.

[18] Canadian Charter of Rights and Freedoms, Part I of the Constitution Act 1982, being Schedule B to the Canada Act 1982 (UK), 1982, c. 11.

fundamental justice.' But in most cases, as Chief Justice Antonio Lamer pointed out, 's. 7 does not offer greater protection than the highly specific guarantee under s. 11(d)'.[19]

The first case interpreting s. 11(d) – and the most important – is the 1985 case of *Valente*.[20] Within a year of the Charter being enacted, a challenge was made to the independence of the Ontario Provincial Court bench. There were eighteen grounds alleged for holding that the judge was not independent. Many of these involved differences from federally appointed s. 96 judges. Salaries, for example, were determined by the executive branch and not by the legislature as with s. 96 judges. Further, removal of a provincial court judge did not, as with s. 96 judges, require a vote by the legislature. Justice Gerald Le Dain, for a unanimous Supreme Court, dismissed the accused's appeal, adopting the test of 'whether the tribunal may be reasonably perceived as independent'.[21] There is, the court stated, no one standard applicable to all courts in Canada.

As to security of tenure, Justice Le Dain held that while the Ontario provision 'falls short of the ideal or highest degree of security',[22]

> it reflects what may be reasonably perceived as the essentials of security of tenure for purposes of s. 11(d) of the Charter: that the judge be removable only for cause, and that cause be subject to independent review and determination by a process at which the judge affected is afforded a full opportunity to be heard. The essence of security of tenure for purposes of s.11(d) is a tenure, whether until an age of retirement, for a fixed term, or for a specific adjudicative task, that is secure against interference by the Executive or other appointing authority in a discretionary or arbitrary manner.

Judicial selection

Judicial selection is directly relevant to judicial independence in the case of the elevation of a judge to a higher court or the selection of a chief justice. There is a blatant conflict of interest for every judge who is interested in moving to a higher court or becoming a chief justice. If the power of selection is solely in the hands of the executive there is a danger that the judge will try to seem attractive to the government and thus be considered for the position. As a former English judge observed: 'A judge who often found against the government, or in some other way

[19] *R* v. *Généreux* [1992] 1 SCR 259 at 310.
[20] *Valente* v. *R* [1985] 2 SCR 673; see Friedland, *A Place Apart*, pp. 8–10.
[21] *Valente* v. *R* [1985] 2 SCR 673 at 689. [22] *Valente* v. *R* [1985] 2 SCR 673 at 698.

displeased the executive, might find that promotion did not come his way.'[23] If that is so, how can we permit the government alone to choose who is to go to a higher court or become a chief justice? I will return to this issue later.

Judicial selection is indirectly related to judicial independence in a general way because the sounder the appointment, the less that disciplinary action will later be needed. Further, weak appointments lower the status of the judiciary in the eyes of the public and create a climate for interference with the necessary independence of the judiciary. Similarly, political appointments that are seen by the public as not based on merit may cause some to worry about the judge's future independence and impartiality on the bench.

Over the years politics was a major factor – if not *the* major factor – in the selection of federal judges in Canada. The formal appointment is made by the cabinet and this necessarily risks introducing strong political considerations into the selection. Prior to 1949 over 50 per cent of the Supreme Court of Canada judges had at some point in their career been elected politicians.[24] Professor R. C. B. Risk looked at all federal judicial appointments in Canada from 1945 to 1965 and concluded that 'all but a few of the judges appointed during [that] period were affiliated with the party in power at the time they were appointed, and most were actively engaged in politics'.[25] In 1957, the Canadian Bar Association recommended that the cabinet be eliminated from the process, but nothing came of this. The Canadian Bar Association kept pushing for change and was joined by the Canadian Association of Law Teachers. The *Landreville* case, which had led to changes in the discipline system, also helped to spur changes in the system of appointing judges. In the early 1970s, future Prime Minister, John Turner, as Trudeau's Minister of Justice, set up the position of Special Adviser on appointments, which was implemented by the subsequent Minister of Justice, Otto Lang, and a number of first-rate appointments were made.[26]

The enactment of the Charter in 1982 and the realization by the public that judges would play an increasingly important role in policy decisions helped to create a positive climate for changing the system. In 1985, both

[23] Friedland, *A Place Apart*, p. 255.

[24] Friedland, *A Place Apart*, p. 236; P. Russell, *The Judiciary in Canada* (Toronto: McGraw-Hill Ryerson, 1987), p. 115.

[25] Friedland, *A Place Apart*, p. 236; J. Willis, 'Methods of Appointing Judges – An Introduction' (1966) 3 *Canadian Legal Studies* 216 at 217.

[26] Friedland, *A Place Apart*, pp. 236–7.

the Canadian Bar Association and the Canadian Association of Law Teachers recommended that nominating councils be established in each province. Nothing was done during Prime Minister Brian Mulroney's first term of office (1984–8). Then in 1988, during Mulroney's second term, the Minister of Justice, Ray Hnatyshyn, who had been advocating changes in the system for many years, set up permanent committees in each province and territory consisting of five members, representative of the bench, the bar and the general public. Applications would now be required and would be sent to the Commissioner for Federal Judicial Affairs, who would submit the names to the applicable committees. The committee would determine whether the person was 'qualified' or 'not qualified'. Only initial appointments, not elevations within the federal judiciary, would be scrutinized by the committees. These were not nominating committees, but screening or vetting committees. Interviews were not done. The result was that the process normally gave the government a reasonably large pool of candidates from which to select judges.[27]

A number of changes were made over the years. In 1991, for example, the classification was changed to 'recommended', 'highly recommended' and 'unable to recommend'. Later, more than one committee was established in both Ontario and Quebec. Each committee would now consist of seven, rather than five, members, the extra two members being chosen by the Minister of Justice. According to the minister, this would 'facilitate the appointment of committees that more fully reflect the diversity of society', but, of course, it gave the minister greater input into the committees. Elevations of provincial court judges were no longer dealt with by the committees.[28]

Professors Peter Russell and Jacob Ziegel studied Mulroney's appointments in his first term and found that just under 50 per cent of those appointed had associations with the Progressive Conservative Party.[29] They did a further study, published in 1991 – after the new committees had been established – and concluded that the 1988 reforms had done 'little to address the basic flaws in the judicial appointment system'.[30] Professor F. L. Morton later conducted a study of Alberta federal

[27] Friedland, *A Place Apart*, p. 240. [28] Friedland, *A Place Apart*, p. 241.

[29] P. Russell and J. Ziegel, 'Federal Judicial Appointments: An Appraisal of the First Mulroney Government's Appointments and the New Judicial Advisory Committees' (1991) 41 *University of Toronto Law Journal* 4 at 19.

[30] Russell and Ziegel, 'Federal Judicial Appointments', at p. 34.

appointments between 1993 and 2000 and also concluded that 'little has changed'.[31]

The process tends to be different at the provincial level. I do not have the space here to analyse in detail the many different systems of selecting judges at the provincial and the territorial level. There is a full description of them in my study for the Canadian Judicial Council.[32] As in the federal system, in all cases the selection is made by the cabinet. Ontario led the way in reform, following the McRuer Royal Commission of Inquiry into Civil Rights, by the establishment of a Judicial Council in 1968 that had as one of its functions 'at the request of the Minister, to consider the proposed appointment of provincial judges and make a report thereon to the Minister'. It reacted to names submitted and did not search out or nominate candidates. The Ontario system was adopted in a number of other provinces. British Columbia also used a Judicial Council, but, unlike Ontario, it gave the Council the responsibility of collecting and recommending names to the Attorney-General.[33]

Quebec adopted a different approach in 1979. Each time a judicial vacancy occurs, the Minister of Justice establishes a selection committee. The vacancy is advertised and applications are sent directly to the committee. All technically qualified candidates are interviewed. The minister is notified of the candidates that the committee considers suitable for appointment and in practice makes the appointment from the list of names supplied. Using interviews was a change from the practice in other parts of the country.[34]

The final provincial scheme to be discussed here is the Ontario Judicial Appointments Advisory Committee, which was set up as a pilot project in 1988 and put on a permanent statutory basis in 1994. Professor Peter Russell was the first chair of the committee, with the majority of the members being lay persons. The committee advertises a vacancy, reviews the applications, establishes criteria to be used by the Committee, interviews a large number of candidates and for each vacancy gives the Attorney-General 'a ranked list of at least two candidates whom it recommends, with brief supporting reasons'. The Attorney-General may appoint 'only a candidate who has been recommended', although the Attorney-General 'may reject the Committee's recommendations and require it to provide a fresh list'.[35]

[31] Morton, 'Judicial Appointments in Post-Charter Canada', p. 68.

[32] Friedland, *A Place Apart*, pp. 243–6. [33] Friedland, *A Place Apart*, p. 243.

[34] Friedland, *A Place Apart*, p. 244. [35] Friedland, *A Place Apart*, p. 245.

In my study for the Canadian Judicial Council, I recommended that the federal government adopt something similar to the Ontario system. The present federal guidelines encourage, but do not require interviews. Perhaps interviews may not be necessary for elevations from the trial court to the Court of Appeal, where the appointees are usually well known by their reputations and written judgments. Surely they should be required for all appointments to the trial division. Canada does not, unlike in England, have probationary appointments. Many of the candidates would not be known to the majority of the committee members. In what other sphere do we make such important decisions without having had at least an opportunity for some of those making the decision to meet with the person to be selected? Certainly not in the academic world.

I also recommended that the committees reviewing superior court applications should play a greater role in narrowing the range of candidates from whom the government can choose. The present system gives the minister too much discretion to bring in non-relevant political considerations. Would it not be better to choose a system in which, say, at least three but not more than six names are put forward for a particular opening? This would tend to narrow the list to the better candidates, but would still give the minister a fair degree of flexibility in making appointments.[36]

Stephen Harper's Conservative government has, however, recently gone in the opposite direction. In 2006 it eliminated the category of 'highly recommended', which, in effect, gives the government wider scope to appoint who they want. It has also added a police representative to each committee and given the representative from the judiciary on each committee a vote only in the case of a tie. Given that restriction, the government now has the power to control the committees with its right to appoint four representatives to an eight-member committee, where there are seven voting members.[37]

This is politicizing the process more than is desirable. University of Ottawa law professor Ed Ratushny, who has been a student of the process for decades, told the Canadian press: 'It is part of a bigger picture where this government seems to have a strong underlying distrust of the [current] judiciary. I can't imagine what objective they could have in mind, other than to look for lawyers who will be hard-assed, law-and-order judges.'[38] I put it more strongly than is my custom in public statements. As the *Globe and*

[36] Friedland, *A Place Apart*, pp. 258–9. [37] Friedland, *My Life in Crime*, p. 399.

[38] 'Toews Under Fire for Plan to Let Police Play Role in Vetting Judges', *Canadian Press*, 16 November 2006 (QL).

Mail stated: 'University of Toronto professor Martin Friedland, an expert on judicial independence and the committees, said the expansion of Ottawa's control over committees that are supposed to be a check on federal politicking is "shocking, because it's such a blatant attempt to control the outcome".'[39] The Canadian Judicial Council was more circumspect, but still relatively blunt, stating that eliminating the 'highly recommended' category 'raises questions about whether the most qualified individuals will continue to be identified for appointment'. The Council also stated in its press release: 'Because the majority of voting members are now appointed by the Minister, the advisory committees may neither be, nor seen to be, fully independent of the government. This puts in peril the concept of an independent body that advises the government on who is best qualified to be a judge.'[40]

I will now deal with the issue of elevations to a higher court and then appointments to the Supreme Court of Canada. In my view, allowing government unlimited control of elevations poses more dangers to judicial independence than having others examine the merits of an elevation. The existing committee structure may not, however, be the appropriate one to consider elevations. It would be preferable to have a similar body, but with members appropriate for the task, to examine all trial judges who by their reputation, expertise, sound judgement and written reasons are thought to be likely candidates for a position. Applications from sitting judges would not be sought. The committee would recommend a ranked shortlist of names to the government. If the government went outside the list, the fact, but not the names, should be publicly known, perhaps through an annual report of the Commissioner for Federal Judicial Affairs.[41]

A similar committee should be established for the selection of a chief justice. I note that the selection of a United States circuit court chief judge is not in the hands of the government. Again, the universities may provide a possible solution. A search committee for a new dean is established to recommend a name to the board of governors. The committee is normally made up of the various estates interested in the selection.[42]

[39] 'Tories Deny Goal Is to Stack Court System', *Globe and Mail*, 14 February 2007 (A6).

[40] See Canadian Judicial Council, news release, 20 February 2007, available online at: www.cjc-ccm.gc.ca.

[41] Friedland, *A Place Apart*, pp. 255–7.

[42] Friedland, *A Place Apart*, pp. 225–32. These issues are thoroughly discussed in J. Ziegel, 'Promotion of Federally Appointed Judges and Appointment of Chief Justices', in Dodek and Sossin (eds.), *Judicial Independence in Context*, pp. 151–90.

The selection of members of the Supreme Court of Canada has understandably been of particular interest to the public and the press. The policy-making role of the Supreme Court is now reasonably obvious to most observers. Up until very recently the selection was made by the cabinet without any formal involvement of Parliament or an outside committee. In 2006, Marshall Rothstein of the Federal Court of Appeal was selected by Prime Minister Harper to fill the Supreme Court of Canada vacancy created by Justice John Major's retirement. Harper selected Rothstein in 2006 from a list of three names sent to the Minister of Justice by a committee made up of parliamentarians, lawyers and others. The list of three had emerged from a list of six names sent to the committee by the former Liberal government. There was then a hearing before a parliamentary committee in which Justice Rothstein was gently questioned. Unlike an American confirmation hearing, the committee did not vote on the issue.[43]

The procedure followed was strange. The committee that put forward the names should have been the one to interview the candidates to determine whether each person's name should have been put forward. Having the parliamentary committee interview the person already selected by the government is simply a rubber-stamping formality. Moreover, the earlier committee should have been able to suggest names not put forward by the government. There was a further opportunity by the Harper government to refine the system for appointing Supreme Court of Canada judges with the announcement in 2008 of the early retirement from the court of Justice Michel Bastarache. A new procedure was proposed by the government. A parliamentary committee of five – two from the government caucus and one from each of the opposition parties – would in a private session review a list of names put forward by the government and provide a three-candidate shortlist from which the government would choose. The person selected would appear at a public hearing of a parliamentary committee. Politics then took over. The committee did not function effectively and Harper announced that his choice was Tom Cromwell of the Nova Scotia Court of Appeal, who would appear before a parliamentary committee after the election that Harper had called. Politics again intervened, Parliament was prorogued shortly after Harper won the election, and Harper appointed Cromwell without a formal hearing.[44]

[43] Friedland, *My Life in Crime*, p. 398; 'Ottawa's best-kept secret?', *Maclean's*, 2 February 2009, pp. 20–4.

[44] Friedland, *A Place Apart*, pp. 240–2; 'Ottawa's best-kept secret?'.

All in all, I still like the relatively non-political scheme I suggest in *A Place Apart*. In my model, there would be a special nominating committee for each appointment to the Supreme Court. The committee could consist of nominees of the province or provinces traditionally associated with the particular appointment, nominees of legal groups and nominees of the federal government. I had not contemplated that parliamentarians would be on the committee, but it would be open to have them. The committee would present a short, possibly ranked, list of names to the government. Now comes the important part. If the government went outside the list, a public confirmation hearing would be held, perhaps by a joint committee of the House and Senate. There would obviously be strong pressure on the government not to go outside the shortlist of recommended candidates. Such a system would be a compromise between the American system requiring a confirmation hearing for all appointments to the Supreme Court and the Canadian system where, at the time I wrote my study, there were none. The special nominating committee would in a sense be a substitute for a confirmation hearing. It would be a proxy for the public.[45]

Thus far, I have not talked about the possibility of electing judges, as happens in many of the states in the United States. I barely touched on the possibility of the election of judges in *A Place Apart*, stating that 'the existence of elections . . . are not models that appear to have much if any support in Canada', even though they are used for a number of state courts in the United States.[46] A Canadian survey done in 2002 indicated, however, that there is, indeed, a surprising amount of support for electing judges. Two-thirds supported the popular election of judges.[47] It would be a disaster. Few things would be more destructive of the independence of the judiciary than to have judges campaign for office accepting contributions to pay for their campaigns, let alone having to run on a law-and-order platform.

Judicial conduct

The only procedure for removing a superior court judge in Canada today is, as set out in s. 99 of the Constitution Act, 'by the Governor-General on Address of the Senate and House of Commons'. We do not know exactly how a joint address in Canada would work because, since Confederation, we have never had a case in which a superior court

[45] Friedland, *A Place Apart*, pp. 256–7. [46] Friedland, *A Place Apart*, p. 254.
[47] Morton, 'Judicial Appointments in Post-Charter Canada', p. 56.

judge was so removed.[48] A number of federally appointed county and district court (not superior court) judges have been removed, but those judges could be removed by the federal cabinet and did not require a joint address.[49] In all cases thus far involving superior court judges, the judges resigned before Parliament could vote on their removal. Justice Leo Landreville, for example, who as mayor of Sudbury had accepted stock options for supporting a pipeline, resigned in 1967 after a joint committee of the House and the Senate had recommended his removal, but before debate on a motion for an address had commenced.[50] The latest resignation was in 2009, when Justice Paul Cosgrove resigned after the Canadian Judicial Council recommended that he be removed from office.[51] In Cosgrove's case, as in most other cases, he could therefore keep his full pension, having served the requisite number of years as a judge.

In my study I suggested that it would be wise for Parliament to consider the process that would apply to a joint address procedure before a specific case arose. The procedure could include provisions dealing with what parliamentary body or committee would hear the evidence, whether the judge would be entitled to be heard and call witnesses, and what the standard and burden of proof should be. At present, a simple majority in each House suffices. One constitutional amendment that should perhaps be considered is to raise the requirement beyond a simple majority of those voting. The present system, in my opinion, gives Parliament – and therefore the government – too much power. In the United States, two-thirds of the senate has to vote in favour of impeachment.[52]

Provincially appointed judges can in most provinces be removed by the cabinet. In Ontario, however, removal is by the legislature; in Quebec, it is by the Court of Appeal; and in British Columbia it can in effect be by the Judicial Council itself. In my view, removal of a provincially appointed judge is sufficiently important because of its effect on judicial independence that one wants substantial protection of the judge. It would be desirable for each province and territory to consider requiring that a final decision on removal be made either by the legislature or by the Court of Appeal.[53]

As stated above, the awkwardness and the uncertainty of the *Landreville* case helped bring about the creation of the Canadian Judicial Council in

[48] Friedland, *A Place Apart*, p. 77. [49] Friedland, *A Place Apart*, pp. 81–2.

[50] Friedland, *A Place Apart*, pp. 84–7.

[51] Canadian Judicial Council, *Annual Report 2008–2009*, p. 10, available online, at: www.cjc-ccm.gc.ca.

[52] Friedland, *A Place Apart*, pp. 129–30. [53] Friedland, *A Place Apart*, p. 130.

1971. One of the chief justices actively involved in setting up the Council referred to the 'awful fiasco' of the single-commissioner approach in *Landreville*. And John Turner, the then Minister of Justice, stated in an interview:[54]

> We felt that after the Landreville case [the Council] was a better vehicle for the self-discipline of the Bench than the Inquiries Act. And that a lot of these matters could be handled more discreetly at an earlier stage by the judges themselves with the [Council] than allowing an issue to deteriorate and then go public under the Inquiries Act.

The longest chapter in *A Place Apart* is the chapter on discipline. I carefully examined the Canadian Judicial Council's procedures and the Council gave me full access to all of their complaint files. My assessment of their procedures was positive. I stated in the report:[55]

> My overall opinion is that the Judicial Conduct Committee and the Executive Director have dealt with the matters received carefully and conscientiously. I never sensed that any matter was being 'covered up' by the Council after a complaint was made to it.

The procedure followed by the Council is as follows. Complaints can be made in writing against a federally appointed judge by any person, including a litigant, a fellow judge, a chief justice, a politician, a civil servant or the Council itself. Complaints can even be made anonymously. No special form is required. The chair of the Judicial Conduct Committee or one of the vice-chairs deals with the complaints. There is an average of about 170 complaints a year. A large number are complaints about the outcome of the case and not about the conduct of the judge and so the person complaining is advised of the normal appeal process. In about half the cases the judge in question and the judge's chief justice are asked for their comments on the complaint. In the vast majority of cases the issue is disposed of at this initial stage and the chair or vice-chair writes to the complainant explaining what has been decided. In some cases an outside counsel is engaged to investigate the allegation. I played such a role a few years ago in a complex case that required pouring over transcripts and interviewing a number of persons. Over 90 per cent of the complaints are disposed of within ten weeks.[56]

54 Friedland, *A Place Apart*, p. 88. 55 Friedland, *A Place Apart*, pp. 94–5.

56 Friedland, *A Place Apart*, pp. 90–8; Canadian Judicial Council, *Procedures for Dealing with Complaints made to the Canadian Judicial Council about Federally Appointed Judges* (January 2003); *Canadian Judicial Council Inquiries and Investigations By-Laws* (January 2003); *Making a Complaint*; Canadian Judicial Council, *Annual Report 2008–2009*, all available online at: www.cjc-ccm.gc.ca.

If the matter is not disposed of at this early stage, a panel of three to five judges is formed to consider in private whether a formal inquiry is required. A panel is also formed if the chair believes that there should be a reprimand of the judge in question. Judges who are not chief justices take part in these panel decisions. In most cases the file is closed, sometimes accompanied by an expression of concern about the judge's conduct or with a recommendation that the judge receive counselling or other similar remedial action.[57]

The next possible stage is a formal inquiry under the by-laws and rules of the Council. The Council judges who took part in the investigation do not take part in an inquiry. And the judges who participate in an inquiry do not take part in the deliberations of the full Council. Thus, there is a careful separation of investigation and adjudication processes. In my view this is preferable to the structure in some states of the United States of a complete separation of the offices and the personnel of investigation and adjudication.[58]

If the complaint is made to the Council by a provincial attorney-general or by the federal Minister of Justice then a formal inquiry is required.[59] Justice Cosgrove challenged the constitutionality of this aspect of the process, but the Federal Court of Appeal held that it is constitutional.[60] Whether it is desirable is another matter. In my report I took the position that it is desirable to permit the Minister of Justice to demand an inquiry, but questioned whether the provincial attorneys-general should have the same right. A provincial attorney-general can always ask the Council to examine the matter, but then it would be up to the Council to determine whether the matter warrants a full formal inquiry. In my opinion, if a provincial attorney-general wants a public inquiry, he or she should have to persuade the Council to undertake one or the federal Minister of Justice to order one.[61]

There were eight cases noted in my study where a formal inquiry had been initiated under the Judges Act 1985 since the creation of the Council in 1971.[62] There have been six cases since then.[63] As stated

[57] *Procedures for Dealing with Complaints made to the Canadian Judicial Council about Federally Appointed Judges*, at s. 5.3.

[58] *Procedures for Dealing with Complaints made to the Canadian Judicial Council about Federally Appointed Judges*, ss. 9.5, 9.9, 10.1.

[59] Friedland, *A Place Apart*, p. 91. [60] *Canada (A.G.)* v. *Cosgrove* 2007 FCA 103.

[61] Friedland, *A Place Apart*, pp. 96–7. [62] Friedland, *A Place Apart*, p. 97.

[63] Canadian Judicial Council, *Inquiry Committee Decisions*, available online at: www.cjc-ccm.gc.ca.

earlier, none of these fourteen cases led to a formal proceeding in Parliament because some did not result in a recommendation by the Inquiry Committee or by the Council for the removal of the judge or because the judge resigned before Parliament could act.

The Inquiry Committee consists of five or seven members, the majority of whom are members of the Council. Senior lawyers or judges make up the balance of the committee. The by-laws provide for the appointment of an independent counsel who presents the case to the Inquiry Committee as well as for a counsel to the committee. The hearings are open to the public, unless ordered closed by the committee. The Canadian Judicial Council receives the report of the Inquiry Committee and makes a recommendation to the Minister of Justice.[64]

One significant difference between Canadian and American federal disciplinary procedures is that the US federal judiciary initially refers complaints to the chief justice of the circuit to see if the issue can be informally resolved. I think Canada should adopt a similar system. For most matters, that is what is done in universities and other institutions. Deans try to resolve problems involving professors against whom a complaint is made. Why bring out the heavy artillery – and the anxiety it engenders – if it is not necessary? A number of provinces give the chief judge of the provincial court power to attempt to resolve the complaint at the very early stages. This recognizes that except in extreme cases the real purpose of the legislation is to change undesirable conduct, not to discipline the judge.[65]

Provincial disciplinary bodies have the power to impose lesser remedies than removal. Some councils provide for the possibility of suspension without pay. Ontario, for example, permits its Council to order up to a 30-day suspension without pay, and Manitoba provides for the possibility of suspension without pay during the period that the judge is receiving education or treatment.[66] I am not persuaded that such additional powers are needed at the federal level. The Council now recognizes that it has the power to do more than recommend dismissal, although in earlier periods it expressed doubt about having such powers. It can, and does, express its view that the judge should change his or her conduct in some way. This was one of the purposes of establishing the Council, according to my reading of the available evidence. The Council, for example, can say that the judge should get judgments out more

[64] Canadian Judicial Council Inquiries and Investigations By-Laws at ss. 2, 3, 5, 11 and 13.
[65] Friedland, *A Place Apart*, pp. 132–4. [66] Friedland, *A Place Apart*, pp. 105–13.

quickly or recommend that the judge should undertake alcohol treatment or take a particular educational course.[67] Relatively recent changes in the Council's procedures now recognize that this is within the Council's powers.[68] There would, of course, be a strong incentive for the judge not to disregard the Council's view in that repetition of the conduct would normally be treated more seriously by the Council in the future and if persisted in could lead to a recommendation that the judge be removed from office.

I do not have space in this chapter to go over all the inquiries; that would require a full-length book. I will simply touch on several of them. The *Gratton* case[69] in 1994 dealt with the issue of whether a judge who suffered a 'severe and debilitating stroke' could be removed under the discipline powers. The judge did not wish to resign, but hoped to be able to do such things as simple consent applications. The Council held, however, that such incapacity could be considered a lack of 'good behaviour' within the meaning of s. 99 of the Constitution and Gratton resigned. I took the position in my report that it would be better to treat such a case in the same way as it is dealt with in other parts of society, that is, through long-term disability status. We should not assume today that incapacity because of disability is necessarily permanent. The determination of incapacity should be made by the judiciary, and a further replacement appointment authorized after such a determination. This is now the practice in the US federal system. If the incapacitated judge recovers, he or she would return to the bench.[70]

The last inquiry to have been heard was the Cosgrove Inquiry, and that resulted in a recommendation by the Inquiry Committee that Justice Paul Cosgrove be removed from the bench. This was supported by the Council in March 2009. As stated above, Cosgrove then resigned.[71] One of the issues in the *Cosgrove* case dealt with the question of incompetence. The conduct by Cosgrove had taken place in a long murder case. Although the Inquiry Committee expressed the view that 'some of Justice Cosgrove's conduct demonstrated incompetence' which was 'bound to undermine public confidence in the administration of justice' the Council, after citing Professor Shimon Shetreet's view on the subject,

[67] Friedland, *A Place Apart*, pp. 139–40.

[68] *Procedures for Dealing with Complaints made to the Canadian Judicial Council about Federally Appointed Judges* at s. 5.3.

[69] *Gratton* v. *Canadian Judicial Council and Attorney-General of Canada* [1994] 2 FC 769.

[70] Friedland, *A Place Apart*, pp. 79–80.

[71] Canadian Judicial Council, *Annual Report 2008–2009*, p. 10.

took the position that 'whether incompetence can be a ground for removal from office, in any given case, would best be dealt with another day, when the issue is more directly raised'.[72]

In the *Matlow* case the previous year, an Inquiry Committee had recommended that Justice Theodore Matlow be removed from office, but this was not supported by the Council, although they strongly admonished him for his conduct.[73] Justice Matlow had actively opposed a municipal development close to where he lived and then did not recuse himself in a case involving the same municipal body. The Council Report dealt in some detail with the application of the code of conduct, *Ethical Principles for Judges*, published in 1998, that had been prepared by the Council and endorsed by it.[74] I had a chapter on codes of conduct in my report to the Council, which 'strongly recommended a code for the judiciary', stating: 'In my view . . . the US federal code would be a good starting point. The US code is used primarily for guidance and is not as directly tied to discipline as are most of the state codes.'[75]

The code prepared by the Council took that approach, stating:[76]

> The Statements, Principles and Commentaries are advisory in nature. Their goals are to assist judges with the difficult ethical and professional issues which confront them and to assist members of the public to better understand the judicial role. They are not and shall not be used as a code or a list of prohibited behaviours. They do not set out standards defining judicial misconduct.

After citing the above language from the Inquiry Report, the Council understandably concluded that the Inquiry Committee was entitled to take the Ethical Principles document into account in assessing whether the conduct complained of constituted sanctionable conduct. The Council stated that it was relevant in disciplinary matters, and added:[77]

> While the Ethical Principles are not absolutes and while a breach will not automatically lead to an expression of concern by the CJC, much less a

[72] Inquiry Committee established to review the conduct of the Honourable Paul Cosgrove, Report of the Canadian Judicial Council to the Minister of Justice (Ottawa: Canadian Judicial Council, 2009), pp. 15–16.

[73] Canadian Judicial Council, *Annual Report 2008–2009*, p. 9.

[74] Canadian Judicial Council, *Ethical Principles for Judges* (Ottawa, 1998).

[75] Friedland, *A Place Apart*, p. 265.

[76] Canadian Judicial Council, *Ethical Principles for Judges*, p. 3.

[77] Inquiry Committee established to review the conduct of the Honourable Theodore Matlow, *Report of the Canadian Judicial Council to the Minister of Justice* (Ottawa: Canadian Judicial Council, 2008), p. 33.

> recommendation for removal from the Bench, they do set out a general framework of values and considerations that will necessarily be relevant in ... determining whether a judge has met the objective standard of impartiality and integrity required of a judge and in determining whether the challenged conduct meets the objective standard for removal from the Bench.

Both the *Matlow* and *Cosgrove* cases used as the test for removal the language used by the 1990 inquiry into the so-called 'Marshall affair' in which the conduct of a number of appeal court judges in Nova Scotia in the Donald Marshall Jr appeal was the subject of a complaint.[78] The Marshall Inquiry Report had used the following test:[79]

> Is the conduct alleged so manifestly and profoundly destructive of the concept of the impartiality, integrity and independence of the judicial role, that public confidence would be sufficiently undermined to render the judge incapable of executing the judicial office?

The Canadian Judicial Council in its 2008–9 annual report concluded that on the basis of the *Matlow* and *Cosgrove* cases that 'while the overall process worked well, several of the components could be improved'.[80] The Council went on to raise the question 'whether the steps involved in the inquiry process are the best and most efficient way to resolve conduct issues'. So we can expect further thought by the Council into its discipline process.

I concluded my Report on judicial independence by stating:[81]

> This study has analysed a great number of issues relating to the independence and accountability of the judiciary. The judiciary, as the title to this volume suggests, is properly 'a place apart'. That place has a solid historical foundation and a fine edifice. This study suggests some relatively modest renovations in its structure to keep it a strong, respected, and independent institution.

This chapter has been prepared in the same spirit.

[78] Inquiry Committee established to review the conduct of the Honourable Paul Cosgrove, pp. 5–6; Inquiry Committee established to review the conduct of the Honourable Theodore Matlow, p. 22.

[79] Friedland, *A Place Apart*, pp. 102–5.

[80] Canadian Judicial Council, *Annual Report 2008–2009*, p. 5.

[81] Friedland, *A Place Apart*, p. 268.

4

Appointment, discipline and removal of judges in New Zealand

PHILIP A. JOSEPH

This chapter examines the appointment, discipline and removal of judges in New Zealand. Developments over recent years have formalised the procedures for appointing and disciplining judges, including the procedures that might lead to a judge's removal. Previously, appointments to judicial office were shrouded in secrecy and mystery, and the disciplining of judges was meted out *in camera* away from the public eye. That system came under mounting scrutiny and pressure for change, with calls for greater transparency and accountability within the judiciary. Changes introduced from 1999 standardised the appointing procedures and made them more transparent, and established a formal complaints process for investigating complaints of judicial misconduct. These changes codified the procedures, but they still remain more permissive than in most other jurisdictions. Heads of bench lack any direct disciplinary powers over their colleagues and appointments to judicial office remain largely at the discretion of those administering the appointments process. New Zealand has resisted setting up a judicial appointments commission which most other jurisdictions have established.

This chapter falls roughly into two parts. The first part sources the guarantee of judicial independence in New Zealand and examines the procedures for appointing, disciplining and removing judges. The second part contextualises the discussion within New Zealand by identifying several practices that, in the writer's view, compromise the principle of judicial independence.

Appointment of judges

Attorney-General's appointing power

New procedures adopted in 1999 conferred responsibility for judicial appointments on the Attorney-General.[1] Previously, the Minister of Justice had recommended the appointment of District Court judges, which accounted for the majority of judicial appointments. District Courts are the workhorse of the judicial system with around three times the number of judges than in the superior courts. Under the revised procedures, the Attorney-General now makes all appointments to the Supreme Court, Court of Appeal, High Court, Employment Court, District Courts (including Family Courts and Youth Courts) and Environment Court. The Attorney-General also recommends the appointment of up to nine Associate Judges of the High Court.[2] The Attorney-General is guardian of the public interest and exercises an independent function not shared by other ministers. He or she acts independently of partisan political interests and is the formal constitutional link between the judiciary and the government. When recommending appointments, the Attorney-General acts as First Law Officer of the crown rather than as a cabinet minister. Judicial appointments are announced in cabinet but are not discussed.

Two exceptions qualify the Attorney-General's appointing power. The Prime Minister recommends the appointment of the Chief Justice and the Minister of Maori Affairs recommends the appointment of judges of the Maori Land Court. The reason for the first exception is not entirely self-evident, although the standard explanation is that the Chief Justice is head of the judiciary[3] and Administrator of the Government when the Governor-General is overseas or unable to perform the office.[4] The second exception is rather more obvious. Te Puni Kokiri (Ministry of Maori Development) administers appointments to the Maori Land Court as judges must have knowledge of 'te reo Maori, tikanga Maori,

[1] *Judicial Appointments, Report to the Cabinet Strategy Committee*, STO (98) 245, 12 October 1998; *Judicial Appointments: Office of High Court Judge*, Attorney-General's Department, Wellington, 1999. This section on judicial appointments draws principally on P. A. Joseph, *Constitutional and Administrative Law in New Zealand*, 3rd edn. (Wellington: Thomson Brookers, 2007), pp. 789–92.

[2] Judicature Act 1908, s. 26C. [3] Supreme Court Act 2003, s. 18(1).

[4] Letters Patent Constituting the Office of Governor-General of New Zealand (SR 1983/225), cll. 12–14.

and the Treaty of Waitangi'.[5] These matters denote, respectively, Maori language, traditional Maori culture and New Zealand's founding document entered into in 1840 between the crown and Maori. A further exception involves lay persons appointed as community magistrates to hear minor criminal cases in the District Court. The Minister of Justice recommends such persons by reason of their personal qualities, experience and skills.[6]

Transparent and standardised procedures

The changes introduced in 1999 standardised the appointments process under transparent procedures: 'Previously, the appointments criteria were not publicised, judicial vacancies were not advertised, expressions of interest were not called for, candidates were not interviewed, and consultation procedures were ad hoc and uncertain.'[7] The Judicial Appointments Unit in the Ministry of Justice initiates the appointments process when vacancies arise (except for appointments to the Maori Land Court which are administered by Te Puni Kokiri). The unit undertakes consultations to obtain suitable candidates and calls for expressions of interest from practitioners wishing to be considered for judicial office. All names that meet the criteria are held on a confidential database. The Solicitor-General supervises appointments to the superior courts and the Secretary for Justice supervises appointments to the inferior courts. The Judicial Appointments Unit provides administrative assistance throughout the process.

For High Court appointments, the Attorney-General and Solicitor-General each consult a range of persons representative of the professional legal community.[8] These include the Chief Justice, the President of the Court of Appeal, such other judges as the Attorney-General or Solicitor-General choose to consult and the presidents of the New Zealand Law Society and New Zealand Bar Association. Recent Attorneys-General have also consulted the opposition shadow Attorney-General, as symbolic endorsement of the apolitical nature of appointments. In consultation with the Solicitor-General, the Chief

[5] Te Ture Whenua Maori Act (Maori Land Act) 1993, s. 7(2A).
[6] District Courts Act 1947, s. 11A.
[7] Joseph, *Constitutional and Administrative Law in New Zealand*, p. 789.
[8] See *Appointing Judges: A Judicial Appointments Commission for New Zealand?*, Public Consultation Paper, Ministry of Justice, Wellington, April 2004, paras. 26–38.

Justice and President of the Court of Appeal produce a 'long list' of potential candidates, from which a 'short list' is drawn up when vacancies arise. The Solicitor-General verifies the personal integrity of shortlisted candidates, who must undertake not to resume legal practice upon vacating the bench. The shortlist is presented to the Attorney-General, who makes the final decision. If the selected candidate accepts the appointment, it is announced to Cabinet and recommended to the Governor-General.

Appointments to the higher appellate courts occur through judicial promotion. Court of Appeal judges are typically recruited from the High Court Bench and appointments to the Supreme Court from the Court of Appeal Bench. Only five Court of Appeal judges have been appointed directly from the profession during the fifty years that the court has been permanently constituted.[9] All appointments to the Supreme Court have been from the Court of Appeal Bench since the court was established in 2004.

Appointments to inferior courts parallel those to the High Court.[10] Prospective candidates either submit an expression of interest or are invited to accept nomination. The 'expression of interest' form is a formal document for obtaining information about the candidate, including a description of the candidate's legal experience. Candidates also submit a curriculum vitae and swear a statutory declaration as to convictions, disciplinary action, bankruptcy and tax status. Persons and organisations typically consulted are the same as for the appointment of High Court judges. The Secretary for Justice submits a proposed shortlist of candidates to the Attorney-General, who approves the nominations after such consultations as he or she considers appropriate. The shortlisted candidates are interviewed by a panel comprising the Chief District Court Judge, the Head of Bench (for appointments to the Family Court, Youth Courts, Environment Court or Employment Court), the Executive Judge for the region and a representative of the Ministry of Justice. The panel then consults the Solicitor-General and the President of the New Zealand Law Society before making its recommendation to the Attorney-General. The Attorney-General may sometimes

[9] See R. Bigwood (ed.), *The Permanent New Zealand Court of Appeal: Essays on the first 50 Years* (Oxford University Press, 2009).

[10] See 'Judicial Appointments: Office of District Court Judge – March 2010', accessible through the Ministry of Justice website at: www.justice.govt.nz/publications/global-publications/j/judicial-appointments-office-of-district-court-judge/judicial-appointments-office-of-district-court-judge-march-2010.

interview candidates personally before announcing appointments in Cabinet and tendering advice to Government House.

Judicial appointments commission

New Zealand resisted a judicial appointments commission when it formalised its appointments procedures. Views remain divided on the merits of an appointments commission. Thirty years ago, a royal commission on the courts recommended an appointments commission, but the judiciary opposed the initiative and the proposal lapsed.[11] Proposals for a commission resurfaced in the 1990s, following developments in other jurisdictions and concerns about the appointments procedures.[12] Supporters believed a commission would promote efficiencies, allow wider consultation, remove mystique and avoid suggestions of political influence. However, others vigorously opposed a judicial appointments commission. Three past Attorneys-General (Sir Geoffrey Palmer, Paul East QC and Sir Douglas Graham) expressed distrust of a formal bureaucratic structure. Appointing commission members would be highly political, they believed, creating the potential for covert political influence. They also believed that the judicial members of the commission would dominate discussions and entrench a non-representative judiciary, rather than promote diversity within it.[13] These persons recommended improving the existing appointments system without imposing bureaucratic structures.

The proposal to end Privy Council appeals and establish a Supreme Court rekindled interest in an appointments commission. Submitters on the Supreme Court Bill expressed distrust of the appointments process and proposed that a commission would allay fears of political appointments to the new court. In 2004 the Clark coalition government issued a

[11] *Report of the Royal Commission on the Courts* (1978) A.J.H.R. H.2 at pp. 200–2.

[12] See New Zealand Law Society's Courts and Tribunals Committee, 'A Model Judicial Commission for New Zealand', *LawTalk*, Vol. 489, No. 13, 1997, p. 14; T. Eichelbaum, 'The Inaugural Neil Williamson Memorial Lecture: Judicial Independence Revisited' (1997) 6 *Canterbury Law Review* 421 at 429; J. McGrath QC, 'Appointing the Judiciary' [1998] *New Zealand Law Journal* 314; L. Dalziel, 'Who Judges the Judges?' [1998] *New Zealand Law Journal* 333 at 334.

[13] P. East, Speech notes for Lawlink Conference, 19 March 1993, at pp. 8–9; P. East, 'A Judicial Commission' [1995] *New Zealand Law Journal* 189; G. Palmer, 'Judicial Selection and Accountability: Can the New Zealand System Survive?', in B. D. Gray and R. B. McLintock (eds.), *Courts and Policy: Checking the Balance* (Wellington: Brookers, 1995), pp. 84–5.

consultation paper calling for submissions on whether to establish a commission, and what its composition, appointment and balance should be. Two years on, however, the government abandoned any thought of establishing a commission.

Judicial appointments commissions have two goals: to guard against political appointments to the judiciary and to promote gender and ethnicity diversity within it. Can appointments commissions achieve these goals? Opponents argue that a commission simply relocates the potential for political influence through purposeful selection of the membership to reflect a particular political suasion. Opponents also argue that appointments commissions have not rooted out gender and ethnicity imbalance across the common law jurisdictions.[14] In New Zealand, gender imbalance is being addressed under existing procedures without an appointments commission. From 1 July 2006 to 1 January 2011, six of the fourteen appointments to the High Court were women, who now represent 26 per cent of the superior court bench (excluding acting and associate judges). Maori and Pacific Islanders, on the other hand, remain under-represented at all levels of the judiciary.

Disciplining of judges

Constitutional tension

All of the common law judiciaries face a common challenge: how to reconcile the guarantee of judicial independence and demands for judicial accountability. That challenge becomes increasingly urgent as society becomes more vocal and insistent, and the institutional mystique of the judiciary less resistant to popular demand. The shibboleths of the law are less revered than in former times and are more exposed to question. All of the common law jurisdictions have explored reforms that can assuage demands for greater judicial accountability.[15] These demands pose a dilemma: how to dispense justice impartially through an independent judiciary *and* maintain the accountability of judges. In the first

[14] See K. Malleson, *The New Judiciary: Effects of Expansion and Activism* (Aldershot: Dartmouth Publishing, 1999), pp. 103–5; K. Malleson, 'Justifying Gender Equality on the Bench: Why Difference Won't Do' (2003) 11 *Feminist Legal Studies* 1; K. Malleson and P. H. Russell (eds.), *Appointing Judges in an Age of Judicial Power: Critical Perspectives from Around the World* (University of Toronto Press, 2006).

[15] Cf. Lord Brown of Eaton-Under-Heywood, 'The Unaccountability of Judges: Surely their Strength not their Weakness', in C. Forsyth *et al.* (eds.), *Effective Judicial Review: A Cornerstone of Good Governance* (Oxford University Press, 2010), p. 208.

judicial review under New Zealand's statutory procedures for removal of judges, the High Court observed that the removal power 'creates tension between accountability and independence, which the Act aims to address through processes and standards designed to ensure that judges are not lightly removed'.[16] Even where removal is not in issue, judges are sometimes an easy media target. There is no bright-line distinction between promoting judges' accountability and inviting gratuitous attacks on the judiciary. Jibes at judges typically draw rebuke from the law societies and bar associations, although with little discernible effect. The legal profession and the judiciary are typically perceived as a professional 'élite' defending its institutional position.

A belief that judicial appointments lack transparency fuels criticisms. For many 'outsiders', the system produces a self-perpetuating judicial oligarchy that is manifestly unrepresentative of society. Such allegations are not easily fended when regard is had to judges' demographics and the stereotypical judicial profile. A knowledge deficit, too, fuels demands for greater judicial accountability. Judges believe that the greatest threat to judicial independence is a lack of understanding of the judicial role and why a judge's independence is fundamental to it.[17] The principle of judicial independence is not well understood and does not excite public sympathy or concern. Exacting greater judicial accountability poses an untoward threat to judges' independence, which if realised would have major implications for civil society and the rule of law.

Immunity from discipline

The expression 'disciplining judges' is a misnomer. In New Zealand, there are no formal procedures for disciplining judges. Each judge is independent of all other judges, including a judge's Head of Bench (the Chief Justice, the President of the Court of Appeal, the Chief High Court Judge, etc.). Heads of Bench might exercise leadership and a degree of oversight over their judicial colleagues, but they do not enjoy any powers of discipline over them. They may reproach, encourage or warn, but they may not take direct action against a judicial colleague.[18] The only powers

[16] *Wilson* v. *Attorney-General* [2011] 1 NZLR 399 at [41] *per* Wild, Miller and Lang JJ.

[17] Eichelbaum, 'The Inaugural Neil Williamson Memorial Lecture,'; S. Elias, '"The Next Revisit": Judicial Independence Seven Years On' (2004) 10 *Canterbury Law Review* 217.

[18] Palmer, 'Judicial Selection and Accountability', p. 86.

to discipline judges are those exercised under the Judicial Conduct Commissioner and Judicial Conduct Panel Act 2004 (JCCJCPA).

Judicial complaints process

The JCCJCPA codified procedures for investigating complaints of judicial misconduct. In 1999, the judiciary adopted its own internal complaints process and this process augments the procedures under the JCCJCPA. This Act does not empower Heads of Bench to take action, but it does reserve for them a counselling role where a complaint would not warrant inquiry into whether a judge might be removed. The process is essentially voluntary, based on a consensual jurisdiction.[19] The absence of compulsion distinguishes it from most other professional disciplinary regimes.

The JCCJCPA established a Judicial Conduct Commissioner to process complaints.[20] The Act off-sets two aims: to provide an investigative process that might lead to a judge's removal; and to protect judicial independence and rights of natural justice.[21] The Act contemplates two classes of complaint against judges: those alleging inappropriate conduct; and those alleging serious misconduct that might initiate removal proceedings. All complaints must be directed through the commissioner, who conducts a preliminary investigation to ascertain whether a complaint has substance. The commissioner must give notice to the judge and invite the judge's response.[22] All relevant information must be disclosed, including information made available by the complainant.[23] The commissioner must then do one of four things: dismiss the complaint, take no further action, refer the complaint to the Head of Bench or recommend that the Attorney-General appoint a Judicial Conduct Panel to investigate whether the judge should be removed.[24]

Judicial Conduct Panels are *ad hoc*. Membership comprises one lay member and either two judges, or a judge and a retired judge, or a judge (or retired judge) and a legal practitioner. The panel is chaired by the retired judge, or by the judge or more senior judge.[25] Only one Judicial Conduct Panel has been appointed – that to investigate complaints

[19] The options and steps are set out in *Complaints about Judicial Conduct*, Office of the Judicial Conduct Commissioner, Wellington, July 2005.

[20] Sections 7–8. [21] Section 4 (purpose section). [22] Sections 14(1)(3) and 15(2)(4).

[23] Section 15(3). [24] Sections 15(5) and 17. [25] Section 22.

against Supreme Court judge, Justice Bill Wilson.[26] The three options are routinely to dismiss the complaint, take no further action or refer it to the Head of Bench. Where it is determined that a complaint has substance, the 'default option' is referral to the Head of Bench,[27] who must independently determine the merits of the complaint and the best way to deal with it. He or she may admonish, encourage or counsel the judge, who may apologise to the complainant and undertake not to repeat the conduct. This process, while consensual and voluntary, is a solemn one. Having to explain one's behaviour to the Head of Bench will usually prompt serious self-reflection and contrition.[28]

Under the statutory scheme, a panel rather than the commissioner is charged with the fact-finding inquiry. A recommendation by the commissioner that a panel be appointed is 'highly provisional'.[29] It must be founded on an opinion that an inquiry into 'alleged' conduct is 'necessary or justified' and 'if established' the conduct 'may' warrant 'consideration of' removal of the judge.[30] The opinion must be honestly held, reasonably open on the facts available and based on the correct legal standard.[31] The facts alleged must be sufficiently plausible to justify further investigation and the conduct, if established, must be sufficiently serious to warrant consideration of removal from office. 'It is a low threshold,' the High Court observed, 'but a definite one.'[32] Furthermore, the commissioner's recommendation must specifically identify the matters about the judge's conduct that are thought to warrant inquiry, as these matters fix the scope of the panel's inquiry. Section 21 of the JCCJCPA authorises the Attorney-General to appoint a panel to inquire into and report on 'any matter or matters concerning the conduct of a Judge that have been the subject of a recommendation by the Commissioner'.

A complainant who is dissatisfied with the complaints process or outcome may refer the matter to the Judicial Complaints Lay Observer. The lay observer exercises a quasi-appellate role for investigating the

[26] On 31 May 2010, the acting Attorney-General announced that a panel would be appointed but the judge resigned from office before the panel assembled.

[27] *Wilson* v. *Attorney-General* [2011] 1 NZLR 399 at [42] *per* Wild, Miller and Lang JJ.

[28] B. V. Harris, 'Remedies and Accountability for Unlawful Judicial Action in New Zealand: Could the law be Tidier?' [2008] *New Zealand Law Review* 483 at 508.

[29] *Wilson* v. *Attorney-General* [2011] 1 NZLR 399 at [43] *per* Wild, Miller and Lang JJ.

[30] Section 18.

[31] *Wilson* v. *Attorney-General* [2011] 1 NZLR 399 at [44] *per* Wild, Miller and Lang JJ, citing *Rees* v. *Crane* [1994] 2 AC 173 at 193, PC.

[32] *Wilson* v. *Attorney-General* [2011] 1 NZLR 399 at [44] *per* Wild, Miller and Lang JJ.

handling of complaints.[33] He or she may invite the Head of Bench to reconsider a complaint, although the Head of Bench must determine the most appropriate way to proceed. No further recourse is available if the complainant still remains dissatisfied with the outcome. The only disciplinary process backed by compulsion is where a Judicial Conduct Panel is appointed to initiate the process for a judge's removal.

Complaints statistics

Since the complaints procedure has been in operation, the vast majority of complaints have been dismissed as lacking substance.[34] There have been on average 133 complaints per year. Discounting the 'live' complaints as at 31 July (the end of the reporting year), an average of 94 complaints each year have been investigated and disposed of. The number of complaints referred to Heads of Bench was: four in 2008–9; two in 2007–8; none in 2006–7; and none in 2005–6. This represents 2.5 complaints each year, or 2.66 per cent of the complaints investigated.

The Judicial Conduct Commissioner has defended both the record of his office and the voluntary complaints process.[35] The number of complaints categorised as 'dismissed' had been artificially inflated, conveying a skewed impression.[36] Many complaints had been resolved rather than dismissed, but the legislation had not permitted the categorisation of complaints as 'resolved'. A statutory amendment remedied this omission by authorising the commissioner to take no further action on complaints that have been resolved: for example, following an apology from the judge or an explanation from the commissioner. The commissioner noted that over half of all complaints were from self-represented litigants, who did not understand court procedures. Cross-examination, for example, was a time for asking questions, not making submissions.[37] In addition, many complainants challenged the correctness of judicial decisions which could be resolved only through the processes of appeal or review.[38]

[33] The Judicial Complaints Lay Observer, although referred to in the JCCJCPA, is not constituted under any statutory authority. None is needed for an appointment under a consensual complaints system that lacks coercive powers or sanctions.

[34] *Office of the Judicial Conduct Commissioner Annual Report for 2008/2009*, Wellington, New Zealand, p. 4.

[35] See Harris, 'Remedies and Accountability for Unlawful Judicial Action in New Zealand', at p. 507.

[36] C. MacLennan, 'Judicial Complaints Process Defended by Commissioner', *LawFuel*, available at: www.lawfuel.co.nz/news/article.asp?NewsIS=548.

[37] MacLennan, 'Judicial Complaints Process Defended by Commissioner'.

[38] MacLennan, 'Judicial Complaints Process Defended by Commissioner'.

Removal of judges

Superior court judges

Security of tenure

The guarantee of judicial independence was not visited upon the colony from the outset in 1840. The provisions of the Act of Settlement 1701 guaranteeing judicial tenure were not inherited as part of its law.[39] In *Terrell* v. *Secretary of State for the Colonies*,[40] Lord Goddard CJ doubted whether any colony inherited the guarantee. From 1840, judges were appointed at pleasure and could be removed at will. That remained the position until 1858, when the Supreme Court Judges Act introduced security of judicial tenure. Superior court judges held office during good behaviour and could be removed only following an address of both Houses of the General Assembly.[41] The Act also guaranteed judicial salaries during the continuance of a judge's commission.

The guarantee of judicial independence was carried over under successive statutes, until the Constitution Act 1986 consolidated New Zealand's primary constitutional provisions. Sections 23 and 24 guarantee superior court judges protection against (a) arbitrary removal from office and (b) executive interference with judicial salaries. Section 23 reads:

> 23 Protection of Judges against removal from office
> A Judge of the High Court shall not be removed from office except by the Sovereign or Governor-General, acting upon an address of the House of Representatives, which address may be moved only on the grounds of that Judge's misbehaviour or of that Judge's incapacity to discharge the functions of that Judge's office.

Section 23 extends protection to all superior court judges, including judges of the Supreme Court and Court of Appeal who hold concurrent appointment as judges of the High Court.[42] Today, the address of one house, not two, is required for a judge's removal. In 1950, New Zealand abolished its upper house, the Legislative Council, and reconstituted its

[39] See now the Imperial Laws Application Act 1988 affirming the inheritance of some but not all the provisions of the Act of Settlement 1701, 12 & 13 Will III, c. 2.

[40] [1953] 2 QB 482, DC.

[41] Section 32 of the New Zealand Constitution Act 1852 (UK) established the General Assembly as a bicameral legislature comprising the Legislative Council and the House of Representatives. See now the Constitution Act 1986, s. 14 reconstituting Parliament as a unicameral legislature.

[42] Supreme Court Act 2003, s. 20; Judicature Act 1908, s. 57(4).

Parliament as the Sovereign in right of New Zealand and the House of Representatives.[43] For completeness, s. 13 of the Judicature Act 1908 prescribes for superior court judges a statutory retirement age of 70 years, and s. 24 of the Constitution Act 1986 secures their salaries against reduction during a judge's commission.[44]

Security of tenure is the cornerstone of judicial independence. Under s. 23, judges do not hold office during 'good behaviour' (as under the Act of Settlement 1701), but may be removed for 'misbehaviour'. This section removed an ambiguity that had beset the law since the Act of Settlement 1701. Under that Act, it was lawful for the sovereign, upon the address of both Houses of Parliament, to remove a judge and revoke the judge's commission. It was uncertain whether those provisions established a single, exhaustive removal power or two distinct powers. One reading might suggest the former: removal by the crown, on a parliamentary address, on the ground of misbehaviour. But another reading might suggest the latter: removal by the crown on the ground of misbehaviour or removal by the crown, on a parliamentary address, on any ground at all.[45]

Section 23 established a single, exhaustive power, exercisable upon a parliamentary address moved on either of the two grounds (misbehaviour or incapacity). However, s. 23, while circumscribing the removal power, did not establish or codify it. The power is part of the prerogative powers of the crown delegated to the Governor-General in New Zealand.[46] The prerogative to appoint judges imports also the prerogative to remove judges (subject to the grounds specified in s. 23 and the procedures under the JCCJCPA). Conduct as might lead to a judge's removal has never been tested as no address to remove a judge has been moved in the history of the New Zealand Parliament.

Under earlier legislation, superior court judges might be suspended from office, but that power was not carried over under the Constitution Act 1986. The suspension power potentially exposed judges to political retribution and compromised their institutional independence. The power had two separate applications.[47] When Parliament was sitting,

[43] Constitution Act 1986, s. 14. See also the Legislative Council Abolition Act 1950.

[44] For discussion see Joseph, *Constitutional and Administrative Law in New Zealand*, pp. 779–82.

[45] *Constitutional Reform*, Department of Justice, February 1986, Second Report, para. 3.98.

[46] Letters Patent Constituting the Office of Governor-General of New Zealand (SR 1983/225 cl. 3).

[47] Judicature Act 1908, ss. 8–9.

the Governor-General in Council might suspend a judge following a resolution of the House seeking the judge's suspension. There was no limitation on the duration of a suspension initiated by parliamentary address.[48] The power was more constrained in its second application when Parliament was not in session. The duration of the suspension of a judge was limited until the end of the next session of Parliament.[49] The Officials Committee which drafted the Constitution Act 1986 conceded that the suspension power may have been justified when parliamentary sessions were short and intermittent, but saw no reason to retain the power under modern conditions.[50]

Historical precedents

No superior court judge has been removed from office through the formal process. However, three judges have been the subject of formal inquiry. In 1874, Supreme Court judge, Henry Chapman, was accused of bias, but a parliamentary inquiry found the accusations to be unfounded.[51] An inquiry was also held into the behaviour of Supreme Court judge, Worley Edwards, who was appointed to the bench in 1896. Edwards was universally disdained.[52] The Auckland bar resolved that his ill-temper and vindictiveness had imperilled the administration of justice, and called for his removal. However, Edwards pre-empted moves for a parliamentary address by transferring from Auckland to Wellington. Edwards then proceeded to inflame the Wellington bar, which likewise agitated for his removal. He was persuaded to take early retirement under a negotiated government settlement.

A third judge was investigated under the procedures of the JCCJCPA. In *Saxmere Co. Ltd* v. *Wool Board Disestablishment Co. Ltd (No. 2)*,[53] the Supreme Court recalled its earlier judgment in proceedings of the same

[48] *Semble* an indefinite suspension would be impermissible as amounting to removal from office. *Quaere* whether a suspension could be of a duration that took the judge to the statutory retirement age of 72 years (as it then was).

[49] Judicature Act 1908, s. 9.

[50] *Constitutional Reform*, Department of Justice, February 1986, Second Report, paras. 3.102–3.

[51] See P. Spiller, 'The Career of Henry Chapman in Dunedin' (1990) 7 *Otago Law Review* 305 at 315–17; A. P. Stockley, 'Judicial Independence: The New Zealand Experience' (1997) 3 *Australian Journal of Legal History* 145 at 154–5.

[52] Stockley, 'Judicial Independence', at p. 155. See further R. B. Cooke QC (ed.), *Portrait of a Profession: The Centennial Book of the New Zealand Law* (Wellington: Reed, 1969), p. 78; J. L. Robson, *Sacred Cows and Rogue Elephants* (Wellington: GPO Publications, 1987), pp. 254–5.

[53] [2009] NZSC 122; [2010] 1 NZLR 76.

name[54] on the ground of judicial bias. The recall application alleged that Supreme Court judge, Justice Bill Wilson, was conflicted when he sat in the *Saxmere* Court of Appeal proceedings, before his elevation to the Supreme Court. It was alleged that the judge was disqualified from sitting by reason of his close business relationship with counsel for the appellant, in whose favour judgment was given. In its earlier decision, the Supreme Court had rejected the plaintiff's claim of a reasonable apprehension that the judge was biased. But, in *Saxmere (No. 2)*, the Supreme Court reversed that decision after the judge made further disclosures which indicated he owed an 'indirect indebtedness' to counsel.

Three complaints were lodged with the Judicial Conduct Commissioner. These alleged the judge's failure to recuse himself and his subsequent, on-going refusal to make full disclosure of his business interests. The commissioner investigated and recommended that the Attorney-General appoint a Judicial Conduct Panel to conduct further inquiries. The Attorney-General, Hon. Chris Finlayson, who had practised law with the judge before entering Parliament, delegated the decision-making to ministerial colleague, Hon. Judith Collins.[55] On 31 May 2010, Collins announced that a Judicial Conduct Panel would be appointed, comprising the Chief Ombudsman, a Court of Appeal judge and the Chief High Court judge. The judge thereupon announced that he would challenge through judicial review the commissioner's recommendation to appoint a panel.[56] He succeeded in his challenge but resigned from office before the commissioner could remedy his omission (failure to particularise the judge's conduct warranting investigation).

[54] *Saxmere Co. Ltd* v. *Wool Board Disestablishment Co. Ltd* [2009] NZSC 72; [2010] 1 NZLR 35.

[55] Collins was appointed Acting Attorney-General in order to exercise the power of appointment. *Quaere* the power to appoint Collins as Acting Attorney-General when s. 9A of the Constitution Act 1986 provides that the Solicitor-General (or, with the Attorney-General's consent, a deputy Solicitor-General: s. 9C) may exercise any of the powers of the Attorney-General. The exercise of the Attorney-General's powers by the Solicitor-General is original, not delegated. Arguably, s. 9A supersedes any residual prerogative power to appoint a deputy Attorney-General to act in lieu of the Solicitor-General. If the Solicitor-General was also conflicted through his involvement in related proceedings, the decision-making should have been delegated to a deputy Solicitor-General. Note that s. 7 of the Constitution Act 1986 does not assist (ministers by whatever designation may exercise the powers of other ministers). The statutory process speaks throughout to the Attorney-General as First Law Officer, not as minister.

[56] *New Zealand Herald*, 1 June 2010. See *Wilson* v. *Attorney-General* [2011] 1 NZLR 399 *per* Wild, Miller and Lang JJ.

Inferior court judges

Security of tenure

Inferior court judges do not hold the same security of tenure as their superior court counterparts. Inferior courts of limited statutory jurisdiction include District Courts,[57] the Employment Court,[58] the Environment Court,[59] the Maori Land Court,[60] the Maori Appellate Court,[61] Coroners[62] and Courts Martial.[63] Subject to one exception, judges of these courts may be removed by the Governor-General, acting on the advice of the Attorney-General. The constituent statutes of the various courts replicate (with minor variations) the security of tenure provision under s. 7 of the District Courts Act 1947. Section 7 provides that the Governor-General may, 'if he thinks fit, remove a Judge for inability or misbehaviour'. Employment Court judges are the exception. Curiously, these judges enjoy the same security of tenure as High Court judges; they may be removed only following a parliamentary address moved on either ground of misbehaviour or incapacity. Why this exception exists is not immediately apparent.

The words of discretion in s. 7 ('if he thinks fit') do not literally mean what they say. As in other Commonwealth jurisdictions, the Governor-General must, by constitutional convention, exercise the crown's powers on and in accordance with ministerial advice tendered. Until 1999, the Minister of Justice recommended the removal of District Court judges, but that function passed to the Attorney-General when the appointments and removal procedures were standardised. The advice may be tendered on either of two grounds: misbehaviour or inability. These grounds do not replicate exactly those for High Court judges: under s. 7, the latter ground is 'inability', not (as for High Court judges) 'incapacity'.

Historical precedents

There are no New Zealand precedents for the removal of an inferior court judge. However, some caution is needed as resident magistrates' courts have existed in one form or another since the early days of the colony.[64] *Hansard* would not have chronicled a magistrate's removal as no parliamentary address would have been required. In addition, there

[57] District Courts Act 1947, s. 3. [58] Employment Relations Act 2000, s. 186.
[59] Resource Management Act 1991, s. 247.
[60] Te Ture Whenua Maori Act 1993 (Maori Land Act 1993), s. 6.
[61] Te Ture Whenua Maori Act 1993, s. 50. [62] Coroners Act 2006, s. 103.
[63] Armed Forces Discipline Act 1971, s. 118.
[64] See the Resident Magistrates' Court Ordinance 1846 (10 Vict., No. 16).

are several instances of forced resignation from the bench in circumstances that might have justified removal by the Governor-General.

Most complaints against inferior court judges have been resolved out of public view. But there have been exceptions. In 1889, a royal commission was appointed at the request of a district judge and resident magistrate, who sought to clear his name. He was accused of drunkenness and partiality in the administration of justice, but the allegations were quickly dispelled.[65] Most other complaints have been resolved by judges retiring, without the need for formal inquiry. In 1965, the Minister of Justice forced the retirements of two magistrates under veiled threat of dismissal.[66] One magistrate had failing health and had become irascible and difficult to deal with in court. He retired when the district law society lodged a complaint and the minister announced he was proposing an inquiry. The second magistrate also resigned after learning that he was to be investigated. The district law society complained that he interrogated witnesses, was overbearing and prejudged cases. These judges invited complaint, but it is debateable whether the complaints against either would have justified dismissal. The House of Commons has rejected intemperate judicial behaviour as a ground for impeachment.[67]

Further inferior court judges have resigned to avoid public spectacle. Sir Geoffrey Palmer forced the resignations of two District Court judges when he was Minister of Justice from 1984 to 1989.[68] In 1998, another District Court judge resigned after indecency charges were laid against him, resulting in two hung juries.[69] However, the most publicised case of judicial misconduct occurred that same year when two District Court judges were charged with intent to defraud.[70] The judges had claimed over-night allowance expenses while on circuit when they had in fact returned home on each sitting day. One judge pleaded guilty and resigned, the other pleaded not guilty and successfully defended the charges.

That precedent forced a review of the removal procedures. The Solicitor-General advised against the Minister of Justice commencing

[65] See R. H. Quilliam, 'A Taranaki Episode: The Rawson Commission', in Cooke (ed.), *Portrait of a Profession*, pp. 357–61.

[66] Robson, *Sacred Cows and Rogue Elephants*, pp. 256–9.

[67] *Kenrick's Case* 13 Parl. Deb., 2nd Ser., 1375 (1825). See further P. A. Joseph, 'Constitutional Law' [1998] *New Zealand Law Review*, 197 at 202.

[68] Palmer, 'Judicial Selection and Accountability', p. 85.

[69] See Joseph, 'Constitutional Law', p. 198.

[70] See Joseph, 'Constitutional Law', pp. 198–206.

removal proceedings against the judge who was acquitted (Judge Martin Beattie).[71] To revisit the allegations would have entailed second-guessing the jury's verdict and been an unwarranted intrusion into the criminal justice process.[72] The Crown had to prove that Beattie had acted dishonestly with intent to defraud and the jury had returned a verdict of not guilty. The judge testified he had acted honestly in the genuine (if mistaken) belief that he was entitled to make the over-night allowance claims.

'Misbehaviour'

Conduct as would justify removing a judge from office must compromise the integrity of the judicial function.[73] It must be 'so manifestly and totally contrary to the impartiality, integrity and independence of the judiciary' as to shake the public's confidence in the justice system.[74] The standard is an exacting one. Conduct that brings the judicial office into disrepute might properly be characterised as 'misbehaviour', yet fail the standard needed for removal from office.[75] The conduct must be calculated to undermine public confidence in the judge impugned and ultimately in the judiciary itself. The judge must be so afflicted as to be 'incapable of performing the duties of . . . office'.[76]

The conduct overall must be aggregated and assessed. Whereas a single instance of misbehaviour might not trigger removal proceedings, a judge's conduct overall might cumulatively indicate an inability to discharge the office.[77] Removal proceedings against a superior court judge of the Cayman Islands culminated in the Privy Council advising that she be removed from office.[78] Individual instances of misbehaviour

[71] J. J. McGrath QC, *Opinion to the Minister of Justice, Hon. Doug Graham, on whether Proceedings might be Instituted under s. 7 of the District Courts Act 1947 to Remove Judge Beattie from the Bench*, 1 September 1997.

[72] McGrath QC, *Opinion to the Minister of Justice*, para. 25.

[73] *Hearing on the Report of the Chief Justice of Gibraltar: Referral under Section 4 of the Judicial Committee Act 1833* [2009] UKPC 43 at [262].

[74] *Hearing on the Report of the Chief Justice of Gibraltar*, at [263], quoting from *Therrien* v. *Minister of Justice* [2001] 2 SCR 3 at 96 *per* Gonthier J, SCC.

[75] *Hearing on the Report of the Chief Justice of Gibraltar.*

[76] *Hearing on the Report of the Chief Justice of Gibraltar*, quoting from *Therrien* v. *Minister of Justice* [2001] 2 SCR 3 at 96 *per* Gonthier J, SCC.

[77] *Hearing on the Report of the Chief Justice of Gibraltar*, at [264].

[78] *Hearing on the Report of the Tribunal to the Governor of The Cayman Islands: Madam Justice Levers (Judge of the Grand Court of the Cayman Islands): Referral under Section 4 of the Judicial Committee Act 1833* [2010] UKPC 24.

fell short of the required threshold but not their cumulative impact. She had made disparaging or derogatory comments about her judicial colleagues, which had undermined the collegiality of the court. The Privy Council termed this behaviour 'serious misconduct', but not of the standard required to remove her from office.[79] Nevertheless, her overall conduct and demeanour, when assessed cumulatively, showed that she was not fit to hold judicial office. She had routinely ordered the summary arrest of jurors for non-attendance, been discourteous to counsel, discriminated against female complainants, used insensitive and injudicious language and habitually criticised her fellow judges.[80] Specific complaints laid against her included 'racism', 'bias against foreigners', 'bias against women' and 'bias in favour of the defence in criminal cases'.[81] Her actions revealed a pattern of conduct that called for her removal from the bench.

The Beattie incident is the leading New Zealand precedent on the meaning of judicial misbehaviour. The Solicitor-General advised that moral turpitude distinguished 'misbehaviour' from lesser transgressions, which would not justify removal from the bench.[82] Virtually every debate in the British Parliament has affirmed this threshold for removal.[83] Expressions used in parliamentary debates to describe 'misbehaviour' include corruption or corrupt motive,[84] dishonest motive,[85] perversion of justice,[86] abuse of power,[87] badness of heart and corrupt intention,[88] partial and oppressive behaviour,[89] partisan political bias,[90] moral delinquency[91] and corruption or moral turpitude.[92]

79 *Hearing on the Report of the Tribunal to the Governor of The Cayman Islands*, at [127].
80 *Hearing on the Report of the Tribunal to the Governor of The Cayman Islands*, at [10].
81 *Hearing on the Report of the Tribunal to the Governor of The Cayman Islands*, at [8], [134].
82 McGrath, *Opinion to the Minister of Justice*, para 25.
83 S. Shetreet, *Judges on Trial: A Study of the Appointment and Accountability of the English Judiciary* (Amsterdam: North-Holland Publishing, 1976), pp. 139–51, 271–81.
84 See *Baron Page's Case* 7 Parl. Hist. 961 (1722); *Lord Ellenborough's Case* 34 Parl. Deb., 1st Ser., 112 (1816); *McClelland's Case* 40 Parl. Deb., 1st Ser., 852 (1819); *Baron Smith's Case* 21 Parl. Deb., 3rd Ser., 744 (1834); *Lord Abinger's Case* 66 Parl. Deb., 3rd Ser., 1129 (1843).
85 *Lord Abinger's Case* 66 Parl. Deb., 3rd Ser., 1129 (1843).
86 *Torren's Case* 140 Parl. Deb., 3rd Ser., 1561 (1856).
87 *Kenrick's Case* 13 Parl. Deb., 2nd Ser., 1138, 1247, 1350, 1407–8, 1410 (1825).
88 *Lord Abinger's Case* 66 Parl. Deb., 3rd Ser., 1129 (1843).
89 *Lord Abinger's Case* 66 Parl. Deb., 3rd Ser., 1129 (1843).
90 *Sir William Grantham's Case* 160 Parl. Deb., 4th Ser., 369 (1906).
91 *McCardie's Case* 175 HC Deb., 6 (23 June 1924).
92 *Sir William Grantham's Case* 160 Parl. Deb., 4th Ser., 409–10 (1906).

Conviction of a criminal offence involving moral wrongness will clearly satisfy the misbehaviour threshold. In 1830, Sir Jonah Barrington was the first judge to be removed from office following an address of both Houses of the British Parliament.[93] Barrington, a judge of the High Court of Admiralty in Ireland, had embezzled moneys paid into court.[94] Intemperate judicial behaviour, of itself, will not be sufficient.[95] However, the conduct complained of need not involve the judge's official duties. Immoral, scandalous or notoriously improper conduct will meet the threshold.[96] So, too, will persistent and unjustified absence from office or neglect of official duties.[97] The wilfulness of such conduct would infect it with moral obloquy, warranting a judge's removal from office.

Must the judge realise the moral 'wrongness' of the conduct? In response to Beattie's situation, the Solicitor-General answered 'yes' and advised against seeking the judge's removal. His conduct could not amount to misbehaviour if he genuinely believed he was entitled to the overnight allowances.[98] But might a different conclusion be reached?

There are problems in holding steadfastly to a subjective standard. Might a judge who genuinely fails to comprehend the moral wrongness of the action nevertheless be guilty of misconduct? More exacting standards of probity and integrity are demanded of judges than ordinary citizens. A judge who was so outrageously oblivious to the offending (when all ordinary folk would not hesitate to condemn the behaviour) would bring the judiciary into disrepute and undermine public confidence in the administration of justice.[99] Knowingly to make false expenses claims, even under colour of right, might excite public indignation and loss of confidence in the justice system.

The law has progressed since the Solicitor-General delivered his opinion in the Beattie saga. In *Wilson* v. *Attorney-General*,[100] the Full Court made two prescient rulings: first, that it is not appropriate to attempt a rigid categorisation or definition of conduct that might

93 *Barrington's Case* 24 Parl. Deb., 2nd Ser., 484, 965, 1075 (1830).
94 Shetreet, *Judges on Trial*, pp. 143–4.
95 *Sir William Grantham's Case* 160 Parl. Deb., 4th Ser., 369 (1906), at 379.
96 *Kenrick's Case (No. 2)* 14 Parl. Deb., 2nd Ser., 507 (1826).
97 *Barrington's Case* 24 Parl. Deb., 2nd Ser., at 974 (1830); *Baron Smith's Case* 21 Parl. Deb., 3rd Ser., 744 (1834).
98 McGrath, *Opinion to the Minister of Justice*, para. 27.
99 W. Anson, *Law and Custom of the Constitution, Part I*, 3rd edn. (Oxford: Clarendon Press, 1906), p. 222 believed any form of conduct that undermined public confidence would constitute misbehaviour.
100 *Wilson* v. *Attorney-General* [2011] 1 NZLR 399 at [64]–[66] *per* Wild, Miller and Lang JJ.

amount to 'misbehaviour' ('as always, context is everything'[101]); and, second, that moral turpitude, while determinative where it can be established, is not a necessary element of misbehaviour. The court endorsed the Privy Council's decision in *The Cayman Islands* case, which emphasised the cumulative effect of the judge's conduct on the judicial role.[102] The court also endorsed their Lordships' decision in the *Gibraltar* case, where the ultimate question was whether the conduct complained of was likely to destroy confidence in the judge's ability to perform the judicial function.[103] These rulings now properly reflect the standard of 'misbehaviour' recognised throughout the common law jurisdictions.

Incapacity

There are no New Zealand precedents for removing a judge for incapacity (or, for that matter, inability). Most judges, afflicted by mental or physical impairment, would retire rather than suffer the anguish of infirmity or ignominy of removal.

Incapacity and inability are overlapping concepts. Incapacity implies physiological, psychological or cognitive impairment leading to the inability to perform the office of judge. Impairment might result from a debilitating stroke, dementia, clinical depression or a combination of degenerative health conditions. Justice Douglas of the American Supreme Court suffered a stroke that partially paralysed him at the end of his long tenure on the court (1939–75). For eleven months, he doggedly remained on the court, despite his incapacity, but eventually took advice and resigned.[104] Under the US Constitution, incapacity is not in itself a ground for impeachment. Article III, s. 1 enshrines the Act of Settlement 1701 guarantee that judges of the Supreme Court shall hold office during good behaviour.

British precedents have been more expansive and conflated misbehaviour and incapacity. In one case, it was said that 'gross perversion of the law . . . by incapacity' would justify removal.[105] But physical or mental

[101] *Wilson v. Attorney-General* [2011] 1 NZLR 399 at [64] *per* Wild, Miller and Lang JJ.

[102] *Hearing on the Report of the Tribunal to the Governor of The Cayman Islands: Madam Justice Levers (Judge of the Grand Court of The Cayman Islands): Referral under Section 4 of the Judicial Committee Act 1833* [2010] UKPC 24.

[103] *Hearing on the Report of the Chief Justice of Gibraltar: Referral under Section 4 of the Judicial Committee Act 1833* [2009] UKPC 43 at [31].

[104] J. J. Patrick, R. M. Pious and D. A. Ritchie, *The Oxford Guide to the United States Government* (New York: Oxford University Press, 2001), p. 197.

[105] *Torrens' Case* 140 Parl. Deb., 3rd Ser., 1561 (1856).

incapacity must exceed mere aberration. Incapacity implied 'not mere error in the exercise of the judicial function, but the incapacity of a judge who continues so long on the Bench that he is physically unable to discharge his duties'.[106] Another precedent referred to a judge 'in a situation of notorious incapacity from age [and] unfit for his duties'.[107] In those circumstances, Parliament's intervention would be a 'painful necessity'.[108]

Administrative necessity drove the expansive interpretation. Under the Act of Settlement 1701, incapacity *per se* is not a ground to remove a judge. But there are problems with this approach. Chronic alcoholism, for example, might amount to incapacity but not misbehaviour. Alcoholism is a compulsive physiological disease that lacks the element of personal culpability needed to establish misbehaviour. A New South Wales court held that a judge, crippled by a depressive illness and unable to deliver judgments, might be removed for incapacity but not misbehaviour.[109] The court treated his clinical depression as a psychiatric disorder.[110] Chronic alcoholism would logically fall into the same category (incapacity but not misbehaviour). On the other hand, persistent episodes of drunkenness not induced by alcoholism might constitute misbehaviour, without also triggering incapacity as a ground for removal.

Inability

Inability overlaps incapacity, and is largely synonymous with it.[111] This ground implies an intellectual and/or professional inability to perform the judicial office, usually (but not always) stemming from incapacity of one form or another. The constitution of Gibraltar, for example, appends to the ground of 'inability' the rider 'whether arising from infirmity of body or mind or any other cause'.[112] Inability will usually stem from an underlying medical condition (clinical depression, stroke, dementia, etc.). The classical example was the New South Wales judge who was

[106] *Grantham's Case* 160 Parl. Deb., 4th Ser., at 395 (1906)
[107] *Fox's Case*, 45 *Lords Journals* 181 (1805) (discussed by Shetreet, *Judges on Trial*, at 140–1, 274).
[108] *Fox's Case*, 45 *Lords Journals* 181 (1805), *per* Lord Grenville.
[109] *Bruce* v. *Cole* (1998) NSWLR 163 at 175–6, NSWCA.
[110] *Bruce* v. *Cole* (1998) NSWLR 163 at 175.
[111] *Hearing on the Report of the Chief Justice of Gibraltar: Referral under Section 4 of the Judicial Committee Act 1833* [2009] UKPC 43 at [261]–[266].
[112] Gibraltar Constitution Order 2006, s. 64(2). See *Hearing on the Report of the Chief Justice of Gibraltar* [2009] UKPC 43.

unable to deliver his judgments and discharge the judicial workload because he suffered from a depressive illness.[113]

The test is whether a judge, through inability, is unfit for judicial office: 'the phrase "wholly unfitted to perform judicial functions" captures the essence of what the word [inability] means in this context'.[114] Might inability invite a more expansive interpretation than suggested above? Might it include inability *per se*, irrespective of any physiological or cognitive impairment? The rider under the Gibraltar constitution would suggest 'yes': inability might arise from infirmity 'or any other cause'. In *Stewart* v. *Secretary of State for Scotland*,[115] Lord Jauncey of Tullichettle held that unfitness for office might arise from defect in character or quirk of behaviour not amounting to mental illness. A judge's decisions, for example, might be so erratic, perverse or morally outrageous that the judge might be deemed unfit for office. In *Stewart*'s case, Lord Clyde opined that sheriffs might be removed from office because they had failed to do things which it was their duty to do, or had done things which they should not have done or were unable to do things they were required to do.[116]

All three grounds (misbehaviour, incapacity and inability) overlap and telescope into each other. In *Stewart*'s case, the ground of removal was inability, but the court might equally have cited misbehaviour. The sheriff had persisted with 'unacceptable behaviour', despite two previous warnings that his conduct would not be tolerated in perpetuity.[117] The actual ground relied on is less important than the crucial question, whether the judge's conduct was calculated to undermine public confidence in the administration of justice. The determining criterion under each of the grounds is fitness for judicial office.

The legal profession is largely self-regulating. Stories circulate as to why some judges take early retirement. Judges do occasionally exhibit failings which, left unattended, would cause embarrassment and disruption. Heads

113 See above, *Bruce* v. *Cole* (1998) NSWLR 163, n. 110.

114 *Hearing on the Report of the Chief Justice of Gibraltar: Referral under Section 4 of the Judicial Committee Act 1833* [2009] UKPC 43 at [266]. The test is essentially the same for the companion grounds of misbehaviour and incapacity.

115 1998 SC 81 at 86, HL.

116 1996 SC 271 (aff'd 1998 SC 81, HL) at 285 (discussed in *Hearing on the Report of the Chief Justice of Gibraltar: Referral under Section 4 of the Judicial Committee Act 1833* [2009] UKPC 43 at [265]).

117 Discussed in *Hearing on the Report of the Chief Justice of Gibraltar* [2009] UKPC 43 at [266].

of Bench might counsel such judges, who might be persuaded to deploy their talents elsewhere.

Judicial review

Proponents of statutory codification sometimes overlook the consequences of codification – the 'judicialisation' of public process. The actions and recommendations of the Judicial Conduct Commissioner and a Judicial Conduct Panel are susceptible to judicial review.[118] The Constitution Act 1986 and JCCJCPA prescribe the grounds and procedures for removal, which opens a decision to challenge under the Judicature Amendment Act 1972. This statute prescribes the procedure for bringing applications for judicial review of the exercise of a statutory power of decision.[119] Significantly, the first panel appointed under the JCCJCPA was successfully challenged through judicial review. In *Wilson* v. *Attorney-General*,[120] the Full Court held that the commissioner had failed to identify the specific aspects of Justice Wilson's behaviour that were to constitute the matters for the panel's inquiry. The commissioner was directed to reconsider the complaints against the judge and, should he recommend a panel be appointed, to identify with particularity the matter or matters concerning the judge's conduct that should be investigated.

To remove a judge, the commissioner and panel must each independently recommend that inquiry into the alleged conduct is necessary and that 'consideration of the removal of the judge is justified'.[121] A commissioner or panel recommendation, although not a 'decision', is reviewable as the exercise of the power satisfies the justiciability test in New Zealand: the power is public in nature and its exercise has important public consequences.[122] The recommendations required under the JCCJCPA are jurisdictional requisites and an error by either the commissioner or panel would vitiate the decision to remove a judge.[123] Their

[118] *Wilson* v. *Attorney-General* [2011] 1 NZLR 399 at [50] *per* Wild, Miller and Lang JJ.

[119] See generally Joseph, *Constitutional and Administrative Law in New Zealand*, pp. 1106–22.

[120] Joseph, *Constitutional and Administrative Law in New Zealand*, pp. 1106–22.

[121] JCCJCPA, ss. 18(1), 32(2)(b).

[122] *Royal Australasian College of Surgeons* v. *Phipps* [1999] 3 NZLR 1 at 11, CA; *Wilson* v. *White* [2005] 1 NZLR 189 at 196, CA. See, e.g., *Peters* v. *Davison* [1999] 2 NZLR 164, CA (report and recommendations of a commission of inquiry amenable to review).

[123] *Wilson* v. *Attorney-General* [2011] 1 NZLR 399 at [144] *per* Wild, Miller and Lang JJ.

investigations are open to challenge, as would their recommendations and grounds in support. Each must comply with the principles of natural justice and must construe and apply correctly the ground relied upon (misbehaviour, incapacity or inability). The decision of the Governor-General to revoke a judge's commission, acting on ministerial advice, would likewise be open to challenge in proceedings for a declaration. The challenger might name the Governor-General as a party, although the preferred litigation strategy would be to join the commissioner and panel and mount a challenge at an earlier stage of the statutory process (as in the case of Justice Wilson).[124]

Other aspects of the removal process would be protected from challenge. The Attorney-General must address the House of Representatives to seek a judge's removal, and a decision whether or not to move an address would be immune from judicial scrutiny. Proceedings in Parliament are protected by Parliament's privileges of exclusive cognisance and freedom of speech in debate.[125] The decision of the House itself, whether or not to seek the judge's removal, would also be a proceeding in Parliament and protected from review.[126]

Practices compromising judicial independence

Acting or temporary judges

Non-tenured judges who hold acting or temporary warrants raise concerns about institutional independence. Acting or temporary judges are routinely appointed to the Supreme Court, High Court and District Court. In recent years, as many as six High Court judges (approximately one-sixth of the High Court Bench) have held acting or temporary warrants. Acting judges in the Supreme Court are of on-going concern. Acting judges are routinely used where Supreme Court judges must recuse themselves owing to prior involvement in proceedings below.[127] Recusal is problematic as the court's

[124] *Wilson* v. *Attorney-General* [2011] 1 NZLR 399 at [144] *per* Wild, Miller and Lang JJ.

[125] See Joseph, *Constitutional and Administrative Law in New Zealand*, ch. 12 for examination of parliamentary privilege in New Zealand.

[126] Cf. *Mangawaro Enterprises Ltd* v. *Attorney-General* [1994] 2 NZLR 451, HC; *Boscawen* v. *Attorney-General* [2009] 2 NZLR 229, CA (the obligation on the Attorney-General under the New Zealand Bill of Rights Act 1990 to report to the House inconsistent Bills was part of a proceeding in Parliament and protected from scrutiny under Art. 9 of the Bill of Rights 1688).

[127] E.g., Justice Bill Wilson was unable to sit in eight cases in the Supreme Court when he was appointed in 2008: M. Taggart, 'Acting Judges and the Supreme Court of New Zealand' (2008) 14, *Canterbury Law Review*, 217 at 221.

quorum of five judges equals the court's permanent membership.[128] No other final appellate court in the common law jurisdictions has a quorum equal to the number of permanent judges on the court.[129]

Acting or temporary judges might ease the judicial workload, but they should be resisted. Non-tenured judges raise suspicions of executive patronage and favour. Almost all persons appointed to these positions are retired judges who have reached the statutory retirement age of 70 years.[130] The suspicion is that judges approaching the retirement age might placate the government in order to secure a non-tenured appointment upon retirement.[131] In *R* v. *Te Kahu*,[132] the Court of Appeal acknowledged that possibility and conceded that acting judges may not be as fiercely independent as judges on permanent tenure. Their Honours cited Scottish authorities in which temporary sheriffs had failed the requirement of an independent and impartial tribunal as required under Scot's Law by the European Convention on Human Rights 1950.[133]

Renewable fixed-term warrants

The renewable nature of fixed-term warrants exacerbates matters. The term of non-tenured judges is fixed, but their warrants are often renewed. The maximum tenure of acting Supreme Court, High Court and District Court judges, who have reached the statutory retirement age, is two years (or one year for High Court or District Court judges who are 72 years of age or over),[134] and one year for temporary High Court judges (including Associate Judges).[135] A 1- or 2-year renewable tenure is only marginally removed from tenure 'at pleasure'. The warrant of an acting District Court judge may be renewed as many as four times, and the warrant of an acting High Court judge as many times as it is

[128] Supreme Court Act 2003, s. 27(1).

[129] Taggart, 'Acting Judges and the Supreme Court of New Zealand', at 218.

[130] District Courts Act 1947, s. 7; Judicature Act 1908, s. 13.

[131] See J. Varuhas, 'Acting Judges' [2006] *New Zealand Law Journal* 172.

[132] [2006] 1 NZLR 459 at 469, CA.

[133] *Starrs* v. *Procurator Fiscal* (1999) 8 BHRR 1; *Millar* v. *Dickson* [2002] 3 All ER 1041, PC. For further discussion of acting or temporary judges, see *Kearney* v. *Her Majesty's Advocate* [2006] UKPC D1; *Forge* v. *ASIC* (2006) 228 CLR 45, HCA. See also A. Dziedic, 'Forge v. Australian Securities and Investment Commission: The Kable Principle and the Constitutional Validity of Acting Judges' (2007) 35 *Federal Law Review* 129.

[134] Supreme Court Act 2003, s. 23(2); Judicature Act 1908, s. 11A(1); District Courts Act 1947, s. 10A(3).

[135] Judicature Act 1908, ss. 11(1) and 26H.

determined necessary for the due conduct of the court's business.[136] In *R* v. *Te Kahu*,[137] the appellant challenged a non-tenured High Court judge, who had been re-appointed several times following his retirement. The Court of Appeal accepted that his successive re-appointments potentially raised issues of executive patronage, but rejected the challenge as the legislation clearly authorised renewable appointments. In Canada, appointing acting judges at pleasure contravened the guarantee of an independent judiciary under the Canadian Charter of Rights and Freedoms.[138] The Canadian courts have also held that a judge advocate, appointed on a case-by-case basis to preside at courts martial, failed the security of tenure requirement of judicial independence.[139]

Judicial secondment to more highly remunerated courts

Arguments about executive patronage also arise where judges are appointed on fixed-term warrants to sit in courts attracting higher levels of remuneration. Tenured District Court judges are regularly appointed to sit in the Employment Court, which attracts a higher judicial salary than the District Court.[140] The Attorney-General, Hon. Chris Finlayson, recently acknowledged that judicial secondment to the Employment Court was a routine practice. He observed that two District Court judges at that time held temporary warrants to sit in the Employment Court.[141]

Similarly, High Court judges routinely sit in the Criminal and Civil Appeal Divisions of the Court of Appeal and receive the salary of a tenured Court of Appeal judge. These judges may be seconded to the court for periods of up to three months.[142] However, unlike secondments to other courts, this practice does not invite insinuations of executive patronage and favour. Neither the Attorney-General nor any other minister is involved in selecting which judges will qualify for the higher paid work. The Chief Justice, in consultation with the President of the Court of Appeal, nominates the High Court judges who will sit in the Court of Appeal.[143]

The High Court has expressed misgivings about judicial secondments and the guarantee of judicial independence. In *Wikio* v. *Attorney-*

[136] District Courts Act 1947, s. 10(2); Judicature Act 1908, s. 11A(1).
[137] [2006] 1 NZLR 459, CA. [138] *Valente* v. *R* [1985] 2 SCR 673, SCC.
[139] *R* v. *Généreux* [1992] 1 SCR 259, SCC.
[140] G. Colgan, 'Letter' [2007] *Employment Law Bulletin* 93.
[141] NZPD, Vol. 661 (2010), at 9512. [142] Judicature Act 1908, ss. 58A(3) and 58B(3).
[143] Judicature Act 1908, ss. 58A(2) and 58B(2).

General,[144] the court acknowledged that s. 23 of the Constitution Act 1986 was a bulwark against reducing a judge's salary during the judge's commission. MacKenzie J thought it 'at least arguable' that a reduction occurs when the secondment ends and the higher salary ceases to be payable.[145]

Abolition or restructuring of courts

The statutory abolition or restructuring of courts raises concerns about judicial independence. A court might be abolished and its jurisdiction merged into other courts, or restructured with a downsizing of jurisdiction and number of judges. For former Australian judge, Michael Kirby, such possibilities posed a 'grave threat to judicial independence'.[146] He believed that judicial officers whose court was abolished or restructured should be re-appointed to a court of similar rank, with similar salary and benefits of office. Kirby also believed that a judge who declined an offer of re-appointment should receive the emoluments of office until the statutory retirement age. These requirements, he maintained, were an unyielding convention, even if a judge was not personally deserving of re-appointment. The inference otherwise was that judicial tenure was effectively at the will of the executive government.

In *Claydon* v. *Attorney-General*,[147] the Court of Appeal endorsed Kirby's thesis. The court acknowledged that judges whose court was abolished or restructured should be entitled to re-appointment or to continued receipt of the benefits of office (remuneration, allowances, etc.).[148] In an ideal world these judges could look to the guarantee of judicial independence for protection. However, there is little political appetite in New Zealand or elsewhere for 'idealised' arguments about judicial independence. Kirby's thesis held no sway when the Coroners Act 2006 reformed New Zealand's coronial system and disestablished all existing coroner positions. Coroners whose positions were disestablished had been appointed under the Governor-General's warrant and

[144] *Wikio* v. *Attorney-General*, 11 July 2008, MacKenzie J, HC Wellington Civ. 2004–485–2198 at [133]–[135].

[145] *Wikio* v. *Attorney-General*, HC Wellington Civ. 2004–485–2198 at [133].

[146] M. Kirby, 'Abolition of Courts and Non-appointment of Judicial Officers' (1995) 12 *Australian Bar Review* 181 at 205–6.

[147] [2004] NZAR 16, CA.

[148] *Claydon* v. *Attorney-General* [2004] NZAR 16 at 42 (McGrath J), 45 (Glazebrook J) (CA).

were inferior courts.[149] On Kirby's view, the disestablished coroners were entitled to re-appointment, or, failing that, to the benefits of office until the statutory retirement age. On this precedent, Kirby might indeed argue that judicial tenure was ultimately at the whim of the political executive.

Knighthoods

Knighthoods under the Royal Honours system demonstrably raise arguments about executive patronage. What marks out some judges for the Royal largess but not others? Not all superior court judges are knighted. Five of the tenured Supreme Court judges have knighthoods (Dame Sian Elias, Sir Peter Blanchard, Sir Andrew Tipping, Sir John McGrath and Sir William Young) but not the sixth judge (Justice Bill Wilson before he resigned from the court). Sir William Young received his knighthood when he was President of the Court of Appeal, which distinguished him from all of his judicial colleagues on the court. Sometimes, even High Court judges receive knighthoods, either before or following retirement. What distinguishes these judges from the rest? It is not any special judicial quality or selfless public service.

Fifty years ago, a commentator observed the anomaly of some puisne judges receiving knighthoods, while others did not. He made the damning observation that 'a judge is not free from hope of discretionary benefit from the executive'.[150] During the 1930s depression, the Attorney-General requested the superior court judges to refund part of their salaries, but they refused, citing the constitutional guarantee against a diminution in judicial salaries. During that government's term, no judges (current or retired) were conferred knighthoods. The government broke with convention and even refused to knight the senior puisne judge, who received his knighthood only after a change of government.[151] Knighthoods were at the grace and favour of the government and were an instrument for exerting pressure on the judiciary.

The 1930s precedent supports an 'all or nothing' approach to Royal Honours: confer knighthoods on all judges above a certain rank, or confer none at all. In the United Kingdom, knighthoods are automatic for judges of the High Court upon their elevation to the bench.

149 Inferior Courts Procedure Act 1909, s. 2(c).
150 K. J. Scott, *The New Zealand Constitution* (Oxford: Clarendon Press, 1962), p. 164.
151 Scott, *The New Zealand Constitution*, p. 163.

Conclusion

There is no credible reason to doubt the independence of New Zealand's judges. The guarantee of judicial tenure, a respect for the traditions of judicial office and judges' personal integrity safeguard the constitutional position of the judiciary. Judges themselves adhere to a code of conduct that is aimed at preserving their independence and integrity. They exercise high public office and bear a weighty responsibility to avoid public controversy.[152] Practices that might compromise judicial independence (temporary warrants, judicial secondment, knighthoods, etc.) should, as far as possible, be resisted, although these practices do not pose a serious threat to the judiciary's institutional independence. Nor do New Zealand's procedures for appointing judges. Judicial appointments commissions, extolled in some jurisdictions, are of contestable utility. The convention is firmly established that judicial appointments are on merit and are not for political or personal reward. Judicial promotion within the higher judiciary, noted but not discussed in this chapter, poses, at most, a theoretical risk to judicial independence. Judicial promotion is a feature of all legal systems similar to New Zealand's, and has the overwhelming advantage of bringing depth of judicial experience to the appellate role.[153]

If there is any real threat to judicial independence, it stems from the nature of the New Zealand polity. New Zealand is a small jurisdiction with a population of 4,355,000. In governmental and professional circles, it is a 'close' community. New Zealand's institutional life comprises a web of interconnecting personal associations and professional or business interests. Such associations or interests can readily compromise judges who fail to monitor their personal situation and recuse themselves where conflict arises. Supreme Court judge, Justice Bill Wilson, who was under investigation as this chapter was written (but has since resigned from office), attests to the need for on-going vigilance and rectitude in judicial office: 'to do right to all manner of people after the laws and usages of New Zealand without fear or favour, affection or ill will'.[154]

A final and worrying concern entails modern expectations of public accountability. New Zealand formalised its procedures for disciplining judges following calls for greater transparency and accountability in the

[152] Elias, '"The Next Revisit"', at p. 218.

[153] *R* v. *Te Kahu* [2006] 1 NZLR 459 at 470, CA; *Wikio* v. *Attorney-General*, at [113]–[115].

[154] The Judicial Oath as prescribed by the Oaths and Declarations Act 1957, s. 18.

judicial role. Yet exacting expectations of public accountability may eventually compromise the ability of judges to do justice. The judiciary is under intensive media scrutiny, sometimes inviting unwarranted attacks on judges when law-and-order groups object to sentences meted out in criminal trials. Senior judges have warned of the vulnerability of the judiciary to corrosive public attack.[155] These voices lament the judiciary's vulnerability, but are scarcely heard above the clamour for accountability in the judicial role. The need to reconcile the tension between accountability and independence presents the greatest challenge for the next generation of New Zealand judges.

[155] Eichelbaum, 'The Inaugural Neil Williamson Memorial Lecture: Judicial Independence Revisited'; Elias, '"The Next Revisit"'.

5

Appointment, discipline and removal of judges in South Africa

HUGH CORDER

Judicial politics[1] has never been in the news in South Africa as much as it is currently. Scarcely a week passes without a newspaper billboard proclaiming the most recent pronouncement by a superior court judge.[2] This shift in the focus of public life is a direct reflection of the elevation of the judiciary in the constitutional framework since 1994, consequent on the allocation to it of the power of judicial review of legislative action.[3] So, from the establishment of the Constitutional Court (CC) in 1994,[4] judgments dealing with highly contentious social issues or high-profile national figures have featured in news media, mostly indicating public approbation for the work done by the courts. Regrettably, however, the past seven years or so have witnessed particular judges or even courts being cast in an altogether less positive light generated by controversy surrounding the judicial appointments and disciplinary processes which have been in place since 1994.

[1] Throughout this chapter I use this term in the sense of the prominence of the courts and the extent to which judicial behaviour provokes public discussion. I am not speaking here of party political affiliation or activity.

[2] This chapter focuses only on such judges, who number just over 200, because the title 'judge' is not used for the 1,600 or so magistrates who preside in the 'inferior' courts throughout the country. Both in their historical and current mode of operation and governance, magistrates are treated differently from judges, although there is commitment in principle from government to move to a model of a 'single judiciary', in which promotion directly from the ranks of magistrates to judicial office would be possible.

[3] Through the Constitution of the Republic of South Africa Acts 200 of 1993 and 108 of 1996, the 'interim' and 'final' constitutions which aided the transition from racist autocracy to democracy.

[4] The CC was the only innovation in the court structure post-apartheid. It was established to emphasise the break from the pro-executive attitudes which pervaded the jurisprudence of the former highest court, the Appellate Division, in the previous thirty years, and to give the new government the opportunity to appoint the members of what would be a significantly more powerful court.

The purpose of this chapter is to describe such events, setting them critically against the practices of the pre-democratic period in South Africa's history and against the prevailing party political climate. As with every aspect of the 'government' of South African society, critical assessment needs to occur in such contexts, not unduly to celebrate successful innovation nor to seek excuses for lamentable shortcomings, but to emphasise properly the complexities of a society in transition. This is a process which necessitates substantial upheavals of established practices and expectations, in which there is a risk of the loss of what might have been conducive of good governance, in pursuit of systemic renewal and a greater degree of equity and justice. So this is a tale of both good and bad, of confusion and poor management in the face of uncharted territory, and of the constant tensions lingering from the wickedness[5] of the past.

The legacy of the past

The practices followed in the appointment, discipline and removal of judges in South Africa before 1994 were essentially shaped by the country's status as a colony and then Dominion of Great Britain. The fact that two of the four provinces of the Union of South Africa established a century ago had been independent 'Afrikaner/Boer republics' during the second half of the nineteenth century[6] had no lasting impact in this area of constitutional law and practice. This is perhaps fortunate, as President Kruger, with little sense of constitutional propriety, dismissed his Chief Justice after a constitutional crisis in 1896, and generally had shown little understanding of or commitment to the principles of judicial independence and the separation of powers, in contrast to the experience in the Orange Free State.[7]

Thus, according to Westminster constitutional practice, judges were formally appointed by the Governor-General in Council, as head of state,[8]

[5] The use of this adjective to describe South African law under apartheid was pioneered in D. Dyzenhaus, *Hard Cases in Wicked Legal Systems* (Oxford: Clarendon Press, 1991). In this leading study, Dyzenhaus reviewed the judicial record under apartheid, using a Dworkinian model against which to measure the extent of injustice perpetrated through the law as interpreted and applied in the appellate courts.

[6] These were the Orange Free State and the Zuid Afrikaansche Republiek, both of which had been subjugated to British rule at the end of hostilities in the Anglo-Boer War of 1899 to 1902. The Orange River Colony and the Transvaal, as they became known, then united with the Cape Colony and Natal, to form the Union, pursuant to the South Africa Act 1909, 9 Edw. VII.

[7] For a detailed treatment of these histories, see L. Thompson, 'Constitutionalism in the South African Republics' (1954) *Butterworth's South African Law Review* 49–72.

[8] South Africa Act 1909, s. 100.

effectively handing the power of selection of judges to the Minister of Justice in cabinet. So, when a vacancy arose in a court, the relevant head of court would have informed the minister, through the Chief Justice, and would in all likelihood have consulted the leaders of the bar at the seat of the court concerned and his fellow judges. Again, although this is not written down at all, in all likelihood one or two names would have been proposed to the minister for appointment to the bench, and the minister would himself have consulted his trusted advisers before putting one name before cabinet.[9] Except for unusually contested periods in South African history,[10] such processes would probably have elicited little comment from cabinet, and the Governor-General would have had no discretion but to appoint the person so nominated. Such a system of judicial appointments continued essentially unchanged when South Africa became a republic in 1961. The outcome of the process, unsurprisingly given the racist foundation of the constitution, was that only white lawyers, overwhelmingly drawn from the ranks of senior counsel in private practice at the bar, achieved judicial appointment. All but two were male. It was only after the initiation of thorough-going political change in 1990, that two 'Indian' South Africans were appointed to the bench.

As far as discipline was concerned, there were no formal regulatory rules or mechanisms. Complaints about minor judicial indiscretions, such as rudeness to counsel or colleagues, were no doubt dealt with through the 'word in the ear' method by the Judge President or Chief Justice, as heads of court in the various divisions. Similarly, judicial misconduct in the public

[9] The use of the male sex in referring to judges and Ministers until 1994 is deliberate, as all Ministers (except the immediate past Minister), and all judges except two (until 1994) have been men. For a good description of the first fifty years of such an appointment practice, see H. R. Hahlo and E. Kahn, *The Union of South Africa: The Development of its Laws and Constitution* (London: Stevens & Sons and Cape Town: Juta, 1960), pp. 264–7. The provisions of the South Africa Act in regard to the judicial process were supplanted by the Supreme Court Act 59 of 1959 at the end of this period.

[10] Until 1994, the two periods during which the greatest attention would have been paid to judicial appointments by the executive are in the immediate aftermath of Union, at which time the courts' character and basic principles for the discharge of the judicial function were being settled (for greater detail on which, see H. Corder, *Judges at Work* (Cape Town: Juta, 1984), ch. 2), and in the decade following the election to office of the National Party in 1948, during which there was a concerted attempt to ensure that almost all those appointed to the bench, and particularly the highest court, the Appellate Division of the Supreme Court, would be broadly empathetic to the apartheid regime (in this regard, see J. Dugard, *Human Rights and the South African Legal Order* (Princeton University Press, 1978), ch. 2).

domain, or even some form of scandal emanating from a judge's private life, was dealt with informally. There is no evidence of a forced resignation of a judge resulting from peer pressure: indeed, the only four resignations from the bench occurred for reasons related chiefly to events outside the courtroom.[11]

Removal of a judge from office was possible, but only by the State President (Governor-General) as head of state 'upon address of both Houses of Parliament in the same session praying for removal' on the grounds of misbehaviour or incapacity.[12] No such address was made and no judge was dismissed in the period under consideration.

This apparently uncontroversial judicial history in the period 1910 to 1994 belies immense tensions and contradictions which remained largely unspoken, despite the open conflict between the Supreme Court (especially the Appellate Division) and Parliament, until a series of studies of the judiciary as a branch of government appeared in the late 1970s and thereafter.[13] These underlying tensions were a major force for change in this whole area of the law coincidental with the advent of a constitutional democracy in 1994.

The current regime

The legal regime governing the appointment, discipline and removal of judges has undergone substantial change, while the practical outcomes have been less clear-cut. This is particularly the case as regards discipline

[11] Judge Jan Steyn resigned from the Cape Bench in 1977 to head the Urban Foundation, the response of organised capital to the political crisis which erupted after the Soweto riots of 1976. Judge Mervyn King resigned from the Transvaal Bench after only three years on the bench in 1980, ostensibly because of finding judicial work not to his liking, although it was rumoured that he found it politically unpalatable. Judge Laurie Ackermann resigned from the Transvaal Bench in 1987 to take up the Chair in Human Rights Law at Stellenbosch University, it being widely known that he felt it impossible to continue as a judge in a country under emergency rule. He returned to the Cape Bench in 1993, and was appointed to the first bench of the CC in 1994. Judge Anton Mostert resigned in 1979 after clashing directly with State President Botha over an attempted cover-up of government misconduct revealed in the commission of inquiry which Mostert chaired.

[12] See the South Africa Act 1909, s. 101, replaced in this respect by the Supreme Court Act 1959, s. 10(7).

[13] Although there had been several more focused studies of groups of judgments, the pioneering works are A. Sachs, *Justice in South Africa* (London: Heinemann, 1973) (not lawfully available in South Africa due to the fact that Sachs was 'listed' under 'state security' legislation) and Dugard, *Human Rights and the South African Legal Order*.

and removal, in which the effects of the changed regime have yet to be transformed to express the ideals and values of the Constitution.

Those negotiating South Africa's constitutional future in 1993 clearly recognised[14] that the allocation of the judicial review power to the courts would require both strong entrenchment of judicial independence, and also additional measures to ensure a degree of judicial accountability over and above the traditional avenues.[15] Efforts to restore the legitimacy of the courts as a whole, after the battering that they had received in popular perception through the executive-mindedness[16] which characterised particularly the highest court during the state of emergency in the late 1980s, were to be seen in the establishment of the CC as the highest authority on constitutional matters; the exclusion from constitutional jurisdiction of the former highest court, the Appellate Division (since 1997 the Supreme Court of Appeal (SCA)); and in the novel mechanism for the appointment of judges.[17] To achieve the last, a Judicial Service Commission (JSC) was created, with its membership drawn from a relatively broad group of constituencies, and this model has been continued in the final constitution.[18]

Chaired by the Chief Justice, the JSC consists of representatives of the judiciary and of the professional bodies of advocates and attorneys, a teacher of law, the Minister of Justice and Constitutional Affairs, ten serving members of Parliament drawn from both Houses[19] and four members

[14] For an account of these negotiations as they concerned the courts, see R. Spitz and M. Chaskalson, *The Politics of Transition: A Hidden History of South Africa's Negotiated Settlement* (Johannesburg: Witwatersrand University Press, 2000), ch. 11 and L. Du Plessis and H. Corder, *Understanding South Africa's Transitional Bill of Rights* (Cape Town: Juta, 1994), pp. 191–205.

[15] For a discussion in the South African context just prior to constitutional change, see E. Cameron, 'Judicial Accountability in South Africa' (1990) 6 *South African Journal on Human Rights* 251–88.

[16] See generally, S. Ellmann, *In a Time of Trouble: Law and Liberty in South Africa's State of Emergency* (Oxford: Clarendon Press, 1992).

[17] Pragmatism determined the fate of the judges serving at the time: although their 'mass dismissal' and re-appointment was considered, the practical problems that would result and the overwhelming goal of reconciliation dictated that all judges would be entitled to continue in office, subject to swearing allegiance to the new Constitution – see Constitution of the Republic of South Africa, Act 200 of 1993, s. 241.

[18] Constitution of the Republic of South Africa, Act 108 of 1996, s. 178.

[19] The practice until recently was that such members would be designated in proportion to the relative strength of the ruling party and the combined opposition parties in the houses. Thus, the six drawn from the National Assembly would be divided four to two (or even equally) as between the government and the opposition. This practice has now been departed from in regard to the National Council of Provinces (NCOP), as all designees belong to the ruling party.

designated by the President as head of the executive, after consultation with the leaders of opposition parties. Thus, of the twenty-three ordinary members[20] of the JSC, fifteen[21] are selected more for their broadly political views than their standing as lawyers, of whom at least twelve are likely to be loyal in the first instance to the ruling party in Parliament.[22]

Appointing judges

The JSC has a broad mandate, including advising the government 'on any matter relating to the judiciary or the administration of justice',[23] but the function which most frequently propels it into the limelight is its role in the appointment of judges.[24] The procedure for filling vacancies on the bench of all superior courts[25] except the CC, for judicial transfers between courts[26] and for the appointment of administrative heads of court[27] is the same. The JSC secretariat calls for nominations and applications for any existing or anticipated vacancies, candidates fill in a detailed questionnaire relating both to their person and their professional experience, a sub-committee of

20 Two additional members join the deliberations of the JSC *ad hoc* when specific appointments are being made viz. the Judge President and Premier (or nominees) of the province in which an appointment is being made. The question of whether such members should be present when matters other than appointments are being considered is currently before the courts, as the Premier of the Western Cape province is challenging the JSC on review for not inviting her to attend the session at which the decision on whether to pursue the complaint against Judge President Hlophe of the Cape High Court was taken; for more on which, see below.

21 Being the ten MPs, the four presidential nominees and the Minister.

22 Seven of the ten MPs, all four of the presidential nominees and the Minister.

23 See the Constitution of the Republic of South Africa, Act 108 of 1996, s. 178(5). It is important to note that, except when it is considering the appointment of judges, the JSC sits *without* the ten serving members drawn from Parliament, reducing it in size to fifteen in such circumstances.

24 This is provided for generally in Constitution of the Republic of South Africa, Act 108 of 1996, s. 174.

25 These are the High Courts with seats in most of the provinces, the Labour Court and the Labour Appeal Court, the Competition Appeal Court, the Land Claims Court and the Supreme Court of Appeal, which sits in Bloemfontein. The administration of justice is the exclusive concern of the national government.

26 This happens most frequently when serving judges move from a High Court to the SCA or another appellate court.

27 Each of the High Courts, the Labour Appeal Court and the Competition Appeal Court is headed by a Judge President (JP), assisted by at least one Deputy Judge President, while the head of the SCA is styled its President. Collectively, the JPs and the President of the SCA are known as the Heads of Court, and they meet regularly, with the Chief Justice (CJ) as Chair, to discuss the management of the courts.

the JSC[28] compiles a shortlist of candidates to be interviewed, and the whole JSC gathers in April and October each year to interview, deliberate on and recommend those for appointment to the bench. The Constitution provides[29] that 'any appropriately qualified woman or man who is a fit and proper person' may be appointed, except that South African citizenship is an additional criterion for those to be appointed to the CC.[30] The JSC then sends its list of recommendations to the President who, as head of state, must appoint those recommended 'on the advice of' the JSC.[31]

The appointment of justices to the CC is significantly different,[32] reflecting their immense authority as the final arbiter on the reach and distribution of the lawful exercise of power under the Constitution. After the interview stage, the JSC must send a list of appointable nominees to the President, which is greater by three than the number of vacancies to be filled on the court. The President, as head of the executive, may select any nominee from the list, after consulting with the Chief Justice and the leaders of all the parties represented in the National Assembly. If the President is of the view that there are insufficient nominees whom he wishes to appoint, he must advise the JSC of the unacceptability of those candidates, and the JSC must then 'supplement the list with further nominees', from whom the President must appoint the remaining justices. Although this is not explicitly stated, the reference back to the JSC may occur only once; in fact, this step has not proved necessary to date. Similarly, the appointment of the Chief Justice and his deputy must be done by the President (as head of the executive) after consulting the JSC (which interviews the candidates) and the leaders of parties in Parliament, and those of the President and Deputy President of the SCA after consulting the JSC.[33] The final peculiarity is that there must at all times be at least four constitutional justices who were judges prior to their appointment:[34] this was particularly necessary in the early days of the court, but appears to be less so today.

Over the past fifteen years of its existence, the JSC has developed a relatively efficient and fair means of operating in the context of

[28] In a document entitled 'Procedures of the Judicial Service Commission' (WHT29/06/95), this committee is referred to as the 'sifting committee', and defined in para. 1.2 as an '*ad hoc* sub-committee of the Commission constituted from time to time'.

[29] In s. 174(1).

[30] To my knowledge, no non-South African has yet been appointed as a judge.

[31] Constitution of the Republic of South Africa, Act 108 of 1996, s. 174(6).

[32] Details are to be found in Constitution of the Republic of South Africa, Act 108 of 1996, s. 174(4).

[33] See Constitution of the Republic of South Africa, Act 108 of 1996, s. 174(3).

[34] See Constitution of the Republic of South Africa, Act 108 of 1996, s. 174(5).

appointments.[35] After something of a baptism of fire in October 1994, when it interviewed[36] in public session twenty-four shortlisted candidates for the first bench of the CC,[37] the JSC attempted to establish as a general practice that its interviews should take place behind closed doors. This was fiercely resisted inside the ranks of the commission, chiefly by the academic representative, Professor Etienne Mureinik, which led to his expressing forthright criticism in the media, which in turn earned him a public rebuke from the then chair of the JSC, Chief Justice Corbett.[38] Mureinik's view, however, triumphed, and the JSC now generally operates as if it were a court of law[39] when interviewing candidates for the bench, but not when it deliberates on its recommendations. The interviews vary in intensity and

[35] The best treatment of the record of the JSC in this area of its work is to be found in F. Du Bois, 'Judicial Selection in Post-apartheid South Africa', in K. Malleson and P. H. Russell (eds.), *Appointing Judges in an Age of Judicial Power* (University of Toronto Press, 2006), pp. 280–312.

[36] The interviews were carefully presided over by the then Chief Justice, Michael Corbett, who from time to time intervened to ensure the fairness of questioning of different candidates. He did this in accordance with a seven-page document, 'Guidelines for questioning candidates for nomination to the Constitutional Court', dated 26 September 1994, which sets out various selection criteria, as follows: independence, open-mindedness, integrity and courage; diversity, empathy and sensitivity; intellect; fairness, judgement and perceptiveness; stamina and industry; and the (fostering of) vigorous internal debate. The final summary of this document is perhaps worth quoting in full:

> Perhaps the central value of the Constitution is accountability. The judges . . . are accountable to those who are subject to their power; but not through the ballot box. They are accountable through their judgments. The Court is governed not by the discipline of electoral accountability, but by the principle of persuasive accountability: its judgments must be cogent justifications of the rulings that it gives. And they must develop our nascent constitutional democracy in a way which earns the confidence of the nation. It is this responsibility to which the judges of the Constitutional Court must be equal.

[37] Much media attention and public controversy was stimulated by these interviews and by the list of recommended candidates submitted to President Mandela. Perhaps the most detailed contemporary study of this first session is to be found in R. Calland, *A Step in the Right Direction: An Analysis of the Interviews of the Nominees for Membership of South Africa's First Constitutional Court* (University of Cape Town, 1995).

[38] A sense of the toughness of the debate is gathered from the correspondence which took place between Chief Justice Corbett and Professor Mureinik on this matter. I have on file a copy of a twenty-page letter from Mureinik to Corbett dated 8 February 1995, in which he defends his critical comment published in the *Weekly Mail and Guardian* of Friday, 6 January 1995, to which Corbett had reacted by letter to Mureinik on Monday, 9 January.

[39] In other words, members of the public and the media may attend the interview sessions, and report on them, but radio and television are generally not allowed to intrude.

focus, often by reference to answers provided by the candidates to the questionnaire which they must complete on application or nomination, and generally are conducted politely and even-handedly. An apparent departure from prior process was to be seen in the interviews conducted in respect of both constitutional and high court judgeships in the latter part of 2009, however, when a more intrusive and occasionally aggressive set of questions relating to the transformation of the justice system was asked particularly of white candidates.

The quality of those appointed has, with limited exceptions, not drawn public or professional criticism and the JSC has succeeded in quite substantially transforming the demographic profile of the superior court judiciary as regards race,[40] though less successfully as regards sex. From the almost all-white, all-male bench in place in early 1994, the current demographic composition of judicial ranks is as follows:[41] seventy-eight African (sixteen women), sixteen coloured (four women), eighteen Indian (eight women), and ninety-one white (fourteen women) judges. So, of the 203 judges permanently appointed to the bench, just over 55 per cent were broadly 'black', while only just over 20 per cent were female. In addition, all but one of the heads of court are black African men,[42] and this has been the case for several years now. In this context, it should be noted that, when succession to the chief justiceship became an issue[43] relatively early on in the tenure of President Zuma as head of state, he appeared to act unconstitutionally by announcing his preferred nominee before embarking on the required process of consultation outlined above. In the event however, the JSC interviewed his nominee and recommended his appointment, while the leaders of other political parties acquiesced with a degree of protest, and Sandile Ngcobo was duly elevated to the chief justiceship.

One specific aspect of the appointments process has drawn adverse comment, being the apparent requirement of the JSC in its approach in

[40] The race groups devised under apartheid are still widely employed in South Africa, chiefly to assess the progress made in reversing the effects of past unfair discrimination. So 'black' people are styled 'African', people of Asian descent are 'Indians', people of mixed racial descent are 'coloured' and the descendants of those who originated in Europe are 'white'. The first three groups are often described as 'black'; I use the term 'broadly black' to distinguish it from Africans.

[41] According to a response from the Department of Justice to a request from the writer during March 2009.

[42] The only exception being the Judge President of the Competition Appeal Court, Dennis Davis.

[43] Much of the reason for the heightened level of public attention to this matter was the rumour that Judge President Hlophe was to be nominated by President Zuma; on which see more below.

practice that anyone seeking appointment to judicial office must have served some time as an Acting Judge. The practice of appointing senior advocates (barristers) to the bench for a period of one to three months, typically to replace a judge on long leave or to help reduce a backlog of pending trials, has now been part of the administration of justice in South Africa for decades. As well as serving the direct purpose of allowing the court concerned to keep pace with the demands for its services, it has allowed those who are likely at some stage to be considered for judicial appointment a limited opportunity to experience judicial work, thus better informing any subsequent decision as to the person's suitability for judicial office, both from a personal as well as a collegial point of view. There has been no significant controversy about such appointments, and the current Constitution contemplates them 'if there is a vacancy or if a judge is absent'.[44] As regards process, the President must appoint acting justices to the CC on the recommendation of the Minister of Justice, who in turn must act 'with the concurrence of the Chief Justice and the President of the [SCA]'. All other acting appointments are made by the Minister of Justice, 'after consulting the senior judge of the court on which the acting judge will serve'.[45]

The principle of appointing acting judges has drawn adversely critical comment from the UN Special Rapporteur on Judicial Independence. In a report published in 2000,[46] Dato' Param Cumaraswamy, after commenting generally favourably on the state of judicial independence in South Africa, singled out this practice as a source of concern, commenting that the appointment of acting judges[47] 'could adversely affect the independent character' of the court concerned, and amounted to 'short probation'. He duly recommended that the JSC

> should review these acting appointments and determine whether they are consistent with the spirit of section 175 . . . and whether such acting judges could be perceived as independent in the light of international standards and judgments of courts from other jurisdictions.[48]

[44] Oddly enough, this is the reason given for acting appointments only in respect of the CC; in the absence of any such reason in relation to all other judicial appointments, it can be argued at least that the same reasons should apply. See the Constitution of the Republic of South Africa, Act 108 of 1996, s. 175.

[45] Constitution of the Republic of South Africa, Act 108 of 1996, s. 175.

[46] UN (Economic and Social Council) Commission on Human Rights, *Report of the Special Rapporteur on the Independence of Judges and Lawyers, Addendum: Mission to South Africa*, ref. E/CN.4/2001/65/Add 2, dated 25 January 2001.

[47] *Report of the Special Rapporteur on the Independence of Judges and Lawyers*, para. 100.

[48] See para. 109 of the Report.

At the time, most South African lawyers, vigilant to the need for judicial independence, would have been unlikely to be too concerned about this criticism, especially as the capacity afforded by acting appointments to speed up entry to judges' ranks by black or female lawyers was seen as a significant means of transforming the bench,[49] but this may no longer be the case. Some Judges President appear to be using acting judgeships in an unduly selective manner in which race plays a disproportionate part; and in early 2010, the Minister of Justice, with the agreement of the Acting Judge President of one of the less prominent High Courts, appointed as an acting judge for some months the former Acting National Director of Public Prosecutions, the very person who finally dropped all charges of corruption against President Zuma just before the general election of 2009.[50] As service in an acting capacity becomes more strictly required as a criterion for judicial appointment or elevation to an appellate court or perhaps to a more senior role in the management of the judiciary, so does concern for its potential misuse grow. This is an area of judicial appointability that needs to be monitored.

Having considered the process for judicial appointment, focus must shift to security of tenure, removal from office and disciplinary steps short of removal.

Disciplining and removing judges from office

The Constitution is silent on the matter of judicial discipline for conduct which does not warrant removal from office, although the jurisdiction of the JSC to be involved in such processes could be argued to be founded in its authority to 'advise the national government on any matter relating to

[49] See a report by C. Rickard, 'Acting Judges won't be Scrapped from SA Legal System – despite UN Criticism', *Sunday Times* (Johannesburg), 28 January 2001, p. 18 which emphasises exactly this argument in favour of continuing the practice.

[50] The lawyer concerned, Mokothedi Mpshe, initially remained on the establishment of the National Prosecuting Authority; it was only after a furious outcry from the organised legal profession and many opposition politicians that the Minister announced that Mpshe had requested that his service be terminated. A similar event occurred under apartheid when in 1979 an Attorney-General (the then equivalent of the current Provincial Director of Public Prosecutions), who had served as a member of a Commission of Inquiry into a high-profile political matter, Braam Lategan, was elevated to the bench, over the protests of those who argued that prosecutorial approach and experience were entirely unlikely to develop either the skills or the independence of mind needed for judicial service.

the judiciary'.[51] The formal steps regulating removal of a judge from office are clear: a finding by the JSC that the judge concerned 'suffers from an incapacity, is grossly incompetent or is guilty of gross misconduct'; a vote supported by at least a two-thirds majority of the National Assembly calling for the removal of such judge; and the removal of such a judge from office by the President, who must do so if the first two steps are achieved. If the JSC advises the President to do so, he may suspend such a judge from office pending the outcome of the process.[52] In all its activities, the commission may 'determine its own procedure, but [its] decisions ... must be supported by a majority of its members'.[53] It is important to note that the commission sits with attenuated membership (that is, without the ten serving members of Parliament) when not appointing judges.[54] Soon after the establishment of the JSC, Parliament passed the Judicial Service Commission Act,[55] which attempted to provide some detail on its duties and processes, without dealing effectively with the matter of judicial discipline.

Nevertheless, the JSC has from time to time received complaints about judicial rudeness in court or some other indiscretion, and these appear to have been resolved informally[56] by means of the intervention of the head of the court concerned or by the Chief Justice as chair of the JSC. There is one recorded instance of a decision by the JSC to pursue a formal investigation into allegations of improper conduct by a judge, which had the potential to become a recommendation for removal from office. However, the judge concerned resigned on the eve of the JSC meeting at which he would have had to account for his alleged financially improper conduct relating to an arbitration in which he presided after his assumption of office as a judge.[57]

Given the absence of appropriate process or guidelines for disciplinary action against judges, substantial steps were taken informally by the various chief justices as chairs of the JSC over the years to draft a set of

[51] Constitution of the Republic of South Africa, Act 108 of 1996, s. 178(5).

[52] Constitution of the Republic of South Africa, Act 108 of 1996, s. 177.

[53] Constitution of the Republic of South Africa, Act 108 of 1996, s. 178(6).

[54] Constitution of the Republic of South Africa, Act 108 of 1996, s. 178(5).

[55] Act 9 of 1994, as amended.

[56] For example, in the years 2005 to 2007, forty such complaints reached the JSC, only one of which (presumably that against Judge Hussain, see below n. 57) had to be taken further. See the Annual Reports of the JSC for 2006 and 2007, p. 6 in each of the Annual Reports.

[57] The judge concerned was Ismail Hussain of the Transvaal High Court. See the *Annual Report of the JSC for the year ended 30 June 2006*, p. 6, for greater detail.

codes and processes to fill this gap. Thus, draft Rules of Judicial Ethics were circulated for comment,[58] and by early 2004 substantial agreement had been reached between the leadership of the judiciary and the then Minister of Justice on a set of legislative measures which would have dealt comprehensively with, among other things, both judicial indiscretions not warranting removal from office and with the more serious processes attendant on possible impeachment by Parliament. Regrettably, the political leadership of the Justice Ministry changed after the general election of 2004, and the new Deputy Minister of Justice departed from the agreed drafts in significant respects, such that there was grave concern in judicial ranks and more broadly that the independence of the bench would be irreparably undermined. In the event, the outcry elicited by these proposed changes persuaded the government to suspend its plans, and the shift of power within the African National Congress (ANC) in the course of 2008 led to their effective demise. While the apparent abandonment of some of the most objectionable aspects introduced in 2004 has been widely welcomed, the effective stalling of the introduction into law and practice of those elements of the package of proposed measures which enjoyed broad support and which would have ensured procedural guidance and fairness in cases of judicial discipline were sorely missed in the intervening period, leading to much anguish and palpable damage to the public reputation of the judiciary.

The first substantial trigger to the urgent development of clear and predictable processes and policy came in the form of a complaint about the conduct of Judge President John Hlophe of the Cape High Court. It came to light that he had been in receipt of regular monthly payments from an asset management company which had then sought his permission, which he had granted, to sue one of his fellow judges for defamation.[59] Judge Hlophe's initial explanation for these payments was that they had been for expenses incurred in his service as chair of a trust run

[58] This was very much an initiative of Chief Justice Ismail Mohamed, the first black lawyer to hold this post, although much of the work has been continued by Judge of Appeal Louis Harms, referring extensively to the Bangalore Draft Code of Judicial Conduct 2001 adopted by the Judicial Group on Strengthening Judicial Integrity, as revised at the Roundtable Meeting of Chief Justices held at the Peace Palace, The Hague, 25–26 November 2002. For a summary of earlier draft proposals concerning both complaints mechanisms and ethics, see 'Proposals for a Mechanism for dealing with complaints against judges, and for a Code of Ethics for Judges – A report of a Committee chaired by Mr Justice L. Harms' (2000) 117 *South African Law Journal* 377.

[59] Leave to sue a judge in a civil matter must be sought from that judge's Head of Court.

by the company, but the size and regularity of the payments forced him subsequently to concede that they had been in the form of a retainer. Whatever the pretext for the payments, they fell foul of the rule that judges may not receive any remuneration other than what is paid them by the state unless they have the permission of the Minister of Justice to do so.[60] Hlophe claimed that he had such permission from the former minister, by then deceased, but no written record of such permission existed.[61]

At about the same time, Hlophe found himself as a silent concurring member of the majority in a split decision of the Cape High Court, finding for the Minister of Health in an enormously controversial matter concerning the pricing of medicines.[62] Hlophe's fellow judge in the majority was also a black African, while the dissenting judge was a white woman (incidentally Hlophe's Deputy Judge President), and when the judgment was greeted with trenchant criticism, apparently including a rumour that Hlophe had in fact written the judgment which had gone out in the name of the other black judge, Hlophe lashed out at his detractors, alleging that they were motivated by racism. He then submitted in early 2005, direct to the minister and without notice to those named in it, a substantial report on what he described as racist practices within the Cape legal community.

Thus, by 2005 two investigations regarding Judge Hlophe's conduct were under way: a complaint to the JSC concerning his receipt of a retainer from a commercial enterprise which was a party to disputes in his court; and his racism report, which found its way to the jurisdiction of the heads of court. There is much more that could be written on this matter, but this is not the place for it.[63] Suffice to say that the JSC, in October 2007 and by the narrowest majority, finally resolved that it would not pursue a full investigation into the payment of the retainer, while the heads of court issued a report on racism and sexism within the judiciary which, while acknowledging the presence of racist practices and attitudes within the legal profession and courts, noted that those named by Hlophe refuted his allegations. The heads recommended a

60 See the Supreme Court Act, 59 of 1959, s. 11, as well as the Judges' Remuneration and Conditions of Employment Act, 47 of 2001, s. 2(6).

61 Contrary to the practice in almost every other such grant of permission by the Minister, as subsequent enquiries revealed. See Letter to the Director of the Democratic Governance and Rights Unit at the University of Cape Town, dated 9 May 2009.

62 *Minister of Health* v. *New Clicks South Africa (Pty) Ltd (Treatment Action Campaign and Another as Amici Curiae)* 2006 (2) SA 311, CC.

63 For the most complete record of all the causes of Judge Hlophe being in the public eye, see 'Legalbrief Today', available at: http://legalbrief.co.za/index.php?page=HlopheSaga, accessed 30 March 2010.

dispute resolution mechanism for any such incidents of this sort that might arise in the future, as well as strongly endorsing the necessity for judicial training on issues of diversity.[64] The extent to which the latter system has been implemented is not clear, but the public outcry which greeted the unwillingness of the JSC to pursue its investigation was extraordinary, and soon degenerated into allegations that those critical of the JSC's apparent timidity were motivated by racism.

This furore had barely subsided[65] when Judge Hlophe's conduct generated even greater controversy, propelling the highest court into the limelight in an extremely damaging manner. The situation was exacerbated by playing off against the background of the strident political campaign to stop the prosecution for corruption of the then aspirant President of South Africa, Jacob Zuma; indeed, the renewed Hlophe controversy related directly to one of Zuma's court battles. At the end of May 2008, the justices of the CC registered a complaint with the JSC alleging that Hlophe had attempted improperly to interfere with the resolution of an appeal to the CC by Zuma and another, through his meeting two of the justices at his request and discussing aspects of the case with them. The CC issued a press statement to this effect soon after making the complaint, and the legal profession was once more thrown into divisive turmoil. The JSC started its investigations with some energy into whether there was a *prima facie* case for Hlophe to meet, but it soon became enmeshed in bitter division and found itself facing a counter-complaint from Hlophe against the CC justices, alleging unwarranted harm to his dignity and reputation, as well as challenges from Hlophe in court. This dispute became inextricably and to some extent inexplicably associated with the fate of Zuma. In addition, when the JSC finally reached its decision (that it would not pursue in a formal sense the question of whether Hlophe should be impeached, in the face of direct contradictions in the evidence given by him and those on the CC directly involved), it was a body with a substantially changed membership from

[64] The mechanism emphasised speed, mediation and informality, with the creation of local and a national committees to which complaints about racist or sexist practices could be made. See *Report and Recommendations on Racism and Sexism adopted by the Heads of Courts* (dated 23 September 2005).

[65] Indeed, as late as May 2008, questions were being asked about whether Judge Hlophe had declared the retainer as taxable income, and had paid taxes on the relatively substantial amounts paid to him over a five-year period. The answer seems to be that he did so, but retrospectively.

that which had started the investigation.[66] This decision was once again met with substantial shock by many, and two applications for its review are pending in different divisions of the High Court.

I have described these incidents in some detail because they have, in my view, done considerable harm to the precious level of legitimacy earned by the post-apartheid judiciary, in particular the CC, as a secure and independent protector of the Constitution and good governance, and because the arguments raised chiefly in support of Hlophe have plumbed new depths of irrationality. This provides a sobering context in which to review the current state of the law regulating judicial discipline and removal from office. As mentioned above, the package of proposed legislation whose passage was stalled due to unilateral executive intervention in late 2004 had much that was good and mutually agreeable in it, so that its effective delay by almost five years was to be regretted. Finally, however, some elements of the proposed legislation relating to judicial discipline were adopted by Parliament in late 2008, in the form of major revisions of the JSC Act.[67] This amendment leaves little of the original Act in place, adding three new chapters to it whose contents are highly relevant to the subject matter of this chapter in the present volume.

Chapter 2 of the JSC Amendment Act, 20 of 2008, is headed 'Oversight over judicial conduct and accountability of judicial officers', and it contemplates a Judicial Conduct Committee (JCC) as part of the JSC, chaired by the Chief Justice, with the Deputy Chief Justice and four other judges (two of whom must be women) designated by the Chief Justice in consultation with the Minister of Justice (s. 8(1)). The objects of the JCC are 'to receive, consider and deal with complaints' against judges on which it must report to the JSC every six months (s. 10). Part III of Chapter 2 of the Act duly provides for the lodging of complaints about judicial incapacity to perform his or her office, and any wilful or grossly negligent breach of the Judicial Code of Conduct (s. 12) or other wilful or grossly negligent conduct, and their disposal either as 'lesser', which may be summarily dismissed under certain conditions, or by an inquiry held

[66] This was directly the result of the intervening general election, which meant that the Minister of Justice and the four presidential nominees were different. In addition, the acting chair, the President of the SCA (the Chief Justice having to recuse himself as an interested party), was newly in office, as was the academic representative and one of the advocates. The decision was taken by a six to four majority.

[67] In the form of the JSC Amendment Act, 20 of 2008, assented to on 20 October 2008, with its date of commencement 1 June 2010.

by the chairperson or member of the Committee where the misconduct may be serious but non-impeachable, or by the appointment of an investigative tribunal (ss. 15, 16 and 17, respectively).

For present purposes, the most important of these means for resolving allegations about judicial misconduct is the last, details of which appear in Chapter 3 of the Act, headed 'Judicial conduct tribunals'. Here we find provision for the composition of such a tribunal (two judges and one other member) (s. 22), making of rules regulating tribunal procedures (s. 25), the appointment of administrative and investigative support for the tribunal (s. 24), the functions and powers of the tribunal (ss. 27–32) and the obligations of a tribunal as regards its findings and reporting (to the JSC) (s. 33). It is clear that these provisions would allow complaints about judicial misconduct of a serious nature to be expeditiously and fairly investigated and resolved; sanctions for non-compliance with the jurisdiction and the process of a tribunal are serious (s. 34). The role of the Chief Justice in ensuring efficient resourcing and administration of this system is critical, as is the support of a minister committed to the substantive independence of the judiciary.[68]

Finally, a vital part of this new regime for rendering judges accountable for maintaining their integrity and impartiality is to be seen in the clear prohibition on judges holding any other 'office of profit' or receiving payment for any service other than that rendered by virtue of being a judge,[69] and even retired judges would need ministerial permission (after consultation with the Chief Justice) in writing to do so.[70] The minister would be bound to report on the granting of such permission annually to Parliament (s. 11(5)). In addition, judges will henceforth have to disclose their own 'registrable interests', as well as those of their immediate family members, to be held in both public and confidential parts of a Register of Judges' Registrable Interests (s. 13), similar to the regime which has existed for members of Parliament since 1996. While such interests remain to be

[68] See, in particular, the obligations of the Chief Justice in ss. 21 and 25, and those of the Minister in s. 35.

[69] JSC Amendment Act, 20 of 2008, see s. 11(1). This seems to foreclose entirely on a judge 'in active service' receiving any form of payment other than salary, with the exception of royalties for legal books written or edited by the judge concerned. For fuller treatment, see Chapter 23 in this volume.

[70] Section 11(2) thus seeks to apply to retired judges what is the current regime for those in active service. This provision, and especially the need for ministerial as opposed to judicial permission, was strongly opposed by many judges, active and retired, but it is now part of the legislation.

defined,[71] they are certain to include ownership of all forms of property, directorships of corporate entities, the receipt of any gifts and so on.

It seems incontestable that, had this regime existed in law from the time that it was first agreed to by most of those directly affected, much of the controversy which surrounded Judge President Hlophe would not have reached the level it did, and the damage to the legitimacy of the courts would have been reduced. And yet, the key to these issues is the steadfastness of the commitment of both the judicial and executive leadership in the country to a regime that promotes judicial accountability, while simultaneously giving resolute endorsement to judicial independence. It is to an assessment of this aspect of the constitutional regime governing judicial appointments, discipline and removal in South Africa that I turn in the final section of this chapter.

Will form become substance?

The formal provisions in the law governing the appointment, discipline and removal of judges in South Africa seem finally to be falling into place. As a general assessment, it can safely be said that the various statutory provisions, founded as they are on the constitutional guarantees of security of tenure and judicial independence and impartiality, more or less satisfactorily respect the doctrine of the separation of powers. The existence of various sets of written guidelines used by the JSC in discharging its functions is commendable,[72] and the imminent adoption of a court management and administrative system, with the Chief Justice assisted by a substantially expanded office capacity at the helm, is likely to improve operational efficiency. The critical question, naturally, is whether this formally improved structure will translate sufficiently into substantial compliance with the goals and values of the Constitution.

In this respect, I would suggest that the area of judicial appointments provides, with a few exceptions, a rosier picture than that of judicial discipline and removals. As I hope to have demonstrated above, the record of the JSC thus far in appointing qualified and fit and proper

71 Much of the detail in this respect awaits definition through regulations, yet to be made by the Minister, acting in consultation with the Chief Justice, and which will have to be approved by Parliament; see s. 13(5).

72 See the reference to, e.g., 'Rules governing complaints and enquiries in terms of section 177(1)(a) of the Constitution', in the *Annual Report of the JSC 2007*, p. 6, although their exact status in law is less clear, and access to them through the secretariat of the JSC is, in my experience in preparing this chapter, perplexingly difficult.

persons to the bench and in seeking to shift the demographic balance of the superior judiciary is at least good. One should not underestimate the pressures brought to bear on it. The words of then President of the CC, Chaskalson P, in 1999 when reflecting on apparent perceptions of falling standards in the work of the courts, were reported as follows:

> If this kind of gossip was to . . . continue the Judicial Service Commission was going to be destroyed from two sides. One group saying that the perception of the public was that the Bench was a racist white Bench and the other group saying that the Bench was an inferior incompetent body of people and that it was no longer reliable.[73]

The minister is reported to have replied that the commission 'had functioned successfully and it had helped to depoliticise the issue of appointments',[74] and this was certainly the case initially, and probably is so today.

The record of the JSC concerning the high-profile complaints about the conduct of Judge President Hlophe is altogether less inspiring; indeed, it is very disturbing, as there seems to be a fundamental unwillingness to confront seriously and to pursue to their logical conclusion allegations of great moment which go to his fitness to hold judicial office. It is important to emphasise the fact that the complaints emanated in the first instance from a 'black' colleague on the Cape High Court, and in the second instance from the justices of the highest court in the country, overwhelmingly 'black' and under black African leadership. So, on the face of it, race should not be playing a role in the JSC's deliberations and decisions, yet it has surfaced almost immediately in the public furore that has attended each incident and it has come to dominate the discourse. It may be that the 'race card' has been skilfully employed to distract attention from the allegations, and it may also be that racist attitudes play some role in moving participants on all sides of these debates to state their positions in a manner which they would not otherwise employ. Yet it shows how deep the fissures born of the accumulated wickedness of past racist practices run, and how unresolved and indeed unreconciled to the present constitutional enterprise many, again on all sides of the divides, remain.

This view is reflected to some extent in the views and programme of the ruling party. In January 2005, the National Executive Committee of the ANC issued a statement on the transformation of the judiciary, in which it said:

[73] As reflected in the *Report on Activities of the JSC for the year ended 30 June 1999*, para. 6.
[74] *Report on Activities of the JSC for the year ended 30 June 1999.*

> The reality can no longer be avoided that many within our judiciary do not see themselves as being part of the masses, accountable to them, and inspired by their hopes, dreams and value systems. If this persists for too long, it will inevitably result in popular antagonism towards the judiciary and our courts, with serious and negative consequences for our democratic system as a whole.[75]

Now some may argue that this statement was intended to prepare the way for the proposed changes to the 'judiciary bills' described above, and that it should be seen as part of the campaign, then gathering momentum, to ensure that Jacob Zuma was not prosecuted for corruption. However, despite the shelving of the Bills relating to the superior courts a year later, the level of invective which was directed against the courts in their findings against Zuma escalated rapidly over the next three years, and the stand-off between the CC justices and Hlophe is certain to have damaged further both morale in the judiciary as well as the level of their public respect and support. In addition, the CC in particular has been the forum used increasingly by those disappointed by the poor record of delivery of basic services, largely to the urban poor, leading to several findings critical of the executive branch of government[76] and inevitably raising tensions between it and the courts. The fact that it was a judgment of a (white) high court judge which effectively allowed Zuma off the corruption hook[77] is too easily forgotten. So there is, at minimum in my view, cause for concern about the future of judicial independence in substance, not because of some deliberate programme of government to undermine it, but because it may well fall victim to the unresolved tensions of the past.

In this respect, it is instructive to note briefly the history of judicial independence in post-colonial societies elsewhere in 'British' southern and east Africa.[78] While the picture is mixed, with the exception of

[75] See 'Statement of the National Executive Committee of the African National Congress on the Occasion of year 93 of the ANC', Umtata, 8 January 2005, available at: www.anc.org.za/ancdocs/history/jan8-05.html.

[76] See, e.g., *Minister of Health and Another* v. *New Clicks South Africa (Pty) Ltd and Others (Treatment Action Campaign and Another as Amici Curiae)* 2006 (2) SA 311, CC; *Njongi* v. *MEC, Department of Welfare, Eastern Cape* 2008 (4) SA 237, CC; and *Leon Joseph* v. *City of Johannesburg*, Case CCT 43/09, judgment handed down 9 October 2009, as yet unreported.

[77] It is true that this judgment was subsequently overruled by the SCA, and that the formal dropping of the charges was the act of the Acting National Director of Public Prosecution in April 2009, but there can be little doubt in retrospect that the watershed moment was the judgment of Nicholson J on 12 September 2008.

[78] For a study of eleven judiciaries in this region, see L. Van de Vijver (ed.), *The Judicial Institution in Southern Africa: A Comparative Study of Common Law Jurisdictions* (Cape Town: Siber Ink, 2006).

Zimbabwe, where a once independent judiciary was systematically and ruthlessly destroyed by the ruling party under President Mugabe,[79] in general the judiciary at all levels has survived with a degree of independence and impartiality, albeit with the ever-present threat of executive interference should the judges take too critical a stance. So the outlook is not entirely bleak, and the fact of South Africa's 'exceptionalism' could also play a role. By this I mean that the relative level of infrastructural and economic sophistication, the high level of organisation and activity within civil society (such as the trades unions, the media, institutions of higher learning and religious groupings), as well as the strong desire to be seen as a success story, as a leader in Africa and as the competent host of major world events, seen especially against the background of past isolation, are likely to ensure that any attempt consciously to undermine judicial independence through tinkering with appointments and disciplinary measures will be fiercely contested.

What need rather to be monitored with intense scrutiny are more subtle and indirect measures which have the effect of undermining judicial independence as provided for in the Constitution. In this regard, the heaviest responsibility rests on the watchdogs in the legal profession and university law faculties, aided critically by the media, as well as by non-governmental organisations.

[79] For an account of this process, see K. Saller, *The Judicial Institution in Zimbabwe* (Cape Town: Siber Ink, 2004).

6

Appointment, discipline and removal of judges: fundamental reforms in the United Kingdom

KATE MALLESON

When the time comes to identify the most significant legacy of the period of the Labour Government from 1997 to 2010, it is likely that constitutional reform will be a strong contender. Under a broad 'modernisation' manifesto, a raft of changes were introduced which have reshaped the constitutional map of the United Kingdom. Devolution of power to Scotland, Northern Ireland and Wales, the reform of the House of Lords and the incorporation of the European Convention on Human Rights into domestic law are some of the most familiar of these reforms. Equally important, though less widely known, are the profound changes affecting the judicial branch of government. In June 2003, the government announced, unexpectedly, that the office of Lord Chancellor was to be abolished, a new Supreme Court was to be set up and the judicial appointments process radically reformed. At the time, some commentators claimed that these proposals were an attempt on the part of the Government to take control of an increasingly activist judiciary.[1] As the details emerged, however, it became clear that such fears were unfounded. Indeed, one of the most paradoxical and striking features of the reforms was that they effected a fundamental shift of power away from the executive.[2]

At the heart of the new arrangements, finalised in the provisions of the Constitutional Reform Act 2005, was the removal or reform of the central role of the Lord Chancellor in the areas of judicial appointments, complaints, discipline and dismissal. Political opposition to the complete

[1] See, e.g., Lord Alexander, 'Is This a Ruthless Grab for Power?' *The Times*, 1 July 2003, Law section, p. 3.

[2] Department of Constitutional Affairs (2003) *Constitutional Reform: A New Way of Appointing Judges*, available at: www.dca.gov.uk/consult/jacommission, accessed 22 October 2010.

abolition of the office of Lord Chancellor resulted in the retention of the title, but its transformation to something far closer to that of a minister of justice. In particular, the role of head of the judiciary in England and Wales was transferred from the Lord Chancellor to the Lord Chief Justice and the two offices were given a new and unique shared responsibility for matters relating to judicial complaints, discipline and dismissal. At the same time, the power to appoint judges was transferred from the Lord Chancellor to two new judicial appointments commissions: one for judges in England and Wales and a second for the new United Kingdom Supreme Court.

Background to the creation of the new judicial appointments process in England and Wales

The decision in 2003 to reform the judicial appointments process took the legal and political world by surprise.[3] Indeed the Lord Chief Justice himself was unaware of the proposals until they were made public. But the arguments for the creation of a judicial appointments commission were not new, having been debated by academics and policy-makers over a number of years. Moreover, close and recent precedents for a commission-based judicial appointments process existed in the form of the Judicial Appointment Board in Scotland created in 2002[4] and the formulation of the framework for a judicial appointments commission in Northern Ireland.[5] The establishment of the new judicial appointments commission for England and Wales therefore finalised the creation of a more coherent and rational system of judicial appointments in the context of the newly devolved powers of the United Kingdom. This coherence was reinforced by the fact that each of the three regional appointment bodies would, under the Constitutional Reform Act 2005, provide a member of the new Supreme Court judicial

3 For a fuller account see K. Malleson, 'Judicial Reform in the UK: The Emergence of the Third Branch of Government', in A. McDonald (ed.), *Reinventing Britain: Constitutional Change under New Labour* (London: Methuen-Politicos, 2007), pp. 133–50.

4 See A. Paterson, 'The Scottish Judicial Appointments Board: New Wine in Old Bottles?', in K. Malleson and P. H. Russell (eds.), *Appointing Judges in an Age of Judicial Power* (University of Toronto Press, 2006). Details of the Scottish Judicial Appointments Board can be found at: www.judicialappointmentsscotland.gov.uk/judicial/JUD_Main.jsp, accessed 22 January 2010.

5 The framework for establishing a commission was set out in the Justice (Northern Ireland) Act 2002. The Commission started work in June 2005. Details of the Northern Ireland Judicial Appointments Commission can be found at: www.nijac.org/default.htm, accessed 22 January 2010.

appointments commission so as to reinforce its status as a Supreme Court for the United Kingdom.

The arguments put forward by the Government in support of these changes were not based on the claim that the system had failed to appoint competent or independent judges. Instead, the primary rationale referred in relatively unspecific terms to the need for constitutional modernisation: 'Many of the most fundamental features of the system, including the role of the Lord Chancellor, remain rooted in the past.'[6] However, a less articulated but equally important driver behind the changes was the need to ensure that judges continued to be selected on merit and not on a political partisan basis. The presence of political patronage in the judicial appointments process in England and Wales was a recognised feature of the system before the Second World War, but since then it had been widely regarded as free of partisan influences.[7] However, fears were beginning to be expressed in the 1990s that this depoliticisation could not be guaranteed. The effect of the growth in judicial review and the passage of the Human Rights Act 1998 had been to bring an increasing number of politically and socially sensitive issues before the courts, which had led to greater tension between the executive and judicial branches.[8] By 2003, a view was emerging among some senior judges and leading constitutional lawyers that the United Kingdom was in a transitional phase moving from a system based on parliamentary sovereignty to that of a constitutional democracy.[9] This, in turn, gave rise to fears that the conventions which underpinned the constitutional arrangements would come under increasing pressure. The convention that judicial appointments in England and Wales are non-partisan was regarded by some as being neither so long established nor so tightly defined that it could not be undermined. In addition to these long-term fears, there was also a sense that the system needed not only to be free of the danger of political interference, but also visibly seen to be so in order to maintain its legitimacy.

A final and more substantive and pressing rationale for change was the need to tackle the lack of diversity in the composition of the judiciary.[10]

[6] Department of Constitutional Affairs, *Constitutional Reform*, para. 18.

[7] See R. Stevens, *The English Judges: Their Role in the Changing Constitution* (Oxford: Hart, 2005).

[8] See Malleson, 'Judicial Reform in the UK'.

[9] See, e.g., Stevens, *The English Judges*; A. Young, 'Judicial Sovereignty and the Human Rights Act' (2002) 61(1) *Cambridge Law Journal* 53–65; J. Jowell, 'Beyond the Rule of Law: Towards Constitutional Judicial Review' [2000] *Public Law* 671–2.

[10] B. Hale, 'Equality and the Judiciary: Why Should We Want more Women Judges? (2001) *Public Law* 489–99; K. Malleson, 'Prospects for Parity: The Position of Women in the

The narrow background from which the judiciary was drawn, particularly at senior levels, had, by the late 1990s, become its Achilles' heel. Almost the only fact that many people knew about judges in England and Wales was that they were generally elderly, white, male barristers educated at private schools and at Oxbridge. The failure of the Lord Chancellor's Department (as was) to make significant progress in this area, despite the implementation of some important practical changes by the former Lord Chancellors, Lord Mackay and Lord Irvine, prompted a radical change of approach by the Government.[11] The 2003 consultation paper on judicial appointments acknowledged that tackling the lack of diversity in the judiciary would require 'fresh approaches and a major re-engineering of the process for appointment'.[12] During the passage of the Constitutional Reform Bill, considerable time was given to debating how the goal of increasing diversity could be included within the remit of the commission without undermining the principle of selection on merit. The resulting compromise was set out in ss. 63 and 64 which state that the commission must: 'have regard to the need to encourage diversity in the range of persons available for selection for appointments' subject to the overriding principle that selection must be made on the grounds of merit alone.

The form of judicial appointments commissions

The first feature to note about the new appointments system is that it encompasses two commissions: one for the United Kingdom Supreme Court and one for all other ranks of judges in England and Wales. The Supreme Court Commission is a small *ad hoc* body, convened only when a vacancy arises, consisting of the President of the Supreme Court (who chairs it), the Deputy President and one of each of the three United Kingdom appointments commissions or boards (England and Wales, Northern Ireland and Scotland). The Judicial Appointments Commission for England and Wales, in contrast, is a larger, permanent body responsible for appointing all the permanent and most of the fee-paid judges and tribunal members to courts in England and Wales.[13] It has a substantial

Judiciary in England and Wales', in G. Shaw and U. Shultz (eds.), *Women in the Worlds Legal Professions* (Oxford: Hart, 2003).

[11] Department of Constitutional Affairs, *Constitutional Reform*, para. 27.

[12] Department of Constitutional Affairs, *Constitutional Reform*, para. 28.

[13] It does not, however, appoint the lay magistrates who number over 30,000 and deal with the majority of criminal cases in England and Wales. Magistrates are appointed by the Lord Chancellor on the advice of local Advisory Committees.

secretariat, equivalent to the section of the government department which previously carried out the day-to-day judicial appointments work for the Lord Chancellor.

Both the Supreme Court Commission and the Judicial Appointments Commission for England and Wales are technically recommending commissions, leaving the final selection to be made by the Lord Chancellor. The powers of the Lord Chancellor under the 2005 provisions to reject a candidate selected by the commission are, however, very limited. The Lord Chancellor can reject a name only on the ground that the person is not suitable for the office concerned. Similarly, the power to refer a name back to the commission can be exercised only in certain limited circumstances, most notably if there is evidence that the person is not the best candidate on merit.[14]

Nevertheless, even this very limited role has been the subject of ongoing attention. In 2007, the Labour Government proposed removing the Lord Chancellor altogether from the process of selecting the judges below the High Court Bench. This proposal was described by the Government as a 'step in the journey' of a much wider constitutional programme of rebalancing the constitution by handing power from the executive to Parliament and the people.[15] In the event, the Constitutional Renewal Bill 2008, which set out the proposed change to the powers of the Lord Chancellor in the judicial appointments process, did not complete its passage through Parliament and the proposal to remove the Lord Chancellor from the process completely was dropped. Instead, the Constitutional Reform and Governance Bill 2009

[14] The candidate can also be referred back if the Lord Chancellor believes that there is not enough evidence that the person is suitable for the office concerned or particular functions of that office (s. 91(2)(a)). In relation to the selection of candidates for the Supreme Court, the Lord Chancellor can also refer back a name if he believes that there is not enough evidence that if the person were appointed the judges of the Court would between them have knowledge of, and experience of practice in, the law of each part of the United Kingdom (s. 30(2)(c)).

[15] Ministry of Justice, *The Governance of Britain: Judicial Appointments*, October 2007, available at: www.justice.gov.uk/docs/cp2507.pdf, accessed 18 December 2009. The consultation paper set out the statement by the then Prime Minister, Gordon Brown, of his vision of the redistribution of power in the United Kingdom:

> For centuries, they [the Executive] have exercised authority in the name of the monarchy without the people and their elected representatives being consulted. So I now propose that in 12 important areas of our national life, the Prime Minister and the Executive should surrender or limit their powers, the exclusive exercise of which by the Government of the day should have no place in a modern democracy . . . And I propose that the Government should consider relinquishing its residual role in the appointment of judges.

proposed a smaller reduction in the power of the executive through the removal of the vestigial power of the Prime Minister to make the final recommendation to the Queen in relation to the selection of Supreme Court candidates. In practice, this role had been reduced by the 2005 provisions to little more than a rubber stamp, since the legislation did not set out any basis on which the Prime Minister could reject the name provided.[16] It is not yet clear whether the Conservative–Liberal Democrat coalition Government formed in 2010 will seek to revisit the question of the involvement of the executive in the judicial appointments process in the near future.

One significant effect of the erosion of the powers of the Lord Chancellor in relation to judicial appointments has been to shift concern from the potential danger of over-politicisation to that of a democratic deficit. The removal of any meaningful input from the executive in the process has meant that there is no direct democratic link between the judicial appointments process and the electoral system. For this reason, there has been increasing interest in the possibility of introducing some form of parliamentary scrutiny of judicial appointments.[17] While Parliament currently has ultimate responsibility for scrutinising the workings of the judicial appointments commission, it plays no role in individual appointment decisions. Although a number of academics, including this author, gave evidence to the Parliamentary Committee arguing in favour of some parliamentary involvement, the Government concluded that the democratic accountability benefits of such a move were outweighed by the risk of politicisation which it raised.[18] In particular, concerns about the weaknesses of the US system cast a long shadow in the debate on the appropriateness of legislative confirmation in the United Kingdom. The possibility of some form of parliamentary involvement was, however, raised again in a Labour Government consultation paper on judicial appointments in 2007. Although again, the decision was made not to proceed with any parliamentary involvement, the possibility of such a change was given fresh impetus by the introduction of parliamentary hearings for Supreme Court nominees

[16] Constitutional Reform Act 2005, s. 26.

[17] The 2007 government consultation paper sought views on this option (see Ministry of Justice, *The Governance of Britain*, para. 4.33). See also the discussion of the possible role of parliamentary hearings in a report on the subject produced by the UK Parliament Group: A. Horne, *The Changing Constitution: A Case for Judicial Confirmation Hearings?* (2010), available at: www.spg.org.uk/spg-paper-1.pdf, accessed 22 January 2010.

[18] The controversial confirmation hearings of Clarence Thomas and Robert Bork in the United States have cast a long shadow over any proposals for such a process in the United Kingdom. Support for some form of parliamentary scrutiny of this kind is, however, growing. See Horne, *The Changing Constitution*.

in Canada. In 2006, Marshall Rothstein became the first Supreme Court nominee to appear in a televised hearing before an *ad hoc* parliamentary committee. This development in Canada, if followed in future Supreme Court appointments, will no doubt be watched closely in the United Kingdom. Given the ongoing concerns about the democratic deficit in the judicial appointments process it is likely that the issue of parliamentary involvement in the selection of senior judges will be revisited at some point, particularly in the light of the ongoing reforms being introduced to the powers and membership of Parliament itself.

Membership of the Judicial Appointments Commission for England and Wales

During the debate on the Constitutional Reform Bill, the exact make-up of the Judicial Appointments Commission was the subject of intense debate. In particular there was sharp disagreement about how to strike the right balance between the numbers of legal and lay members. It was widely recognised that the latter are the conduit through which new approaches and fresh ideas in appointments are brought onto the commission. Their experience of other selection systems and recruitment methods, in particular, was considered vital to the development of an innovative and effective system and in providing increased legitimacy and a counter to the danger of self-replication which had been such a feature of the judicial appointments system in England and Wales. A key subject of debate in determining the exact balance between lay and legal members was how to reduce the danger that the lay members might defer inappropriately to the legal insiders, particularly senior judges. Supporters of the role of lay members argued strongly that this could be achieved only by appointing an equal number of lay and legal members, as is the case in Scotland, or a majority of lay members, as is the case on the Judicial Appointments Advisory Committee in Ontario. In the event, this view did not prevail and the composition of the commission in England and Wales is much more heavily legally dominated than these bodies, consisting of six lay people, five judges, one solicitor, one barrister, one magistrate and one tribunal member. One factor mitigating the strong legal presence is the fact that the chair of the commission must be a lay member.[19]

[19] The JAAC in Ontario and the JAB in Scotland also both have lay chairs. The first chair of the Judicial Appointments Commission is Baroness Usha Prashar, First Civil Service Commissioner between 2000 and 2005.

While there were strong differences in opinion about the best balance between lay and legal members on the commission, there was very little support for including members of Parliament. By statute, no Member of Parliament can be appointed to the commission. This approach is not universal. The South African Judicial Service Commission and the Judicial Appointments Commission in Israel, for example, both include members of the legislature as a means of enhancing the democratic legitimacy of the system. The absence of any elected representatives heightens the issue of democratic legitimacy raised above.

Just as important as the make-up of the commission members is the question of how they are appointed and by whom. Many commissions in other jurisdictions, including the Scottish Judicial Appointment Board, leave the selection of the members wholly to the executive. In contrast, the Lord Chancellor appointed the commissioners for England and Wales after consultation with an advisory body consisting of the Lord Chief Justice, the chair of the commission and an additional lay member appointed by the Lord Chancellor. In relation to the judicial and legal members the Lord Chancellor must also consult the judicial council and legal governing bodies, respectively. Although the posts are advertised and selected through open competition, little information is publicly available about the exact details by which the appointments are made.

The record of the judicial appointments commissions to date

The Judicial Appointments Commission for England and Wales made its first appointments in 2006. In the first three years of the commission's work, all the names which it put forward to the Lord Chancellor were approved. However, in 2010 the commission recommended the appointment of Sir Nicholas Wall to the post of President of the Family Division. The then Lord Chancellor, Jack Straw, referred the decision back to the commission. It, in turn, resubmitted his name after which he was duly appointed. No information was made public by the Lord Chancellor or the commission as to why Sir Nicholas had been referred back and why he had been resubmitted, leading to speculation in the press that the Lord Chancellor had sought to block his appointment because of earlier critical comments Sir Nicholas had made publicly about the resourcing of the Family Courts. The lack of transparency in the process means that it is not possible to assess whether there is any basis for this claim.

Another area in which the new judicial appointments process has attracted criticism, particularly in the early years, concerned delays in processing applications.[20] Given the size of the system which the commission inherited, with over 900 appointments being made each year, it was perhaps not surprising that it suffered from teething problems. These were inevitably exacerbated by the fact that in its first two years the commission was also instituting many changes to the application and selection processes. However, more substantive and ongoing concerns of the new system have been expressed about the type and quality of the appointments made. On the one hand, it has been argued that the greater emphasis on interview skills and competencies has sometimes excluded highly talented applicants who would have been appointed under the old system.[21] On the other hand, there is evidence that, despite changes to the process, there has been little real increase in the background and make-up of those selected.

This last criticism is particularly significant given the central importance of diversity in the rationale for setting up the commission. In 2009, the former Lord Chancellor, Jack Straw, acknowledged in evidence to Parliament that progress in increasing diversity had been disappointing. In the same year a report by the Equalities and Human Rights Commission on women in power concluded that at current rates of progress, it would take fifty-five years to achieve gender equality in the judiciary.[22] In response to these concerns, an Advisory Panel on Judicial Diversity was established in 2009 to 'identify the barriers to a more diverse judiciary and to make recommendations to more speedily achieve a judiciary that is more representative of the community'. The Panel's report was produced in 2010. It recommended a fundamental shift in approach from a focus on selection processes towards a judicial career.[23] The report provided relatively few details as to how this shift was to be undertaken and it is not yet clear whether any of its recommendations will be taken forward by the Conservative–Liberal Democrat Government.

Concern about progress on diversity issues in judicial appointments has not been limited to appointments to the judiciary in England and Wales. The first appointments of the Supreme Court Commission were disappointing for those who hoped that the three new appointments made in 2009 would include justices from outside the traditional candidate pool, in

[20] 'Ministers are Blamed for Shortage of Judges', *The Times*, 10 September 2007.

[21] See S. Sedley, 'On the Move', *London Review of Books*, 8 October 2009, pp. 3–5.

[22] Equalities and Human Rights Commission, *Sex and Power* (London: EHRC, 2008).

[23] *The Report of the Advisory Panel on Judicial Diversity*, March 2010, available at: www.justice.gov.uk/publications/judicial-diversity-report.htm.

particular the appointment of a second female justice and/or a candidate from a black or minority ethnic background. Given that the eligibility rules do not require that justices are recruited from the Court of Appeal and are wide enough to include many senior practitioners and academics, there was inevitable criticism of the fact that three white, male members of the Court of Appeal were the first appointments to the Supreme Court, albeit that one of these appointed was, for the first time, a former solicitor rather than a former barrister. In 2010, this issue again became the subject of controversy when it became known that a senior barrister, Jonathan Sumption QC, had been shortlisted for the twelfth vacancy on the court. Strong objections were voiced from some members of the Supreme Court and the Court of Appeal to the appointment of a candidate who had not previously been a member of one of the UK higher courts. The outcome of the selection process was that a member of the Court of Appeal, Sir John Dyson, was elevated to fill the vacancy.

An important consequence of this incident was to highlight the very central role which judges occupy, formally and informally, in the selection of the judiciary, particularly at the upper levels. Given the dangers of self-replication which are present when the selection of any group is left to its current members, the prospects of significant change in the composition of the judiciary in England and Wales and the UK Supreme Court look very slim while the current arrangements remain in place.

Discipline and removal

The institutional changes to the judicial appointments process implemented in 2006 have been mirrored by similarly far-reaching changes to the system of judicial complaints, discipline and removal. The details of the new arrangements were initially determined in an agreement (the 'Concordat') negotiated in private between the then Lord Chancellor, Lord Falconer, and the then Lord Chief Justice, Lord Woolf. Between 2003 and 2005 the two met regularly to determine how the many functions previously undertaken by the Lord Chancellor would be carried out in future as the Lord Chief Justice took on the role of the head of the judiciary.[24] The fact that such a vital constitutional issue as the responsibility for judicial complaints, discipline and removal should have been determined in this way, without public debate, is perhaps

[24] This process was described by Lord Woolf in his valedictory speech in 2005 as one of 'almost continuous dialogue' over two years.

indicative of the lack of public engagement in England and Wales with constitutional issues concerning the judiciary. Yet despite the questionable process by which the new arrangements were created, the outcome was both innovative and impressive. At first glance the Concordat looks like nothing more than a carve-up of power between the judicial and executive branches of government. In fact, what it created was a unique form of constitutional partnership, in which the two branches of government share in the decision-making affecting the governance of the judiciary and the running of the courts through the allocation of decision-making powers 'with appropriate constraints and mutual consultation'.[25]

Removal

To understand the effects of the provisions of the Concordat on the power to remove judges in England and Wales, a distinction needs to be made between senior judges, those above the High Court, and posts in the lower judiciary. The former have been largely unaffected by the changes. Under the Act of Settlement 1701, High Court judges and above hold office 'during good behaviour' and can be dismissed only by a motion of both houses of Parliament. The only High Court judge to be removed in this way to date was an Irish judge, Sir Jonah Barrington, in 1830, for embezzling fees paid into court.[26] The definition of misbehaviour as limited to such criminal behaviour is now a strong convention and any attempt to institute proceedings for anything less serious would be very unlikely to succeed.

Below the High Court, responsibility for the removal of a judge rested, before 2005, in the hands of the Lord Chancellor. He could dismiss a judge up to and including circuit judges on the grounds of 'incapacity

[25] Lord Falconer commented in 2004 that the Concordat 'lays down the right kind of partnership between the executive and the judiciary, with clear roles for each within the framework of the separation of powers of both' (HL Deb., 12 February 2004, Vol. 657, col. 1216). Lord Woolf similarly noted: 'A spirit of partnership between the judiciary, the legislature and the executive is essential if the judiciary are to meet the changing needs of society' (Squire Centenary Lecture, Cambridge University, 3 March 2004). See also speech of the senior presiding judge, Lord Justice Thomas, 'The Judicial and Executive Branches of Government: A New Partnership', Institute of Advanced Legal Studies, London, 10 November 2005.

[26] See S. Shetreet, *Judges on Trial: A Study of the Appointment and Accountability of the English Judiciary* (Oxford: North Holland Publishing, 1976).

and misbehaviour'.[27] In practice, the exercise of this power was similarly restricted to misconduct which amounted to criminal behaviour, having only been used once in recent times, against a Circuit judge caught smuggling whiskey and cigarettes in 1983. In cases involving other serious misconduct the threat of action was usually enough to induce a resignation.

Before 2005, the process for removing a judge was not set out in statute and left a wide measure of discretion to the Lord Chancellor. The inadequacy of these arrangements were highlighted in 1989 when a Circuit judge, James Pickles, was threatened with dismissal proceedings over public comments which he made about a trial over which he had presided. Judge Pickles refused to attend a hearing which the then Lord Chancellor had arranged to consider the matter and threatened judicial review of the process on the grounds that the Lord Chancellor was 'complainant, prosecutor, judge and jury'.[28] Whatever the merits of that particular case, the failings of the disciplinary and dismissal procedure in terms of due process were clearly highlighted. Only the fact that such public conflicts were so rare allowed the system to continue for another sixteen years.

Under the terms of the Concordat as set out in the Constitutional Reform Act 2005 the power to remove or suspend a judge below the High Court continues to rest with the Lord Chancellor.[29] However, before this power can be exercised the Lord Chancellor must consult with the Lord Chief Justice. In addition, a tribunal must be established, either by the Lord Chancellor after consulting the Lord Chief Justice or by the Lord Chief Justice after consulting the Lord Chancellor, to enquire into the allegation against the judge. Removal may occur only if the tribunal has reported to the Lord Chancellor recommending that the judge be removed on the ground of misbehaviour or inability to perform the functions of the office.[30] Each review body consists of four members: two judicial office holders and two lay persons. The members of the

[27] Courts Act 1971, s. 17(4).

[28] For a review of the Judge Pickles case, see J. Rozenberg, *The Search for Justice* (London: Hodder & Stoughton, 1994).

[29] Constitutional Reform Act 2005, s. 134(2).

[30] A new provision gives the Lord Chief Justice the power, exercisable with the agreement of the Lord Chancellor, to suspend a senior judge from office while she or he is subject to proceedings for an address for their removal in Parliament (s. 108(6)); the Lord Chief Justice may suspend other holders of judicial office while they are under investigation for an offence (s. 108(7)).

tribunal are appointed by the Lord Chancellor after consultation with members of the senior judiciary.

To date, the establishment of such a tribunal had led to one case in which a judge was removed. In 2009, a district judge was dismissed by the Lord Chancellor after the tribunal recommended her removal for, among other things, 'inappropriate, rude and petulant' behaviour to solicitors appearing before her. The decision represented a significant departure from the earlier more limited interpretation of misbehaviour as being restricted to criminal activity. Nevertheless, this change has not, to date, given rise to expressions of concern that this new approach leaves the independence of the judiciary inappropriately weakened. Instead, the general consensus has been that the public has a right to expect that judges should be dismissed where they are found, though a fair and rigorous investigation, to have failed to meet basic standards of competence and professionalism.

Complaints and disciplinary procedures

Traditionally, the judicial discipline system was essentially self-regulatory in that it was largely left to the individual judge to determine what constituted acceptable and unacceptable behaviour, with support and advice from their peers. Only where this judicial self-control failed in a serious way, did responsibility for discipline then fall to the Lord Chancellor.[31] Moreover, under the Courts Act 1971 there was no action less draconian than dismissal which the Lord Chancellor could invoke in response to poor judicial conduct. By convention, he could admonish a judge whose behaviour had been criticised and issue a public rebuke. In practice, it was very rare for a reprimand to be made public. Moreover, there was no requirement that the complainant be informed that any action had been taken.

This informal system could survive only in a small, highly homogeneous legal world in which demands for judicial accountability were limited. It was also completely dependent on the unique and pivotal role of the Lord Chancellor. The radical reform of that office and the transfer of the role of head of the judiciary to the Lord Chief Justice meant that structural change was required. More generally, the informal complaints and disciplinary system was increasingly incompatible with the creation of more developed forms of accountability within the rest of the legal

[31] D. Pannick, *Judges* (Oxford University Press, 1988), p. 76.

system. Formal grievance mechanisms through Citizens' Charters and access to ombudsmen are now an inherent feature of government. The public have been encouraged to consider themselves as consumers of the legal system with rights to expect a minimum level of service and to complain if they do not receive it. In addition, the development of independent disciplinary and complaints procedures in the professions, including both branches of the legal profession, increasingly stood out in marked contrast to the arrangements for the judiciary.[32]

The combined effect of these internal and external pressures was to increase demand for more formalised and open procedures through which to set minimum standards of judicial behaviour, investigate complaints and provide corrective action when a judge's conduct is found to have been at fault. One possible approach which was considered at the time the new judicial appointments process was set up was to give this task to the Judicial Appointments Commission and to expand its remit to cover this role. Instead, it was decided to create a unique constitutional arrangement whereby responsibility for judicial discipline was shared between the Lord Chancellor and Lord Chief Justice. While the final decision on dismissal remains with the Lord Chancellor, under the Constitutional Reform Act 2005 the Lord Chief Justice has the power, exercisable only with the agreement of the Lord Chancellor, to give a judicial office holder formal advice about a disciplinary matter, or a formal warning or reprimand.[33] In addition, the Lord Chief Justice (with the agreement of the Lord Chancellor) may suspend a judge who is subject to criminal proceedings, serving a sentence imposed in criminal proceedings or has under certain circumstances been convicted of an offence.[34]

The Act also created an Office of Judicial Complaints (OJC), which has the role of receiving complaints about judges and for advising and supporting the Lord Chancellor and Lord Chief Justice in their responsibilities for the complaints and discipline system. Between 2007 and 2008 the OJC received 1,437 complaints against judicial office-holders, 61 per cent of which related to judicial decisions, which are outside the scope of the OJC. Disciplinary action, following investigations, was taken

[32] In 1996, the Law Society established the Office of Supervision of Solicitors including lay members, in response to criticism of its failures to deal with the rising numbers of complaints against solicitors. Similarly, in 1997, the bar set up a formal complaints machinery headed by an independent lay complaints commissioner.

[33] Constitutional Reform Act 2005, s. 108(2). The Lord Chief Justice can continue to give informal advice as before.

[34] Section 108(4), (5).

in forty-nine cases.[35] Controversy has arisen over the degree of openness around the individual cases. Details of each case have, to date, not been published on the grounds that this could undermine the judges' authority in the courtroom. However, in 2009, *The Guardian* brought an action under the Freedom of Information Act 2000, arguing that the public had a right under the statutory provisions to have more information about the cases. Although the action did not succeed, the Ministry of Justice agreed that, in future, there would be a 'presumption' that members of the judiciary who were dismissed for misconduct should be identified. However, the Lord Chancellor reserved the right to conceal their name 'on a case-by-case' basis.

The work of the OJC, and indeed the Judicial Appointments Commission, is also now subject to the review and scrutiny of a new body – the Judicial Appointments and Conduct Ombudsman, whose role is to investigate complaints about the judicial appointments process and the handling of matters involving judicial discipline or conduct. Applications to the Ombudsman can be made by candidates for judicial office about the way in which their application for appointment has been handled, provided they have already made a formal complaint to the Judicial Appointments Commission, or they are complainants about judicial behaviour who are not satisfied with the way their complaint has been handled by the OJC. The Ombudsman can also investigate complaints from judges about the work of the OJC. The remit of the Ombudsman is limited to identifying procedural failure or some other maladministration.[36] She or he has the power to set aside a disciplinary finding where there has been maladministration that makes it unreliable.[37]

In addition to the creation of these formal mechanisms for dealing with and overseeing complaints and discipline, a new guide to judicial conduct has been produced by the Judges' Council which is designed to act as a code of conduct and covers the issues normally found in judicial codes of conduct in other jurisdictions, such as commercial activities undertaken by judges and relations with the media.[38] The development

[35] Twenty-one of the forty-nine judicial office-holders subject to disciplinary action were disciplined for not fulfilling their judicial duty. Twelve were disciplined for inappropriate behaviour or comments, seven for motoring offences, and three each for discrimination, criminal convictions and misuse of judicial status. Full details at: www.judicialcomplaints.gov.uk, accessed 22 January 2010.

[36] Section 110(1). [37] Section 111(5).

[38] Judges' Council, *Guide to Judicial Conduct*, October 2004, available at: www.judiciary.gov.uk/docs/judges_council/judicialconduct_update0408.pdf, accessed 22 January 2010.

of the new guide to judicial conduct represents one further step away from the informal system of self-regulation towards the creation of common and open standards of professional conduct against which the behaviour of individual judges can be measured.

Conclusion

The most significant common feature of the recent and radical changes to the systems of judicial appointments, discipline and dismissal is that far from being a grab for power on the part of the Government as some commentators initially feared, the reforms are rare examples of the executive giving away a source of political control and potential patronage. Changes in both areas have the potential to secure judicial independence, to promote greater diversity on the bench and to enhance the legitimacy of the judiciary. However, the early record of the Judicial Appointments Commission in England and Wales has been patchy. Some of the problems identified in the new system, such as the delays in dealing with applications, can be put down to teething problems, but others, most particularly in relation to increasing diversity, are more worrying and suggest the continuing impact of underlying structural and regulatory flaws. Unless there is evidence of significant change in the composition of the judiciary in the near future, it is likely that the Judicial Appointments Commission will lose public confidence and support. Given that the origins of the problems lie to a great extent outside the commission's control, being rooted in the composition and working arrangements of the legal profession and even the legal education system before it, this is no small task. But the difficulties which the commission faces in creating a judicial appointments process which selects independent, talented and diverse judges is partly mitigated by the fact that it has inherited a system in which the job of judging is still highly prized and the quality of applicants is very high.

In one important respect the reform of the judicial appointments process and the disciplinary system are closely related. If the judicial appointments process achieves its aim of creating a genuinely more diverse judiciary, this change will be more deep-rooted than simply the adding to the bench a few token lawyers who happen to be non-white, female, gay or disabled. Instead, it will lead to the creation of a judiciary which is made up of individuals who are drawn from a wide range of legal careers, social backgrounds, lifestyles, experiences and attitudes. Such a judiciary will gain public confidence and legitimacy, but it will lose the binds of shared attitudes and behaviour which flow from being a highly homogeneous group. One consequence of this will be a greater need for more open debate about the detailed rules of judicial conduct which can be enforced by a very effective complaints and discipline system. That system has, to date, relied heavily on the striking homogeneity of the judiciary to ensure conformity to certain sets of behaviour with almost no debate about the boundaries of judicial conduct, either on or off the bench. The new framework for complaints, discipline and removal has been under relatively little pressure to date. On paper, the system appears both robust and appropriate with the capacity to strike the right balance between judicial independence and accountability. Only if and when the system is tested more rigorously will we know whether it will prove to be equally effective in practice.

7

Judicial selection, removal and discipline in the United States

MARK TUSHNET

The United States has many systems of judicial selection, discipline and removal. The national courts (sometimes called the federal courts) and the fifty states differ quite substantially along these dimensions. This chapter describes the federal court system in some detail and provides a broad-brush overview of state judicial systems. There are perhaps two modest common characteristics among all these systems: (1) judicial selection in all the systems is, with minor exceptions, tightly connected to ordinary politics and judges individually or through their hierarchies play a relatively small role in judicial selection and removal; and (2) judges are initially appointed from the practicing bar at almost every level, with no strong expectation of promotion within the judicial hierarchy.

The national courts of the United States

The national court system in the United States has four tiers.[1] Initial decisions in many administrative matters, including immigration cases and disputed claims for payments to the disabled, are made by "administrative law judges." These judges are appointed through merit-based processes within the administrative agency or bureaucracy they serve, although political appointees sometimes intervened in those processes in the Bush administration, and they are subject to discipline and removal through typical civil service mechanisms. Within the federal courts the lowest tier is occupied by "magistrate judges," appointed within each district by the local judges and serving eight-year renewable terms. Magistrate judges make preliminary rulings in cases assigned to them

[1] Most authors assert that the national court system has three tiers, but J. Resnik, "Tiers" (1984) 57 *Southern California Law Review* 837, shows that assertion's inaccuracy.

by trial judges, make recommendations to those judges on dispositive questions and may try criminal cases, mostly minor offenses, with the defendant's permission.

The second tier consists of the federal district courts. Each state contains one or more districts, defined geographically, with one or more district judges. District judges are expected to serve within their districts, although with special permission they can be assigned for individual cases or for short periods to serve elsewhere, including service on the federal appeals courts. Above the district courts are the federal courts of appeals, called circuit courts. Eleven circuit courts are organized geographically, hearing appeals from the district courts in the several states within the circuits. In addition, the circuit court for the District of Columbia hears appeals from cases within the District (the nation's capital) and is an important venue for appeals from federal administrative agencies. Finally, a specialized Court of Appeals for the Federal Circuit hears appeals in patent and international trade cases arising throughout the nation; it also has jurisdiction over appeals from decisions by the federal civil service system. The courts of appeals typically sit in panels of three judges, although in extraordinary cases the entire court of appeals will hear or rehear a case *en banc*. At the peak of the national judicial hierarchy is the Supreme Court, consisting of nine justices. It has jurisdiction over all cases decided by the federal courts of appeals and over cases involving national law, including constitutional law, decided by state courts. It always sits as a bench of nine.

Appointment

The US Constitution provides that federal judges – from the district courts to the Supreme Court – be nominated by the President and confirmed in their positions by the Senate. Once confirmed, they serve "during good behavior," which is understood to mean that, unless removed by impeachment (discussed below), federal judges serve until they die or choose to retire.[2] During the twentieth century, Congress enacted statutes providing incentives for older judges to take part-time status without loss of salary or pension benefits. Judicial independence is

[2] A minor strand of scholarship defends the proposition that "good behavior" is different from life tenure to the extent that it allows for removal from office by a process other than impeachment, if that process is administered by judges rather than legislators. That scholarship has never had significant impact on the general understanding of the constitutional provisions.

further promoted by a constitutional guarantee that judicial salaries cannot be reduced after appointment, and the Supreme Court has held that this guarantee is absolute, prevailing even over government-wide salary reductions or freezes.[3] The Supreme Court has never considered on the merits a case challenging a legislative failure to adjust judicial salaries upwards to take inflation into account, but the consensus among commentators is that the Constitution does not require such adjustments. The national legislature controls the budget for the national judicial system, and has on rare occasions used its power over budgets to communicate disapproval of court, particularly Supreme Court, decisions.

The involvement of the President and the Senate in judicial appointments inevitably gives that process a political cast. The form that the politics of judicial selection takes differs for the different levels of courts, and has differed over time as well.[4] Political influence on judicial selection almost certainly affects judicial behavior after appointment. Studies over the past decade have regularly shown that on issues where the major US parties divide over legal policy, such as anti-discrimination law and criminal law, judges appointed by presidents of different parties divide "along" party lines as well. This effect is particularly pronounced on the courts of appeals when panels are composed of three judges appointed by the same President.[5] These effects occur not because of direct political intervention but because senators and presidents have become increasingly sensitive to the general ideological commitments of those they nominate and appoint to the federal courts. As a result the federal judiciary mirrors, albeit imperfectly, the national legislature's views on divisive issues of legal policy.

For most of US history, appointments to the district and circuit courts were ordinary patronage appointments, with the senators for the states in which the courts sat using whatever criteria they chose to reward political supporters with judicial positions, and with the President deferring to the senators' choice.[6] This tradition continues to some extent

[3] *United States* v. *Will* 449 US 200 (1980).

[4] For an overview of the selection process, see S. A. Binder and F. Maltzman, *Advice and Dissent: The Struggle to Shape the Federal Judiciary* (Washington: Brookings Institution Press, 2009), which describes in more detail many of the aspects of the nomination process sketched here.

[5] See J. P. Kastellac, "Panel Composition and Voting on the U.S. Courts of Appeals Over Time," 2008, available at: http://papers.ssrn.com/sol3/papers.cfm?abstract_id= 1012111.

[6] See D. S. Rutkus, "CRS Report for Congress: Role of Home State Senators in the Selection of Lower Federal Court Judges," March 6, 2008, available at: www.policyarchive.org/bitstream/

today; when the President's political party has no senators in a particular state, the local party leaders play the role that senators do in other states. Some senators now convene judicial selection committees to develop lists of potential nominees to the district courts within their states, and sometimes invite lawyers interested in a judicial position to express their interest to these committees. Federal judges do not, however, sit on these commissions. The consensus among observers is that these committees are strongly influenced by political considerations, using some minimum notion of professionalism to screen out the least qualified among the applicants, but otherwise paying attention to a potential nominee's political support. Often the recommendations made by these committees are confidential, which allows the senator to recommend the appointment of someone not approved by the committee, subject to whatever political cost might occur if the departure from the recommendation is leaked to the press. Important among the political matters considered by the committees and the senator is demographic diversity on the local bench. Presidents continue to defer to senators' choices for district judges.

Because the federal courts of appeals encompass several states, the selection process for judges on those courts differs somewhat from that of district judges.[7] By tradition positions on each court of appeals are informally allocated to specific states, and breaching that tradition can be politically costly to a President. When the tradition is respected senators play the same role as they do with respect to the district courts, although the President can sometimes play a larger role in suggesting potential nominees, and there have been several appellate judges appointed as a result of their service to the national administration either as fund-raisers or in more official positions. Because the District of Columbia has no representation in the Senate, the President has the dominant role in nominating judges to the Court of Appeals for the District of Columbia Circuit.

For most of US history the Senate has routinely confirmed nominees for district and circuit courts, although individual senators have occasionally communicated their displeasure over prospective nominees directly to the White House before the nomination became final. Over

handle/10207/19209/RL34405_20080306.pdf?sequence=2; S. Goldman, *Picking Federal Judges: Lower Court Selection from Roosevelt through Reagan* (New Haven, CT: Yale University Press, 1997); N. Scherer, *Scoring Points: Politicians, Activists, and the Lower Federal Court Appointment Process* (Stanford University Press, 2005).

[7] See D. Songer, R. S. Sheehan, and S. B. Haire, *Continuity and Change on the United States Courts of Appeals* (Ann Arbor, MI: University of Michigan Press, 2000).

the past generation, the Senate has become more assertive in confirming nominations. Senators use a "blue slip" – a note to the Committee on the Judiciary saying that they have objections to going forward with a confirmation – to delay the process, and sometimes this will be enough to force the withdrawal of the nomination. The overall effect of the Senate's new assertiveness has been to extend the length of time that nominations are pending before confirmation, with only minor effects on the confirmation rate. Still, the fact that more nominations are withdrawn or never made because of anticipated resistance by the Senate is both novel and politically significant. It has probably meant that recent presidents have had to make careful calculations about the extent to which they are willing to use their limited political resources to push for particular nominees rather than for other policies in their general platforms.

There are no formal qualifications required for appointment to the federal courts. District judges have varied backgrounds. Some have served as judges in state courts; others come from the private bar; still others have been government lawyers, with former prosecutors having a notably large share of appointments to the federal district courts, while public defenders and lawyers similarly specializing in criminal defense have a notably small share. Similar diversity in background characterizes court of appeals judges, although recently an increasing number of court of appeals judges have been "promoted" from the district courts.

Nomination and confirmation of Supreme Court justices is also political, but, of course, different because the stakes are higher and presidents play the dominant role. Presidents pick nominees to satisfy political demands on them, and senators vote to support or oppose confirmation to satisfy the sometimes different political demands they face.[8] The politics of Supreme Court nominations are the same as whatever processes characterize policy-making when the nomination occurs, and those processes change over time.

Some aspects of the politics of nominations are discussed below.

Short-term politics

On occasion presidents use nominations to achieve short-term political goals. In 1956 President Dwight Eisenhower, a Republican, had to fill a vacancy while he was running for re-election. He and his advisors

[8] For discussions of the selection process, outlining the different roles of the White House and the Department of Justice and developments in recent decades, see D. A. Yalof, *Pursuit of Justices: Presidential Politics and the Selection of Supreme Court Nominees* (University of Chicago Press, 1999); M. Comiskey, *Seeking Justices: The Judging of Supreme Court Nominees* (Lawrence, KA: University Press of Kansas, 2004).

wanted to shore up his support among urban Catholics in the northeast, so he nominated New Jersey Supreme Court Justice, William Brennan, a Catholic, for the position. This is usually a minor factor in the nomination process, though, because Supreme Court vacancies open up pretty much at random.

Patronage

In the 1880s, politics was dominated by patronage, with government structured around parties as dispensers of patronage. And so Supreme Court nominations were patronage appointments. Perhaps the most dramatic example, obscure today, is the Senate's rejection of President Ulysses S. Grant's nomination of Ebenezer Hoar to a Supreme Court vacancy. Hoar was eminently qualified, having served as a supreme court judge in Massachusetts and as Grant's Attorney-General. Despite this, the Republican-dominated Senate rejected Republican President Grant's nominee because Senate leaders wanted the position to go to someone associated with their faction within the Republican Party.

The politics of representation

Throughout US history, presidents have used Supreme Court nominations to ensure that interests of political importance to them are represented on the court. For much of the nation's history the most important dimension of representation was regional. Presidents wanted to make sure that people throughout the country could realistically think that the President and his party represented them, and one way of sending that message was to maintain regional representation on the Supreme Court. Regional representation had disappeared as a concern by the end of the twentieth century, but other dimensions of representation remained important. For some time religious representation played a role in ensuring that there would be a "Jewish" and at least one "Catholic" seat on the court, but today religious representation appears to have become a minor concern. Representation of women and ethnic minorities such as Hispanic Americans and African Americans remains important; the number of women on the Supreme Court increased to three in 2010.

Ideology

In the early twenty-first century, Supreme Court nominations are about judicial ideology. Presidents and senators ask themselves, is this candidate for appointment a judicial conservative or a judicial liberal? The focus on ideology is a relatively recent development, tied to the challenge mounted by Republicans in the late 1960s to the Democrats and the Supreme Court headed by Chief Justice Earl Warren, himself a liberal Republican who had been the party's vice-presidential candidate in 1948. Republicans presented voters with their constitutional vision, quite distinct from that of the Warren Court. As the Republican Party grew more conservative, Republican presidents could confine their attention to nominees who, they thought, were likely to be reliably conservative. The Democratic Party did not move as decisively or as quickly to ideological homogeneity.

Surrounding the parties are interest groups. Traditional interest groups have sometimes played an important role in Supreme Court nominations. Labor unions joined with the National Association for the Advancement of Colored People to defeat President Herbert Hoover's nomination of Judge John J. Parker in 1930, for example.[9] Generally, though, those interest groups have stood in the background. The gradual transformation of the parties in the final twenty-five years of the last century produced a new type of interest group, organized to promote an ideology rather than the pocketbook interests of its supporters. Starting with the nomination of Robert Bork in 1987, ideological interest groups have conducted vigorous campaigns around Supreme Court nominations. Their effects are unclear; the Bork nomination failed because of generally unfavorable political circumstances for President Reagan, and the interest-group attacks on Judge Bork might not have made much difference. But, as the parties became increasingly homogeneous, ideological interest groups found that judicial nominations were a useful focus for their fund-raising efforts and perhaps for some public education. Confirmation hearings have become quite contentious since the Bork nomination, but contentiousness is not intrinsic to the process. Rather, it results from the particular array of parties and their platforms in the contemporary United States, with one ideologically homogeneous party with significant commitments on issues of constitutional interpretation, the Republicans, facing a somewhat less homogeneous party with somewhat weaker commitments to such issues. Were the party structure to change, so would the way in which confirmation hearings are conducted.

[9] See K.W. Goings, *The NAACP Comes of Age: The Defeat of Judge John J. Parker* (Bloomington, IN: Indiana University Press, 1990).

Removal and discipline

Serving during good behavior, that is, for life, federal judges can be removed from office only by impeachment, a process initiated by the preferring of "charges" by a majority vote in the House of Representatives and concluded by conviction by a two-thirds majority in the Senate. Early in the nation's history the standards for impeachment were clarified when the Senate refused to convict Supreme Court Justice Samuel Chase, against whom charges of unjudicial behavior had been brought. Although some of Chase's actions involved the way he ran his courtroom when sitting as a trial judge, a large portion of the charges rested on Chase's legal rulings with which the House of Representatives (and President Thomas Jefferson) disagreed. The failure of Chase's impeachment has been taken to mean that federal judges cannot be removed from office merely because the House and Senate disagree with a judge's rulings on questions of law, including constitutional law, and no serious efforts to do so have occurred in modern times. Impeachment has occurred only when a federal judge has been charged with criminal misconduct, typically corruption, such as bribe-taking. Ordinarily the impeachment process follows a criminal prosecution; in one notable instance a federal judge was acquitted of the corruption offense in his criminal trial, but was then impeached and removed from office based on the same underlying behavior as well as a charge that he had lied while testifying in the criminal trial.[10]

Federal judges are subject to the ordinary criminal law, even for misconduct in connection with their office. The stringency of the impeachment process has had effects on other processes of judicial discipline. In essence, federal judges discipline each other, sensitive to the fact that judges vary widely in the way in which they do, and lawfully may, handle cases and run their courtrooms and that disappointed litigants sometimes attribute their losses to judicial misconduct rather than to the lack of merit to their claims. In 1970, the Supreme Court refused to intervene when a circuit court acted without express statutory authorization to remove cases from the docket of a truly eccentric district judge.[11] A decade later Congress provided that authorization by creating the first formal system for judicial discipline, leaving it in the hands of the judges. The Judicial Conduct and Disability Act 1980 allows anyone

[10] The judge, Alcee Hastings, then ran for and won a seat in the House of Representatives, where he continues to serve.

[11] *Chandler* v. *Judicial Council of the Tenth Circuit* 398 US 74 (1970).

to file a complaint with the Circuit Court clerk, alleging conduct "prejudicial to the effective and expeditious administration" of judicial business. The Chief Judge of the Court of Appeals, whose position is achieved solely through seniority, reviews the complaint and can appoint an investigative committee. The Circuit's Judicial Council, which consists of a mix of trial and appellate judges in the circuit, can then impose discipline ranging from a private or public censure through removal of cases from the judge's docket to a request that the judge voluntarily retire. In extreme cases, the Circuit Council can refer the case to the Judicial Conference, which consists of judges from all the courts of appeals and over which the Chief Justice presides, which can recommend impeachment.

Prodded by congressional criticism, Chief Justice William Rehnquist appointed a committee headed by Justice Stephen Breyer to examine the effectiveness of the process of judicial discipline. Reporting in 2006, the committee found that the system generally worked well, and that most of the system's mistakes were procedural rather than substantive. According to the report, "almost all complaints are filed by prisoners or litigants" rather than by attorneys, and that "almost all complaints are dismissed by the chief judge." It did not suggest that these dismissals were mistaken or that real misconduct went unaddressed. Of more than five thousand complaints considered between 2001 and 2005, only thirty-two resulted in "corrective action," although another forty-two were terminated with no action needed because of "intervening events," such as the retirement or death of the judge against whom the complaint was made. Special committees investigated fifteen cases, imposed public censure twice, private censure once, and "other discipline" once. The Breyer Committee did find that a substantial fraction of "high visibility" cases were mishandled procedurally and recommended modest improvements in the handling process.

Federal judges are rarely disciplined because they are generally quite well-qualified and temperate in their behavior. The screening provided by the nomination and confirmation process helps to reduce the probability that an injudicious judge will take the bench. In addition, the relatively small number of federal judicial positions – at present there are 179 authorized positions on the courts of appeals and 678 on the district courts, in a nation with more than 1 million lawyers – makes the pool of those qualified for a position on the federal bench quite rich, and reduces the chances that the selection process will lead to the choice of a judge who will ultimately deserve discipline.

Resignations before ordinary retirement age have historically been rare, and remain so. Since the late twentieth century judicial salary increases have been tied to salary increases for members of Congress, and because those members are reluctant to face voter disapproval for excessive salary increases the salaries of members of Congress and therefore of federal judges have not kept pace with inflation.[12] Coupled with the increasing appointment of federal judges at relatively young ages – in their thirties and forties – this has led to a somewhat elevated number of resignations before retirement age. There are no restrictions on the employment pursued by federal judges who resign or retire, and some former federal judges return to the practice of law.

The state courts

Most adjudication in the United States occurs in state courts. Court organization in the fifty states (and the District of Columbia, which has its own set of local courts as well as a federal district court and court of appeals) varies substantially, and only the broadest generalizations are possible. State courts usually have four tiers. At the lowest level are municipal or police courts handling minor criminal and sometimes civil matters; they rarely deal with difficult legal issues but they are often the point of contact that most ordinary people have with the judicial system. Some are staffed by lay judges or lawyers, who serve part-time while maintaining their private legal practices. The bulk of significant criminal and civil cases is initially heard in state trial courts, which go by various and sometimes surprisingly misleading names. In New York, for example, the trial court is called the Supreme Court. Nearly every state has an intermediate appellate court and every state has a highest court for appeals. Here too names vary: New York's highest court is the Court of Errors and Appeals, Massachusetts' is the Supreme Judicial Court.

Selection

The most distinctive feature of judicial selection in the state court systems is the widespread use of elections to choose judges, or to retain judges who were initially appointed to their positions. Roughly half the states select judges through elections; the others typically have judges

[12] *Williams* v. *United States* 535 US 911 (2002).

appointed by the state's chief executive, usually choosing from a list submitted by a judicial nominating commission.[13] In many states in the latter group, the appointed judges must run for retention within a few years of initial appointment.

States adopted systems of judicial elections beginning in the 1830s, and the practice gradually spread. The reasons for moving from systems in which judges were appointed to those in which they were elected were twofold.[14] Not surprisingly, one was the migration of ideas of democratic responsibility from the legislature and executive branches to the judicial branch. Such ideas had real purchase in the United States, where courts with the power of constitutional review regularly intervened in matters of substantial political controversy, and where even ordinary private law decisions often had significant and visible policy impacts. In addition, judicial elections were initially seen as a way of promoting the rule of law by removing judicial selection from the hands of politicians, who were thought to be using judicial appointments as a form of patronage to the point of possible corruption. Voters, it was thought, would be more attentive to professional norms than to the needs of political "machines" as they chose judges. Criticism of election of judges began in the 1850s and has persisted, particularly among legal elites, but no substitute has yet attracted widespread support, in part precisely because substitutes for elections pit professional elites against the deep populism of the American public.

Only a few states follow the national model of judicial selection by the state's chief executive, and only a few have unlimited terms for judges. Terms of office for state high courts range from six to fifteen years, with eight to twelve years being the most common. There are generally no restrictions on a judge's post-tenure employment. Most states set mandatory retirement ages for judges, usually at seventy years. Typically, the chief executive has the power to name a judge to fill a vacancy that has arisen from a retirement or resignation, with the chief executive's power sometimes limited by a requirement that one house of the state legislature must confirm the appointment. At some point these appointed judges must face the electorate. Most judges at every level are drawn

[13] For an overview, see L. Berkson, updated by R. Caulfield, *Judicial Selection in the United States: A Special Report* (American Judicature Society, 2004), available at: www.ajs.org/selection/docs/Berkson.pdf.

[14] J. Shugerman, *The People's Courts: The Rise of Judicial Elections and Judicial Power in America* (Cambridge, MA: Harvard University Press, 2011).

from the practicing bar; "promotions" from lower to higher courts are rare. The practice backgrounds of judges vary, although a substantially larger number have been prosecutors than have represented criminal defendants as a major component of their practice.

Judicial elections have various forms. The predominant one is the "retention" election for a sitting judge. Retention elections ask voters to decide whether a named judge should remain in office, without an opposing candidate on the ballot. The system of initial appointment based on recommendations from a nominating commission, followed by a retention election, was first adopted in 1940 in Missouri, and is therefore generally known as the Missouri plan. Typically, the nominating commissions do not include sitting judges from any level of the judicial system; rather, practicing lawyers dominate the commissions, which often also include one or more "public" members who are not members of the bar but who typically have some professional experience connected to the court system. A judge's first retention election usually occurs within a few years of initial appointment, and additional retention elections occur after some fixed period, such as eight years.

The actual practice of judicial nominating commissions is intensely local, and generalizations are difficult. The commissions are almost certainly sensitive to the political concerns of the appointing chief executive, but they have the power to limit the chief executive's choice to the list they submit, which gives them some independent power. Judges chosen by a Missouri-type system are probably somewhat more qualified in standard professional terms than judges chosen in contested elections, although the difference in "merit" is probably small.

Judges hold their seats in retention elections at exceedingly high rates, largely because the elections are uncontested and in part because judicial elections have historically been much less visible than elections for legislative and executive positions. This does not mean, though, that judges in states with retention elections are unaware of the possibility of losing office because of popular dissatisfaction with their performance, and in particular with some specific rulings they might make. Over the past decades several judges on the highest courts in California and Tennessee lost retention elections when opponents organized campaigns against their retention focusing on decisions in which the judges had ruled against the imposition of capital punishment either generally or in especially notorious cases. Judges throughout the country know of these defeats. The Missouri plan thus does not eliminate the way in which elections may reduce the orientation of judges solely to the "rule of law," although it may mitigate the effects of elections on that orientation.

In other states judicial elections are contested, that is, two or more candidates seek the position. Again typically, one candidate is an incumbent who has been appointed to the seat. Contested judicial elections are either non-partisan, with the candidates not identified by party on the ballot, or partisan. Candidate selection in partisan elections is done through the mechanisms used for all other elections: nominating conventions or primary elections. Again because of the low visibility of judicial elections, local party leaders play an especially important role in choosing nominees for trial and intermediate appellate courts, a smaller one in connection with state high courts. Even in non-partisan elections parties sometimes play an important role because they have the resources to mobilize voters in what have usually been low visibility elections. The party label, of course, plays an important part in partisan judicial elections, where often the only thing voters know about candidates is their party affiliation. Some degree of "self-nomination" also occurs: a lawyer decides to become a judge and assembles the resources to run for office, often financing the campaign out of personal funds. Sometimes these self-nominated candidates succeed for unusual reasons. The lore about judicial elections includes stories about how some judges have been elected simply because they shared a surname with some important political or public figures; voters with essentially no information about the candidate's professional background or qualifications use the family name as a signal about the candidate's position, imputing the positions taken by family members to the candidate even though the candidate may not actually be related to the family.

For many years judicial elections attracted little attention except from advocates of "good government," who opposed judicial elections in principle as interfering with merit-based selection, and by scholars and political theorists, who treated such elections as embodying a tension between democratic theory and some versions of the "rule of law." Toward the end of the twentieth century judicial elections in one state after another became highly visible. The most important cause lay in the substantive private law state high courts began to articulate, and in associated procedural rules. Partly for doctrinal reasons, partly for "ideological" or philosophical ones, and partly for political reasons, state high courts expanded the circumstances under which injured plaintiffs could recover substantial awards from private corporations, both as to substance and through procedural innovations such as expansive ideas about when and how "classes" of plaintiffs could join together in a single lawsuit.

The composition of state high courts began to matter, to both the plaintiffs and the corporate bar. In the US legal system plaintiffs' lawyers are usually paid on a "contingency fee" basis, receiving a portion of the damages awarded to plaintiffs. They therefore have a direct financial interest in expansive liability rules, and through their organizations – for many years, named associations of "trial lawyers," but actually consisting almost exclusively of lawyers for plaintiffs in private law litigation – began to contribute substantial amounts to the campaigns of judicial candidates who they believed would continue to expand liability rules. Largely in response, but sometimes independently, lawyers for corporate defendants began to contribute similar amounts, and the cost of some judicial campaigns escalated dramatically.[15]

Contested judicial elections, and occasionally retention elections, sometimes focused on the private law questions that generated the large campaign contributions, with one side emphasizing how the judges were siding with ordinary people and the other emphasizing the ways in which expansive liability rules impaired the economy. More often, though, the campaigns used criminal law issues as the stalking horse for the underlying issues, because judges who frequently favored plaintiffs in private law litigation favored criminal defendants in decisions that sometimes could be cast as threats to public safety. Forms of advertising that were common in campaigns for legislative and executive positions – television advertisements, "negative" and "attack" advertisements – spread to judicial campaigns. Most attention focused on campaigns for state high courts, but occasionally elections for intermediate and trial court positions became highly contested.

The escalating cost of judicial elections has fueled renewed criticism of judicial elections as such, but at present the movement to curtail the scope of judicial elections has achieved little. Public financing of judicial campaigns has been adopted in a few states, which ameliorates the problems associated with such campaigns.

Removal and discipline

State court judges can be removed from office if they lose retention or contested elections. In addition, some states allow "recall" elections in which voters can remove a judge from office during his or her term, but

[15] For some details on the campaign costs in judicial elections, provided by an advocacy group, see "Justice at Stake Campaign, The New Politics of Judicial Elections 2006" (Washington, DC, 2007), available at: www.justiceatstake.org/media/cms/NewPoliticsofJudicialElections2006_D2A2449B77CDA.pdf.

these provisions have fallen into desuetude. Relying on British practices, about one-third of the states allow for removal of judges by legislative address, but this mechanism too has not been used successfully in recent decades.

Nearly every state provides for judicial removal by means of impeachment and conviction, typically for one of a list of offenses such as "malfeasance" or "gross misconduct." According to one study, "In the last 15 years, only two state judges have been impeached, only one has been convicted, and only five more have been involved in impeachment investigations."[16]

The near absence of removal by means of impeachment does not indicate that there are few problems of judicial performance in the states. In light of the large numbers of state court judges and the high variability in their quality, problems of judicial performance – ranging from straightforward corruption to mistreatment of litigants and court personnel, including sexual harassment and racial insensitivity – are far from rare. They are dealt with by judicial conduct commissions, typically composed of judges, lawyers, and non-lawyer public members. Ordinarily judges hold only a minority of the seats on these commissions. The study quoted above found that "In 2006, as a result of state judicial discipline proceedings, 12 judges were removed from office; 11 judges resigned or retired in lieu of discipline . . .; 1 judge was required to retire." More than one hundred additional judges received some form of public discipline, including suspensions without pay and public admonitions, reprimands, and warnings.[17]

Public discipline short of removal from office may have some effects on a judge's decision to seek re-election, although, even so, more than a few judges who have been disciplined are re-elected. In addition, judicial conduct commissions appear to have rather high thresholds for finding improper conduct. Although many complaints against judges involve their conduct in the courtroom and in judicial chambers rather than their decisions, judicial conduct commissions are concerned that disciplinary rulings might interfere with judicial independence, which they seem to construe as including the judge's power to organize the courtroom as he or she wishes.

[16] American Judicature Society, "Methods of Removing State Judges," available at: www.ajs.org/ethics/eth_impeachement.asp.

[17] American Judicature Society, "Methods of Removing State Judges."

Conclusion

Institutional change in judicial selection and removal is difficult, in part because it is constrained to some degree by explicit constitutionally entrenched rules. One can discern two trends that may have some impact over the next decades.

A career judiciary appears to be emerging in the federal courts

Increasingly, district judges have served as magistrate judges, and court of appeals judges as district judges. Historically, Supreme Court justices have come to the court from a wide range of prior positions. Charles Evans Hughes had been Governor of New York; William Howard Taft, President of the United States; and Earl Warren, Governor of California. Numerous senators have been appointed to the Supreme Court. Today's Supreme Court has only one justice who held an important position in the national government, whether in the executive branch or Congress, and every other justice had been a court of appeals judge when nominated. Some substantial amount of prior judicial experience may have become an implicit qualification for a seat on the Supreme Court, although we can expect occasional deviations. A significant portion of the federal judiciary is likely to consist of people with careers as judges and little else.

Two recent Supreme Court decisions have increased elite discomfort with state systems of judicial elections

Republican Party of Minnesota v. *White* held that the First Amendment's protection of free speech barred states from enforcing judicial codes of ethics stating that judicial candidates could not announce their positions on issues (not on specific cases) likely to come before them as judges.[18] The court's rationale was straightforward: judicial elections are elections like any other, and political speech, which occurs when candidates seek elective office, is at the heart of the First Amendment. Coupled with the increasing amounts of money spent on campaigns for judicial office, and the migration of advertising techniques common in other campaigns – advertisements attacking a candidate for some mis-step earlier in his or her career, for example. The *White* decision challenged the idea that

[18] *Republican Party of Minnesota* v. *White* 536 US 765 (2002).

judicial elections were compatible with the ideal of a politically neutral rule of law.

In *Caperton* v. *A. T. Massey Coal Co., Inc.*, the court held that the constitutional guarantee of "due process" was violated when a state supreme court judge cast the decisive vote in a high-stakes case in favor of a litigant who had spent a large amount of money (more than US$3 million) on advertisements supporting the judge's election.[19] The court's decision emphasized the case's dramatic facts and suggested that its holding would rarely lead to the disqualification of judges in cases involving litigants who had made less substantial campaign contributions. Yet, by finding that spending on a candidate's behalf could produce a constitutional violation, the court cast more doubt on judicial elections as such. After the *Caperton* decision retired Supreme Court Justice Sandra Day O'Connor sponsored a public education initiative aimed at eliminating judicial elections. That initiative is unlikely to succeed in the short run, but we can expect some perhaps modest reductions in the scope of judicial elections over the next decades.

[19] *Caperton* v. *A. T. Massey Coal Co., Inc.* 129 S.Ct. 2252 (2009).

PART III

8

Judges' freedom of speech: Australia

JOHN M. WILLIAMS

In April 2001 High Court Justice Michael Kirby addressed a university graduation ceremony in Adelaide. In what was described as a 'passionate defence of Australia's public education system' the judge called upon the Commonwealth government to boost funding for state schools.[1] Not surprisingly his call was roundly endorsed by the Australian Education Union and praised by the Opposition spokesperson Mr Michael Lee as a timely intervention. The Attorney-General, Mr Daryl Williams, and the Prime Minister, Mr John Howard, bluntly responded to this incursion into a public policy debate by a member of the judiciary. The Attorney-General said that:

> While I am a supporter of the judiciary raising community awareness about legal issues by explaining the roles of the courts and taking the lead in defending themselves, I do not support judges commenting publicly on political contentious issues.[2]

The Prime Minister was less restrained in his condemnation of Justice Kirby's actions:

> The comments that Mr Justice Michael Kirby made at the weekend regarding school funding were a direct intervention into a partisan political debate. It's not appropriate for a High Court judge to involve himself in something that is so blatantly and obviously a matter of debate between the two political parties.[3]

Reflecting on the incident on the eve of his retirement from the High Court in 2009, Justice Kirby conceded that the intervention was 'a mistake, looking

1 'Kirby sounds alarm on school funding', *The Australian*, 28 April 2001, p. 8.
2 'PM's attack on judge a first', *The Australian*, 2 May 2001, p. 2.
3 'PM's attack on judge a first', *The Australian*, 2 May 2001, p. 1.

back on it'.[4] Nevertheless he believed there was value in engaging with the public as a sitting judge.

> I have tried to engage the Australian community and talk about the law and about its directions and about its problems, problems of being a judge, the decision-making process. So that you've got to put into the balance the occasional error, for which I say *mea culpa*, against the value of a more transparent approach to the law.[5]

Michael Kirby was atypical of the Australian judiciary in his willingness to engage with the community on an array of judicial and human rights issues.[6] Yet the 2001 speech, and the political rebuke that was visited upon the 'occasional error', only highlights the tightrope that judicial officers walk when they enter into the public domain.[7] Even discussion of the relatively uncontroversial role of the courts and the administration of justice is an invitation to politicians and commentators to respond. Reason and dialogue may be expected, though ill-tempered and irrational responses are not unknown. What is certain is that the judicial officer is unlikely to be afforded the courtesy of the last word.

This chapter is divided into three parts. The first will outline Australia's constitutional arrangements highlighting the place of the judiciary and the protection of rights such as the freedom of expression. The second part will focus upon the influence that the 'Kilmuir rules' have had on the Australian approach to extra-curial commentary and the theoretical arguments that have been made for the relaxation of the previous reluctance to speak out. The final part will discuss what protections are available to the judiciary from unreasonable criticism and the constitutional dimension to the Australian debate.

The judiciary and Australia's legal system

Australia's constitutional arrangements represent an amalgamation of its legal heritage overlayed upon a federal structure. The framing of the

4 'Justice Michael Kirby steps down from the High Court', ABC Radio National, The Law Report, 3 February 2009, available at: www.abc.net.au/rn/lawreport/stories/2009/2480107.htm.

5 'Justice Michael Kirby steps down from the High Court', ABC Radio National.

6 See I. Freckelton, 'Introduction: Appealing to the Future', in I. Freckelton and H. Selby (eds.), *Appealing to the Future* (Sydney: Thomson Reuters, 2009), pp. 5–6.

7 M. McMurdo, 'Should Judges Speak Out or Just Shut Up?', Queensland Business Institute, Brisbane, 16 October 2001, p. 11, available at: www.sclqld.org.au/qjudiciary/profiles/mamcmurdo/publications.

Australian Constitution took place in the decade of the 1890s, with the Commonwealth of Australia coming into existence on 1 January 1901.[8] Prior to that date the six colonies had established, to various degrees, self-governing polities based upon the Westminster system of responsible government and parliamentary democracy. In bringing about a greater union of the colonies the framers looked to the federal template of the United States as a means of maintaining relative independence of the new states as well as the creation of a nation.

There are a number of distinct features of Australia's constitutional arrangements that assist in understanding the place of the judiciary within the system. Some of these represent deliberate choices by the framers and others have emerged, largely unpredicted by the drafters, over the century. Whether planned or the result of the organic interaction with the necessities of history these factors have helped to shape the role and function of the judiciary in contemporary society and contextualise the general reticence on the part of the judiciary to exercise their right as individuals to speak out.

By far the most striking feature of Australia's constitutional system is, when compared with other countries, the absence at the federal level of an entrenched freedom of speech guarantee. As the former Chief Justice of the High Court, Sir Owen Dixon, famously commented to an American audience in 1942 when comparing the two constitutions:

> The framers of the Australian Constitution were not prepared to place fetters upon legislative action, except and in so far as it might be necessary for the purpose of distributing between the States and the central government the full content of legislative power. The history of their country had not taught them the need of provisions directed to the control of the legislature itself.[9]

The faith of the framers in responsible government did not exclude from the Constitution the inclusion of some substantial express guarantees.[10] In this regard the Constitution contains, in certain circumstances, a guarantee of trial by jury, protections against acquisitions of property on other than just terms, a guarantee of religious freedom and a prohibition against discrimination by one state against the residents of another

[8] J. A. La Nauze, *Making of the Australian Constitution* (Melbourne University Press, 1974).

[9] O. Dixon, 'Two Constitutions Compared', in S. Woinarski (ed.), *Jesting Pilate* (Melbourne: Law Book Co., 1965), p. 102.

[10] See generally, R. French, 'Protecting Human Rights without a Bill of Rights' (2010) 19 *Commonwealth Lawyer* 28.

state.[11] These few express rights or guarantees are not the total protection offered to Australian citizens by the Australian Constitution. In broad terms a written constitution with a constitutionally entrenched and independent judiciary has proven to be a significant protection of rights.[12] Notwithstanding the lack of an express protection of speech, the High Court in the 1990s found implicit in the Constitution a limited guarantee of 'political communication' relating to government and governmental matters.[13] This development and its impact on the role of judges will be discussed in the third part of this chapter.

Absent a bill or charter of rights at the Commonwealth level (and until recently the state or territory) the protection of the right to free speech has been left to the common law and the parliaments. As the High Court noted in *Lange*:

> Under a legal system based on the common law, 'everybody is free to do anything, subject only to the provisions of the law', so that one proceeds 'upon an assumption of freedom of speech' and turns to the law 'to discover the established exceptions to it'.[14]

The 'established exceptions', such as the law of defamation, have changed content and application over time. Obviously, there is a balance to be struck between the absolute right of individuals to publicise issues of concern and the countervailing right to protect individual reputation or institutional integrity. Setting that balance is often guided by interpretative principles of the courts or by constitutional or statutory instruments.[15]

In two Australian jurisdictions the rights of citizens have been codified with the passage of bills or charters of rights. The Australian Capital Territory in 2004 enacted the Human Rights Act 2004 (ACT). Informed by the UK Human Rights Act 1998 the Act protects many civil and political rights, including the freedom of expression.[16] These rights 'may

[11] Sections 80, 51 (xxxi), 116 and 117.

[12] *Street* v. *Queensland Bar Association* (1989) 168 CLR 461, 521–2 *per* Deane J.

[13] *Australian Capital Television Pty Ltd* v. *Commonwealth* (1992) 177 CLR 106 and *Nationwide News Pty Ltd* v. *Wills* (1992) 177 CLR 1.

[14] *Lange* v. *Australian Broadcasting Corporation* (1997) 189 CLR 520 at 564 citing with approval *Attorney-General* v. *Guardian Newspapers Ltd (No. 2)* [1990] 1 AC 109 at 283.

[15] See, e.g., *Coco* v. *R* (1994) 179 CLR 427 in terms of interpretation of statutes to require clear and unambiguous language to limit common law rights and the Defamation Act 2005 (NSW) and Defamation Act 2005 (SA) with regard to the balancing of competing rights through statutory means.

[16] Human Rights Act 2004 (ACT), s. 16.

be subject only to reasonable limits set by Territory laws that can be demonstrably justified in a free and democratic society'.[17] The Human Rights Act is predicated upon a 'dialogue' model between the Supreme Court and the ACT Government. The Court issues to the government a declaration of incompatibility when ACT legislation is inconsistent with the full realisation of a human right.[18] The Government in turn may act to rectify the incompatibility or justify its policy decision to the Parliament.[19]

In 2006, the Victorian Parliament enacted the Charter of Human Rights and Responsibilities Act 2006. Like the ACT model the Victorian Charter protects freedom of expression.[20] It also uses the balancing test of 'reasonable limits as can be demonstrably justified in a free and democratic society based on human dignity, equality and freedom' to adjudicate between competing policy choices.[21]

Notwithstanding the concerns of some, an outbreak of rights litigation in the ACT or Victoria has not occurred. This, in part, is explained by the structural design of the Acts that are primarily directed at parliamentary practice and policy formulation rather than the traditional individual advocate as the right-holder.[22]

In summary, Australia's legal structure has supported freedom of speech and other rights through a combination of the common law, statutory instruments and interpretation, and a limited set of constitutional guarantees. It is against this backdrop that the right of all Australians (including judicial officers) are supported when entering into public discussion. In the next section of this chapter I will explore the reticence on the part of judicial officers to exercise their rights to speech and the debate that exists as to the soundness of this self-limiting ordinance.

Framing the debate: the Kilmuir rules and beyond

On 14 July 1955 the Director-General of the BBC, Sir Ian Jacobs, wrote to Lord Chancellor Kilmuir to request the involvement of members of the judiciary in a radio series on 'great judges of the past'.[23] This rather innocuous request became the catalyst for a statement of policy about the

[17] Human Rights Act 2004 (ACT), s. 28(1). [18] Human Rights Act 2004 (ACT), s. 32.
[19] Human Rights Act 2004 (ACT), s. 33. [20] Section 15. [21] Section 7(2).
[22] For an account of the schemes see C. Evans and S. Evans, *Australian Bills of Rights – The Law of the Victorian Charter and the ACT Human Rights Act* (Chatswood: LexisNexis Butterworths, 2008).
[23] A. W. Bradley, 'Judges and the Media – The Kilmuir Rules' [1986] *Public Law* 383 at 385.

interaction between the judiciary, the media and the public. In introducing the publication of the correspondence, A. W. Bradley noted that 'the public status of judges . . . is partly founded upon rules of law, but to a large extent also upon an untidy mass of non-legal rules, customary practices and political expectations, which may be conveniently identified as constitutional conventions'.[24] Undoubtedly, in 1955 the custom and practice was one of stoic silence and professional distance by the judiciary from any possible controversy.

In response to the request Lord Chancellor Kilmuir stated:

> It is, I think, agreed that there are positive advantages to the public when serious and important topics are dealt with through the medium of broadcasting by the highest authorities. We are likely, for example, to get a better assessment of the qualities of some eminent Judge of the past through an existing member of the Judiciary than from anyone else.
>
> But the overriding consideration . . . is the importance of keeping the Judiciary in this country insulated from the controversies of the day. So long as a Judge keeps silent his reputation for wisdom and impartiality remains unassailable: but every utterance which he makes in public, except in the actual performance of his judicial duties, must necessarily bring him within the focus of criticism. It would, moreover, be inappropriate for the Judiciary to be associated with any series of talks or anything which could be fairly interpreted as entertainment: and in no circumstances, of course, should a Judge take a fee in connection with a broadcast.[25]

Notwithstanding that the Kilmuir rules have never formally been part of the Australian judicial custom they have undoubtedly framed the debate in this country. Subsequent commentaries on the issue have inevitably referred to them either to acknowledge their underlying value or to question their relevance to contemporary Australia. While they remain the high watermark for judicial reticence, they continue to serve as a readily recognised point for those who wish to debate the wisdom of judicial officers exercising their rights as a citizen to speak out on matters of public concern.

The Kilmuir rules caution restraint primarily upon the basis of avoidance of controversy. Unsaid in this formulation is an articulation of the underlying principles that should guide the extra-curial utterances. In this sense the rules are defensive and merely an assertion of good practice rather than a reasoned account of the limitations, and perhaps obligations, that fall upon the judicial officers.

[24] Bradley, 'Judges and the Media'. [25] Bradley, 'Judges and the Media', at p. 385.

It is possible to derive some general guidance from constitutional principle about the appropriateness of judges speaking out. In what follows I will develop these arguments by recourse to two overlapping principles: the separation of powers and the maintenance of the rule of law. As will be seen these twin principles have been deployed by proponents of restraint comment as well as those who wish to encourage greater public involvement.

The first of these principles, the separation of powers, rests on the institutional arrangements and customs associated with judicial independence. Classically, this separation of powers is referenced to Alexander Hamilton's articulation that the judiciary was the weakest branch of government. As he famously stated:

> It may truly be said to have neither FORCE nor WILL, but merely judgment; and must ultimately depend upon the aid of the executive arm even for the efficacy of its judgments.[26]

Like the United States, the Australian judiciary is supported by robust structural arrangements. The Commonwealth Constitution provides that federal judges are appointed by the Governor-General in Council and

> shall not be removed except by the Governor-General in Council, on an address from both Houses of the Parliament in the same session, praying for such removal on the ground of proved misbehaviour or incapacity.[27]

Further, the remuneration of a judge cannot be diminished during the term of his or her office.[28]

At the state level the position varies, though generally judges hold their office subject to a vote of both houses of the state parliament praying for their removal. In some states, like New South Wales, the grounds have been stipulated in the Constitution. So, for example, the New South Wales Constitution requires there to be 'proved misbehaviour or incapacity' on the part of the judge.[29]

The separation of the judiciary from the executive and legislature is completed at the federal level by the exclusive vesting of 'judicial power' in the High Court and other federal courts.[30] This strict separation of

[26] J. Madison, A. Hamilton and J. Jay, *The Federalist Papers* (Harmondsworth: Penguin, 1987), Federalist Paper 78, p. 437.

[27] Section 72(ii) [28] Section 72(iii).

[29] Constitution Act 1902 (NSW), s. 53(2). See J. Crawford and B. Opeskin, *Australian Courts of Law*, 4th edn. (Melbourne: Oxford University Press, 2004), pp. 68–9.

[30] The section does go on to also vest judicial power in 'such other courts as it invests with federal jurisdiction'.

power has proved to be critical in the development of the jurisprudence relating to Australian federalism, and has in turn supported an approach to constitutional interpretation focused upon legalism.[31] The notion that the safest path to interpretation of the Constitution is a form of 'strict and complete legalism', to use Dixon's formulation, has proved to be a powerful theme in Australian jurisprudence. At its core the Dixonian approach linked legalism to public confidence in the court and its role in the Australian polity.[32]

The state level does not mirror the Commonwealth in terms of the vesting of state judicial power. State constitutions do not enforce a strict separation of powers and a number of non-judicial functions have, mainly for historical reasons, been undertaken by the courts or members of the courts.[33] These include the chief justice acting as Lieutenant-Governor in some states or the supreme courts undertaking functions that involve non-judicial functions.[34] Increasingly, a greater integration between the Commonwealth and state judicial branches has hardened this historical flexibility.

It is the separation of powers and the protection of the judicial office that has prompted some commentators to support a more adventurous stance on the part of judicial officers towards speaking out. Writing in the context of the Canadian 'Justice Berger affair', Professor Jeremy Webber addressed the theoretical dimension of extra-judicial comments by a judge.[35] Webber approached the question from the twin perspectives of the capacity of the judiciary to threaten the 'autonomy of the legislature and executive' and the ability of the 'executive and legislative' to threaten autonomy of the judiciary. On the first perspective Webber concluded that:

> Mere extra-judicial comment, although it may embarrass the legislature and executive authorities in the same way that the comments of any respected citizen might, cannot result in the subjection of law-making or law-executing to the will of the appointed judiciary. Thus, there is no reason, on this basis alone, to restrict extra-judicial comments.[36]

[31] L. Zines, *The High Court and the Constitution*, 5th edn. (Sydney: Federation Press, 2008), ch. 17.

[32] Zines, *The High Court and the Constitution*, p. 597.

[33] *Kable* v. *Director of Public Prosecutions (NSW)* (1996) 189 CLR 51 at 117–19 *per* McHugh J.

[34] For instance, in South Australia the members of the Supreme Court constitute the Boundaries Commission: Constitution Act 1934, s. 78.

[35] J. Webber, 'The Limits to Judges' Free Speech: A Comment on the Report of the Committee of Investigation into the Conduct of the Hon. Mr Justice Berger' (1994) 29 *McGill Law Journal* 369.

[36] Webber, 'The Limits to Judges' Free Speech', at pp. 380–1.

As to the second perspective, Webber acknowledged that at times extra-judicial comments may provoke retaliation by the executive, and that the judiciary must be careful in making comments that would be seen as an abandonment of the judicial process of decision-making in favour of the legislative or executive decision-making process. However, acknowledging these concerns, he also argued that there was enough protection to support a judge's right to speak out. He said:

> Institutions exist precisely to separate the exercise of judicial duties from action in one's personal capacity: these include the physical arrangements of the courtroom, the ceremonial robes and procedures, the professional ethics of judges, and the various formal devices (procedural rules, rules of evidence, the need to justify one's decisions, control by an appellate court). The mere extra-judicial expression of opinion, then, cannot be said to raise a reasonable suspicion that judicial decision-making has been subverted.[37]

It should be acknowledged that Webber does not advocate an unbridled commentary by judicial officers. Rather, by returning to first principles he was able to propound a more relaxed approach to extra-curial comment based upon the separation of powers and the protections that it creates. What is of interest in the Webber formulation is that it inverts the usual separation of powers argument. That is, the separation of powers, and the protection that it offers, is highlighted as a source of authority to speak rather than an indicator for silence.

The Canadian Charter of Rights and Freedoms 1982 clearly influences the debate within that country as to the nature of public dialogue and the central role of the judiciary in resolving complex legal issues that have overt political content. However, the separation of powers doctrine is common to both Australia and Canada and the approach offered by Webber does provide an institutional argument for the relaxation of the reticence of judicial officers to be involved in public discussions. Notwithstanding the constitutional supports for the independence of the judiciary, this of itself is not enough to guard against the court's loss of reputation. As Sir Ninian Stephen commented, 'an independent judiciary, although a formidable protector of individual liberty, is at the same time a very vulnerable institution, a fragile bastion indeed'.[38]

[37] Webber, 'The Limits to Judges' Free Speech', at p. 384.

[38] N. Stephen, 'Southey Memorial Lecture 1981: Judicial Independence – A Fragile Bastion' (1981) 13 *Melbourne University Law Review* 334 at 338.

This notion of fragility links to the second principle. Constitutions divide power for a number of theoretical and practical reasons. Arguably, the greatest of these is to protect and advance the rule of law (and thus the liberty of the citizen). That the law can be both known and accepted is fundamental to our understanding of the rule of law. Professor Joseph Raz, for one, expressly linked the independence of the judiciary with the rule of law. For Raz 'it is futile to guide one's action on the basis of the law if when the matter comes to adjudication the courts will not apply the law and will act for some other reasons'.[39] That the law is accepted rests largely upon the confidence that the public have in the integrity of the institutions that make and declare the law. For the judiciary this manifests in a number of requirements. In particular, that the judicial officer is free of the control of the other arms of the state and approaches any dispute without bias or prejudice. Again as Sir Ninian stated:

> What ultimately protects the independence of the judiciary is the community consensus that that independence is a quality worth protecting, the citizen being better served if the judiciary is preserved from domination by those more overtly powerful elements of governments, on whose support the judiciary is dependent, yet which exercise of power the judiciary is charged with keeping within the bounds prescribed by law.[40]

This second principle of the rule of law, resting on public confidence, does not automatically dictate judicial tapestry. The Kilmuir rules suggest that a degree of mystery about the judiciary and its function will be needed to maintain confidence in the institution. However, public confidence can be fostered by explaining the judicial process as much as avoiding the public. This has become the contemporary approach in Australia, and its rise coincided with a marked change in attitude on the part of the judiciary and the executive.

In the 1990s, during the era of the Mason Court, a new openness about the role and function of the High Court emerged.[41] In particular, Sir Anthony Mason attempted to explain his understanding of the preferred judicial method of courts of final appeal. In eschewing many of the stultifying aspects of legal formalism Mason stated that:

> It is now accepted that, at the appellate level at least, judges do make law when they extend, qualify or re-shape a principle of law . . . Judges do not

[39] J. Raz, 'The Rule of Law and Its Virtue' (1977) 93 *Law Quarterly Review* 195 at 201.

[40] N. Stephen, 'Southey Memorial Lecture 1981', at p. 339.

[41] C. Saunders, 'The Mason Court in Context', in C. Saunders (ed.), *Courts of Final Jurisdiction: The Mason Court in Australia* (Sydney: Federation Press, 1998), p. 3.

> carry out this responsibility in a vacuum, by shutting their eyes to contemporary conditions. They must have an eye to the justice of a rule, to the fairness and the practical efficacy of its operation in the circumstances of contemporary society. A rule that is anchored in conditions which have changed radically with passage of time may have no place in the law of today.[42]

The articulation of this change in approach necessitated further explanation, and at times reassurance, that the judicial sky was not about to fall in because of the revelation that judges make choices and subsequently law. As Professor Geoffrey Lindell, the editor of the *Mason Papers* noted:

> The extra-judicial addresses and writings demonstrate a concerted attempt to cultivate a greater public understanding of the work performed by the courts and they foreshadow the need for judges to undertake that role themselves in a way that transcends the medium of the written judgment.[43]

To take such a step into the public forum, in an attempt to explain the judicial process, was not one to be taken lightly. As Mason acknowledged the value of 'judicial reticence' was that it 'insulated the judiciary from controversy'. Considering the merits of the previous approach Mason argued that:

> Judicial reticence has much to commend it: it preserves the neutrality of the judge, it shields him or her from controversy and it deters the more loquacious members of the judiciary from exposing their colleagues to controversy. Judges are not renowned for their sense of public relations.[44]

Judicial public relations were put on a new footing in 2002. The then Attorney-General, Daryl Williams, withdrew from the established convention that the Attorney-General would defend the judiciary from unreasonable criticism and attack. Williams stated the new position:

> In my view, the Attorney-General's relationship with the judiciary must be approached in a principled and coherent way that preserves the separation of powers and maintains public confidence in the justice system. Australian Attorneys-General are elected members of Parliament, answerable to their party colleagues, Parliament and the

[42] A. Mason, 'Future Directions in Australian Law' (1987) 13 *Monash Law Review* 149 at 158.

[43] G. Lindell (ed.), *The Mason Papers* (Sydney: Federation Press, 2007), p. 2.

[44] A. Mason, 'Judicial Independence and the Separation of Powers – Some Problems Old and New' (1990) 13 *University of New South Wales Law Journal* 173 at 181.

> electorate. They are not, and cannot be, independent of political imperatives . . .
>
> Nonetheless, to me it is clear that, in the Australian context, it is up to the judiciary to take the lead in defending themselves and their courts against criticism. My views fully recognise the courts as the third branch of government, capable of taking action to defend themselves against unjust criticism.[45]

This new approach prompted a discussion about how, and when, the judiciary should speak for itself and what was the previous convention as it related to the Attorney-General.[46] Undoubtedly, this new set of circumstances has influenced the Australian judiciary and has emphasised a greater self-reliance in terms of dealing with the public.

The Australian response

The contemporary Australian debate regarding judicial officers speaking out ranges from near prohibition to a more liberalised norm that focuses on the rights of the 'citizen judge'. On balance, the Australian judiciary has endorsed a cautious acceptance that there are circumstances when judicial officers are free to speak out, but this should be approached with great care and awareness of the need to support the integrity of the institution.

Those who have engaged in this discussion highlight the fundamental principles of the separation of powers and the need to maintain public confidence in the judiciary and the functions that it performs. The maintenance of public confidence, as noted, has been deployed as an argument for both greater engagement and judicial silence. Sir Daryl Dawson, a member of the High Court in the 1980s, refused numerous media requests to be interviewed. He reasoned that the primary 'function of a judge is to judge cases' and an open court and published reasons provide enough evidence of the operation of the law.[47] To add to the primary function by undertaking media interviews emphasises, according to Dawson, the 'individual personality' over 'the process of the law'.[48]

[45] D. Williams, 'The Roles of the Attorney-General' (2002) 13 *Public Law Review* 252 at 261.

[46] R. McColl, 'Reflections on the Role of the Attorney-General' (2003) 13 *Public Law Review* 20; L. King, 'The Attorney-General, Politics and the Judiciary' (2000) 74 *Australian Law Journal* 444.

[47] D. Dawson, 'Judges and the Media' (1987) 10 *University of New South Wales Law Journal* 17 at 18.

[48] Dawson, 'Judges and the Media'.

In similar terms the former President of the New South Wales Court of Appeal, Athol Moffitt, criticised fellow New South Wales Supreme Court Justice, James Wood, for public statements made about drug laws in that state. In criticising Justice Wood's intervention Justice Moffitt cautioned that judges who entered into politically disputed areas risked the independence of the judiciary and public confidence.[49]

Consistent with the views of Mason, the Chief Justice of South Australia, John Doyle, suggested that the maintenance of public confidence may necessitate greater involvement of the judiciary in explaining their role and function. This is the least contentious area of judicial dialogue. As Doyle stated:

> My starting point is that fundamental principle supports the proposition that the judiciary has a responsibility to foster public support for judicial independence, and to enhance public confidence in the judicial system by engaging in communication with the public, if that communication will achieve those objectives.[50]

While there is disagreement among the judiciary as to whether public discourse will damage judicial independence (especially in areas that do not relate to the administration of justice) there is no disagreement that there are some actions that are inconsistent with judicial office. For instance, the judiciary should not associate themselves with partisan political activities such as endorsing a political party or policy.[51] Similarly, activities or statements that would give rise to an apprehension of bias or prejudice must be avoided.[52]

Where judicial commentators are divided is upon the rights accorded to the judge as a citizen, on the one hand, and the institutional obligations that fall upon an individual once they have taken up judicial office, on the other. Chief Justice Gleeson outlined this tension between the citizen judge and the individual as a member of a court. He said:

> Like other members of the community, individual judges will, on occasion, disapprove of some of the laws enacted by Parliament. Provided their capacity to administer the law impartially is not compromised, they are

[49] A. Moffitt, 'Judges, Royal Commissioners and the Separation of Powers' (2000) *Quadrant* 36.

[50] J. Doyle, 'Should Judges Speak Out?', Judicial Conference of Australia, Uluru, 2001, p. 2, available at: www.jca.asn.au/attachments/doyle.pdf.

[51] J. Thomas, *Judicial Ethics in Australia*, 3rd edn. (Sydney: LexisNexis Butterworths, 2009), pp. 181–3.

[52] J. Thomas, *Judicial Ethics in Australia*, p. 72.

> free to criticise the law, and to propose change. In fact, judges regularly point out defects in the law, and make proposals for law reform. Many Australian courts have established procedures for drawing to the attention of Parliaments, and Law Reform Commissions, suggestions for changes in the law. Judges are often especially well placed to understand, and comment upon the implications of, legislative measures. The qualification earlier expressed, however, is important.

Impartiality is a condition upon which judges are invested with authority. Judges are accorded a measure of respect, and weight is given to what they have to say, upon the faith of an understanding by the community that to be judicial is to be impartial. Judges, as citizens, have a right of free speech, and there may be circumstances in which they have a duty to speak out against what they regard as injustice. But to deploy judicial authority in support of a cause risks undermining the foundation upon which such authority rests.[53]

The rights of a judge as a citizen are acknowledged at international law. As well as the rights expressed in the foundational international instruments the role of the judiciary has had specific recognition. In the 'Basic Principles on Independence of the Judiciary', adopted by the Seventh United Nations Congress on the Prevention of Crime and the Treatment of Offenders in Milan in 1985 and endorsed by the General Assembly, those rights are outlined.[54] These state that:

> Freedom of expression and association
>
> 8. In accordance with the Universal Declaration of Human Rights, members of the judiciary are like other citizens entitled to freedom of expression, belief, association and assembly; provided, however, that in exercising such rights, judges shall always conduct themselves in such a manner as to preserve the dignity of their office and the impartiality and independence of the judiciary.
>
> 9. Judges shall be free to form and join associations of judges or other organizations to represent their interests, to promote their professional training and to protect their judicial independence.

The strongest advocate of the citizen judge approach is Keith Mason, the former President of the Court of Appeal of New South Wales. While not suggesting that all judges are *obliged* to speak (indeed, he wished that many would not) he argued that: 'Surely a person who is a judge is free as

[53] M. Gleeson, 'Judicial Legitimacy', speech given to the Australian Bar Association Conference, New York, 2 July 2000 www.hcourt.gov.au/speeches/cj/cj_aba_conf.htm.

[54] Resolutions 40/32 of 29 November 1985 and 40/146 of 13 December 1985, available at: www2.ohchr.org/english/law/indjudiciary.htm.

a citizen to describe laws as "unjust" without betraying the judicial oath or putting judicial independence at risk.'[55] As well as the skill and insights associated with 'hammering out truth' judges have a right to contribute to the 'marketplace of ideas' like other citizens. Moreover, in certain circumstances judges may have an overriding moral objection to certain laws that compel them to speak out.[56]

In responding to Keith Mason, Chief Justice Doyle, focused upon the obligations that fell upon the individual once they took up judicial office. While favouring public engagement, even on contentious issues such as sentencing, he preferred that the issue of the administration of justice should be approached from an institutional standpoint (and usually through the head of jurisdiction). Individual interventions, according to Doyle, may be counter-productive in that they may conflict with institutional response and hamper an overall strategy of informing the public.[57]

Beyond the administration of justice issues, which directly involve the work of the courts, Doyle noted that there were 'issues of the day' that moved members of the judiciary to speak out. In recent times these have included the coming Australian republic, attitudes to homosexuality, mandatory sentencing and statements about reconciliation between Aboriginal and non-Aboriginal Australians. While Doyle did not suggest that judicial participation in these matters was never appropriate, he emphasised the overarching responsibility of the judicial officer to maintain public confidence in the courts. He said:

> Of course, we have the individual rights of all other Australians, but acceptance of judicial office brings with it certain restraints. Perhaps the acceptance of fetters on our right to participate in public debate is one of the restraints that goes with judicial office, in the interests of maintaining public confidence in our capacity to adjudicate dispassionately, fairly and soundly. On the other hand, perhaps I am a neo-Kilmuirean, afraid to let the public know the truth, that within our numbers very different views are held on many issues, and that outside our field of expertise we are usually no smarter than the rest of society.[58]

The President of the Queensland Court of Appeal, Margaret McMurdo, in her contribution to the question came to the inevitable conclusion that

[55] K. Mason, 'Should Judges Speak Out?', available at: www.lawlink.nsw.govau/lawlink/supreme_court/ll_sc.nsf/pages/SCO_speech_mason_090401.

[56] Mason, 'Should Judges Speak Out?'. [57] Doyle, 'Should Judges Speak Out?', at p. 5.

[58] Doyle, 'Should Judges Speak Out?', at p. 7.

different judicial officers will exercise their own discretion and choice as to if, or when, they will make extra-judicial statements.[59] She provided three principles to guide her colleagues:

> First, a judge should not engage in public discussion about a case which the judge is hearing or in which the judge has delivered judgment . . .
>
> Second, if speaking or writing extra-judicially, judges must be cautious not to breach the doctrine of the separation of powers . . .
>
> Third, judges' public pronouncements must not lead to a perception of bias or lack of impartiality which could require judges to withdraw from cases.[60]

The approach of Justice McMurdo concentrated on the exercise of the primary function of the judge and the need not to make statements that would frustrate the administration of justice.

The question as to what is the appropriate approach to engaging in public comment by judicial officers will be an ongoing discussion within Australia. While there are some obvious areas which cross a line and endanger the credibility of the individual judge (and thus the collective authority of the judiciary), at the margins there are differing opinions based upon reasonably held views of the competing principles. The closest to an agreed approach among the Australian judiciary is set out in the *Guide to Judicial Conduct*. The *Guide*, which was first published in 2002, was the result of consultation with judicial officers and was approved for publication by the Council of Chief Justices. The *Guide* is designed to give practical guidance to judicial officers and covers an array of situations where judicial officers must consider questions of impartiality, judicial independence, integrity and personal behaviour.[61] The *Guide* acknowledges that the 'preferred position' of the majority of judicial officers surveyed is that judges, 'subject always to the priority to be given to judicial duties and other necessary restraints – should be, and be seen to be, involved in the community in which they live, and should enjoy the fundamental freedoms of other citizens'.[62] On the issue of public comment by judges it makes the following points:

> Many aspects of the administration of justice and of the functioning of the judiciary are the subject of public consideration and debate in the

[59] McMurdo, 'Should Judges Speak Out or Just Shut Up?', at p. 18.
[60] McMurdo, 'Should Judges Speak Out or Just Shut Up?', at p. 9.
[61] The Australian Institute of Judicial Administration, *Guide to Judicial Conduct*, 2nd edn. (Victoria, 2007), p. 3.
[62] *Guide to Judicial Conduct*, p. 1.

media, at public meetings and at meetings of a wide range of interest groups.

Appropriate judicial contribution to this consideration is desirable. It may contribute to the public's understanding of the administration of justice and to public confidence in the judiciary. At the least it may help to dispose of misunderstanding, and to correct false impressions.

Considerable care should be exercised to avoid using the authority and status of the judicial office for purposes for which they were not conferred. Points to bear in mind when considering whether it is appropriate to contribute to public debate on any matter include the following:

- A judge must avoid involvement in political controversy, unless the controversy itself directly affects the operation of the courts, the independence of the judiciary or aspects of the administration of justice.
- The place at which, or the occasion on which, a judge speaks may cause the public to associate the judge with a particular organisation, group or cause.
- There is a risk that the judge may express views, or be led in the course of discussion to express views, that will give rise to issues of bias or prejudgment in cases that later come before the judge even in areas apparently unconnected with the original debate. A distinction might be drawn between opinions and comments on matters of law or legal principle, and the expression of opinions or attitudes about issues or persons or causes that might come before the judge.
- Expressions of views on private occasions must also be considered carefully as they may lead to the perception of bias.
- Other judges may hold conflicting views, and may wish to respond accordingly, possibly giving rise to a public conflict between judges which may bring the judiciary into disrepute or could diminish the authority of a court.
- A judge, subject to the restraints that come with judicial office, has the same rights as other citizens to participate in public debate.
- A judge who joins in community debate cannot expect the respect that the judge would receive in court, and cannot expect to join and to leave the debate on the judge's terms.[63]

The *Guide*'s practical advice to judicial officers acknowledges that there is value in the judiciary engaging in discussion of the administration of justice, and it attempts to balance the competing rights of the judge with the institutional requirements of public confidence in the process. The caution displayed in the *Guide* is reflective of the historic reticence of the judiciary and the overarching sentiment to avoid needless public controversy.

[63] *Guide to Judicial Conduct*, p. 23.

Criticism of the court and the constitutional guarantee

A final aspect of the freedom of speech of the judiciary in Australia is the issue of the constitutional protection afforded to judicial officers. The judiciary, like the other public institutions, are the subject of review and criticism. It would be misleading to think that sharp critique and unreasonable comment is a recent phenomenon in Australia. Even before the High Court came into existence in 1903 its judges were condemned by the radical journal *Tocsin* as 'plutocratic socially and Conservative politically'.[64] Yet, unsurprisingly, it is the contemporary attacks that have come to dominate recent literature in the area. Justice Kirby, writing in 1998, highlighted the level of abuse heaped on the court during his tenure. As he said in:

> recent High Court decisions, the court and the justices were labelled 'bogus', 'pusillanimous and evasive', guilty of 'plunging Australia into the abyss', a 'pathetic ... self-appointed [group of] Kings and Queens', a group of 'basket-weavers', 'gripped ... in a mania for progressivism', purveyors of 'intellectual dishonesty', unaware of 'its place', 'adventurous', needing a 'good behaviour bond', needing, on the contrary, a sentence to 'life on the streets', an 'unfaithful servant of the Constitution', 'undermining democracy', a body 'packed with feral judges', 'a professional labor cartel'.[65]

While the right of judicial officers to speak out is the subject of internal discussion within the judiciary, an important aspect of political communication is the protection afforded to judges by Australia's legal system. It is not the intention of this chapter to deal with the extensive legal protections that are afforded to the judiciary such as contempt proceedings. These are outlined and discussed in detail by leading Australian authors.[66] However, there is one aspect of the debate that does impinge upon the willingness of judicial officers to engage in public discussion and that is the constitutional protection that may be accorded to those who criticise the courts.

[64] H. Adnerson, *The Tocsin: Contenting the Constitution* (Maryborough: Red Rooster Press, 2000), p. 120.

[65] M. Kirby, 'Attacks on Judges – A Universal Phenomenon (1998) 72 *Australian Law Journal* 599 at 601 (references omitted).

[66] E. Campbell and H. P. Lee, *The Australian Judiciary* (Cambridge University Press, 2001), ch. 8 and E. Campbell and H. P. Lee, 'Criticism of Judges and Freedom of Expression' (2003) 8 *Media and Arts Law Review* 77.

In 1992, the High Court articulated an implied guarantee linked to the text and structure of the Australian Constitution. This related to a guarantee of political communication about government and governmental matters. One of the first cases to develop the principle exemplifies the relationship between the judiciary and public criticism. On 14 November 1989, a freelance journalist attacked the Commonwealth Arbitration Commission as regulating Australian workers through 'a vast bureaucracy in the ministry of labour and enforced by a corrupt and compliant "judiciary" in the official Soviet-style Arbitration Commission'.[67] In publishing these comments the newspaper committed an offence under the relevant Act in that it 'did by writing use words calculated to bring the Australian Industrial Relations Commission into disrepute'.[68] By majority the High Court held that the provision was invalid in that it was disproportionate to the objectives it was attempting to achieve. The constitutional guarantee has developed over the subsequent decade and in *Lange* a two-limb test of invalidity was articulated.[69] As recently stated in 2004 the test is:

> First, does the law effectively burden freedom of communication about government or political matters either in its terms, operation or effect? Second, if the law effectively burdens that freedom, is the law reasonably appropriate and adapted to serve a legitimate end [in a manner] which is compatible with the maintenance of the constitutionally prescribed system of representative and responsible government and the procedure prescribed by s. 128 for submitting a proposed amendment of the Constitution to the informed decision of the people (hereafter collectively 'the system of government prescribed by the Constitution'). If the first question is answered 'yes' and the second is answered 'no', the law is invalid.[70]

The *Lange* test has been significant given its influence on public discourse and criticism of government. There have been a number of cases where judicial officers have commenced defamation actions against commentators and newspapers and the *Lange* defence has been raised.[71] This, in turn, has prompted the question of whether or not judicial officers are involved in governmental activities. The question was

[67] *Nationwide News Pty Ltd* v. *Wills* (1992) 177 CLR 1 at 62.

[68] Industrial Relations Act 1988 (Cth), s. 299(1)(d)(ii).

[69] *Lange* v. *Australian Broadcasting Corporation* (1997) 189 CLR 520.

[70] *Coleman* v. *Powers* (2004) 220 CLR 1 at 50 *per* McHugh J.

[71] E.g., *Herald & Weekly Times Ltd* v. *Popovic* (2003) 9 VR 1 and *John Fairfax Publications Pty Ltd* v. *O'Shane* [2005] NSWCA 164.

considered, though not resolved, in *APLA Ltd* v. *Legal Services Commission for New South Wales*.[72] The case involved a challenge to regulations that prohibited advertising of legal services in New South Wales. A number of constitutional grounds were advanced to challenge the validity of the regulations, including that the law infringed the guarantee of political communications. The ground was unsuccessful because advertising related to commercial activities rather than governmental matters.[73]

Justice McHugh, like the other members of the court, rejected the submission based on the implied guarantee of political communications. In considering the issue he concluded that there was nothing in the *Lange* judgment that 'supports the proposition that the exercise of judicial power is within the freedom recognised by *Lange*. *Lange* concerned the conduct of a politician'.[74] In the course of his judgment Justice McHugh came to a distinction between communication that attracted the guarantee and communication that did not:

> Discussion of the appointment or removal of judges, the prosecution of offences, the withdrawal of charges, the provision of legal aid and the funding of courts, for example, are communications that attract the *Lange* freedom. That is because they concern, expressly or inferentially, acts or omissions of the legislature or the Executive Government. They do not lose the freedom recognised in *Lange* because they also deal with the administration of justice in federal jurisdiction. However, communications concerning the results of cases or the reasoning or conduct of the judges who decide them are not ordinarily within the *Lange* freedom.[75]

Justice McHugh went on to acknowledge that:

> The distinction between communications concerning the administration of justice that are within the *Lange* freedom and those that are not may sometimes appear to be artificial. But it is a distinction that arises from the origins of the constitutional implication concerning freedom of communication on political and government matters.[76]

The distinction that Justice McHugh has drawn is too sharp. The doctrinal arguments about the origins of the guarantee artificially separate

[72] (2003) 224 CLR 322.

[73] (2003) 224 CLR 322 at 360. As Gleeson CJ and Heydon J noted: 'The regulations do not, in their terms, prohibit communications about government or political matters. They prohibit communication between lawyers and people . . . Such communications are an essentially commercial activity' (at 351).

[74] (2003) 224 CLR 322 at 360. [75] (2003) 224 CLR 322 at 361. [76] (2003) 224 CLR 322.

the relationship between the three arms of the states. Leaving this point behind, there is a more significant issue to be confronted and that is the degree to which the courts should be seen as separate from the accountability principle that underscores the constitutional guarantee. No doubt the courts are accountable through the mechanisms of open justice, appellant review and published reasons. Yet accountability must also extend to criticism, even strident criticism, of the judiciary and its operation. As Justice Sackville noted when considering the current state of the jurisprudence 'the independence of the judiciary does not justify conferring on judges greater protection than that enjoyed by elected representatives or public officials'.[77]

Conclusion

Australians live in an age where criticism of public institutions is the norm. The Kilmuir rules and the assumptions they contain appear otherworldly from our perspective. They rest on a belief that the courts could command respect through status and public confidence which was assured by the diligent execution of the judicial function.

This chapter has outlined the general relaxation in attitude towards judicial officers speaking out. It is now uncontroversial that the courts have a role to play in explaining to the public their part in the administration of justice. Such an approach is consistent with a greater openness about the judicial process and a desire on the part of the courts to maintain and foster public confidence.

The wisdom of individual judges entering into public discussions of issues beyond the immediate concern of the judiciary is contested terrain in Australia. There is a healthy debate among judicial officers as to the rights that they hold as citizens and the obligations that befall them upon taking the oath of office. The chapter has outlined and considered the theoretical arguments that have been advanced for the adherence to silence or greater engagement in public discourse. The rule of law, the separation of powers and the need for public confidence in the 'fragile bastion' are arguments that have been advanced by all sides of the discussion. The debate has served to highlight that at the margins there is no definitive answer and that judicial officers, guided by a mature sense of the nature of Australia's public culture,

[77] R. Sackville, 'How Fragile are the Courts? Freedom of Speech and Criticism of the Judiciary' (2005) 31 *Monash University Law Review* 191 at 211.

will need to strike their own balance between the obligations of office and their rights as a citizen.

Australia has been well served by an independent and respected judiciary. There is no reason to think that greater engagement with the public by the judiciary, especially on topics relating to the administration of justice, will diminish that respect. Indeed, it is anticipated that the opposite will be the case.

9

Judges and free speech in Canada

KENT ROACH

Canada provides an interesting case study of the interaction of free speech and the judiciary in large part because of the impact of the Canadian Charter of Rights and Freedoms (henceforth 'the Charter') on the topic. The Charter was enacted as a constitutional bill of rights in 1982. Subject to demonstrably justified reasonable limits that are prescribed by law, the Charter protects freedom of expression. It also recognises the importance of judicial independence and impartiality by providing a right to a fair and public hearing by an independent and impartial tribunal. In addition, it protects equality rights.

The Charter has had a significant liberating effect on critical speech about the judiciary and on extra-judicial free speech by sitting judges. Today, judges in Canada make extra-judicial speeches on matters of public controversy that would have been unacceptable in the pre-Charter era. Canadian judges can now discuss labour, health, national security and criminal justice policy and the treatment of disadvantaged groups and justifiably claim that they are focusing on issues that relate to the administration of justice.

Although the Charter has tilted the balance in the direction of freedom of expression with respect to extra-judicial speech, it has had the curious effect of supporting new limits on speech from the bench. Those who object to speech from the bench invoke constitutional concerns that can compete with freedom of expression. They argue that judicial speech threatens the impartiality of the judiciary, including the need for judges to respect equality rights. In this sense, the Charter has emerged as a double-edged sword with respect to judicial speech.

Although some argue that increased limits on judicial speech in court can be justified because 'a judge should be careful to treat all people equally and fairly in accordance with the principles enshrined in the

Charter',[1] the increased focus on regulating speech from the bench represents a reversal from traditional restraints that focused on extra-judicial speech but did not attempt to regulate speech from the bench.[2] As will be seen, three judges in Canada have effectively been removed from office over the last fifteen years for what they did or said from the bench, and a fourth has been removed because of a combination of judicial and extra-judicial conduct. These cases can be contrasted to the most famous pre-Charter case in which Thomas Berger resigned from the bench because of a politically controversial extra-judicial speech. Today, Canadian judges enjoy more freedom than did Justice Berger to engage in extra-judicial speech. At the same time, they are far from immune from sanctions with respect to speech made in the discharge of their judicial duties. A perceived need to maintain judicial impartiality has led to the removal of a few judges for what they have said on the bench despite concerns that frank speech from the bench is required for both free speech and judicial independence.

This chapter will examine the growing jurisprudence in decisions by courts and various disciplinary or judicial councils of judges concerning the limits of critical free speech about the judiciary and about judicial free speech. It will also examine the question of what is the best methodology for providing future guidance about the limits of judicial free speech. These methodologies include the provision of ethical guidelines for judges, decisions by judicial councils about complaints against individual judges, use of intermediate sanctions short of dismissal and reliance on appeals and other legal processes as a means of responding to improper judicial speech from the bench.

Increasing critical speech about the judiciary: the demise of the contempt offence of scandalising the court

Unlike in the United Kingdom, where the offence had fallen into desuetude, there were a number of successful contempt of court prosecutions in Canada for scandalising the court before the Charter. For example, in 1976, a federal minister was convicted of the offence for declaring that a judgment dismissing a prosecution brought by his ministry was a 'silly

[1] W. MacKay, 'Judicial Free Speech and Accountability: Should the Judges Be Seen and Not Heard' (1993) 3 *National Journal of Constitutional Law* 159 at 241.

[2] E. Ratushny, 'Speaking as Judges: How Far Can They Go?' (1992) 11 *National Journal of Constitutional Law* 293 at 323–4.

decision . . . a complete shock and a complete disgrace'.[3] In 1982, the Law Reform Commission of Canada rejected arguments to abolish the offence and proposed a new statutory offence of insulting judges or attacking the integrity, independence or impartiality of the judicial process.[4]

Despite this support for fairly robust restrictions on critical speech about the judiciary, the offence of scandalising the court was essentially abolished under the Charter. The decisive case arose when a lawyer, Harry Kopyto, who had represented a client who had long campaigned against the police, responded very negatively when a civil law suit against the police was dismissed in 1985 as statute-barred. Kopyto told a reporter: 'This decision is a mockery of justice. It stinks to high hell . . . The courts and the RCMP are sticking so close together you'd think they were put together with Krazy Glue.'[5] The lawyer was found guilty of the common law offence of scandalising the court. His conviction was quashed on appeal, with the majority of the Ontario Court of Appeal holding that the common law offence could no longer be justified as a reasonable limit on freedom of expression under the Charter.

Justice Cory recognised that 'hyperbole and colourful, perhaps even disrespectful language, may be the necessary touchstone to fire the interest and imagination of the public, to the need for reform, and to suggest the manner in which that reform may be achieved'.[6] Relying in part on authority under the American Bill of Rights, as well as the idea that 'the courts are not fragile flowers that will wither in the hot heat of controversy', he held that the criminalisation of speech about the courts, however long accepted in countries without bills of rights, could be justified as a reasonable limit on freedom of expression only if the state could demonstrate 'a clear and present danger to the administration of justice'.[7]

In the wake of this decision, no attempts have been made to reformulate the scandalising the court offence or to criminalise free speech about the courts. Criticisms of court decisions and the judiciary are part of political discourse in Canada. Guidelines from the Canadian Judicial Council warn that 'judges must henceforth be prepared to endure almost

[3] *R* v. *Ouellette* (1976) 32 CCC (2d) 149, Que. CA.

[4] Law Reform Commission of Canada, *Contempt of Court* (Ottawa: Supply and Services, 1982), pp. 60–1.

[5] As quoted in *R* v. *Koypto* (1987) 37 CCC (3d) 1 at 7–8, Ont. CA.

[6] *R* v. *Koypto* (1987) 37 CCC (3d) 1 at 14.

[7] *R* v. *Koypto* (1987) 37 CCC (3d) 1 at 29.

any form of out of court criticism'.[8] The desire of judges to respond to such criticisms has probably played a role in liberalising the Canadian approach to extra-judicial speech.

The Berger affair

Any account of the limits of extra-judicial speech must start with the Berger affair. Before his appointment to the bench, Thomas Berger was a leading lawyer who represented Aboriginal people in many landmark cases. As a judge, he chaired an innovative public inquiry that focused on the adverse effects that the construction of a pipeline would have on Aboriginal people in Canada's north. In 1981, he made a speech at a university and wrote an op-ed article in a national newspaper that criticised an initial constitutional agreement because of its omission of protection for Aboriginal and treaty rights and a veto for Quebec on future constitutional change. Justice Berger's interventions in the constitutional debate attracted much attention, including a complaint by Prime Minister Trudeau that it was improper for a sitting judge to make such remarks and that he hoped that 'the judges will do something about it'.[9] They did.

A sitting judge made a strongly worded complaint to the Canadian Judicial Council (CJC). The CJC was created in 1971 as a body composed of Chief and Associate Chief Justices and some other senior judges. It has authority to hear complaints about the conduct of federally appointed judges on and off the bench.[10] Complaints are considered by an executive committee of judges. In more serious cases, panels are convened and they have the power to make recommendations for removal from office that are then considered by the full CJC. The inquiries and the full CJC issue lengthy decisions in such cases.[11] In all cases where the CJC has recommended removal from office, the judge in question has resigned without the constitutional requirement of a joint resolution of both houses of Parliament being necessary.

A three-judge inquiry was appointed in the Berger affair and delivered its judgment in March 1982. The panel took a fairly absolutist approach

[8] As quoted in M. L. Friedland, *A Place Apart: Judicial Independence and Accountability in Canada* (Ottawa: Canadian Judicial Council, 1995), p. 32.

[9] Friedland, *A Place Apart*, p. 98.

[10] Such judges in Canada include judges of the superior courts and courts of appeal in each province. There are provincial judicial councils with similar powers in each province.

[11] See www.cjc-ccm.gc.ca/english/index_fn.asp.

against judicial speech on matters of political or constitutional controversy. It rejected Justice Berger's defence that his remarks related to matters of conscience that transcended partisan politics and his Chief Justice's argument that the inquiry process threatened judicial independence. The panel equated the freedom of judges from political interference with the freedom of politicians 'from judicial intermeddling in political activities' and reasoned that 'judges, of necessity, must be divorced from all politics . . . they are gagged by the very nature of their independent office'.[12] The panel concluded that Justice Berger's remarks were 'unwise and inappropriate', and suggested that a judge who felt compelled to intervene in contentious matters should resign from the bench. The panel only declined to recommend Berger's removal from office because this was the first time that the CJC had dealt with such an issue and it would not 'be fair to set standards *ex post facto* to support a recommendation for removal in this case'.[13] The full CJC took a more forgiving approach and concluded that while Justice Berger's 'actions were indiscreet, they constitute no basis for a recommendation that he be removed from office'. It warned, however, that 'members of the Judiciary should avoid taking part in controversial political discussions except only in respect of matters that directly affect the operation of the courts'.[14]

The matter should have been put to rest at that point, but in September 1982, Chief Justice Bora Laskin gave a speech in which he argued that 'unbelievably, some members of the press and some in public office in this country, seem to think that freedom of speech for the judges gave them the full scope of participation and comment on current political controversies, on current social, and political issues. Was there ever such ignorance of history or principle?' Laskin criticised Berger and suggested that a judge who wants to speak out on political issues 'is best advised to resign from the bench'.[15] Justice Berger did just that less than a year later.

The Berger affair remains a matter of controversy. Laskin's biographer is critical of both Berger's speech on political matters and Laskin's subsequent intervention, which he concludes was done in 'an excessive and entirely inappropriate manner'.[16] Peter Russell, a leading Canadian

[12] Report of the Committee of Investigation to the Canadian Judicial Council (1983) 28 *McGill Law Journal* 380 at 389 and 391.

[13] Report of the Committee of Investigation to the Canadian Judicial Council, at 391–2.

[14] Report of the Committee of Investigation to the Canadian Judicial Council, at 379.

[15] As quoted in P. Girard, *Bora Laskin Bringing Law to Life* (University of Toronto Press, 2005), pp. 521–2.

[16] Girard, *Bora Laskin Bringing Law to Life*, p. 525.

commentator on the judiciary, has expressed concerns that Justice Berger acted improperly by intervening in matters of political controversy. At the same time, he criticised the 'heavy-handed' nature of the formal inquiry.[17] Jeremy Webber has critiqued the CJC's approach for discounting the value of allowing judges to make extra-judicial statements on matters affecting the constitution and the administration of justice as opposed to partisan politics. He also argues that Justice Berger's comments did not demonstrate a prejudice that would threaten his impartiality.[18] Wayne Mackay has argued that the CJC's approach gave insufficient weight to Justice Berger's freedom of expression, and was effectively abandoned in the 1990s as judges made speeches on a wide variety of topics.[19]

The inquiry's approach is absolutist in tone in stressing that a complete gag on contentious extra-judicial speech comes with judicial appointment. The full CJC took a somewhat more liberal approach, but its exemption for judicial speech that directly affected the operation of the courts can be criticised as overly narrow. An exemption only for speech about the courts, including issues relating to salaries and benefits, also runs the risk of being self-serving. The CJC's present ethical principles more generously contemplate that judges can take part in controversial political discussions affecting 'fundamental aspects of the administration of justice'.[20] Under the Charter, the range of matters that relate to the administration of justice has expanded as courts make decisions on a broad range of political and social matters. Neither the inquiry decision nor the CJC's decision in the Berger affair account for the constitutional protection of freedom of expression or attempt to reconcile this right with the demands of judicial impartiality or independence. Like the common law offence of scandalising the court, the Berger affair is best viewed as a historical touchstone rather than one that reflects contemporary standards on the limits of freedom of expression.

[17] P. Russell, *The Judiciary in Canada: The Third Branch of Government* (Toronto: McGraw-Hill Ryerson, 1987), pp. 87–8.

[18] J. Webber, 'The Limits to Judges' Free Speech: A Comment on the Report of the Committee of Investigation into the Conduct of the Hon Mr Justice Berger' (1984) 29 *McGill Law Journal* 369.

[19] W. Mackay, 'Judicial Free Speech and Accountability: Should Judges Be Seen but not Heard?' (1991) 3 *National Journal of Constitutional Law* 159 at 180.

[20] CJC, *Canadian Ethical Principles for Judges* (Ottawa: Canadian Judicial Council, 1998) at 29, 42.

Beyond Berger: the expanding limits of free extra-judicial speech

The CJC, which generally receives about 150 complaints a year, has summarily dismissed complaints made against Justice Bertha Wilson and Chief Justice Beverly McLachlin about extra-judicial speeches they have made on matters such as whether female judges have made a difference and criminal justice policy.[21] Because such complaints never go to full public inquiry, they tend not to result in fully reasoned public defences of judicial free speech.

A more serious case involved a complaint brought against Justice McClung after he wrote a letter to a national newspaper criticising Supreme Court of Canada Justice L'Heureux-Dubé for criticism she made of one of his judgments in a sexual assault case. Justice McClung's letter criticised Justice L'Heureux-Dubé for a 'graceless slide into personal invective' and delivering 'personal convictions' from 'her judicial chair'. He also conducted a press interview in which he affirmed disparaging remarks about the complainant in the sexual assault case. A panel of the CJC expressed disapproval of the letter and interview, but also held that a full inquiry was not required because the sending of the letter was 'an impetuous and isolated incident which does not warrant further consideration' and that the judge's comments both on and off the bench did not display bias against women. At the same time, the CJC dismissed a complaint brought against Justice L'Heureux-Dubé for the 'strong language' she had used in her judgment criticising Justice McClung for embracing myths and stereotypes about complainants in sexual assault cases.[22]

In 1995, J. C. Angers, the Chief Justice of the New Brunswick Court of Appeal, wrote an open letter to the Prime Minister and Members of Parliament opposing the government's measures to increase gun control as abolishing 'property rights without trial, hearing or compensation'.[23] The CJC panel expressed strong disapproval of the letter, but refused to refer the complaint to an official inquiry on the basis that the conduct could not justify dismissal. It concluded: 'we believe your conduct has

21 J. Sopinka, 'Must a Judge be a Monk? Revisited' (1996) 45 *University of New Brunswick Law Journal* 167.

22 CJC, *Annual Report 1999–2000*. p. 22. For criticisms of the CJC's approach see H. Lessard, 'Farce or Tragedy? Judicial Backlash and Justice McClung' (1999) 10(3) *Constitutional Forum* 65. For a defence see E. Ratushny, 'Speaking as Judges: How Far Can They Go?' (1992) 11 *National Journal of Constitutional Law* 293 at 400ff.

23 The open letter is found at (1996) 45 *University of New Brunswick Law Journal* 185.

not seriously prejudiced the political process and that you should be able to put your feelings aside and judge matters that come before you fairly and impartially'.[24] The panel maintained that although the Charter had been enacted since the Berger decision, it had not changed the traditional rule against judges making partisan political statements. At the same time, the panel noted that it was not deciding whether the judge had a Charter right to make the statements he did.

The Angers panel decision written by Chief Justice McEachern, who had defended Justice Berger, also appeared to distinguish the Berger decision by noting that while Justice Berger was commenting 'on matters of high constitutional importance', Justice Angers had made 'a highly partisan attack upon a proposal which, if carried forward into legislation, could well come frequently before you for interpretation or enforcement'.[25] Despite this difference, Justice Anger's case did not reach the final stage of consideration by the full CJC. It is difficult to escape the conclusion that the Angers affair represents a more lenient, albeit still disapproving, approach to controversial political speech by judges than the Berger affair.

The CJC has also disapproved of the conduct of Justice Flynn, who made comments to a press reporter about a controversial land deal that was made by cottage owners, including his wife, in an apparent attempt to avoid the application of a new law. In this case, a formal inquiry was held and concluded that Justice Flynn had acted improperly when he 'spoke out on matters of a very controversial political nature which, moreover, were likely to come before the Superior Court of which he was a member'.[26] Nevertheless, the inquiry found that removal from office was not justified because of

> the irreproachable career of the judge in question, the isolated nature of the incident complained of, the unlikelihood of a similar incident reoccurring, the judge's acknowledgment of his remarks, his letter and the acknowledgment made by his counsel that the judge in question made a mistake in making the statements complained of to the journalist. We remain convinced that the judge in question retains his independence and complete impartiality to continue deciding matters brought before him now and in the future.[27]

[24] The panel's conclusions are found at (1996) 45 *University of New Brunswick Law Journal* 185 at 188.

[25] (1996) 45 *University of New Brunswick Law Journal* 185 at 187.

[26] Report of the Inquiry Regarding Judge Flynn, 12 December 2002 at para. 71, available at: www.cjc-ccm.gc.ca/cmslib/general/conduct_inq_flynn_ReportIC_ 200303_fn.pdf.

[27] Report of the Inquiry Regarding Judge Flynn, para. 77.

Justice Flynn did not receive as harsh treatment as Justice Berger did even though his speech was arguably more inappropriate for a judge than Justice Berger's.

Cases combining extra-judicial speech and on the bench conduct

Cases that involve both extra-judicial and judicial speech demonstrate how a judge's extra-judicial speech can affect his or her performance on the bench. As will be seen, the outcome of these cases is consistent with the thesis that the Canadian experience after Berger and the Charter has been less forgiving of controversial judicial speech on the bench than off the bench.

Justice Andrée Ruffo of the Court of Quebec was a controversial and, in some quarters, popular judge known for her outspoken views both on and off the bench about the need for greater protection of the rights of children. Over her judicial career, a number of complaints were made against her including by her Chief Justice and by those who worked in various child protection agencies that appeared before her in court. In 2005, the Quebec Court of Appeal upheld an inquiry decision holding that Justice Ruffo should be removed from her position on the provincially appointed court. The specific complaint alleged that Justice Ruffo had acted improperly on the bench by not revealing a friendship with a possible witness and meeting privately with a witness without telling the parties. Nevertheless, the Court of Appeal's decision took a broader approach that also examined the judge's extra-judicial activities, which included paid speeches and appearing in an advertisement. The Court of Appeal recognised that judges had a right to freedom of expression both on and off the bench, but also stressed that the right must 'be reconciled with and, as needed, prioritised in relation to the constitutional right to judicial independence and the institutional protection of the judiciary as a whole'.[28] In the end, the Court of Appeal stressed that 'Respect for and confidence in the judicial task and the correlative duty to act in a reserved manner demand that judges remain apart from any turmoil or controversy that is likely to taint the image of impartiality that their conduct must project.'[29] The Court of Appeal held that Justice Ruffo's media appearance criticising the discipline process was 'unacceptable',[30] as was her signing of petitions to be sent to governments and her acceptance of a

[28] *Re Ruffo* 2005 QCCA 1197 at para. 56. [29] *Re Ruffo* 2005 QCCA 1197 at para. 410.
[30] *Re Ruffo* 2005 QCCA 1197 at para. 228.

fee for a talk at a commercial trade show. Although this case articulates limits on extra-judicial speech, it is also noteworthy that the removal decision mainly concerned improper conduct on the bench.

The most recent example of a case that combined allegations of improper conduct on and off the bench was the case of Justice Ted Matlow of the Ontario Superior Court. Justice Matlow was found by an inquiry to have engaged in improper conduct by organizing and leading community opposition to a development near his home, by promoting media attention to the campaign and by using intemperate language and allegations of misconduct as part of the campaign. In such interactions, the judge had signed letters with his judicial title. The inquiry also found related misconduct on the bench, because Justice Matlow had sat on cases involving similar matters. The inquiry panel reached the conclusion that these findings were of such gravity that they justified Justice Matlow's removal from office. The CJC, however, in a divided decision, ruled that the conduct did not justify Justice Matlow's removal from the bench. The CJC held that some of Justice Matlow's actions would be protected by freedom of expression.[31] At the same time, the CJC stressed that a judge cannot invoke fundamental freedoms 'in order to avoid the constitutional obligations inherent in holding judicial office'.[32] It strongly condemned Justice Matlow's use of intemperate language and his use of his judicial title in his campaign against development near his house.[33]

Consistent with the thesis advanced in this chapter that there has been greater tolerance in recent years for judges who make controversial extra-judicial as opposed to judicial statements, the majority of the CJC stressed that Justice Matlow's misconduct occurred off the bench:

[31] The majority of the CJC stated:

> In their role as private citizens, judges are not obliged to defer to all municipal actions simply because they also happen to be judges. Promoting public scrutiny and accountability through a vigilant media is an integral part of a Parliamentary democracy. Consequently, to suggest that inviting media scrutiny of a municipal decision challenged by a judge in his or her role as a private citizen means that he or she has necessarily placed himself or herself in a position incompatible with the due execution of the judicial office is an unduly general proposition that admits of no exceptions or refinements irrespective of the circumstances.

Report of the CJC to the Minister of Justice, 31 December 2008 at para. 110, available at: www.cjc-ccm.gc.ca/cmslib/general/Matlow_Docs/Final%20Report%20En.pdf.

[32] Report of the CJC to the Minister of Justice, para. 87.

[33] Report of the CJC to the Minister of Justice, para. 121.

> Without in any way excusing Justice Matlow's conduct, it related to actions off the Bench in pursuit of his private interests. Given the evidence before us, we expect that Justice Matlow will refrain from any similar conduct in the future now that the nature and gravity of his inappropriate behaviour has been brought home to him. We also believe that Justice Matlow will be impartial in continuing to decide matters brought before him in the future.[34]

These conclusions, however, discount how Justice Matlow's extra-judicial actions placed him in an arguable conflict of interest in a series of court cases. The majority of the CJC stressed that Justice Matlow's failure to inform parties of his involvement or to take steps to remove himself from related cases was done in good faith, but the minority of the CJC agreed with the inquiry that they constituted a failure to properly exercise his judicial office. Unlike the *Ruffo* case discussed above, the *Matlow* case was seen as a case involving extra-judicial misconduct and the judge in question remained on the bench.

The CJC's decision in the case is also noteworthy for the forging of intermediate sanctions short of dismissal in the form of requiring Justice Matlow to write letters of apology and obtain pre-approval for any further participation in public debate. On the one hand, there are strong arguments about the need for alternatives to the drastic and blunt remedy of dismissal. On the other hand, the intermediate sanctions placed some burdens on the judge's continued freedom of expression.

The limits of judicial speech from the bench: threats to judicial independence?

The need to respect judicial independence would normally counsel more latitude for comments made by judges in the discharge of their judicial duties as opposed to extra-judicial speech. In addition, improper speech from the bench can be addressed through appeals. One mechanism that cannot, however, be used is a libel or defamation action given the immunity enjoyed by judges in their judicial work. In what follows, it will be seen that there has been an increasing trend to disciplining judges for improper speech on the bench.

One of the most well-known attempts to discipline a judge for what he or she said on the bench was the fallout from the wrongful conviction of Donald Marshall Jr. A five-judge panel of the Nova Scotia Court of

[34] Report of the CJC to the Minister of Justice, para. 183.

Appeal stated in their judgment that any miscarriage of justice in the case was 'more apparent than real', in part, because of its conclusion that Mr Marshall committed perjury and did not admit to being engaged in a robbery at the time of the killing. A subsequent public inquiry appointed by the government attempted to compel the judges to explain their reasons for making these statements and also to explain why one of the judges sat on the case despite being Attorney-General at the time that Marshall was originally convicted. The judges refused to testify before the public inquiry and the Supreme Court held that judicial independence protected them from being compelled to testify.[35] The public inquiry criticised the judges in the case for their remarks and the Nova Scotia Attorney-General subsequently invoked statutory powers to require a full inquiry to be conducted by the CJC to determine whether there were grounds to justify the removal of the judges from office.

The CJC inquiry expressed 'strong disapproval' of the Court of Appeal's statement that any miscarriage of justice in the case was more apparent than real. At the same time, the inquiry held that the judges' finding that Marshall has been involved in a robbery was one that it could have honestly made given the evidence and the judicial role in determining credibility. The inquiry concluded that while the judges had erred and acted inappropriately in not recognising a manifest injustice, their conduct did not render them incapable of executing their office impartially and independently with continued public confidence. One judge in concurring reasons stressed the importance of judges being able to be candid in their reasons for judgment.[36] Several academic articles were critical of the CJC inquiry for what they perceived as excessive leniency towards the judges.[37] As will be seen, subsequent CJC inquiries would be less lenient.

An inquiry in 1996 concluded that the removal of Justice Jean Bienvenue of the Quebec Superior Court was justified in the light of a series of comments he made during a murder trial. The judge criticised the jury both before and after the verdict, including its refusal to bring in a first-degree murder conviction. During the sentencing of the female accused, the judge commented that women when they 'degrade themselves . . . sink to depths to which even the vilest man could not sink'. He also commented at

[35] *MacKeigan* v. *Hickman* [1989] 2 SCR 796.

[36] Report to the CJC, August 1990, available at: http://cjc-ccm.gc.ca/cmslib/general/conduct_inq_HartJonesMacdonald_ReportIC_199008_fn.pdf.

[37] See the symposium at (1991) 40 *University of New Brunswick Law Journal* 262ff.

sentencing that the victim had died a painful death as compared with Jews in the concentration camps who had died 'without suffering'. The inquiry stressed that the judge's comments about women 'convey a sexist stereotype that both idealises and demeans women' and adopted 'a bias that denies the principle of equality before the law and brings their impartiality into question'.[38] One judge dissented and stressed the importance of judicial independence. He also stressed that the judge had made apologies to the affected groups and had not intended to insult women or Jews. The judge subsequently resigned. The majority's decision in this case underlined that judges can be removed because of comments made from the bench and that Charter-based concerns about both freedom of expression and judicial independence could in some contexts be outweighed by considerations about the importance of judicial impartiality and respect for equality values.

Similar themes are found in the case of Judge Moreau-Bérubé, who in the course of sentencing commented that 'if a survey were taken in the Acadian Peninsula, of the honest people as against the dishonest people, I have the impression that the dishonest people would win. We have now got to the point where we can no longer trust our neighbour next door or across the street. In the area where I live, I wonder whether I'm not myself surrounded by crooks.' She apologized in open court a few days later stating that she 'certainly had no intention of impugning the honesty of my fellow citizens of the Acadian Peninsula'.[39] An inquiry was held in which two of the panel found that there was misconduct, but that it was not so destructive of impartiality and public confidence so as to require removal. A third panellist found no misconduct. The matter was then considered by the entire New Brunswick Judicial Council which had jurisdiction because the judge had been appointed by the province. The Council found that the judge should be removed from office because her comments had undermined public confidence and created a reasonable apprehension that she would not be impartial.

The Supreme Court of Canada upheld the Judicial Council's decision. Justice Arbour stated for the court that 'while it cannot be stressed enough that judges must be free to speak in their judicial capacity, and must be perceived to speak freely, there will unavoidably be occasions where their actions will be called into question'.[40] The court deferred to

[38] Bienvenue Report to the CJC, June 1996, at p 50 available at: www.cjc-ccm.gc.ca/cmslib/general/conduct_inq_bienvenue_ReportIC_199606_fn.pdf.

[39] *Moreau-Bérubé* v. *New Brunswick (Judicial Council)* [2002] 1 SCR 249 at paras. 3 and 4.

[40] *Moreau-Bérubé* v. *New Brunswick (Judicial Council)* [2002] 1 SCR 249 at para. 59.

the Judicial Council, stating that it was 'acutely sensitive to the requirements of judicial independence' including the danger of chilling unpopular expression by judges, but also that the Council as a regulatory body for judges 'must also be equally sensitive to the reasonable expectations of an informed dispassionate public that holders of judicial office will remain at all times worthy of trust, confidence and respect'.[41] The court did not deal directly with the merits of the judge's removal or the appropriate balance between the competing values at stake, but rather deferred to the Judicial Council's role and expertise in striking such a balance.

The removal decision can be questioned on the basis that it gives insufficient weight to the values of both free expression and judicial independence. The Council's findings of a reasonable apprehension of bias can also be questioned given the nature of the remarks and the judge's apology and clarification of her remarks. Judge Moreau-Bérubé's comments were less corrosive of judicial impartiality than those that Justice Bienvenue made about women and Jews. Nevertheless, the case remains a valid and judicially approved precedent of how a judge's remarks on the bench can lead to removal from office because of the perceived effects of those remarks on the judge's continued impartiality.

The latest case of discipline for comments made on the bench in Canada involved Justice Paul Cosgrove, who entered a stay of proceedings after a two-year murder trial on the basis of over 150 violations of the Charter. The stay was subsequently overturned on appeal, with the Ontario Court of Appeal severely criticising Justice Cosgrove on the basis that he made 'numerous legal errors as to the application of the Charter. He made findings of misconduct against crown counsel and police officers that were unwarranted and unsubstantiated. He misused his powers of contempt and allowed investigations into areas that were extraneous to the real issues in the case.'[42] Following the court's statements that the appeal process itself does not remedy harm to the integrity of the judiciary, the Attorney-General of Ontario used his powers to make a complaint to the CJC which triggers a mandatory inquiry. The inquiry concluded that Justice Cosgrove had inappropriately aligned himself with defence counsel giving rise to an apprehension

[41] *Moreau-Bérubé* v. *New Brunswick (Judicial Council)* [2002] 1 SCR 249 at para. 72.

[42] *R* v. *Elliott* (2003) 179 OAC 219 at para. 166, CA. For a recent decision in which the same Court of Appeal severely criticised a judge for engaging in 'personal diatribes' about the inefficacy of prison in deterring drug crimes see *R* v. *Song* 2009 ONCA 896 at paras. 11–13.

of bias and what it termed an 'anti-Crown bias'.[43] The five-person inquiry concluded, with one dissent, that Justice Cosgrove's conduct had created 'a reasonable and irremediable apprehension of bias' and that he had abused his judicial powers.[44]

The full CJC confirmed this decision and in doing so placed considerable reliance on the *Moreau-Bérubé* precedent discussed above. A distinguishing feature of the *Cosgrove* case, however, is the focus on the merits of the judge's decisions. Even though his judgment was overturned on appeal, the CJC unanimously found that Justice Cosgrove's dismissal was required because of concerns about his impartiality. This decision, when combined with the CJC's decision a few months earlier in the Matlow matter, underlines that the CJC at present seems considerably more lenient to inappropriate speech by judges off the bench than inappropriate speech and conduct in the course of discharging their judicial duties. The CJC concluded that Justice Cosgrove's conduct threatened his continued impartiality on the bench in a manner that Justice Matlow's did not. Nevertheless, there are reasons to be concerned about the *Cosgrove* case. It comes perilously close to removing a judge for legal errors and incompetence. In addition, any lack of impartiality in this case can be distinguished from those found in the *Bienvenue* and *Moreau-Bérubé* cases because they related to the conduct of the individual litigants before him and were not based on ascribed characteristics of groups such as women, minorities or the residents of a particular community. Finally, Justice Cosgrove was found to be removable from office for the way in which he performed his assigned judicial duties, whereas Justice Matlow made a voluntary decision to use his judicial office in a campaign against development in his neighbourhood.

The need for alternatives to a case-by-case approach tied to dismissal

As the above survey reflects, the decision of judicial councils in individual cases has emerged over the last two decades as the dominant means of deciding the limits of judicial free speech. Although a case-by-case approach will be required if abuses of judicial speech are tied to the remedy of removal, it will be suggested below that there are better ways

[43] Report of the Inquiry Concerning Justice Cosgrove, November 2008 at para. 74, available at: www.cjc-ccm.gc.ca/cmslib/general/Report%20 to%20CJC%202008-11-27.pdf.

[44] Report of the Inquiry Concerning Justice Cosgrove, para. 189.

to provide advance guidance to judges through the use of ethical and other guides.

Most complaints are dismissed without a formal inquiry or a public judgment because of legitimate concerns about confidentiality. Nevertheless, such an approach creates a danger that the case law is skewed to the more serious cases and this could chill freedom of expression. In some cases where judges have engaged in high profile speech, it may be helpful for the CJC to provide fuller explanations about why such speech is acceptable.

The deferential approach taken by the courts to decisions by judicial councils in the *Moreau-Bérubé* and *Ruffo* cases suggests that more thought needs to be given to how those councils deliberate and reach their decisions. The dominance of Chief Justices and Associate Chief Justices in the CJC might perhaps be rethought to include more puisne judges and lay representatives. Although the preferred positions of Attorneys-General in triggering a formal inquiry has recently been upheld from a Charter challenge that it infringed judicial independence,[45] it also needs to be rethought especially in cases such as *Cosgrove* where the complaint was an alleged anti-crown bias. Although the Attorney-General has special responsibilities for the administration of justice, he or she is also an active litigant before the courts. Judicial councils themselves can be expected to be able to discern those cases where the public interest in the administration of justice requires a full inquiry.

The deferential approach taken by the courts towards judicial councils is based on an assumption that judicial councils are best suited to reconcile the competing demands of judicial independence and judicial integrity. The judicial community, however, is small and can be influenced by a judge's reputation and the collective embarrassment that an errant judge can cause to his or her colleagues. The assumption that judicial councils are in the best position to reconcile all the competing values could break down when judges who are subject to discipline are seen by their fellow judges as outsiders or are embarrassments to the judiciary. In such cases, those who sit on judicial councils may be tempted to support dismissal over less drastic sanctions.

The Supreme Court in *Moreau-Bérubé* has indicated that the discipline of judges is designed to respond to harms to the judiciary that are not addressed by the appeal process. This observation makes logical

[45] *Attorney-General of Canada* v. *Cosgrove* 2007 FCA 103.

sense, especially in cases where a judge has engaged in a pattern of persistent misconduct. Nevertheless, there is a danger that courts and councils may underestimate the benefits of appeals in restoring public confidence about the judiciary and in educating judges about proper conduct. For example, the effects of the Ontario Court of Appeal's overturning of Justice Cosgrove's decision to stay proceedings and its severe criticism of his actions did not feature prominently in either the inquiry or CJC decision that recommended his removal from the bench. Appellate courts should be aware of the harm that improper judicial speech can cause to reputations and may be in a position to compensate for the inability of adversely affected individuals to bring defamation actions. Judges who make derogatory comments about groups or demonstrate a bias towards certain parties would also be vulnerable to recusal motions even in the absence of judicial discipline. It would be ironic if stricter standards were applied in cases that seek a judge's permanent removal from office than his or her recusal in an individual case.[46] Although discipline can have a residual role, especially in cases of persistent misconduct, judicial councils should not be too quick to underestimate the salutary effects of a stern reversal on appeal to the integrity of the judiciary and to the reform of most errant judges.

In addition to appeals, judicial councils should also be careful to take into account the effects of judicial apologies in restoring public confidence in the judiciary and in helping to prevent a repeat of misconduct. In both the *Moreau-Bérubé* and *Bienvenue* cases, more weight could have been given to the judge's apologies to those groups who may have been offended by the judicial speech. The CJC's recent decision in *Matlow* also opens the possibility of intermediate sanctions as an alternative to the 'capital punishment' of dismissal from the bench. It will be recalled that Justice Matlow was required by the CJC to write letters of apology and to seek prior approval of further engagement in public debates. Although the value of forced apologies can be questioned, a 'probation' sanction allows judges to receive mentoring and guidance about how they reconcile freedom of speech with the demands of their office.

The need for better advance guidance for judges

The complaints jurisprudence is growing more complex. The CJC deserves credit for increasing the transparency of the inquiry process

[46] *R* v. *S (RD)* [1997] 3 SCR 484 (no reasonable apprehension of bias when trial judge commented that police officers had been known to over-react when dealing with non-white groups).

by posting not only the decisions, but all supporting material on its helpful website. That said, complex jurisprudence may not provide optimal guidance for judges. In addition the *Moreau-Bérubé* and *Matlow* cases demonstrate the additional complexity caused when the full Judicial Council departs from recommendations made by inquiry panels.

An alternative form of guidance is provided by ethical principles issued by the CJC in 1998. Unfortunately, however, these principles are less helpful than they might be. Both the Supreme Court and the CJC have made clear that ethical principles should not be seen as codes of conduct or misconduct.[47] Nevertheless, it might be helpful to amend the ethical principles to provide some concrete examples of speech that is clearly proper and improper.

Even if the principles were interpreted more as a code of conduct, they will not answer all the questions. For example, the principles suggest that judges should avoid 'taking part publicly in controversial political discussions except in respect of matters directly affecting the operation of the courts, the independence of the judiciary or fundamental aspects of the administration of justice'.[48] Given the pervasive influence of the Charter, it could be argued that many matters of political controversy, including the issues raised by Justice Berger, relate to the administration of justice. On the other hand, the ambit of speech relating to the courts and the administration of justice could be interpreted more narrowly. To their credit, the principles recognise their own indeterminacy and contemplate that judges in particular cases can obtain advisory opinions on their meaning. Such advance decisions also provide an opportunity for peer mentoring of judges about the limits of their free expression.

The CJC ethical principles represent an advance over the approach articulated by the CJC panel in the Berger affair, because they focus on the effects of speech and related activities on judicial impartiality. The commentary to the principles, however, also suggests that judges should avoid speech that 'may unnecessarily expose the judge to political attack or be inconsistent with the dignity of judicial office'.[49] Such concerns, however, might suggest that judges should avoid all controversial speech even on matters relating to the administration of justice. The focus

[47] *Ruffo* v. *Conseil de la magistrature* [1995] 4 SCR 267. But see also G. Jackson, 'The Mystery of Judicial Ethics: Deciphering the "Code"' (2005) 68 *Saskatchewan Law Review* 1.

[48] Canadian Judicial Council, *Ethical Principles for Judges* (1998), Principle 6.

[49] *Ethical Principles for Judges*, at p. 41.

should be on the effect of judicial speech on judicial impartiality and not on the fact that judicial speech may be controversial or expose the judge to political attack. Under the Charter, judges are already fair game for political attack.

In addition to more explicit and more consistent ethical principles, public debate about the limits of judicial speech should be encouraged. The Berger affair spawned much commentary, most of it critical, and the influence of these critiques can be seen in a number of decisions that have taken a more liberal approach to controversial extra-judicial speech. Similarly, the Marshall affair spawned critical commentary and the influence of these critiques can be seen in the stricter approach that has been taken in recent years to judicial speech on the bench. Critical commentary can contribute to a healthy process of continual incremental adjustment to the balance that is struck between the values of free speech and judicial independence and impartiality in this difficult area.

Conclusion

Canada provides an interesting case study of the effects that constitutional guarantees of freedom of expression and of judicial independence and impartiality can have on speech about and by the judiciary. The Charter has had the most decisive effect with respect to critical speech about the judiciary as it has invalidated the common law contempt offence of scandalising the court that, before the Charter, was used more frequently in Canada than in other democracies with respect to criticisms of the judiciary. Although the impact is more indirect, the Charter has also likely had a liberating effect with respect to extra-judicial speech. Judges in Canada, often led by justices of the Supreme Court, frequently exercise their right to free speech and have made public speeches that have at times resulted in controversy. This seems appropriate in a free and democratic society where judges make important decisions on matters of policy and when their decisions are often strongly criticised in public debate.

Since the Berger affair, judges in Canada have been more likely to be removed from the bench for controversial speech made on the bench than for extra-judicial speech. Most recently, Justice Cosgrove had to resign from the bench because of his conduct in a case, whereas Justice Matlow was allowed to stay on the bench even though he improperly used his judicial title in a campaign against a development near his home. Although judges should not enjoy immunity from discipline for anything they say on the bench, judicial councils may have underestimated the chilling effects that removal decisions may have on judicial candour and independence. In addition, judicial councils should be careful not to underestimate the salutary effects of successful appeals and apologies by judges in restoring public confidence in judicial impartiality and in educating judges about the real limits that remain on their free speech rights.

The Canadian experience demonstrates increased recognition of the importance of freedom of expression with respect to criticism of the judiciary and extra-judicial speech by judges. At the same time, there has been a willingness to limit judicial speech in the name of preserving judicial impartiality. The limits on such judicial speech are not abstract. They have led to the removal of four Canadian judges for speech and conduct from the bench.

10

Judges and free speech in New Zealand

GRANT HAMMOND

Lord Atkin once memorably remarked that 'Justice is not a cloistered virtue; she must be allowed to suffer the scrutiny and respectful even though outspoken comments of ordinary men.'[1] His Lordship had in contemplation, in a contempt case, a bipartite problem: those who administer the law, and with the cloak of the protections afforded that role, may, and must where necessary and appropriate, make strong comment in the course of determining a controversy. And persons outside the circle of those administering justice are entitled to make 'respectful' but just as outspoken comment or replies about the 'public act done in the seat of justice'.[2] Those propositions are not in doubt.

The question the equation as thus stated does not answer is, what is the position of a judge who feels impelled to make some observations as to what is happening within the justice system itself, or some particular aspect of it, outside of the formal confines of a given case or judgment? Should the judge confine his or her observations purely to the discharge of particular judicial obligations in that given case? If not, under what circumstances *is* it permissible and appropriate for an individual judge to offer particular commentary of a more general character?

This chapter addresses these issues in three parts. First, I set out the 'formal' position in New Zealand. Second, I then outline some contemporary controversies to illustrate the problems arising in this subject area in New Zealand. Third, I endeavour to address whether there are principled grounds for permitting extra-judicial comment, and how far a judge may properly go outside of a particular case he or she is charged with determining.

[1] *Ambard* v. *Attorney-General for Trinidad and Tobago* [1936] AC 322 at 335, PC.
[2] *Ambard* v. *Attorney-General for Trinidad and Tobago* [1936] AC 322.

An overview of the New Zealand position

Historical constraints on judges

The historic position in New Zealand was much like the position in Australia and the United Kingdom. Although New Zealand never formally adopted the Kilmuir rules, in practice, in the mid-1950s and for perhaps twenty years thereafter, the New Zealand judiciary acted very much in conformance with those rules, the essence of which was often said to be a doctrine of judicial neutrality.[3]

Over perhaps the last quarter-century, however, some judges have occasionally chosen to make extra-judicial comment, sometimes ranging quite broadly. More recently, there have been some tense exchanges involving senior members of the judiciary, on the one hand, and the executive, on the other, as to whether judges have crossed the line and inappropriately intruded into the political arena.

There are no specific statutory provisions in New Zealand which inhibit a judge from making public comment on a matter that is not before him or her. The principal argument against a judge doing so has to be advanced as one of inference: that is, as a logical consequence from the statutory role of that judge. This might be termed a 'formal constraint' and has long been thought to be the subject of 'convention'.

As to less formal 'internal constraints', the present position is summarised in the Judges' Bench Book, issued under the hand of the Chief Justice of New Zealand, which is distributed to all higher court judges in New Zealand. It provides:

(a) Participation in public debate

> If a matter of public controversy calls for a response from the judiciary or a particular court, it should come from the Chief Justice or Head of Jurisdiction or with his or her approval. In other cases it may be beneficial to public debate for judges to provide information relating to the administration of justice and the functions of the judiciary. Such participation is desirable but requires care. In particular, a judge must avoid political controversy unless the controversy is about judicial function. It is important to avoid using judicial office to promote personal views and to avoid the appearance of

[3] Perhaps the best discussion of the Kilmuir rules and their demise is to be found in G. R. Rubin, 'Judicial Free Speech versus Judicial Neutrality in Mid-Twentieth Century England: The Last Hurrah for the Ancien Regime?' (2009) 27 *Law and History Review* 373.

capture by particular organisations or causes. It is important to avoid expressing opinions on matters which may arise in litigation and which may lead to concern about the impartiality of the judge.

(b) Submissions or evidence to Parliamentary Select Committees

It is not inappropriate for a judge to make a submission or give evidence before a Parliamentary Select Committee on a matter affecting the legal system. It is important to avoid entering upon matters of a political nature and to bear in mind the need to maintain judicial independence from the Legislative and Executive branches of government. It is important for the head of jurisdiction to be consulted before embarking upon a submission.

(c) Comment on judicial decisions

Judgments must stand without further clarification or explanation. Where a decision is subject to inaccurate comment, any appropriate response should be from the Chief Justice or Head of Jurisdiction. Generally the most effective response is to get the full text of the judgment into the public arena promptly.

Policing judicial free speech

As to the important question of who is to police – if there is to be any policing at all – judicial free speech in New Zealand, traditionally complaints about judges went to the Head of Bench. The Head of Bench would deal with that matter as he or she saw fit, but against the background of established conventions, including that of judicial neutrality.

That matter of process has become potentially complicated by the enactment of the Judicial Conduct Commissioner and Judicial Conduct Panel Act 2004. Under s. 12 of that statute any person may make a complaint about the 'conduct of a judge'. Conduct is not defined. And s. 11(1) is explicit that the Judicial Conduct Commissioner must receive and deal with every complaint made under the Act about the conduct of a judge regardless of whether the subject matter of the complaint arises in the exercise of the judge's judicial duties or otherwise. The breadth of the statutory provisions are such that, conceivably, judicial speech, whether in court or out, could be the subject of the disciplinary procedures and steps which can be taken under that Act.

The Bill of Rights and judicial free speech

The issue of judicial free speech in New Zealand is further complicated by the general law relating to free speech under the New Zealand Bill of

Rights Act 1990 (Bill of Rights). Section 14 of the Bill of Rights, the starting point for the legal protection of free speech in New Zealand, protects freedom of expression in these terms:

> Everyone has the right to freedom of expression, including the freedom to seek, receive, and impart information and opinions of any kind in any form.

This right has been described by the New Zealand Court of Appeal as 'being of the highest importance in a modern democracy'[4] and 'as wide as human thought and imagination'.[5]

Do judges enjoy the benefit of s. 14? Commentators agree that the wording particular to each right protected in the Bill of Rights determines who enjoys its benefit. Accordingly, the benefit of freedom of expression is enjoyed by 'everyone'.[6] More generally, s. 29 provides that the benefit of the Bill of Rights applies, 'so far as practicable', to all natural persons. On this basis it can be said that *prima facie* judicial free speech is protected by the Bill of Rights.

This literal reading of the statutory text is bolstered by a consideration of international instruments relevant to the present context.[7] In particular, Article 9 of the United Nations Basic Principles on the Independence of the Judiciary (Basic Principles)[8] confirms that judges are entitled to freedom of expression – as provided for in the Universal Declaration of Human Rights – just as citizens are.

There may be something in the point noted by Butler and Butler, however, that given that the purpose of the Bill of Rights is to limit government power, it may appear contradictory that agents of the state enjoy its benefit also.[9] Their suggested reconciliation is to emphasise 'as

[4] *Hosking* v. *Runting* [2005] 1 NZLR 1, CA at [178].

[5] *Moonen* v. *Film and Literature Board of Review* [2000] 2 NZLR 9 at [15].

[6] A. Butler and P. Butler, *The New Zealand Bill of Rights Act. A Commentary* (Wellington: LexisNexis, 2005), at 5.10.1; P. Rishworth *et al.*, *The New Zealand Bill of Rights* (Melbourne: Oxford University Press, 2003), p. 71.

[7] Given the Bill of Rights' genesis in international law, part of its purpose is to 'affirm New Zealand's commitment to the International Covenant on Civil and Political Rights' (ICCPR): Long Title, international instruments are considered useful interpretative aids in specific contexts. See the well-known example *Simpson* v. *Attorney-General (Baigent's case)* [1994] 3 NZLR 667, CA, where both the UDHR's and the ICCPR's provisions were an important feature of the finding that Bill of Rights breaches could attract compensation.

[8] Basic Principles on the Independence of the Judiciary, GA Res. 40/32 and GA Res. 40/146 (1995).

[9] Butler and Butler, *The New Zealand Bill of Rights Act*, at 5.12.2.

far as practicable' s. 29's limitation: the state and its agents may enjoy the Bill of Rights' protection, but that enjoyment may be subject to special considerations.[10]

A final note on the scope of the benefit of the Bill of Rights is that it applies only in respect of acts done by the legislative, executive, or judicial branches of government,[11] or, more broadly, acts done in some public capacity.[12] In other words judicial free speech may be protected by the Bill of Rights only against constraints imposed by such acts.

The Bill of Rights itself imposes two 'self-regarding' constraints (self-regarding because they do not require reference to others' rights) on freedom of expression: 'reasonable limits' and 'practicability'. Freedom of expression is limited by 'such reasonable limits prescribed by law as can be demonstrably justified in a free and democratic society'.[13] For example, judicial free speech is limited in some cases by statutory suppression reminders. Butler and Butler[14] suggest that s. 29 and its 'practicability' requirement is a further limitation on the extent to which public officials enjoy the benefit of the Bill of Rights' protection. It may be that constitutional convention, for example, the principle of comity, might be such a limit on judges' freedom of expression.

The Basic Principles suggest two further self-regarding constraints: neutrality and preserving the impartiality and dignity of judicial office.

As for other-regarding constraints, the Bill of Rights applies to acts of the judicial branch of government.[15] This means for present purposes that others may claim Bill of Rights protection in respect of acts of the judicial branch of government. Judges are constrained by dint of their office from making utterances that infringe on an individual's rights as protected by the Bill of Rights, unless that infringement is a reasonable limit in s. 5 terms. There is a difficult question as to whether s. 3 means this constraint applies to all acts done by an individual holding a judicial warrant, or whether acts done in a personal capacity are excluded.

It will be apparent from the foregoing that the Bill of Rights has overlaid what were already quite difficult issues with further layers of complexity.

[10] Butler and Butler, *The New Zealand Bill of Rights Act*, at 5.12.–3. [11] Section 3(a).

[12] Section 3(b) is more specific. See also *Ransfield* v. *The Radio Network Ltd* [2005] 1 NZLR 233, HC.

[13] Section 5. [14] Butler and Butler, *The New Zealand Bill of Rights Act*, at 5.12.3.

[15] Section 3.

The judiciary as the third arm of government

New Zealand statute law provides that the judiciary is a branch of the government of New Zealand.[16] This may be thought to have some significance for judicial free speech. A branch of government could hardly be expected to be like the submarine service and 'Run Silent, Run Deep' (though perhaps the judiciary operates that way sometimes!). 'Branch of government' implies some obligation to speak. The executive and parliamentary branches of government have their own rules and conventions, but it is worth observing that they too have some controversies about where the edges of their roles begin and end; and debates about the limits of speech of individual participants are not unknown.

New Zealand controversies

This section covers four incidents which may be regarded as typical of the sort of things which have arisen in New Zealand in recent years. One is an example of the Chief Justice of New Zealand speaking out on criminal justice matters; another is an example of a trial judge speaking out on a contentious matter not before him in a particular case; one relates to criticism of particular judges, but those judges perhaps not being able to respond; and the fourth relates to an unmitigated ongoing attack on judges to which judges seem powerless to respond.

The Chief Justice speaks out: sentencing

The Rt Hon. Dame Sian Elias, Chief Justice of New Zealand, was invited to deliver the 2009 Shirley Smith Address. This is an annual lecture promoted by the Women in Law Committee of the Wellington Branch of the New Zealand Law Society. By way of context, Shirley Smith was a former Wellington legal practitioner. She was the daughter of a respected High Court judge. She was the first woman law lecturer in a New Zealand university. She entered the profession as a sole practitioner. Much of what she did was *pro bono* representation for the poorly paid and afflicted. Most of her work was in the area of criminal law. She wrote letters to newspaper editors. She was not averse to breaking into print about the futility of escalating sentences. For instance, in November 1999

[16] See the Constitution Act 1986 and the New Zealand Bill of Rights Act 1990, s. 3(a).

she wrote a letter to the editor of *The Dominion* newspaper in Wellington expressing her abhorrence of a bill increasing sentences.[17] She said:

> To provide only a prison at the bottom of the cliff is not a solution. Criminals will just go on falling into it, at great cost to the community.
>
> We have to find out why blameless babes become criminals. Writing as a lawyer who has read many probation reports I have no doubt that their life experience has been the cause. Society creates criminals, society must look at the conditions that create them.

The Chief Justice took those observations as a theme for her invited address. For the first dozen or so pages of a formally reasoned and documented paper the Chief Justice traced the way in which hopeful strategies for penal reform have given way to professional pessimism and community loss of confidence in those working in the criminal justice sector.[18] She traversed why this was so. She then turned to the inexorable rise in the size of the prison population and the cost of keeping people incarcerated. She considered what might be done by way of community education, intervention to improve the management of prisoners on parole and the awful statistics relating to the proportion of people with severe personality disorders or serious mental illness within prison.

Nothing which had been said to that point might be thought likely to have crossed any particular line. This was a head of bench – indeed, by statute the head of the judiciary in New Zealand[19] – identifying certain problems, and the fact that the penal system in New Zealand has not been able to rectify them any better than in any other jurisdiction. So far so good.

What caused a great deal of debate came right at the end of the paper. It is as well to use the particular words uttered by the Chief Justice. She asked whether the real drivers of the increased prison population depend upon the insistence 'that risk be managed by a policy of containment'.[20] She said:[21]

> My last suggestion may be controversial. I do not know whether it is practical or politically acceptable, but I think it needs to be considered. We need to look at direct tools to manage the prison population if overcrowding is not to cause significant safety and human rights issues.

[17] S. Smith 'Kneejerk Reaction', *The Dominion*, 17 November 1999, edn. 2, p. 12.

[18] The address has been reproduced as Dame S. Elias, 'Blameless Babes' (2009) 40 *Victoria University of Wellington Law Review* 581.

[19] Supreme Court Act 2003, s. 18(1). [20] Elias, 'Blameless Babes', p. 594.

[21] Elias, 'Blameless Babes', pp. 593–4.

> Other countries use executive amnesties to send prisoners into the community early to prevent overcrowding. Such solutions will not please many. And I am not well placed to assess whether they are feasible. But the alternatives and the costs of overcrowding need to be weighed . . .
>
> I question whether that strategy can responsibly be maintained. Changing it will require public acceptance that risk cannot be eliminated and that the costs we are absorbing to try to do so are disproportionately expensive. If we are not prepared to relax the pressures to contain risk in the discretionary decisions as to bail and parole, then the only other immediate options may be to confront the length of sentences directly. That could be achieved by statutory changes to bring down the parole component of the sentence (effecting an overall reduction in sentence), statutory modification of the policy of containment of risk in the current bail legislation, and early release amnesty. Are we ready for solutions such as these? If not, we will have to keep building prisons and diverting resources into incapacitation, a strategy that Shirley Smith had no doubt would not work.

The official reaction to the Chief Justice's speech was swift and condemnatory. The Minister of Justice, the Hon. Simon Power, commented sharply and publicly: 'It is the judiciary's job to apply the law set by Parliament . . . This government was elected on the sentencing policy. Judges are appointed to apply it. The Chief Justice's speech does not represent government policy in any way, shape or form.'[22]

The Prime Minister of New Zealand, the Hon. John Key, told a national television audience on the *Breakfast* show on TV1, on Monday 20 July 2009: 'Releasing the speech puts [the Chief Justice] over the line and that was really the point that the Minister of Justice [made] . . . There's a line there and hopefully politicians don't stray one side and the judiciary don't stray the other.' Speaking later that day on a public radio channel, the Prime Minister said Dame Sian had strayed 'into the Justice Minister's area'.[23]

[22] Reported in R. Tiffin, 'Irate Power tells Chief Justice to Butt out of Policy', *The New Zealand Herald*, 17 July 2009, A2. It should be added that this was not the first time that the Chief Justice had come under political fire. In 2003, the then Deputy Prime Minister in the Labour administration, the Hon. Dr Michael Cullen sharply reacted to another address by the Chief Justice which is now published as 'Sovereignty in the 21st Century: Another Spin on the Merry-go-round' (2003) 14 *Public Law Review* 148. Dr Cullen warned against judges developing new limits on the power of Parliament and 'the confusion that can be caused by an activist Judge'. See his comments, 'Parliamentary Sovereignty in the Courts' [2004] *New Zealand Law Journal* 243 and 'Parliament: Supremacy over Fundamental Norms?' (2005) 3 *New Zealand Journal of Public International Law* 1.

[23] Reported in New Zealand Press Association, 'Chief Justice Crossed Line on Prisons – Key', *New Zealand Herald Online*, 20 July, 2009, available at: www.nzherald.co.nz.

In Parliament, the Labour Opposition spoke out in defence of the Chief Justice. Charles Chauvel, Labour's Associate Justice spokesperson said 'it is a convention, and, in fact, a duty, for members of the judiciary, including the head of the judiciary, to speak out on matters of important public policy in the justice sector'.[24]

There followed an astonishing outpouring of newspaper editorials and commentary. There were outraged cries from the Sensible Sentencing Trust (a victims' rights organisation) that the Chief Justice should resign. Even quite moderate letter writers took the substance of her points, but thought that the Chief Justice had overstepped the line. For instance, one letter to the Editor of the *New Zealand Herald* said:[25]

> While not in conflict with much of what Chief Justice Sian Elias had to say about crime and punishment, I feel she has dangerously breached the separation of Executive and judiciary. Hers was essentially a political sociological essay.

Academic commentators were guarded. A commentary by Associate Professor Andrew Geddis in the *New Zealand Herald* on 22 July 2009 pretty much followed the title to that piece: 'Stick to your knitting principle, a knotty one to apply'.

The President of the New Zealand Law Society, Mr John Marshall QC, on behalf of the legal profession in New Zealand, said that the Chief Justice did not criticise any specific government policy.[26] But Sir Douglas Graham, a former Attorney-General and Justice Minister said the present minister was right to remind the Chief Justice that she had stepped over the line:[27]

> If there is any doubt whether on the one hand you want the Chief Justice to feel free to speak and, on the other, comply with constitutional convention, then she should simply comply. She should comply with constitutional convention, rather than err on the side of liberality . . . The Executive [Cabinet] of government does not trample into the realms of the judiciary. The rules exist so that the judiciary is free to get on with judging and the Executive gets on with governing.

Senior newspaper editorials, on the whole, recognised the force in what the Chief Justice had said, but several suggested she had gone 'over the line'.

[24] NewsTalk ZB, 18 July 2009. [25] 29 July 2009; 656 NZPD 5249.

[26] Reported in G. Armstrong, 'Lawyers Rally behind Chief Justice', *Sunday Star Times*, 19 July 2009, p. A2.

[27] Armstrong, 'Lawyers Rally behind Chief Justice'.

Cartoonists had very good copy:

Figure 10.1 Tom Scott, *The Dominion Post*, 22 July 2009, p. B5.

Figure 10.2 Peter Bromhead, *The New Zealand Herald*, Sunday, 19 July 2009, p. 54.

It is now over a year since that incident occurred, and it seems to have dropped off the public radar altogether. It may be thought significant that a recent address in London by the President of the Court of Appeal, Sir William Young,[28] also expressing concern about the drift of the current sentencing policy, went largely unnoticed in New Zealand.

Public advocacy by a trial judge

It is widely agreed that the Adoption Act 1955 is out of date in New Zealand. Among the many criticisms of it is that only married couples and individuals can legally adopt a child. In 2000, the New Zealand Law Commission recommended lifting that adoption ban. It suggested that there was not enough evidence to show that being adopted by a same sex couple was against a child's best interests. A proposed member's bill drafted by a Green MP, the Hon. Kevin Hague, to change the law in this respect was entered into the New Zealand Parliamentary ballot process.[29]

Judge von Dadelszen has many years' service as a Judge of the Family Court. Delivering a speech, the judge came out strongly in favour of the proposed legislation. Fairfax Media became aware that the judge has a daughter in a same sex relationship who could benefit from the changes the judge advocated. This then attracted sharp media commentary, though on nothing like the scale which had attended the sentencing comments of the Chief Justice.

In the only parliamentary comment, the Hon. Peter Dunne MP, the leader of the United Future Party (very much a family values party) said that legalising gay adoption would be contrary to the mainstream view. But, he said, 'The judge was "as entitled to his views as anyone else".'[30]

Given the comparatively mild reaction to Judge von Dadelszen's speech, what explains the difference in response in the 'Blameless Babes' incident? If it was merely a matter of constitutional principle – judges stepping on politicians' toes – that so outraged Elias CJ's critics, then surely there should have been a similar response here?

[28] Sir W. Young, 'The Effects of Imprisonment on Offending: A Judge's Perspective' (2010) *Criminal Law Review* 3.

[29] The procedure relating to this ballot process enables private Members' Bills (from whatever party) to be 'drawn' and entered onto the Parliamentary Order Paper, and to proceed through the House of Representatives, if they can gain support.

[30] Reported in 'Daughter's Status not Relevant, says Judge', *Taranaki Daily News*, 24 August, 2009, p. 4.

There are other examples too which seem to demonstrate an even starker disparity in treatment. Two senior judges, of the Family Court and Youth Court, respectively, are both given to regular and sometimes quite forthright media comment, yet the response is often positive. This may suggest that the issue is not what the limit of judicial free speech is in principle, it is instead what is politically tolerable, and that depends on the content of the speech.

A conclusion that the limits on judicial free speech are essentially politically constrained would help to explain the contrasting response to the Chief Justice, as presumably the Chief Justice is perceived to have more influence, or rather, is feared by politicians to have more, over the population at large.

Theoretical support for this kind of conclusion can be found in Matthew Palmer's article, 'New Zealand Constitutional Culture'.[31] Palmer takes a 'constitutional realist' approach to understanding New Zealand's constitutional arrangements, arguing that these arrangements are determined by the 'beliefs and behaviour' of constitutional actors.[32] Identifying features of New Zealand's constitutional culture are, according to Palmer, authoritarianism, egalitarianism and pragmatism.[33] Associated norms of representative democracy and parliamentary sovereignty combine with these cultural orientations to generate a generally held 'fundamental suspicion' of judges; particularly of their perceived power to 'frustrate the will of a democratically elected government'.[34]

Newspaper attacks on judges

The most controversial 'surveys' of judges in New Zealand have been published by *The Independent*, a business newspaper. In September 1994, a survey was taken of lawyers, including apparently senior counsel who remained anonymous, of the High Court and Court of Appeal judges. The Supreme Court of New Zealand was not then in existence.

The Rt Hon. Sir Thomas Eichelbaum, the then Chief Justice of New Zealand, said it was 'unprecedented in New Zealand for lawyers to speak

[31] M. Palmer, 'New Zealand Constitutional Culture' (2007) 22 *New Zealand Universities Law Review* 565.

[32] Palmer, 'New Zealand Constitutional Culture'.

[33] Palmer, 'New Zealand Constitutional Culture', p. 576.

[34] Palmer, 'New Zealand Constitutional Culture', p. 586.

out critically in public of judges in this way'.[35] Critics responded that the judiciary was demanding blind and uncritical respect for fear of opening the judicial system to the public gaze.

The editor, Jenni McManus, prefaced the 'results' of *The Independent*'s 2009 repeat survey with her observations that:[36]

> Judges are empowered to sit in judgement on all of us. But who judges the judges . . . most readers welcome the opportunity to learn more about judges; their habits, intellectual and judicial abilities, and their foibles – information previously confined to Chambers parties and barristers robing rooms.

The 2009 survey results were not altogether kind. To get a flavour of the gutter-type comments made, it is unfortunately necessary to reproduce some of them. It was said of the Chief Justice that she had been:[37]

> promoted beyond her abilities and tried to take on too much, meaning the business of the Court is not being dealt with expeditiously. Has a very good brain but did not have much of a practice before being appointed to the bench.

The President of the Court of Appeal, Sir William Young, was said to be,[38]

> arrogant, with a high opinion of himself. Makes off-the-cuff comments that are not necessarily justified but can be damaging . . . I'm not sure if we're lucky to have him or he's lucky to have the job.

For present purposes, the significant thing about these sorts of bilious outpourings is that judges felt unable or were unwilling to respond, and doubtless that was complicated by the disgraceful attack on the heads of bench. In 1994, some judges contemplated suing, but were talked out of it by colleagues. In relation to the 2009 piece, some fifteen years later, the then Chief Justice said nothing publicly. And, whatever they thought privately, or said among themselves, the judges took no steps. The Attorney-General made no comment.[39] The President of the New

[35] Reported in J. McManus, 'Special Report: Judging the Judges', *The Independent*, 21 May 2009, p. 7.

[36] McManus, 'Special Report: Judging the Judges'.

[37] McManus, 'Special Report: Judging the Judges', p. 8.

[38] McManus, 'Special Report: Judging the Judges', p. 8.

[39] For a recent discussion of when an Attorney-General should comment, see J. Plunkett, 'The Role of the Attorney-General in Defending the Judiciary' (2010) 19 *Journal of Judicial Administration* 160; and Hon. Justice Priestley, 'Chipping Away at the Judicial Arm' (2009) 17 *Waikato Law Review* 1.

Zealand Law Society, Mr John Marshall QC, wrote to the Chief Justice on 26 May 2009, in a letter which was distributed to all judges, indicating that the New Zealand judiciary had the full confidence and support of the profession. Mr Marshall said:[40]

> The article does not reflect well on either *The Independent* or on the lawyers who gave their views under the cloak of anonymity. Frankly, I am disappointed to hear that senior barristers have apparently chosen to make comments, some of a hurtful nature, about our judiciary when, as officers of the court, they have a duty to uphold the rule of law.

Concerted attacks by individuals: the Siemer saga

Mr Vincent Siemer has over the last several years been engaged in concerted litigation against superior court judges in New Zealand. At the time of writing there are some fifty-nine judgments relating to Mr Siemer in the High Court, Court of Appeal and Supreme Court with the prospect of more to come. He has also engaged in vituperative media attacks on the New Zealand judiciary.

It all came about this way. Mr Siemer, an American citizen, was the managing director of Paragon Oil. Paragon is a company which purifies and refurbishes oil used in transformers and hydraulic systems. In late 2000, Mr Stiassny was appointed by the court as Paragon's receiver. Paragon had gone into receivership, by consent, in the context of a claim by Mr Siemer of oppressive conduct by the other shareholders. As it transpired, the present author made orders in Mr Siemer's favour transferring shares held by other shareholders to Mr Siemer.[41] After Mr Siemer became the sole shareholder in Paragon the receivership terminated, in August 2001. One of the terms of the compromise agreement was a confidentiality clause. Mr Siemer had, and still maintains, various complaints about Mr Stiassny's conduct of the receivership. Despite the confidentiality agreement, he began to conduct a public campaign against him. For instance, in April 2005 Mr Siemer rented a large billboard in a prominent position in central Auckland which referred to Mr Stiassny in various critical ways and then referred viewers

[40] Letter from John Marshall QC, President New Zealand Law Society to The Rt Hon. Dame Sian Elias, Chief Justice of New Zealand regarding *The Independent* article, 'Judging the Judges', 26 May 2009.

[41] *Siemer* v. *Paragon Oil Systems Ltd* (2001) 9 NZCLC 262, 693, HC.

to a website which was distinctly critical of Mr Stiassny's conduct, and of judges who had found for him.[42]

This set in train the extraordinary number of proceedings, some of which are still before the Supreme Court of New Zealand. There were all sorts of interlocutory proceedings, injunction proceedings and contempt proceedings. As regrettably can happen, when things went against him, Mr Siemer turned his fire on the judiciary. As the present author had occasion to remark in one *Siemer* case, a 'deeply disturbing feature' of these proceedings was that:[43]

> Mr Siemer has in the past, and to this day, lashed out at judicial officers who have the burden of endeavouring to adjudicate on the various aspects of the claims which have come before our courts. Lord Reith once famously remarked, 'When people feel deeply, impartiality is bias' (*Into the Wind* (1949)). Doubtless all litigants feel deeply about their cases and they can be bitterly disappointed when a ruling or decision does not go in their favour. What is inexcusable is to assert that the judge is corrupt or to make what are nothing more than wild-eyed and unsustainable allegations, simply because they lost.

Ultimately, Mr Siemer was sentenced to a term of imprisonment for contempt. When he had served that term he renewed his attacks on the judiciary, quite unabated. It is not appropriate to refer to the matters that are presently still before the courts, including the Supreme Court of New Zealand, but the Siemer saga introduces another element into the problem of attacks on judges and the ability or inability of judges to respond: much of this attack was electronic and hence hard to police, and it circulated widely outside of New Zealand.

A principled approach towards judicial free speech

Free speech in general

Most of the arguments proffered with respect to judicial free speech seem to operate at the level of an intuitive 'this is not the sort of thing judges ought to be doing'. The concern seems to be with the damage which might be seen to the judicial role if judges 'cross the line'. This is not particularly attractive, let alone compelling, reasoning. It is simply a visceral approach. The issue needs to be approached from the basis of

42 www.stiassny.org.

43 *Siemer* v. *Ferrier Hodgson* [2007] NZCA 581; [2008] 3 NZLR 22 at [31].

first principles: ought there to be a line? Is there a line? And if so, why is it put in the place it apparently is?

Looked at from the point of view of first principle a good place to start is with the general justifications for free speech. We can then turn to whether there are some distinct features of the judicial role which can legitimately be thought to impact upon the general principle.

Freedom of speech and expression is thought by many – perhaps an overwhelming number – of people to have some kind of special status among the truly cherished liberties of individuals. It ranks right up behind the right to life itself: the ability to communicate by speech is said to be precisely what differentiates humankind from other life forms.

If freedom of speech has this place in the pantheon of human values, it follows that if speech is to be restricted the reasons for restriction must be distinctly more compelling than we would ordinarily accept as a basis for government or other restraining conduct generally.[44] A slight gain in total welfare will not do: there would have to be in some sense a very real overall welfare gain.

The justifications for an overarching free speech principle fall, broadly, into two categories. First, there are consequentialist arguments. Free speech is seen to be valuable because it serves some other value or interest – such as the pursuit of truth or democratic self-governance or justice.[45] The second broad argument is a deontological one. That is, the consequences of the exercise of free speech are disregarded. What is stressed instead is the intrinsic importance of speech to each *individual*.

To take the consequentialist arguments first, the argument from truth is usually most closely associated with John Stuart Mill.[46] It is in a sense an avoidance of mistake argument. If some truth about something is to be attained, all individuals must have unrestricted access to the views and opinions of others and enjoy freedom of self-expression. Established opinion may then be tested. The Millian view finds its firmest legal expression in the famous 'marketplace of ideas' propounded by Justice Holmes' dissent in *Abrams* v. *US*:[47]

[44] F. Schauer, *Free Speech: A Philosophical Inquiry* (Cambridge University Press, 1982).

[45] I am indebted to E. Barendt, *Freedom of Speech* (Oxford: Clarendon Press, 1985); see also T. Campbell, 'Rationales for Freedom of Communication', in T. Campbell and W. Sadurski (eds.), *Freedom of Communication* (Dartmouth: Ashgate, 1994).

[46] See C. L. Ten, *Mill on Liberty* (Oxford: Clarendon Press, 1980).

[47] *Abrams* v. *US* (1919) 250 US 616 at 630.

> When men have realized that time has upset many fighting faiths, they may come to believe even more than they believed the very foundations of their own conduct that the ultimate good desired is better reached by free trade in ideas – that the best test of truth is the power of the thought to get itself accepted in the competition of the market, and that truth is the only ground upon which their wishes safely can be carried out.

This sort of approach confers a very wide – perhaps the widest – degree of immunity upon speakers in general, and certainly upon the media. There is no justification for interfering with speech that is possibly true even if highly prejudicial, nor with the intemperate or ill-informed.

A difficulty with this approach is that some downside has to be accepted. For the particular freely expressed view may be a positive instigation to do something very bad. What is to be done about that, and in what contexts, can be a very difficult question. What if *The Independent* publishes an editorial which says: 'Our New Zealand judges are so bad that the people should rise up and displace them all'? Even the Millian thinker has to concede that there are *some* limits to free speech, which explains why even Justice Holmes was prepared to accept wartime restrictions.

There are philosophical difficulties too with this approach. First, there is the assumption that somehow there is an objective truth just waiting to be 'discovered' by free debate. But frequently this will relate to issues of morality or politics, which are contestable. Second, even when a truly revealed idea comes forward, that is not to say that it will become somehow accepted simply because of its rational force. We 'accept' something for all sorts of quite diverse reasons.

The argument from democracy puts a very high value on deliberative democracy, and unencumbered political discussion. The value of free speech is that it is seen as perhaps the principal means by which the citizens of a democratic state can acquire information about the functioning of government. This argument goes all the way back to the views of James Madison, the author of the First Amendment to the United States Constitution. In its simplest terms it is an argument for 'political truth'.[48]

It is only a short step from the political truth argument to a similar thesis with respect to 'justice'. Thus, for instance, in *R* v. *Felixstowe JJ ex p. Leigh*,

[48] This sort of notion has been prominent in Canadian jurisprudence: see *Edmonton Journal* v. *Alberta* (1989) 64 DLR 4th 577, SC, at 607–8; and *Dagenais* v. *Canadian Broadcasting Corporation* (1995) 120 DLR 4th 12, SC, at 36–7.

Watkins LJ described the court reporter as a person of vital significance in opening up the administration of justice to public scrutiny and comment.[49] The European Court of Human Rights has a similar thesis:[50]

> Whilst the mass media must not overstep the bounds imposed in the interests of the proper administration of justice, it is incumbent upon them to impart information and ideas concerning matters that come before the courts just as in other areas of public interest.

A difficulty with the political truth argument, and arguments for truth about justice, is that they are vulnerable to majoritarian decisions to restrict speech. Assume, for instance, that our elected representatives close all criminal courts to the media and members of the public alike. That could not be resisted by a pure appeal to the argument from democracy or justice. That is why there is such a strong argument for entrenching free speech principles in bills of rights.

Turning now to the intrinsic values of a free speech principle – that is, intrinsic to individuals – these relate principally to self-determination or fulfilment.[51] The interest is needed if individuals are to develop their capacities and realise their own individual potential. Expression is in this form an integral part of self.

This argument too has found judicial acceptance. Thus, famously, Justice Brandeis said in *Whitney* v. *California*: 'Those who won our independence believed that the final end of the state was to make men free to develop their faculties.'[52] The European Court of Human Rights early on emphasised the development of each individual in a freedom of expression context in *Handiside* v. *UK*.[53]

A more sophisticated argument of a non-consequentialist variety has been advanced by Ronald Dworkin, which turns on the proposition that government should treat all its adult members as responsible moral agents. He says that government cannot:[54]

> [insult] its citizens and [deny] their moral responsibility, when it decrees that they cannot be trusted to hear opinions that might persuade them to dangerous or offensive opinion. We retain our dignity, as individuals,

[49] *R* v. *Felixstowe JJ ex p. Leigh* [1987] 1 All ER 551, QB.

[50] *Sunday Times* v. *UK* (1979–80) 2 EHRR 245 at 280.

[51] See T. M. Scanlon, 'Freedom of Expression and Categories of Expression' (1979) 40 *University of Pittsburgh Law Review* 519 at 544–5.

[52] *Whitney* v. *California* (1927) 274 US 357 at 374.

[53] *Handiside* v. *UK* (1979–80) 1 EHRR 737.

[54] R. Dworkin, *Freedoms of Law: The Moral Reading of the American Constitution* (Cambridge, MA: Harvard University Press, 1996), p. 200.

> only by insisting that no-one – no official and no majority – has the right to withhold an opinion from us on the ground that we are not fit to hear it and consider it.

It cannot be confidently asserted at this time that there is any one basis on which we could all agree as to a 'free speech principle', yet clearly there is common ground that it *is* a very valuable principle and that there ought to be profound distrust as to any regulation of speech.

Judicial free speech

Turning now to the position of the judiciary, in terms of general principle, there has to be a very powerful argument for truth in justice, just as there is for exposure of the truth in politics. Within the context of a case a judge may feel impelled to say that the particular operation of a particular statute in that case has to be observed, and he or she will give effect to that law in his or her judgment. But it is by no means unknown for courts of the highest authority, as well as trial judges, to point out that the statute is having some kind of untoward effect, or creating what most people would regard as an injustice. Whether to make any observations of that kind is a most difficult matter for a judge, but it has never been suggested that there is an absolute prohibition on such observations.

Illustrations in New Zealand include the following. In early 2010 *The Dominion Post*, in Wellington, reported that Judge Saunders had criticised a proposed 'three strikes law' during a sentencing hearing in the Christchurch District Court, noting it might have produced an unduly harsh outcome had it applied to the case before him (although it appears the judge may have misunderstood the precise application of the proposed law, which reveals a judicial hazard in commenting!).[55]

In *R* v. *Pora*[56] Thomas J used strong language to describe retrospective legislation increasing the minimum non-parole period for those convicted of murder involving 'home invasion'. In his judgment the offending provision was, amongst other things, 'repugnant to the rule of law'.[57] In the end the specific provision fell victim to a conflicting general provision consistent with the presumption against retrospectivity.

In *Accident Rehabilitation and Compensation Insurance Corporation* v. *Tarr*[58] the respondent had to cease employment because of incapacity.

[55] J. Hartevelt, 'Judge's Swipe at "3-strikes" law', *The Dominion Post*, 21 January 2010, p. 5.
[56] *R* v. *Pora* [2001] 2 NZLR 37, CA. [57] *R* v. *Pora* [2001] 2 NZLR 37, CA, at [123].
[58] *Accident Rehabilitation and Compensation Insurance Corporation* v. *Tarr* [1996] 3 NZLR 715, HC.

He was entitled to weekly compensation under accident compensation legislation. His entitlement was to be calculated by reference to his 'weekly earnings', which for Mr Tarr were defined by the legislation in this way:

> the earnings of that person other than earnings as an employee in the most recent income year . . . last ended before the commencement of the period of incapacity as shown in an income tax return divided by the number of weeks in that income year.

During the previous year he had worked as a self-employed person for forty-one weeks and as an employee for the remainder. His weekly entitlement therefore was determined by dividing his earnings over the forty-one-week period by fifty-two, the number of weeks in the income tax year. The effect was to disregard eleven weeks' worth of earnings in the calculation, thereby, somewhat arbitrarily it would appear, reducing his weekly compensation entitlement. The judgment of the court referred to the 'manifest injustice'[59] of this provision, but said the court was bound to apply the 'clear statutory language'[60] and there was 'no basis for the Court to look for a method of avoiding the injustice that result[ed]'.[61]

If it is accepted that a judge can comment on the operation of the law within a case, on what basis is it to be said that the fundamental value of free speech is to be confined *outside* the courtroom? Recall that, on the argument advanced in this chapter, the justification for restraint has to be a very powerful one: something that engages the total welfare of citizens.

The justification which seems to be advanced – if it is articulated at all – is that judges do not pronounce upon contested questions of public policy. But the fact of the matter is that judges do, in cases and outside them! For at least the last fifty years, and increasingly over the last decade or so, judges have been invited to give public lectures, write books and put their views 'out there' much in the manner contemplated by Justice Holmes.[62] They may make fools of themselves, their arguments may be

[59] *Accident Rehabilitation and Compensation Insurance Corporation* v. *Tarr* [1996] 3 NZLR 715, HC, at 720.

[60] *Accident Rehabilitation and Compensation Insurance Corporation* v. *Tarr* [1996] 3 NZLR 715, HC.

[61] *Accident Rehabilitation and Compensation Insurance Corporation* v. *Tarr* [1996] 3 NZLR 715, HC.

[62] At the time of writing this chapter, I was involved in an appeal relating to tax avoidance. I note that in 2005 Lord Hoffmann published an article criticising certain judgments of

shown to be completely fallacious and unquestionably there will be occasions on which the executive is downright irritated by what has been said, but none of these kinds of things would seem to come anywhere near the level required for something approaching a blanket restraint. And there is an obvious distinction between not doing something at all, under a *per se* restraint, and doing it, but rather badly or ill advisedly or without sufficient care.

The ability to respond

Speech is a form of communication. Today there are fewer utterances, even by authority figures, of a unilateral kind. There are still some very formal occasions on which what could be called a 'unilateral speech' is delivered. But in most contexts, speech is part of a continuing dialogue. This, of course, fits with the notions of why we have free speech at all: individual development; the advancement of democratic government; and the pursuit of justice. Judges who proffer up some kind of observations on 'the system' or 'the particular workings of the system' could not reasonably expect others not to be able to reply.

However, perhaps the most difficult matter for judges today is a perceived inability to respond to personal attacks. This is a difficult issue. Traditionally, judges have not responded at all to that kind of attack. If there is to be a response, the expectation is that the head of bench or, in some circumstances, the Attorney-General will respond on their behalf.[63] In relation to particular judgments, the principle has always rightly been – and still is – that a judgment speaks for itself, for better or for worse.

But what of the situation in which neither the head of bench, nor the Attorney, nor the bar sees fit to do anything? The profession could do much better than it does in supporting the judiciary, as well as criticising

his colleagues in the House of Lords (L. Hoffmann, 'Tax Avoidance' (2005) 2 *British Tax Review* 197). Does it make a difference that this grew out of a lecture delivered at the Centre of Commercial Law Studies on the occasion of its twenty-fifth anniversary? Of interest here also is the trend to publishing collections of lectures given by senior judges: see, e.g., T. Bingham, *The Business of Judging. Selected Essays and Speeches* (Oxford University Press, 2005).

[63] The current New Zealand Cabinet Manual provides at para. 4.8: 'The Attorney-General is the link between the judiciary and executive government. The Attorney-General recommends the appointment of judges and has an important role in defending the judiciary by answering improper and unfair public criticism, and discouraging ministerial colleagues from criticising judges and their decisions.'

it, but it is not often heard from.[64] The expectation then still seems to be that the judge will not respond. That is, that somehow the bile comes with the territory, and the judge must just swallow it. The ability of a judge to live with that fact varies from individual to individual. It is not unheard of for judges to choose to leave the bench, *sub silentio* as it were, having been in a real sense hounded out of office.

One would have thought that better institutional responses might be found. For instance, when the Judicial Conduct Commissioner scheme was set up in New Zealand this author at one point suggested that judges ought perhaps to be able to make a complaint to the commissioner about what had been said about them, and that the commissioner might have powers (not unlike some press councils) to at least require the publication of a correction. That particular suggestion got no traction; indeed, no explanation was offered for why it did not.

In any event, very much as a convention in New Zealand today the position is still that a judge is expected not to respond to personal criticism. There is in a sense an exception to this for what might be termed 'legal argument'. It is not unknown for a judge in a periodical, or text, to take issue with something that commentators have said as to the validity or strength of an argument which had been adopted by a judge even in a case. No objection seems to be taken to that, presumably on the footing that this is simply part of an ongoing argument about what the law is on a particular point, and therefore of public benefit.

Conclusion

The older order, based on a 'convention' of a largely visceral nature, is clearly changing in New Zealand. The shape of a newer, and more nuanced order is still emerging. Quite where the lines will be drawn in the future are somewhat indistinct. But it may be thought healthy, and something to be encouraged, that more judges are prepared to speak out on the health of the justice system as such. There is no defensible principle which can be raised against them doing so. Personal attacks will likely always come with the territory, and can realistically be repelled only by institutional responses.

[64] See Priestley, 'Chipping Away at the Judicial Arm'.

11

The judiciary and freedom of speech in South Africa

IAIN CURRIE

What limits are placed on speech about the judiciary in South Africa and what are the limits on speech by the judiciary? Like the other South African chapters in this volume, in answering these questions this chapter contrasts the old and the new orders. Under the *ancien régime*, a legal system premised on a racially exclusive variant of Westminster constitutionalism, the South African judiciary was shielded from much of the adverse criticism that its service to such a system would otherwise have invoked. The judiciary was a beneficiary of statutory and executive measures designed to stifle opposition and shore up an illegitimate state edifice. On occasion though, the judges took on a more active role in silencing their critics by means of the contempt power. The result, in the estimation of one of the most perspicacious observers of this period, was that

> the right to address oneself freely to all aspects of the administration of justice has ... become essentially a 'fugitive and cloistered virtue' in South Africa, resulting in the situation today [1978] that substantial pockets of decision-making in that vast administration are untouched by meaningful comment, dissent and scrutiny.[1]

On the other side of the coin, the judiciary itself assiduously followed Westminster conventions of aloofness from political controversy.

This state of affairs came to an end when the old order was succeeded by a system of constitutional democracy with judicial review and with a Bill of Rights giving strong protection to the civil liberties protecting

[1] B. van Niekerk, 'The Uncloistering of the Virtue: Freedom of Speech and the Administration of Justice – A Comparative Overview' (1978) 95 *South African Law Journal* 362 at 362. The phrase is from Milton, *Areopagitica* (1644): 'I cannot praise a fugitive and cloistered virtue, unexercised and unbreathed, that never sallies out and seeks her adversary, but slinks out of the race, where the immortal garland is to be run for, not without dust and heat.'

political speech. The consequence of the exercise of the judicial review power under the new Constitution has been a thoroughgoing transformation of the legal parameters of judicial free speech in South Africa.[2] But, at the same time, there has also been a transformation of the social and political context within which the judiciary does its work. As Hugh Corder's chapter (Chapter 5) in this volume has shown, the greatly expanded powers accorded to the judicial branch under the new Constitution have brought the judiciary firmly and routinely into the arena of bare-knuckled political contestation.[3] The combined effect of the loss (or disavowal) of the protective legal carapace enjoyed by the judiciary under the previous dispensation and the increasingly immoderate criticism and attack to which it has become subject may, over time, result in a weakening of the judicial institution in South Africa. At the same time, while the South African judiciary is more willing to defend itself extra-curially than it was in the past, the old conventions of detachment that kept the judiciary out of the public arena have not entirely lost their grip.

Judicial free speech under the old regime

The Truth Commission legal institutional hearing

On 27, 28 and 29 October 1997, the Truth and Reconciliation Commission of South Africa sat to hear oral testimony in an 'institutional hearing' on the role played by the South African judiciary, the legal profession and the law schools between 1960 and 1994. The Truth Commission's principal mandate was to investigate the causes, nature and extent of gross violations of human rights that had taken place during this period, the climactic years of the country's three-century-old racial conflict.[4] The institutional hearings were intended to provide the commission with a sense of the broad historical, social and political context in which human rights violations had occurred; to help it understand, as the commission put it, 'how, over the years, people who considered themselves ordinary, decent and God-fearing found themselves turning a blind eye to a system which impoverished, oppressed and violated the lives and very existence of so many of their

[2] This is van Niekerk's useful short-hand term, meaning free speech broadly concerning the administration of justice, by the judiciary and about the judiciary. Niekerk, 'The Uncloistering of the Virtue', p. 363.

[3] See Chapter 5, this volume.

[4] The Commission was established by the National Unity and Reconciliation Act 34 of 1995.

fellow citizens'.[5] Sectors of society that had exercised influence during those years and that had, at times, been criticised for complicity with the apartheid system – the media, business, prisons, the churches, the legal system and the health sector – were invited to attend the hearings and present their views.

For the legal community hearing, the commission's invitation asked organisations and individuals to address a number of questions and issues relevant to the conduct of the legal profession during the apartheid era. Some of these were focused on the judiciary: for example, were attempts made to undermine judicial independence; what was the relationship between the judiciary and the government during this period; what role was played by judicial discretion in the deciding of cases; how were members of the judiciary appointed?[6] The point of the hearing, the commission's invitation emphasised, was not 'to establish guilt or hold individuals responsible . . . The hearing is an attempt to understand the role the legal system played in contributing to the violation and/or protection of human rights and to identify institutional changes required to prevent those abuses which occurred from happening again.'[7]

To the commission's disappointment, neither branch of the judiciary, judges or magistrates, attended the hearings. Some individual judges made written submissions; no member of the magistracy was heard from.[8] Why had the judges not appeared? The official set of arguments justifying the reluctance of the judiciary to testify before the commission can be found in a 1996 letter to the commission by then Chief Justice, Michael Corbett.[9] A general accounting by the judiciary for its conduct during the apartheid period would undermine an important principle, Corbett argued. This was the independence of the judiciary: 'a judge must enjoy independence from

[5] Truth and Reconciliation Commission of South Africa, *Report*, vol. 4 (Cape Town: Juta, 1998), p. 1.

[6] Truth and Reconciliation Commission of South Africa, *Report*, p. 94.

[7] Truth and Reconciliation Commission of South Africa, *Report*, p. 95.

[8] Kahn reports that the Magistrates' Commission (a statutory body which was the rough equivalent of the Judicial Service Commission) had earlier written to the Truth and Reconciliation Commission (TRC) in legalistic and somewhat defensive terms to say that it could not decide on whether participation in the TRC process would be beneficial because there was no clarity about the exact allegations, the accused and 'which section of the legal system stands accused'. E. Kahn, 'The Truth and Reconciliation Commission, and the Bench, Legal Practitioners and Legal Academics: Prefatory Remarks by the Editor' (1998) 118 *South African Law Journal* 15 at 16.

[9] M. M. Corbett, 'Presentation to the Truth and Reconciliation Commission' (1998) 115 *South African Law Journal* 17. The letter responds to an invitation by the TRC to respond to allegations that had been made in a written presentation entitled 'Injustice under apartheid judiciary'.

the legislature, from the executive, from any other body or authority which could be tempted to influence his decisions'. This did not mean, he continued, that judges are unaccountable, but rather that they are accountable in a narrow and specialised sense of the term. A judge

> is accountable to a superior court of appeal; he performs his duties openly and in public and is thus subject to daily scrutiny and criticism; and in the last resort there is impeachment. Outside these parameters, however, a judge may not be called upon to account for his or her judgments or to debate and justify before, for instance, governmental bodies or commissions.[10]

The commission was critical of this stance, arguing that the voluntary participation of the judges in the special and never-to-be-repeated circumstances of the hearing could not create a precedent adverse to judicial independence. Given the importance of the occasion, written submissions were not enough, Archbishop Desmond Tutu, the commission's chairman, declared at the beginning of the hearing; the judges ought to have appeared in person.[11] Summarising its views in its Report, the commission echoed Tutu's rebuke, declaring that, by absenting themselves from the hearing, the judiciary had missed the opportunity to make the powerful symbolic gesture of 'showing themselves publicly and humbly to be accountable . . . to the South African nation it serves'.[12] Indeed, the absence of the judges drew stinging criticism from the other participants at the hearing, the Minister of Justice pointedly remarking that he had not considered himself above accepting the commission's invitation and that President Mandela himself would willingly have appeared if he had been invited.[13]

Though the reasons for their non-appearance were undoubtedly more complex than the 'independence' argument would suggest,[14] Corbett's

[10] Corbett, 'Presentation to the Truth and Reconciliation Commission', p. 20.

[11] D. M. Davis, G. J. Marcus and J. Klaaren, 'The Administration of Justice' 1997 *Annual Survey of South African Law* 788.

[12] Truth and Reconciliation Commission of South Africa, *Report*, pp. 107–8.

[13] D. Dyzenhaus, *Judging the Judges, Judging Ourselves: Truth, Reconciliation and the Apartheid Legal Order* (Oxford: Hart, 1998), pp. 29–30. Dyzenhaus attributes the confrontational tone of the subsequent hearings, in part, to the decision of the judges to absent themselves and the impression this created 'that the judges considered themselves beyond the reach of truth and reconciliation' (p. 87).

[14] Dyzenhaus (*Judging the Judges*, p. 38) finds the 'independence' justification unconvincing, pointing out that Corbett's successor, Chief Justice Ismail Mahomed stated that judges were free to appear before the Commission. Moreover, many judges, Corbett included, made written submissions to the Commission responding to the questions posed in its invitation. Other reasons were, Dyzenhaus thinks, at play, notably the fear of

letter can nevertheless be taken as representative of the views of the legal establishment on the commission's enterprise. The affronted and defensive tone adopted by some of the other judicial respondents indicates that the South African judiciary was not particularly accustomed to scrutiny of this type, and that many judges thought that the record of the judiciary under apartheid did not require defending or explaining. Certainly, during the days of apartheid the independence and quality of the Supreme Court of South Africa and its judges were often spoken of in admiring terms by the government and its apologists.[15] Initially, even liberal opponents of the regime considered the courts to be islands of justice and respect for human rights in the midst of the routine repressiveness of the other organs of the South African state. Faced with a government and a legislature determined to impress their racist ideology on all aspects of life and to stifle all dissent to this process, the Supreme Court appeared to advance somewhat less objectionable values. While an autocratic government set about shutting down South Africa's limited democratic institutions, the Supreme Court was thought by some to live on in principled and unhindered independence. This independence had survived the political transition and was a crucial asset to the new democratic order; it should not, so the argument went, be compromised by the unseemly spectacle of the judges appearing before the Truth Commission to confess their past sins.

Though it is unlikely, however, that the high reputation of the superior courts extended much beyond elite and official circles, this view went largely unchallenged in South African political and legal discourse. With hindsight, the fact that much of the legal establishment could insouciantly view itself as untainted by apartheid is remarkable. Most people who experienced state repression at first hand in all likelihood saw the courts as complicit in the laws they were enforcing. Racial discrimination was defined by law and enforced by the courts. The systematic political repression and stifling of opposition by the government was principally conducted through the mechanism of the law and, again, was enforced

a rift between 'old order' judges and more progressive recent appointments if the latter were to appear before the Commission and use it as a platform to criticise the former.

15 G. Marcus, 'Respect for the Courts: Myth and Reality' (1985) 1 *South African Journal of Human Rights* 236. See, e.g., the written submission of Mr Justice C. S. White to the Truth Commission: 'During the apartheid years the judiciary was the one leg of government which was virtually devoid of international criticism and which was respected by the populace. If this investigation results in the lowering of that high esteem, it would have done more harm than good'. 'Submissions: The Judiciary in the Republic of Transkei' (1998) 115 *South African Law Journal* 65 at 65.

by the courts.[16] The inevitable result was that the judiciary and the courts came to be seen in most peoples' minds as instruments of oppression. Yet the judiciary was shielded from this unpalatable reality by a number of factors. First, radical oppositional views were censored and opponents of the regime persecuted in terms of a panoply of internal security laws.[17] This left only a narrow space for 'legitimate' oppositional activity and speech. In this space, criticism of the judiciary was further subject to common-law restrictions. Grouped under the broad heading of contempt of court, the South African common law included two offences aimed at the protection of the administration of justice. These were the offence of 'scandalising the court' (call it 'scandalising contempt') and a prohibition on the publication of speech tending to prejudice or interfere with the administration of justice in proceedings that were *sub judice* ('*sub judice* contempt'). As will be canvassed in the next section, during the apartheid period the interpretation and application of these offences had the effect of suppressing comment critical of the judiciary and, more broadly, of the political order.

Contempt of court during the apartheid era

For much of the apartheid period, the legal academy was markedly constrained in its criticism of the judiciary and, indeed, of the apartheid legal system as a whole.[18] Academic publications tended to avoid politically controversial issues and to conduct discussion of judicial decisions

[16] See I. Mahomed, A. Chaskalson, P. Langa, H. J. O. van Heerden and M. M. Corbett, 'The Legal System in South Africa 1960–1994: Representations to the Truth and Reconciliation Commission' (1998) 115 *South African Law Journal* 21 at 22–8. The sentiments expressed by Archbishop Tutu at the commencement of the legal institutional hearing can be taken as representative: 'The black experience of the law. Virtually every encounter with the law for blacks in the old dispensation was one calculated to develop in us a contempt, indeed a hatred for the law because every such encounter was virtually designed to demean, to humiliate, to dehumanise the black person since by definition a law you had had no part in its making was not likely to be favourable towards you.' Transcript of Legal Hearings, Johannesburg, 27–29 October 1997, available at: www.justice.govza/trc/special/legal/legal.htm, accessed 28 February 2010.

[17] J. Dugard, *Human Rights and the South African Legal Order* (Princeton University Press, 1978), ch. 6, p. 150. In addition to general restrictions on freedom of assembly, a specific legislative prohibition on demonstrations near court buildings was enacted in 1982: Demonstrations In or Near Court Buildings Act 71 of 1982.

[18] See, 'Truth and Reconciliation Commission Submissions by the Society of University Teachers of Law and Certain Law Schools' (1998) 115 *South African Law Journal* 101.

with a rhetoric of elaborate deference and diffidence.[19] In such an atmosphere, an article on the death penalty published over two parts of the *South African Law Journal* in 1969 and 1970 was unusual both in its tone and the forthrightness of the challenge it posed to the judiciary of the time.[20] But so was its author unusual; Barend van Niekerk, at the time a senior lecturer at the Wits Law School, was a man who some years earlier had 'undergone a Pauline conversion. From a staunch Nationalist he changed to a liberal humanist.'[21] The flamboyance and passion with which he expressed these convictions made van Niekerk a quite singular figure in the South African legal academy of the period; as Ellison Kahn memorably put it, 'unlike the typical white South African of liberal sentiments and humanitarian ideals, [van Niekerk] did not handle reality delicately with a pair of tongs'.[22] The article was a wide-ranging attack on the death penalty in principle and on its enthusiastic embrace in apartheid South Africa, a country which, at the time of van Niekerk's research, conducted almost half of the world's executions.[23] It was an unacknowledged fact that there were stark racial disparities in the application of the death penalty; van Niekerk was bold enough to highlight these.[24] At one point in his research, van Niekerk had surveyed the bar with a questionnaire, asking advocates who had been involved in capital cases whether 'you consider, for whatever reason, that a Non-European tried on a capital charge stands a better chance of being sentenced to death than a European?'.[25] The results were ambiguous.

[19] See the assessment by E. Cameron, 'Lawyers, Language and Politics: In Memory of J. C. de Wet and W. A. Joubert' (1993) 110 *South African Law Journal* 51 at 59ff.

[20] B. van Niekerk, '... Hanged by the Neck Until you are Dead: Some Thoughts on the Application of the Death Penalty in South Africa' (1969) 86 *South African Law Journal* 457 and (1970) 87 *South African Law Journal* 60. An earlier article by A. S. Mathews and R. C. Albino, 'The Permanence of the Temporary' (1966) 83 *South African Law Journal* 16 which was critical of the judicial response to the introduction of detention without trial had earned a rebuke from the Chief Justice, L. C. Steyn. See Dugard, *Human Rights and the South African Legal Order*, pp. 290–2.

[21] From the obituary by E. Kahn, 'In Memoriam: Barend van Niekerk' (1981) 98 *South African Law Journal* 402 at 404.

[22] Kahn, 'In Memoriam: Barend van Niekerk', at 409.

[23] van Niekerk (1969), '... Hanged by the Neck Until you are Dead', p. 458.

[24] See Dugard, *Human Rights and the South African Legal Order*, p. 127: 'Of the 2,470 persons executed [between 1910 and 1975], less than 100, it is estimated, were white; no white has yet been hanged for the rape of a black; and only about six whites have been hanged for the murder of blacks. Conversely, blacks convicted of the murder or rape of whites are usually executed.'

[25] van Niekerk (1969), '... Hanged by the Neck Until you are Dead', p. 467.

He then asked 'If your answer to the previous question is "yes" . . . do you think that the differentiation shown to the different races as regards the death penalty is conscious and deliberate?'. The results were, in van Niekerk's summary, damning: 'a considerable majority of replying advocates, almost 50 per cent in fact, believe that justice as regards capital punishment is meted out on a differential basis to the different races, and 41 per cent who so believe are also of the opinion that such differentiation is "conscious and deliberate"'.[26]

These unpalatable conclusions resulted in van Niekerk's prosecution for contempt of court.[27] He was acquitted after a trial on the basis that he did not have the requisite intention to commit the crime. However, the presiding judge went on to make a series of remarks to the effect that the published statements could, objectively speaking, be viewed as being contempt of court because 'a reasonable person reading the article . . . could possibly hold the judges and the administration of justice in low esteem' since the judges could no longer be 'universally thought of as impartial'.[28] Writing six years later, Dugard noted that this warning had had its intended chilling effect: no research into the effect of race on the judicial process was published in South Africa in the years between the van Niekerk prosecution and the Dugard article.[29]

This was not the end of van Niekerk's legal travails, however. In October 1971, Ahmed Timol, a young Communist Party activist, had died while held under the indefinite detention provisions of the Terrorism Act 1967. He had jumped, police said, from the tenth floor window of security police headquarters in Johannesburg while being interrogated.[30] Timol's death led to widespread outrage and protest; at one such protest meeting held in Durban, Barend van Niekerk, by then a professor at the University of Natal Law School, criticised the institution of indefinite detention without trial in solitary confinement and the

[26] van Niekerk (1969), '. . . Hanged by the Neck Until you are Dead', p. 467.

[27] The prosecution was apparently brought on the complaint of the Judge President of the Transvaal, Mr Justice P. M. Cilliè. Dugard, *Human Rights and the South African Legal Order*, pp. 292–3.

[28] *S* v. *van Niekerk* 1970 (3) SA 655, T, 658–9, quoted by Dugard, *Human Rights and the South African Legal Order*, p. 293.

[29] Dugard, *Human Rights and the South African Legal Order*. E. Kahn, at the time the editor of the *South African Law Journal*, commented that the judgment meant that 'as an editor I would have to be more careful in future of a possible breach of the law. I had learned my lesson.' Kahn, 'In Memoriam: Barend van Niekerk', p. 406.

[30] See the account of the subsequent inquest by G. Bizos, *No One to Blame? In Pursuit of Justice in South Africa* (Cape Town: David Philip Publishers, 1998), ch. 1.

attitude of lawyers and the judiciary to evidence obtained by its use. Indefinite solitary confinement of a detainee was torture, van Niekerk, argued. 'Cannot our judiciary', he asked, 'in effect kill one aspect of the usefulness of the Terrorism Act for our authorities? They can do so by denying, on account of the built-in intimidatory effect of unsupervised solitary confinement, practically all creditworthiness to evidence procured under those detention provisions.'[31]

The speech resulted in van Niekerk being charged with contempt of court and with attempting to defeat or obstruct the course of justice. The contempt charge went to both forms of the offence: it was alleged that the remarks had scandalised or insulted the judicial institution. In addition, according to the indictment, van Niekerk's speech was intended to prejudice and influence proceedings in *S* v. *Hassim and others*, a criminal trial that was then ongoing in the Pietermaritzburg Supreme Court in which the accused and several state witnesses had been held as Terrorism Act detainees under the conditions criticised by van Niekerk.[32] The trial court acquitted van Niekerk on the charge of scandalising the court, but convicted him of contempt for publishing comments that had the tendency to prejudice or interfere with the *sub judice* proceedings in *Hassim*. On appeal, the Appellate Division, in a judgment given by Chief Justice Ogilvie Thompson, upheld the conviction for breach of the *sub judice* rule and, further, held that the exhortation to 'kill' the usefulness of evidence obtained from Terrorism Act detainees by denying it 'practically all creditworthiness', constituted the offence of attempting to defeat or obstruct the course of justice.

A court less hostile to the content of van Niekerk's remarks might well have found differently. As Dugard has shown, on both its treatment of the facts and its interpretation of the law, the Appellate Division went to some lengths to find against van Niekerk.[33] Van Niekerk had not mentioned the *Hassim* trial and the protest meeting at which he spoke had been called on another issue, the death of Ahmed Timol. Moreover, the Appeal Court conceded, there was no evidence of a risk of prejudice to the *Hassim* trial since, according to Ogilvie Thompson CJ, 'it may ... unhesitantly, be assumed that ...[the judge and assessors in *Hassim*'s case] would not in

[31] See, Dugard, *Human Rights and the South African Legal Order*, pp. 294–5.

[32] Dugard, *Human Rights and the South African Legal Order*, p. 296.

[33] Dugard, *Human Rights and the South African Legal Order*, pp. 298–9. See also J. Dugard, 'Judges, Academics and Unjust Laws: The van Niekerk Contempt Case' (1972) 89 *South African Law Journal* 271.

fact have been in any way whatever influenced by appellant's ... exhortation, even if it had been brought to their attention'.[34] But this was irrelevant, the court held. The test to be applied was whether 'the statement or document in issue tends to prejudice or interfere with the administration of justice in a pending proceeding'. Setting the scope of the *sub judice* rule so widely, as Dugard put it at the time,

> seriously stifles academic and press comment on the administration of justice. If the law as it now stands is rigorously enforced it will bring practically all comment on matters before the courts or on matters still to come before the courts to an end, because most newspaper or law journal comments not only have the tendency to influence courts in pending or future proceedings, but they are deliberately intended to do so.[35]

In the course of his all too short academic career, van Niekerk was to return again and again to the issue of judicial free speech; his treatment at the hands of the courts had made the issue, in Kahn's estimation, an *idée fixe* in his mind.[36] The result is a body of work that, though it may not meet the conventional academic standard of disinterest, is encyclopaedic on the subject and well worth revisiting for the breadth of its scholarship and for its uncommon wit. In a magisterial two-part article in the *South African Law Journal*, van Niekerk surveyed the comparative jurisprudence on the subject and his resultant verdict on the South African law was, predictably enough, damning. The law and practice of the South African courts in relation to contempt had a 'debilitating effect' on 'crucial social interests'.[37] The rules on *sub judice* contempt in particular had reached their 'purest' state in the South African application, constituting 'an effective ban on any kind of public comment made out of court that may conceivably affect the deliberations of a court ... on the supposition that nothing extraneous should exert any influence on its independent decision-making processes'.[38] Things have changed, as the next section will outline, but there is enduring

[34] *S* v. *van Niekerk* 1972 (3) SA 723, A. In *S* v. *Harber* 1988 (3) SA 396, A the Appellate Division confirmed that actual influence was irrelevant; instead the test was whether, if the facts set out in the impugned publication were to be accepted by the tribunal, they could influence the proceedings before it.

[35] Dugard, *Human Rights and the South African Legal Order*, pp. 299–300.

[36] Kahn, 'In Memoriam: Barend van Niekerk', p. 408. van Niekerk had also been successfully sued for defamation by a cabinet minister for his criticism of an apparent racial disparity in sentencing: *South African Associated Newspapers* v. *Estate Pelser* 1975 (4) SA 797, A.

[37] van Niekerk, 'The Uncloistering of the Virtue', p. 538.

[38] Niekerk, 'The Uncloistering of the Virtue', p. 548, citing as authority (no surprise) *S* v. *van Niekerk* 1972 (3) SA 723, A.

interest in van Niekerk's account of the extent to which judicial free speech is 'at least as much restricted by informal restrictions and taboos as by formal restrictions'.[39] Academics and lawyers in South Africa, van Niekerk thought, had adopted the British custom of avoidance of criticism of the judiciary, a 'factor that induces lawyers to indulge in various forms of sycophancy in and out of court';[40] the press tended to follow suit and the judiciary contributed 'a stream of extracurial pronouncements by judges deprecating criticism of judges'.[41]

Judicial free speech in the post-1994 era

Reconsideration of the contempt power

We have seen that the South African judiciary was a passive beneficiary of politically repressive measures that had the effect of inhibiting free speech in general. With the arrival of constitutional democracy, most of these have been removed and the result has been a flourishing of expression, particularly in the political sphere. The impact of the new constitutional order on the common-law restrictions on judicial free speech presents a somewhat more mixed picture.

In its first year of existence, the newly established Constitutional Court of South Africa had occasion to consider the scope of its contempt powers, if any. The occasion was its decision in *Executive Council, Western Cape Legislature* v. *President of the Republic of South Africa*, a case of considerable moment as it was the first in which the court was called to decide on the constitutionality of a provision of a law of the post-1994 democratic Parliament. After dealing with the main issues in the case, Chaskalson P turned to consider a side matter:[42]

> On the morning of the 8th September [1995] a report appeared in *Die Burger* of a speech made the previous evening by the Third Applicant. According to the report the speech was delivered in the Sarepta Community Hall in front of an enthusiastic crowd of the Third Applicant's political supporters who had come from far afield to hear him.[43]

[39] Niekerk, 'The Uncloistering of the Virtue', p. 555.

[40] Niekerk, 'The Uncloistering of the Virtue', p. 559.

[41] Niekerk, 'The Uncloistering of the Virtue', p. 565.

[42] *Executive Council, Western Cape Legislature* v. *President of the Republic of South Africa* 1995 (4) SA 877, CC.

[43] *Executive Council, Western Cape Legislature* v. *President of the Republic of South Africa* 1995 (4) SA 877, CC, at [116].

The third applicant was Mr Pieter Marais, who was a member of the Western Provincial Executive, and the speech was made at the time that the decision of the Constitutional Court was still pending. He was reported to have said that: 'The Western Cape government has an outstanding chance to win the case in the Constitutional Court, unless the court makes a political decision.'[44] Marais subsequently withdrew the remark insofar as it could be interpreted as intending 'to insult the Constitutional Court, or insinuate that party political considerations could have an influence on the court's decision'.[45] But the issue of Marais' remarks was pursued by the respondents, who argued that 'the reported statement constituted a serious contempt of Court, whether on the basis of a contempt tending to prejudice the outcome of a case or one scandalising the Court'.[46] Chaskalson P, speaking for the court on this aspect of the case, was disapproving but declined to invoke the contempt power. The statement, he said,

> undermines not only this Court, but constitutionalism itself, of which this Court is a guardian. Having regard to the high political office held by ... [Marais], the consequences of a statement impugning the integrity of this Court might have been particularly harmful. All citizens are free to attend Court, to listen to proceedings, to comment on them and on the judgments given and to criticise such judgments, even vigorously, where it is appropriate to do so, but it is irresponsible to make unfounded statements which impugn the integrity of the Court. I leave the matter there.[47]

A comment on the court's treatment of this controversy in the *Annual Survey of South African Law* was critical of the summary procedure used to investigate the respondents' complaint, since the words complained about were uttered *ex facie curiae*.[48] Marais was not convicted of contempt, nevertheless, the authors felt, 'he ended up with something that resembled a conviction albeit unattended by any sanction'.[49] Moreover,

[44] *Executive Council, Western Cape Legislature* v. *President of the Republic of South Africa* 1995 (4) SA 877, CC, at [116].

[45] *Executive Council, Western Cape Legislature* v. *President of the Republic of South Africa* 1995 (4) SA 877, CC, at [117].

[46] *Executive Council, Western Cape Legislature* v. *President of the Republic of South Africa* 1995 (4) SA 877, CC, at [119].

[47] *Executive Council, Western Cape Legislature* v. *President of the Republic of South Africa* 1995 (4) SA 877, CC, at [122].

[48] D. M. Davis, G. Marcus and J. Klaaren, 'The Administration of Justice, Law Reform and Jurisprudence', 1995 *Annual Survey of South African Law* 728 at 733.

[49] Davis, Marcus and Klaaren, 'The Administration of Justice, Law Reform and Jurisprudence', p. 733.

it was doubtful that the speech that had occasioned the court's attention could be considered contemptuous, unless measured by the hyper-sensitive standard of the apartheid-era jurisprudence. 'It would be extremely unfortunate', concluded the authors, 'if the observations of Chaskalson P had a "chilling effect" on criticism of the Constitutional Court.'[50]

These concerns turned out to be unfounded and, indeed, the court's reaction to the Marais incident stands out as exceptional in that it has not again made any attempt to censure speech critical of it, even though there have been recent examples which make Marais' remarks look positively thoughtful and measured.[51] Moreover, as soon as it was presented with the opportunity to reconsider the contempt jurisprudence, the Constitutional Court distanced itself from the old-era approach. In *S* v. *Mamabolo*,[52] the Constitutional Court heard an appeal against the conviction of an official of the Department of Correctional Services, who had been summarily tried and convicted for contempt

[50] Davis, Marcus and Klaaren, 'The Administration of Justice, Law Reform and Jurisprudence', p. 735.

[51] Perhaps the highest profile incident arose from a speech made in June 2008 by Gwede Mantashe, the Secretary-General of the ANC. Mantashe expressed his view that 'the movement is under siege and counter-revolutionary forces are regrouping'. He proceeded to list various instances of this 'regrouping', at which point he made the following remarks about the Constitutional Court, which was at the time embroiled in the Hlophe saga (discussed in Chapter 5, this volume) and about to decide a crucial appeal in the corruption case against the President of the ANC, Jacob Zuma. 'The smokescreen, comrades', Mantashe said, 'round the so-called Hlophe case, whose intention is to drag the name of the president of the ANC in the mud. The reality of what we call the Hlophe case in that court ... it's a psychological preparation of society for them to pounce. So when they pounce on our president we should be ready at that point in time. Our revolution is in danger and we must stand and defend it with everything we have.' The remarks, interpreted to mean that the Constitutional Court was part of the 'counter-revolutionary' forces threatening the democratic movement, caused widespread dismay. See Franz Kruger, 'You said it Mantashe', *Mail & Guardian*, 14 October 2008. Mantashe denied that this had been his meaning and the government stepped in to disavow allegations of disrespect for the judiciary, but considerable damage was done by the tenor of the remarks; many commentators and the public on the blogosphere enthusiastically endorsed the 'counter-revolutionary' charge. There can be little doubt that this incident, and the many other instances of court-bashing that took place at the time had a negative impact on the court. In his recent memoir, Justice Albie Sachs comments briefly and wryly on the incident: 'I was 73 years old and ... on long leave as a Ford Foundation Scholar in Residence, when I discovered I was a counter-revolutionary.' A. Sachs, *The Strange Alchemy of Life and Law* (Oxford University Press, 2009), p. 274.

[52] *S* v. *Mamabolo (E-TV, Business Day and the Freedom of Expression Institute Intervening)* 2001 (3) SA 409, CC.

following comments on an ongoing case as reported in a newspaper. The comments, made by the accused when asked why a warrant for the release of a prisoner had not been carried out, were to the effect that the judge issuing the warrant 'had made a mistake'. He was summoned by the judge he had referred to and, after a summary trial, convicted of making a 'scandalous comment' which 'impugned on the integrity of this court'.[53]

In overturning the conviction, the Constitutional Court embarked on a reconsideration of the offence of scandalising contempt in a constitutional democracy.[54] Certainly, the right to freedom of expression justified considerable latitude for speech about the judiciary, particularly given the power judges wielded under the new Constitution and the role they played in matters that were frequently politically controversial. But to be balanced against these considerations was the fact of the relative institutional weakness of the judiciary; it had 'no constituency, no purse and no sword'.[55] More than the other branches of the state, the judiciary relied for its effectiveness on a positive public perception of its integrity and it was therefore particularly vulnerable to unwarranted attacks on that integrity, a vulnerability exacerbated by the particular methods of judicial decision-making and its style of conducting itself:

> courts have over the centuries developed a method of functioning, a self-discipline and a restraint which, although it differs from jurisdiction to jurisdiction, has a number of essential characteristics. The most important is that judges speak in court and only in court. They are not at liberty to defend or even debate their decisions in public.[56]

The balance was struck by reformulating the test for scandalising contempt, in the process abandoning the 'tendency to prejudice' standard of *S* v. *van Niekerk* and similar cases: instead, to justify a conviction, the court must be satisfied that 'the publisher of the offending statement brought about a particular result. In the case of scandalising the court that result must have been to bring the administration of justice into disrepute.'[57]

This reformulation allowed the court to avoid the conclusion that the offence was unconstitutional; the offence could be retained, though, as the court admitted, once reformulated in this way, the test 'will not lightly result in a finding that the crime of scandalising the court has been committed'.[58] The possibility of a conviction for scandalising contempt only in the most

[53] *S* v. *Mamabolo* 2001 (3) SA 409 at [11].
[54] *S* v. *Mamabolo* 2001 (3) SA 409 at [15].
[55] *S* v. *Mamabolo* 2001 (3) SA 409 at [16].
[56] *S* v. *Mamabolo* 2001 (3) SA 409 at [18].
[57] *S* v. *Mamabolo* 2001 (3) SA 409 at [44].
[58] *S* v. *Mamabolo* 2001 (3) SA 409 at [45].

serious cases of likely damage to the administration of justice meant that the offence remained a limitation of freedom of expression, but one that was sufficiently attenuated to be justifiable.

A similar reconsideration of the scope of the offence of *sub judice* contempt was subsequently undertaken by the Supreme Court of Appeal in the *Midi Television* case.[59] The matter involved attempts to prevent the broadcast of a television documentary dealing with a lurid murder case pending in the courts. The Cape High Court interdicted broadcast of the programme (which included interviews with several people likely to be state witnesses in the trial), but the interdict was set aside on appeal.

The definition of the offence had to be revisited, the court held, to strike a better balance between the constitutional right to comment freely on the administration of justice and the need to protect against prejudice or interference with the legal process. As with scandalising contempt, this balance turned on an abandonment of the old 'tendency to prejudice' standard and replacing it with a higher threshold of risk:

> a publication will be unlawful, and thus susceptible to being prohibited, only if the prejudice that the publication might cause to the administration of justice is demonstrable and substantial and there is a real risk that the prejudice will occur if publication takes place . . . [I]f a risk of that kind is clearly established, and if it cannot be prevented from occurring by other means, a ban on publication that is confined in scope and in content and in duration to what is necessary to avoid the risk might be considered.[60]

What has been the result of these speech-regarding reformulations of the scope of the contempt rule? Critics of the *Mamabolo* decision have expressed regret that the court did not take the opportunity to dispense with the offence of scandalising contempt altogether.[61] Despite the court's reassurances that the threshold it had set would not easily be reached, since *Mamabolo* there have been two reported convictions for scandalising. In *S* v. *Bresler*, the accused in a traffic matter made statements in his appeal documents attacking the magistrate who had convicted him and decrying the state of the administration of justice more generally; this was 'bush law', 'an insane verdict', the magistrate was 'second rate' and presided over 'a Mickey Mouse court', and so on.[62]

59 *Midi Television (Pty) Ltd t/a E-TV* v. *Director of Public Prosecutions (Western Cape)* 2007 (5) SA 540, SCA.

60 *Midi Television (Pty) Ltd* v. *Director of Public Prosecutions* 2007 (5) SA 540 at [19].

61 S. Hoctor, 'The Right to Freedom of Expression and the Criminal Law: The Journey Thus Far' (2005) 26 *Obiter* 459 at 465.

62 *S* v. *Bresler* 2002 (4) SA 524, CC.

Following *Mamabolo*, Satchwell J held, there had to be far greater tolerance of statements critical of the judiciary than there had been in the past. Nevertheless, there were limits; statements that were 'downright harmful to the public interest by undermining the legitimacy of the judicial process as such are not permitted'.[63] Convicting the accused for contempt, the court held that his speech fell into the category of egregious statements identified in *Mamabolo*; his comments targeted a particular judicial officer to the extent of impeding his ability to carry out his judicial functions and they 'maligned all the courts of this country and … attacked the very basis of the administration of justice and the right of all members of this society to trust therein and rely thereupon'.[64]

In *S* v. *Moila*, the accused's comments also had the character of racist rantings about the judge who had issued an eviction order against him and about the judiciary in general.[65] In a 'press statement' sent to all and sundry, the accused railed against the judge, stating that his decision had been racially inspired, that he was 'demented with a whiff of power', he had acted outside the law and that the judgment was 'evil' and a 'miscarriage of justice'. The accused announced that 'I will not comply with … [the] Court order until [Judge] Bertelsmann interprets the law lawfully. If it takes a jail term to measure my conviction, so let it be.'[66] The accused continued indefatigably in this vein in a series of letters and documents over the course of a year. Convicting the accused on ten counts of contempt, the court referred to the following remarks of Kotzé J in the venerable case of *In re Phelan* (1877–81):

> nothing can have a greater tendency to bring the administration of justice into contempt than to say, or suggest, in a public newspaper, that the Judge … instead of being guided by principle and his conscience, has been guilty of personal favouritism, and allowed himself to be influenced by personal and corrupt motives, in judicially deciding a matter in open Court.

These two decisions, the only reported cases of prosecutions for scandalising contempt post-*Mamabolo*, illustrate that there is some utility for the courts in retaining the capacity to use the contempt power to discipline irrational and self-serving speech by disappointed litigants like the accused in *Moila*. That said, there seems to be no inclination for the courts or the prosecution services to attempt to censure the sort of speech that van Niekerk had been prosecuted for under the old regime, that is, critical

[63] *S* v. *Bresler* 2002 (4) SA 524 at 531, quoting *S* v. *Mamabolo* 2001 (3) SA 409 at [32].
[64] *S* v. *Bresler* 2002 (4) SA 524 at 543–4.
[65] *S* v. *Moila* 2006 (1) SA 330, T. [66] *S* v. *Moila* 2006 (1) SA 330, T at 337.

speech made with a more broadly political motive. For example, commenting on a High Court decision that had denied the ANC intellectual property protection for the phrase 'Congress of the People', the Secretary-General of the organisation is reported to have described the two black judges who made the decision as 'apartheid apologists', and to have said that he could not understand why the two black judges did not 'know historical facts'.[67] These comments elicited much criticism, but no suggestion was made that they constituted the crime of scandalising the courts.[68] As for *sub judice* contempt, there has been no reported instance of a prosecution since the *Midi Television* decision.

Speech by judges

In most jurisdictions, the independence of the judiciary is thought to require judges to keep themselves detached from political and social controversies. This has always been the South African position too. 'A measure of aloofness attaches to judicial office', was how Chief Justice Ogilvie Thompson put it in 1972, 'it behoves a judge to . . . endeavour at all times to avoid creating, however unintentionally, any impression that he holds views which might, albeit perhaps unwarrantedly, be construed as evidence of some sort of prejudice regarding, or prejudging of, some issue, which, directly or indirectly, conceivably fall for decision in his court'. As a consequence, the Chief Justice continued, 'the expression in public, and in particular in the Press or other media, by judges of opinions on controversial issues, whether or not such issues have political overtones, is to be deprecated'.[69] Stated this widely, this principle leaves little scope for judges to make extra-curial pronouncements on

[67] 'Mantashe Lashes out at Black Judges', *Cape Argus*, 14 December 2008.

[68] Other court decisions on political issues have elicited outright avowals of defiance. It was reported that a High Court decision interdicting the singing of an inflammatory song was described by the President of the ANC Youth League as granted by an 'untransformed justice system, the same one that had functioned during apartheid'. These comments were endorsed by the veterans' association of the liberation army, Mkhonto we Sizwe, who reportedly said, 'There is no way we will stop singing the song. The judge is ignorant'. 'MK-veterane, jeugliga val regbank aan', *Beeld*, 5 April 2010.

[69] The speech, made at the centenary celebrations of the Northern Cape Division of the Supreme Court of South Africa is reported in (1972) 89 *South African Law Journal* 23 at 32. It is quoted in R. Goldstone, 'Do Judges Speak Out?' (1994) 111 *South African Law Journal* 258 at 259. See also the similar views of Ogilvie Thompson's predecessor, Chief Justice L. C. Steyn, 'Regsbank en Regsfakulteit' (1967) 30 *Tydskrif van die Hedendaagse Romeins-Hollandse Reg* 101.

any but the blandest and most uncontroversial of topics. It was frowned upon even for judges to write a letter to the press. Ellison Kahn summed up the attitude of the times with reference to the motto attributed to Benjamin Jowett, Master of Balliol College: 'Never regret, never explain, never apologise'.[70]

This attitude, a matter of custom rather than rule,[71] meant that judicial statements on politically controversial topics were extremely rare.[72] It meant also that judges who might have been so inclined were unable to speak critically about the manifest injustices of the apartheid era.[73] Of course, this silence reinforced the impression that much of the judiciary was at best quiescent about and, at worst, willing participants in an oppressive system.[74]

Much has changed since 1994. To a far greater extent than under the old regime, South African judges now routinely give speeches at, and participate in, academic conferences, give speeches to university students and address gatherings of the legal profession. Such events have seen judges strongly criticise matters relating to the administration of justice and law reform.[75] A High Court judge even hosts a weekly television discussion show called 'Judge for Yourself', in which he chairs debates

[70] E. Kahn, 'Extra-judicial Activities of Judges', 1980 *De Jure* 188, 217.

[71] As H. Corder (Chapter 5, this volume) points out, prior to the establishment of the Judicial Service Commission in 1994 there were no formal rules or mechanisms governing judicial conduct.

[72] Even extra-curial comments that pertained to the administration of justice were considered improper. See, e.g., the incident reported by J. R. L. Milton, 'The Administration of Justice, Law Reform and Jurisprudence' 1970 *Annual Survey of South African Law* 444 at 450–1.

[73] See the response by judges to calls that they should condemn 'unjust laws', as reported by B. van Niekerk, 'The Administration of Justice, Law Reform and Jurisprudence', 1967 *Annual Survey of South African Law* 444 at 456–7. Calls for judges to register a protest, said Mr Justice J. D. Cloete of the Eastern Cape Division, could undermine the status of the judiciary. If so, the people making the calls 'should be stopped'.

[74] The TRC, in its findings concluded that 'the most common form of subservience [of the judiciary and legal profession to the system] can be captured in the maxim *qui tacet consentire*'. Truth and Reconciliation Commission of South Africa, *Report*, p. 101. See also the comments by four Appeal Court judges on the issue of the 'silence of the judiciary' in their submission to the TRC: J. S. Smalberger, C. T. Howie, R. M. Marais and D. G. Scott, 'Submission on the Role of the Judiciary' (1998) 115 *South African Law Journal* 42 at 48–9: 'There are many who believe that more could, and should, have been said [against apartheid]. We count ourselves among them.'

[75] E.g., the reaction of many judges to controversial proposed amendments to the Constitution relating to the powers of the Executive over the administration of the court system resulting in the withdrawal of the proposals. 'Government Backs off Controversial Judicial Bills', *Cape Times*, 31 July 2006.

about current affairs. But such appetite for the limelight is rare, and most judges prefer it seems to maintain a low profile. The limits of free speech by judges, still much constrained by convention and custom, is now governed also by a legal rule. The Judicial Service Commission Act 9 of 1994 was amended in 2008 to flesh out the commission's constitutional powers to discipline the judiciary. The Act now provides a mechanism for the investigation and adjudication of complaints against judges, which may be brought, *inter alia*, on the grounds that a judge's conduct is 'incompatible with or unbecoming of the holding of judicial office, including any conduct that is prejudicial to the independence, impartiality, dignity, accessibility, efficiency or effectiveness of the courts'.[76] Further detail is intended to be provided by a Code of Judicial Conduct to be compiled by the Chief Justice in consultation with the Minister of Justice. This will replace the informal 'Guidelines for Judges' which have been in place for a decade.[77] As to the limits of free speech, the Guidelines contain an ethical prohibition on judges becoming involved in 'political controversy or activity' and of membership of a political party or secret organisation.[78]

Justice Edwin Cameron's book, *Witness to AIDS*, contains a highly illuminating meditation on these rules and guidelines in relation to a concrete case, his own. On numerous platforms, Cameron, who was at the time an Appeal Court judge, directly confronted the catastrophic 'AIDS-denialism' that had gripped the South African Government during the Mbeki administration.[79] He did so while accepting that 'judicial office requires those assuming it to accept some limitation on how openly and fully they can participate in public debate on contentious current political issues'.[80] But he was also, as his account goes, mindful of the conclusions of the Truth Commission that the judges during apartheid had failed in their duty not to collaborate in injustice 'by omission, silence and inaction'.[81] Cameron's interventions in the debate on this political issue were undoubtedly close to or even beyond the limits of judicial free speech even in the liberalised post-1994 era. In his account

[76] Section 14(4)(e) of the Judicial Service Commission Act.

[77] See, 'Proposals for a Mechanism for Dealing with Complaints Against Judges, and for a Code of Ethics for Judges – A Report of a Committee Chaired by Mr Justice L. Harms' (2000) 117 *South African Law Journal* 377 at 406 ('Guidelines'). See, further Chapter 23, this volume.

[78] 'Proposals for a Mechanism for Dealing with Complaints Against Judges', rule 18.

[79] E. Cameron, *Witness to AIDS* (Cape Town: Tafelberg, 2005).

[80] Cameron, *Witness to AIDS*, p. 149. [81] Cameron, *Witness to AIDS*, p. 152.

of his decision to speak out, he stresses his personal circumstances with the implication that his decision is not generalisable. As he describes his situation, Cameron felt personally impelled to enter the political arena, it was morally impossible for him to remain silent in the face of an injustice comparable with those that had been investigated by the Truth Commission:

> When the agony of denialism beset our country, I felt I was called to witness. I felt called to account for my survival in a country in which hundreds of thousands were dying unnecessary deaths . . . This provided that rare justification that is needed for a judge to become involved in political contention.[82]

For the sake of completeness, I should mention a related body of law that has not received much attention in the case law since 1994 and which is still, on the face of it, under the sway of the old inclination towards excessive deference to judicial sensibilities. This is the law of contempt *ex facie curiae*. This species of the contempt power also clearly merits a systematic reweighting of the principles underlying it in favour of freedom of speech; a fact that might underlie the apparent reluctance of the courts to invoke the power in the post-apartheid era.

[82] Cameron, *Witness to AIDS*, p. 155.

12

Judges and free speech in the United Kingdom

KEITH D. EWING

On 22 July 1977, the Secretary of State for Scotland (Mr Bruce Millan) laid an order before Parliament removing Sheriff Peter Thomson from judicial office, the order to take effect on 6 December 1977. The said order was made under a statutory procedure which empowered the Secretary of State to remove a Sheriff on the ground that the latter was 'unfit for office by reason of inability, neglect of duty or misbehaviour', a power which could be exercised only after an investigation by the Lord President of the Court of Session and the Lord Justice Clerk, the two most senior judges in Scotland.[1] In this case the complaint against Sheriff Thomson was that he had published a pamphlet entitled 'Scottish Plebiscite – Report by Sheriff Peter Thomson', proposing a referendum on Scottish Home Rule. This was not the first time Sheriff Thomson had engaged in political action. In 1974 he had circulated voting cards with questions about the establishment of a Parliament in Scotland, along with a return envelope addressed to himself as 'The Returning Officer'. On being given notice of this earlier incident, the then Secretary of State requested an investigation to be conducted by the Lord President and the Lord Justice Clerk, with which, to the evident irritation of the senior judges, Sheriff Thomson refused to cooperate, or even acknowledge. The judges reported that although Sheriff Thomson's conduct was 'incompatible with his judicial office', he was nevertheless not unfit for office 'in view of his otherwise satisfactory service', though they did add that if the Sheriff should engage in any similar activity in the future, 'it might be extremely difficult to resist the conclusion that his fitness for his office was at an end'.[2]

[1] Sheriff Courts (Scotland) Act 1971, s. 12.

[2] This account is drawn from a parliamentary statement by Mr Millan on 25 November 1977: HC Debs., 25 November 1977, cols. 922–5 WA.

On 25 November 1977, Mr Millan informed the House that the publication of the pamphlet had made it necessary to 'request a further investigation by the judges' on Sheriff Thomson's fitness for office. Once again,

> the judges wrote to Sheriff Thomson, informing him that they were undertaking an investigation into his fitness for office and inviting him to make written representations, and to appear before them either personally or by counsel. As in 1974, Sheriff Thomson did not acknowledge the invitations, and neither made written representations nor appeared before the judges.[3]

The Lord President and the Lord Justice Clerk nevertheless conducted their investigations in the absence of Sheriff Thomson and reported to the Secretary of State that 'the publication of the pamphlet could only be regarded as a repetition of the kind of activity condemned in the earlier report and in clear defiance of the warning then given to the Sheriff', adding that 'in the light of the previous similar conduct of the Sheriff, his refusals to heed warnings and advice, and his apparent disrespect for authority, it would be unrealistic to hope that he would never do anything of the kind again'. It was thus concluded that 'because of his misbehaviour', Sheriff Thomson was 'no longer fit to hold his judicial office'.[4] On receipt of this report, the Secretary of State gave Sheriff Thomson an opportunity to comment upon it before deciding what steps to take, another invitation to which the Sheriff refused to respond. Acting on the report of the senior judges the Secretary of State then proceeded to dismiss Thomson under the procedure in the Sheriff Courts (Scotland) Act 1971, s. 12.[5]

By no means everyone was impressed by the handling of this affair, or persuaded that Thomson was guilty of misconduct such as to justify his removal from office. A motion was moved to annul the order of dismissal,[6] with the debate taking place on 6 December 1977, in the course of which the leading backbencher who moved the motion thought it 'important to remember that in the pamphlet Sheriff Thomson does not campaign for or propose any constitutional change in Scotland. What he proposes is that the people of Scotland be given the opportunity to express their opinion on what constitutional change, if any, they would like'.[7] Moreover, 'in the

[3] HC Debs., 25 November 1977, col. 924.

[4] HC Debs., 25 November 1977. The text of the letters is to be found at HC Debs., 30 November 1977, col. 245 WA.

[5] HC Debs., 25 November 1977, cols. 924–5 WA.

[6] HC Debs., 6 December 1977, col. 1288.

[7] HC Debs., 6 December 1977, col. 1289 (Dennis Canavan).

pamphlet Sheriff Thomson attempts to be as impartial as possible in putting forward his proposals', it being noted also that the Sheriff claimed that his activity was of 'a non-party and non-partisan nature', and that he had 'not been a member of any party or partisan organisation for at least 22 years'.[8] This led to the following direct challenge:

> Can the Secretary of State tell me what political activity Sheriff Thomson has ever indulged in that has interfered, or was in danger of interfering, with his impartiality as a judge? There is nothing in this pamphlet which suggests that his impartiality as a judge was being impaired. There is nothing biased in the pamphlet. There is nothing partisan in it.[9]

In responding to this challenge, the Secretary of State suggested that impartiality was not an issue, but that wider concerns were at stake which touched the propriety of judicial conduct. According to the Secretary of State, where a judge 'takes part publicly in discussion or argument on a subject which may be politically controversial, not as the result of an invitation by the Government to undertake a public duty but of his own accord, in my view he is entering upon dangerous ground'.[10] Although 'this is no doubt an area in which it is extremely difficult to lay down hard and fast rules', a line was said to have been crossed when a judge 'goes beyond even expressing private opinions about a controversial matter and takes the form of involving his judicial office in the controversy'.[11] In this case, the Sheriff

> referred to himself on an earlier occasion as 'The Returning Officer', and as recently as July of this year he published an advertisement in a Scottish newspaper for a public meeting to discuss the plebiscite, complete with a picture of himself in judicial wig and gown. Therefore, there has been a deliberate association of his judicial office with this particular political campaign.[12]

Judicial independence and judicial impartiality

The removal of Sheriff Thomson is the only occasion in modern times in which a judge has been removed from office because of things said outside the course of his or her judicial office. Apart from thus being unique, the case is also important for bringing into sharp relief conflicting views about the role of judges in society, and the boundaries of

[8] HC Debs., 6 December 1977, cols. 1289–90 (Dennis Canavan).
[9] HC Debs., 6 December 1977, col. 1293 (Dennis Canavan).
[10] HC Debs., 6 December 1977, col. 1305.
[11] HC Debs., 6 December 1977. [12] HC Debs., 6 December 1977, col. 1307.

judicial propriety. There was a clear conflict on display in the House of Commons on the motion to annul the removal order between (a) those backbenchers who supported the Sheriff, and (b) the senior judges and ministers who wanted him out. This was a conflict between, on the one hand, a concern that the judge should be constrained only by a requirement that he or she should do nothing that would undermine his or her capacity to act with impartiality in a particular case, and, on the other hand, a more general constraint of indeterminate scope about the inherent nature and dignity of the judicial office. On this latter view there are certain boundaries which should not be crossed, even if the conduct in question is unlikely to have any bearing on the impartiality of the judge in specific proceedings. These latter considerations are sometimes wrapped around principles such as the separation of powers and judicial independence. Crudely, the role of the court is to apply and develop the law, not to seek to otherwise influence its content. This is not to deny that the judicial function may require that judges should engage publicly with controversial matters when performing their official duties, which may in turn lead to the expression of contested views and to engagement in politically sensitive areas. Nevertheless, these are well within the proper scope of the judicial function, though they may give rise to concern when a judge uses the bench as a pulpit, as seemed often to be the case with Lord Denning.[13]

It may be thought that the constitutional changes introduced in the United Kingdom would reinforce the view of the government in the Thomson case, and strengthen the claim that the need for judicial restraint is based not so much on the need for impartiality in a particular case, but on the need to maintain a sense of propriety based on the role of the judge in society and the nature of his or her role, in the context of which impartiality is an issue, but a secondary issue. As far as these constitutional changes are concerned, there are two that lead inexorably to the case for judicial restraint in terms of political activity in the widest sense of the term, to include not only partisan party political activity, but also criticism or approval of the government (whether British or foreign), or the support for or opposition to contentious public policy proposals, where this is unrelated to the performance of judicial duties. Perhaps the most significant of these changes is the growing separation of law and politics in the sense of a growing formal and institutional separation of judges from the political process. Thus, we now have a new

[13] HC Debs., 6 December 1977, cols. 1291–2.

Supreme Court to replace the Appellate Committee of the House of Lords, and we now have new statutory rules which prohibit Supreme Court justices from active membership of the legislature.[14] Having thus been denied a platform for their personal views by being excluded from the House of Lords, it would now be curious if senior judges could find other platforms for the expression of personal views. It was surely not membership of the legislature *per se* that was incompatible with the requirements of judicial office, as much as what might be said or done in consequence of such membership.

But not only do we now have a formal separation of function, we also have a strengthening of constitutional principle to underpin that clearer separation of function. The Constitutional Reform Act 2005 imposes a duty on the Lord Chancellor, other ministers of the crown and all with responsibility for matters relating to the judiciary or otherwise to the administration of justice to 'uphold the continued independence of the judiciary'.[15] It is unclear whether this applies to judges individually, though presumably they too have 'responsibility for matters relating to the judiciary or otherwise to the administration of justice'. This would suggest that they too have not only a professional responsibility, but also a statutory duty to do nothing that would undermine their independence, in addition to and apart from any common law obligation (considered below) not to do anything that would compromise their impartiality. It is important to emphasise that there is a difference between independence and impartiality, as the Canadian Judicial Council has most impressively pointed out, drawing on Supreme Court of Canada jurisprudence.[16] So while the two principles overlap,

> Independence of the judiciary refers to the necessary individual and collective or institutional independence required for impartial decisions and decision-making. Judicial independence thus characterises both a state of mind and a set of institutional and operational arrangements. The former is concerned with the judge's impartiality in fact; the latter with defining the relationships between the judiciary and others, particularly the other branches of government, so as to assure both the reality and the appearance of independence and impartiality.[17]

But not only is there a duty on the part of the judges individually and collectively to do nothing that would undermine their own

[14] Constitutional Reform Act 2005, s. 137. [15] Constitutional Reform Act 2005, s. 3.

[16] *Valente* v. *R.* [1985] 2 SCR 652.

[17] Canadian Judicial Council, *Ethical Principles for Judges*, p. 8.

independence or that of the judiciary as a whole, paradoxically there is also an obligation on the part of the government to intervene when that duty is compromised by judges who stray beyond their brief. This is a matter to which we return.

The rules on judicial speech

In the light of the foregoing it is perhaps curious that the current rules relating to judicial public engagement appear to have been relaxed rather than strengthened in recent years, with the apparent emphasis of the principles *as applied* being located narrowly in ideas of judicial impartiality, rather than more widely in considerations of judicial independence. These principles are currently to be found in two places. The first is in the self-regulatory codes drafted by the judges themselves, though these principles are as much concerned with freedom of association and assembly as with freedom of expression. *The Guide to Judicial Conduct* was 'drafted by a working group of judges set up by the Judges' Council, under the chairmanship of Lord Justice Pill and published by the Judges' Council following extensive consultation with the judiciary'.[18] First created in 1873, the Judges' Council has been re-invigorated in recent years partly as a result of the changes introduced by the Constitutional Reform Act 2005 and the responsibilities of the Lord Chief Justice to be found therein. The duties of the Judges' Council (which is broadly representative of the judiciary as a whole) is to advise the Lord Chief Justice on a range of matters, including judicial independence, career development, terms and conditions of employment (including pay and pensions) and the *Guide to Judicial Conduct*.[19] It thus performs a number of tasks of a classical trade union nature, with the right to 'form or join associations of judges or participate in other organisations representing the interests of judges' being expressly recognised by the *Guide*.[20] It is also consulted by the government about court resources and claims 'recently [to have] selected three judicial members of the Judicial

[18] *Guide to Judicial Conduct* (2008), p. iii, available at: www.judiciary.gov.uk/NR/rdonlyres/6AA2E609-537A-4D47-8B11-02F86CD30851/0/judicialconduct_update0408.pdf. The corresponding *Guide to Judicial Conduct* (2009) for Supreme Court justices is available at: www.supremecourt.gov.uk/docs/guide_to_judicial_conduct.pdf.

[19] On the Judges' Council, see J. Thomas, 'The Judges Council' [2005] *Public Law* 608. See also A. W. Bradley and K. D. Ewing, *Constitutional and Administrative Law*, 14th edn. (Harlow: Pearson Longman, 2007), p. 394.

[20] *Guide to Judicial Conduct* (2008), p. 25.

Appointments Commission pursuant to paragraph 7(7) of the Constitutional Reform Act'.[21]

In keeping with the fine traditions of good trade unionism, the standards set in the *Guide* are permissive rather than restrictive; but they are also highly ambiguous as befits principles intended to guide the conduct of those by whom they have been written. On the one hand, 'a judge, like any other citizen, is entitled to freedom of expression, belief, association and assembly', provided that 'in exercising such rights', a judge 'always conducts himself or herself in such a manner as to preserve the dignity of the judicial office and the impartiality and independence of the judiciary'.[22] It is not thought to be inconsistent with judicial propriety for a judge to:

- write, lecture, teach and participate in activities concerning the law, the legal system, the administration of justice or related matters;
- appear at a public hearing before an official body concerned with matters relating to the law, the legal system, the administration of justice or related matters;
- serve as a member of an official body, or other government commission, committee or advisory body, if such membership is not inconsistent with the perceived impartiality and political neutrality of a judge; or
- engage in other activities if such activities do not detract from the dignity of the judicial office or otherwise interfere with the performance of judicial duties.[23]

The scope for freedom of expression is thus wide, the existing standards simply ventilating the claim made by the Secretary of State during the Thomson affair that this is 'an area in which it is extremely difficult to lay down hard and fast rules'.[24] The crucial phrase – in the first bullet point above – 'the law, the legal system, the administration of justice or related matters' is not defined, with engagement in these activities being restrained only by a need to ensure that they do not interfere with 'the proper performance of judicial duties', another statement which begs more questions than it answers.

On the other hand, however, there are suggested restraints on judicial speech (which as already suggested appear not to be informed by considerations of judicial independence, but mainly with the needs of

[21] www.judiciary.gov.uk/about-the-judiciary/the-judiciary-in-detail/index/judges-council.
[22] *Guide to Judicial Conduct* (2008), p. 23. [23] *Guide to Judicial Conduct* (2008), p 25.
[24] HC Debs., 6 December 1977, col. 1305.

impartiality). To this end, two concerns are highlighted. The first reflects a well-established principle of the constitution that judges should disengage from the political process, and 'must forgo any kind of political activity', which means that they are required 'on appointment [to] sever all ties with political parties'.[25] To this end, in turn, 'an appearance of continuing ties such as might occur by attendance at political gatherings, political fundraising events or through contribution to a political party, should be avoided'.[26] Equally, the need for abstinence 'also involves not participating in public demonstrations which, by associating the judge with a political viewpoint or cause, may diminish his authority as a judge and create in subsequent cases a perception of bias'.[27] But apart from partisan political activity (which is unlikely), a second concern addresses more general considerations. Another application of the principle of impartiality (albeit 'one difficult to define and apply in specific situations')[28] is that 'the expression of views out of court that would give rise to issues of perceived bias or pre-judgment in cases that later come before the judge'. It is also pointed out that:

> If a judge is known to hold strong views on topics relevant to issues in the case, by reason of public statements or other expression of opinion on such topics, possible disqualification of the judge may have to be addressed, whether or not the matter is raised by the parties. The risk will arise if a judge has taken part publicly in a controversial or political discussion. It will seldom, if ever, arise from what a judge has said in other cases.[29]

Challenging the government

These guidelines were drafted in the wake of the major re-organisation of the judiciary as part of the recent constitutional changes in the United Kingdom. But to the extent that they probably reflect standards, expectations and ambiguities already in force, the limited impact that self-regulation has on judicial free speech was most spectacularly revealed by the lecture delivered at the University of Cambridge by the then Lord Chief

[25] *Guide to Judicial Conduct* (2008), p. 9. The last example of this (though it was some time ago now) was the Avonside affair in 1968 (referred to in the Thomson debate above) in which a Scottish Court of Session judge was forced by the weight of adverse public opinion to give up a role in an inquiry on the constitution established by the Conservative Party, then in Opposition. The position would have been different had it been a government-appointed inquiry, as also reinforced by the minister in the Thomson debate above.

[26] *Guide to Judicial Conduct* (2008), p. 9. [27] *Guide to Judicial Conduct* (2008), p. 10.

[28] *Guide to Judicial Conduct* (2008). [29] *Guide to Judicial Conduct* (2008), p. 13.

Justice (Lord Woolf) on 'The Rule of Law and a Change in the Constitution' in early March 2004. Although modestly published in the *Cambridge Law Journal*,[30] this was a very public event which attracted a good deal of media attention and political comment,[31] inevitable given that it was (in judicial terms) an outspoken attack on the government's proposals for judicial reform generally, and its proposals to restrict the right to judicial review in certain asylum and immigration cases, in particular. It was a source of great irritation that major changes to the judiciary (including the abolition of the traditional roles of the Lord Chancellor) were to be made without first consulting the judiciary, and that this had been announced in a government press release.[32] According to Lord Woolf, the government had failed to appreciate sufficiently that the Lord Chancellor 'played a pivotal role in coordinating the three arms of government. Nor had sufficient attention been paid to the fact that, because of his membership of the Cabinet, the Lord Chancellor was able to act as 'a lightening conductor at times of high tension between the executive and the judiciary'.[33]

Lord Woolf then took aim at the creation of the new Supreme Court, which would not in fact be a supreme court as the 'new court will be subordinate to the will of Parliament as expressed in legislation and will have no jurisdiction to hear Scottish criminal appeals'. Indeed, 'among the Supreme Courts of the world, our Supreme Court will, because of its more limited role, be a poor relation', with a 'first class Final Court of Appeal' being replaced by 'a second class Supreme Court'.[34] Lord Woolf had other concerns, including the resources to be made available to the new court, being 'particularly unhappy about the suggestion that the running costs will be recouped by imposing a surcharge on court fees'.[35] All of which led him in turn to believe that the decision to create the new court should be deferred, claiming that to push ahead would be 'inconsistent with the desirability of achieving constitutional change by consensus'.[36] According to Lord Woolf

> The reason for having a Final Court of Appeal separate from the House of Lords is largely symbolic. However, symbols can have unexpected results.

[30] Lord Woolf, 'The Rule of Law and a Change in the Constitution' (2004) 63 *Cambridge Law Journal* 317. It is also published on the Cambridge University Law Faculty website at: www.law.cam.ac.uk.
[31] See the very full account in *The Daily Telegraph*, 4 March 2004.
[32] Woolf, 'The Rule of Law and a Change in the Constitution', p. 320.
[33] Woolf, 'The Rule of Law and a Change in the Constitution', p. 320.
[34] Woolf, 'The Rule of Law and a Change in the Constitution', p. 326.
[35] Woolf, 'The Rule of Law and a Change in the Constitution', p. 326.
[36] Woolf, 'The Rule of Law and a Change in the Constitution', p. 327.

> Separating the House of Lords in its legislative capacity from its activities as the Final Court of Appeal, could act as a catalyst causing the new court to be more proactive than its predecessor. This could lead to tensions. Although the Law Lords involvement in the legislative chamber is limited, the very fact that they are members of the legislature does provide them with an insight and understanding of the workings of Parliament to a greater extent than will be possible if they are no longer part of the House of Lords.[37]

From great issues of constitutional principle and architecture, Lord Woolf concluded by training his guns on an unrelated matter of immediate controversy affecting asylum and immigration. The judges took particular exception to a provision in the Asylum and Immigration Bill, which provided for the creation of an Asylum and Immigration Tribunal to deal with asylum and immigration appeals. Quite whether the grave concern and excessive Dicey-esque hyper-ventilation could be justified is another matter altogether: other common law jurisdictions operate comfortably with specialist tribunals, this one was to be presided over by a High Court judge, and wide exclusion clauses (even ones giving tribunals the power to determine their own jurisdiction) are not unknown in the United Kingdom, even on matters relating to human rights.[38] Yet despite having sat on their hands in the past, for whatever reasons on this occasion the judges found their voice, with Lord Woolf saying that the measure was 'fundamentally in conflict with the rule of law and should not be contemplated by any government if it had respect for the rule of law',[39] and that indeed that it was a 'blot on the reputation of the Government and [would] undermine its attempts to be a champion of the rule of law overseas'.[40] So serious were these measures that they could lead to 'a loss of confidence in the commitment of the government to the rule of law',[41] with attempts to justify the proposals being 'specious and unsatisfactory'.[42] Lord Woolf's parting shot was that 'if this clause were to become law, it would be so inconsistent with the spirit of

[37] Woolf, 'The Rule of Law and a Change in the Constitution', p. 326.

[38] See Regulation of Investigatory Powers Act 2000, and before that the Interception of Communications Act 1985, among others.

[39] Woolf, 'The Rule of Law and a Change in the Constitution', p. 328.

[40] Woolf, 'The Rule of Law and a Change in the Constitution', p. 329.

[41] Woolf, 'The Rule of Law and a Change in the Constitution', p. 329.

[42] Woolf, 'The Rule of Law and a Change in the Constitution', p. 329. Lord Woolf also disclosed publicly that the judges had expressed their concerns to the Home Office privately in the course of 'extensive consultations'. However, it appears that having listened to the judges and noted their concerns that its initial proposals contained a number of loopholes, the government had moved to close the loopholes rather than abandon the measure, which perhaps explains the judicial anger.

mutual respect between the different arms of government that it could be the catalyst for a campaign for a written constitution'.[43]

Courting controversy

It is difficult to imagine a more political speech by a senior judge than this; but it is equally difficult to argue that it was an improper intervention at the time it was delivered, at least in relation to Lord Woolf's first two concerns (the changing nature of the role of Lord Chancellor and the creation of the Supreme Court).[44] More difficulty is presented by less strident interventions at the same time on different issues, illustrating the narrow restraints under which judges operate. The first is a lecture by Lord Hope delivered as the Essex Law Lecture in association with global law firm Clifford Chance on 28 January 2004, just over a month before Lord Woolf's stirring intervention. This was a powerful attack on the use of torture, at a time when there was great concern about the conduct of the US government at Guantanamo Bay. In a very scholarly presentation, subsequently published in the *International and Comparative Law Quarterly*,[45] Lord Hope traced the use and abolition of torture in English and Scots law, making clear that 'the position which the law takes is not now in doubt': 'evidence which has been obtained by the use of any form of inducement or pressure is inadmissible. There are no exceptions to this rule.'[46] Nothing wrong with that perhaps, until it is appreciated that the admissibility of torture evidence and the circumstances in which it is to be admitted was making its way up through the courts to the House of Lords, in a case in which Lord Hope would sit (and indeed cite his own article).[47] And while we might applaud the sentiments, quite whether it was proper for a judge to criticise the US government for what was happening at Guantanamo Bay is another matter for debate:

> We must not allow the smiling charming faces of our American allies to divert us from seeking to discover the reality of what is being done by their interrogators. History tells us that we must lead by example if we wish to root out evil practices. That example must be shown on both sides of the Atlantic. How can we expect to eliminate torture elsewhere if there

[43] Woolf, 'The Rule of Law and a Change in the Constitution', p. 329.

[44] This is perhaps less so in relation to the Asylum and Immigration Bill where the proper forum to discuss such matters would be in a court in the context of litigation.

[45] D. Hope, 'Torture' (2004) 53 *International and Comparative Law Quarterly* 807.

[46] Hope, 'Torture', p. 803. [47] *A* v. *Home Secretary (No. 2)* [2005] UKHL 71.

> is no sure way of knowing whether or not it has been practised at Guantanamo Bay by the Americans?[48]

A second – but altogether even more notable – intervention was Sir Stephen Sedley's speech at the University of Leicester in November 2004 advocating the introduction of a national DNA database, arguing in a *London Review of Books* article published shortly thereafter that 'the case is growing for a national database holding the DNA profile of everyone living in or entering the country', and arguing further that 'in a society disturbed not only by serious crime but by the possibility of people being mistakenly acquitted or convicted of it, the potential gain represented by a comprehensive national DNA register is considerable'.[49] It appears that this was not a spoof and that Sir Stephen was serious, with his comments repeated on the BBC two years later, and widely reported in the press under the headline 'Judge wants everyone in UK on DNA database'.[50] Sedley's views certainly created a storm, and were said to have provoked anger on the part of civil liberties groups as 'a chilling proposal, ripe for indignity, error and abuse'.[51] The government felt obliged to respond, with the Prime Minister's office defending the existing database (already the largest in the world), but playing down suggestions that it could be expanded along the lines proposed, while the Home Office thought that Sedley was 'underestimating the practical issues, logistics, civil [liberties] and ethical issues' involved.[52] This intervention was also notable not only for the nature of the proposal, but because both the 2005 and 2007 contributions were made (1) just after the House of Lords had upheld the Court of Appeal (which had included Sedley) that the existing DNA database did not violate Convention rights,[53] but (2) before the European Court of Human Rights had published its unanimous disagreement with the British courts that the DNA database engaged Convention rights and that the database as then constituted violated these rights.[54] More to the point, it is not known when Sedley

[48] Hope, 'Torture', p. 831. See the even more outspoken and widely reported remarks by Lord Steyn in the F. A. Mann Lecture: *The Guardian*, 26 November 2003; *The Independent*, 26 November 2003.

[49] S. Sedley, 'Short Cuts', *London Review of Books*, 20 January 2005, p. 24. See also letter, *London Review of Books*, 3 March 2005.

[50] *The Guardian*, 5 September 2007.

[51] BBC News, 5 September 2007. See also *The Independent*, 6 September 2007.

[52] BBC News, 5 September 2007.

[53] *R (S)* v. *South Yorkshire Chief Constable* [2004] UKHL 39, [2004] 1 WLR 2196.

[54] *S and Marper* v. *United Kingdom* [2009] 48 EHRR 50.

formed his views about the DNA database, but the timing of the speech was such that it would be impossible for the litigants who had appeared before him in the Court of Appeal to do much about it, except perhaps nurse an even more exaggerated sense of grievance.

A third intervention of note did not involve criticism of the government or its allies, nor did it advance a radical proposal on a controversial topic. Rather, it involved vigorous criticism of fellow judges,[55] though again a common theme was the fact that the author played a part in the litigation to which the comments related. In a lecture at King's College London,[56] Lord Bingham – then the senior Law Lord – took issue in strong terms with three colleagues who had sat with him in a bench of nine judges convened to consider whether the Hunting Act 2004 was a valid Act of Parliament,[57] a preposterous question in the British system. Although the challenge to the Act failed, three of the judges (Lords Steyn and Hope and Baroness Hale) confronted the sovereignty of Parliament with eccentric obiter suggestions that there may be certain common law restraints on the power of Westminster.[58] Lord Bingham did not address these questions in his judgment, but he directly contradicted them in what was a most scholarly lecture, drawing on a rich vein of historical material,[59] and addressing limits on the sovereignty of Parliament mistakenly said by some to arise from EU law, devolution and the Human Rights Act 1998, as well as the suggested limitations which popped up in the speeches of his three colleagues in the *Jackson* case. In relation to the last, Lord Bingham was unable to 'accept that [his] colleagues' observations [we]re correct'. Indeed

> The British people have not repelled the extraneous power of the papacy in spiritual matters and the pretensions of royal power in temporal in order to subject themselves to the unchallengeable rulings of unelected judges. A constitution should reflect the will of a clear majority of the

55 On which, see also the public criticism of Lord Hoffmann by Lord Steyn: *The Daily Telegraph*, 26 November 2004. Lord Hoffmann's change of mind to reflect a position closer to that of Lord Steyn was to earn him a public rebuke from Tony Blair. See n. 80 below.

56 Lord Bingham, 'The Rule of Law and the Sovereignty of Parliament', 1 November 2007. The lecture may be downloaded at: www.kcl.ac.uk/news/news_details.php?news_id=672&year=2007. It is also published in (2008) 19 *King's Law Journal* 223 and in T. H. Bingham, *The Rule of Law* (London: Penguin, 2010).

57 *R (Jackson)* v. *Attorney-General* [2005] UKHL 56, [2006] 1 AC 262.

58 For a powerful critique (referred to by Bingham), see R. Ekins, 'Acts of Parliament and the Parliament Acts' (2007) 123 *Law Quarterly Review* 91.

59 Much of it drawn from J. Goldsworthy, *The Sovereignty of Parliament* (Oxford: Clarendon Press, 1999).

> people, and a constitutional change of the kind here contemplated should be made in accordance with that will or not at all.[60]

These are remarks that would divide public lawyers, though it is unclear how many would tend to support the *Jackson Three*. But the significance of the remarks for present purposes lies in the fact that the senior law lord should find it appropriate in a public forum to criticise fellow judges for something said in the course of a decision, and should do so in a way that left no room for doubt about his views on a question of fundamental importance to the government and constitution of the country. The intervention was all the more remarkable for the fact that the lecture addressed a matter which conceivably could arise for consideration in a court of which Lord Bingham was a member, this having become a lively issue of contemporary constitutional law.

Impartiality as a boundary and the boundary of impartiality

The foregoing give some flavour of the type of public engagement in which senior judges are now involved. The examples are not selected at random, but to illustrate that it is now considered acceptable for judges to use public space to attack the government, to criticise foreign governments and to disagree in robust terms with each other. (Another example of the last is Lord Hoffmann's valedictory criticisms of the European Court of Human Rights.)[61] As such, these examples illustrate the point that in the British system there does not appear to be any significant restraint based on the nature of the judicial office or the constitutional principles that the office is designed to uphold. Judges are generally free to speak, subject only to the requirements of fairness and impartiality which pervade the *Guide to Judicial Conduct*. But even here the bar appears to be set very high, so that although these latter principles are reinforced by the rule against bias in administrative law,[62] it would be highly unusual for a judge to be disqualified on this ground for anything said in an extra-judicial capacity. The point is best illustrated by the extra-judicial comments of Lord McCluskey, a more senior Scottish judge than Sheriff Thomson, who in 1986 had given the BBC's flagship

60 Bingham, 'The Rule of Law and the Sovereignty of Parliament', p. 24.

61 *The Guardian* , 6 April 2009.

62 See *R* v. *Bow Street Metropolitan Stipendiary Magistrate ex p. Pinochet Ugarte (No. 2)* [1999] UKHL 52, [2000] 1 AC 119. See A. W. Bradley and K. D. Ewing, *Constitutional and Administrative Law*, 15th edn. (Harlow: Pearson Longman, 2010), pp. 688–9.

Reith Lecture, in which he had powerfully opposed the gathering campaign for a Bill of Rights which led to the enactment of the Human Rights Act 1998.[63] The consequences of Lord McCluskey's subsequent unrestrained attack on the Human Rights Act 1998 in the year following its enactment in a series of valedictory newspaper articles in the Scottish press,[64] reveals that (1) while the rule against bias can lead to disqualification, (2) the reason for disqualification will not be the words spoken or the beliefs held, but (3) the manner of their expression. As such, it is not a rule against bias or partiality, but a rule against misjudgement in the forceful expression of views.

At the time his articles were published, Lord McCluskey was presiding in a complicated criminal prosecution of three Dutchmen whose defence relied heavily on their Convention rights. One of the articles complained of 'appeared a little over a week after the Appeal Court gave judgment on the first stage of the appellants' appeal, less than a week after they refused leave to appeal to the Privy Council and at a time when the court had directed that the next stage of the appellant's appeal was to proceed on 6 March'.[65] The accused complained that Lord McCluskey was biased and ought to be disqualified from hearing the rest of the case, which he refused to accept. The Criminal Appeal Court disagreed, and issued a blistering decision which could leave no one in any doubt about their disapproval of Lord McCluskey as they warmly endorsed the 'skilful arguments' of the Dutch lawyer for the accused who, referring to the articles,

> pointed to the negative view of the Convention which came through in the ironic reference to it going 'by the splendidly attractive name of the European Convention on Human Rights'. He went on to submit that the tone of the references to the Strasbourg Court, which expounds the Convention, as 'including those Andorrans and Ukrainians' appeared nationalist – suggesting that the author regarded the Court and its judgments as inferior to the Scottish courts and their judgments. This was of no little significance in a case where the Appeal Court was being asked to apply judgments of the European Court of Human Rights. Similarly, by likening the introduction of the Convention into Scots law to the introduction of a Trojan Horse, in the shape of a revolutionary instrument for change, Lord McCluskey was conjuring up the picture of a deceitful stratagem being used to introduce into the citadel of Scots law an alien force which would attack the defending

[63] J. H. McCluskey, *Law, Justice and Democracy* (London: Sweet & Maxwell, 1987).

[64] *Scotland on Sunday*, 6 February 2000.

[65] *Hoekstra* v. *H. M. Advocate* [2000] Scot.HC 32 at para. [11].

> soldiers. There was an implicit suggestion that this alien force would be introducing a revolution which would change the established and better ways of the native Scots law. The immediate results of the introduction of the Convention in Scotland had been 'devastating' – implying that it had laid waste areas of national law.[66]

In the light of the foregoing, it was no surprise that the court should conclude that 'the article, published very shortly after the decision in the appeal, would create in the mind of an informed observer an apprehension of bias on the part of Lord McCluskey against the Convention and against the rights deriving from it';[67] the court also making clear, however, that the other two judges who had sat with McCluskey were not in any way 'infected' by his views.[68] Yet – as already suggested – what is particularly interesting about this case is not that Lord McCluskey had criticised the Human Rights Act, but that he had done so in an inappropriate manner. There would have been no disqualification and no impartiality if he had revealed himself in less strident terms:

> in reaching this conclusion, we attach particular importance to the tone of the language and the impression which the author deliberately gives that his hostility to the operation of the Convention as part of our domestic law is both long-standing and deep-seated. The position would have been very different if all that Lord McCluskey had done was to publish, say, an article in a legal journal drawing attention, in moderate language, to what he perceived to be the drawbacks of incorporating the Convention into our law. Judges, like other members of the public and other members of the legal profession, are entitled to criticise developments in our law, whether in the form of legislation or in the form of judicial decisions. Indeed criticism of particular legislative provisions or particular decisions is often to be found in judges' opinions. Similarly, judges may welcome particular developments in our law. It is well known that in their extra-judicial capacity many prominent judges – not only in England – publicly advocated incorporation of the Convention and equally publicly welcomed the Government's decision to incorporate. But what judges cannot do with impunity is to publish either criticism or praise of such a nature or in such language as to give rise to a legitimate apprehension that, when called upon in the course of their judicial duties to apply that particular branch of the law, they will not be able to do so impartially.[69]

[66] *Hoekstra* v. *H. M. Advocate* [2000] Scot.HC 32 at para. [18].
[67] *Hoekstra* v. *H. M. Advocate* [2000] Scot.HC 32 at para. [22].
[68] *Hoekstra* v. *H. M. Advocate* [2000] Scot.HC 32 at para. [24].
[69] *Hoekstra* v. *H. M. Advocate* [2000] Scot.HC 32 at para. [23].

The one-dimensional nature of judicial independence

So while the McCluskey case reveals that there are boundaries to judicial free speech, paradoxically it also reinforces the freedom of the judge to speak out on a wide range of questions. Paradoxical in the sense that the rule against bias seems to protect the right to express partisan or partial opinions before or after a case, provided it is done with a measure of restraint. Paradoxical, too, in the sense that the rule against bias in this sense is being used not to protect the impartiality of the judge, but effectively to protect the independence of the judiciary in the same way as the statutory procedure in the Sheriff Courts (Scotland) Act 1971 was used in the Thomson case. And paradoxical further in the sense that a framework of rules and principles based on the independence of the judiciary invites consideration of a much wider range of restraints which address not only the manner of expression but the fact of expression. At the moment the relationship between judicial independence and free speech is one-dimensional, creating expectations about the conduct of government ministers rather than expectations about the conduct of judges. Thus, by strong convention such criticism was forbidden and the few examples over the years of judges being attacked by the government served only to underline the strength of the convention.[70] There is a sense, however, that criticisms by ministers have been made with increasing frequency, as the principles of constitutional propriety appeared to change under the New Labour government. In one notable incident, the then Home Secretary (David Blunkett) was said to have 'implicitly criticised a judge in 2003 for upholding the right of six asylum-seekers to receive support from the National Asylum Support Service', writing a strongly-worded article under the headline 'It's time for judges to learn their place'.[71]

More recently, one of Mr Blunkett's successors as Home Secretary as well as the then Solicitor-General criticised the Cardiff Recorder for imposing a life sentence with a minimum tariff of five years and 108 days on a convicted paedophile (Craig Sweeney), while making it clear when passing sentence that the individual in question would be released only 'when and if there is no risk of you re-offending'. Joining in a media frenzy against the sentence (in which other politicians played a part), the Home Secretary attacked the judge on the ground that the sentence was too lenient, the Solicitor-General

[70] See Bradley and Ewing, *Constitutional and Administrative Law*, 15th edn., pp. 370–1.

[71] House of Lords Constitution Committee, 'Relations Between the Executive, Judiciary and Parliament', HL Paper 151, 2006–7, para. 44.

claiming on BBC television that the judge was wrong.[72] These concerns were reinforced by the fact that the criticisms of the Cardiff Recorder took place after the Constitutional Reform Act 2005 had come into force, which, as already pointed out, imposed a duty on the Lord Chancellor to defend the independence of the judiciary. In an important report of the House of Lords Constitution Committee, the Lord Chancellor's duty to defend was said to be stronger than the duty of all other ministers to uphold that independence, 'giving him a special enforcement role in relation to the rest of the government'.[73] In a review of this incident, the Committee concluded that:

> The Sweeney case was the first big test of whether the new relationship between the Lord Chancellor and the judiciary was working properly, and it is clear that there was a systemic failure. Ensuring that ministers do not impugn individual judges, and restraining and reprimanding those who do, is one of the most important duties of the Lord Chancellor.[74]

The Committee recommended that in order to prevent problems of this kind in the future, the *Ministerial Code* should be amended 'to include reference to the constitutional conventions which ought to govern public comment by ministers on judges'.[75]

This has not been done. It is, nevertheless, important that judges are protected from media criticism by politicians, and important too that the Lord Chancellor and other ministers are fully mindful of their constitutional and legal responsibilities. Indeed, in the view of the House of Lords Constitution Committee, 'the Lord Chancellor's duty, as the defender of judicial independence in the Cabinet, is both to ensure that ministers are aware of the need to avoid attacking individual judges and to reprimand them if they breach this principle'.[76] Such attacks serve only to diminish the role of the judge, they are often ill-informed and motivated by dubious concerns, and they tend to feed what has sometimes been vicious press comment.[77] Although there are notionally common law rules for dealing with the

[72] HL Paper 151, 2006–7, paras. 45–6. [73] HL Paper 151, 2006–7, para. 39.

[74] HL Paper 151, 2006–7, para. 49. [75] HL Paper 151, 2006–7, para. 50.

[76] HL Paper 151, 2006–7, para. 42.

[77] The House of Lords Constitution Committee reported that after the sentence in the *Sweeney* case, the *Sun* criticised 'the arrogance of judges in their mink-lined ivory towers who leave the rest of us to cope with the real crisis of soaring crime', adding that 'judges are a law unto themselves'. The *Daily Express* branded the judiciary as 'deluded, out-of-touch and frankly deranged', 'combining arrogance with downright wickedness', suggesting that 'our legal system has not only lost touch with public opinion but with natural justice itself . . . [sentencing] now bears no relation at all to the seriousness of the crime' (HL Paper 151, 2006–7, para. 46).

last,[78] these have generally fallen into disuse and it has been a long time since anyone was convicted for scurrilous abuse of a judge. But as already suggested, concerns about judicial independence cannot be one-dimensional, the duty to uphold the independence of the judiciary applies to both the government and the judges themselves. To this end, the Lord Chancellor has an obligation not only to ensure that ministers do not violate the principle, but also to ensure that judges do not do the same. While careless speech by ministers on popular television programmes may take them across the line, so may carefully constructed public speeches by judges on controversial subjects. It is not clear whether that responsibility of the Lord Chancellor is currently being fully discharged by allowing judges themselves to decide when it is appropriate to speak in public and in what circumstances. Nor is it clear whether the duty of the judges collectively to uphold judicial independence is fully met by a self-serving code of conduct and self-serving common law rules characterised principally by their elasticity.

Conclusion

The problems of frustrated politicians criticising judges perhaps reflects a great contradiction on the part of a government which helped to unleash judicial power, but was manifestly unprepared for what the consequences might be. A measure of that frustration is to be found in the memoirs of the architect of that power, with Tony Blair reflecting on the decision of the House of Lords in *A* v. *Home Secretary*[79] and the outspoken remarks of Lord Hoffmann that he could not 'credit how a sensible person could say anything quite so grossly stupid'.[80] Political attacks on judges are perhaps also a reflection of the extent to which the judicial role has been politicised in recent years, with judicial decisions sometimes irritating governments and sometimes creating difficulty for the effective implementation of government policy, however exaggerated, misguided or wrong these concerns might be. Nevertheless, it is clear that the constitutional changes since 1997 have soured the relationship between government and judiciary, and while

[78] See *R* v. *Gray* [1900] 2 QB 36; *R* v *New Statesman ex p. DPP* (1928) 44 TLR 301; *Ambard* v. *Attorney-General for Trinidad and Tobago* [1936] AC 322; and *R* v. *Metropolitan Police Commissioner ex p. Blackburn (No. 2)* [1968] 2 QB 150. See most recently, *Anwar Respondent* [2008] HCJAC 36, 2008 SLT 710.

[79] [2004] UKHL 56 (the so-called *Belmarsh* case in which the House of Lords ruled the detention without trial of international terrorist suspects to be incompatible with the ECHR. Lords Hoffmann and Scott expressed themselves in strong terms).

[80] T. Blair, *A Journey* (London: Random House, 2010), p. 568.

it is widely recognised that a measure of tension between the two branches of government is both desirable and healthy, it is also clear that new lines need to be drawn to define a new settlement in the relationship between the two branches of government.

While the conduct of government has rightly been subject to criticism (the House of Lords Constitution Committee being the most appropriate forum for such criticism), it is not clear whether in the long term the current rules on judicial free speech are set with sufficient humility about the propriety of the judicial role or whether the current focus on impartiality in legal proceedings is an adequate basis for extra-judicial conduct. This is not to say that *in extremis* the judges may need to speak out where they feel their institutional position is under threat or not treated with sufficient seriousness or gravity by the government – as in the manner of Lord Woolf in relation to at least some (though perhaps not all) of the content of his Squire lecture. But even here there are now clearly defined channels which ought to be used at least in the first instance for ventilating such concerns, with the Constitutional Reform Act 2005 having introduced a procedure whereby the 'chief justice of any part of the United Kingdom may lay before Parliament written representations on matters that appear to him to be matters of importance relating to the judiciary, or otherwise to the administration of justice, in that part of the United Kingdom'.

In other cases, the obligations relating to judicial independence raise questions about how far judges should be permitted to go in their extra-judicial activity and whether there is a need to get closer to the standards on display during the Thomson affair with which this chapter began. If impartiality is not the only constraint, there may be a need for clearer rules to determine the circumstances in which judges should be free to speak under cover of 'the law, the legal system, the administration of justice or related matters': it is not clear why a Court of Appeal judge should be free to advocate controversial restraints on civil liberties, while a Scottish sheriff should be sacked for advocating a referendum on home rule for Scotland at a time when a government bill (the Scotland Bill) was making precisely such arrangements. If – contrary to the argument in this chapter – impartiality is the only constraint, it is in any event not clear why litigants should be content with a process in which judges nail strong colours to the mast, whether before or after litigation has taken place. But perhaps what is needed above all is Guidelines that are not drafted by the people to whom they are designed to apply. No institution of government should have the power to make and administer its own rules. Not even the judges.

13

The criticism and speech of judges in the United States

CHARLES GARDNER GEYH

American judges live in interesting times. A confluence of events, some centuries in the making, others more recent, has put judges at the center of many of the most politically charged disputes in the United States, which has exposed them to withering criticism and proposals to curb their discretion from the political right, to a lesser extent from the political left, and from fringe groups that defy classification. American judges have bemoaned their plight, and with their implicit and sometimes explicit support, state and national bar organizations have created commissions, issued reports, and developed programs aimed at defending judges from attack. Private organizations have emerged to criticize court critics and align themselves with state and federal judiciaries to the end of promoting fair and impartial courts. Faced with opposition from court defenders who decry what they regard as unwarranted threats to the judiciary's independence, court critics have rejoined that they are merely seeking to promote meaningful judicial accountability to the public that judges serve.

For their part, judges themselves have acquired new, ill-defined rights to speak out on issues of the day, which has liberated them to an as yet uncertain extent from ethics restrictions on their speech and enabled them to respond more effectively to their critics. At the same time, it portends to thrust them further into the political limelight, thereby diminishing the differences that separate judges from public officials in the so-called "political branches" of government, and arguably making them even more inviting targets for their detractors.

The "freedom of speech" in the United States, as it applies to what judges and their critics say, is a potentially sprawling topic. It could well canvas the speech and expressive conduct of judges and their detractors in myriad contexts from the courtroom, to the newsroom, the bar-room, and the bedroom. This chapter, however, will focus on speech pertaining to the cases judges decide, and the flashpoints that have occurred in the public conversation between judges and court observers over the issues embedded in those cases. In so doing, it will de-emphasize speech and expressive conduct arising in the personal lives of judges that can get them into trouble with the public and disciplinary bodies: the drunken reveler on New Year's Eve who says things he should not; the spurned lover who threatens the object of her affection; or the avid golfer who joins a local country club that excludes women.

This chapter will tackle its topic in three parts. First, it will address the causes and effects of the recent campaign to criticize the decision-making and curb the discretion of state and federal judges. Second, it will discuss the role of judges in responding to the developments detailed in the first part of the chapter – the applicable ethics restrictions on judicial speech and the recently declared right of judges to announce their views, which may trump some ethics restrictions on judicial speech. Third, and finally, it will explore the likely impact of these events in the future.

The criticism of judges in the United States

The First Amendment to the US Constitution provides that Congress shall pass no law abridging the freedom of speech. The First Amendment has been read broadly to prohibit not only Congress, but also the President and administrative agencies from abridging the freedom of speech.[1] In addition, the Supreme Court has interpreted the Fourteenth Amendment, which provides that "no state shall deprive its citizens of life liberty or property without due process of law," as rendering the First Amendment freedom of speech applicable to state governments.[2] In short, with exceptions largely irrelevant to this context, the right of citizens to criticize the decisions of state and federal judges is nearly absolute.[3]

Ostensibly, judges have a common law right to sue their detractors for defamation. As a legal matter, however, judges are public figures, and as

[1] J. Kinsler, "Circuit-Specific Application of the Internal Revenue Code: An Unconstitutional Tax," (2004) 81 *Denver University Law Review* 113 at 136.

[2] *Gitlow* v. *New York* 268 US 652 (1925), 666.

[3] For a general discussion of exceptions to the first amendment, see E. Chemerinsky, *Constitutional Law: Principles and Policies*, 3rd edn. (New York: Aspen, 1997); L. H. Tribe, *American Constitutional Law*, 3rd edn. (St. Paul: West Publishing, 1999).

such are entitled to recover for defamation only if their critics' statements were knowingly false or made with reckless disregard of the truth – an exacting standard calculated to give breathing room to the First Amendment.[4] As a practical matter, a judge who sued his or her critics would expose him- or herself to accusations of being too thin-skinned and intent on silencing his or her detractors, which would likely offset whatever reputational gains could be achieved by a favorable verdict. In short, defamation is an unattractive and, hence, largely unused remedy.

The net effect is that, apart from criminal threats on a judge's life, the "right" to criticize judges is largely unconstrained by law. The limits of appropriate criticism are thus circumscribed largely by less formal norms. The primary norms at issue relate to judicial independence and judicial accountability: the desirability of protecting judges from criticism that could interfere with their independent, impartial judgment, on the one hand, and the desirability of subjecting judges to criticism that could hold them better accountable to the public they serve, on the other.

Judicial independence and accountability do have a footing in constitutional law, and to that extent are more than "informal" norms. For example, the independence of federal judges is protected by a guarantee of tenure "during good behavior" and a prohibition on diminution of salary, while judicial accountability is promoted by an impeachment mechanism.[5] In state systems, independence is often guaranteed by constitutions that explicitly provide for a separate and independent judicial branch of government, while accountability is typically promoted through some form of popular judicial election.[6] As distinguished from simple criticism, courts have ruled that imposing some controls on judges or judicial systems – such as mandatory sentencing guidelines – is unconstitutional, while the propriety of other controls, such as stripping courts of subject-matter jurisdiction to hear controversial issues, is still debated.[7] When it comes to criticism *per se*, however, including criticism embodied in threats to control the courts in ways that, if implemented,

[4] *New York Times Co.* v. *Sullivan* 376 US 254 (1964); Chemerinsky, *Constitutional Law*, pp. 850–2.

[5] United States Constitution, Art. III, s. 1; Art. IV.

[6] C. G. Geyh, "Elastic Nature of Judicial Independence," in G. Griller (ed.), *The Improvement of the Administration of Justice*, 7th edn. (Chicago, IL: ABA Publishing, 2002), p. 167.

[7] *United States* v. *Booker* 543 US 220 (2005); E. Chemerinsky, *Federal Jurisdiction*, 5th edn. (New York: Aspen, 2007), p. 173.

might or might not be constitutional, the debate tends to focus more on whether the criticism is out of line, than on whether it is unconstitutional. For that reason, the debate over when healthy, accountability promoting criticism degenerates into independence threatening intimidation typically takes place above the constitutional floor.

Criticism of judges and their decisions is, at one level, perpetual: critics will vent whenever a disagreeable decision is reported. At another level, however, it is cyclical: concerted campaigns to control perceived judicial excesses come and go in waves driven by political realignments. When a new political order replaces the old, holdover judges of the old regime may be targeted by leaders and followers of the new. Accountability (or its equivalent) is the watchword of those who seek to replace or chasten judges of the former regime, while independence is the *nom de guerre* for those who defend judges from attack. Gradually, equilibrium is restored as holdover judges become outnumbered by new judges, court critics lose interest, and court defenders gain ground.

There have been at least half a dozen such cycles in American history:[8] when President Thomas Jefferson ushered in the first transition of political power from the Federalists to the Republicans in 1802; when President Andrew Jackson rode a populist wave into the White House in 1828; when the "Radical Republicans" took control of Congress in the aftermath of the Civil War; when the Populists and Progressives challenged conservative courts at the turn of the twentieth century; when Franklin D. Roosevelt took on the Supreme Court whose decisions threatened his New Deal agenda in the 1930s; and when critics challenged perceived excesses of the Warren Court, culminating in the election of President Richard Nixon in 1968. To explore the criticism of courts today, however, this chapter focuses on the most recent cycle of anti-court sentiment in the United States. While the cycle began in earnest in the mid-1990s, when the Republican Party regained control of Congress in 1994, its roots run deeper, with at least five underlying causes.

First, state and federal courts have gradually moved more directly into the political spotlight. Commentators have variously written of a "litigation explosion" in which litigants have sought relief from courts that they could not get from legislatures, and a "law explosion" in which legislatures have greatly expanded the range of statutory remedies

[8] C. G. Geyh, *When Courts & Congress Collide: The Struggle for Control of America's Judicial System* (Ann Arbor, MN: University of Michigan Press, 2006), pp. 23–50.

available to litigants. In either case, it has put the courts in the position of implementing often controversial public policies.[9] At the federal level, the frequency with which the US Supreme Court has declared Acts of Congress and state legislatures to be unconstitutional has increased significantly over time, thereby inviting attacks from disgruntled legislators and the voters they represent. At the state level, as the US Supreme Court became more conservative and less sympathetic to the causes of social reform groups in the last quarter of the twentieth century, reformers turned increasingly to state courts for relief. The resulting "rediscovery of state constitutions" has put state supreme courts at the front and center of many national debates as never before.[10]

Second, the political reawakening of evangelical conservatives, beginning in the 1970s, has polarized American politics and sometimes demonized American judges. Issues on the agenda of evangelical conservatives are among the most hotly contested in American politics and include ending abortion rights, prohibiting gay marriage, and permitting prayer and other religious observances in public schools and public places more generally. For Christian conservatives, these agenda items are moral absolutes, which reduce, if not eliminate, opportunities to avoid confrontation through compromise with the social reform groups who oppose their agenda, and infuse criticism of judicial rulings adverse to their cause with a religious fervor.[11]

Third, the public has gradually internalized the lessons of legal realism and become more skeptical of claims that independent judges follow the law. The legal realists of the early twentieth century challenged the proposition that judicial decision-making was a mechanical process in which judges simply applied the law; rather, they argued, judges, like others, were influenced by their backgrounds – their sense of fairness informed by their education, experiences, ideologies, and so on. As a movement, legal realism ran its course in the 1930s, but it continued to influence the way scholars in other disciplines (such as political science) and, ultimately, the public think about what judges do. Today, a majority of Americans surveyed continues to think that it is very important for

[9] Whether this is a problem of the courts' own making, or one that has been thrust upon them by litigants and legislatures, remains disputed and beyond the scope of this chapter. See *Justice in Jeopardy*, American Bar Association Commission on the 21st Century Judiciary, 2003, pp. 13–14.

[10] ABA, *Justice in Jeopardy*, p. 15.

[11] Geyh, *When Courts & Congress Collide*, p. 272; J. Morone, *Hellfire Nation: The Politics of Sin in American History* (New Haven, CT: Yale University Press, 2004).

judges to decide cases on the basis of the law and facts alone, and yet a majority also thinks that judges are deeply ideological and often base decisions on their feelings despite saying that they are following the law.[12] While this has not translated into a crisis of confidence in American courts, it has made the public more receptive to the arguments of court critics that judges are too often captive to ideological influences.

Fourth, intermediate appellate courts have gradually become courts of last resort in most cases, which has limited the dockets of highly visible supreme courts to fewer, more controversial and politically charged cases. In the federal system, appeals as of right to the Supreme Court were eliminated in the 1980s, which has left the court to hear a much smaller number of cases: cases in which the law is typically uncertain, the outcome is hotly contested, and where the opportunities for ideology to influence the decisions of the justices are correspondingly greater.[13] A similar phenomenon has occurred in state systems, as states gradually established intermediate appellate courts throughout the twentieth century and reduced or eliminated mandatory appeals as a means to relieve docket congestion for their supreme courts.[14] As a consequence, the flagship courts for the states and nation publish a disproportionate number of divisive opinions on politically charged topics that invite criticism. At the same time, because intermediate appellate courts have become the courts of last resort in the vast majority of cases, they too have become more attractive targets for criticism.

Fifth, the Internet has enabled information about judicial decisions to be communicated quickly and unfiltered. Controversial decisions by remote courts that would never have come to national attention through traditional media can be communicated instantaneously to a worldwide audience of critics affiliated with court-watch groups. Moreover, the Internet allows for reporting and commentary on cases, both prominent and obscure, that is unchecked by journalistic conventions or standards. The Internet has thereby created a new medium for incendiary criticism of judicial decisions.

[12] K. Bybee, "The Rule of Law is Dead! Long Live the Rule of Law!," in C. Geyh (ed.), *What's Law Got To Do With It: What Judges Do, Why They Do It, and What's at Stake* (Palo Alto, CA: Stanford University Press, forthcoming 2011), p. 34.

[13] 28 USC 1254; M. Cordray, "The Supreme Court's Plenary Docket" (2001) *Washington & Lee Law Review* 58 at 751.

[14] P. Carrington, D. Meador, and M. Rosenberg, *Justice on Appeal* (St. Paul: West Publishing, 1976), p. 150.

These disparate developments have contributed to a new wave of criticism directed at the US courts. Most notable, perhaps, has been the national campaign against "liberal judicial activism," launched by social and political conservatives in the mid-1990s. An inaugural event in this campaign was a controversial ruling by federal District Judge Harold Baer, suppressing evidence in a drug case.[15] The ruling was issued as the 1996 election cycle was getting underway, and provided Republican presidential candidate (and then senator) Robert Dole with an opportunity to criticize liberal judges appointed by incumbent President Bill Clinton. House and Senate Republicans joined Dole in threatening the District Judge with impeachment if he did not reverse his ruling, and the President's press secretary suggested that the President might ask for the judge's resignation if he did not reverse his ruling. The judge reversed his ruling.

In the years that followed, House Republicans threatened to impeach "liberal activist" judges; they introduced legislation to deprive federal courts of subject-matter jurisdiction to hear cases on controversial topics such as gay marriage, public displays of the Ten Commandments, and the constitutionality of the phrase "one nation, under God" in the Pledge of Allegiance; and they threatened to cut the judiciary's budget and to disestablish uncooperative courts.[16] In the Senate, after a federal judge's family was murdered in 2005 by a party who appeared before the judge, one Republican senator effectively attributed the event to judicial activism, asserting that when "judges are making political decisions, yet are unaccountable to the public . . . it builds up and builds up and builds up to the point where some people engage in violence."[17]

In a most peculiar episode in 2005, Congress intervened in a dispute between the husband and parents of a long-comatose woman, Theresa Schiavo. Florida state courts found that she was in a persistent vegetative state, sided with the husband, and ordered the woman's feeding tube removed. Responding to angry social conservatives who characterized the Florida decision as state-sanctioned murder, Congress enacted special legislation conferring jurisdiction on the federal courts to hear the *Schiavo* case. When the federal courts quickly affirmed the state court ruling, sponsors of the legislation were furious: the federal courts had

[15] *United States* v. *Bayless* 921 F.Supp. 211, SDNY 1996.

[16] Geyh, *When Courts & Congress Collide*, p. 3.

[17] M. Dowd, "Judge Lefkow: My Family Lost Its Safety," *Fox News*, 2005.

"thumbed their nose at Congress and the President," declared the House majority leader, and warned that "the time will come for the men responsible for this to answer for their behavior."[18]

At the state level, disgruntled legislatures have cut judicial budgets in retaliation for unwelcome judicial rulings.[19] A number of states have proposed to end or curtail judicial review.[20] And judges have been threatened with impeachment or discipline for rendering adverse decisions. In 2005, for example, shortly after the Massachusetts Supreme Court held that the state's constitution guaranteed the right of gays to marry, several state legislators filed a petition to remove the court's Chief Justice. The petition asserted that the Chief Justice had predetermined the outcome of the case and imposed pressure on her fellow justices to join her decision in an effort to "promote their values and those of 'their like-minded friends in the communities they socialize in'."[21]

Apart from threats by public officials, conservative pundits have berated "activist" state and federal judges for decisions on a range of issues, from abortion rights and gay marriage, to criminal sentencing and the death penalty because, in the words of one commentator, "judges have become the tool of an outlandish liberal fringe that has violated the graves of the Founding Fathers."[22] Various websites have done the same – one going as far as to imply that judges who uphold abortion rights should be assassinated.[23] Religious organizations have hosted annual prayer vigils decrying judicial activism and promoting the selection of conservative judges, one explaining that "the future of the judiciary is perhaps the most important domestic priority facing the country at this time."[24]

One startling grass-roots initiative was the so-called Judicial Accountability Initiative Law (JAIL) movement, which formed chapters in several states, and launched a successful petition drive to place a

[18] C. Hulse and D. Kirkpatrick, "Even Death Does not Quiet Harsh Political Fight," *New York Times*, April 1, 2005, p. A1.

[19] J. Douglas and R. Hartley, "The Politics of Court Budgeting in the States: Is Judicial Independence Threatened by the Budgetary Process?" (2003) 63 *Public Administration Review* (July/August), 441.

[20] E. F. Van Tassel, "Challenges to Constitutional Decisions," in *Justice in Jeopardy*, Appendix E, pp. 7–8.

[21] S. Helman, "Romney Rips SJC's Justices on Values," *The Boston Globe*, 2005, p. 1.

[22] C. Tucker, "Religious Extremists Seek Their Own 'Activist Judges,'" Charleston, *Sunday Gazette-Mail*, April 3, p. 3.

[23] "The Nuremburg Files," www.christiangallery.com/atrocity/index.html, p 1.

[24] J. Lampman, "Bringing the Case Against Judges," *The Christian Science Monitor*, 2005, p. 1.

proposed constitutional amendment on the South Dakota ballot in 2006. The measure would have created special grand juries to evaluate the conduct of judges and strip them of immunity from civil suit or criminal prosecution if they were found to have deliberately disregarded the law.[25] The measure was resoundingly defeated, in large part because of an opposition campaign coordinated by the South Dakota Bar, which took the position that "exposing judges to a grand jury every time a litigant may disagree with them is just an attempt to intimidate judges and improperly influence justice."[26]

Liberal attacks on conservative judges have been more muted, with one glaring exception. The Supreme Court's decision in *Bush* v. *Gore*,[27] which split five to four along ideological lines, effectively declared George W. Bush the winner of the 2000 presidential election and provoked a firestorm of criticism from the political left.[28] For the most part, however, liberal critics of conservative judges have concentrated their efforts in the federal judicial selection process.

Some of the most virulent criticism of judges has occurred in the course of judicial selection.[29] In the federal system, circuit and Supreme Court nominees of President George W. Bush were branded conservative extremists by Democratic senators, who exploited a range of procedural devices – most notably the filibuster – to thwart confirmation. Republican senators (when they were in the majority) threatened to retaliate by ending filibuster rights, and when Bill Clinton was president, challenged his nominees as "liberal activists" and delayed hearings and votes on their confirmation.

In state systems, judicial election campaigns have been the forum of choice for some of the most strident court-directed animus. In states that elect judges in partisan and non-partisan races, the rates at which incumbent Supreme Court justices are challenged has been increasing over time.[30] In recent years, incumbent judges have been criticized, challenged, and sometimes defeated for their votes in cases raising

[25] V. Consul, "Thinking Boldly . . . J.A.I.L.ing Judges," *Nevada Lawyer* 14 (2006) 8.

[26] R. Acello, "South Dakota to Vote on Putting Judges on Trial," *ABA Journal*, e-Report, January 13, 2006.

[27] 531 US 98 (2000).

[28] V. Bugliosi, "None Dare Call it Treason," *The Nation*, February 5, 2001.

[29] Geyh, *When Courts & Congress Collide*, pp. 212–22.

[30] M. G. Hall, "Competition as Accountability in State Supreme Court Elections," in M. Streb (ed.), *Running for Judge: The Rising Political, Financial, and Legal Stakes of Judicial Elections* (New York University Press, 2007), p. 172.

issues from abortion and the death penalty, to gay marriage and water rights.[31]

The more significant development in state judicial selection, perhaps, has been a dramatic increase in the amount of money spent in Supreme (and sometimes lower) Court races.[32] Multi-million dollar campaigns, once unheard of, are now relatively commonplace.[33] The driving force behind this influx has been the "tort reform" issue.[34] Groups intent on limiting the liability of defendants in tort cases, most notably the US Chamber of Commerce, have spent enormous sums on like-minded judicial candidates, while pro-plaintiff groups, most notably trial lawyers, have done the same for their candidates.[35] The result has been an expensive, high-stakes battle for control of state supreme courts. While some of the money at issue has been contributed to the candidates directly, much of it has been spent by the groups themselves in independent campaigns.[36] In these independent campaigns, advertising dollars are sometimes spent attacking judges for their decisions on tort-related issues or for their alliance with the interest groups sponsoring their campaigns.[37] It is not uncommon, however, to see tort reform groups run attack adverts against the candidate they oppose on unrelated issues, such as crime or victims' rights, that are more likely to resonate with the electorate.[38]

The role of judges in responding to criticism

The authority of judges to respond to their critics is governed by ethics rules, modeled in varying degrees upon the American Bar Association's (ABA) Model Code of Judicial Conduct, which was first promulgated in

[31] C. G. Geyh, "Why Judicial Elections Stink" (2003) 61 *The Ohio State Law Journal* 43 at 49–50.

[32] See C. Bonneau, "The Dynamics of Campaign Spending in State Supreme Court Elections," in M. Streb (ed.), *Running for Judge: The Rising Political, Financial, and Legal Stakes of Judicial Elections* (New York University Press, 2007), pp. 63–4; R. Caulfield, "The Changing Tone of Judicial Campaigns as a Result of White," in Streb (ed.), *Running for Judge*, p. 37; M. Streb, "The Study of Judicial Elections," in Streb (ed.), *Running for Judge*, pp. 1–2.

[33] Streb, "The Study of Judicial Elections," in Streb (ed.), *Running for Judge*, p. 2.

[34] D. Goldberg, "Interest Group Participation in Judicial Elections," in Streb (ed.), p. 80.

[35] Goldberg, "Interest Group Participation in Judicial Elections," in Streb (ed.), p. 78.

[36] Goldberg, "Interest Group Participation in Judicial Elections," in Streb (ed.), pp. 78–9.

[37] Goldberg, "Interest Group Participation in Judicial Elections," in Streb (ed.), pp. 81–2.

[38] Goldberg, "Interest Group Participation in Judicial Elections," in Streb (ed.), pp. 82–3; E. Heller and M. Ballard, "Hard-Fought, Big Money Judicial Races: U.S. Chamber of Commerce Enters Fray with Ad Money," *National Law Journal*, 2000, p. 42.

1972, and subsequently revised in 1990 and 2007.[39] In state systems, violation of applicable ethics rules subjects judges to discipline, ranging from private reprimands to removal from office.[40] In the federal system, the Code of Conduct for United States judges is stated in hortatory terms, but when disregarded can, in appropriate cases, lead to discipline (limited to means short of removal, given that impeachment is the sole means that the US Constitution provides for removal of federal judges).

On the one hand, codes of conduct authorize judges to teach, speak, write, and testify before governmental bodies on law-related matters, which enable them to speak out on the legal issues of the day.[41] On the other hand, codes constrain judicial speech in significant ways, and curtail the authority of judges to respond to their critics.

The preamble to the 2007 Model Code reflects its animating principles:

> Judges should maintain the dignity of judicial office at all times, and avoid both impropriety and the appearance of impropriety in their professional and personal lives. They should aspire at all times to conduct that ensures the greatest possible public confidence in their independence, impartiality, integrity, and competence.

These principles have given rise to a number of rules that restrict judicial speech, to the end of promoting judicial independence, impartiality, and integrity. Model rule 2.10 is of the most immediate relevance. Section (A) of that rule imposes significant limits on what judges can say about pending and impending cases:

> A judge shall not make any public statement that might reasonably be expected to affect the outcome or impair the fairness of a matter pending or impending in any court, or make any nonpublic statement that might substantially interfere with a fair trial or hearing.

Note that as written, the rule restricts judges from commenting on cases pending not only in their courts, but in *any* court, so that judges are foreclosed from opining on pending cases in other jurisdictions and

[39] The precursor to the *Code of Judicial Conduct* was the *Canons of Judicial Ethics*, which the ABA published in 1924. Unlike the *Code*, which established enforceable standards of conduct, the *Canons* were intended as hortatory guidelines: J. Alfini, S. Lubet, J. Shaman, and C. G. Geyh, *Judicial Conduct and Ethics*, 4th edn. (Newark: Matthew Bender, 2007), section 1.03.

[40] Alfini, Lubet, Shaman, and Geyh, *Judicial Conduct and Ethics*, section 1.04.

[41] *Model Code of Judicial Conduct*, rule 3.1, Comment 1; rule 3.2.

court systems.[42] Rule 2.10(E) adds that "subject to the requirements of paragraph (A), a judge may respond directly or through a third party to allegations in the media or elsewhere concerning a judge's conduct in the matter." Although section (E) gives judges some latitude to respond to their critics, that latitude is subject to section (A), which is generally understood to forbid judges from commenting outside of the courtroom on pending cases, other than to explain court procedures.[43] While there are cases in which courts have declined to sanction judges for responding to their critics in pending cases, such cases remain exceptional.[44] Rather, the norm remains for judges to let their written opinions do the talking, and otherwise avoid responding directly to their critics. As the Chief Judge of New York's highest court explained:

> To secure an impartial forum, even for their most vocal critics, and to assure the dignity of the judicial process, judges by and large must stay out of the fray. They do not duel with public officials about the correctness of their decisions; they do not conduct press conferences about cases; and they have no call-in radio and television shows to explain their rulings. They rely on their decisions, whether written or oral, to speak for themselves.[45]

Given longstanding norms against judges answering their critics, critics may challenge judges who buck the norm. Thus, for example, when presidential candidate Senator Robert Dole threatened District Judge Harold Baer with impeachment for suppressing evidence in a cocaine case, Second Circuit Judge Jon O. Newman (among others) criticized the threats as inimical to judicial independence.[46] Dole responded to Newman's statement by chiding the judge for commenting on the matter, asserting that "Judges, unlike elected officials such as Senators, perform what your statement calls their 'important responsibilities in a constitutional democracy' in the courtroom, not in the court of public opinion."[47]

With respect to statements concerning future, as distinct from pending or impending, cases, rule 2.10(B) prohibits judges from making

[42] Alfini, Lubet, Shaman, and Geyh, *Judicial Conduct and Ethics*, section 10.06D.

[43] Rule 2.10(D) states that "notwithstanding the restrictions in paragraph (A), a judge may make statements in the course of official duties, may explain court procedures, and may comment on any proceeding in which the judge is a litigant in a personal capacity."

[44] D. M. Schaffzin, "Memorandum on Ethical Constraints," in *Uncertain Justice: Politics and America's Courts* (New York: The Century Foundation Press, 2000), pp. 173, 176–83.

[45] J. Kaye, "Safeguarding a Crown Jewel: Judicial Independence and Lawyer Criticism of Courts" (1997) 25 *Hofstra Law Review* 703 at 712.

[46] J. Newman, "The Judge Baer Controversy" (1997) *Judicature* 158.

[47] Newman, "The Judge Baer Controversy," p. 161.

"pledges, promises or commitments that are inconsistent with the impartial performance of the adjudicative duties of judicial office" in regard to "cases, controversies, or issues likely to come before the court." As discussed below, this restriction leaves room for judges to announce their views on issues likely to arise in future cases, subject to the uncertain lines that separate an announcement of views from a pledge, promise or commitment, and a future case from an impending one.

While not a focus of this chapter, it is worth noting that ethics codes circumscribe the rights of judges to express their views or associate themselves with others in myriad other ways. Rule 1.2 operates as a guiding principle that regulates judicial speech and conduct when the judge is on and off duty: "A judge shall act at all times in a manner that promotes public confidence in the independence, integrity, and impartiality of the judiciary, and shall avoid impropriety and the appearance of impropriety." The judge's freedom to criticize participants in the litigation process is circumscribed by rule 2.8(B), which states that "a judge shall be patient, dignified, and courteous to litigants, jurors, witnesses, lawyers, court staff, and others with whom the judge deals in an official capacity." Rule 2.8(C) singles out jury verdicts for special protection, stating that "a judge shall not commend or criticize jurors for their verdict other than in a court order or opinion in a proceeding." Rule 3.2 prohibits judges from testifying before governmental bodies except on specified subject matter; rule 3.5 prohibits judges from using or disclosing non-public information acquired in a judicial capacity; and rule 3.6 prohibits judges from affiliating themselves with organizations that practice invidious discrimination. Finally, Canon 4 imposes significant restrictions on a judge's political speech: subject to exceptions (depending on how they are selected), judges must not make speeches on behalf of political organizations, publicly endorse or oppose other candidates, identify themselves as candidates of a political organization, or knowingly or recklessly make false or misleading statements.[48]

With respect to public employees generally, the First Amendment limits the authority of governmental employers to discipline or remove employees for their speech on matters of public interest relevant to their work. As the Supreme Court explained in the context of a case involving the dismissal of a public school teacher for publishing a letter critical of his school board: "The problem in any case is to arrive at a balance between the interests of the [employee] as a citizen, in commenting upon

[48] *Model Code of Judicial Conduct*, rule 4.1.

matters of public concern and the interest of the State, as an employer, in promoting the efficiency of the public services it performs through its employees."[49]

As far as judges are concerned, however, it has generally been accepted that the state's interest in preserving judicial impartiality, independence, and integrity justifies wide-ranging restrictions on judicial speech and association, and that judges must accept such restrictions as the price of being a judge. As one treatise on judicial conduct explains:

> There are many First Amendment protections that are available to ordinary citizens but that judges must forgo upon assuming office. For example, judges are prevented from endorsing political candidates, a practice that lies at the very heart of the First Amendment. They also may not solicit charitable contributions, hold office in certain organizations, or discuss certain pending or impending litigation. All of these activities would be protected by the Constitution if undertaken by members of the public, but they are prohibited to judges for the purpose of insuring the dignity, integrity, and impartiality of the judiciary . . . [I]n order to foster the proper functioning of our courts, it is necessary for those who take the bench to covenant to adhere to "standards of conduct more stringent than those acceptable for others."[50]

There are, however, limits to the state's authority to restrict judicial speech in the name of promoting judicial impartiality, independence, and integrity. At issue in *Republican Party of Minnesota* v. *White*[51] was an ethics rule in the Minnesota Code of Judicial Conduct, fashioned after a clause in the 1972 Model Code of Judicial Conduct, which forbade judicial candidates from announcing their views on disputed legal and political issues. Minnesota argued that the rule was needed to preserve the impartiality of judicial candidates who would later decide the issues upon which they took positions as candidates. The Supreme Court disagreed and declared the "announce clause" unconstitutional. Because the rule imposed a content-based restriction on a judge's speech, the court explained, it could survive constitutional scrutiny only if it was narrowly tailored to serve a compelling state interest. Here, the court reasoned, barring judicial candidates from announcing their views on disputed issues was not narrowly tailored to promote impartiality: if impartiality meant a lack of bias against parties, the rule did not directly promote impartiality because it prohibited speech about issues, not parties; and if

49 *Pickering* v. *Board of Education* 391 US 563 (1968) at 568.
50 Alfini, Lubet, Shaman, and Geyh, *Judicial Conduct and Ethics*, section 10.06A.
51 536 US 765 (2002).

impartiality meant open-mindedness, the rule was under-inclusive, because it barred speech on legal and political issues during election campaigns, but not before or after.

The reach of the Supreme Court's decision in *White* remains unclear. Broadly read, *White* implies that every code of conduct restriction on judicial speech must survive the exacting test of strict scrutiny, which bodes ill for many rules limiting judicial speech and association. Read narrowly, *White* simply gutted a vague and excessive ban (so vague and excessive that the ABA had removed a comparable clause from its 1990 Model Code) on election-related speech, where the need for robust First Amendment protection is arguably greatest.

In the years since, the lower courts have been called upon to apply *White* to other rules and in different settings, with inconsistent results. Some courts have invalidated rules barring judges from making pledges, promises, or commitments;[52] others have upheld them.[53] Some courts have struck down rules prohibiting judges from engaging in partisan activities of various kinds;[54] others have upheld them.[55] Some courts have invalidated rules that prohibited judges from soliciting campaign contributions from donors directly.[56] At least one circuit has held that rules prohibiting judicial candidates from making false or misleading statements are overly broad and unconstitutional.[57] Most cases applying *White* have concerned rules restricting judicial speech or association in the context of judicial elections. One important exception was a Mississippi case in which the state supreme court held, in light of *White*, that it was unconstitutional to discipline a judge for writing a letter to his local newspaper arguing that gays and lesbians should be institutionalized.[58]

At a minimum, however, *White* made clear that judges have a right to take public positions on disputed legal issues they are likely to decide – at

52 *Duwe* v. *Alexander* 490 F.Supp. 2d 968 (WD Wis. 2007); *North Dakota Family Alliance, Inc* v. *Bader* 361 F.Supp.2d 1021 (DND 2005); *Family Trust Found of Ky* v. *Wolnitzek* 345 F.Supp.2d 672 (ED Ky. 2004).

53 *In re Kinsey* 842 So.2d 77 (Fla. 2003), cert. denied, 540 US 825 (2003); *In re Watson* 794 NE 2d 1 (NY 2003).

54 *Republican Party of Minnesota* v. *White*, 361 F. 3d 1035 (8th Cir. 2004); *In the Matter of William A. Vincent, Jr*, 172 P.3d 605 (NM 2007); *Carey* v. *Wolnitzek* No. 3:06-cv-00036, 2006 WL 2916814 (ED Ky. October 10, 2006).

55 *Simes* v. *Arkansas Judicial Discipline & Disability Comm'n* 247 SW 3d 876 (Ark 2007).

56 *Kansas Judicial Watch* v. *Stout* 440 F.Supp. 2d 1209 (D Kan 2006).

57 *Weaver* v. *Bonner* 309 F. 3d 1312 (11th Cir., 2002).

58 *Mississippi Commission on Judicial Performance* v. *Wilkerson* 867 So. 2d 1006 (Miss. 2004).

least with respect to matters that are not pending or impending. The Supreme Court's five to four decision in *White* notwithstanding, many state judges remain concerned that judicial candidates who take positions on matters likely to come before them later undermine the appearance, if not the reality, of their impartiality and remain loath to share their views.[59] *White* does not *require* judges to state their positions on issues of the day, but it puts pressure on them to do so when interest groups submit questionnaires soliciting the candidates' views, accompanied by express or implied threats to campaign against candidates who do not comply. Unsurprisingly, then, states that have reacted to *White* by relaxing their restrictions on judicial speech the most, are witnessing campaigns that turn, to an increasing extent, on debates over the legal issues those judges are likely to decide.[60]

Ultimately, *White* is a product of, and contributor to, the political currents that have shaped the most recent cycle of anti-court sentiment. Underlying *White* is a perspective shared by many court critics – that judges are not all that different from other "politicians." In *White*, the court's majority accused the dissent of "greatly exaggerating the difference between judicial and legislative elections." The majority reasoned that:

> Complete separation of the judiciary from the enterprise of "representative government" might have some truth in those countries where judges neither make law themselves nor set aside the laws enacted by the legislature. It is not a true picture of the American system. Not only do state-court judges possess the power to "make" common law, but they have the immense power to shape the States' constitutions as well.[61]

Insofar as the differences between judges and other public officials is illusory, so, too, arguably, is the justification for judicial independence. In other words, to the extent that independent judges are not uniquely committed to following the law – to the extent that they, like other politicians, are influenced by their ideological preferences – why should they be any freer from direct political accountability for their views than other public officials?

59 P. White, "Preserving the Legacy: A Tribute to Chief Justice Harry L. Carrico, One Who Exalted Judicial Independence" (2004) *University of Richmond Law Review* 38 at 624; B. Ogunro, "How Can the Integrity of Judicial Elections Be Safeguarded After White?" (2003) 20 *Communications Lawyer* 21.

60 Caulfield, "The Changing Tone of Judicial Campaigns as a Result of White," in Streb (ed.), *Running for Judge*, pp. 55–6.

61 *Republican Party of Minnesota* v. *White*, 536 US 765 at 784 (2002).

The future

There is an irony underlying the American debate over judges and their decisions. Those most critical of judges are often the most keen to see judges defend themselves and their decisions, while those most inclined to think that judges have been unfairly maligned are the most apt to retain restrictions on judges' authority to fight back. Court critics are deeply skeptical of the notion that independent judges can be trusted to follow the law, and regard the purported differences between judges and other elected officials as overblown. If judges are subjected to the rough and tumble of the political process, it will increase the likelihood that the views judges bring to the bench are acceptable to their "constituents." To ensure that the public and their elected representatives know where their judges stand on the issues of the day, enabling judges to debate those issues and defend their decisions is critical.

The legal establishment, in contrast, has decried efforts to make "politicians" of judges and has sought to "depoliticize" or "take politics out" of their selection and oversight. Court defenders worry that subjecting the decisions of judges to public or political controls will undermine judges' impartiality and lead them to do what is popular, rather than what the law requires. And so they have struggled to keep judges and their decisions insulated from such controls, in part by preserving norms against judges announcing or defending their views outside of the courtroom, by retaining rules restricting judicial speech and association, and by continuing to call for an end to judicial elections.

Looking toward the future, it is probably safe to say that "depoliticizing" the judiciary is not a viable option. Over a century ago, Roscoe Pound decried "putting courts into politics," but attributed the phenomenon to "an age in transition," that would pass with time.[62] A century later, judicial politics remains a feature in the landscape of American government that is, if anything, even more prominent. Cyclical, partisan attacks on judges continue apace. Despite recurrent calls to evaluate nominees to the federal bench on the basis of merit alone, nominee ideology has become a focal point of the confirmation process. In state systems, the mid-twentieth century movement to "depoliticize" judicial selection by replacing contested elections with "merit selection" systems (in which judges are appointed from a commission-approved pool of

[62] R. Pound, "The Causes of Popular Dissatisfaction with the Administration of Justice" (1906) 40 *American Law Review* 729.

candidates and later stand for retention election) has stalled, in part because merit selection systems themselves are seen as politicized.

Quietly, almost imperceptibly, the legal establishment has begun to recognize that judicial politics is a force to be managed, rather than a pestilence to be exterminated. While deeply concerned about politically motivated attacks on judges, the ABA and other organizations have applauded rather than condemned "criticism" as such, and have focused their efforts on discouraging threats and intimidation. Recognizing the inevitability of unfair criticism, they have sought to counter, rather than end it, by proposing the establishment of bar and citizen groups that will respond to unjust criticism of judges when it arises – an approach that circumvents the ethical dilemmas that occur when targeted judges respond for themselves. And while the ABA remains opposed to the contested election of judges, it has reoriented its focus toward ameliorating what it regards as the baneful effects of elections by, for example, proposing public financing for judicial campaigns – in recognition of the political reality that in the current climate, judicial elections are here to stay.

Most telling of court defenders' recent efforts to manage judicial politics in lieu of purging politics from the process is the campaign for disqualification reform. Rather than prevent judges from taking positions on legal issues in judicial campaigns and otherwise, which the Supreme Court has ruled contravenes the First Amendment, the ABA has proposed to let judges speak, but require them to withdraw later from any case in which their prior statements call their impartiality into question. In response to *White*, the ABA revised its Model Code of Judicial Conduct in 2003 to require disqualification when "The judge, while a judge or a judicial candidate, has made a public statement, other than in a court proceeding, judicial decision, or opinion, that commits or appears to commit the judge to reach a particular result or rule in a particular way in the proceeding or controversy." Eleven states to date have since adopted this clause.[63]

In a similar vein, the ABA Model Code calls for disqualification of a judge when litigants or lawyers who contribute more than a specified amount to a judge's election campaign later appear before that judge – an approach that allows the political process to move forward while seeking to ameliorate its effects on litigation. While two states employ related

[63] Judicial Disqualification Project, "Taking Judicial Disqualification Seriously" *Judicature* 92 (July–August 2008), p. 15.

provisions, none to date have adopted the ABA Model,[64] but that may change in the aftermath of the 2009 US Supreme Court decision in *Caperton* v. *A. T. Massey Coal Co., Inc.*[65] In *Caperton*, a state Supreme Court justice declined to disqualify himself from a case in which the defendant's CEO had spent over US$3 million in support of the justice's election campaign while the case was pending. The justice in question ultimately cast the deciding vote in a three to two decision in favor of the defendant that reversed a judgment on a jury verdict for the plaintiff. A sharply divided Supreme Court held that the justice's failure to disqualify himself violated the plaintiff's constitutional right to due process of law. *Caperton* concerned a party's independent expenditures on a judicial candidate's behalf, while the ABA Model Code provision only regulates contributions made directly to the judge's campaign, but the decision may well prompt wider-ranging disqualification reform across the states.

Conclusion

Criticism of judges – including shrill and intemperate criticism – is a part of the American political tradition, and claims that judges are under attack now to a greater extent than in the past are unsupportable. It is nevertheless true that the confluence of events giving rise to the latest cycle of anti-court sentiment has a unique dynamic: the judicial selection process has fixated on how would-be judges will decide ideologically driven issues; judges have acquired a "right" to take public positions on those very issues; and interest groups have spent unprecedented sums of money to influence the selection of judges whose views on those issues are compatible with their own. In such an environment, pleas to "depoliticize" the judiciary seem increasingly unrealistic and are gradually being supplanted by proposals to manage judicial politics in ways that concede to political reality, while seeking to preserve the essentials of an independent and impartial judiciary.

[64] Judicial Disqualification Project, "Taking Judicial Disqualification Seriously," p. 14.
[65] 129 S.Ct. 2252 (2009).

PART IV

14

Judges, bias and recusal in Australia

COLIN CAMPBELL

Although an allegation of *actual* bias may certainly be brought against a judge in an Australian court,[1] it is not necessary, in circumstances where there are concerns about a judge's lack of impartiality, for such an allegation to be made out in order for the judge to be disqualified from hearing the matter in question. Rather, under Australian law a judge may be disqualified if it can be demonstrated that a 'fair-minded lay observer might reasonably apprehend that the judge might not bring an impartial mind to the resolution of the question that the judge is required to decide'[2] (the 'reasonable apprehension of bias test').

Furthermore, allegations of actual bias in Australian courts in respect of judges are rare.[3] Rather, due to the relative ease of demonstrating that a reasonable apprehension of bias may exist with regard to a judge (compared with proving that he or she *is* actually biased),[4] and also, possibly, due to the lower risk of offending a judge by arguing for the former rather than the latter,[5] a party who has concerns about a judge's impartiality will normally seek to demonstrate that there is a reasonable apprehension of bias in relation to the judge, rather than that the judge is actually biased.[6]

For that reason, the reasonable apprehension of bias test will be the focus of this chapter. To begin, the way in which the test operates will be briefly outlined. Next, the purposes said to be achieved by the test will be explained. Then, consideration will be given, in succession, to each of

1 *Ebner* v. *Official Trustee* (2000) 205 CLR 337 at 344 *per* Gleeson CJ, McHugh, Gummow and Hayne JJ.
2 *Ebner* v. *Official Trustee* (2000) 205 CLR 337 at 344.
3 *Ebner* v. *Official Trustee* (2000) 205 CLR 337 at 370 *per* Kirby J.
4 See the text accompanying nn. 51–4 below.
5 *Ebner* v. *Official Trustee* (2000) 205 CLR 337 at 370 *per* Kirby J.
6 *Ebner* v. *Official Trustee* (2000) 205 CLR 337 at 370.

the following: the role played by the so-called fair-minded lay observer in the operation of the reasonable apprehension of bias test; the relevance of the judge's possession of a financial interest in the outcome of the matter; and, finally, the role played, in relation to the reasonable apprehension of bias test, by the notions of waiver and necessity. In respect of each of these matters an examination will be made of, *inter alia*, the extent to which the courts' approach gives effect to what are said to be the underlying purposes of the reasonable apprehension of bias test.

The operation of the test

A party alleging the existence of a reasonable apprehension of bias in respect of a judge, whether before an appellate court, or to the judge him- or herself in seeking the judge's recusal, must go through three steps. First, the party must identify 'what it is said might lead [the] judge . . . to decide [the] case other than on its legal and factual merits'[7] (the 'matter suggesting bias').[8] In *Webb* v. *R*[9] Deane J identified 'four distinct, though overlapping',[10] categories of matter suggesting bias. Subsequently, the High Court, while declining to 'decide upon the comprehensiveness of such categorisation',[11] suggested that 'it provides a convenient frame of reference'.[12] The categories identified by Deane J were:

- an 'interest',[13] whether 'pecuniary or otherwise',[14] and whether 'direct or indirect',[15] in the proceedings;
- 'conduct'[16] either 'in the course of, or outside, the proceedings';[17]
- an 'association',[18] including 'some direct or indirect relationship . . . or contact [between the judge and] a person or persons interested in, or otherwise involved in, the proceedings';[19] and

[7] *Ebner* v. *Official Trustee* (2000) 205 CLR 337 at 345.
[8] This is a term adopted in this chapter, rather than a term of art.
[9] (1994) 181 CLR 41.
[10] *Ebner* v. *Official Trustee* (2000) 205 CLR 337 at 348 *per* Gleeson CJ, McHugh, Gummow and Hayne JJ.
[11] *Ebner* v. *Official Trustee* (2000) 205 CLR 337 at 349.
[12] *Ebner* v. *Official Trustee* (2000) 205 CLR 337 at 349.
[13] *Webb* v. *R* (1994) 181 CLR 41 at 74 *per* Deane J.
[14] *Webb* v. *R* (1994) 181 CLR 41 at 74.
[15] *Webb* v. *R* (1994) 181 CLR 41 at 74.
[16] *Webb* v. *R* (1994) 181 CLR 41 at 74.
[17] *Webb* v. *R* (1994) 181 CLR 41 at 74.
[18] *Webb* v. *R* (1994) 181 CLR 41 at 74.
[19] *Webb* v. *R* (1994) 181 CLR 41 at 74.

- 'extraneous information',[20] including knowledge, possessed by the judge, 'of some prejudicial but inadmissible fact or circumstance'.[21]

Second, and 'no less important',[22] the party alleging the existence of a reasonable apprehension of bias must then articulate that which is said to be 'the logical connection between the [matter suggesting bias] and the feared deviation from the course of deciding the case on its merits'.[23] Hence, for instance, the 'bare assertion that a judge ... has an "interest" in litigation ... will be of no assistance until the nature of the interest, and the asserted connection with the possibility of departure from impartial decision making, is articulated'.[24]

Third, once the matter suggesting bias has been identified and the logical connection between that matter and the feared deviation articulated, the party must argue that there is an ensuing apprehension of bias and that that apprehension is reasonable.[25]

As a 'matter of prudence and professional practice',[26] judges should disclose to the parties before them 'interests and associations'[27] (and also, presumably, any possession by the judge of extraneous information) 'if there is a serious possibility'[28] that any of these is 'potentially disqualifying'.[29] However, the failure by a judge to make such disclosure will not, '*of itself*, give a litigant any right to have the judge desist from further hearing the matter or to have the ultimate decision in the matter set aside'.[30] The judge's failure to disclose, though, will be one matter that is taken into account in determining whether the reasonable apprehension of bias test is made out.[31]

[20] *Webb* v. *R* (1994) 181 CLR 41 at 74. [21] *Webb* v. *R* (1994) 181 CLR 41 at 74.

[22] *Ebner* v. *Official Trustee* (2000) 205 CLR 337 at 345 *per* Gleeson CJ, McHugh, Gummow and Hayne JJ.

[23] *Ebner* v. *Official Trustee* (2000) 205 CLR 337 at 345.

[24] *Ebner* v. *Official Trustee* (2000) 205 CLR 337 at 345.

[25] *Ebner* v. *Official Trustee* (2000) 205 CLR 337 at 345.

[26] *Ebner* v. *Official Trustee* (2000) 205 CLR 337 at 360.

[27] *Ebner* v. *Official Trustee* (2000) 205 CLR 337 at 360.

[28] *Ebner* v. *Official Trustee* (2000) 205 CLR 337 at 360.

[29] *Ebner* v. *Official Trustee* (2000) 205 CLR 337 at 360.

[30] *Ebner* v. *Official Trustee* (2000) 205 CLR 337 at 360 (emphasis added).

[31] *Ebner* v. *Official Trustee* (2000) 205 CLR 337 at 360.

A judge should certainly not 'automatically'[32] or 'too readily'[33] accede to an application that he or she is subject to a reasonable apprehension of bias, and so recuse him- or herself too readily from hearing a matter. If judges were to recuse themselves in such circumstances, parties would be tempted to make meritless applications for recusal, in the hope of obtaining a judge 'thought to be more likely to decide the case in their favour'[34] or to gain the 'strategic advantage'[35] that might be secured by 'the interruption of lengthy proceedings . . . and the delays consequent upon obtaining a fresh start in a busy court or tribunal'.[36] Such a state of affairs would be 'intolerable'.[37]

Rather, a judge is obliged to recuse him- or herself from hearing a matter only if, in his or her view, there is a 'real possibility that his [or her] participation in a case might lead to a reasonable apprehension of . . . bias'.[38] That is not to say, however, that this is the only circumstance in which a judge may appropriately choose to recuse him- or herself. In 'a case of real doubt',[39] where the application for recusal is 'based upon a substantial ground for contending that the judge is disqualified from hearing . . . the case'[40] a judge 'may decide not to sit in order to avoid the inconvenience that could result if an appellate court were to take a different view on [the matter of disqualification]'.[41] Matters relevant to that assessment would include, *inter alia*, 'the stage at which an objection is raised [and] the practical possibility of arranging for another judge to hear the case'.[42]

If an appellant is successful in arguing, as a ground of appeal, that a reasonable apprehension of bias attaches to the judge below, the matter

32 *Livesey* v. *New South Wales Bar Association* (1983) 151 CLR 288 at 294 *per* Mason, Murphy, Brennan, Deane and Dawson JJ.
33 *Johnson* v. *Johnson* (2000) 201 CLR 488 at 504 *per* Kirby J.
34 *Re JRL ex p. CJL* (1986) 161 CLR 342 at 352 *per* Mason J.
35 *Johnson* v. *Johnson* (2000) 201 CLR 488 at 504 *per* Kirby J.
36 *Johnson* v. *Johnson* (2000) 201 CLR 488 at 504.
37 *Ebner* v. *Official Trustee* (2000) 205 CLR 337 at 348 *per* Gleeson CJ, McHugh, Gummow and Hayne JJ.
38 *Livesey* v. *New South Wales Bar Association* (1983) 151 CLR 288 at 294 *per* Mason, Murphy, Brennan, Deane and Dawson JJ.
39 *Ebner* v. *Official Trustee* (2000) 205 CLR 337 at 348 *per* Gleeson CJ, McHugh, Gummow and Hayne JJ.
40 *Ebner* v. *Official Trustee* (2000) 205 CLR 337 at 348.
41 *Ebner* v. *Official Trustee* (2000) 205 CLR 337 at 348.
42 *Ebner* v. *Official Trustee* (2000) 205 CLR 337 at 348.

will normally be remitted for a retrial of the substantive action by a court free of apprehended bias.[43] Where an appellant raises a number of grounds of appeal, only one of which is apprehended bias, the appellate court must deal with the issue of bias first,[44] even if the ground of bias is sought to be relied upon only in the alternative.[45] The court must deal with the ground of bias first because 'apprehended bias strikes at the validity and acceptability of the trial and its outcome'.[46] If the ground of apprehended bias is made out, the appellate court must remit the matter, even if, were the appellant successful on one of the other grounds, he or she would obtain the substantive result that he or she desired.[47] The appellate court should put the party making an allegation of apprehended bias 'to an election on the basis that if the allegation … is made out, a retrial will be ordered irrespective of possible findings on other issues'.[48]

The test's purposes

The reasonable apprehension of bias test serves two immediate purposes. One is to protect against the occurrence of *actual* bias, and so to give effect to the 'fundamental'[49] and 'basic'[50] principle that an adversarial trial be conducted by a tribunal that is actually 'independent and impartial'.[51] The reasonable apprehension of bias test protects against the occurrence of actual bias, even more effectively than would an actual bias test, by obviating the need for the applicant to make arguments pertaining to 'the actual thought processes of the judge'[52] and, rather,

43 *Concrete Pty Ltd* v. *Parramatta Design and Developments* (2006) 229 CLR 577 at 611 *per* Kirby and Crennan JJ.

44 *Concrete Pty Ltd* v. *Parramatta Design and Developments* (2006) 229 CLR 577 at 611.

45 *Concrete Pty Ltd* v. *Parramatta Design and Developments* (2006) 229 CLR 577 at 611.

46 *Concrete Pty Ltd* v. *Parramatta Design and Developments* (2006) 229 CLR 577 at 611.

47 *Concrete Pty Ltd* v. *Parramatta Design and Developments* (2006) 229 CLR 577 at 611.

48 *Concrete Pty Ltd* v. *Parramatta Design and Developments* (2006) 229 CLR 577 at 611.

49 *Ebner* v. *Official Trustee* (2000) 205 CLR 337 at 343, 348 *per* Gleeson CJ, McHugh, Gummow and Hayne JJ.

50 *Ebner* v. *Official Trustee* (2000) 205 CLR 337 at 345.

51 *Ebner* v. *Official Trustee* (2000) 205 CLR 337 at 343.

52 *Ebner* v. *Official Trustee* (2000) 205 CLR 337 at 345.

permitting the bias ground to be made out simply if there are factors present that might objectively suggest bias.[53]

As indicated above, in arguing that there is a reasonable apprehension of bias, the applicant would certainly need to identify the matter suggesting bias, and the logical connection between that matter and the feared deviation from impartial decision-making. However, unlike an applicant alleging actual bias, an applicant arguing that there had been a contravention of the reasonable apprehension of bias test would not face the burdensome[54] task of proving that the judge, in making his or her decision *actually* would be, or *actually* had been, improperly influenced by the matter or matters in question. Rather, it would be necessary only for the applicant to demonstrate that it might reasonably be apprehended that the judge *might* be biased.

The reasonable apprehension of bias test would presumably catch at least most – if not all – of the cases of actual bias that would be caught by an actual bias test. If it could be demonstrated in the circumstances of a case that the judge would *actually* be, or had *actually* been, biased in making a particular decision, then it is difficult to see how those circumstances would not give rise to the reasonable apprehension that he or she *might* be biased.

Additionally, the reasonable apprehension of bias test would also catch cases of actual bias that would not be caught by an actual bias test. In circumstances where the judge *was* actually biased, but it could not be proved that the judge possessed the requisite mental state for actual bias, it is entirely possible, if not likely, that the external facts – the possession, for instance, by the judge of an interest of some kind in the outcome of the case – would nonetheless give rise to a reasonable apprehension of bias in the necessary sense.

Thus, as far as catching of cases of actual bias is concerned, the reasonable apprehension of bias test operates in a prophylactic fashion.[55] By recognising 'the possibility of human frailty'[56] and permitting the ground of bias to be made out by reference to matters that *might* tempt a judge to act improperly (but which have not necessarily done so) the test

[53] *Ebner* v. *Official Trustee* (2000) 205 CLR 337 at 345.

[54] *Webb* v. *R* (1994) 181 CLR 41 at 52 *per* Mason CJ and McHugh J. See also M. Groves, 'The Rule Against Bias' (2009) 39 *Hong Kong Law Journal* 485 at 494.

[55] M. Conaglen, 'Public–Private Intersection: Comparing Fiduciary Conflict Doctrine and Bias' (2008) *Public Law* 58 at 75.

[56] *Ebner* v. *Official Trustee* (2000) 205 CLR 337 at 345 *per* Gleeson CJ, McHugh, Gummow and Hayne JJ.

operates expansively to catch not only most of the cases of actual bias that would be caught by an actual bias test, but also some cases of actual bias that would not be caught by such a test.

The other immediate purpose of the reasonable apprehension of bias test, so it is claimed, is to guard against the *appearance* of bias, even in cases where the judge in question is not actually biased. In respect of both immediate purposes, but especially the latter, it is claimed by the courts that the reasonable apprehension of bias test serves the broader purpose of maintaining and promoting public confidence in the administration of justice.[57]

It is, though, important to be very careful in understanding the role actually accorded by the judges to the notion of public confidence in this context. Certainly, if the public at large had an awareness of the cases in which judges had recused themselves, or in which appeals had been successful, because of the operation of the reasonable apprehension of bias test, it could plausibly be argued that the test actually serves to promote public confidence in the administration of justice. Hence, for instance, if the public were aware of such cases, it could sensibly be suggested that by requiring a judge to disqualify him- or herself from hearing a case if the apprehension could reasonably be entertained that he or she were biased, the test guards against the sense of disquiet that could arise if he or she were permitted to preside over the case despite the presence of circumstances suggesting the possibility of bias.

However, there is no reason to think that anything other than a minute fraction of the population has even the slightest awareness of the cases in which judges recuse themselves, or appeals are successful, because of the operation of the reasonable apprehension of bias test, or are even aware of the reasonable apprehension of bias test itself. But if the vast bulk of the population is entirely ignorant of the cases in which, but for the operation of the reasonable apprehension of bias test, there might be apprehended (or even actual) bias, and of the test itself, it simply cannot be the case that the court's reliance on that test actually has any significant impact on public confidence in the administration of justice.

[57] *Johnson* v. *Johnson* (2000) 201 CLR 488 at 493 *per* Gleeson CJ, Gaudron, McHugh, Gummow and Hayne JJ; *Ebner* v. *Official Trustee* (2000) 205 CLR 337 at 359 *per* Gleeson CJ, McHugh, Gummow and Hayne JJ, at 364 *per* Gaudron J; *Webb* v. *R* (1994) 181 CLR 41 at 75 *per* Deane J; *Re JRL ex p. CJL* (1986) 161 CLR 342 at 351 *per* Mason J.

Accordingly, it is very unlikely that when the judges say the reasonable apprehension of bias test serves to promote public confidence in the administration of justice, they are talking about what the test actually does. A more charitable understanding of the judges' meaning here is that they are making use of the notion of public confidence in the independence and integrity of the judiciary in a hypothetical sense: they are saying that *if* the public *were* aware of the test and its operation, public confidence in the administration of justice *would* be protected. It follows, so the argument would go, that because public confidence in the administration of justice is normatively desirable, a test pertaining to bias, that *would* have the effect of maintaining and promoting such confidence, *if* it were widely known about, is normatively desirable too.

In relation to the normative role played by the notion of public confidence in respect of the reasonable apprehension of bias test, it is important to appreciate that the apprehension in question – in determining whether there is a reasonable apprehension of bias – is, supposedly at least, not that of the court but, rather, that of a fair-minded *lay* observer[58] (or rather, and more strictly, that which the court takes to be the apprehension of the fair-minded lay observer).[59] The rationale is that it will be more useful for the court, in determining whether the test would guard against disquiet on behalf of the public (were the public to be aware of the test and its operation), to have regard to what it thinks would be 'the reaction of the ordinary reasonable member of the public to the irregularity in question'[60] than to whether the court itself would reasonably apprehend bias.

The fair-minded lay observer in action

In considering the application of the reasonable apprehension of bias test, it is important to have regard to three matters in relation to the fair-minded lay observer, as that notion is understood by the courts: those aspects of the situation that the fair-minded lay observer will consider in determining whether he or she apprehends bias on the part of the judge; the meticulousness (or otherwise) with which he or she will carry out that consideration; and the amount of knowledge he or she has about both the substantive law the subject of the case in question, and also the operation of the judicial process.

[58] *Webb* v. *R* (1994) 181 CLR 41 at 51 *per* Mason CJ and McHugh J.

[59] *Webb* v. *R* (1994) 181 CLR 41 at 52. [60] *Webb* v. *R* (1994) 181 CLR 41 at 51.

What the fair-minded lay observer will consider

In respect of the first matter, the fair-minded lay observer will have regard to 'all the relevant circumstances',[61] including, *inter alia*, the facts of the substantive case, in the context of which the allegation of bias has arisen.[62] In a case where the apprehension of bias is alleged to have been created by the conduct of the judge in dealing with the case, the fair-minded lay observer will consider not just the particular conduct in question but, rather, the whole trial[63] and even, if necessary, the resulting judgment.[64] Accordingly, while 'some statements, or some behaviour, may produce an ineradicable apprehension of prejudgment',[65] 'on other occasions ... a preliminary impression created by what is said or done may be altered by a later statement'.[66]

The meticulousness of the fair-minded lay observer's consideration

In respect of the second matter, the meticulousness with which those circumstances will be considered, there is some judicial comment to the effect that the fair-minded lay observer will not undertake the task of considering whether he or she reasonably apprehends bias with any great exactitude. Hence, according to Kirby J, the fair-minded lay observer will 'have neither the time nor the inclination to explore the facts at length'.[67] Rather, he or she will adopt a 'broad brush'[68] in making the relevant assessment, and will form 'an impressionistic, and to some extent,

[61] *Johnson* v. *Johnson* (2000) 201 CLR 488 at 508 *per* Kirby J; *Re JRL ex p. CJL* (1986) 161 CLR 342 at 371–2 *per* Dawson J.

[62] See, e.g., the knowledge of the facts accorded to the fair-minded lay observer in *Concrete Pty Ltd* v. *Parramatta Design and Developments* (2006) 229 CLR 577 at 585–612 and especially, 604–11 *per* Kirby and Crennan JJ.

[63] *Concrete Pty Ltd.* v. *Parramatta Design and Developments* (2006) 229 CLR 577 at 636 *per* Callinan J; *Johnson* v. *Johnson* (2000) 201 CLR 488 at 494 *per* Gleeson CJ, Gaudron, McHugh, Gummow and Hayne JJ.

[64] *Concrete Pty Ltd* v. *Parramatta Design and Developments* (2006) 229 CLR 577 at 636 *per* Callinan J; *Vakauta* v. *Kelly* (1989) 167 CLR 568 at 579 *per* Dawson J.

[65] *Re JRL ex p. CJL* (1986) 161 CLR 342 at 372 *per* Dawson J.

[66] *Johnson* v. *Johnson* (2000) 201 CLR 488 at 494 *per* Gleeson CJ, Gaudron, McHugh, Gummow and Hayne JJ. But cf. *British American Tobacco Australia Services Ltd* v. *Claudia Jean Laurie* [2011] HCA 2 at para. 145 *per* Heydon, Kiefel and Bell JJ.

[67] *Raybos Australia Pty Ltd* v. *Tectran Corporation Pty Ltd (No. 9)*, NSWCA, 27 November 1990, unreported, Kirby J, at 20, extracted in *Australian National Industries Pty Ltd* v. *Spedley Securities Pty Ltd* (1992) 26 NSWLR 411 at 420 *per* Kirby J.

[68] *Raybos Australia Pty Ltd* v. *Tectran Corporation Pty Ltd (No. 9)*, NSWCA, 27 November 1990, unreported, at 20.

superficial, opinion based upon a consideration of the broad features of the allegation made'.[69] His or her view as to whether he or she apprehends bias will certainly not be made 'upon a detailed exploration of [or] ... lengthy rumination about'[70] the allegation's merits.

In practice, however, and notwithstanding these comments, the courts tend to attribute to the fair-minded lay observer, for the purpose of ascertaining whether there is an apprehension of bias, a significant degree of engagement with the details of the case at hand. Hence, for instance, in *Smits* v. *Roach*,[71] the appellants, who were solicitors, and who had *formerly* acted for the respondents, were suing the respondents for the legal costs and expenses to which they claimed to be entitled in preparing a negligence action on behalf of the respondents against another firm of solicitors, Freehills.

In turn, the respondents' action against Freehills was on-going, with the respondents now being represented in that action by (still) another firm of solicitors. If the respondents' action in negligence against Freehills ended up being successful – a matter not decided when the action between the appellants and the respondents was being heard – then the respondents would be able to recover from Freehills the reasonable legal costs that they, the respondents, had incurred in prosecuting their claim against Freehills, including the bulk of any sum for which they, the respondents, were held to be liable in the primary action. In other words, if the appellants were successful in the primary action against the respondents, then Freehills would be subject to a *contingent* liability, in respect of the amount for which the respondents had been held liable in preparing the case against Freehills. In the event that the respondents were successful, eventually, against Freehills in the negligence action, then the respondents could recover from Freehills at least the bulk of any money that they, the respondents, were held to owe to the appellants in the primary action.

It was argued by the appellants in the primary action that a reasonable apprehension of bias appertained in respect of McClellan J, the judge hearing the case, because his brother was, at that time, Chairman of Partners at Freehills. The court rejected the appellant's arguments to that effect and the reasons it provided for doing so reflect, on the part of the

[69] *Raybos Australia Pty Ltd* v. *Tectran Corporation Pty Ltd (No. 9)*, NSWCA, 27 November 1990, unreported, at 20.

[70] *Raybos Australia Pty Ltd* v. *Tectran Corporation Pty Ltd (No. 9)*, NSWCA, 27 November 1990, unreported, at 20.

[71] (2006) 227 CLR 423.

fair-minded lay observer, if not 'fine ... analysis'[72] then at least an engagement with the facts that is more than superficial and impressionistic. Hence, no apprehension of bias was held to lie in respect of the judge, it was claimed, because 'the evidence did not disclose any demonstrable relationship between',[73] on the one hand, the sums claimed by the appellant to be owed to them by the respondent in respect of the work done in preparing the case against Freehills, and on the other hand, 'any amount that Freehills ultimately might be called upon to bear in respect of the costs attributable to the Freehills litigation up until the time that the Roach interests retained new solicitors';[74] any portion of that liability attaching to the judge's brother, one of eighty partners in the firm, 'would probably need to be divided by at least 80';[75] and in any case, any liability would probably be covered by insurance.[76]

That which the fair-minded lay observer is taken to know

In cases involving the application of the reasonable apprehension of bias test, the fair-minded lay observer is attributed by the court with knowledge about the law pertaining to the substantive matter in the context of which the allegation of bias has arisen and also with knowledge of the judicial process.

The attribution to the fair-minded lay observer of knowledge of the former kind is rarely remarked upon by the courts, or expressly acknowledged, but must rather be inferred from the conclusions which are deemed to be reached by the fair-minded lay observer. Hence, for instance, in *Smits* v. *Roach*, in order to have made a determination as to whether he or she apprehended bias, the fair-minded lay observer must have appreciated, *inter alia*, that a client can engage a solicitor to do legal work for the client; that a solicitor may be able to sue a client in respect of legal work done on behalf of the client for which payment has not been received; that a client can sue a solicitor on the basis that the solicitor has done legal work, undertaken on behalf the client, negligently (whatever it is that is meant by doing legal work 'negligently'); that if a party is successfully sued then financial damages are likely to be awarded

[72] *Smits* v. *Roach* (2006) 227 CLR 423 at 464 *per* Kirby J.
[73] *Smits* v. *Roach* (2006) 227 CLR 423 at 443 *per* Gleeson CJ, Heydon and Crennan JJ.
[74] *Smits* v. *Roach* (2006) 227 CLR 423 at 443 *per* Gleeson CJ, Heydon and Crennan JJ.
[75] *Smits* v. *Roach* (2006) 227 CLR 423 at 443.
[76] *Smits* v. *Roach* (2006) 227 CLR 423 at 443.

against that party, in favour of the party that sued; that law firms are partnerships; that if a partnership is successfully sued the partners may suffer financially; that, to an extent at least, any suffering by the partners will be distributed among the partners; and that law firms may be able to obtain insurance against at least certain kinds of claims in negligence. There is no reason to think that *Smits* v. *Roach* is atypical in terms of the degree or sort of knowledge about the legal issues arising in the substantive case that is attributed to the fair-minded lay observer. Accordingly, it seems that, as occurred in that case, the fair-minded lay observer will be accorded sufficient knowledge about the legal issues pertaining to the substantive case to understand the legal and factual background pertaining to the allegation of bias.

In respect of the latter kind of legal knowledge – that relating to the judicial process – the fair-minded lay observer – at least according to the courts – will certainly not be accorded the same degree of familiarity with the legal process as would be possessed by 'a litigation lawyer'.[77] However, the fair-minded lay observer will have at least some awareness of 'ordinary judicial practice',[78] including the tendency for contemporary judges 'responding to a need for more active case management, [to] intervene in the conduct of cases'[79] to a much greater extent than would have occurred in earlier times. Accordingly, judges 'who, in exchanges with counsel, express tentative views which reflect a certain tendency of mind are not, on that account alone to be taken [by the fair-minded lay observer] to indicate prejudgment'.[80]

The fair-minded lay observer and the general public – a critique

It is plain that the fair-mined lay observer is a 'fiction'[81] and a 'hypothetical construct'[82] that has been arrived at by the courts without regard, empirically, to when, in particular situations, members of the public would actually apprehend bias. However, it does not necessarily follow

[77] *Concrete Pty Ltd* v. *Parramatta Design and Developments* (2006) 229 CLR 577 at 635 *per* Callinan J.

[78] *Johnson* v. *Johnson* (2000) 201 CLR 488 at 493 *per* Gleeson CJ, Gaudron, McHugh, Gummow and Hayne JJ.

[79] *Johnson* v. *Johnson* (2000) 201 CLR 488 at 493.

[80] *Johnson* v. *Johnson* (2000) 201 CLR 488 at 493.

[81] *Johnson* v. *Johnson* (2000) 201 CLR 488 at 506 *per* Kirby J; *Smits* v. *Roach* (2006) 228 ALR 262 at 289 *per* Kirby J.

[82] *Smits* v. *Roach* (2006) 227 CLR 423 at 456 *per* Kirby J.

from that observation that, were the reasonable apprehension of bias test and its operation widely known about, the test would fail to promote public confidence in the administration of justice by virtue of guarding against the apprehension of bias. It may be, for instance, that members of the public would note, and take comfort from, the relative assiduousness and sophistication accorded by the courts to the fair-minded lay observer in the operation of the reasonable apprehension of bias test.

But, in the absence of a theory for determining the counterfactual views held by members of the public, and for distilling such views so that a representative view, to be accorded to 'the public', could be arrived at, any conclusions in this regard must necessarily be speculative. It could equally be argued, for instance, that the public might regard the fair-minded lay observer, as conceptualised by the courts and as employed in the reasonable apprehension of bias test, as too forgiving of judges in respect of when bias is apprehended. Hence, as seen above, the fair-minded lay observer will have regard 'to all the relevant circumstances' pertaining to an application of bias, with the result that a reasonable *prima facie* apprehension of bias that arises in respect of, for instance, a particular statement, may be displaced when considered in the context of the whole trial. It is not outrageous to suggest, for instance, that 'the public' (however that notion is conceived), being alert to the importance of the judicial role and the dangers of bias and, perhaps, these days being more cynical about societal institutions than previously,[83] might be of the view that an apprehension of possible bias, created by a single statement made presumably in unguarded fashion, cannot in any circumstances be displaced by subsequent comments, that may be made in contrived fashion to achieve just that end.

Similarly, unlike the fair-minded lay observer who, it seems, will not be prepared to apprehend bias on the basis of anything short of a meticulous examination of the facts, it may be the public would be of the view that it is so important to guard against judicial bias, that the judge should recuse him- or herself if even a superficial examination of the facts suggests the possibility of bias. Along similar lines, it might be that the public would not share the view that seems to be held by the fair-minded lay observer that behaviour which ostensibly suggests bias does not, in fact, do so in cases where the behaviour conforms to common

[83] *Raybos Australia Pty Ltd* v. *Tectran Corporation Pty Ltd (No. 9)*, NSWCA, 27 November 1990, unreported, Kirby J, at 20, extracted in *Australian National Industries Pty Ltd* v. *Spedley Securities Pty Ltd* (1992) 26 NSWLR 411, 420 *per* Kirby J.

judicial practice.[84] The public, which would presumably be made up largely of 'outsiders'[85] to legal culture, may adopt a more sceptical approach.

The consequence of this uncertainty is that it is very difficult to ascertain the extent to which, if the public did know about the reasonable apprehension of bias test and the circumstances in which it operates, the test would serve to promote public confidence in the administration of justice by reason of guarding against the appearance of bias. In similar fashion, it is difficult to know the precise extent to which the reasonable apprehension of bias test would promote public confidence in the administration of justice, if the test were widely known about, by virtue of its capacity to catch cases of actual bias. Certainly, as suggested above, the feature of the reasonable apprehension of bias test that contributes most to the capacity of the test to catch cases of actual bias is its 'objective' nature – the fact that it does not require consideration to be given to the internal mental state of the judge in question. However, if it is the case that the fair-minded lay observer, as conceptualised by the courts, would apprehend bias in a narrower range of circumstances than would the public – a matter which we do not know – then, presumably, the reasonable apprehension of bias test, making use of the fair-minded lay observer, would catch cases of actual bias in a narrower range of circumstances than it would if the circumstances in which the fair-minded lay observer apprehends bias were more closely aligned with the circumstances in which the public would apprehend bias.

Pecuniary interests

Having examined the role played by the fair-minded lay observer in the reasonable apprehension of bias test, consideration will now be given to the position that pertains in Australian law where the rule against bias is claimed to have been breached as a result of a judge having a direct financial interest in the outcome of the case he or she is hearing. Specifically, the question will be addressed whether, if the judge does have such an interest, he or she is automatically disqualified from

[84] See, e.g., *Johnson* v. *Johnson* (2000) 201 CLR 488 at 493 *per* Gleeson CJ, Gaudron, McHugh, Gummow and Hayne JJ.

[85] *Gillies* v. *Secretary of State for Work and Pensions* [2006] 1 All ER 731 at 745 *per* Baroness Hale, referred to in M. Groves, 'The Rule Against Bias' (2009) 39 *Hong Kong Law Journal* 485 at 494.

hearing the matter in question. In the jointly heard appeals of *Ebner* v. *Official Trustee in Bankruptcy*; *Clenae Pty Ltd* v. *Australia*; *New Zealand Banking Group Ltd* ('*Ebner*')[86] the High Court of Australia ruled definitively on just that matter.

The majority, comprising Gleeson CJ, McHugh, Gummow and Hayne JJ, rejected the argument 'that there is a separate and free-standing rule of automatic disqualification which applies where a judge has a direct pecuniary interest, however small, in the outcome in the case over which the judge is presiding'.[87] Rather, said the majority, the matter must be assessed by reference to the normal reasonable apprehension of bias test.[88] Callinan J agreed with the reasoning of the majority.[89] Gaudron J, by way of contrast, followed the approach adopted earlier by Deane J, that a judge would be automatically disqualified from hearing a case if he or she had a direct pecuniary interest in the outcome of proceedings.[90] Kirby J held, even more strictly, that a judge would be automatically disqualified from hearing a matter if he or she had a direct pecuniary interest either in 'the subject matter of, or in a party to, litigation'.[91]

The majority relied on both pragmatic and principled reasons in coming to its conclusion that there was no automatic rule of disqualification. With regard to the former, the court argued that the rule of automatic disqualification, contended for by the appellants, would not always be capable of precise application. Hence, for instance, there would be cases where it was not apparent whether or not a judge's interest in the outcome of a case would be 'direct' in the requisite sense.[92] Nor, indeed, would it always be apparent whether a judge possessed an 'interest' in the outcome of a case,[93] as opposed, for example, to having an impermissible association with someone connected with the case. Hence, at least in the view of the majority, what 'looks like a bright-line rule draws a line which is far from bright'.[94]

In respect of its objections of the latter kind, the court contended that even if it were possible in all cases to identify whether a judge had an

86 (2000) 205 CLR 337.

87 (2000) 205 CLR 337 at 356 *per* Gleeson CJ, McHugh, Gummow and Hayne JJ.

88 (2000) 205 CLR 337 at 356–7. 89 (2000) 205 CLR 337 at 396 *per* Callinan J.

90 (2000) 205 CLR 337 at 366 *per* Gaudron J.

91 (2000) 205 CLR 337 at 394 *per* Kirby J. But cf. the judge's comment on p. 390, where he says that he 'would adhere to the settled authority of this Court as most recently explained by Deane J in *Webb* v. *R* . . . There is a "special class" of case where a judge is disqualified where he or she has a 'direct pecuniary interest in the outcome of the proceedings.'

92 (2000) 205 CLR 337 at 352 *per* Gleeson CJ, McHugh, Gummow and Hayne JJ.

93 (2000) 205 CLR 337 at 357. 94 (2000) 205 CLR 337 at 352.

'interest' in the outcome of a case that was 'direct' there was 'no reason, in principle' why the rule of automatic disqualification 'should be limited to interests that are pecuniary, or why, if it were so limited, it should be limited to pecuniary interests that are direct'.[95] Nor is it 'logical to have one rule applying to disqualification for interest and a different rule applying to disqualification by association'.[96]

The case principally relied on by the appellants in arguing for the rule of automatic disqualification was *Dimes* v. *Proprietors of the Grand Junction Canal*,[97] decided in 1852. The majority in *Ebner* emphasised that the same result as was reached in *Dimes*, pertaining to the disqualification of the Lord Chancellor, would have been arrived at by the application of the reasonable apprehension of bias test, 'had it then existed'.[98] The majority also emphasised that *Dimes* certainly did not hold that 'the mere fact of ownership [by a judge hearing a case] of shares in a listed company which is a litigant means that the judge has a direct pecuniary interest in the outcome of the litigation'.[99] Rather, *Dimes* 'and the cases which have followed it'[100] all recognised that 'there is a difference between having an interest in the outcome of a case, and [merely] having an interest in a party to the case'.[101] The reasonable apprehension of bias test 'directs attention'[102] to that difference by requiring 'articulation of the connection between the asserted interest and the disposition of the cause which is alleged'.[103]

It is interesting to note that the majority's rejection of a rule of automatic disqualification on the basis of a financial interest is by no means unequivocally consistent with all of the purposes underlying the reasonable apprehension of bias test, even though, pursuant to that rejection, cases that would otherwise have been decided by reference to the rule of automatic disqualification will be decided by reference to the reasonable apprehension of bias test. Hence, as was argued above, one purpose of the reasonable apprehension of bias test is to catch cases of *actual* bias. But a rule of automatic disqualification for judges with direct financial interests

[95] (2000) 205 CLR 337 at 356–7. [96] (2000) 205 CLR 337 at 35.
[97] (1852) 3 HLC 759, 10 ER 301.
[98] *Ebner* v. *Official Trustee* (2000) 205 CLR 337 at 356 *per* Gleeson CJ, McHugh, Gummow and Hayne JJ.
[99] *Ebner* v. *Official Trustee* (2000) 205 CLR 337 at 357.
[100] *Ebner* v. *Official Trustee* (2000) 205 CLR 337 at 357.
[101] *Ebner* v. *Official Trustee* (2000) 205 CLR 337 at 357.
[102] *Ebner* v. *Official Trustee* (2000) 205 CLR 337 at 357.
[103] *Ebner* v. *Official Trustee* (2000) 205 CLR 337 at 357.

in the outcome of a matter, operating *alongside* the reasonable apprehension of bias test, would be even more effective at catching cases of actual bias than would the reasonable apprehension of bias test operating alone. Hence, there might plausibly be some cases where the judge's direct interest in the outcome of a matter he or she was hearing was sufficiently modest that the reasonable apprehension of bias test might not be contravened, but in which, nonetheless, the judge actually *was* biased. In such circumstances (and as long as the interest was known about), the existence of a rule of automatic disqualification would ensure that the judge would be required to recuse him- or herself or, if the judge refused, any ensuing decision could be appealed. As Kirby J noted in *Ebner*, the rule of automatic disqualification 'concentrates the law's attention upon the *fact* of the integrity of the adjudicator'.[104] It follows, that to the extent that the ability of the law to catch cases of actual bias would promote the broader purpose of achieving public confidence in the administration of justice, the rejection of the automatic rule of disqualification would, at least to *some* degree, retard that promotion.

However, the argument does not go all one way, particularly in respect of public confidence in the administration of justice. Little credit would be reflected upon the courts if it were known that, for the purpose of determining the legal rights of litigants before them, the courts were relying on tests that could not always be applied consistently, and which were unprincipled. While keeping in mind the qualification that it is very difficult to gauge exactly what the public's reaction would be, it nonetheless does not seem too unreasonable to suggest that the public might gain some comfort if aware that the automatic disqualification test was rejected by the High Court of Australia because (in their view at least) it was flawed in just these ways.

Waiver and necessity

Finally, consideration will be given to the doctrines of waiver and necessity. Pursuant to the doctrine of waiver, a party can relinquish its ability to object to the hearing of a case by a particular judge by virtue of apprehended or actual bias on the part of the judge.[105] The waiver can be

[104] *Ebner* v. *Official Trustee* (2000) 205 CLR 337 at 388 *per* Kirby J. Emphasis in original.

[105] See, M. Groves, 'The Rule against Bias', in M. Groves and H. P. Lee (eds.), *Australian Administrative Law, Fundamentals, Principles and Doctrines* (Cambridge University Press, 2007), pp. 327–8.

made expressly[106] – as will often occur at the beginning of a proceeding when the judge discloses his or her interest – or can occur impliedly.[107] Waiver of the latter sort will have occurred if a party to a proceeding has not objected to the hearing of the matter by a particular judge as soon as the party became aware of the matters suggesting the possibility of bias.[108]

Under the doctrine of necessity, a judge will not be required to recuse him- or herself from hearing a matter if, even though a reasonable apprehension of bias pertains to the judge in respect of hearing the matter either there is no other available judge who sensibly can hear the matter,[109] or if the same objection, pertaining to bias, could be raised in respect of all other decision-makers.[110] What is most notable about both doctrines is that their application can have the result that a judge will be permitted to hear a case, even if the fair-minded lay observer would reasonably apprehend bias in respect of the hearing of the case by that judge.

Constitutional implications

In *Ebner* Gaudron J held, *inter alia*, that the appearance of impartiality is a 'defining feature'[111] of judicial power under Chapter III of the Australian Constitution. Strictly, given the well-established presence of waiver and necessity in Australian law, that cannot be correct. The need to rely on waiver and necessity arises only in circumstances where there is a reasonable apprehension of bias to begin with. But if the appearance of impartiality were actually a 'defining feature' of judicial power then, in circumstances where there was an apprehension of bias, there could be no judicial power. There could be no judicial power because a defining feature of judicial power – the appearance of impartiality – would not be present. But if there were no judicial power, there could be nothing in respect of which the doctrines of waiver or necessity could operate.

106 Groves, 'The Rule against Bias', Groves and Lee (eds.), *Australian Administrative Law, Fundamentals, Principles and Doctrines*, pp. 327–8.

107 See E. Campbell and H. P. Lee, *The Australian Judiciary* (Cambridge University Press, 2001), p. 145; M. Groves, 'The Rule against Bias' in Groves and Lee (eds.), *Australian Administrative Law, Fundamentals, Principles and Doctrines*, p. 328.

108 Campbell and H. P. Lee, *The Australian Judiciary*, p. 145.

109 See, e.g., *Ebner* v *Official Trustee* (2000) 205 CLR 337 at 359 *per* Gleeson CJ, McHugh, Gummow and Hayne JJ.

110 See Campbell and Lee, *The Australian Judiciary*, p. 145.

111 *Ebner* v. *Official Trustee* (2000) 205 CLR 337 at 362 *per* Gaudron J. See also Campbell and Lee, *The Australian Judiciary*, pp. 146 and 151 for discussion of this issue.

Rather, the appearance of impartiality is better described as a paradigmatic feature of judicial power under Chapter III: that is, a feature that is typically possessed by judicial power under Chapter III, and which we expect to be possessed by judicial power, but which is not necessarily possessed by judicial power. Gaudron J's misdescription in this regard led her to speak overly broadly about the operation of Chapter III in respect of judicial power under the Constitution. Hence, in a passage endorsed by Kirby J,[112] Gaudron J stated that Chapter III 'operates to guarantee that matters in federal jurisdiction are determined by a court constituted by a judge ... who appears to be impartial'.[113] But, as has been demonstrated, that guarantee is subject to exceptions. Hence, if the litigants have waived their right to object to the apprehension of bias, or if the doctrine of necessity is in operation, Chapter III offers no such guarantee.

The underlying purposes of the reasonable apprehension of bias test

As is the case with respect to the rejection, by the majority in *Ebner* of an automatic rule of disqualification in the case of financial interests, the reliance by the courts on the doctrines of waiver and necessity is by no means supported by each of the purposes underlying the reasonable apprehension of bias test. As established above, the disqualification of judges in respect of whom bias is reasonably apprehended, pursuant to the reasonable apprehension of bias test, will necessarily result in the disqualification of some judges who are actually biased. The consequence of the operation of the doctrines of waiver and necessity, then – pursuant to which judges, in respect of whom a reasonable apprehension of bias pertains, may nonetheless continue to hear a matter – is that some judges who are actually biased, and who would otherwise be disqualified, will not be disqualified. Accordingly, the doctrines of waiver and necessity run counter to the purpose of the reasonable apprehension of bias test of preventing judges who are actually biased in respect of particular proceedings from presiding over those proceedings. And, as mentioned above, to the extent that the ability of the law to catch cases of actual bias would help to promote public

112 *Ebner* v. *Official Trustee* (2000) 205 CLR 337 at 372 *per* Kirby J; *Smits* v. *Roach* (2006) 227 CLR 423 at 465 *per* Kirby J.

113 *Ebner* v. *Official Trustee* (2000) 205 CLR 337 at 362 *per* Gaudron J.

confidence in the administration of justice, a limitation upon its ability to catch such cases of bias would hinder that promotion, at least to some extent.

Similarly – and subject to the reservation expressed above – it is difficult to see how the doctrine of necessity can do anything other than undermine public confidence in the administration of justice, to the extent that that confidence is advanced by the appearance of impartiality. The doctrine of necessity necessarily permits judges, in respect of whom a reasonable allegation of bias clearly pertains, to preside over a case.

It is not so clear that the doctrine of waiver would undermine public confidence in the administration of justice, by virtue of permitting judges in respect of whom an apprehension of bias pertains to hear a case. Hence, for instance, the public might be of the view that any apparent lack of impartiality on the part of a judge in respect of whom waiver has occurred could not be too serious, because the person who provided the waiver would be a party appearing before the judge. That person, so the argument would go, would be best placed to assess his or her own interests in the light of any apparent lack of impartiality, and if that person was of the view that the perceived lack of impartiality of the judge was too grave, he or she would not have granted the waiver to begin with. Difficulties arise here, however, as a result of it being unclear what degree of sophistication should be attributed to the general public. Hence, for instance, a public with a slightly greater degree of sophistication than that just envisaged might appreciate that in certain cases at least, a party might waive his or her objection to apprehended bias on behalf of the judge for reasons that had nothing to do with a lack of concern about that bias. For example, a party might refrain from making an application that the judge recuse him- or herself on the basis of even apprehended bias because of a concern about the adverse consequences that might follow if the judge did not accede to the application, and was offended by the very making of the application; or, a party with limited funds might not make an application of apprehended bias, particularly if the matters that would give rise to the apprehension did not arise until well after the commencement of the proceedings because, with the costs already expended, the party would be unable to afford to pay for a rehearing; or a party simply might not have the emotional energy to contemplate a rehearing of what might be a lengthy case – they might just want the matter over with.

However, again, the argument does not go all one way. It seems that, in the view of the courts at least, the efficacy of the courts in disposing of matters contributes to public confidence in the judiciary.[114] Accordingly, it does not seem unreasonable to suggest that the public's confidence in the administration of justice would be undermined if a party were able, for instance, to hold his or her complaint about apprehended bias in reserve, until the very end of possibly a very lengthy trial, after considerable resources had been expended by both the court and the parties, and then, in the event of an unfavourable outcome, could make an application for disqualification. But just that outcome would be possible if the courts did not recognise *implied* waiver. Similarly, it is not outrageous to suggest that public confidence in the administration of justice might be deleteriously affected if a party's legal rights were unable to be vindicated by reason of there being no judge able to hear that case as a result of an apprehension of bias pertaining to the only judge who could suitably hear the case, or such an apprehension pertaining to all of the relevant court's judges.

Conclusion

The ultimate purpose of the reasonable apprehension of bias test, so claims the Australian High Court, is to maintain and promote public confidence in the administration of justice. In this chapter it has been argued that the extent to which the test could serve that purpose, even hypothetically – if the test and its operation *were* widely known about – is unclear. Hence, for example, it is uncertain to what extent the views of the fair-minded lay observer, from whose putative perspective the courts seek to ascertain whether bias would be apprehended in respect of a judge, would coincide with those of the public, however that notion is conceived. Certainly, the Australian courts, while keen to emphasise that the views of the fair-minded lay observer should not depart from the public,[115] have not developed any sort of theory for the purpose of determining the extent of such coincidence.

Uncertainty also surrounds the extent to which public confidence in the administration of justice would be maintained and promoted by the court's rejection of a rule requiring the automatic disqualification of a judge who has a financial interest in the outcome of a matter he or she is hearing, and by the approach adopted by the courts to the doctrines of

[114] *Ebner* v *Official Trustee* (2000) 205 CLR 337 at 359 *per* Gleeson CJ, McHugh, Gummow and Hayne JJ.

[115] *Webb* v. *R* (1994) 181 CLR 41 at 51 *per* Mason CJ and McHugh J.

waiver and necessity. Even assuming the court could arrive at a coherent conception of that which constitutes the public, cogent arguments can be made not only in favour of, but also against, the notion that the court's positions in these areas might, if widely known about, maintain and promote public confidence in the administration of justice.

Such uncertainty prompts the question as to what extent the maintenance and preservation of public confidence in the administration of justice – even hypothetically – *should* be regarded by the Australian High Court as the ultimate purpose of the reasonable apprehension of bias test, and its related legal rules. A comprehensive answer to that question would require, in addition to the analysis presented here, an examination, from an external perspective, of whether that purpose is in fact normatively attractive.[116] But the difficulties involved in ascertaining whether the Australian law pertaining to bias advances the purpose it purportedly serves, at least give cause to wonder whether that purpose should be reconceived.

[116] For a critique of 'public confidence' as a guiding principle for the development of judicial doctrine in another context, see E. Handsley, 'Public Confidence in the Judiciary: A Red Herring for the Separation of Judicial Power' (1998) 20 *Sydney Law Review* 183.

15

Judges, bias and recusal in Canada

LORNE SOSSIN[1]

In Canada, as in other jurisdictions, natural justice has included in the injunction that, 'No one may be the judge in his or her own cause'.[2] This rule began with a concern for self-dealing and pecuniary interests, but has evolved to include a range of biases, including attitudinal ones.

The essence of bias is a closed mind, or put differently, the absence of an open mind – as one judge observed: 'bias represents a predisposition to decide an issue or cause in a certain way which does not leave the judicial mind perfectly open to conviction'.[3]

In Canada, bias has developed both as a legal component of fairness, in which every litigant is entitled to an impartial and independent judge,[4] and an ethical requirement, whereby a failure to recuse in the face of a conflict of interest may lead to a finding that the judge acted unethically, and in extreme circumstances, could justify the removal of the judge.

Whether expressed as a legal or ethical requirement, the result should be the same: a biased judge will be disqualified from hearing and deciding the matter to which the bias relates.[5] Unlike other standards which

[1] This chapter draws on material published in 'Judges', a chapter co-authored with P. Bryden, in A. Dodek and J. Hoskins (eds.), *Canadian Legal Regulation in the 21st Century* (Toronto: LexisNexis, 2009) (looseleaf), ch.16. I am grateful to Phil, and to my previous co-author, the late Justice Kenneth Lysyk, for their insights on the regulation of judges.

[2] *Nemo debet esse judex in propria sua causa*, which was considered an established rule of law by Coke in the *Earl of Derby's Case*, 12 Co. Rep. 114, in about 1610. The maxim was cited as *nemo judex in causa sua debet esse* in *Brosseau* v. *Alberta (Securities Commission)* [1989] SCJ No. 15, [1989] 1 SCR 301 at 309, SCC.

[3] *R* v. *Bertram* [1989] OJ No. 2123 at 51, HCJ.

[4] While Canadian Courts will speak of independence and impartiality as both components of procedural rights, as judicial independence in Canada is covered elsewhere in this volume, I will focus this analysis on judicial impartiality.

[5] See P. Bryden, 'Legal Principles Governing the Disqualification of Judges' (2003), 82 *Canadian Bar Review* 555 at 564 and 572.

may be expressed as a spectrum or continuum, impartiality tends to be understood as a 'bright line' test. As Madame Justice L'Heureux-Dubé stated in *2747–3174 Québec Inc* v. *Québec (Régie des permis d'alcool)*,[6] 'the concept of impartiality should be seen as a dichotomy involving two states: that of bias and that of impartiality. The only choice in such a dichotomy is between bias and impartiality, meaning that there is no intermediate obligation and thus no continuum.'

This chapter explores the law relating to the bias of judges in Canada. First, I examine the legal definition of bias developed in Canada and discuss the development of Canada's 'reasonable apprehension of bias' standard. Second, I explore the application of bias to various concrete settings in order to understand the nature and scope of the protection. I suggest that while the standard of judicial impartiality in Canada is well defined and widely accepted, its application demonstrates how this standard is in flux, particularly as the make-up of Canadian society and the role of the judge evolve. Finally, I canvass the judge's duty to recuse in circumstances where bias may be apprehended and the consequences where the judge does not do so, both as a matter of law and as a matter of judicial ethics.

Defining bias

Bias may be defined in many ways. Inherently, it is a concept that has objective and subjective elements. It is difficult to argue with the proposition that all parents are biased when assessing the conduct of their own children. Bias, however, usually arises as an issue in settings that are less clear-cut. Can a judge of Asian origin impartially consider a claim of racial discrimination against a citizen of Asian origin? Can a judge who is not of Asian origin impartially consider such a claim? It is plausible to answer either question in a way that renders every judge biased. To answer these questions, it is first necessary to employ a definition of bias.

Bias in Canada has been defined functionally in the following manner:

> Bias as applied to a person or tribunal exercising judicial functions is a state of mind disqualifying the person affected from adjudicating impartially in respect of the subject-matter under consideration. It is not a concrete fact but is an inference to be drawn from relevant facts. The facts from which bias may be implied take a wide range and include not only financial interest, however slight, by any member of the tribunal in the

[6] [1996] SCJ No. 112, [1996] 3 SCR 919, SCC.

> result of the adjudication; or relationship of any such member within a prohibited degree to a party to the litigation; but any other interest in or relation to the litigation, which should be assumed to affect any member of the tribunal with prejudice or partiality in relation thereto.[7]

The result of bias is therefore partiality. A biased judge may not only render the decision in a matter unfair, and therefore a reversible error, but may also contravene the litigant's right to an impartial tribunal under the Charter of Rights and Freedoms.[8] Furthermore, as Lubet has emphasized, a public perception of widespread bias in the judiciary would threaten the rule of law itself:

> In a democracy, the enforcement of judicial decrees and orders ultimately depends upon the public co-operation. The level of co-operation, in turn depends upon a widely held perception that judges decide cases impartially ... Should the citizenry conclude, even erroneously, that cases were decided on the basis of favouritism or prejudice rather than according to law and fact, then regiments would be necessary to enforce judgments.[9]

The leading decision in Canada on the test for bias is the Supreme Court's decision is *Committee for Justice and Liberty* v. *Canada (National Energy Board).*[10] In an application for disqualification of certain members of the board, it was alleged that those members were biased as a result of their co-authorship of an inquiry report that came to conclusions about the subject matter of the instant hearing. Laskin CJ stated his view of the test to be applied:

> This court in fixing on the test of reasonable apprehension of bias, as in *Ghirardosi* v. *Minister of Highways for British Columbia* and again in *Blanchette* v. *CIS Ltd* (where Pigeon J said at pp. 842–3 that, 'a reasonable apprehension that the judge might not act in an entirely impartial manner is ground for the disqualification') was merely restating what Rand J said in *Szilard* v. *Szasz* at pp. 6–7 in speaking of the 'probability or reasoned suspicion of biased appraisal in judgment, unintended though it may be'. This test is grounded in a firm concern that there be no lack of public confidence in the impartiality of adjudicative agencies, and I think that

[7] *Re Perry* [1929] PEIJ No. 3, 51 CCC 105, 109–10, SCJ.

[8] Constitution Act 1982, Schedule B, s. 11(d).

[9] S. Lubet, 'Judicial Ethics and Private Lives' (1984–5) 79 *Northwestern University Law Review* 983 at 986, cited in A.W. MacKay, 'Judicial Ethics: Exploring Misconduct and Accountability for Judges' (1995), available at: cjei.org/publications/mackay.html. See also generally Canadian Judicial Council, *Ethical Principles for Judges*, at www.cjc-ccm.gc.ca/cmslib/general/news_pub_judicialconduct_Principles_1998_fn.pdf, ch. 6, 'Impartiality'.

[10] [1978] 1 SCR 369.

> emphasis is lent to this concern in the present case by the fact that the National Energy Board is enjoined to have regard for the public interest.[11]

Courts have more frequently made reference to the formulation of de Grandpre J, who dissented on the facts in the same case:

> the apprehension of bias must be a reasonable one, held by reasonable and right minded persons, applying themselves to the question and obtaining thereon the required information. In the words of the Court of Appeal, that test is 'what would an informed person viewing the matter realistically and practically – and having thought the matter through – conclude'.[12]

While an awkward formulation, this standard asks a reviewing judge to consider whether the conduct of the judge in question would have given rise to an apprehension of bias in a reasonable person. Thus, the standard has come to be known as the 'reasonable apprehension of bias' standard, applied both to the question of whether there was a reversible error as a breach of procedural fairness, and to the question of whether the Charter of Rights guarantee of impartiality has been breached.

Apprehension suggests that there 'might' be bias or that there is a 'suspicion' of bias.[13] The degree of probability of bias required is not entirely clear. In *R* v. *S (RD)*,[14] a case discussed below, Cory J (in what is arguably the unanimous opinion of the court on this point) states agreement with the comment of de Grandpre J in *Committee for Justice and Liberty*: 'I can see no real difference between ... "reasonable apprehension of bias", "reasonable suspicion of bias", or "real likelihood of bias". The grounds for this apprehension must, however, be substantial'.[15] Cory J, therefore, expresses the obiter view that 'substantial' grounds for the apprehension are sufficient, even if no assessment of probability is made. However, he goes on to note that the English and Canadian case law supports the proposition that a 'likelihood' or 'probability' of bias must be shown.

While the reasonable apprehension of bias standard includes a subjective element, it is bracketed by the bounds of reasonableness.

[11] [1976] SCJ No. 118, [1978] 1 SCR 369 at 391, SCC.

[12] [1976] SCJ No. 118, [1978] 1 SCR 369 at 394, SCC.

[13] One American formulation is a 'significant doubt' of impartiality: *Pepsico, Inc.* v. *McMillan*, 764 F.2d 458 (7th Cir., 1985). See also P. Bryden, 'Legal Principles Governing the Disqualification of Judges' (2003) 82 *Canadian Bar Review* 555, where it is argued that the conceptual tools used in addressing issues of judicial impartiality fail us precisely in the marginal cases where reasonable people could disagree on whether or not a judge ought to be disqualified (p. 557).

[14] [1997] 3 SCR 484, 530, SCC.

[15] [1978] 1 SCR 369 at 39–95, SCC.

Irrational imaginings in this sense cannot give rise to a reasonable apprehension of bias. The probability of bias or partiality must be a realistic one, as perceived by an outside observer. In this test, the perceptions of the litigants themselves, while not irrelevant, cannot be determinative. Furthermore, the possibility of bias is not to be assessed from the point of view of the reviewing judge. Rather, the judge is to look to the reasonable person. In an increasingly multicultural and diverse community, however, the reasonable person may be an increasingly elusive standard. This becomes apparent as the analysis shifts to the application of this standard in a range of concrete settings.

Applying the law of bias

The reasonable apprehension of bias standard has been applied in Canada for over a generation. Below, I explore some of the concrete settings in which its scope and nature have been elucidated. The discussion below is intended to illustrate the application of bias, and its implications, rather than provide an exhaustive review.

Pecuniary interest

As stated above, the law of bias in Canada began with the point of departure of preventing a judge from obtaining a private pecuniary or financial benefit from the exercise of the judge's office. While it is probably true that judicial bias based upon pecuniary interest is no longer considered to be analytically different from other types of bias, pecuniary interest continues to be assessed by a very strict standard.[16] The classic

[16] In England a distinction is drawn between cases in which a judge has a personal interest, in which case the judge is automatically disqualified, and other cases in which disqualification flows for a reasoned perception that the judge may be unable to adjudicate impartially. *R* v. *Bow Street Metropolitan Stipendiary Magistrate, ex p. Pinochet Ugarte (No. 2)* [2000] 1 AC 119, HL; *Porter* v. *Magill* [2002] 2 AC 357, HL. The Supreme Court of Canada has observed that:

> Whatever the case in Britain, the idea of a rule of automatic disqualification takes a different shade in Canada, in light of our insistence that disqualification rest either on actual bias or on the reasonable apprehension of bias, both of which, as we have said, require a consideration of the judge's state of mind, either as a matter of fact or as imagined by the reasonable person.

Wewaykum Indian Band v. *Canada* [2003] SCJ No. 50, [2003] 2 SCR 259, 2003 SCC 45 at 72, SCC.

formulation is that any pecuniary interest, however small, will disqualify the judge.[17] Canadian courts, like their English counterparts, have been extremely reluctant to engage in an assessment of whether the financial interest in question is sufficiently significant that a reasonable person would conclude that the existence of the interest would influence the decision-maker. Where a judge held stock in a company, for example, a reasonable person would perceive bias if the judge adjudicated in a dispute materially affecting the interests of the company. That said, pecuniary bias must be assessed in its context. Today, every judge through mutual funds likely has some small financial stake in a wide range of companies and other funds. Such modest and widely held interests can no longer be sufficient to justify disqualification. While the size and significance of a judge's financial interest will always be relevant, the judge's own control over those interests also will be relevant.

A judge with numerous financial interests may be seen to have lost in some degree his or her judicial independence. As Shetreet observes:

> In short, independence of the judiciary implies not only that a judge should be free from governmental and political pressure and political entanglements but also that he should be removed from financial or business entanglements likely to affect, or rather to seem to affect, him in the exercise of his judicial functions.[18]

In *Essex (County) Roman Catholic Children's Aid Society* v. *P (T)*,[19] the trial judge was married to an associate lawyer in the firm representing the society. The opposing parties based their application for disqualification not on the personal or family connection in itself, but on the possibility that the judge would favour the society in an attempt to protect his spouse's advancement in the firm representing the society. After careful review of the older authorities, including those prohibiting any pecuniary interest, 'however small', the judge dismissed the disqualification application, stating that 'a real likelihood of bias does not exist in the circumstances of this case'.[20]

In *Commentaries on Judicial Conduct*, authored by the Canadian Judicial Council in 1991, it stated that:

> The only certain statement of a Canadian rule is that a significant, direct pecuniary interest in the litigation will disqualify. Remoteness of interest

[17] *R* v. *Rand* (1866) LR 1 QB 230 at 232; *R* v. *Justices of Sunderland* [1901] 2 KB 357 at 367, CA.
[18] S. Shetreet, *Judges on Trial* (North Holland: Amsterdam, 1976), pp. 17–18.
[19] [1989] OJ No. 606 (Prov. Ct.). [20] [1989] OJ No. 606 at 19.

> may be an issue but it is unclear to what extent, if any, the rule applies to an insignificant interest. Even remote, or insignificant pecuniary interest, which does not disqualify *per se* may, in some circumstances, give rise to a reasonable apprehension of bias.[21]

The majority of the Federal Court of Appeal in *Re Energy Probe and Atomic Energy Control Board*[22] rejected an argument that a member of the Atomic Energy Control Board should be disqualified from hearing Ontario Hydro's application for renewal of its operating licence for a nuclear power plant because he was the president of a company that supplied cable to companies running nuclear power plants, including Ontario Hydro. The majority came to this conclusion because the board member had no direct financial interest in the outcome of the renewal application.[23]

Financial interests may also involve the personal relationships of the judge, as opposed to the financial interests involved in the matter under adjudication.[24]

A judge may be allowed to hear a case even where he or she has a direct financial interest in the outcome through an invocation of the doctrine of necessity. This may occur when courts must adjudicate on issues concerning judicial salaries and taxation and the constitutional validity of systems used to establish judicial salaries. The Supreme Court stated in *R* v. *Campbell*[25] that the doctrine of necessity should not be used if the outcome of its usage would be to sanction a substantive injustice.[26]

Group membership

Judges may avoid some potential allegations of conflict of interest by a policy of non-involvement in business or other groups. However, judges are always, at a minimum, citizens and taxpayers. The latter group membership was raised unsuccessfully as a conflict in *Bekar* v.

21 Canadian Judicial Council, *Commentaries on Judicial Conduct* (Cowansville, Quebec: Yvon Blais, 1991), p. 62.

22 (1984) 15 DLR (4th) 48, FCA.

23 For an overview of the emerging *de minimus* exception to disqualification for financial interests in Commonwealth court as well as an interesting discussion of the impact of different types of financial interest, see P. Bryden, 'Legal Principles Governing the Disqualification of Judges' (2003) 82 *Canadian Bar Review* 555 at 574–80.

24 *Slater Financial Inc.* v. *Carrefour Ltd Partnership* [1996] OJ No. 3127, CA.

25 [1998] 1 SCR 3, SCC.

26 R. Tracey, 'Disqualified Adjudicators: The Doctrine of Necessity in Public Law' [1982] *Public Law* 628.

Thrower,[27] a decision of the British Columbia County Court. The appellant in that case intended to run for municipal office on a platform of tax increases, but his nomination forms were rejected by the returning officer. That decision was unsuccessfully appealed to a provincial court judge. On further appeal, the appellant argued that the provincial court judge had, as a ratepayer, a financial interest in seeing the appellant's nomination rejected. The appeal court applied the standard of the reasonable person and dismissed this ground of appeal.

It is also self-evident that a judge will be a member of the group of judges of the jurisdiction. If a judge appears as a plaintiff or defendant before a trial judge of the same court, it might be alleged that professional association (and perhaps personal acquaintance) could lead to bias. Some provinces address this possibility in legislation by requiring that any proceeding involving a provincial court judge be heard by a superior court judge.[28]

A suggestion that an Alberta judge might receive preferential treatment in his own jurisdiction was made in a *forum conveniens* hearing held in Ontario.[29] The judge had been sued for negligence in performing legal services rendered prior to his elevation to the bench. There was some connection between the subject matter of the action in both Alberta and Ontario. The Ontario judge hearing the application ruled that while the simple fact that the defendant was an Alberta judge would not disqualify another Alberta judge from hearing the case, this issue was a factor that justified an order that the matter be heard in Ontario.[30] This decision suggests that a specific factual foundation will be required before a 'fellow judge' disqualification motion can succeed.

Judges are also put in a position of self-interest when adjudicating disputes that arise from the decision-making of judicial compensation tribunals. In *Newfoundland Assn of Provincial Court Judges* v. *Newfoundland*,[31] this issue was canvassed by the Newfoundland Court of Appeal which held that a public sector salary freeze was constitutionally inapplicable to judges. Green JA, writing for the majority, characterized it as 'unseemly' and 'disquieting' for judges to enlist the support of another judge in advancing a legal claim for compensation against the government. However, Green JA

27 [1989] 42 MPLR 85, BC C.Ct.

28 E.g., see County Court Act, RSBC 1979, c. 72, s. 28 (repealed by SBC 1989, c. 40, s. 18.

29 *Occidental Chemical Corp.* v. *Sovereign General Insurance Co.* [1997] OJ No. 6294, 32 OR (3d) 277, Gen.Div.

30 *Occidental Chemical Corp.* v. *Sovereign General Insurance Co.* [1997] OJ No. 6294 at 283.

31 *Newfoundland Assn of Provincial Court Judges* v. *Newfoundland* [2000] NJ No. 258, 191 DLR (4th) 225 at 141–6 and 321–2, CA.

nonetheless asserted that judges cannot be deprived of a forum to raise such challenges, and absent some constitutional or legislative amendment creating a different route of appeal from decisions of judicial compensation tribunals, those challenges must be heard, if at all, in court.

The potential for conflict where a judge adjudicates a dispute between a judicial association and the crown regarding the recommendation of a Judicial Compensation Commission was addressed in *Bodner* v. *Alberta*.[32] In *Bodner*, the Government of Alberta had rejected the recommendation of a Judicial Compensation Commission on the appropriate salaries for JPs. The Alberta Court of Appeal rejected the government's justification for this action and concluded that the lower level of compensation which the provincial government intended to impose on JPs violated the constitutionally protected standards of judicial independence. In its submissions, the government had contended that any additional financial obligations imposed on it by the court would have to come from the overall court services budget. In the light of this assertion, the court addressed the perception that its own resources may be at stake in its decision. Paperny JA framed the conflict in the following terms:

> On reflection, however, I remain concerned by what I consider to be the basic propositions being advanced by government and, if correct, the consequences that logically flow from them. They are as follows:
>
> 1. If the government has to pay the Commission's recommended salary increase, money will be removed from court services to do so.
> 2. In responding to the salary increases of judicial officers, the government can legitimately remove other monies allocated to the courts.
>
> In justifying the first proposition, the government affidavit states that Justice is going through a period of economic restraint. Why this is so is unclear ... In the absence of a legitimate rationale for this position, a reasonable person might conclude that its purpose or effect was to apply pressure to the decision-maker, in turn, casting doubt on its impartiality ... The public perception of judicial independence is of utmost importance. Confidence in our judicial system is fundamental to democracy. If a court is perceived to be subject to financial sanction for decisions it makes, public confidence will, justifiably, be diminished. Where the court is faced with the loss of services to it, if it fails to grant the order requested, it is reasonable to conclude that public trust in institutional impartiality is adversely affected.[33]

[32] 2003 ABCA 102, 327 AR 77, CA.

[33] *Newfoundland Assn of Provincial Court Judges* v. *Newfoundland* [2000] NJ No. 258, 191 DLR (4th) 225 at 26–9.

Consequently, Paperny JA recused herself from deciding the government's application, noting that it fell to the Supreme Court to resolve the impasse, 'where any deleterious effect on impartiality and independence is of lesser magnitude'.[34]

While judicial associations advocate on behalf of judges before government, they do not constitute an 'association' of public servants. As a result, dues paid to judicial associations cannot be deducted as 'annual union, professional or like dues' within the meaning of the Income Tax Act.[35] That said, in the eyes of the reasonable person, a judge ruling on whether an association of judges should be treated as a professional association could well be seen as giving rise itself to a conflict.

Personal relationships

In addition to pecuniary benefits and group affiliations, judges may be perceived to be biased based on their various personal relationships.

In *Canada (Minister of Citizenship and Immigration)* v. *Tobiass*,[36] a meeting took place between the Chief Justice of the Federal Court and the Assistant Deputy Attorney-General for Canada. The purpose of the meeting was to express the latter's concern at the slow pace of certain cases being heard by the Associate Chief Justice of the Federal Court. In addition to the meeting, correspondence was exchanged. Counsel representing the other parties to the cases were neither made aware of the meeting nor copied with the correspondence. In his letter to the Assistant Deputy Attorney-General, the Chief Justice stated that he and the Associate Chief Justice appreciated the 'urgency of dealing with these matters as expeditiously as the Government would like'. When this letter was eventually copied to counsel opposing the crown in the matters in question, they brought a motion for a stay of proceedings on the ground that the meeting and the correspondence demonstrated a bias by the Federal Court in favour of the crown's interests.

The Supreme Court of Canada held that a reasonable observer apprised of the circumstances would conclude that the justices of the Federal Court were unduly influenced by a senior officer of the government. However, if the hearings were to continue under another judge,

[34] *Newfoundland Assn of Provincial Court Judges* v. *Newfoundland* [2000] NJ No. 258, 191 DLR (4th) 225 at 31.

[35] *Crowe* v. *Canada* [2002] TCJ No. 113, 112 ACWS (3d) 980, Tax Ct.

[36] [1997] 3 SCR 391.

with no further direction from the Chief Justice or the Associate Chief Justice, there was no likelihood that the undue influence would continue. Accordingly, a stay of proceedings was not required. The remedy chosen by the Supreme Court indicates that while a reasonable apprehension of bias was identified, it was not found to extend to the Federal Court as a whole. The apprehended bias was implicitly found to be personal, or relationship-based, not institutional.

Canadian courts have, however, clearly rejected the argument that the collegial relationships judges inevitably have with their fellow judges form a basis for disqualification. In *Mugesera* v. *Canada (Minister of Citizenship and Immigration)*,[37] for example, the Supreme Court of Canada rejected a motion seeking a permanent stay of all deportation proceedings concerning the applicant. One of the grounds alleged in support of the motion was that all members of the court were 'contaminated' by the presence on the court of Madam Justice Abella. Madam Justice Abella had voluntarily recused herself because her husband, in his capacity as chair of the War Crimes Committee of the Canadian Jewish Congress, a party to the proceedings before the Supreme Court of Canada, had at one point conveyed representations about the case to the Minister of Citizenship and Immigration. The court rejected this line of argument in the following terms:

> No reasonable person would think, after Abella J voluntarily recused herself, that her mere presence on the Court would impair the ability of the balance of its members to remain impartial. If there is a duty on the part of one member of our Court to recuse him- or herself, it is an astounding proposition to suggest that the same duty automatically attaches to the rest of the Court or compromises the integrity of the whole Court. To reach that conclusion would be to ascribe a singular fragility to the impartiality that a judge must necessarily show, and to the ability of judges to discharge the duties associated with impartiality in accordance with the traditions of our jurisprudence.[38]

Counsel should not appear before a judge where there is a spousal relationship between them. Such a situation is intolerable on both the ground of reasonable apprehension of bias and for evidentiary reasons. A co-habiting judge and counsel could never eliminate the possibility or suspicion that privileged or inadmissible evidence was being communicated. For example, would all parties have confidence that a settlement offer would not be revealed over the dinner table?

[37] 2005 SCC 39. [38] 2005 SCC 39 at 15.

A tenuous claim of family-related bias was made in *Middelkamp* v. *Fraser Valley Real Estate Board*.[39] Counsel argued that the judge might be biased because the opposing party was represented by a law firm of which the judge's ex-husband was a member. The judge and her ex-husband had separated ten years earlier. Her Ladyship noted that she 'had no ongoing relationship, social or otherwise' with her ex-husband, and dismissed this argument.

Courts have also rejected allegations of bias where the brother of a judge was a member of a large law firm which acted for the defendant in the case.[40]

Judges are drawn from the legal profession and, inevitably, have pre-existing relationships with members of the bar who may appear before them. The bars of most provinces in Canada have developed a 'rule of thumb' to eliminate the most obvious situations. Where a member of a law firm is elevated to the bench, no other member of the firm may appear before that judge for a specified period of two to five years after the elevation. This is a rule of professional conduct applicable to lawyers and not judges, although in practice judges may feel bound to disqualify themselves, even if a former colleague before them wishes to proceed.

Generally speaking, the Canadian rule is that a judge should not sit on a case in which his former firm was directly involved as counsel of record or in any other capacity.[41]

The Nova Scotia Court of Appeal had the opportunity to consider the issue of a continuing friendship between a lawyer and a judge in the case of *R* v. *Smith & Whiteway Fisheries Ltd*.[42] The trial judge and the crown prosecutor had been law partners until seven years prior to the trial. After the trial had concluded, and the accused convicted, defence counsel discovered that the prosecutor and the trial judge had maintained a friendship after the latter's elevation to the bench. The Court of Appeal

[39] (1993) 83 BCLR (2d) 257, CA.

[40] *G. W. L. Properties Ltd* v. *W. R. Grace & Co. of Canada Ltd* (1992) 74 BCLR (2d) 283, CA. See also *Makowsky* v. *John Doe* [2008] BCJ No. 576, 2008 BCCA 112, CA, in which the court ruled that a trial judge was not required to disqualify himself simply because his son, who had no involvement with the case, was employed by the fifty-lawyer firm representing one of the parties; and *Microsoft Corp.* v. *United States* (2000) 530 US 1301, USSC, in which Chief Justice Rehnquist concluded that his son's representation of Microsoft in antitrust litigation unrelated to the Microsoft case before the United States Supreme Court did not render it necessary for him to disqualify himself.

[41] See Canadian Judicial Council, *Ethical Principles for Judges*, Commentary 6. E19(a).

[42] 133 NSR (2d) 50 at 57, CA.

found that a reasonable person would not consider the relationship as described to raise a reasonable apprehension of bias.

The relationship between the judge and counsel may be a negative one. A lawyer who has lodged a complaint with the Canadian Judicial Council against a judge may be concerned about whether his or her clients will receive something less than a fair hearing before that judge in the future. In *Allain Sales & Services Ltd* v. *Guardian Insurance Co. of Canada*,[43] for example, the applicant's solicitors had, three years before, complained to the Council about the judge scheduled to hear the application. The complaint was soon withdrawn, but the judge continued a practice of not hearing the solicitors' trials. When the application came before the judge sitting in Motions Court, he declined to recuse himself. His view was that a reasonable outside observer would not think that an old withdrawn complaint would act to override the presumption that the judge would carry out his oath to act impartially.[44]

Prejudice and attitudinal bias

As a general rule, judges in Canada are encouraged to limit their statements of opinion to their written judgments and to avoid being drawn into public debates or controversies. A key reason that expressions of judicial opinion are generally found only in judgments is a desire to avoid any suggestion of prejudice. Judges seek to maintain at least the appearance of a system in which no decision is made until all evidence and argument has been presented. In the case of Ruffo J of the Court of Quebec, Youth Division,[45] it was alleged that Her Honour's strong publicly expressed views about the youth welfare system made it impossible for the province's youth welfare administrators to receive a fair hearing before her.

Following several candid interviews with Supreme Court of Canada Justice Bastarache, which appeared in *The Lawyers Weekly* in three instalments in January and February of 2001, complaints were lodged with the Canadian Judicial Council by the Atlantic Policy Congress of First Nation Chiefs and the Ontario Criminal Lawyers' Association. The

[43] (1996) 180 NBR (2d) 338, QB.

[44] See also *S (P)* v. *C (AJ)* (1993) 101 DLR (4th) 345, CA. where it was stated that a complaint against the trial judge is a serious ground for disqualification, but not necessarily sufficient. The court in that case raised the possibility of 'dishonest manoeuvres' if a complaint were to result automatically in a recusal.

[45] *Ruffo* v. *Conseil de la Magistrature* [1995] 4 SCR 267.

complaints alleged that Bastarache J expressed personal views on issues which had come before the Supreme Court of Canada and which were likely to come before the Court in the future, particularly with respect to aboriginal rights and criminal law. While not expressing a view on whether Bastarache J should recuse himself from future cases dealing with the views expressed in the interviews, the Judicial Conduct Committee of the Canadian Judicial Council concluded that the interviews did not create a bias that would affect Bastarache J's capacity to carry out his judicial functions. In explaining this conclusion in a letter to Bastarache J, Chief Justice Richard Scott, Chairperson of the Judicial Conduct Committee, stated:

> I am satisfied that your statements were made honestly and in good faith to encourage a better understanding of the differences in judicial approach which gave rise to divisions of opinion in the Court. Your purpose was not to proselytise or to act as a public advocate for the views which you expressed, but only to explain why you hold them. While your personal motives were laudable, some of your comments were of a nature that could be expected to cause controversy. It is clearly preferable for judges to exercise restraint when speaking publicly.[46]

In *Chrétien* v. *Canada (Gomery)*,[47] the Federal Court of Canada found that statements made to the media by Mr Justice Gomery in his capacity as the Commissioner of Inquiry into the Sponsorship Program and Advertising Activities did give rise to a reasonable apprehension that Justice Gomery had prejudged certain issues before the inquiry and was not impartial towards former Prime Minister Chrétien. It is noteworthy that the court took the view that even though a public inquiry may have the purpose of educating and informing the public, it is not appropriate for a judge who is serving as a Commissioner of Inquiry to become an active participant in the media.[48]

Less clear-cut cases will arise in which the judge makes no overt statement of opinion, but at the same time displays hostility to one side or the other. In this type of situation, the judge might question witnesses aggressively, or comment on the abilities of counsel. Whether obvious judicial antipathy crosses the line into a demonstration of prejudice depends, of course, upon context and degree. Again, the test to be applied is that of the reasonable and fully informed member of the

[46] Canadian Judicial Council, News Release, 'Judicial Conduct Committee Chairperson closes file involving Mr Justice Bastarache', 16 March 2001.

[47] 2008 FC 802, FCC. [48] 2008 FC 802 at 104–6.

public: would such a person come to the conclusion that a fair result might not be reached?

Concerns over bias in judicial opinions extend to comments made outside the courtroom. For example, during an address to the Canadian Club in Vancouver on 8 February 2002 on the subject of 'Aboriginal Rights: International Perspectives', Chief Justice McLachlin stated that:

> There are two major challenges facing Canada today in the area of aboriginal rights – completing the unfinished business of treaty negotiation and interpreting disputes about the meaning of treaties. These issues are the direct product of the British legal framework in the colonial era, which affirmed the right of conquered peoples to their lands, subject to the negotiation of treaties with the Crown.

Aboriginal groups objected to the 'conquered peoples' references in this speech and Dene National Chief Bill Erasmus filed a formal complaint with the Canadian Judicial Council by letter, dated 18 February 2002. This letter asserted that the remarks of the Chief Justice 'have created an apprehension of bias in relation to treaty and aboriginal rights issues' that warranted removal from office.[49] The Council subsequently advised the complainant that it had closed its file on this matter, without issuing a news release or otherwise commenting publicly on its disposition of the complaint.

In responding to complaints arising from a letter written by Justice McClung of the Alberta Court of Appeal to the *National Post*,[50] which contained disparaging remarks about Madam Justice L'Heureux-Dubé of the Supreme Court of Canada, the Canadian Judicial Council characterized judicial speech in the following fashion:

> Speech is one form of conduct. It may be an expression of rudeness towards a litigant or counsel which falls below the standard of demeanour and courtesy expected of a judge. It may express racism, religious intolerance or sexism which is incompatible with the judicial role. Judicial speech is often the basis on which the public forms impressions of the impartiality, competence and integrity of the judiciary. Judges are given the special duty and privilege of passing judgment on fellow human beings. The public has a justifiable expectation that they will be temperate, fair and wise in what they have to say.[51]

The issue of alleged bigotry in a judgment arose in a case in the Halifax Youth Court that was eventually heard in the Supreme Court of

49 S. Bailey, 'Chief Justice Irks Native Group', *London Free Press*, 9 February 2002, A9.

50 *National Post*, 26 February 1999.

51 Canadian Judicial Council, Letter to Mr Justice McClung, 19 May 1999, File No. 98–128.

Canada.[52] A young black person was accused of assaulting a white police officer. The police officer testified that the accused had ridden his bicycle into the officer's legs as the police officer was effecting an arrest of the accused's friend. The accused denied striking the officer with the bicycle, and testified that the police officer had arrested him for the sole reason that he had persisted in talking to his friend even after the officer had told him to 'shut up'.

The Youth Court judge, who also happened to be the first black woman appointed to the bench in Nova Scotia, acquitted the accused. She did not specifically set out any reason based upon the testimony as to why she might have preferred one version of events over another. Instead, she expressed her view that 'police officers do overreact, particularly when they're dealing with non-white groups. That, to me, indicates a state of mind right there that is questionable . . . I do accept the evidence of [the accused] that he was told to shut up or he would be under arrest. That seems to be in keeping with the prevalent attitude of the day.'[53] The summary conviction appeal judge and the Nova Scotia Court of Appeal agreed that a new trial for the accused was required. It was held on those appeals that the judge's comments revealed a form of bias that rendered her decision unsustainable. The order for a new trial was appealed by the accused youth to the Supreme Court of Canada.

The accused's appeal was heard by a nine-judge bench of the Supreme Court, and four judgments were written. In summary, Major and Sopinka JJ and Lamer CJC would have upheld the order for a new trial, on the ground that the trial judge had generalized or stereotyped in determining the credibility of the police officer, creating an irreparable defect in the verdict. Cory and Iacobucci JJ considered the trial judge's generalizations unfortunate, but held that the verdict was supportable if her oral judgment was read in its entirety. McLachlin and L'Heureux-Dubé JJ held that there was nothing objectionable in the trial judge's statements. Gonthier and La Forest JJ agreed with the judgment of Cory and Iacobucci JJ with respect to the general law of bias, and with the judgment of McLachlin and L'Heureux-Dubé JJ as it approved of the trial judge's statements. In the result, the appeal was allowed by a six-to-three margin, and Cory J's general explication of the law of bias was approved by seven of the nine members of the court. Five Supreme Court Judges considered the trial judge's comments unfortunate or objectionable; four did not.

[52] *R* v. *S (RD)* [1997] 3 SCR 484, SCC. [53] *R* v. *S (RD)* [1997] 3 SCR 484 at 494.

As noted above, there was little disagreement in the Supreme Court of Canada about the basic tenets of the law relating to bias when the issue was raised in *R* v. *S (RD)*. Bias was said to be the quality of not being open to persuasion. The formulation of de Grandpré J in *Committee for Justice and Liberty*,[54] being that of the reasonable apprehension of a reasonable and informed person, was again adopted.[55] Cory J went on to emphasize the presumption of judicial impartiality arising out of the judge's oath, which results in a heavy onus being placed on the party who alleges bias.

This case demonstrates the ways in which judicial impartiality attempts to grapple with the changing nature of Canadian society. Just as the Youth Court judge assessed credibility in the light both of the evidence and her own experience as a black woman in Nova Scotia, so judges drawn from a variety of other racial, ethnic and cultural communities, including the historical majority communities in Canada, will rely on their own experiences to adjudicate as well. As the make-up of the judiciary changes, the nature of impartiality will have to adapt.[56]

Concerns are sometimes raised about statements made by judges prior to their appointment to the bench which are said to indicate a predisposition on the part of the judge to decide a case in a particular manner. Many judges have written books or articles commenting on areas of the law with which they are familiar. Likewise, many judges have played an active role in politics or in advocacy organizations prior to taking judicial office. As a general rule, Canadian courts are reluctant to assume that because earlier in his or her career a judge has expressed views about a legal issue or engaged in advocacy in support of a cause, the judge is incapable of adjudicating impartially with respect to that issue or cause.

Recusal

In Canada, a judge is under an ethical and legal obligation to recuse him- or herself in any case in which an issue of bias (or apprehension of bias) might arise. The judge may do this on her or his own motion, and need

[54] [1978] 1 SCR 369 at 394–5, SCC. [55] [1997] 3 SCR 484 at 530, SCC.

[56] For discussion, see L. Sossin, 'Should Canada Have a Representative Supreme Court?', SC Working Paper, 2009, No. 7, Special Series on the Federal Dimensions of Reforming the Supreme Court of Canada, Institute of Intergovernmental Relations, School of Policy Studies, Queen's University, available at: www.queensu.ca/iigr/working/SCC/SCCpapers/SossinFINAL.pdf. See also L. Sossin, 'Discretion and the Culture of Justice' (2006) *Singapore Journal of Legal Studies* 356–84.

not (and should not) wait for the matter to be raised by one of the parties. This self-disqualification is known as recusal. A judge may recuse him- or herself despite the express wishes of all parties that the judge continues. From the judge's point of view, the consent of the parties is not determinative, although consent will count against an appellant if bias is raised on appeal. Generally, this is a matter left to the discretion of the judge, though the Quebec *Code of Civil Procedure* contains a scheme of *recusation* rules that specify in some detail the circumstances in which a judge should not hear a case.[57] The Canadian Judicial Council has set out the following non-binding statement of principles with respect to recusal:

1. Judges should disqualify themselves in any case in which they believe they will be unable to judge impartially;
2. Judges should disqualify themselves in any case in which they believe that a reasonable, fair minded and informed person would have a reasoned suspicion of conflict between a judge's personal interest (or that of a judge's immediate family or close friends or associates) and a judge's duty.
3. Disqualification is not appropriate if: (a) the matter giving rise to the perception of a possibility of conflict is trifling or would not support a plausible argument in favour of disqualification; or (b) no other tribunal can be constituted to deal with the case, or because of urgent circumstances, failure to act could lead to a miscarriage or justice.[58]

Thus, the failure to recuse may give rise both to a legal challenge by the losing party to the litigation seeking to reverse the decision, and to a complaint against the judge for breaching this ethical obligation. In the matter of *SOS–Save Our St Clair Inc.* v. *Toronto (City)*,[59] Mr Justice Matlow refused to recuse himself from a dispute involving the City's development plans for a neighbourhood when he was active in opposing the City's development plans in a nearby part of the City. The court initially ruled against the city, but when the city's solicitor filed a complaint with the Canadian Judicial Council on the issue of the judge's failure to recuse, the other two judges on the original panel took the unusual step of vacating the judgment on grounds of a reasonable apprehension of bias. Ultimately, the Canadian Judicial

[57] Articles 234 and 235 of the Quebec *Code*.

[58] Canadian Judicial Council, *Ethical Principles for Judges*, Principle 6.E, 'Conflicts of Interest'.

[59] (2005) 18 C.P.C. (6th) 286, Ont. Div.Ct.

Council found that Justice Matlow had engaged in misconduct by failing to recuse, but stopped short of recommending his removal on this basis.

While failing to recuse can have serious implications for both the case and for the judge, the same may apply where a judge does decide to disqualify him- or herself. When Mr Justice Jean-Guy Boilard decided to withdraw from the 'Hell's Angels' trial, the subsequent judge, Mr Justice Pierre Beliveau of the Quebec Superior Court, had no other choice but to dissolve the jury because they had been compromised. Judge Beliveau said that it would be better to start a new trial that would last six months than it would be to add several months to the proceedings.[60]

Justice Boilard's decision to recuse himself from the case led the Attorney-General of Quebec to ask the Canadian Judicial Council to carry out an inquiry into the judge's conduct and whether it constituted misconduct or grounds for removal. The Inquiry Committee concluded that although his decision to withdraw was improper, it was not grounds for his removal from the bench.[61] The Council itself, on the other hand, decided that there was nothing in the record to rebut the presumption that Mr Justice Boilard had acted in good faith in making a discretionary decision, and therefore his decision to disqualify himself was not capable of constituting 'misconduct' or 'placing himself in a position incompatible with the due execution of his office' within the meaning of the Judges Act 1985. The Council concluded:

> While some may disagree with Justice Boilard's decision to step aside, it was his decision to make. It is the individual responsibility of every judge to determine, in good faith, when there are circumstances that render him or her unable to hear or continue to hear a particular case. He or she is not required to consult with any other person, including his or her Chief Justice. In the end, it was Justice Boilard, acting in good faith, who was required to decide his capacity to continue.[62]

A judge typically should recuse him- or herself where the matter before that judge is one in which he or she acted or was involved with prior to

[60] Tu Thanh Ha and A. Lawlor, 'Judge Pulls Plug on Hells Angels Trial', *Globe and Mail*, 7 August 2002.

[61] Report to the Canadian Judicial Council of the Inquiry Committee Appointed Pursuant to s. 63(3) of the Judges Act to Conduct an Inquiry Concerning Mr Justice Jean-Guy Boilard with Respect to the Decision Made by Him on July 22, 2002 to Abandon the Conduct of the Trial in *R* v. *Beauchamp*, p. 4.

[62] Report to the Canadian Judicial Council of the Inquiry Committee Appointed Pursuant to s. 63(3) of the Judges Act, pp. 3–4.

becoming a judge. For example, in *Authorson* v. *Canada*,[63] Justice Iacobucci of the Supreme Court took no part in the hearing as he played a role in the matter being adjudicated when he was Deputy Minister of Justice prior to his appointment to the court. This arose again in the case of *Wewaykum Indian Band* v. *Canada*.[64]

After the judgment in this case was rendered by the Supreme Court of Canada, the aboriginal band which had lost its claim for compensation relating to a land claim, raised a complaint over Justice Binnie's participation in the case. Justice Binnie had written the unanimous judgment of the court in the case. The basis of the complaint was that Justice Binnie, while Associate Deputy Minister of Justice eighteen years earlier, had allegedly been aware of documents and strategy relating to the case. Justice Binnie, while having some general recollection of the issues, did not recall specifically taking part in any decision-making regarding the government's position or strategy in the case. Following the complaint, the Supreme Court took the unusual step of ordering a hearing on the issue of the potential conflict to consider whether to vacate the court's earlier judgment in the case. In the course of that hearing, the two most salient issues for the court appeared to be the fact that Justice Binnie had no recollection of direct involvement in the case (leading Major J to question how a judge could be expected to recuse himself when he had no knowledge of a conflict) and the fact that Justice Binnie's prior tenure in the Department of Justice was known prior to the original hearing of the case and the aboriginal bands had raised no concern over a possible conflict at the time.

The motion to vacate the earlier judgment was heard on 23 June 2003 and all remaining eight members of the court decided that it should be dismissed.[65] They concluded that in the circumstances of this case, no reasonable apprehension of bias was established and, hence, Supreme Court Justice Binnie was not disqualified from hearing the appeals or participating in the judgment. The court concentrated on two factors: his limited administrative and supervisory role, and that his role of Associate Deputy Minister dated back over fifteen years. Based on those factors, the court concluded that a reasonable person, viewing the matter realistically, could not conclude that Justice Binnie's ability

[63] Justice Iacobucci's recusal is discussed in K. Makin, 'Judge Seen as Absolved of any Bias', *Globe and Mail*, 31 May 2003, p. A6.

[64] *Wewaykum Indian Band* v. *Canada* [2002] 4 SCR 245, 2002 SCC 79.

[65] *Wewaykum Indian Band* v. *Canada* [2003] SCJ No. 50, SCC.

to remain impartial was unconsciously affected. In addition, the court decided that even if the involvement of a single judge had given rise to a reasonable apprehension of bias, it was not reasonable to conclude that the remaining eight judges were also biased or tainted.[66]

Conclusion

The law in Canada relating to judicial bias and recusal is at once clear and unsettled. It is clear because for purposes both of legal and ethical accountability, the standard of impartiality which has been adopted, that of the reasonable apprehension of bias, has found widespread acceptance. It is unsettled because the application of that standard remains very much in flux. To highlight just two of the ways in which this flux is apparent, first, the reasonable apprehension of bias standard is shifting as Canada becomes a more heterogeneous and multicultural community, and, second, it is a standard which is shifting as the role of the judge in the community is growing. In this sense, unlike judicial independence more broadly, which has a static quality, judicial bias and recusal should be seen as dynamic categories, whose nature and scope is changing over time.

[66] See A. Dodek, 'Constitutional Legitimacy and Responsibility: Confronting Allegations of Bias after *Wewaykum Indian Band* v. *Canada*' (2004) 23 *Supreme Court Law Review* 165.

16

Judicial recusal in New Zealand

GERARD McCOY

At the end of the nineteenth century[1] the New Zealand Court of Appeal was bristling with righteous indignation at the mere conception that a superior court judge could be disqualified for bias; for by the very fact of sitting the judge had already honourably concluded (from a Panglossian perspective) that no impediment of bias existed. The early cases looked single-mindedly towards a current and direct financial interest[2] as being the exclusive basis for judicial disqualification. Only that narrowly drawn category of bias could interfere with the sworn duty of a judge: 'nothing short of direct pecuniary interest will so disqualify a judge of a court of record of superior or general jurisdiction such as is this Court'.[3] Over time the austerity of the original test was relaxed so that a direct pecuniary interest did not exist where it was 'so remote as to be fanciful',[4] or where the interest depended on a number of contingencies.[5] But where a court fine for breach of a by-law would be paid under legislation to a borough council, a councillor of that body who held office as a Justice of the Peace was disabled from issuing a summons upon the information of the council.[6] A decision of a Compensation Court was invalidated because one of the parties before the court was represented by a partner

1 *Steinmann* v. *De Courte* (1899) 17 NZLR 805 at 811, CA.

2 An employee of a city was disqualified as an independent statutory assessor of compensation owed by the city: *Joseph* v. *Mayor of Wellington* (1885) 3 NZLR 291, SC.

3 *Steinmann* v. *De Courte* (1899) 17 NZLR 805 at 811, CA.

4 *Cook* v. *Patterson* [1972] NZLR 861, 865, CA. Information against a bookmaker for wilfully trespassing on a racecourse and refusing to leave when warned, was sworn before a Justice of the Peace who was a steward of the racing club which leased the racecourse. Prendergast CJ concluded that the information was a nullity because the justice was disqualified by his pecuniary conflict of interest. Also, *Ryan* v. *Stanford* (1897) 15 NZLR 390, 399 following *R* v. *Gibbon* (1880) 6 QBD 168.

5 *Panel on Takeovers and Mergers* v. *Cheung Kai Man William* [1995] 3 HKC 517, PC.

6 *Whitten* v. *Pennell* [1918] NZLR 762, which accords with *Ryan* v. *Stanford* (1897) 15 NZLR 390.

in the same law firm as a lay member of the court, the lawyer's fee being paid into the joint partnership account.[7] Indirect pecuniary interests engage an expansive protean notion. They may arise from a relationship (rather than from a contractual or financial connection) and extend to cases of potential advantage, benefit or liability.[8] Where a magistrate had been lawfully engaged in financial business transactions with a person up until the day before that person sought from the magistrate a liquor licence, remarkably it somehow survived scrutiny.[9] The myopic focus applied, namely, that there was no current conflict of interest involved, was quite unreal. It asked the wrong question. A clinical, temporal distraction wrongly succeeded. It was implausible in the extreme that one night's sleep altered the appearance of anything, although it was literally no longer a current pecuniary association.

Vocational introspection: judicial self-examination

The self-discipline and self-criticism required of judges extends in Justice Frankfurter's words to the 'incertitude that one's own views are incontestable'.[10] Judicial bias may be subliminal, unconscious, insidious or may be because 'a fixed idea is apt to become master'.[11] Justice Bertha Wilson of the Supreme Court of Canada quoted[12] Lord Macmillan's description of the mind of a judge as being 'a mass of prepossessions inherited and acquired, often none the less dangerous because unrecognized by their possessor'. There is a continuous and positive obligation on a judge therefore 'to discover and to suppress his prejudices'.[13] This requires introspection to yield insight allowing a detached critical self-examination of the apparent verities which the judge takes for granted.

7 *In re Skene's Award* (1904) 24 NZLR 591. In *Auckland Education Board* v. *Haselden* (1898) 17 NZLR 277 a decision of a Teacher's Court of Appeal was set aside as one member as president of the Teacher's Institute, had in that capacity undertaken to pay any costs awarded against the teacher.

8 *Calvert & Co.* v. *Dunedin City Council* [1993] 2 NZLR 460, 471; *Re Greene and Borins* (1985) 18 DLR (4th) 260.

9 *Ex p. Frethey, In re O'Driscoll's Application* (1902) 21 NZLR 317, CA.

10 G. R. Winters (ed.), *Handbook for Judges* (Des Moines, IA: American Judicature Society, 1975), p. 4.

11 *Quill* v. *Isitt* (1892) 10 NZLR 663 at 675 *per* Denniston J.

12 B. Wilson, 'Will Women Judges Really Make a Difference?' (1990) 28 *Osgoode Hall Law Journal* 507 at 508.

13 F. Frankfurter, 'The Appointment of a Justice', in P. Kurland (ed.), *Felix Frankfurter on the Supreme Court* (Cambridge, MA: Belknap Press of Harvard University Press, 1970), pp. 211, 216.

Confidence: price of unbiased justice

It is platitudinous that justice must be rooted in confidence.[14] Because the judiciary is one leg of the tripod of government[15] the acceptance of judicial authority and its structural integrity is dependent on the judiciary's own ability and responsibility to surpass the expectations of the very law over which it has stewardship.[16] Whether that authority is actually vindicated is measured by the notional informed observer. A premium is put on appearance as that externality engages sensibilities and will therefore demand more for satisfaction than cosy, acculturated legal logic. To Lord Hewart CJ is usually attributed the declamation that 'Justice should not only be done, but should manifestly and undoubtedly be seen to be done'.[17] But a reappointed New Zealand judge, Edwards J,[18] had much earlier emphasised the same irreducible obligation in the aphorism: 'The principle is that the administration of justice must not only be pure, but must seem pure.'[19] This captures the essence of recusal decision-making.

Deciding the test for recusal

For about a hundred years, the New Zealand superior courts oscillated between applying a test of either the reasonable suspicion or apprehension of bias,[20] without closely examining the worldly view of the perspective of the detached observer; a judge, it was concluded, necessarily embodied the virtues of the ideal notional person, a perfect anthropomorphic extrapolation. A mid-point between suspicion and apprehension, namely, of a real likelihood of bias, was occasionally adopted as the putative test.[21] The

[14] *Metropolitan Properties Co. (FGC) Ltd* v. *Lannon* [1969] 1 QB 577 at 599 *per* Lord Denning MR; *Saxmere Co. Ltd* v. *Wool Board Disestablishment Co. Ltd* [2010] 1 NZLR 35 at [92] McGrath J correctly emphasises that a specific advantage of a test based on perceptions is that the approach 'gives significant weight to the need for public confidence in the integrity of the judicial system'.

[15] In New Zealand, Part 4 of the Constitution Act 1986 makes this explicit.

[16] K. Bokhary, 'The Rule of Law in an Evolving Democracy', 19 June 2010, Honourable Society of the Inner Temple, 'Democracy's Illusions: Challenges to the Rule of Law?', p. 1.

[17] *R* v. *Sussex Justices ex p. McCarthy* [1924] 1 KB 256, 259.

[18] See *Attorney-General* v. *Mr Justice Edwards* (1891) 9 NZLR 321, CA for *quo warranto* proceedings, finding his original supernumerary appointment lawful. However, it was reversed in *Buckley* v. *Edwards* [1892] AC 387, PC; but his judgments were valid by the *de facto* judge doctrine: *In re Aldridge* (1893) 15 NZLR 361, CA.

[19] *Ex p. Frethey, In re O'Driscoll's Application* (1902) 21 NZLR 317 at 368, CA.

[20] *English* v. *Bay of Islands Licensing Committee* [1921] NZLR 127 at 133, SC.

[21] *Muir* v. *Franklin Licensing Committee* [1954] NZLR 152, 156, SC.

decisive influence had been *Dimes* v. *Proprietors of the Grand Junction Canal*[22] with its rigid insistence that a farthing's influence was fatal. In *R* v. *Camborne Justices ex p. Pearce*[23] the English court opted for a real likelihood of bias as the correct test and the New Zealand courts willingly followed, notwithstanding that the local landscape was strewn with conflicting decisions as to the contemporary test. Until very recently, New Zealand law as to recusal had been dominated by attempts to configure the appropriate test for judicial bias. Various permutations were adapted and adopted which essentially aligned with its English counterpart. Decisional law identified the earlier alternative tests of reasonable suspicion of bias or real danger or likelihood of bias as tending to produce no practical conflict in the outcome.[24] The Privy Council, shortly before being disestablished as the final court for New Zealand, baulked at delivering a definitive judgment as to what was the test for judicial recusal,[25] in the absence of a specific decision of the Court of Appeal, as to whether the test in *R* v. *Gough*[26] should be adjusted to realign the emphasis to the perspective of the fair-minded observer rather than from the view of the court.[27] On either test,[28] the Court of Appeal had held[29] that the recusal application there failed. Earlier, in *Riverside Casino Ltd* v. *Moxon*,[30] Gault J had emphasised that 'where the possibility of bias can be actually excluded appearances will be irrelevant. However, where actual bias cannot be excluded, the danger or possibility of bias can still be held

[22] (1852) 3 HLC 759, 10 ER 301. In *Ebner* v. *Official Trustee in Bankruptcy* (2000) 205 CLR 337 the High Court of Australia held that a judge was not automatically disqualified by having an indirect pecuniary interest in the outcome of the proceeding. Followed in *Saxmere Co. Ltd* v. *Wool Board Disestablishment Co. Ltd* [2010] 1 NZLR 35, SCNZ.

[23] [1955] 1 QB 41.

[24] *Mutual Finance Ltd* v. *Equiticorp Industries Group Ltd* [1993] 3 NZLR 650 at 654, CA *per* Cooke P. *BOC New Zealand Ltd* v. *Trans Tasman Properties Ltd* [1997] NZAR 49 at 55, *per* Gault J: 'A reasonable objective observer invested with knowledge of the material facts will not easily distinguish between a reasonable possibility and a reasonable suspicion.' Stephen Sedley, 'When Should a Judge not be a Judge?', *London Review of Books*, 6 January 2011: 'The first main difficulty is to decide what makes someone else's cause the judge's own.'

[25] *Man O'War Station Ltd* v. *Auckland City Council (No. 1)* [2002] 3 NZLR 577, PC.

[26] [1993] AC 646, HL which had been followed in *Auckland Casino Ltd* v. *Casino Control Authority* [1995] 1 NZLR 142, CA and *Riverside Casino Ltd* v. *Moxon* [2001] 2 NZLR 78, CA.

[27] To adopt the approach in *Porter* v. *Magill* [2002] 2 AC 357.

[28] Lord Steyn emphasised at p. 583, that the distinction 'is a fine one'.

[29] After consideration of *President of the Republic of South Africa* v. *South African Rugby Football Union* 1999 (4) SA 147 at 177 and *Locabail (UK) Ltd* v. *Bayfield Properties Ltd* [2000] QB 451, CA.

[30] [2001] 2 NZLR 78 at 88, para. [31].

to arise from appearances.' A firm and realistic standard which ensured public confidence was warranted.

Privy Council extirpates biased appellate practice

In *R* v. *Taito*[31] the Privy Council invalidated a long-standing practice of the Court of Appeal in which substantive criminal appeals were dismissed on the papers, without an appearance by either party, upon a decision having been made by three judges that the prospective appeals had insufficient chance of success for legal aid to be granted. The outcome of the decision on legal aid was the effective decision too on the appeal itself. Lord Steyn in emphasising that this 'extra-legal approach' was structurally unlawful and violative of constitutional rights, also concluded that dismissing the substantive appeals on the papers involved the 'participation of a Judge who had concluded that legal aid should not be granted, would have suggested to a fair-minded and informed observer that the Judge was not independent'.[32] That conflation of duties was impermissible and meant the decision was tainted with ineradicable bias.

Distinctive New Zealand jurisprudence

Apart from eventually settling on the appropriate test only in 2009, the subject of judicial recusal had only been lightly tilled. The deep underlying issues were either bypassed or ignored. It was the erudite and challenging monograph[33] by Grant Hammond in 2009 that provoked the need to conceptualise the long hidden fundamentals. That work emphasised the judicial responsibility of soul-searching tested against context-specific perceptions. The New Zealand law of recusal had been, however, relatively sedate until the tumultuous events of the *Saxmere*[34] litigation and its unended sequels, described below. Distinctive features of the New Zealand jurisprudence relate to the eclectic yet discerning adoption of overseas authority, a liberal acceptance of the admissibility

[31] [2003] 3 NZLR 577, PC. [32] [2003] 3 NZLR 577 at 598.

[33] G. Hammond, *Judicial Recusal: Principles, Process and Problems* (Oxford: Hart, 2009). The author is a distinguished Justice of the New Zealand Court of Appeal and formerly a professor of law in New Zealand, Canada and the United States, and recently President of the New Zealand Law Commission. See (2010) 69 *Cambridge Law Journal* 205–6 for a laudatory book review.

[34] *Saxmere Co. Ltd* v. *Wool Board Disestablishment Co. Ltd* [2010] 1 NZLR 35; *Saxmere Co. Ltd* v. *Wool Board Disestablishment Co. Ltd (No. 2)* [2010] 1 NZLR 76.

of evidence from bystanders[35] as to their impression of what had transpired in court, the focus on a more nuanced test engaging the appropriate frame of reference for the informed observer and the practical consequences of proven bias,[36] including the burden of costs.[37]

Locus to challenge: judges recusing too easily

Judges jumping ship too early has also become a recognised phenomenon across the common law jurisdictions. When an inferior court judge prematurely or unjustifiably ejects from the seat of adjudication, by wrongly acceding to a recusal submission, or by an act of personal self-abnegation, a superior court may by judicial review put the judge back in the saddle.[38] The judge is neither a party[39] nor an intervener[40] in appeals

[35] *R* v. *Morris* [2001] 1 NZLR 1, CA. In *Williams* v. *Willems*, High Court Hamilton, A62/00, 21 March 2001, Hammond J at [87] noted that while leave was required to adduce evidence of observers, 'such evidence is permissible, and even common-place, in this type of appeal'. A scandalous affidavit filed in support of recusal will be ordered removed from the court's file, but retained by the Registrar pending contempt or disciplinary proceedings against the responsible solicitor: *Steinmann* v. *De Courte* (1899) 17 NZLR 805 at 806, 815 (*mala fide* attempt to 'frighten' Edwards J by gratuitous reference to his wife's plight as defendant in breach of contract case).

[36] If an appeal is allowed on the ground of bias, the ordinary course, barring some special reason to the contrary, is to order a rehearing: *EH Cochrane Ltd* v. *Ministry of Transport* [1987] 1 NZLR 146 at 153, CA *per* Cooke P.

[37] Hammond, *Judicial Recusal*, p. 104 – the author notes that one civil case was quashed on appeal and ordered to be retried because 'the trial Judge's conduct has inflicted these substantial additional costs on the parties', and the New Zealand Government agreed to bear the costs.

[38] *Police* v. *Wanganui District Court* [2009] NZAR 97 and *Hosking* v. *Tauranga District Court* [2009] NZAR 712 (where self-made recusal determinations wrongly succeeded); *Nattrass* v. *Attorney-General* [1996] 1 HKC 480 (where a prosecution application had wrongly succeeded); *Secretary for Justice* v. *Chan Hung Yip* [1999] 1 HKLRD 555 (where a defence application wrongly succeeded); *Re Polities, ex p. Hoyts Commission Pty Ltd* (1991) 65 ALJR 445, HCA (where Commissioner ejected too soon).

[39] The invariable position is that the judge abides the decision of the superior courts: *R* v. *Thornton* (1898) 67 LJQB 249, CA. However, anomalously, a coroner appeared by counsel to justify herself when proceedings to quash an inquest were instituted: *Re Sutherland (Deceased)* [1994] 2 NZLR 242; *Coroner's Court* v. *Newton* [2006] NZAR 312, CA deciding that as a constitutional imperative, costs against a judicial officer are only awarded in extreme circumstances.

[40] *Vakalalabure* v. *State (Justice Shameem Intervener)* [2006] NZAR 741, Fiji SC (a trial judge applied to intervene in an appeal from her decision on the basis that one of the judges hearing the appeal was actually biased against her). In *Locabail (UK) Ltd* v. *Bayfield Properties Ltd* [2000] QB 451 at 480, CA it was held that a judge was automatically disqualified 'if there were personal friendships or animosity between the Judge and any member of the public involved in the case'.

or judicial reviews from a recusal decision. The judge ought to scrupulously abide by the decision of the superior courts with disinterest. To recuse for an insubstantial reason would lead to the intolerable conclusion that individual parties to litigation could strategically influence the composition of the bench.[41] It has been suggested that it is uncertain whether a person who is not, strictly speaking, an interested party before the court may apply for the judge to be recused.[42] Some authority exists for the proposition that an allegation of bias raises an issue intended to benefit the public as a whole, so the recusal evaluation process is valid even if instigated by a non-party.[43] But this is entirely suspect. If the relevant party is aware of all material facts and makes an informed decision, that election to continue precludes extraneous persons seeking to impeach that decision or its legal consequences. A person who has no right in any event to be heard in the underlying litigation, has no locus to raise a recusal application or to assert bias.[44]

Saxmere: judicial bias, judicial misconduct?

A somewhat mundane dispute about funding between the Wool Board and Saxmere was the setting for rounds of litigation that were to scar the legal system. At first instance, uneventfully, the action was resolved in the High Court in favour of Saxmere. The Board appealed to the Court of Appeal and Saxmere cross-appealed. One of the justices who heard and determined the appeal was Wilson J, who, as a highly-regarded silk, had been directly appointed to that court.[45] The appellant Board was represented by Alan Galbraith QC, an eminent advocate. Wilson J prior to the appeal telephoned counsel for Saxmere and disclosed that he and Mr Galbraith had some

41 *Ebner* v. *Official Trustee in Bankruptcy* (2000) 205 CLR 337 at 20 *per* Gleeson CJ, McHugh, Gummow and Hayne JJ.

42 R. E. Flamm, *Judicial Disqualification: Recusal and Disqualification of Judges*', 2nd edn. (Berkeley, CA: Banks & Jordan Law Publishing, 2007 [1996]), (1996), p. 496.

43 *Kellogg* v. *Martin* 810 SW.2d 302 (1991); *Re Tip-Pa-Hans Enterprises Inc.* 27 BR 780, 785 (BC WD Va 1983): 'Such prohibitions are plainly intended not merely for the general parties to a suit, but for the general interests of justice, by preserving the purity and impartiality of the Courts, and the respect and confidence of the people for their decisions.' This is distinguished in *Vakalalabure* v. *State (Justice Shameem Intervener)* [2006] NZAR 741 at 763, Fiji SC.

44 *Eves* v. *Hambros Bank (Jersey) Ltd* [1996] 1 WLR 251, 255, PC; *R* v. *Secretary of State for the Environment ex p. Kirkstall Valley Campaign Ltd* [1996] 3 All ER 304 at 323 *per* Sedley J. See also below n. 56 herein where Cooke P is less absolute on this issue.

45 Wilson J was only the seventh ever direct permanent appointment to the Court of Appeal.

mutual but unspecified business association. The informality of that communication was probably in conformity with the prevailing ethos between the senior judiciary and the relatively small and congenial inner bar. However, this conversation, its detail and extent, remain in issue.[46] The appeal proceeded without any objection by Saxmere or its counsel to Wilson J's participation. William Young P delivering the reserved and unanimous judgment of the court reversed the decision in the High Court, with the Board wholly succeeding and Saxmere's cross-appeal wholly failing. An application by Saxmere to the Supreme Court itself for leave to appeal to it was dismissed on the basis that the judgment of the Court of Appeal was unimpeachable.[47] It appeared to be all over for Saxmere.

However, some time later investigation revealed that there was appreciably more to that business association between the judge and counsel than had been earlier disclosed. Armed with (incomplete) fresh evidence, Saxmere made an unprecedented second application to the Supreme Court for leave to appeal from the decision of the Court of Appeal, now on the new basis of the apparent bias of Wilson J. This had the colour of *Pinochet*[48] all over it. The Supreme Court decided that the nature of the allegation and its intrinsic seriousness justified the granting of leave to appeal.[49] As Lord Atkin had said, 'Finality is a good thing, but justice is a better.'[50] The Supreme Court invited Wilson J to make a written statement[51] to it for the purposes of the appeal. (By now the internecine complications were close to breaking point as Wilson J had already been rapidly promoted from the Court of Appeal to the position of one of the five permanent justices of the Supreme Court.[52]) The Attorney-General was now granted leave to intervene in the appeal.

46 A. Beck, 'Litigation' [2010] *New Zealand Law Journal* 97.

47 *Saxmere Co. Ltd* v. *Wool Board Disestablishment Co. Ltd* [2007] NZSC 88.

48 *R.* v. *Bow Street Metropolitan Stipendiary Magistrate ex p. Pinochet Ugarte (No. 2)* [2000] 1 AC 119.

49 *Saxmere Co. Ltd* v. *Wool Board Disestablishment Co. Ltd* (2008) 19 PRNZ 132.

50 *Ras Behari Lal* v. *King-Emperor* (1933) 50 TLR 1, 2, PC.

51 This procedure was recommended in *Man O'War Station Ltd* v. *Auckland City Council* [2001] 1 NZLR 552, CA. Evidence is inadmissible from the impugned judge to explain his or her conduct and motives. No attempt to predict or inquire into the actual thought processes of a judge is lawful. Wilson J provided the Supreme Court with a written statement replying to the affidavits filed in the Supreme Court concerning his relationship with Counsel. *Saxmere Co. Ltd* v. *Wool Board Disestablishment Co. Ltd* [2010] 1 NZLR 35 at 14 *per* Blanchard J.

52 Wilson J was permanently appointed to the Supreme Court on 1 February 2008. As a later consequence of the imbroglio, William Young P was in June 2010 appointed under a hitherto unused statutory provision as a sixth permanent Justice of the Supreme Court.

The evidence gathered by Saxmere demonstrated that the judge and counsel were sole partners or shareholders in an equine stud. It was a really significant enterprise with revenue in the millions of dollars and it owned livestock and land. The details remained fuzzy, but the core nature of the business association was now much better understood, albeit still imperfectly. The Chief Justice recused herself from hearing the appeal as she and Wilson J were, ironically, in business together in yet another equine venture. The remaining three permanent justices[53] sat to hear the appeal with two former members[54] of the court complementing it to form the full quorum.

Saxmere (No. 1): Supreme Court

The Supreme Court delivered its judgment[55] four months after argument. After a close analysis of the competing strands of common law authority the court adopted the decision of the High Court of Australia in *Ebner* v. *Official Trustee in Bankruptcy*,[56] that, subject to waiver[57] and necessity, a judge was disqualified if a fair-minded lay observer might reasonably apprehend[58] that there was a real and not remote possibility that the judge might not bring an impartial mind to the resolution of the question the judge was required to decide. The highest court had pronounced the definitive legal test.

[53] Blanchard, Tipping and McGrath JJ. [54] Gault and Anderson JJ.

[55] *Saxmere Co. Ltd* v. *Wool Board Disestablishment Co. Ltd* [2010] 1 NZLR 35 on 3 July 2009.

[56] (2000) 205 CLR 337, HCA.

[57] G. McCoy, 'Inferior Courts Procedure Act' [2009] *New Zealand Law Journal* 373 at 374 noting a statutory waiver provision, which applies to a defined class of non-superior courts and certain tribunals. Reed J admonished in *New Zealand Sheep-Farmers Agency Ltd* v. *Mosley and Hill* [1932] NZLR 949 at 969, CA, 'if it elects, as it has done, to stand by for a period of some five weeks, it waives the right to move for prohibition; it cannot have it both ways – it cannot stand by, hoping for a favourable judgment, and when disappointed move for the writ'. The section validates and upholds any waiver or acquiescence, being unequivocal conduct or concurrence by inaction. Waiver or acquiescence by the parties is fatal to subsequent challenge, which also applies to the appearance of bias. However, Cooke P emphasised in *Auckland Casino Ltd* v. *Casino Control Authority* [1995] 1 NZLR 142, 152, CA, adopting *Goktas* v. *Government Insurance Office of New South Wales* (1993) 31 NSWLR 684, 686–7 *per* Kirby P, that 'displays of blatant bias, likely to undermine public confidence in the system of administration of justice, should not necessarily be capable of private waiver; while in criminal cases private waiver would not normally be possible at all'.

[58] *Auckland Casino Ltd* v. *Casino Control Authority* [1995] 1 NZLR 142 at [91] where McGrath J emphasises that the test 'aligned the common law with the international human rights jurisprudence'.

The Supreme Court identified from the affidavits filed and the statement of Wilson J that judge and counsel had been close personal friends for many years and had together with others been involved in the establishment of the horse stud. The judge and counsel each were 50 per cent shareholders and directors in a company which owned 41 per cent of the land on which the thoroughbred business was carried on.[59] Blanchard J concluded that the objective observer would have equally concluded that there was no evidence that the judge was 'beholden to Mr Galbraith because of the business dimension of their relationship'. Blanchard J noted by contrast[60] that a disqualifying situation

> might theoretically exist if, for example, the Judge had been lent money by counsel or was dependent on counsel in order to meet some liability. However, the materials placed before the Court revealed nothing of this kind. There is nothing to indicate any indebtedness by the Judge to Mr Galbraith, nor any indication of any inability of their joint company, Rich Hill Ltd., to meet its obligations.

Tipping J saw the issue as whether 'it could reasonably be thought that the Judge was dependent on Mr Galbraith's continuing friendship and association in the shared business interests to the extent that he may have unconsciously favoured Mr Galbraith's client'.[61] McGrath J, with what eventually proved to be real prescience noted, that a 'financial association can have elements that introduce a degree of dependency that will provide the necessary logical connection between the association between a Judge and counsel and its capacity to influence the decision in a particular case'.[62] The Supreme Court unanimously concluded, on the facts as they were then known to the court, that the *Ebner* test for disqualification for apparent bias was not reached. It seemed that once again Saxmere had finally failed.

[59] *Saxmere Co. Ltd* v. *Wool Board Disestablishment Co. Ltd* [2010] 1 NZLR 35 at [16].

[60] *Saxmere Co. Ltd* v. *Wool Board Disestablishment Co. Ltd* [2010] 1 NZLR 35 at [25]. Gault and Anderson JJ concurred in short judgments with the other judges.

[61] *Saxmere Co. Ltd* v. *Wool Board Disestablishment Co. Ltd* [2010] 1 NZLR 35 at [44].

[62] *Saxmere Co. Ltd* v. *Wool Board Disestablishment Co. Ltd* [2010] 1 NZLR 35 at [111]. Adopting *Aussie Airlines Pty Ltd* v. *Australian Airlines Pty Ltd* (1996) 135 ALR 753 where the test was whether the judge was 'beholden' by some fear, favour or some capacity to exercise power in relation to their association; 'such situations may arise if, for example, a Judge is indebted to counsel, or has otherwise been financially assisted by counsel, in respect of significant sums payable at call'. Article 101 of the Italian Constitution requires that 'Judges shall be beholden only to the law': *Maestri* v. *Italy* (2004) 39 EHRR 38.

Some time after the judgment had been delivered the apparently indefatigable Saxmere interests and their intrepid counsel applied to the Supreme Court to recall its judgment. The judgment had, however, been perfected and sealed. The basis of this application included the fact that even more material information had been sleuthed and that additional disclosures had also now been made by Wilson J relating to the nature of the business interests and relationship. His revelation was indubitably precipitated by the contents of paragraph 25 of the Supreme Court judgment. That 'crucial paragraph'[63] expressly stated that there was no evidence that Wilson J was indebted or beholden to the Queen's Counsel. It remains as yet obscure as to what immediate steps, if any, Wilson J took upon reading paragraph 25 of the judgment of the Supreme Court.

Saxmere (No. 2): Supreme Court recalls its sealed judgment

The Supreme Court heard the application[64] to recall its earlier judgment and three days later set it aside, allowed the appeal of Saxmere and remitted the original proceedings to the Court of Appeal for a fresh determination by a different panel of judges. It was not perturbed by any possible want of jurisdiction itself, concluding rather brusquely that jurisdiction existed in the exceptional circumstances, basing itself on an earlier decision,[65] although the judgment there had not been sealed. The reasoning is scarce and staccato. While the result as to jurisdiction is correct, the court in its haste did not tarry to leave more than a flimsy signpost of the path it had travelled.

Prior to the hearing of the substantive recall application, Wilson J sought leave to provide yet a further statement to the Supreme Court.

63 B. Robertson, 'Judicial Ethics' [2010] *New Zealand Law Journal* 121.

64 *Saxmere Co. Ltd* v. *Wool Board Disestablishment Co. Ltd (No. 2)* [2010] 1 NZLR 76. Only four of the original justices sat as Gault J was unavailable. The recall application was heard on 24 November 2009. What transpired between 3 July 2009 when the first judgment was delivered and the hearing of the recall decision is now part of the subject matter of a formal judicial conduct inquiry. See *Wilson* v. *Attorney-General (Judicial Conduct)* [2010] NZAR 434 in which Wilson J unsuccessfully applied for interim relief, pending a substantive judicial review proceeding instituted by him of the decision of the Acting Attorney-General to accept the recommendation of the Judicial Conduct Commissioner to appoint a Judicial Conduct Panel to inquire into the circumstances of the Saxmere litigation and his conduct.

65 *Horowhenua County* v. *Nash (No. 2)* [1968] NZLR 632, 633.

This was done and, indeed, was even further supplemented by him[66] – being by now the judge's fourth or fifth attempt at written[67] disclosure. In *Ebner*,[68] the High Court of Australia analysed the 'duty' to disclose as one of imperfect obligation, without legal significance beyond its potential relevance as casting 'some evidentiary light on the ultimate question' of whether bias was factually established as perception or actuality. The Supreme Court appeared to palliate, if not wholly excuse, the deficiencies in the judge's earlier disclosure(s), on the basis that as no reported decision existed in New Zealand on apparent bias based on the relationship between a judge and counsel,[69] such that perhaps 'the Judge had not anticipated the view which we would form on the applicable principles in that connection'.[70] That really is too tender. There was no special subset of conduct between judge and counsel which could mean that the ordinary rules of apparent bias were somehow modified or displaced by its subject matter. It was not the bare relationship between bench and bar that was in issue, but was in context the undisclosed double helix commercial relationship that imperilled the appearance of justice. As was said in *Ebner*: 'It is not logical to have one rule applying to disqualification for interest and a different rule applying to disqualification for association.'[71]

The new evidence garnered by Saxmere and the drip-feed disclosures by the judge together now established that the original scenario of the company being seen as a passive land-holding entity, in which the judge and counsel made equal contributions as shareholders to the share capital and any loan capital of the company, was wholly unsustainable. The real position demonstrated that there was an imbalance in the shareholder's accounts (in which the judge was in significant

66 *Horowhenua County* v. *Nash (No. 2)* [1968] NZLR 632 at [6]–[7]. Wilson J's additional disclosures were a response to the suggestion 'he had not made a full disclosure before the earlier hearing'.

67 The judge had made some oral disclosure to Mr Galbraith QC's opponent before the hearing in the Court of Appeal.

68 *Ebner* v. *Official Trustee in Bankruptcy* (2000) 205 CLR 337 at [70] *per* Gleeson CJ, McHugh, Gummow and Hayne JJ.

69 See *Re A Barrister* [1987] HKLR 442, where a barrister was convicted of professional misconduct for travelling to, and spending the weekend in, Macau together with a Deputy District Court Judge while appearing before that judge. All expenses were shared equally and the case was never discussed.

70 *Saxmere Co. Ltd* v. *Wool Board Disestablishment Co. Ltd (No. 2)* [2010] 1 NZLR 76 at para [13].

71 *Ebner* v. *Official Trustee in Bankruptcy* (2000) 205 CLR 337 at [54] *per* Gleeson CJ, McHugh, Gummow and Hayne JJ.

comparative debt) and that the judge had also not actually made any payment of the bank debt, such that the aggregate sum of almost NZ$243,000 was owed by him to counsel. The Supreme Court was 'of the clear opinion that the objective lay observer could reasonably consider that, notwithstanding that background, the Judge was at the relevant time beholden'[72] to counsel, such that the unconscious effect of apparent bias with his creditor appearing before him as counsel, could not be safely dispelled.

The Supreme Court also lamented that a further material circumstance had not been brought to its attention at the first appeal. It transpired that the company was preparing to participate in the settlement of a sale and purchase in which it had contracted to buy a parcel of land to enlarge the horse stud. The company had put in place arrangements to borrow that price on the security of its existing land. The court noted therefore that: 'The Judge and Mr Galbraith must have been reliant upon one another, during the very time when the *Saxmere* judgment was reserved in the Court of Appeal, for mutual cooperation to enable the funding and completion of the purchase of the additional land.' This, too, was yet a further basis for setting aside the original judgment.

The wake of *Saxmere (No. 2)*: Judicial Conduct Panel

Formal complaints against Wilson J were made to the statutory Judicial Conduct Commissioner. After seeking the advice of Gleeson CJ of Australia and perhaps prompted by a public revelation that a former acting justice of the Supreme Court[73] had himself laid a complaint with the commissioner against Wilson J for the *Saxmere* conduct, the commissioner concluded under s. 18 of the Judicial Conduct Commissioner and Judicial Conduct Panel Act 2004[74] that he would recommend to the Acting Attorney-General that a Judicial Conduct Panel be appointed. Wilson J has now exercised the right available to every person under the law and become a protagonist by instituting judicial review proceedings challenging the lawfulness of the decision of the

[72] *Ebner* v. *Official Trustee in Bankruptcy* (2000) 205 CLR 337 at [17] *per* Gleeson CJ, McHugh, Gummow and Hayne JJ.

[73] His application to seek joinder as an interested party was granted, but as an additional defendant was refused: *Wilson* v. *Attorney-General (Judicial Conduct) (No. 2)* [2010] NZAR 509.

[74] Section 4 of the Act states that its purpose 'is to enhance public confidence in, and to protect the impartiality and integrity of, the judicial system'.

Acting Attorney-General under s. 21 of the Act to constitute a Judicial Conduct Panel,[75] by arguing that there was on any basis insufficient culpable conduct by him that could possibly justify his dismissal from office.[76] That claim failed. The Full Bench held that moral turpitude was not required. But it was also held the Commissioner wrongly took into account irrelevant matters. His decision was quashed and he was directed to reconsider the evidence. Thereafter, Wilson J resigned his office.

There can be little doubt that the appearance of confidence in Wilson J, as notionally held by the informed observer, would have been badly, if not irretrievably, dented by the unedifying episodes revealed (that observer though, may be unduly influenced by the media sensationalism). But the cachet and prestige of the Supreme Court itself must have been inadvertently wounded as collateral damage. The clear pedagogical lesson must be that niggardly, ungenerous judicial disclosure may be as misleading as it is incomplete. The vulnerability of the parties before the court is their dependence on the timeliness, comprehensiveness and reliability of the judicial disclosure. A stammering reluctance or spasmodic failure to be full and frank in the disclosure, plainly exposes a judge to the condemnation of having made, at minimum, a stupendous lack of judgement – which could amount, in brazen circumstances, to a repudiation of the essential criterion in the job description. A judge holds public office and considerations of privacy must be subordinate to the greater interest of the fundamental rights of the litigants before the judge to a fair trial – a constitutional right. The obligation on a judge, self-referential of the very authority to adjudicate, is to pre-empt a situation in which an allegation of withholding material information in the context of a recusal scenario can be plausibly advanced against that judge.

[75] *Wilson* v. *Attorney-General* [2011] 1 NZLR 399. The Attorney-General recused himself from the statutory decision on the basis of the appearance of bias as previously he and Wilson J had been partners for some years together in the same firm of barristers and solicitors.

[76] P. Joseph, *Constitutional & Administrative Law in New Zealand*, 3rd edn. (London: Thomson, 2007) at pp. 774–5 details the crucial lineage from the Act of Settlement 1700 (English) which provides that judicial tenure was held during good behaviour: *quamdiu se bene gesserint*. The constitutional importance of this issue mandates that only serious wrongdoing would qualify to remove a judge; the culpability would need to be intentional with foresight as to its consequences, otherwise the conduct would not be proportionate to the sanction of removal: *Rees* v. *Crane* [1994] 2 AC 173, PC.

A real question arises from the *Saxmere* saga as to in which quarter the burden of wasted legal costs for the entire episode should fall. This is exacerbated because it is now verified that the same combination of judge and counsel was also involved in at least four other separate cases during Wilson J's short tenure in the Court of Appeal. The issue there is indistinguishable from those circumstances giving rise to the actual *Saxmere* disqualification. On the face of it the same outcome must inexorably ensue. The costs of all of this and the necessary rehearings will be massive as they were each very significant commercial law matters. One solution, if not actually the only honourable one, is that legislation be enacted indemnifying all the blameless parties for all the costs thrown away.[77]

The informed observer in New Zealand: indigenous characteristics

The informed observer is the yardstick for recusal decisions. This person is imputed with knowledge of the law, its values and 'traditions and culture'.[78] A fair understanding of the ordinary workings of the judicial system ought to comprehend the professional and honourable values within it, fortified by a judicial oath and by the ethical responsibilities shouldered by officers of the court. But as McGrath J appositely observed: 'Public perception of the judiciary was not advanced by attributing to fair-minded members of the public a knowledge of law in judicial process that ordinary experience suggested was not the case.'[79] The informed observer approaches the relevant question in issue with a 'complex and contextualised understanding of the issues in the case'.[80]

[77] E. Campbell and H. P. Lee, *The Australian Judiciary* (Cambridge University Press, 2001), p. 97; *Rawlinson* v. *Rice* [1997] 2 NZLR 651, CA where this is contemplated, noted in Hammond, *Judicial Recusal*, p. 104. Saxmere ultimately lost: [2010] NZCA 513, [2011] NZSC 12.

[78] *Taylor* v. *Lawrence* [2003] QB 528 at [61] *per* Lord Woolf CJ. But Lord Steyn in *Lawal* v. *Northern Spirit Ltd* [2004] 1 All ER 187 at [22] acknowledged that the observer 'may not be wholly uncritical of this culture'. Any custom must pass the test of reasonableness to be valid: *Wolstanton Ltd and A-G of Duchy of Lancaster* v. *Newcastle-under-Lyme Corporation* [1940] AC 860, HL. The catechism set out in *Locabail (UK) Ltd* v. *Bayfield Properties Ltd* [2000] QB 451 at [25] of relationships and associations not ordinarily objectionable is pragmatic yet not definitive. It has been criticised as a statement of policy rather than being grounded in fact: K. Malleson, 'Safeguarding Judicial Impartiality' (2002) 22 *Legal Studies* 53 at 62.

[79] *Saxmere Co. Ltd* v. *Wool Board Disestablishment Co. Ltd* [2010] 1 NZLR 35 at [62] adopting the approach of Mason CJ and McHugh J in *Webb* v. *R* (1994) 181 CLR 41 at 50–2, HCA.

[80] *R* v. *S (RD)* [1997] 3 SCR 484 at [48] *per* L'Heureux-Dubé and McLachlin JJ.

The observer is 'neither complacent nor unduly sensitive or suspicious',[81] such that a balanced, intelligent yet critical view is taken. The observer is not a colourless, squeamish or impetuous individual, but rather an individual invested with a healthy dose of realism, neither unduly benevolent nor cynical. To such a person, though, the judicial oath is not a mere ritualistic incantation. The heightened and subjective sensitivities of an individual embroiled in the dispute are certainly not the criterion for recusal.[82] In one case, the appellant in person had in advance of the Court of Appeal hearing written to the assigned[83] judges unsuccessfully seeking confirmation of whether they were or had been members of a range of groups including the Church of Scientology.[84]

Impetuous and temperamental behaviour and actual bias

In *Re Royal Commission on Thomas Case*,[85] after the grant of a free pardon for murder to Mr Thomas a statutory commission of inquiry sat to inquire into and report on the circumstances leading to the convictions. Proceedings were taken to quash the royal commission on grounds including that the chairman had been so robust, interventionist and gruelling in his questioning that bias or predetermination was made out. The Court of Appeal in dismissing (by a whisker) the challenge emphasised that for the legal test for bias 'it is appearances that matter'.[86] In an inquisitional tribunal and the courts, the right to express tentative views may be an indispensable attribute of a fair hearing. It is only where the evidence discloses that the court or tribunal has 'adopted a fixed view, ceasing to be amendable to proper argument'[87] that predetermination is made out. A foreshadowed possible conclusion does not establish a

[81] *Johnson* v. *Johnson* (2000) 201 CLR 488 at [53] *per* Kirby J. In *R* v. *Spear* [2001] 2 WLR 1692 at [31] the court integrated the vision of the hypothetical observer with the strictures of Art. 6 of the ECHR and posed the test of a reasonable man, apprised of all the relevant facts about the particular case and the general practice. See, too, *Deacons* v. *White & Case Ltd* (2003) 6 HKCFAR 322 *per* Ribeiro PJ.

[82] *Inform Group Ltd* v. *Fleet Card (NZ) Ltd* [1989] 3 NZLR 293, 298, CA *per* Richardson J.

[83] In *Smith* v. *Attorney-General* CA 555/2008, [2010] NZCA 258, Hammond J adroitly rejected a recusal application directed at all three justices, on the basis that the panel was not drawn by lot, rejoinding at [14] that 'a lottery is not what is presently required by law'.

[84] *Collier* v. *Attorney-General* [2002] NZAR 257, CA: valid though as to membership of Cabinet: *Davidson* v. *Scottish Ministers* [2005] SC (HL) 7.

[85] [1982] 1 NZLR 252, CA.

[86] *Re Royal Commission on Thomas Case*[1982] 1 NZLR 252 at 277.

[87] *Re Royal Commission on Thomas Case*[1982] 1 NZLR 252 at 279.

foreclosed mind. Unless 'irretrievably committed'[88] the decision-maker has not predetermined the issue. An open mind is not to be confused with an empty one.[89] An allegation of excessive questioning by a trial judge is more easily sustainable if it is a trial by jury,[90] as the complaint may also appear to usurp the separate function of the jury. Cooke P emphasised that issues of bias or judicial intervention may overlap and are ultimately an application of the constitutional right to a fair trial.[91] A judge who displays impatience, frustration or rudeness does not necessarily display bias.[92] While that type of behaviour is unseemly, it does not mean that the judge had actually or apparently favoured one party or witness over another. There are, not unexpectedly, very few cases of actual judicial bias.[93] In part, this is because a softer finding of the appearance of bias suffices for disqualification.

Bias: relations between opposing lawyers and judges

There are even fewer cases closely analysing the disqualifying perils in a relationship between a judge and a legal practitioner. But derivative value can be drawn from the approach applied in testing the safety of

[88] *CREEDNZ Inc.* v. *Governor-General* [1981] 1 NZLR 172, 179 *per* Cooke J.

[89] G. McCoy, 'Public Law Potpourri' [2009] *New Zealand Law Journal* 352 at 360.

[90] *EH Cochrane Ltd* v. *Ministry of Transport* [1987] 1 NZLR 146, CA. In *Attorney-General of Hong Kong* v. *Siu Yuk Shing* [1989] 1 WLR 236 at 241, PC, Lord Griffiths contrasted the reduced role of prejudice in a trial by judge alone.

[91] *EH Cochrane Ltd* v. *Ministry of Transport* [1987] 1 NZLR 146 at 148.

[92] *Chau Siu Woon* v. *Cheung Shek Kong* [2010] 3 HKLRD 49, CA; cf. *Incorporated Owners of Finance Building* v. *Bright Hill Management Consultants Co. Ltd* [2010] 3 HKLRD 1, CA where the judge used pejorative words and phrases in an intemperate manner directed at a litigant in person, and presumptive bias was established.

[93] Where prohibitionists were elected as the majority of members of a Liquor Licensing Committee, their decision to effect the closing of all licensed premises in their district showed they were incapable by bias of exercising a lawful discretion: *Isitt* v. *Quill* (1893) 11 NZLR 224, CA. Their election pledge was to do just what they decided. Their actions were 'as remote as can well be conceived from the ideal of a judicial body': *Quill* v. *Isitt* (1892) 10 NZLR 663 at 668, SC. See: *R* v. *Handley* (1921) 61 DLR 656, where a magistrate refused to recuse despite the fact he had broken the defendant's nose in an altercation only a few weeks earlier; *Satharasinghe* v. *Juriansz* (1964) 66 NLR 490, Ceylon SC, where after hearing defence counsel a magistrate immediately read out a judgment he had written, signed and dated more than two weeks earlier; *Balis* v. *R (No. 2)* (1994) 75 A Crim R 515, where a judge told another that he would revoke bail when a particular application came before him. Actual bias existed when a lay member of the Insider Dealing Tribunal (presided over by a High Court judge) ironically leaked information about the deliberations of the Tribunal at a school reunion: *Francis Cheung* v. *Insider Dealing Tribunal* [2000] 1 HKLRD 807, CA.

the appearance of justice between legal practitioners. In *R* v. *Szabo*[94] a conviction was quashed in which the female prosecuting counsel had lived together with the defence counsel for almost a year, just until two months before the commencement of the relevant criminal trial in which they were opposed. The defendant was convicted and based on information slowly accrued, learned that his lawyer and prosecuting counsel had occupied the same motel room (platonically) over the weekend following the trial and that the lawyers' relationship re-blossomed a few months thereafter. Grounds for recusal are not confined, as had been sometimes stated, to 'something antecedent'[95] to the commencement of the hearing, but also engage what transpires during the hearing and indeed after it. The whole continuum of the litigation must be evaluated. In quashing the conviction, Thomas JA in *Szabo* accepted that a proper analogy could be drawn between the test for apparent bias of judicial decision-makers and allegations of disquiet concerning the conduct of counsel,[96] as each play an inseparable part in the proper administration of justice and the need for public confidence in the process is no less. By inherent jurisdiction[97] superior courts have the power to control and regulate who may appear as counsel and solicitors before them. In *Thurlow* v. *Clements*[98] the modern test for the appearance of bias in judges was assimilated to the determination of whether a legal practitioner was disabled from further acting for a party, because of his appearance of lack of independence and objectivity which his conduct had engendered. This test for bias, applying to all legal professionals within the legal system, has been used analogously in determining whether a trustee had a conflict of interest, noting that an interest in one spouse was

[94] (2000) 112 A Crim R 215, Qld.CA, De Jersey CJ and Davies JA concurring. See also *R* v. *Butt* [1996] Crim L R 910, CA.

[95] *Healey* v. *Rauhina* [1958] NZLR 945, 951; *Gould* v. *Wily* [1960] NZLR 960, 961.

[96] (2000) 112 A Crim R 215 at [48] and more importantly at [59]. This conforms with the New York State Bar Association Committee opinion 660 (39(a)–93) which provides 'the appearance of partiality in the administration of justice is so strong that a couple who date frequently should not be permitted to appear opposite one another in criminal cases'. While directed only at opposing counsel the same conclusion must follow from a judge in such a relationship with counsel before the court.

[97] *Black* v. *Taylor* [1993] 3 NZLR 403, CA.

[98] [2010] NZAR 172, HC. Cf. *Geveran Trading Co. Ltd* v. *Skjevesland* [2003] 1 WLR 912, 925 at [48], *per* Arden LJ The fact that the compromised solicitor might instruct an independent counsel was no salvation: *Boland* v. *Yates Property Corporation Pty Ltd* (1999) 167 ALJR 575, HCA.

capable[99] of creating an interest in the other. But a lawyer, unlike a judge, represents and promotes the interest of a party. The principle that it was immaterial that the conflicting interest was held by a trustee beneficially or as trustee for others[100] ought equally apply to a judge. A trustee as a fiduciary, a legal practitioner as an officer of the court and a judge as a sworn impartial public officer exercising judicial power should all be answerable to the same version of confidence that the informed observer would naturally expect them to meet.

Other judicial decision-makers: arbitrators and jurors

Arbitrators can be removed by a superior court if they act with bias.[101] A barrister having acted for a group of parties in other litigation earlier will not necessarily be disqualified as an arbitrator later involving the parties. But an arbitrator with a direct financial interest in the disputed outcome is hopelessly disqualified.[102] The general saving provision[103] for informalities affecting jurors cannot salvage the verdict of a biased juror. In *Tibbets* v. *Attorney-General of the Cayman Islands*[104] the Privy Council advised that applying the test in *Porter* v. *Magill*[105] with the nuance that the fair-minded and reasonable observer is neither unduly complacent or naive nor unduly cynical or suspicious,[106] it was not established that there was a real possibility that one of the jurors was biased in favour of one of the witnesses (and therefore against the appellant). The suggested additional requirement in *R* v. *Khan and Hanif*[107] that the appellant also

[99] *Collinge* v. *Kyd* [2005] 1 NZLR 847. The subjective evidence of a trustee that he was uninfluenced by the interest is inadmissible: *Parker* v. *McKenna* (1874) LR 10 Ch App 96 at 124–5 *per* James LJ.

[100] *Transvaal Land Co.* v. *New Belgian (Transvaal) Land and Development Co.* [1914] 2 Ch 488. A judge who holds a bond has a pecuniary stake in the project or has a right in it: *Collinge* v. *Kyd* [2005] 1 NZLR 847, 859; cf. *In re the Wanganui Licensing Committee* (1892) 10 NZLR 583 at 595 which is wrongly decided.

[101] For a case of actual bias see the xenophobic and racist comments of the removed arbitrator in *Catalina (Owners)* v. *Norma (Owners)* (1938) 61 Ll LR 360, DC *per* Charles and Du Parcq JJ.

[102] *Grey District Council* v. *Banks* [2003] NZAR 487.

[103] Section 33, Juries Act 1981. A judge may discharge a juror who is not disinterested: s. 22 (1); *Williams* v. *The Great Western Railway Co.* (1858) 28 LJ Exch 2; *R* v. *McCallum and Woodhouse* (1988) 3 CRNZ 376, CA; *R* v. *Te Pou* [1992] 1 NZLR 522, CA. For predetermination by a juror: *R* v. *Morris* [2001] 1 NZLR 1 at 4, CA.

[104] [2010] UKPC 8. [105] [2002] 2 AC 357.

[106] *R* v. *Abdroikof* [2007] 1 WLR 269, HL at [15] *per* Lord Bingham.

[107] [2008] 2 Cr App R 161, CA.

had to establish that the putative observer would consider that such partiality might have affected the outcome of the trial, where the allegation was one of partiality towards a witness (by contrast with a party), was expressly disapproved.

Prior judicial decision-making: basis for recusal?

Prior decision-making as a judge of fact in relation to a party in a separate matter, in particular a criminal trial,[108] is presumptively disabling and vitiates the trial where the party's 'known history could safely postulate' decisive inculpatory inferences. However, in a split trial to disbelieve a witness as to liability does not debar the same judge later determining quantum issues involving the same witness.[109] But where a judge has expressed an opinion in a separate case either about a question of fact which constituted a live and significant issue in the subsequent case, or about the credit of a witness whose evidence was material on such a question of fact, the risk of disqualification is engaged and must be evaluated.[110] The determination that there existed a *prima facie* case (even if expressed in forthright terms) or findings of fact given in interlocutory judgments[111] will not debar a judge from adjudicating at the substantive trial, unless the opinions antagonistic or favourable to the parties demonstrated prejudgment. The five Law Lords in *Re Lonrho Plc*[112] recused themselves upon a submission that a contempt proceeding they had initiated in the course of an appeal before them should not also be determined by them, being 'reluctant to leave Lonrho with a sense of grievance, however misguided'. This is too gallant by half and is unsupportable as an illustration of the proper disciplined principle. A misguided perception should not be given credence. Sometimes an appellate

[108] *Butler* v. *Norris* [1937] NZLR 743, SC; *Small* v. *Police* [1962] NZLR 488, SC; *Police* v. *Pereira* [1977] 1 NZLR 547, SC. Mahon J at 557 in quashing the convictions wryly observed that an appearance existed that 'the decision was founded in part on the knowledge of the magistrate that the proclivities of the appellant exactly matched the allegations against him'.

[109] *Inform Group Ltd* v. *Fleet Card (NZ) Ltd* [1989] 3 NZLR 293.

[110] *Livesey* v. *New South Wales Bar Association* (1983) 151 CLR 288 at 300.

[111] *Thornton Hall Manufacturing Ltd* v. *Shanton Apparel Ltd* [1989] 3 NZLR 304, 316, CA. Cf. *Australian National Industries Pty Ltd* v. *Spedley Securities Pty Ltd* (1992) 26 NSWLR 411, NSWCA, where the majority held that the strong opinions expressed against the credibility or credit of certain witnesses led to disqualification.

[112] [1990] 2 AC 154 at 178, HL referred to by Wylie J in *Thornton Hall Manufacturing Ltd* v. *Shanton Apparel Ltd* [1989] 3 NZLR 304 at 320, CA.

court may itself be unable to unanimously agree on a recusal application.[113]

Necessity: exception to the rule against bias

Parliament has occasionally authorised a statutory decision-maker that has a rival financial interest to an applicant before it to impartially determine substantive matters.[114] Necessity invalidates bias.[115] The rules of natural justice, though, can be excluded only by 'express words or by patent necessary implication'.[116] Where the Commissioner of Patents applied by statute on behalf of the crown for certain trade marks, the issue arose whether the Assistant Commissioner, being the officer holding the statutory power and responsibility for determining applications for registration, was debarred from adjudication. Necessity supplied the authority[117] and invalidates the perception of bias.

Bias: recusal in domestic bodies

New Zealand law recognises that a lawful and comprehensive appeal process in a domestic body or administrative decision may cure an initial want of natural justice or other administrative law error at first instance.[118] Expulsion of club members in breach of natural justice and minimum standards of fairness has proved to be a fertile ground for

[113] *Thornton Hall Manufacturing Ltd* v. *Shanton Apparel Ltd* [1989] 3 NZLR 304, CA.

[114] *Layton Wines Ltd* v. *Wellington South Licensing Trust (No. 2)* [1977] 1 NZLR 570. Wild CJ at 577 holding a corporate person cannot be a judge in its own cause either.

[115] *Between the Parishes of Great Charte and Kennington* (1743) 2 Str 1173; *Jeffs* v. *New Zealand Dairy Production and Marketing Board* [1965] NZLR 522, 535–6, CA.

[116] *Rich* v. *Christchurch Girls High School Board of Governors (No. 1)* [1974] 1 NZLR 1, 9, CA, *per* McCarthy P.

[117] *R* v. *Hardy* [2003] NZIPOTM 4. The applications were refused: see also *O'Kane* v. *Alcyon Shipping Co. Ltd* (1960) 24 DLR (2d) 119. In *Mayor of Auckland* v. *Speight* (1898) 16 NZLR 651, CA and in *Campbell* v. *AMP Society* (1906) 23 WN (NSW) 50 all the Supreme Court judges had investments with the insurance company concerned and necessity required them to sit as every other judge was similarly placed. See also, *The Judges* v. *Attorney-General (Saskatchewan)* (1937) 53 TLR 464, PC.

[118] *Reid* v. *Rowley* [1977] 2 NZLR 472 at 481, CA; *Calvin* v. *Carr* [1980] AC 574 at 595–6, PC; *Slipper Island Resort Ltd* v. *Number One Town and Country Planning Appeal Board* [1981] 1 NZLR 143 at 145, CA, 'a decision reached by a procedure in breach of natural justice is appealable'; *Nicholls* v. *Registrar of the Court of Appeal* [1998] 2 NZLR 385 at 436, CA; *Malkit Singh* v. *Attorney-General* [2000] NZAR 136 at 138–40, CA.

administrative law.[119] The stewards of a jockey club[120] are not precluded from decision-making even if the club or a steward have a direct or indirect pecuniary interest in the outcome of a protest, as this conflict is validated by the implied terms for joining the club or attending the races. Until *Church* v. *Commerce Club of Auckland*[121] it was generally considered[122] that only actual bias would disqualify a decision-maker in a domestic club scenario. Earlier New Zealand authority on this point was, however, both sparse and lacking in close analysis. The pertinent features include the contractual or consensual nature of the club and the fact that the executive of the club who decide the fate of the alleged miscreant will often have had personal interactive experience with the member, in fulfilment of the associational tenets of the club. It therefore appears that the price of membership carries the necessary implication that members have waived *inter se* objections on the basis of prior knowledge. By contrast, a closed and predetermined mindset would disqualify as lacking the minimum essential for fair and honourable decision-making. No member has waived his or her right to object to the closed mind of a judge of fact. A member will usually have a proprietary right in the club upon its dissolution, as well as reputational rights.[123]

Bias: recusal in local and central government decisions

In challenges to local government decision-making asserting that councillors were biased, the pragmatic approach adopted under New Zealand law has been to evaluate whether 'they had closed their minds and were

[119] *Law* v. *The Wellington Working-Men's Club and Literacy Institute* (1911) 30 NZLR 1198; *Perry* v. *Fielding Club Inc.* [1929] NZLR 529 (denial of right to cross-examine accuser); *Henderson* v. *Kane* [1924] NZLR 1073; *Millar* v. *Smith* [1953] NZLR 1049; *Byrne* v. *Auckland Irish Society Inc.* [1979] 1 NZLR 351 (expulsion without notice; damages awarded).

[120] *Ellis* v. *Hopper* (1858) 28 LJ Ex 1 (steward not debarred from adjudicating protest in a race on which he had a wager, this species of interest must have been foreseen); *O'Brien* v. *Boyle* (1893) 13 NZLR 69 at 77, SC (no disqualification unless 'actually actuated by improper or discreditable motives'.

[121] [2006] NZAR 494, HC. Venning J declined to follow *Maloney* v. *New South Wales National Coursing Association Ltd* [1978] 1 NSWLR 161 and *Whittle* v. *Australian Miniature Pony Society Inc.* (1995) 57 FCR 252.

[122] *Armstrong* v. *Kane* [1964] NZLR 369. Cf. *Chan Ho Har Wane Daisy* v. *Deep Water Bay Golf Club* [1992] 2 HKC 604 *per* Bokhary J.

[123] *Baroness Baillieu* v. *Foreign Correspondents' Club, Hong Kong* [2009] 5 HKLRD 557, CA, *per* Stock VP.

no longer giving genuine consideration to the issues'.[124] Where a local body completely surrendered its powers of independent judgment as a statutory tribunal because of its intense collaborative assistance to a party before it, actual bias by way of predetermination to grant the application was established.[125] A court has no discretion to refuse relief when actual bias is demonstrated.[126] In *Travis Holdings Ltd* v. *Christchurch City Council*,[127] Tipping J held that an applicant alleging that a public body had fettered its statutory discretion by contract or by predetermination needed to establish actual predetermination rather than just its appearance. The reasoning impelling this conclusion was that the test for challenges to decision-making and decisions of ministers of the crown and central government should also apply to decisions of local government. The elevated standard of judicial bias was completely inappropriate.[128] As it is self-evident that ministerial or departmental policy cannot be regarded as disqualifying bias,[129] the fact that a local government body or member has advocated a scheme or supported it as a matter of policy or of electoral husting advocacy does not itself disqualify. It will be a matter of fact and degree. The tipping-point is proof of actual predetermination. An advance contract by the decision-maker to grant or refuse contested planning permission is plainly actual bias.[130] Where an objection to a proposal was made by a company of which five of the twelve councillors were shareholders, the court held that the successful opposition decision should be quashed and reconsidered by non-shareholders unless the statutory quorum of the council could not be attained without the shareholder-councillors: *Meadowvale Stud Farm Ltd* v. *Stratford County Council*.[131] In *R (Lewis)*,[132] Pill LJ emphasised that it would be 'damaging to the democratic process' and

[124] *Loveridge and Henry* v. *Eltham County Council* (1985) 5 NZAR 257, 264, applying *Rigg* v. *University of Waikato* [1984] 1 NZLR 149, 221, that local government councillors are affected by a 'personal motive' when their interest is 'greater than that of the public at large'.

[125] *Anderton* v. *Auckland City Council* [1978] 1 NZLR 657 at 698.

[126] *Re O'Driscoll ex p. Frethey* (1902) 21 NZLR 317 at 342 *per* Stout CJ.

[127] [1993] 3 NZLR 32 at 47.

[128] *Friends of Turitea Reserve Society Inc.* v. *Palmeston North City Council* [2008] 2 NZLR 661 *per* Baragwanath J; *R* v. *Secretary of State for the Environment ex p. Kirkstall Valley Campaign Ltd* [1996] 3 All ER 304, 320j–321a *per* Sedley J; *R (Lewis)* v. *Redcar and Cleveland Borough Council* [2009] 1 WLR 83 at [62], [65]–[66] *per* Pill, Rix and Longmore LJJ.

[129] *Fowler and Roderique Ltd* v. *Attorney-General* [1987] 2 NZLR 56.

[130] *Fairland Overseas Development Ltd* v. *Secretary for Justice* [2007] 4 HKLRD 949 at [84].

[131] [1979] 1 NZLR 342, SC. [132] See above n. 128.

inconsistent with the 'constitutional position' to quash decisions of local councillors on the basis of a closed mind 'without powerful evidence'. Predisposition is not predetermination.[133]

Epilogue

Implausible claims of bias of administrative decision-makers are now commonly deployed before the courts as a makeweight or strategic submission designed for forum-shopping purposes. Similar forensic momentum may now be seen in the number of direct applications made to judges of the superior courts for recusal. What was once almost unheard of has now become commonplace. Tendentious submissions of disqualifying bias are now made with irresponsible ease: the currency of judicial recusal has become debased.

The judges too have willingly let the bar be lowered. The Court of Appeal wrongly acceded to a submission that because one of them had acted as counsel for the appellant thirty-two years earlier (the judge having no memory of this early foray as a barrister), the appeal should be heard by a different panel.[134] The reasoning that the judge 'may be subconsciously affected by his previous professional relationship' is flaccid and preoccupied by an oversensitivity that is not part of the informed onlooker's make-up. A lawyer who kept her bias objection up her sleeve, though, was correctly held to have waived her right to object later as being fully aware of the legal consequences of her choice not to deploy her objection earlier.[135] Although it would be trespassory for an informed bystander to determine waiver, the calculated strategem there would have been plainly offensive to the expectations of the ordinary person on the sideline. Recusal choices have consequences.

[133] G. McCoy, 'Public Law Potpurri' [2009] *New Zealand Law Journal* 352 at 356.

[134] *R* v. *Reekers* [2011] NZCA 125 at [15].

[135] *Sisson* v. *Canterbury District Law Society* [2011] NZCA 55 at [44]–[47] adopting the principle but distinguishing the result in *Smith* v. *Kvaerner Cementation Foundation Ltd* [2007] 1 WLR 370 (CA) at [29].

17

Judges, bias and recusal in South Africa

KATE O'REGAN AND EDWIN CAMERON

The South African Constitution confers extensive powers on the South African judiciary to uphold the rule of law. In so doing, it stipulates that courts must be independent and subject only to the Constitution and to the law, which judges must apply impartially and without fear, favour or prejudice.[1]

Judicial impartiality is thus a principle at the forefront of the Constitution, but it was also deeply embedded in South African common law. Roman-Dutch law (derived substantially from Roman law) recognised the principle that no one should be a judge in his (or her) own cause[2] and afforded a remedy, the *exceptio recusationis*, to enforce it. In the era of parliamentary sovereignty before the new democratic dispensation, the courts conferred perhaps the strongest protection they could on the common law requirement of judicial impartiality: they held that it could be excluded only by an express provision in an Act of Parliament.[3] The Roman-Dutch law principle is substantially similar to the English common law principle of judicial impartiality and, accordingly, Commonwealth jurisprudence on judicial impartiality has been influential in South African courts.

In the sixteen years since the adoption of the Constitution, there have been a number of cases in both the Constitutional Court (the highest court on constitutional matters[4]) and the Supreme Court of Appeal (the highest court save in constitutional matters[5]) relating to judicial impartiality and recusal. These decisions make plain that the legal basis of the principle of

1 Section 165(2) of the South African Constitution.

2 *Nemo in sua causa iudex potest*: D 2.1.10. See also Voet 5.1.47 and the full discussion in *SA Motor Acceptance Corporation (Edms) Bpk* v. *Oberholzer* 1974 (4) SA 808, T, at 811B–813H; *BTR Industries SA (Pty) Ltd* v. *MAWU* 1992 (3) AA 673, A, at 688E–689A (citing the discussion in *Oberholzer* with approval).

3 *Council of Review, South African Defence Force* v. *Mönnig* 1992 (3) SA 482, A.

4 Section 167(3)(a) of the Constitution. 5 Section 168(3) of the Constitution.

judicial impartiality in South Africa is now to be found in the Constitution, but that pre-constitutional authority remains relevant to the development of the constitutional law principle.[6]

This chapter is divided into three parts: first, we describe the general approach to recusal in South African law; second, we consider certain specific factual circumstances in which the recusal of judicial officers has been sought; and third, we consider the procedure in recusal applications and allegations of bias, including the effect on the proceedings of a conclusion that a judge was biased or reasonably apprehended to be biased.

General approach to recusal

As in many Commonwealth countries, it is generally accepted that there are two circumstances in which a judge must recuse him- or herself. The first is where the judge is actually biased or has a clear conflict of interest, and the second is where a reasonable person, in possession of the facts, would harbour a reasonable apprehension that the judge is biased.[7] It is perhaps surprising that there has been little recent judicial discussion of the test for actual bias in South African case law, given the attention this question has received in other jurisdictions in the last few decades.[8] Even in other jurisdictions, cases are rare.[9] A close familial relationship with a party (though not necessarily his or her legal representative)[10] will

6 See, e.g., *President of the Republic of South Africa* v. *South African Rugby Football Union* (hereafter '*SARFU*') 1999 (4) SA 147, CC, at para. 48; *S* v. *Roberts* 1999 (4) SA 915, SCA, at paras. 32–4; *South African Commercial, Catering and Allied Workers Union (SACCAWU)* v. *I & J Ltd* 2000 (3) SA 705, CC, at para. 11.

7 See the discussion below on the relationship between the 'reasonable apprehension' test and the 'real likelihood' test applicable in the United Kingdom.

8 See *R* v. *Bow Street Metropolitan Stipendiary Magistrate ex p. Pinochet Ugarte (No. 2)* [2000] 1 AC 119, 1999 (1) All ER 577, HL; *Locabail (UK) Ltd* v. *Bayfield Properties Ltd* [2000] QB 451, 2000 (1) All ER 65, CA; *Ebner* v. *Official Trustee in Bankruptcy* (2001) 205 CLR 337 at paras. 141–63 (*per* Kirby J, dissenting, holding that any 'real' direct pecuniary interest that is not *de minimis* operates as an automatic disqualification to sitting). See also the helpful discussion in G. Hammond, *Judicial Recusal: Principles, Process and Problems* (Oxford: Hart, 2009), ch. 4.

9 In *Ebner* v. *Official Trustee in Bankruptcy* (2001) 205 CLR 337, Kirby J noted that 'It is rare indeed for this defect to be claimed, doubtless for reasons which include prudence, politeness and difficulty of proof' (para. 109).

10 In the Constitutional Court, former Chief Justice Chaskalson sat in cases in which his son appeared: see for one instance, *SARFU* [1999] ZACC 9, 1999 (4) SA 147, 1999 (7) BCLR 725. One of the present authors, however, recused herself on occasions when her spouse appeared before the court.

clearly be a ground for recusal on the grounds of actual bias.[11] The ordinarily accepted principle is that a direct financial interest will also disqualify a judge, but there has been no thorough judicial consideration of this issue nor of the question of a *de minimis* rule. There has been some judicial support for the idea that a remote or insignificant financial interest should not give rise to a need for recusal.[12] The Constitutional Court in *Bernert* v. *Absa Bank Ltd*[13] has now authoritatively held that recusal is necessary only where a realistic possibility exists that the outcome of the proceedings will affect a judge's shareholding in a company litigating before the court.

Commonwealth jurisprudence suggests an emerging sense that the primary protection for the constitutional principle of judicial impartiality subsists in the judicial duty to recuse if a reasonable person would have a reasonable apprehension that the judge is biased. As Lord Bingham of Cornhill CJ commented in *Locabail (UK) Ltd* v. *Bayfield Properties Ltd*:

> in practice, the most effective guarantee of the fundamental right recognised at the outset of this judgment is afforded not (for reasons already given) by the rules which provide for disqualification on grounds of actual bias, nor by those which provide for automatic disqualification, because automatic disqualification on grounds of personal interest is extremely rare and judges routinely take care to disqualify themselves, in advance of any hearing, in any case where a personal interest could be thought to arise. The most effective protection of the right is in practice afforded by a rule which provides for the disqualification of a judge, and the setting aside of a decision, if on examination of all the relevant circumstances the court concludes that there was a real danger (or possibility) of bias.[14]

For somewhat similar reasons, a majority of the Australian High Court has discountenanced a rule providing that a judge is automatically disqualified from hearing a case where the judge has a direct pecuniary interest in the outcome of the case, no matter how small. The court held that such situations would better be dealt with by the rule of the reasonable apprehension of bias.[15]

[11] See *SA Motor Acceptance Corp* v. *Oberholzer* 1974 (4) SA 808 at 811A.

[12] See *BTR Industries SA (Pty) Ltd* v. *Metal and Allied Workers Union* 1992 (3) SA 672, A, at 694 I and the judgment of Kirby J in *Ebner* v. *Official Trustee in Bankruptcy* (2001) 205 CLR 337 at paras. 165–8.

[13] [2010] ZACC 28 at paras. 47–52.

[14] *Locabail (UK) Ltd* v. *Bayfield Properties Ltd* [2000] QB 451, 2000 (1) All ER 65, CA at para. 16.

[15] See *Ebner* v. *Official Trustee in Bankruptcy* (2001) 205 CLR 337 at para. 54, but see the dissent by Kirby J at paras. 141ff.

As the recusal jurisprudence in recent years in South Africa has been in the main concerned with the reasonable apprehension test, it may be that there is an emerging consensus among practitioners that this is the pre-eminent legal principle governing the question of bias and judicial recusal, save in circumstances where there is a clear familial relationship between the judge and a litigant or some other clear example of disqualification. In such cases, however, as Lord Bingham noted, judges may be expected ordinarily to recuse themselves anyway and no dispute will arise.

The difficulties with an absolute disqualification for any financial interest are easily described. Many cases will arise where judges have an indirect financial interest in the outcome of the proceedings. Early in its existence, for example, the Constitutional Court had to adjudicate a direct access challenge to the entire system of progressive taxation, an issue in which every taxpayer (and therefore every judge) ineluctably has an interest. The case was dismissed on procedural grounds and no judgment was written. Similarly, judges will often themselves have an interest in challenges to municipal rates as ratepayers.[16] There have been several such challenges in South Africa, but to our knowledge no judge has ever recused him- or herself, nor has any application been made for a judge's recusal on the ground of the judge's financial interest as a ratepayer.[17] Such cases, of course, could well be dealt with under the head of reasonable apprehension of bias should a litigant harbour anxiety, though the principle of necessity – which holds that judges should not decline to hear a case where no alternative is readily available – might oblige a judge about whom there is a reasonable suspicion to sit.[18]

The test of reasonable apprehension of bias was authoritatively established by the Constitutional Court in *President of the Republic of South Africa* v. *South African Rugby Football Union* (hereafter '*SARFU*') as follows:

> whether a reasonable, objective and informed person would on the correct facts apprehend that the judge has not and will not bring an impartial mind to bear on the adjudication of the case, that is, a mind open to persuasion by the evidence and the submissions of counsel. The reasonableness of the apprehension must be assessed in the light of the oath of office taken by the judges to administer justice without fear or

[16] See *Fedsure Life Assurance Ltd* v. *Greater Johannesburg Transitional Metropolitan Council* 1999 (1) SA 374, CC.

[17] See the similar discussion raised by the majority judgment in High Court of Australia in *Ebner* v. *Official Trustee in Bankruptcy* (2001) 205 CLR 337 at para. 41.

[18] See Hammond, *Judicial Recusal*, p. 32 and ch.12.

> favour; and their ability to carry out that oath by reason of their training and experience. It must be assumed that they can disabuse their minds of any irrelevant personal beliefs or predispositions. They must take into account the fact that they have a duty to sit in any case in which they are not obliged to recuse themselves. At the same time, it must never be forgotten that an impartial Judge is a fundamental prerequisite to a fair trial and a judicial officer should not hesitate to recuse herself or himself if there are reasonable grounds on the part of the litigant for apprehending that the judicial officer, for whatever reasons, was not or will not be impartial.[19]

Before the adoption of the principle of 'reasonable apprehension of bias', there had been some discussion in the South African case law as to whether the test should be whether a 'real likelihood' (or 'real danger') of bias has been established. This is the test in the English courts.[20]

In one case before the Appellate Division (the pre-constitutional Supreme Court of Appeal), the question of which test should be adopted was left open,[21] but shortly thereafter the issue was decided in *BTR Industries SA*. This concerned a bitter labour dispute about a mass dismissal of strikers. The presiding judicial officer in the industrial court proceedings during the course of the hearing attended and spoke at a management labour forum that the employer's industrial relations advisers had organised. The union then sought his recusal on the ground that his conduct gave rise to a reasonable apprehension of bias. The judicial officer refused, and the High Court supported this stand; but the Appellate Division endorsed the challenge and set aside the proceedings.

Hoexter JA found that the test adopted in England – that recusal is required only where there is a 'real likelihood' of bias – is more exacting than the test of reasonable apprehension or suspicion of bias.[22] He preferred the latter on the basis that it better cultivated the root principle underlying the requirement of judicial impartiality, that justice must not only be done, but must be seen to be done.[23] He emphasised that determining whether there was a reasonable suspicion[24] of bias required

[19] *SARFU* 1999 (4) SA 147 at para. 48. [20] See *R* v. *Gough* [1993] AC 646, HL.

[21] *Council of Review, South African Defence Force* v. *Mönnig* 1992 (3) SA 482, A, at 490.

[22] *BTR Industries (Pty) Ltd* v. *MAWU* 1992 (3) SA 673, A, at 693 I.

[23] *BTR Industries (Pty) Ltd* v. *MAWU* 1992 (3) SA 673, A, at 694G–5A.

[24] The test was originally formulated as whether a 'reasonable suspicion' of bias existed. The noun 'apprehension' in place of 'suspicion' has been preferred in later cases because of the 'inappropriate connotation' that might flow from 'suspicion'. See *SARFU* 1999 (4) SA 147 at para. 38; and *SACCAWU* 2000 (3) SA 705 at para. 15, fn. 24.

consideration of context, and should not be undertaken *in vacuo*.[25] The facts before the court, he found, sharply illustrated the difference between the two approaches. On the English test, no case for recusal would have been made out, while on the reasonable suspicion of bias test, the judicial officer ought to have recused himself.[26] This exposition contrasts somewhat with English authority that suggests that the two tests will ordinarily produce the same result.[27]

In applying the test of reasonable apprehension of bias, a court must take into account the following considerations (nearly all alluded to in the reasoning in *SARFU* and each of which we discuss more fully below): absolute neutrality is a chimera; the judicial oath of office coupled with the professional expertise of a judge imply that an applicant seeking the recusal of a judge must produce clear and cogent evidence; judicial officers have a duty to sit in matters that come before them and should not lightly recuse themselves; the question of whether a reasonable apprehension exists must be determined on the facts as they appear to the court; and the double reasonableness requirement of the test which emphasises its objective, not subjective, character.

The chimera of absolute neutrality[28]

It has long been recognised that no judge can be absolutely neutral. Judges are unavoidably influenced by the society in which they live. But Martha Minow has noted the difference between prior knowledge and prejudice:[29]

[25] *BTR Industries (Pty) Ltd* v. *MAWU* 1992 (3) SA 673, A, at 695C–D.

[26] *BTR Industries (Pty) Ltd* v. *MAWU* 1992 (3) SA 673, A, at 696I–J.

[27] See *Locabail (UK) Ltd* v. *Bayfield Properties Ltd* [2000] QB 451, 2000 (1) All ER 65 at para. 17 (the two tests would 'in the overwhelming majority of cases' lead to the same outcome).

[28] See *SACCAWU* v. *I & J Ltd* 2000 (3) SA 705 at para. 14 where the Constitutional Court used the metaphor of a 'chimera' in this context in the following manner:

> 'absolute neutrality' is something of a chimera in the judicial context. This is because judges are human. They are unavoidably the product of their own life experiences, and the perspective thus derived inevitably distinctively informs each judge's performance of his or her judicial duties. But colourless neutrality stands in contrast to judicial impartiality – a distinction the *SARFU* decision itself vividly illustrates. Impartiality is that quality of open-minded readiness to persuasion without unfitting adherence to either party, or the judge's own predilections, preconceptions and personal views – that is the keystone of a civilized system of adjudication.

[29] M. Minow, 'Stripped Down like a Runner or Enriched by Experience: Bias and Impartiality of Judges and Jurors' (1992) 33 *William and Mary Law Review* 1201–18.

> None of us can know anything except by building upon, challenging, responding to what we already have known, what we see from where we stand. But we can insist on seeing what we are used to seeing, or else we can try to see something new and fresh. The latter is the open mind we hope for from those who judge, but not the mind as a sieve without prior reference points and commitments. We want judges and juries to be objective about the facts and the questions of guilt and innocence but committed to building upon what they already know about the world, human beings and each person's own implication in the lives of others. Pretending not to know risks leaving unexamined the very assumptions that deserve reconsideration.[30]

Thus understood, impartiality is a habit of mind and a professional duty that needs to be cultivated: a habit of not insisting on seeing what we expect to see, but rather seeking to see things afresh. In applying the recusal test, therefore, a court must accept that judges are not 'colourlessly neutral'[31] but have life experiences that influence their perspective. The open mind that judicial impartiality requires calls upon judges to be aware of their own predilections as far as is possible and to listen to evidence and argument open to the possibility of being persuaded by either side.

The presumption of judicial impartiality: onus to produce convincing evidence

The reasoning in *SARFU* accepts that judges who have taken an oath of office to administer justice without fear or favour can ordinarily disabuse their minds of irrelevant personal beliefs or predispositions.[32] In *SACCAWU* v. *I & J Ltd*,[33] the Constitutional Court held that this principle entailed two consequences: that a person seeking recusal bears the onus of rebutting the presumption of judicial impartiality; and that the presumption is not easily dislodged but requires cogent or convincing evidence.[34]

The duty to sit

Like other Commonwealth courts, the South African courts have acknowledged that a judge has a duty to hear a case unless required to recuse him- or herself. In *SARFU*, the court cited the following comments from the High Court of Australia with approval:

[30] Minow, 'Stripped Down like a Runner or Enriched by Experience', p. 1217.
[31] *SACCAWU* v. *I & J Ltd* 2000 (3) SA 705 at para. 14.
[32] See also *S* v. *Radebe* 1973 (1) SA 796, A, at 813.
[33] *SACCAWU* v. *I & J Ltd* 2000 (3) SA 705.
[34] *SACCAWU* v. *I & J Ltd* 2000 (3) SA 705 at para. 13.

> Although it is important that justice must be seen to be done, it is equally important that judicial officers discharge their duty to sit and do not, by acceding too readily to suggestions of appearance of bias, encourage parties to believe that by seeking the disqualification of a judge, they will have their case tried by someone thought to be more likely to decide the case in their favour.[35]

In the case of the Constitutional Court, the court held that given 'the intricate procedure to appoint a balanced and representative bench' of that court, each of the judges of the court bears a particular responsibility to adjudicate each case unless disqualified from doing so.[36]

The situation of the Constitutional Court is particularly difficult, as the court in *SARFU* noted,[37] because it is a court of eleven judges, with a quorum of eight.[38] If the recusal of more than three judges is successfully sought, the court is no longer quorate. The question that would then arise is whether the court may sit with fewer than eight judges (despite the constitutionally stipulated quorum), whether acting judges could be appointed to fill the temporary vacancies or whether under the doctrine of necessity the disqualified judges might for limited or more purposes be obliged (and therefore constitutionally entitled) to sit. Section 175(1) of the Constitution provides that the President may appoint (on the recommendation of the Minister of Justice with the concurrence of the Chief Justice) an acting judge of the Constitutional Court if 'there is a vacancy or if a judge is absent'. Does recusal result in a judge being 'absent'? These questions have never been determined, although a matter in which they arose was recently enrolled for hearing. It was subsequently withdrawn.[39]

Determination of reasonable apprehension of bias on facts

The question of whether there is a reasonable apprehension of bias must be determined on the facts before the court. So in considering an application for recusal, a court should ignore incorrect assertions.[40] A challenge based on inaccurate information can therefore not succeed.

35 *Re JRL ex p. CJL* (1986) 16 CLR 342 at 352.

36 *SARFU* 1999 (4) SA 147 at para. 46. In this regard, the court quoted with approval a judgment of the US Supreme Court, *Laird* v. *Tatum* 409 US 824 (1972) at 837–8, where Rehnquist CJ made similar remarks concerning associate justices of the US Supreme Court.

37 *SARFU* 1999 (4) SA 147 at paras. 9 and 47.

38 Section 167(2) of the Constitution.

39 *Hlophe* v. *Langa* CCT 40/2009.

40 *SARFU* 1999 (4) SA 147 at para. 45.

Double reasonableness requirement

The South African test, like the Canadian, has a 'double' reasonableness requirement. The apprehension of bias must be a reasonable one in the mind of a reasonable observer. Although the two 'reasonablenesses' can be telescoped into one – since a reasonable person by definition will not entertain unreasonable or ill-informed apprehensions – the duplication has been said not only to ensure that the threshold for establishing apprehended bias is high,[41] but also that 'mere apprehensiveness' on the part of a litigant is not enough.[42] A court must determine that objectively a reasonable litigant would entertain an apprehension that on the facts is reasonable. A subjective anxiety on the part of a litigant, even if genuine, will not suffice for recusal if it is not grounded on facts sufficient to give rise to a reasonable apprehension of bias in the mind of a reasonable litigant.

Specific factual circumstances in which recusal has been sought

Colleagues on same bench

It is common practice in South Africa that where a judge is a litigant, the case will not be heard by one of his or her colleagues from the same bench. So, where a judge from the Free State High Court is a litigant, a judge from a different High Court will ordinarily hear the case. This practice stemmed from a decision in *SA Motor Acceptance Corporation (Edms) Bpk* v. *Oberholzer*.[43] In this case a magistrate was a litigant in his own district. The matter came before one of his colleagues who refused an application to recuse himself. The appellate court held that he should have recused himself. It invoked a passage from Justinian's Code indicating that a judicial officer should not be a judge in his (or her) own case, or in a case of his (or her) children or those with whom he associates.[44] The court held that if a judicial officer presided over a case in which one of his or her colleagues was a party it would give rise to a reasonable apprehension of bias.

The race of the judicial officer

Can a litigant in South Africa ask a judicial officer to recuse him- or herself on the ground that the accused is of a different race to the judicial officer?

41 See *SACCAWU* v. *I & J Ltd* 2000 (3) SA 705 at paras. 16–17, citing with approval Cory J in *R* v. *S (RD)* (1997) 118 CCC (3d) 353, SCC, at para. 113.

42 *SACCAWU* v. *I & J Ltd* 2000 (3) SA 705.

43 1974 (4) SA 808, T.

44 '*vel ceteris quos secum habet*' D.2.1.10 (Ulpian).

This arose sharply for decision in *S* v. *Collier*.[45] The accused argued that the white magistrate presiding in his trial erred in refusing to recuse himself because a black litigant may reasonably apprehend that a white judicial officer will be biased on grounds of race. The argument was dismissed. In a related question, a judge in Namibia whom leading politicians had publicly attacked as a 'colonialist' who was guilty of 'anti-black thinking' during a criminal trial,[46] raised *mero motu* the question whether he should recuse himself. On the basis that a judge has taken an oath of office to carry out his or her duties as judge, he found that he should not.[47]

Political associations before appointment

In *SARFU*, the applicant for the recusal of five judges of the court based some of his reasoning on the fact that four of the judges had been members of the African National Congress (ANC) before appointment, although they had all resigned upon appointment. It was argued that their prior political affiliation gave rise to a reasonable apprehension that they would be biased in favour of the President of the country, the president of the ANC, against whom the applicant was litigating. This argument was rejected. The court reasoned that all judges are expected to put party political loyalties behind them upon appointment. It also reasoned that given South Africa's history it would have been 'surprising if many candidates for appointment to the bench had not been active in or publicly sympathetic towards the liberation struggle'.[48] The court concluded that prior political affiliation would not be a ground for recusal 'unless the subject matter of the litigation arises from such association or activities'.[49]

Conduct of the proceedings

As in most Commonwealth jurisdictions, a judicial officer's conduct during the proceedings may found review or appeal proceedings afterwards. There is a close overlap here between the rules governing recusal, and the constitutional right to a fair trial.[50] The latter is entrenched in respect of civil trials in s. 34 ('Everyone has the right to have any dispute

[45] 1995 (2) SACR 648.

[46] *S* v. *Heita* 1992 (3) SA 785, Nm. The nature of the remarks made against the judge is described at 786.

[47] *S* v. *Heita* 1992 (3) SA 785 at 796D–E.

[48] *SARFU* 1999 (4) SA 147 at para. 75.

[49] *SARFU* 1999 (4) SA 147 at para. 76.

[50] See *S* v. *Basson* 2007 (1) SACR 566, CC, at para. 24.

that can be resolved by the application of law decided in a fair public hearing before a court or, where appropriate, another independent or impartial tribunal or forum') and in respect of criminal trials in s. 35 of the Constitution (rights of those arrested, detained and accused).

A judicial officer presiding over criminal proceedings is not merely an umpire, and the criminal proceedings are not a game. The judge is there to ensure that justice is done.[51] Thus, as the Supreme Court of Appeal recently remarked:

> Fairness of court proceedings requires of the trier to be actively involved in the management of the trial, to control the proceedings, to ensure that public and private resources are not wasted, to point out when evidence is irrelevant, and to refuse to listen to irrelevant evidence. A supine approach towards litigation by judicial officers is not justifiable either in terms of the fair trial requirement or in the context of resources.[52]

On the other hand, a judicial officer must strive to ensure that those involved in the trial perceive the conduct of the trial to be fair. These potentially countervailing requirements mean that a judicial officer must walk the 'thin dividing line between managing a trial and getting involved in the fray'.[53]

Expression of a preliminary view about the evidence to a witness or counsel will not ordinarily give rise to a reasonable perception of bias.[54] Indeed, it will generally be difficult for a litigant to establish bias on the basis of the conduct of a judge during a trial.[55] A litigant will succeed in establishing bias only if it is clear that the conduct complained of does not arise from mere impatience or irritation on the part of the judge, but indeed from what may reasonably perceived to be bias.[56] But where a judge's intervention and questioning is so sustained and aggressive as to place him or her in the arena of conflict, and to cloud the judicial vision, a reasonable impression of bias will be created.[57]

[51] *R* v. *Hepworth* 1928 AD 265 at 267.

[52] *Take and Save Trading CC* v. *Standard Bank of SA Ltd* 2004 (4) SA 1, SCA, at para. 3.

[53] *Take and Save Trading CC* v. *Standard Bank of SA Ltd* 2004 (4) SA 1 at para. 4.

[54] See *R* v. *Silber* 1952 (2) SA 475 (A) at 481 where Schreiner JA commented as follows: 'Indeed a court may in a proper case call upon a party to argue out of the usual order, thus clearly indicating that its provisional view favours the other party, but no reasonable person, least of all a person trained in the law, would think of ascribing this provisional attitude to, or identifying it with, bias.' See also *Sager* v. *Smith* 2001 (4) All SA 401 (A) at para. 25.

[55] See also *S* v. *Basson* 2007 (3) SA 582, CC, at para. 35.

[56] *S* v. *Basson* 2007 (3) SA 582 at para. 36.

[57] *S* v. *Rall* 1982 (1) SA 828 (A) at 832–4, applied in *S* v. *Le Grange* 2009 (2) SA 434, SCA, at para. 13, pointing out that 'Partiality has both an attitudinal and behavioural component' (para. 22).

An example of a reasonable apprehension of bias is *Moch* v. *Nedtravel (Pty) Ltd t/a American Express Travel Services*.[58] The applicant sought the recusal of a judge on the grounds that the judge had a strained relationship with her lawyer. In his judgment dealing with this, the judge found that the applicant had been an untruthful deponent and had acted in bad faith and for an ulterior purpose. No oral evidence had been led in the proceedings, which were disposed of entirely on affidavit. The appeal court held that in the light of the conclusions of the judge on the evidence in the recusal application, the litigant had reasonable ground to believe that the judge would not determine the main proceedings with an open mind. The court, therefore, found that the judge ought to have withdrawn from the proceedings.

Where the judicial officer gets so involved in the fray that it results in a reasonable apprehension of bias, the ordinary, but not inflexible,[59] procedure is for a dissatisfied litigant to pursue the complaint by way of appeal or review once the proceedings are complete. As Schreiner JA observed in *R* v. *Silber*:

> The grounds related purely to what had happened in the course of the trial. Neither counsel has been able to find any reported case in which an application for recusal has been made in the course of a trial on the ground that the judicial officer has shown bias by his conduct of the proceedings. And this is not surprising, since the ordinary way of meeting any apparent bias shown by the court in its conduct of the proceedings would be by challenging his eventual decision in an appeal or review.[60]

Procedure in matters concerning recusal

Where there is no call for recusal

A judge must consider whether there is any bar to sitting in a particular matter. To do so, the judge must consider whether he or she is 'personally disabled from bringing a fair and impartial judicial mind to the case'.[61] In considering this question, a judge must take account of the duty to sit in every matter absent a legal bar.

[58] 1996 (3) SA 1, A.

[59] See *Moch*'s case discussed in the previous paragraph where leave to appeal against a refusal of a recusal application was granted. See also the discussion of procedure below.

[60] 1952 (2) SA 475, A, at 481.

[61] *SARFU* 1999 (4) SA 147 at paras. 33–4.

Should a judge consider that there is a fact relevant to whether he or she may be considered to be impartial, it is a practice in many South African courts (particularly the Constitutional Court and Supreme Court of Appeal) for the judge to ask the registrar to write to the litigants to draw their attention to that fact. A judge will ordinarily do this when he or she considers that the fact does not require recusal, but that it may be one to which in fairness parties' attention should be drawn. This was done, for example, in *Fedsure Life Assurance Ltd* v. *Greater Johannesburg Transitional Metropolitan Council*[62] where the registrar informed the parties that several judges were ratepayers in the city whose rates awards were under challenge. No recusal application followed.[63]

Applications for recusal

Should a party consider that a judge is actually biased or that there is a reasonable apprehension of bias, the party may initiate an application for recusal. Again, as a matter of practice, an application will not normally be launched until a meeting with the judge and counsel for the other parties at which the judge's attention is drawn to the issue.[64] The judge will then have to consider whether he or she is disqualified from sitting in the matter.

If the judge considers there are no grounds for recusal, he or she will communicate that, at which stage the application for recusal may be brought. The application will ordinarily be accompanied by an affidavit setting out the grounds. The application will be served on other parties. In South African law, an application for recusal is ordinarily determined by the judge involved.[65] As will become plain, however, leave to appeal may be sought against a refusal. Moreover, an improper failure to recuse will ground a review or appeal.

Where the application is made against one or more members of the Constitutional Court, the application will be considered both

[62] 1999 (1) SA 374, CC.

[63] Conversely, the problems that may arise if this practice is not scrupulously followed are illustrated by *Bernert* v. *Absa Bank Ltd* [2010] ZACC 28, where the litigant's legal representative was told orally of one judge's shareholding in the bank shortly before the hearing started. After judgment adverse to the litigant was handed down, the litigant alleged a perception of bias. The Constitutional Court rejected the challenge.

[64] *SARFU* 1999 (4) SA 147 at para. 50.

[65] See the interesting and novel suggestion in Hammond, *Judicial Recusal*, ch. 9, that a judge other than the judges whose recusal is sought should determine the recusal application.

individually by each judge whose recusal is sought as well as collectively by the whole court.[66] The court has left open the question of what should happen should there be a disagreement between a majority of the court and one judge whose recusal was sought.[67]

Effect of unlawful failure to recuse

The effect of an improper failure to recuse from proceedings when grounds for recusal exist vitiates the proceedings.[68] The result is that the proceedings will be set aside and must start afresh. An appeal or a review on different grounds will not remedy the illegality of the proceedings on the recusal ground, save if the appeal or review set aside the proceedings.[69]

In *SARFU*, the Constitutional Court noted that where one member of a bench should not have heard a matter, the effect is that the hearing is rendered void.[70] It referred to *R* v. *Bow Street Metropolitan Stipendiary Magistrate ex p. Pinochet Ugarte (No. 2)*.[71]

Appeals against the refusal of a recusal application

An unsuccessful applicant for recusal may seek leave to appeal.[72] In considering whether leave should be granted immediately, rather than at the end of the proceedings, a court will take into account the fact that proceedings before a court that is improperly constituted are null and void. A countervailing principle, however, is that piecemeal appeals should, where possible, be avoided.

It is clear that any waiver concerning recusal must be clear and unequivocal.[73] This rule is similar to that in the United Kingdom.[74]

66 *SARFU* 1999 (4) SA 147 at paras. 33–4.

67 *SARFU* 1999 (4) SA 147 at para. 34.

68 See *R* v. *Milne & Erleigh* (6) 1951 (1) SA 1 (A), 6H; *Moch* v. *Nedtravel (Pty) Ltd t/a American Express Travel Services* 1996 (3) SA 1 (A) at 13H; *Council of Review, South African Defence Force* v. *Mönnig* 1992 (3) SA 482 (A) at 495B–C.

69 See *Council of Review, South African Defence Force* v *Mönnig* 1992 (3) SA 482, A, at 495.

70 *SARFU*, 1999 (4) SA 147 at para. 32.

71 *R* v. *Bow Street Metropolitan Stipendiary Magistrate ex p. Pinochet Ugarte (No. 2)* [2000] 1 AC 119, 1999 (1) All ER 577, HL.

72 *Muller and Cloete* v. *Lady Grey Divisional Council* 1929 EDL 307; *SA Motor Acceptance Corp Bpk* v. *Oberholzer* 1974 (4) SA 808, T, at 810F.

73 See *SACCAWU* v. *I & J Ltd* 2000 (3) SA 705 at para. 5; *Bernert* v. *Absa Bank Ltd* [2010] ZACC 28 at paras. 73–6.

74 See *Locabail (UK) Ltd* v. *Bayfield Properties Ltd* [2000] QB 451, 2000 (1) All ER 65 at para. 15.

Accordingly, an applicant may reserve his or her right to raise the recusal point on appeal or review after the proceedings have been concluded. Accordingly, the Supreme Court of Appeal and the Constitutional Court have both recently warned that there is not a right to an immediate appeal when an application for recusal is refused.[75] Whether or not leave to appeal will be granted in the midst of proceedings depends on the facts. It may be that where the ground for recusal does not relate to the conduct of the proceedings, but is extraneous to the proceedings, leave to appeal is more likely to be granted.

However, even where the facts fall short of establishing waiver, the Constitutional Court has held that it is not in the interests of justice to permit a litigant who awaits the outcome of a hearing, holding a recusal challenge in reserve, to pursue that challenge.[76]

Conclusion

The principle that judges must act impartially and without fear, favour or prejudice is foundational to South Africa's constitutional order. In developing a jurisprudence based on this constitutional principle, South African courts are fortunate to have both South African common law jurisprudence upon which to build as well as the jurisprudence of many other jurisdictions, particularly in the Commonwealth, as this chapter has illustrated. Cultivating a habit of impartiality and open-mindedness is a continuing task for judicial officers in every democratic state. Nowhere is that task more important or difficult than in recusal applications. It will indubitably be made easier by studying how judicial colleagues in other jurisdictions have addressed the questions raised by recusal applications.

[75] See *Take and Save Trading CC* v. *Standard Bank of South Africa Ltd* 2004 (4) SA 1 at para. 4; *SACCAWU* v. *I & J Ltd* 2000 (3) SA 705 at paras. 4–5.

[76] *Bernert* v. *Absa Bank Ltd* [2010] ZACC 28 at paras. 73–6.

18

Judges, bias and recusal in the United Kingdom

CHRISTOPHER FORSYTH

The fundamental nature of the rule against bias

Nemo judex in re sua is both an ancient and fundamental principle of English law.[1] A judge is disqualified from determining any case in which he or she may be, or may fairly be suspected to be, biased. The word 'bias' comes from the tendency of a bowl to turn in one direction of another. It thus means simply an improper predisposition of a judge to decide in one way or another.[2] But if the fundamental nature of the rule is well recognised, its application and reach is less clear. The law is set about by some subtle distinctions which have been unstable and uncertain in the recent past. The law is now relatively clear, but the way in which it is applied is still open to debate and discussion.

This chapter will start with a consideration of two interlinked but important themes necessary for an understanding of the law. The first of these is the question of whether the rule is, in truth, a rule against bias at all or whether it is a rule against the appearance of bias. Judicial views have differed on this in the past eighteen years but, as will be seen, the

[1] Indeed, it was in the context of a judge being a judge in his own cause that Coke made his famous statement in *Dr Bonham's Case* (1610) 8 Co. Rep. 107a, 118a, 77 Eng. Rep. 638, 652 that 'the common law will controul acts of Parliament and sometimes adjudge them to be utterly void' when the Act was 'against common right or reason'. And see Hobart CJ in *Day* v. *Savadge* (1614) Hobart 85, who said 'even an Act of Parliament made against natural equity, as to make a man judge in his own case, is void in itself, for *jura naturae sunt immutabilia* and they are *leges legum*'. But subsequent cases have made clear that if the Act appoints a judge to be a judge in his or her own cause the Act will prevail over the common law: *Parish of Great Charte* v. *Parish of Kennington* (1742) 2 Strange 1173; 93 ER 1107, 1108. See J. Goldsworthy, *The Sovereignty of Parliament* (Oxford: Clarendon Press, 1999), pp. 197ff for discussion of the true import of *Dr Bonham's Case*. The ancient origin of the rule against bias may lie in the canon law. See A. Le Sueur, S. A. De Smith, H. Woolf and J. Jowell, *De Smith's Judicial Review of Administrative Action*, 6th edn. (London: Sweet and Maxwell, 2007), p. 502.

[2] *Flaherty* v. *National Greyhound Racing Club Ltd* [2005] EWCA Civ. 1117 at para. 28.

issue is now largely settled in favour of the view that it is the appearance of bias that is predominant.[3] This result is keyed into the primary purpose[4] that lies behind the rule against bias: it is to protect and secure public confidence in the administration of justice.

The second and related question is what then is the test of the appearance of bias? Here a balance has to be struck between fanciful or far-fetched allegations of bias, which should not be allowed to disrupt the administration of justice, and the serious apprehension of bias, which justifies the quashing of an otherwise exemplary judicial decision. Will a 'reasonable possibility' of bias, a 'real likelihood' of bias or a 'real danger' of bias be required to be apprehended? Here again the law has recently become relatively settled in favour of the 'real danger' test. But crucial to this settlement, as will be seen, is the point of view from which the test is applied. Is it to be applied from the point of view of the judge, after the event, and in possession of all the facts? Or is the test to be applied from the point of view of 'the fair-minded and well-informed observer', who, it seems, may be less well informed than the judge.

The rule against bias is a rule against the appearance of bias

From at least the nineteenth century until the early 1990s it was clear that the rule against bias was a rule against the appearance of bias. In the *locus classicus*, *Dimes* v. *Proprietors of the Grand Junction Canal*,[5] the Lord Chancellor, Lord Cottenham, had affirmed a number of decrees made by

[3] As we shall see, although this is clear in law there remains a spirited scholarly preference among some scholars for the contrary view.

[4] There are, indeed, other purposes that justify the rule against bias. A partial judge is not, of course, an independent judge – thus, the rule against bias buttresses the independence of the courts. And a partial judge will make decisions contrary to the weight of the evidence, etc. So the rule against bias secures better decisions. And it would be pointless to attempt to secure public confidence in the administration of justice if, in fact, the administration of justice was flawed by partial decisions. But, as will become plain as the discussion proceeds, securing public confidence in the administration of justice is the most prominent purpose of the rule underlying the most prominent changes in the law in recent years. Note the distinction drawn by Baroness Hale in *Gillies* v. *Secretary of State for Work and Pensions* [2006] UKHL 2, [2006] 1 WLR 751, HL, at para. 38: 'Impartiality is not the same as independence, although the two are closely linked. Impartiality is the tribunal's approach to deciding the cases before it. Independence is the structural or institutional framework which secures this impartiality, not only in the minds of the tribunal members but also in the perception of the public.'

[5] (1852) 3 HLC 759.

the Vice-Chancellor in favour of a canal company in which Lord Cottenham was a shareholder to the extent of several thousand pounds.

Lord Cottenham's decrees were set aside by the House of Lords even though it was accepted that his decision was not affected by his interests as a shareholder. Lord Campbell said in canonical words:

> No one can suppose that Lord Cottenham could be, in the remotest degree, influenced by the interest that he had in this concern; but, my Lords, it is of the last importance that the maxim, that no man is to be a judge in his own cause, should be held sacred. And that is not to be confined to a cause in which he is a party, but applies to a cause in which he has an interest ... And it will have a most salutary influence on [inferior] tribunals when it is known that this high Court of last resort, in a case in which the Lord Chancellor of England had an interest, considered that his decree was on that account a decree not according to law, and was set aside. This will be a lesson to all inferior tribunals to take care not only that in their decrees they are not influenced by their personal interest, but to avoid the appearance of labouring under such an influence.[6]

In *Dimes* the offending interest was pecuniary but the same principle applied where the interest was non-pecuniary, as was made clear in the equally famous Court of Appeal decision of *R* v. *Sussex Justices ex p. McCarthy*.[7] What had happened was that a solicitor was acting for a client who was suing a motorist for damages caused in a road accident. The solicitor was also acting clerk to the justices before whom the same motorist was convicted of dangerous driving arising out of the same accident. He retired with the justices when they were considering their verdict. Although it was proved that the justices had not in fact consulted the clerk and that he had scrupulously refrained from saying anything prejudicial, the conviction was set aside. Lord Hewart CJ expressed the essence of the rule:

> The question therefore is not whether in this case the deputy clerk made any observation or offered any criticism which he might not properly have made or offered; the question is whether he was so related to the case in its civil aspect as to be unfit to act as clerk to the justices in the criminal matter. The answer to that question depends not upon what actually was done but upon what might appear to be done. Nothing is to be done which creates even a suspicion that there has been an improper interference with the course of justice.[8]

[6] (1852) 3 HLC 759 at 793. [7] [1924] 1 KB 256. [8] [1924] 1 KB 256 at 259.

Or, more pithily, the Lord Chief Justice also said: 'justice should not only be done, but should manifestly and undoubtedly be seen to be done'.[9]

Given these authorities, few propositions could have been considered more firmly established than that the rule against bias was a rule against the appearance of bias. And then in 1993 came the decision in *R* v. *Gough*,[10] a case concerning the impartiality of a juror which re-orientated the law. What had happened was that there were two brothers Gough (Robert and David (also known as Steve)). Robert stood trial for conspiracy to rob. David had originally been committed for trial with Robert but the evidence against him, it was said, was too weak and he was discharged.

But David remained closely linked to the trial of his brother. He was the person with whom Robert was alleged to have conspired. He was mentioned several times in evidence, his address was read out to the jury and a photograph of him and his brother was shown to the jury. After the verdict of guilty was brought in against Robert, his brother David started shouting and protesting from the public gallery. And at that point one of the jurors recognised David as her next-door neighbour! She subsequently made an affidavit to the effect she had known him as 'Steve' and the connection was entirely unknown to her until after the verdict. A reasonable observer who knew of the connection between juror and the defendant would, it seems likely, have apprehended a danger of bias. But to the judge looking at the matter on appeal and with the benefit of the juror's affidavit it would have been plain that the connection had no effect on the verdict. Would the appearance or the reality prevail?

When the matter came before the House of Lords, Lord Goff noted that:

> Since however the court investigates the actual circumstances, knowledge of such circumstances as are found by the court must be imputed to the reasonable man; and in the result it is difficult to see what difference there is between the impression derived by a reasonable man to whom such knowledge has been imputed, and the impression derived by the court, here personifying the reasonable man.[11]

This change of perspective – from the point of view of the reasonable observer to that of the court in possession of all the relevant evidence –

[9] *R* v. *Sussex Justices ex p. McCarthy* [1924] 1 KB 256 at 259. See also Atkin LJ in *Shrager* v. *Basil Dighton Ltd* [1924] 1 KB 274 at 284 ('Next to the tribunal being in fact impartial is the importance of its appearing so').

[10] [1993] AC 646, HL. [11] [1993] AC 646 at 667–8.

led Simon Brown LJ in the Court of Appeal to conclude in a later case[12] that, 'by the time the legal challenge comes to be resolved, the court is no longer concerned strictly with the appearance of bias but rather with establishing that there was actual although unconscious bias'.[13] '[If] despite the appearance of bias,' Lord Bingham said, 'the court is able to examine all the relevant material and satisfy itself that there was no danger of the alleged bias having in fact caused injustice, the impugned decision will be allowed to stand.'[14] These remarks may be measured against the classic statement that 'justice should not only be done, but should manifestly and undoubtedly be seen to be done'[15] to reveal the extent to which *Gough* had re-orientated the law in this area.

There are subtleties in this re-orientation that are not often explored. As the passage quoted from Lord Goff's speech shows, he considers that the reasonable observer will be in possession of the same information as the judge. If that is right, there is no difference between the test of the reasonable observer and that of the reasonable judge; and that insight drives Lord Goff's judgment. But the crucial point, if the test against bias is to serve the purpose of securing public confidence in the administration of justice, is that the fair-minded member of the public, sitting in the public gallery, and whose confidence the rule seeks to secure and enhance, will often not be in possession of the same information as the judge. Only rarely will there be a full investigation on appeal or review and it will become clear, as it did in *ex p. McCarthy* and *Gough*, that the connection between the defendant and the judge (using that word to cover both the justices' clerk and a juror) could not have affected the outcome. Far more commonly, the fair-minded member of the public will become aware of a connection between the judge and a party and his or her suspicions will be aroused, but they will never be resolved or stilled. The observer will never learn the crucial fact that shows that the connection had no influence on the decision; he or she will simply be left with the festering appearance of bias. The rule against bias exists to

[12] *R* v. *Inner West London Coroner ex p. Dallaglio* [1994] 4 All ER 139. For criticism, see B. Rayment, 'Bias after Dallaglio' [1996] *Judicial Review* 102 (Rayment).

[13] *R* v. *Inner West London Coroner ex p. Dallaglio* [1994] 4 All ER 139 at 152.

[14] *R* v. *Inner West London Coroner ex p. Dallaglio* [1994] 4 All ER 139 at 162.

[15] *R* v. *Sussex Justices ex p. McCarthy* [1924] 1 KB 256 at 259. Lord Bingham MR's remark that: '[This] famous aphorism ... is no longer, it seems, good law': (*R* v. *Inner West London Coroner ex p. Dallaglio* [1994] 4 All ER 139 at 162) is mistaken. Appropriately, Lord Bingham (then in the House of Lords) later approved *ex p. McCarthy* (in *R* v. *Abdroikov, Green and Williamson* [2007] UKHL 37, [2007] 1 WLR 2679 at para. 14).

secure that person's confidence in the administration of justice and so must look at the question from the observer's point of view.

Moreover, very frequently a judge will often have to apply the test (typically when asked to recuse him- or herself) before the decision has been taken. In these circumstances it cannot be known that the impugned connection in fact had no influence on the decision. All that can be relied upon is appearances. The elevated view from the House of Lords, after the event and in possession of all the facts, is only rarely the point of view from which the rule against bias has to be applied.

But *Gough* was not to stand unchallenged for long. The point was this: the jurisprudence of the European Convention on Human Rights insists that the appearance of bias, even if there is no actual bias, is sufficient to taint a decision as a breach of Article 6(1).[16] In the jurisprudence of the European Court of Human Rights, the concept of impartiality is tested both subjectively – was there in fact bias?[17] – and objectively – were there guarantees in place to exclude any legitimate doubt as to the impartiality of the tribunal?[18] The importance of the appearance of impartiality has often been stressed by the European Court of Human Rights, which has stated that what 'is at stake is the confidence which the courts in a democratic society must inspire in the public and, above all, as far as criminal proceedings are concerned, in the accused'.[19] Thus, the *Gough* change of approach in disregarding the hallowed principle that justice must be seen to be done, introduced a discrepancy between the Convention and the common law in ensuring impartial decision-making. That discrepancy would have been less pressing had it not been for the enactment of the Human Rights Act 1998 which gave effect in domestic law to the relevant provisions of the Convention. But since the 1998 Act a discrepancy became if not intolerable very difficult.

So the House of Lords, in recognition of this discrepancy, has now in *Lawal* v. *Northern Spirit Ltd*[20] made 'a modest adjustment' to the real danger test to ensure consistency between the Convention and the

[16] Which, in brief, provides that in the determination of their 'civil rights and obligations' or of any 'criminal charge' against them, everyone is entitled to a hearing 'by an independent and impartial tribunal established by law'.

[17] This is, of course, only established very rarely.

[18] *Piersack* v. *Belgium* A53 (1982) and *Hauschildt* v. *Denmark* A 154 (1989).

[19] *Fey* v. *Austria* A 255-A (1993) at para. 30.

[20] [2003] UKHL 35 following a dictum in *Porter* v. *Magill* [2001] UKHL 67, [2002] 2 WLR 37, HL (discussed R. Williams, 'Wilful Misconduct – The House of Lords' Decision in *Porter v Magill*' (2002) 61 *Cambridge Law Journal* 249; J. Rowbottom, 'Homes for Votes, Bias, and Political Purposes' (2002) 118 *Law Quarterly Review* 364). The 'modest adjustment' was first proposed in *In re Medicaments and Related Classes of Goods (No. 2)* [2001] 1 WLR 700, CA.

common law. The case concerned a leading counsel, a Recorder, who had been appointed by the Lord Chancellor to serve as a part-time judge in the Employment Appeal Tribunal. He was briefed to appear before an Employment Appeal Tribunal which included lay members who had previously sat with him in his role as judge. The test of bias laid down was 'whether the fair-minded and informed observer, having considered the facts, would conclude that there was a real possibility that the tribunal was biased'.[21] Applying this test the House of Lords concluded that it was reasonably possible that that observer might consider that the Recorder's submissions would carry particular weight, perhaps subconsciously, with the lay members with whom he had sat in the past.[22]

This change in the test – and the shift in perspective – was firmly based in the necessity of ensuring public confidence in the administration of justice.[23] The House of Lords made clear though that the 'fair-minded and informed observer' would adopt a 'balanced approach'[24] and was 'neither complacent nor unduly sensitive or suspicious'.[25] Lord Hope in a later case has given a full description of the 'fair-minded and informed observer' in these words:[26]

> The fair-minded and informed observer is a relative newcomer among the select group of personalities who inhabit our legal village and are available to be called upon when a problem arises that needs to be solved objectively. Like the reasonable man whose attributes have been explored so often in the context of the law of negligence, the fair-minded observer is a creature of fiction. Gender-neutral ... she has attributes which many of us might

It is now accepted that there is no difference between the Art. 6(1) test and the common law: *R* v. *Abdroikov, Green and Williamson* [2007] UKHL 37, [2007] 1 WLR 2679 at para. 14 *per* Lord Bingham, and *Lawal* v. *Northern Spirit Ltd* [2003] UKHL 35, [2004] 1 All ER 187 at para. 14 *per* Lord Steyn.

21 The cited words come from Lord Phillips's judgment in *In re Medicaments and Related Classes of Goods (No. 2)* [2001] 1 WLR 700 at para. 85, adopted by Lord Hope in *Porter* v *Magill* [2001] UKHL 67 at para. 103 and Lord Bingham in *Lawal* v. *Northern Spirit Ltd* [2003] UKHL 35 at para. 14. The test is discussed by S. Hanif, 'The Use of the Bystander Test for Apparent Bias' [2005] *Judicial Review* 78.

22 That this was a reasonable apprehension in such circumstances was shown by the specific rules that precluded part-time judges in Employment Tribunals from appearing before Employment Tribunals containing lay members with whom they had previously sat.

23 The Strasbourg jurisprudence (as well as the traditional common law) stressed this. See, for instance, *Belilos* v. *Switzerland* (1988) 10 EHRR 466 at para. 67.

24 *Lawal* v. *Northern Spirit* [2003] UKHL 35 at para. 14.

25 Lord Bingham in *Lawal* v. *Northern Spirit Ltd* [2003] UKHL 35 adopting a phrase of Kirby J in *Johnson* v. *Johnson* (2000) 200 CLR 488 at para. 53.

26 *Helow* v. *Secretary of State for the Home Department and Another (Scotland)* [2008] UKHL 6 at paras. 1–3.

> struggle to attain to. The observer who is fair-minded is the sort of person who always reserves judgment on every point until she has seen and fully understood both sides of the argument. She is not unduly sensitive or suspicious . . . Her approach must not be confused with that of the person who has brought the complaint. The 'real possibility' test ensures that there is this measure of detachment. The assumptions that the complainer makes are not to be attributed to the observer unless they can be justified objectively. But she is not complacent either. She knows that fairness requires that a judge must be, and must be seen to be, unbiased. She knows that judges, like anybody else, have their weaknesses. She will not shrink from the conclusion, if it can be justified objectively, that things that they have said or done or associations that they have formed may make it difficult for them to judge the case before them impartially. Then there is the attribute that the observer is 'informed'. It makes the point that, before she takes a balanced approach to any information she is given, she will take the trouble to inform herself on all matters that are relevant. She is the sort of person who takes the trouble to read the text of an article as well as the headlines. She is able to put whatever she has read or seen into its overall social, political or geographical context. She is fair-minded, so she will appreciate that the context forms an important part of the material which she must consider before passing judgment.

It has been made clear that the 'fair-minded and informed observer can be assumed to have access to all the facts that are capable of being known by members of the public generally, bearing in mind that it is the appearance that these facts give rise to that matters, not what is in the mind of the particular judge or tribunal member who is under scrutiny'.[27] It is important that fanciful and unmeritorious allegations of bias are discouraged and that proper regard is had to the context in which the issue arises. The remark by Lord Bingham that 'the administration of justice requires higher standards today than was the case even a decade or two ago'[28] has been a harbinger of more exacting standards. We shall consider the application of the 'fair-minded and informed observer' in more detail below.[29]

[27] *Gillies* v. *Secretary of State for Work and Pensions* [2006] UKHL 2, [2006] 1 WLR 751, HL, at para. 17 *per* Lord Hope.

[28] *Lawal* v. *Northern Spirit Ltd* [2003] UKHL 35 at para. 22.

[29] *Gillies* v. *Secretary of State for Work and Pensions* [2006] UKHL 2, [2006] 1 WLR 751 may serve as an example of the application of the test. The medical member of a disability appeal tribunal had provided and continued to provide reports on behalf of the Benefits Agency in disability living allowance and incapacity benefit cases. She was not disqualified. The fair-minded observer would have 'no reason' to believe she would have any predisposition to prefer the reports of the medical examiners. The test was also applied in *Feld* v. *London Borough of Barnet* [2004] EWCA Civ. 1307 (fair-minded observer would not apprehend bias where second internal review of decision to offer accommodation to homeless person carried out by same person who carried out first review).

The test of bias for judicial officers

If it is now clear that we are concerned with appearance and that we will be looking from the point of view of the 'fair-minded and informed observer' the questions remains: what is the test of apparent bias? This question has a tangled history, although the modern test, set out below, is now relatively clear.

Much confusion has been caused in the past by the concurrent use of differently formulated tests for disqualifying bias. In the past many judges have laid down and applied a 'real likelihood' formula, holding that the test for disqualification is whether the facts, as assessed by the court, give rise to a real likelihood of bias;[30] and this test has naturally been emphasised in cases where the allegation of bias was far-fetched.[31] Other judges have employed a 'reasonable suspicion' test, emphasising that justice must be seen to be done, and that no person should adjudicate in any way if it might reasonably be thought that he or she ought not to act because of some personal interest.[32] In one case it was even said that the rule for judges of all kinds was that they must be free from even unreasonable suspicion of bias.[33]

In many cases both tests led to the same result, since 'likelihood' was given the meaning of possibility rather than probability. For if there was no real possibility of bias, no reasonable person would suspect it. But other judicial statements, more naturally, equated 'likelihood' with 'probability',[34] so that the two tests became different, and courts confronted with them felt obliged to elect between them. In 1954, a Divisional Court, after reviewing authorities, decided firmly in favour of real likelihood.[35] But in 1968, the Court of Appeal decided equally

[30] R v. *Rand* (1866) LR 1 QB 230; *R* v. *Sunderland Justices* (1901) 2 KB 357; *Frome United Breweries Co.* v. *Bath Justices* [1926] AC 586; *R* v. *Camborne Justices ex p. Pearce* [1955] 1 QB 41; *Hannam* v. *Bradford Corporation* [1970] 1 WLR 937.

[31] See *R* v. *Camborne Justices ex p. Pearce* [1955] 1 QB 41.

[32] The numerous decisions include *R* v. *Gaisford* [1892] 1 QB 381: *R* v. *Sussex Justices ex p. McCarthy* [1924] 1 KB 256; *Cooper* v. *Wilson* [1937] 2 KB 309 at 324, 344; *Metropolitan Properties Co. (FGC) Ltd* v. *Lannon* [1969] 1 QB 577.

[33] *Eckersley* v. *Mersey Docks and Harbour Board* [1894] 2 QB 667.

[34] *R* v. *Barnsley Licensing Justices ex p. Barnsley and District Licensed Victuallers' Association* [1960] 2 QB 167 at 187 *per* Devlin LJ: *Metropolitan Properties (FGC) Ltd* v. *Lannon* [1969] 1 QB 577 at 599 *per* Lord Denning MR.

[35] *R* v. *Camborne Justices ex p. Pearce* [1955] 1 QB 41. See similarly, *R* v. *Nailsworth Licensing Justices ex p. Bird* [1953] 1 WLR 1046.

firmly in favour of reasonable suspicion,[36] although Lord Denning MR interwove this with the other test. This decision reasserted 'justice must be seen to be done' as the operative principle. But 'it left a legacy of some confusion'[37] in 'a somewhat confusing welter of authority'.[38]

In 1993 in *Gough*[39] the House of Lords affirmed the 'real likelihood' test in a criminal case, though preferring to state it in terms of 'real danger', so as to emphasise that 'the court is thinking in terms of possibility rather than probability of bias'. This assessment of the response of the 'fair-minded and informed observer' is in essence a return to the old test of reasonable suspicion. But its application in any particular case is a matter of judgment.

Automatic disqualification in certain cases

The case concerning Cottenham LC, described above, is an example of the rule that a direct pecuniary interest disqualifies the decision-maker. It became the rule that any direct pecuniary interest, however small, was a disqualification,[40] and this rule was applied rigorously.[41] Indeed, in a prominent modern case, *R* v. *Bow Street Metropolitan Stipendiary Magistrate ex p. Pinochet Ugarte (No. 2)*,[42] the House of Lords has affirmed that the principle of automatic disqualification in fact extends beyond pecuniary and proprietary interests. It applies equally where the judge is himself a party or has a relevant interest in the subject matter of the litigation, even if he has no financial interest in its outcome. The case concerned an appeal before the House of Lords in which the Crown Prosecution Service sought to overturn the quashing by the Divisional Court of extradition warrants made against a former head of state. Amnesty International (AI) was given leave to intervene in the

[36] *Metropolitan Properties (FGC) Ltd* v. *Lannon* [1969] 1 QB 577.

[37] *R* v. *Gough* [1993] AC 646, HL, *per* Lord Goff.

[38] *Hannam* v. *Bradford Corporation* [1970] 1 WLR 937 *per* Widgery LJ.

[39] [1993] AC 646. But where a juror knew vital witnesses and did not reveal this to the court, a real danger was found: *R* v. *K*, *The Times*, 14 April 1995. See also, *R* v. *Wilson and Strason* (1996) 8 Admin. LR 1.

[40] *R* v. *Rand* (1866) LR 1 QB 230; *R* v. *Meyer* (1875) 1 QBD 173; *R* v. *Farrant* (1887) 20 QBD 58; *R* v. *Barnsley Licensing Justices ex p. Barnsley and District Licensed Victuallers' Association* [1960] 2 QB 167.

[41] See, e.g., *R* v. *Cambridge Recorder* (1857) 8 E & B 637. In *R* v. *Farrant* (1887) 20 QBD 58 it was held that a magistrate who made a bet on the result of the case would be disqualified for pecuniary interest.

[42] [1999] UKHL 52, [2000] 1 AC 119.

proceedings before the House of Lords. Unknown to the representatives of the former head of state at the time, one of the law lords was in fact an (unpaid) director and chairperson of Amnesty International Charity Ltd (AICL), a company under the control of AI which was formed to carry out the charitable parts of AI's activities. The law lord, who did not disclose his links with AI, had no financial interest in the outcome and was not a party to the proceedings, but the 'substance of the matter is that AI . . . and AICL are all various parts of an entity or movement working in different fields towards the same goals'.[43] This was enough to automatically disqualify the law lord; and the matter was reheard before a differently constituted Appeal Committee. The circumstances of this case were most unusual; it is difficult to see what other non-pecuniary interests will suffice other than the obvious one where the judge is a party.[44]

The application of the test of bias

The law that emerges from the account above is relatively clear. In assessing whether a judicial decision is tainted by bias the court will ask whether a 'fair-minded and informed observer' would apprehend or suspect a 'real danger' of bias (this last phrase connoting possibility of bias rather than probability). In certain circumstances – where the judge has a pecuniary interest in the outcome of the decision or has so associated him- or herself with a party that he or she may be equated with that party – the disqualification will be automatic.

But if the law is clear, its application may be another matter. Fortunately, the decided cases provide significant guidance. In the first place, a line must be drawn between genuine and fanciful cases. The leading case is *Locabail (UK) Ltd* v. *Bayfield Properties Ltd*[45] in which a specially constituted Court of Appeal, speaking with the special authority of the Lord Chief Justice, the Master of the Rolls and the

[43] *R* v. *Bow Street Metropolitan Stipendiary Magistrate ex p. Pinochet Ugarte (No. 2)* [1999] UKHL 52, [2000] 1 AC 119 at 135 *per* Lord Browne-Wilkinson.

[44] The automatic disqualification rule was held inapplicable in *Meerabux* v. *Attorney-General of Belize* [2005] UKPC 12, [2005] 2 WLR 1307, PC (complaint made to Governor-General by Bar Association alleging misbehaviour by judge; constitutional Advisory Council convened to consider complaint chaired by another judge who was (as required by law) a member of Bar Association); no 'personal or pecuniary' interest found, no automatic disqualification.

[45] [2000] 2 WLR 870 (CA).

Vice-Chancellor and hearing several cases together where there had been a challenge to the impartiality of the judge, gave far-reaching guidance. In one of these cases a deputy High Court judge was held not disqualified because the solicitors' firm of which he was a partner was, without his knowledge, involved in related litigation. And a judge who was the director of a property company, which was the landlord of one of the parties, was not disqualified.[46] The judge did not know of this link, but even if he had known there could in the circumstances 'not be a real danger of bias'. The judge added: 'The interest was so minimal, that no reasonable and fair-minded person sitting in court would have considered there was a real as opposed to a fanciful danger of a fair trial not being possible.'[47] On the other hand, in another of the cases heard together, the judge had expressed himself vigorously but properly in law journal articles on the legal issues that subsequently arose before him. He had crossed 'the ill-defined line' and the Court of Appeal concluded that there was a real danger that 'a lay observer with knowledge of the facts' would not have excluded the possibility of unconscious bias.[48] Judicial criticism of the law must in the future be expressed in measured and restrained language.

Perhaps more important than these particular examples is the general guidance given by the Court of Appeal. The court laid down that, while everything will depend upon the facts and the nature of the issue to be decided, objections could not be based on religion, ethnic or national origin, gender, age, class, means or sexual orientation of the judge. Nor, ordinarily, would the judge's educational, social, employment or service background, nor his political associations, professional associations (for example, membership of an Inn of Court), membership of social, sporting or charitable bodies (including Masonic associations), prior judicial decisions or views expressed in textbooks, lectures or articles, nor the fact that he or she had in

[46] *R* v. *Bristol Betting and Gaming Licensing Committee ex p. O'Callaghan* (heard with the *Locabail* case). See similarly, *R* v. *Mulvihill* [1990] 1 WLR 438 (bank robber's appeal on the ground that judge held shares in the bank robbed failed since no one could reasonably suspect unfairness).

[47] [2000] 2 WLR 870 at 906.

[48] *Timmins* v. *Gormely* (heard with the *Locabail* case). The phrase 'ill defined line' comes from *Vakauta* v. *Kelly* (1989) 167 CLR 568 at 571. Similarly, a senior Scottish judge who had published a newspaper article which painted a vivid but negative picture of the impact of the European Convention on Human Rights and Fundamental Freedoms on the law, created a 'legitimate apprehension' in defendants that he would not act impartially in the protection of their Convention rights, and his decision was set aside (*Hoekstra* v. *Lord Advocate* [2001] 1 AC 216, PC).

the past received instructions from a party (or the parties' legal representatives) be relevant. But a history of personal friendship or animosity between the judge and a member of the public associated with the case (for example, as party or witness) may disqualify the judge.[49]

This approach has the robust smack of common sense about it and firmly discards flimsy and fanciful allegations of bias. It has been most influential. Consistent with this approach was the case of a judge who was disqualified since he had known a witness for 30 years.[50] On the other hand, the judge who was, at all relevant times, a member of the International Association of Jewish Lawyers and Jurists (which published a magazine that contained some 'fervently pro-Israeli' articles[51]) was not disqualified from hearing an application to apply for leave to appeal against refusal of asylum by the Palestine Liberation Organisation (PLO) supporting applicant.[52] An application that the Lord Chief Justice constitute a special panel of judges 'with proven sensitivity and understanding of religious issues' to hear cases involving religious rights predictably failed (notwithstanding support from a former Archbishop of Canterbury).[53] But in a bold decision a judge was not disqualified in a case where one party's solicitors were already acting for the judge in relation to his will.[54]

This last mentioned case stretches the unsuspicious nature of the fair-minded observer quite far. The judge in fact met with the solicitors to execute a codicil to his will on the same day as he heard closing speeches and the day before he gave judgment. Moreover, the judge disclosed that he was a client of the solicitors only after the fourth hearing of the case; and in fact no bill was rendered by the solicitors for the work done. The 'legal traditions and culture of this jurisdiction' said Lord Woolf would be known to the fair-minded observer who would consequently not suspect bias.[55] This case prompts the comment that the apprehensions of the fair-minded observer might not be the only factors in play. The Court of Appeal being imbued with the 'legal traditions and culture of this jurisdiction' was doubtless confident that no improper

[49] *Locabail (UK) Ltd* v. *Bayfield Properties Ltd* [2000] QB 451, CA.

[50] *AWG Group Ltd* v. *Morrison* [2006] EWCA Civ. 6, [2006] 1 WLR 1163, CA.

[51] *Helow* v. *Home Secretary* [2008] 2 UKHL 62 at para. 5 *per* Lord Hope.

[52] *Helow* v. *Secretary of State for the Home Department and Another (Scotland)* [2008] 2 UKHL 62.

[53] *McFarlane* v. *Relate Avon Ltd* [2010] EWCA Civ. B1.

[54] *Taylor* v. *Lawrence (Appeal: Jurisdiction to Reopen)* [2002] EWCA Civ. 90, [2003] QB 528 (no 'significant injustice' justifying reopening of appeal).

[55] *Taylor* v. *Lawrence (Appeal: Jurisdiction to Reopen)* [2002] EWCA Civ. 90, [2003] QB 528 at para. 60.

communication took place between the judge and the solicitors when attending to the codicil; and so upheld the decision. But this represents a shift back to the *Gough* law and potentially undermines public confidence in the administration of justice.

More difficult too is the leading decision of the House of Lords, *R* v. *Abdroikov, Green and Williamson*,[56] where their Lordships' House was divided in the application of the test (although in full agreement as to what the test was). Each of these cases involved a challenge to the impartiality of a juror in the trials at which each defendant had been convicted. In two of the cases a police officer was one of the jury and in the other a crown prosecutor acted as a juror. In one of the policeman cases the House of Lords unanimously dismissed the appeal, since there was no particular link between the police witnesses in the case and the juror and the case did not turn on a clash between the evidence of the police witnesses and the defendant. But in the second policeman case there was a clash between the evidence of the defendant and the police witnesses and it might reasonably be thought, held the majority, that the policeman juror might give greater weight to the evidence of the police officers who came from the same local force (although not known to each other). With the crown prosecutor the juror was sitting in judgment on a prosecution brought by his or her employer which again led, held the majority, to an apprehension of bias. The minority taking either a more robust view of the fair-minded observer or recognised that Parliament in making provision for policemen and prosecutors (as well as many others including judges) to sit on juries in the Criminal Justice Act 2003 had not intended them to be too easily excluded.

These differences of view in the House of Lords depend upon the detailed circumstances of each case. It is not surprising given the open texture of the test that the courts should from time to time be divided in its application. But this has led to a spirited criticism of the changes in the common law and a strong call for a return to the law as laid down in *R* v. *Gough*.[57]

Waiver

The right to object to a disqualified judge may be waived, and this may be so even where the disqualification is statutory.[58] But it has to be clear that

[56] [2007] UKHL 37, [2007] 1 WLR 2679.

[57] See A. A. Olowofoyeku, 'Bias and the Informed Observer: A Call for a Return to Gough' (2009) 68 *Cambridge Law Journal* 388.

[58] *Wakefield Local Board of Health* v. *West Riding and Grimsby Rly Co.* (1865) 1 QB 84.

the person alleged to have waived his or her right to object to a judge 'has acted freely and in full knowledge of the facts'.[59] And if counsel has advised the applicant inadequately as to his or her right to object to a judge, the applicant will not be taken to have waived the right to object.[60] The court normally insists that the objection shall be taken as soon as the party prejudiced knows the facts which entitle him or her to object. If, after the party or his or her advisers know of the disqualification, they let the proceedings continue without protest, they are held to have waived their objection and the determination cannot be challenged.[61] In the past this rule has been strictly applied, so much so that the practice was to refuse a quashing order unless it was specifically shown in the affidavits that the applicant had no knowledge of the disqualifying facts at the time of the proceedings.[62] But in one case, where the litigant had appeared in person before the justices, a quashing order was granted even though he knew the facts at the trial, since he did not know that he was entitled to raise his objection then, and there can be no waiver of rights of which the person entitled is unaware.[63]

Recusal[64]

It may be that one of the parties will draw a judge's attention to some relevant connection between the judge and one of the parties or the subject matter of the dispute. Or it may be that the judge him- or herself

[59] *R* v. *Bow Street Magistrate ex p. Pinochet (No. 2)* [2000] 1 AC 119, 1999 (1) All ER 577, HL, at 137 *per* Lord Browne-Wilkinson.

[60] *Smith* v. *Kvaerner Cementation Foundations Ltd* [2006] EWCA Civ. 242 (counsel, in good faith, had conveyed a 'vigorous recommendation of the qualities of his head of chambers' (the disqualified adjudicator) which made it difficult for the applicant to object). See also *Jones* v. *DAS Legal Expenses Insurance Co.* [2003] EWCA Civ. 1071 for detailed guidance on judicial conduct when this issue arises.

[61] *R* v. *Byles ex p. Hollidge* (1912) 77 JP 40: *R* v. *Nailsworth Licensing Justices ex p. Bird* [1953] 1 WLR 1046; *Thomas* v. *University of Bradford (No. 2)* [1992] 1 All ER 964 (waiver of correct procedure); *R* v. *Lilydale Magistrates' Court ex p. Ciccone* [1973] VR 122; and see *R* v. *Antrim Justices* [1895] 2 IR 603; *Tolputt (H.) & Co. Ltd* v. *Mole* [1911] 1 KB 836; *Corrigan* v. *Irish Land Commission* [1977] IR 317; *Locabail (UK) Ltd* v. *Bayfield Properties Ltd* [2000] QB 451, CA ('It is not open to [the litigant] to wait and see how her claims . . . turned out before pursuing her complaint of bias . . . [She] wanted to have the best of both worlds. The law will not allow her to do so' *per* Lord Woolf MR, Lord Bingham LCJ and Scott V-C).

[62] *R* v. *Williams ex p. Phillips* [1914] 1 KB 608; *R* v. *Kent Justices* (1880) 44 JP 298.

[63] *R* v. *Essex Justices ex p. Perkins* [1927] 2 KB 475.

[64] See generally, G. Hammond, *Judicial Recusal: Principles, Process and Problem* (Oxford: Hart Publishing, 2009) especially in regard to the process of recusal.

becomes aware of the matter before any of the parties. When this occurs the judge must clearly consider the matter, apply the test of the fair-minded observer, and if it is apprehended that there is a real danger of bias, the parties must either waive their right to object or the judge must recuse him- or herself.[65] Where there is 'real ground for doubt, that doubt should be resolved in favour of recusal'.[66] 'Where the hearing has not yet begun,' said the Court of Appeal in another case, 'there is scope for the sensible application of the precautionary principle. Prudence normally leans on the side of being safe rather than sorry.'[67]

A court reviewing a decision of a judge not to recuse him- or herself will consider a written statement of explanation by the judge, justice or juror as the case may be. The court is not, however,

> necessarily bound to accept such statement at its face value. Much will depend on the nature of the fact of which ignorance is asserted, the source of the statement, the effect of any corroborative or contradictory statement, the inherent probabilities and all the circumstances of the case in question . . . There can, however, be no question of cross-examining or seeking disclosure from the judge. Nor will the reviewing court pay attention to any statement by the judge concerning the impact of any knowledge on his mind or his decision . . . it is for the reviewing court and not the judge whose impartiality is challenged to assess the risk that some illegitimate extraneous consideration may have influenced the decision.[68]

These principles were duly applied in 2007 in the decision of the Court of Appeal in *Howell & Others* v. *Lees Millais & Others*.[69] The case established no fresh principle and was simply an egregious and rather embarrassing example of judicial lack of impartiality. What had happened was that the judge had been in discussions with a solicitors' firm over the possibility that the judge would be employed by the firm. In the event agreement was not reached and the discussions ended with intemperate emails from the judge. The judge remarked in an email to the senior partner 'I am not very impressed with you or your firm at the moment and I do not think the tone of your emails enhances the position.' Shortly

65 Recusal 'not a discretionary case management decision' in which inconvenience might outweigh the breach of impartiality. *AWG Group Ltd* v. *Morrison* [2006] ECWA Civ. 6, [2006] 1 WLR 1163 at [5].

66 *Locabail UK Ltd* v. *Bayfield Properties Ltd* [2000] QB 451 at [25]; and see *AWG Group Ltd* v. *Morrison* [2006] ECWA Civ. 6, [2006] 1 WLR 1163 at [5].

67 *AWG Group Ltd* v. *Morrison* [2006] ECWA Civ. 6, [2006] 1 WLR 1163 at [9].

68 *Locabail UK Ltd* v. *Bayfield Properties Ltd* [2000] QB 451 [19].

69 [2007] EWCA Civ. 720.

thereafter the firm in question found themselves representing a client before the judge.

Inevitably, an application for recusal was made and the transcript of the hearing as the Court of Appeal remarked 'does not make entirely happy reading'. The judge in effect cross-examined the partner who gave evidence of the discussions with the judge and the reasons for their breakdown. There followed several 'extraordinary exchanges' between the judge and counsel for the firm concerning the breakdown of the discussions as well as the past contact (and dispute) between the judge and the firm. The judge displayed little judicial temperament. The judge duly refused the application that he recuse himself and the matter went to the Court of Appeal.

The Master of the Rolls concluded as follows:

> The judge's contribution to these exchanges seems to me to be intemperate. In short, the cross-examination of [the partner] and the approach adopted by the judge in the course of [counsel's] submissions provides strong support for [the] submissions that the fair-minded and informed observer having considered the facts would conclude that there was a real possibility that the judge was biased against [the firm] and its partners, one of whom is the first claimant in the application. When this evidence is put together with the content and tone of the emails sent by the judge . . . I am quite satisfied that this is a case in which the judge should have recused himself. This is not to my mind a case which is close to the borderline but a case in which there is no doubt that the test laid down in the authorities is satisfied.[70]

The Master of the Rolls is plainly quite right. It was as plain as a pikestaff that the judge should have recused himself. The whole incident was embarrassing to the English judiciary, but at least such incidents are very rare. After the decision of the Court of Appeal the Lord Chief Justice referred the judge's conduct to the independent Office for Judicial Complaints (OJC) amid speculation that the judge would resign. On 18 April 2008, the OJC announced that it had found that misconduct had been established against the judge. Consequently, the Lord Chief Justice reprimanded the judge (who remains in office).

Conclusions

That the UK's judges do, on the whole, take their decisions impartially is not in doubt. This impartiality is undoubtedly a buttress to their independence. The cases discussed in the preceding pages where judicial

[70] [2007] EWCA Civ. 720 at para. 25.

decisions were overturned on the ground that an appearance of bias was shown, may truly be considered exceptional and egregious. But we should not become complacent and should recall how easily and unexpectedly the learning of centuries was set aside and the law re-orientated in *Gough*. Intriguingly enough, it was the Human Rights Act 1998 lurking in the background that required the 'modest adjustment' that reversed the effect of *R* v. *Gough* and returned the common law to the path of rectitude.

Moreover, it should be frankly recognised that there are uncertainties in the application of the 'fair-minded and well-informed observer' test. It is inevitable that courts will sometimes be divided on its application. But some of the cases discussed above tempt one to wonder whether the observer is having so much knowledge imputed to him or her in order to ensure that the administration of justice is not too gravely disrupted. There is a strong public interest in the proper dispatch of judicial business, and that is threatened if fanciful allegations of bias are given too much weight. But that issue should not be addressed by imputing unrealistic amounts of knowledge to the 'fair-minded and well-informed observer'.

19

Bias, the appearance of bias, and judicial disqualification in the United States

W. WILLIAM HODES

American society is deeply conflicted – perhaps it would be more accurate to say schizophrenic – with respect to the role that both elected and appointed judges should play (and should be allowed to play) in the governance of a constitutional democracy with a long tradition of judicial review.

On the one hand, Americans of every political stripe and every social stratum are quick to "go to law" to achieve vindication (or establishment) of their rights, eagerly egging judges on as they craft novel remedies for the perceived ills of society. Sooner or later, it seems, every issue of social policy, from the most fundamental to the most trivial, will be presented to an American court for adjudication.[1]

On the other hand, when a day in court ends badly for a party, or when onlookers find a judicial decision to be foolhardy, Americans are just as quick to complain that an activist judicial branch is taking over the country and supplanting the rest of government, rather than enforcing the law as laid down by the political branches and performing its historical constitutional function of providing needed checks and balances.

In these situations, critics assert that they know all too well what "role" the judges are playing: they are giving free rein to their personal preferences, ideologies, and individual prejudices, and imposing those values on the rest of us, under the pretense that that is what "the law" requires.

[1] To be fair, it should be remembered that although questions great and small are pervasively *presented* to the courts for adjudication in the United States, the courts do not always oblige with an on-the-merits answer. Indeed, despite frequent criticism of the courts – especially federal courts – for excess "meddling" in the political affairs of the country, robust prudential and constitutional justiciability doctrines ensure that many issues are remitted back to the political system for resolution.

Alternatively – and more to the point of this chapter – losing parties or court critics sometimes assert that the infelicitous result can be explained only by the judge's bias or partiality, whether the bias is personal, political, ideological, racial, class-based, gender-based, or based on a catch-all "appearance of bias."

When such a charge is merely sour grapes, it should be ignored. But when it has merit the administration of justice has gone off the rails, and corrective action must be taken. Furthermore, if there is a demonstrated risk of partiality *in advance* of a decision being made, it would be not merely prudent, but imperative, to take prophylactic action to separate the judge in question from the opportunity to render a biased decision.

That, in turn, can be accomplished by disqualifying the judge or requiring the judge to self-disqualify with respect to particular cases, or by not appointing or electing the judge in the first place.

The first of these, disqualification of judges for bias, is the chief subject of this chapter. However, as will be seen, the connection between judicial disqualification and judicial selection – especially if the selection is through contested elections – is so strong in the contemporary United States that the latter subject cannot be ignored in a chapter on the former.

Impartiality as a necessary element of the judicial function

The signature theme of the Model Code of Judicial Conduct (CJC) as revised by the American Bar Association in February 2007, is to promote and require the "independence, integrity, and impartiality" of the judiciary; dozens of provisions are couched in those terms explicitly. Although there is some overlap between what became known during the drafting process as the "3 I's," each is separately defined in the terminology section that precedes the substantive Rules.

With respect to disqualification for bias, however, impartiality is necessarily the key factor among the three. Indeed, Rule 2.11, "Disqualification," refers *only* to impartiality. Once impartiality has been established as a *sine qua non* for judicial officers – and the 2007 CJC is hardly the first or only source of such a standard – it becomes critical to get right an operational definition of "partiality" or "bias." Thus, a second order debate must rage over exactly what level and what kind of bias should "count" as sufficiently egregious to be disqualifying. Moreover, if prophylactic action is contemplated, it is important as well to calibrate correctly the level of risk that bias will actually infect decision-making.

Set the bar too low, and citizens generally will develop contempt first for individual judges, then for the judiciary as a whole, and then for the rule of law itself. Set the bar too high, however, and the system becomes dysfunctional. Parties will gin up claims of bias as a method of judge-shopping, and judges – especially elected judges – leery of becoming embroiled in controversial cases, will "confess" to a watered down bias in order to duck their responsibility to decide, increasing the workload of their colleagues at the same time.[2]

This chapter will first survey the history and current state of play as regards judicial impartiality and both disqualification and disciplinary sanctions for bias. As will be seen, similar but not identical standards were developed for state and federal judges, on roughly the same timetable. In addition, federal constitutional doctrines sounding in fairness and due process of law were layered on top of this baseline. The temptation to skewed decision-making can be so strong, and the deck so severely stacked, that a supposedly "judicial" proceeding becomes a sham proceeding instead, one that is essentially "lawless."

Second, this chapter will consider the impact of two decisions of the US Supreme Court and their still developing aftermath. The more recent of the two, *Caperton* v. *A. T. Massey Coal Co., Inc.*,[3] specifically dealt with the federal constitutional overlay described immediately above. By a vote of 5–4, the court held that massive campaign expenditures – repeatedly, but incorrectly, referred to as massive campaign contributions – by a party in a pending case were so likely to skew the judgment of the favored candidate, that disqualification of that (winning) candidate – now sitting on the deciding state Supreme Court – was constitutionally required.

The other case was *Republican Party of Minnesota* v. *White*,[4] which established, also by a 5–4 vote, the free speech right of candidates for elective judicial office to "announce their views" on disputed legal and political issues, *even if those issues might later come before a successful candidate while sitting on the bench.*

[2] See Model Code of Judicial Conduct, Rule 2.7, "Responsibility to Decide": "A judge *shall* hear and decide matters assigned to the judge, *except* when disqualification is *required* by Rule 2.11 or other law" (emphasis supplied). The tension between Rules 2.7 and 2.11, and the awkward position into which they can thrust sitting judges, is discussed later in this chapter.

[3] 129 S.Ct. 2252 (2009). [4] 536 US 765 (2002).

This chapter will conclude with the perhaps surprising prognostication that even as respects disqualification, it will be *White* that will most clearly shape future developments, not *Caperton*. The key factor in the area of judicial disqualification will not be bias and lack of impartiality *per se*, but rather the sensibilities of both voters and candidates, where judges must campaign for election or re-election, or present themselves to the voters for an up or down retention vote of confidence.

Inevitably, as candidates more and more openly state their views on controversial issues, litigants with opposing views will insist that the former candidate – now a judge sitting on their cases – is "biased" and must be disqualified.[5] Once again, the definition of what does and does not "count" as bias or impartiality will take center stage.

The common law approach to judicial bias and the influence of American Legal Realism

At common law, and in the United States well into the twentieth century, the concept of judicial bias was a narrow one, and disqualification for bias was largely unheard of. This was not an accident, but a reflection of the dominant understanding of what it meant to *be* a judge in the first place. The very idea of a judge was that of a professional who had foresworn partisanship, and had pledged to serve only the law, and then only as a neutral observer.

In this view, judges were not infallible, but their mistakes were attributable to a failure of craft or a lack of proper study or analysis, not favoritism. Judges were not "for" or "against" anybody, but would follow an objectified legal path wherever it led, even if the path was poorly lit and bumpy. A "biased" judge was close to an oxymoron, because upon ascending the bench each judge had *by definition* put aside his or her own passions and prejudices. Thus, a judge ruling for or against this

[5] At the end of Chapter 13 of this book, "The Criticism and Speech of Judges in the United States," Professor Charles Gardner Geyh briefly notes this consequence of the *White* decision. As he explains, the ABA amended its Model Code of Judicial Conduct in 2003 to *require* judges, on pain of discipline, to disqualify themselves if they had made a campaign or other public speech that "commits *or appears to commit* the judge to reach a particular result or rule in a particular way in the proceeding or controversy" (emphasis supplied). That language was carried forward into Rule 2.11(A)(5) of the 2007 CJC. It might be said that this chapter begins where Professor Geyh left off with respect to that issue.

party or that found no pleasure in it; it was what fidelity to the law required.

During his Senate confirmation hearings in 2005, Chief Justice John Roberts famously compared the function of a judge making each decision with that of a baseball umpire calling each pitch a ball or a strike. That analogy is discussed in more detail below, but his almost as famous exchange with Senator Richard Durbin of Illinois is perhaps an even more telling statement of the traditional view of judging with respect to fidelity to the law rather than to the interests of any particular litigant or class of litigants.

After Senator Durbin had posed a series of hypotheticals about whether there were causes to which Judge Roberts would not have lent his legal talents *as a lawyer*, Judge Roberts somewhat bemusedly explained that although individuals choose to become lawyers for their own good reasons, he had become a lawyer to promote and vindicate the rule of law itself. While some might disparage this as a kind of "hired gun" mentality, Roberts added, that approach fails to appreciate "an ennobling truth about the legal system: that lawyers serve the rule of law, above and beyond representing particular clients."

When Senator Durbin apparently still failed to grasp the point that the role of an advocate in "expanding freedom" or "restricting rights" is entirely different – by definition – from that of a judge *adjudicating* a case in which freedom or rights might be expanded or restricted, Judge Roberts continued as follows:

> I had someone ask me in this process – I don't remember who it was, but somebody asked me, you know, "Are you going to be on the side of the little guy?"
>
> And you obviously want to give an immediate answer, but, as you reflect on it, if the Constitution says that the little guy should win, the little guy's going to win in court before me. But if the Constitution says that the big guy should win, well, then the big guy's going to win, because my obligation is to the Constitution. That's the oath.
>
> The oath that a judge takes is not that, "I'll look out for particular interests, I'll be on the side of particular interests." The oath is to uphold the Constitution and laws of the United States. And that's what I would do.

The traditional view of judging was challenged and modified – but certainly not replaced – by the American Legal Realism school of thought that dominated legal education so thoroughly in the period roughly between the World Wars that today's law professors all learned their craft at the feet of law professors who themselves learned from the original masters. We are all legal realists now.[6]

The key precept of American Legal Realism is that notwithstanding the invocation of supposedly immutable, predetermined, and transcendent or "neutral" principles of law, the law is instead indeterminate and crowded with opportunities for the exercise of discretionary judgment. Judges are not law-spouting computers, but university-trained lawyers who bring with them to the bench all manner of life experiences, philosophies, habits of thought, cultural values, personality traits, and intellectual prowess.

A corollary principle is that *within the range of discretionary judgment* – the interstices of the law – judges are *not* neutral, but incrementally "make new law" to fit new situations, according to their *own* understanding of how discretion *ought* to be exercised. Thus, because two judges faced with the same situation will often make different judgment calls, judicial decision-making is in fact influenced, to one extent or another, by the identity of the judicial decision-maker.

This is not an indictment of all or most judges as biased or unprincipled, and it does not countenance a broad free-fire zone in which judges will make discretionary policy judgments according to their own personal preferences. Instead, Legal Realism epitomizes the richness of the traditional judicial role, properly understood and stripped of its obscurantist cant. Very likely, Chief Justice Roberts had this in mind when he used the baseball umpire analogy during his confirmation hearings.

That analogy has often been mocked by critics who complain that the then judge was being disingenuous and trying to have it both ways: it is easy to make the seemingly modest claim that one is "merely" judging each pitch to be a ball or a strike – by analogy, judging whether each aspect of a case is or is not required by law – *if one also has some ability to define what the law is*! We are all legal realists now.

But the analogy is more apt than critics give Roberts credit for, because baseball – unlike, say, tennis[7] – has almost as much discretion built-in to

[6] That was the often quoted first sentence of J. W. Singer, "Legal Realism Now" (1988) 76 *California Law Review* 465. Professor Singer's point, in a long review essay of Laura Kalman's 1986 book, *Legal Realism at Yale*: 1927–1960, was that the basic tenets of Legal Realism had so thoroughly dethroned formalism, that all later modes of legal thought in the United States were derived, at least to some extent, from those basics.

[7] The author of this chapter was for several years certified as an umpire by the United States Tennis Association. In tennis, there is no discretion in line calls; each ball is either "in" or it is "out," and the definition of "in" requires tennis umpires to live by the adage that "a ball that is 99% out is 100% in."

the decision-making process as the law does. Although the official rulebook defines a "strike" as a pitch that crosses any part of home plate at a height no higher than halfway between the batter's shoulders and his belt, and no lower than the hollow behind his kneecap, different umpires will apply the height requirement slightly differently.

Pitchers, batters, and baseball managers all understand that some umpires enforce a smaller strike zone than others, and this is considered to be acceptable "judging" of pitches, *as long as each umpire applies his version of the strike zone consistently throughout the game, and to both teams equally.*

The analogy to judging legal issues is obvious: there is no improper bias, as long as each individual judge brings his or her own discretion to bear *consistently*, and without regard to which party is favored or burdened in the process. Thus, while it would be wrong for Judge Roberts or any other judge to rule against "the little guy" in the face of the judge's genuinely held view that the law actually favors that guy, it would be just as wrong for the same judge to abandon his genuinely held view of what the law requires, merely to give a break to the little guy and even up the won–lost statistics.

In the hands of its students and practitioners, Legal Realism is not a crude and reductionist way of thinking. A banker's son does not, as a judge, always rule in favor of banks in commercial paper cases, and a female divorce court judge does not always award custody to the mother rather than the father. It is most definitely not the case – despite what one constantly reads in the crude and reductionist press in the United States – that judges from a particular political party always rule the same way as other judges from the same party, or in favor of members of their party.[8]

There are abundant constraints on the freedom of judges to disregard "the law" in favor of personal preference, including training, tradition, moral values, pride in craft, fear of reversal, and more. The zone of discretionary judgment is surprisingly narrow, even at the Supreme Court level, where at least the constraint of being embarrassed by frequent reversals has been removed. In a typical year, cases decided by a 9–0 vote constitute the plurality, and the justices are split no worse than 7–2 over 60 percent of the

[8] One of the best known counter-examples is *United States* v. *Nixon* 418 US 683 (1974), in which Richard Nixon, the Republican President of the United States, was brought down by a unanimous (8–0) Supreme Court that included four Republicans, three of whom had been appointed by Nixon himself.

time.[9] We tend to remember most clearly the 5–4 cases, because they are usually the most controversial and tendentious.[10]

In any event, although genuine differences about non-settled and still developing issues of law should not count as "bias" under traditional theories of judging or under Legal Realism or its follow-ons, judicial bias against individual litigants certainly can exist, and the legal system has developed several methods of removing that threat to the integrity of the administration of justice.

Standards for disqualification and for discipline of judges in the contemporary United States

Two closely related but nonetheless distinct remedies can be brought to bear when a judge has exhibited bias or prejudice in a particular case, or where the risk of bias is too great to be ignored. As in the case of misbehaving lawyers, a judge can be subjected to discipline or can be disqualified from proceeding further in the matter (or both).

With respect to disciplinary action against state court judges, the baseline is typically set and enforced by the highest court in each state of the United States, through adoption of a code of judicial conduct, almost always based on the American Bar Association's Model Code of Judicial Conduct (CJC), most recently revised in 2007.[11] Federal judges

[9] According to SCOTUSblog.com, the figures for October Terms 2005 through 2008 were 72 percent, 62 percent, 66 percent, and 54.5 percent. In the October Term 2009, which ended in July 2010, 40 percent of the cases were decided by 9–0 votes, 24 percent by 8–1 or 7–2 votes, and only 19 percent were decided 5–4.

[10] Critics of one of the most controversial 5–4 decisions in recent memory, *Bush* v. *Gore* 531 US 98 (2000), forget – or pretend to forget – that it wasn't a 5–4 decision! In *Gore* v. *Harris* 772 So.2d 1243 (Fla. 2000), the Florida Supreme Court, by a 4–3 vote, ordered a further manual recount of the votes cast in the recent presidential election, *but only in certain counties that candidate Al Gore and his lawyers had selected as likely to yield a more favorable outcome*. Candidate George Bush appealed to the US Supreme Court, arguing that through that ruling the State of Florida had violated his rights under the Equal Protection Clause of the US Constitution. The first task of an appellate court is to affirm or reverse, and *Bush* v. *Gore* reversed *Gore* v. *Harris* by a vote of 7–2, not 5–4. The Supreme Court *then* divided 5–4 with respect to the question of what remedy should be applied in light of the reversal.

[11] The ABA first promulgated its Model Code of Judicial Conduct in 1972 – a Code that was meant to have the force of law after adoption in each jurisdiction. Prior to that, judicial ethics was largely governed by reference to the hortatory Canons of Judicial Ethics, published by the ABA in 1924. Although not legally enforceable *per se*, the Canons were treated seriously, and often formed the basis for common law judicial rulings on disqualification.

(other than justices of the Supreme Court) are subject to the Code of Conduct for United States Judges, which is enforced administratively.[12] This Code of Conduct is similar in many ways to the CJC, but also contains some significant differences that are discussed below.

In the state courts, disqualification of the judge can be sought by a party to a lawsuit or the judge can initiate disqualification, according to statute or court rule or both. Although the CJC applies directly only to cases of judicial discipline, courts almost universally borrow heavily from those rules to set the substantive standard for disqualification as well. Moreover, because the *failure* of a judge to disqualify him- or herself when he or she should have is a disciplinary offense under Rule 2.11, in that instance the two standards converge completely.

Disqualification of federal judges for bias (or interestedness) is the subject of two federal statutes that have also gradually converged with each other, and with the standard for judicial discipline. What is now codified as 28 USC s. 455 is a direct descendant of the English common law and of a statute passed during George Washington's first term as President. Originally, s. 455 was limited to situations in which a judge had a financial stake in the outcome of a case, or had earlier appeared as counsel for one of the parties. Interestedness remained the focus of the statute through a series of amendments stretching into the twentieth century, as the statute's reach was extended to cover the interests of the judge's spouse, family members, and former law partners, and also to require disqualification when a judge was related to a party or a party's lawyer.

Finally, in 1974, not long after the ABA promulgated its Model Code of Judicial Conduct in 1972, Congress added to s. 455 a variation of the CJC requirement that a judge disqualify him- or herself when "his impartiality might reasonably be questioned," thus bringing disqualification for bias into the statute for the first time. Moreover, as noted above, the Code of Conduct for United States Judges had been adopted in 1973; it too had a provision requiring disqualification (on pain of

[12] The Code of Conduct for United States Judges was first adopted in 1973, and is both promulgated by and enforced by the Judicial Conference of the United States, which is chaired by the Chief Justice of the United States and composed of the chief judges of each of the US Courts of Appeal and a US District Court judge elected from each of the eleven regional judicial circuits. Because the US Constitution specifies that federal judges can be removed from office or suffer a reduction in compensation only by action of the US Senate, after impeachment by the House of Representatives, the Judicial Conference can impose lesser sanctions only.

administrative sanction) for lack of impartiality, also borrowed from the CJC.

28 USC s. 144 was first adopted in 1911, and it dealt with disqualification for bias right from the start. Under s. 144, a party files an affidavit (through counsel) alleging specifically described "personal bias or prejudice," and must attach a certificate of counsel stating that the affidavit has been filed in good faith. The trial court judge receiving the affidavit is permitted to assess its timeliness and sufficiency only, not the underlying facts stated, but what constitutes sufficient "personal bias or prejudice" to trigger the statute has generally been given a strict and narrow construction.[13]

Traditionally, bias has been measured by individualized and personal concerns, for purposes of both disqualification and discipline. Is the judge closely related by blood or marriage to a litigant or lawyer? Does the judge have a direct financial stake in the outcome? Could the judge's own finances be impacted by a decision, even if he or she has no stake in the immediate case at hand? Today, these concerns still resonate, but ideological or "issue" bias has more and more been added to the mix, even though the fact that a judge harbors particular views on legal issues should be no more disqualifying or ethically troubling than a baseball umpire's tendency to favor a larger or a smaller strike zone.

It is in this context of issue bias that the different ways in which "impartiality" can be defined come back into view. Under the Model Code of Judicial Conduct, Rule 2.11(A) states that "a judge *shall* disqualify himself or herself in any proceeding in which the judge's impartiality *might reasonably be questioned*" (emphasis supplied), and then gives a non-exclusive list of examples of situations in which that might be

[13] The first significant test of s. 144 came in *Berger* v. *United States* 255 US 22 (1921), a prosecution of German-born socialists under the Espionage Act after the First World War. In their affidavit submitted to the trial judge before trial, the defendants alleged that he had said, among other things, that "if anybody has said anything worse about the Germans than I have I would like to know it so I can use it," and, addressing a defendant of German extraction in another case, "your hearts are reeking with disloyalty." Not surprisingly, the Supreme Court held that the affidavits were sufficient to show personal bias, but even so three justices dissented, pointing out that most of the judge's remarks were directed to a defendant who had been *convicted* under the same Act, and was being *sentenced*. In the view of the dissenters, the judge's words, though intemperate, did not evince a bias against Germans generally. The trial judge in the case was Kenesaw Mountain Landis, who is otherwise famous in American law for almost single-handedly creating the concept of "appearance of impropriety," when, without resigning his position as a federal judge, he became Commissioner of Baseball.

so. In addition to the traditional situations involving financial and other relationships to parties or lawyers in the case, what is now Rule 2.11(A)(5) – the substance of which was not added to the CJC until 2003 – requires judges to disqualify themselves if they have previously made a campaign or other public speech that "commits *or appears to commit* the judge to reach a particular result or rule in a particular way in the proceeding or controversy" (emphasis supplied).

Canon 3C of the Code of Conduct for United States Judges is structured in the same way, includes the "might reasonably be questioned" triggering language, but pointedly *omits* any reference to campaign or other extra-judicial speech. Where the challenge to a judge's impartiality is based upon "issue bias," this difference is likely to lead to different results in many real-world situations.

In addition, while the standard for mandatory self-disqualification is distressingly vague under both sets of norms, it may be even more so under the CJC, without regard to the First Amendment problems inherent in requiring disqualification, *on pain of discipline*, on the basis of campaign or other public speech.

Disqualification is required under both codes if the judge's impartiality "might reasonably be questioned," but what is the baseline for determining reasonableness? How much knowledge of the facts must the hypothetical person who is "questioning" the judge's impartiality have? How deep an inquiry must be made to learn those facts? And – most important of all – how much understanding of the role of an independent judiciary is assumed; how much understanding of the law?

In this regard, the disparate explanations of the even vaguer term "appearance of impropriety" given in the Comments to the CJC and Commentary to the federal Code of Conduct are instructive and perhaps suggestive of how the basic disqualification standard might be applied.

Canon 2 of the federal Code requires federal judges to avoid impropriety and the appearance of impropriety, but no specific provision under Canon 2 refers to those terms. The Commentary to Canon 2A, however, states that "An appearance of impropriety occurs when reasonable minds, *with knowledge of all the relevant circumstances disclosed by a reasonable inquiry*, would conclude that the judge's honesty, integrity, impartiality, temperament, or fitness to serve as a judge is impaired" (emphasis supplied).

In the 2007 iteration of the ABA's Model Code of Judicial Conduct, avoiding "the appearance of impropriety" was for the first time explicitly prohibited by an enforceable rule, Rule 1.2, "Promoting Confidence in the Judiciary." Comment [5] to Rule 1.2 states, in part, "The test for appearance of impropriety is whether the conduct would create in reasonable minds a perception that the judge violated this Code or engaged in other conduct that reflects adversely on the judge's honesty, impartiality, temperament, or fitness to serve as a judge."

The much less demanding test for "reasonableness" in the CJC, omitting the qualifying language italicized above in the federal Code's understanding of the term, if also applied to pure disqualification matters, will put judges in such an awkward position under Rule 2.11 that they may be able to launch a constitutional attack on the disqualification regime.

It should not be forgotten, after all, that although Rule 2.11 of the CJC speaks of "disqualification," it is a rule of discipline – the discipline to be meted out by an arm of the state government in any state that has adopted the Model Code of Judicial Conduct without significant amendment.

The difficulty is made worse when Rule 2.11 is considered together with Rule 2.7(A), which commands that "A judge *shall* hear and decide matters assigned to the judge, *except* when disqualification is required by Rule 2.11 or other law" (emphasis supplied).

In tandem, these Rules draw a sharp line of demarcation that is, moreover, designed to leave no lacunae. As a default proposition, judges must not shrink from deciding whatever cases or controversies come before them in the normal course of events. That is what they are paid to do (from the public fisc, no less), and that is their contribution to the public good. But when disqualification is required, the public need to avoid bias in the courts trumps the traditional "duty to sit."

If a judge fails to disqualify him- or herself when disqualification is required, he or she is subject to discipline under Rule 2.11. But if a judge disqualifies him- or herself when disqualification was not "required" by Rule 2.11, then the judge violates Rule 2.7. When the impact of the vague and overbroad language of Rule 2.11 is factored in, judges have been placed squarely between Scylla and Charybdis.

Federal constitutional protection against exceptionally biased decision-making in the state courts

By a large margin, most judges in the United States sit on state courts, and are therefore regulated – as to both disqualification and discipline – by the highest court in each state. In a few instances, however, the US Supreme Court has intervened to say that the pressures on a judicial officer *not* "to hold the balance nice, clear and true" between litigants is a denial of the Due Process Clause of the Fourteenth Amendment as to the party likely to be disfavored. This puts a constitutional floor under the state-based systems regulating judicial bias, and the Supreme Court has repeatedly made clear that mere kinship or personal bias would not suffice to trigger the Due Process Clause; those are left to the state legislatures and courts to work through.

The seminal and still most obvious and easiest to understand case was *Tumey* v. *Ohio*,[14] which first used the "nice, clear and true" catch-phrase. In *Tumey*, mayors of small towns were authorized to sit as judges to hear (without a jury) cases involving petty criminal offenses under the Ohio alcoholic beverages laws.

Under the Ohio regime, convicted defendants would pay a small fine, and these fines would be paid in part into the town's treasury, and in part to the mayor personally as a stipend for taking on the additional duty of sitting as a judge. Of course, as the Supreme Court readily saw, the stipend was actually for taking on the additional duty of *convicting* defendants, because absent a conviction there would be no fine and no stipend.[15]

The only other significant case in this line – until 2009 – was *Aetna Life Ins. Co.* v. *Lavoie*.[16] In that case, Justice T. Eric Embry of the Alabama Supreme Court had voted with the majority of a closely divided court to uphold a punitive damages award against Aetna for bad faith refusal to pay a claim under a health insurance policy. At the same time, the justice was himself the lead plaintiff in a class action pending in the lower courts of Alabama against the health insurance carrier for all state employees (including not only Justice Embry, but presumably all of his colleagues on the Alabama Supreme Court). The class, claiming that the carrier pervasively delayed and refused to pay valid claims, sought punitive as well as compensatory damages.

The US Supreme Court reversed the Alabama Supreme Court's decision against Aetna because of Justice Embry's refusal to disqualify himself, but, significantly, only after *rejecting* a claim that the justice was biased or prejudiced toward insurance companies generally, as

[14] 273 US 510 (1927).

[15] In a later case, *Ward* v. *Monroeville* 409 US 57 (1972), a similar statutory scheme involving traffic fines was invalidated on the same grounds, even where the mayor did not personally receive part of the fine; the temptation for the executive officer of the town to raise revenue while wearing a supposedly neutral hat was too great.

[16] 475 US 813 (1986).

evidenced by statements he had made at his deposition in the class action. That ground for disqualification was unknown at common law, the court reminded, and was a matter for the states to regulate by statute or court rule, and could essentially never rise to the constitutional level.

But it is not hard to see why Justice Embry's participation in the *Lavoie* decision was *Tumey*-like in its self-interestedness: although the justice could not gain directly at Aetna's expense, a ruling against Aetna on the availability of punitive damages in Alabama would significantly enhance his leverage against the defending carrier in the case in which he was the lead plaintiff. Thus, Aetna was entitled to have this justice removed from decision-making in *its* case as a matter of fundamental fairness.[17]

The Supreme Court had a more difficult time, however, putting limits on the *Lavoie* rule, and this may have come back to haunt it in the *Caperton* case in 2009, discussed immediately below. In *Lavoie*, the question was asked why only Justice Embry, and not the other members of the Alabama Supreme Court (who were also members of the class in the suit against the state's health insurance carrier), was required to be disqualified. In response, the US Supreme Court simply asserted that the other justices had only a "slight" pecuniary interest, whereas Embry's was "direct, personal, substantial, [and] pecuniary."[18]

Earlier in the opinion, the court had conceded that it was impossible to know if Justice Embry had actually been influenced by the pendency of the class action, but said that a "possible temptation" was sufficient to require disqualification – again citing *Tumey*. Ultimately, the court had to content itself with the hellishly vague proposition that "justice must satisfy the appearance of justice" in order to comport with the Due Process Clause. If that is the standard, there is no standard; whatever "appears" to a majority of the Supreme Court to be "not justice," or a "possible temptation" to injustice, will be struck down.

In *Caperton* v. *A. T. Massey Coal Co., Inc.*,[19] another justice of a state Supreme Court (West Virginia) was ordered disqualified from a case by the US Supreme Court on the basis of the due process analysis developed in *Tumey* and *Lavoie*, but not because of anything that the justice did,

[17] Interestingly, twenty years earlier Eric Embry had been lead trial counsel for the defense in the landmark First Amendment case *New York Times Co.* v. *Sullivan* 376 US 254 (1964), which established an extremely high bar for public figures to overcome in prosecuting libel cases. Defending the *New York Times* against an elected City Commissioner was not a popular thing to do in Montgomery, Alabama in the 1960s.

[18] 475 US at 826 (quoting from the *Tumey* decision).

[19] 129 S.Ct. 2252 (2009).

and not because of anything more substantial, ultimately, than the "appearance" that an injustice might have been done.

The case began in 2002 in the state courts of West Virginia, when Hugh Caperton and his small development and coal sales firms sued Massey Coal, one of the largest coal producers in the world, for business torts, including fraudulent misrepresentation and interference with contractual relationships. A jury found for Caperton, and awarded $50 million in damages, including punitive damages. When the case eventually made its way to the West Virginia Supreme Court of Appeals and was decided in 2007, a 3–2 majority found that Massey had indeed engaged in misconduct and that the jury's verdict was supported by the facts. The majority nonetheless reversed the jury verdict, on the basis of two subtle and perhaps novel procedural and jurisdictional issues.

A lot had happened between the end of the proceedings in the trial court and the decision in the state Supreme Court, in particular, the November 2004 election in which Brent Benjamin unseated (by a comfortable margin) Justice Warren McGraw, who was seeking re-election. As it turned out, Don Blankenship, the CEO of Massey Coal, had donated a small amount to Benjamin's campaign, but had spent over $3 million on independent expenditures such as anti-McGraw television spots.[20] Indeed, Blankenship spent more than the campaign committees of both candidates combined.

As the case made its way to the West Virginia Supreme Court of Appeals, Caperton not surprisingly picked up the meme that had been developed by the press in and out of the state: Massey and its CEO had purchased (or at least seen to the election of) their own personal justice to sit on their pending $50 million case. Caperton now repeatedly moved to disqualify Justice Benjamin, and he repeatedly denied the motion, eventually explaining that he had no "direct, personal, substantial, pecuniary interest in this case," quoting the language from the *Lavoie* case, and that bowing to a standard based on appearances "seems little more

[20] Those unfamiliar with American election law will be forgiven for thinking that there is no substantive difference between "contributions" and "expenditures." As all justices of the Supreme Court well knew, however, that distinction has been the single most important distinction in the regulation of political campaigns since the Supreme Court made it so over thirty years ago in *Buckley* v. *Valeo* 424 US 1 (1976). In a nutshell, *Buckley* established the proposition that while contributions to a candidate's campaign may be regulated to some extent, a supporter of a candidate may make his or her *own* expenditures without limit – if not coordinated with the campaign – because such expenditures are the equivalent of pure political speech, and thus entitled to the highest level of protection under the First Amendment.

than an invitation to subject West Virginia's justice system to the vagaries of the day – a framework in which predictability and stability yield to supposition, innuendo, half-truths, and partisan manipulations."[21]

The US Supreme Court held, as it had in *Tumey* and in *Lavoie*, that disqualification was constitutionally required. But Justice Anthony Kennedy's opinion for the 5–4 majority left unanswered many questions as to exactly what combination of facts and circumstances led to that conclusion. Indeed, in his dissent Chief Justice Roberts asked forty of them – twice the number allotted in the common parlor game.

Certainly, Justice Benjamin would not be tempted to skew toward Massey in the hope that a win for Massey would bring him direct pecuniary gain (as had been the case in *Tumey*). Nor – absent a criminal quid pro quo arrangement that the Supreme Court specifically assumed did *not* exist – was there a way in which skewing toward Massey would bring future collateral benefits (as had been the case in *Lavoie*).

Thus, in order to find that disqualification of Justice Benjamin was required, the Supreme Court had to extend the rationale of the previous cases and accept Caperton's claim that Benjamin would be unable to resist the temptation to repay the "debt of gratitude" that he owed to Blankenship, a temptation that is "inherent in human nature." We are all psychologists now.

After noting Justice Benjamin's conscientious efforts to examine his own motives, and without making any finding that actual bias existed, the Supreme Court adopted what it said was an objective standard: whether, "under a realistic appraisal of psychological tendencies and human weakness, [Benjamin's possible desire to reward Blankenship's company] poses such a risk of actual bias or prejudgment that the practice must be forbidden if the guarantee of due process is to be adequately implemented."[22]

Turning to the facts of the *Caperton* v. *A. T. Massey Coal Co., Inc.* case itself, Justice Kennedy incorporated by reference the "appearance of impropriety" and "impartiality might reasonably be questioned"

[21] Justice Benjamin's opinion denying disqualification was quoted by the US Supreme Court, 129 S.Ct. 2252 (2009) at 2259.

[22] *Caperton* v. *A. T. Massey Coal Co., Inc.* 129 S.Ct. 2252 (2009) at 2263. The language was taken from *Withrow* v. *Larkin* 421 US 35, 47 (1975), a case in which the court unanimously *rejected* the claim of a physician charged with misconduct that the Wisconsin Medical Examining Board violated his due process rights when it combined both investigatory and adjudicatory functions.

language of the ABA Model Code of Judicial Conduct discussed earlier in this chapter. But in rehearsing why it might be reasonable to question Justice Benjamin's impartiality, Justice Kennedy referred several times to Blankenship's extraordinary "contributions" to Benjamin's campaign (which in fact were no more than anyone else's), and even suggested that Blankenship had helped "direct" the campaign (when in fact merely *coordinating* efforts with a campaign is strictly forbidden to people making independent expenditures).

Finally, brushing aside abundant evidence that Justice McGraw would have lost badly to Brent Benjamin even without any independent action by Don Blankenship, Justice Kennedy concluded, "Just as no man is allowed to be a judge in his own cause, similar fears of bias can arise when – without the consent of the other parties – a man *chooses the judge in his own cause*."[23]

Justice Kennedy's fear of the possible corrupting effects of independent expenditures seems especially odd, in light of his opinion for himself and the four *Caperton* dissenters in *Citizens United* v. *Federal Election Commission*,[24] less than eight months later. In *Citizens United*, the court permitted a long-standing federal ban on corporate and labor union contributions to electoral campaigns to stand, but invalidated restrictions on independent expenditures (by anyone) as violative of the First Amendment.

The burden of the *Caperton* and *Citizens United* decisions, read together, seems to be that Don Blankenship not only did nothing wrong in the West Virginia elections of 2004, but that he had a First Amendment right to spend as much as he wished of his own or even Massey Coal's money to defeat McGraw and to elect Benjamin (as long as he did not coordinate his efforts with the Benjamin campaign).

Yet Justice Benjamin, who did not know Blankenship and was powerless to interfere with his constitutionally protected activities in any event, was required to disqualify himself from hearing *Massey Coal* cases[25] – not only

[23] 129 S.Ct. 2252 (2009) at 2265 (emphasis added). [24] 130 S.Ct. at 876.

[25] Actually, Justice Benjamin sat on several other cases in which Massey Coal was a party without any objection or motion to disqualify being filed. In some of those cases he voted *against* the interests of Massey, including one in which he voted to deny review, thus permitting a $243 million verdict against Massey to stand. See Ronald Rotunda, 'Judicial Disqualification in the Aftermath of Caperton v. A. T. Massey Coal Co.' (2010) 60 *Syracuse Law Review* 247 at 270–1. As Professor Rotunda further reported, the state of West Virginia also opposed Massey Coal in cases pending before Justice Benjamin, but did not seek to remove him. This is striking, in light of the fact that the Attorney-General of West Virginia at the time was Darrell McGraw, the brother of former Justice Warren McGraw, who was defeated by Benjamin in the 2004 election.

by the Constitution, but presumably on pain of discipline under the West Virginia Code of Judicial Conduct. Moreover, the damage to his reputation will never be fully repaired; in the popular culture he will always be known as "the West Virginia justice that Massey Coal purchased for $3 million in order to win a $50 million case."

The protection of judicial campaign speech under the First Amendment and the uneasy place of judicial elections within American democracy

The constitution rights of judges and candidates for judicial office, rather than litigants, were at stake in *Republican Party of Minnesota* v. *White*.[26] The court struck down the so-called "announce" (or "do *not* announce") clause that originally appeared in the 1972 ABA Model Code of Judicial Conduct, and was still in force in Minnesota long after it had been removed from the CJC and from the disciplinary rules of most states. Under the "announce" clause a candidate for judicial office (including incumbents running for re-election or retention) was prohibited from "announc[ing] his or her views on disputed legal or political issues."

In a 5–4 decision, the Supreme Court in *White* held that content-based government bans of this kind on one of the purest forms of political speech could not pass muster under the First Amendment. In particular, the restriction was so underinclusive as to render it unsuitable for actually accomplishing any legitimate purpose: a lawyer could write or speak about anything he or she liked, up until the day he or she filed candidacy papers.

Although this was first and foremost a free speech decision, it is likely to figure prominently in future developments regarding disqualification of judges for perceived bias against litigants or classes of litigants. Because the State of Minnesota defended the "announce" clause on the ground that it was necessary to prevent candidates from literally broadcasting their prejudgments on the merits of future cases in order to curry favor with the voters, the *White* opinion necessarily had to discuss judicial bias.

Unfortunately, although the "announce" clause was indeed designed to maintain the independence and impartiality of judicial candidates by taking even implicit campaign promises off the table, it instead highlighted the awkward place that judicial elections themselves occupy in American democratic theory.

[26] 536 US 765 (2002).

If candidates may not even state their "views" on the issues of the day in the public square, what basis would voters have to choose between candidates? Under the regime of the "announce" clause, candidates often contented themselves with vapid generalities about "serving the community" and "the majesty of the law," while others, sadly, made overt racial and ethnic appeals by legally changing their names to sound more (or less) Italian, Polish, Jewish, or Latino, depending on the demographics of the electorate. Of course, in the majority of states that held partisan elections, the dominant reason for favoring a candidate was often simply a matter of party affiliation.

But if voters have little or no basis for making informed choices between candidates, what is the point of having elections in the first place, other than to satisfy a "feel-good" sense of community? The answer may lie in an observation made by Professor Charles Gardner Geyh in Chapter 13 of this book, "The Criticism and Speech of Judges in the United States," that even people without training in the law have internalized the core teachings of Legal Realism.

Because, under Legal Realism, it *matters* which judge decides which case, voters demand the opportunity to elect judges who will do their bidding, just as they are accustomed to voting for legislative and executive branch officials on the basis of the policies they have promised to implement and the results they have promised to deliver. But this is a grave misunderstanding of the role of the judiciary. Judges do not "represent" anyone, they cannot promise results in advance (without rightfully being charged with bias and disqualified), and in constitutional litigation, moreover, they must sometimes make decisions that are avowedly *against* the will of the majority.

Unfortunately, the version of Legal Realism employed by the public at large and by the popular press is a crude one, and incorrectly assumes that judges have essentially full freedom to decide cases according to their personal views. Thus, voters will grasp at any clue to try to determine who they want on the bench, and the "announce" clause was a ham-handed attempt to deny "illicit" information to the voters.

Oddly, however, although the public favors judicial elections, presumably for the reasons outlined above, the notion that judicial elections may ultimately be largely for show is borne out by a symposium article written by Professor Geyh shortly after the *White* decision was handed down. According to his "Axiom of 80," which he derived from reliable sociological data and then rounded up or down slightly to achieve rough symmetry: 80 percent of the US population favors judicial elections,

80 percent of the US population does not vote in judicial elections and does not know who the candidates are, and 80 percent of the US population believes that those who contribute money to judicial campaigns receive more favorable treatment in court than those who do not.[27]

By the time that *Republican Party of Minnesota* v. *White* was decided in 2002, most jurisdictions had abandoned the "announce" clause anyway, and had adopted a prohibition on making statements "that commit or appear to commit the candidate with respect to cases, controversies or issues that are likely to come before the court." As noted earlier in this chapter, during the 2007 revision to the Model Code of Judicial Conduct, this language was carried forward, but moved to Rule 2.11(A)(5), *a rule governing disqualification*.

At the same time, more attention was being paid to the "pledges and promises" clause, which originally prohibited a candidate from making "pledges or promises of conduct in office other than the faithful and impartial performance of the duties of the office." The Supreme Court expressed no view on that clause in *White*, but it was discussed at some length in the exchanges between the majority and dissenting opinions. The upshot is that it appeared likely, but by no means certain, that a restriction narrowly targeted at campaign promises to decide specific cases in specific ways would be upheld.

Almost immediately after the *White* case was decided, the American Bar Association amended the CJC to make the "pledges and promises" clause more specific. The new language, which was incorporated without further change into Rule 4.1 of the 2007 Code, prohibited both sitting judges and judicial candidates from making "pledges, promises, or commitments that are inconsistent with the impartial performance of the adjudicative duties of judicial office." The 2007 Comments also attempted to spell out in more detail the difference between mere statements of personal views (which are permitted on the authority of *White*), and "specifically undertaking to reach a particular result," which is a prohibited pledge or promise.

When all of these provisions are considered together, the close linkage between judicial campaigns and later disqualification becomes clear. The *White* decision freed up candidates to state their personal views on a wide variety of topics, including contested legal issues of the day. Because, according to Justice Antonin Scalia's opinion for the court,

[27] See C. G. Geyh, 'Why Judicial Elections Stink' (2003) 64 *Ohio State Law Journal* 43 at 52–5.

even a strongly stated view did not evince bias against any particular *party*, there should be no concern of lack of impartiality.[28]

It is true that a party whose case depended on the opposite view prevailing would be more likely to lose on that issue, but that would be true with respect to all such parties equally. (Some baseball umpires, it will be recalled, favor a smaller strike zone than others, but they apply it equally to all pitchers and all batters.)

During a heated campaign, however, not everyone will agree whether or not a particular statement has crossed over the line and become an improper pledge or promise of specific results. A rival candidate may take the matter up with the disciplinary authorities (after losing *or* winning the election), and members of the public may complain as well. But the much more likely prospect in today's hyper-sensitive world is that a litigant will later seek the winning candidate's disqualification *under Rule 2.11(A)(5)*. The same campaign speech that might land a candidate in hot water for making a promise of specific results, could also be characterized by a litigant's lawyer as a series of statements "that commit *or appear to commit* the candidate with respect to cases, controversies or issues that are likely to come before the court." Once "appearances" are put back in play, the old questions about whose sensibilities and on what knowledge base must be revisited again. And the jeopardy facing elected judges will increase again, because judges are required as a matter of judicial ethics to disqualify *themselves* even before the motion is made.

It is not too much to say that the relative freedom that the Supreme Court gave to candidates to speak out on legal and political issues in the *White* case may be undermined by a glut of disqualification motions and self-disqualifications, consuming additional judicial resources, disrupting the functioning of the courts, and likely tarnishing the reputation of many good judges.

It will not be too long – one or two election cycles at the most – before the Supreme Court will have to weigh in again and decide whether disqualification for "issue bias" will be the exception or the rule. If robust campaign speech can be purchased only by more and more frequent disqualifications, the 80 percent of Americans who want to elect judges (but do not care enough to vote) might finally begin to soften their enthusiasm for an elected judiciary.

[28] *Republican Party of Minnesota* v. *White* 536 US 765 at 774–7 (2002).

PART V

20

Judges and non-judicial functions in Australia

PATRICK EMERTON AND H. P. LEE

Judges in Australia are not confined to the performance of judicial functions only. As judges at federal and state levels are held in very high regard by the general public, governments at both levels have from time to time sought to have judges perform non-judicial functions.

Australian judges have engaged in a broad spectrum of non-judicial or extra-judicial activities.[1] There have been a few historical instances of judges accepting ambassadorial appointments. A Justice of the High Court of Australia, Sir Owen Dixon, served as Ambassador to the United States; Chief Justice John Latham was Minister Plenipotentiary in Japan; and Justice Fox of the Federal Court served as Ambassador of Australia for Nuclear Non-Proliferation and Safeguards. The Director of the Australian Security Intelligence Organisation (ASIO) was at one stage a federal judge; likewise the Chair of the National Crime Authority. Federal judges have been appointed as President or Deputy President of the Administrative Appeals Tribunal (AAT), a tribunal performing 'administrative' functions. Judges have been entrusted with the non-judicial function of authorising warrants for the interception of communications, and more recently with the issuance of detention and questioning orders in relation to terrorism investigations. The use of judges, federal and state, in conducting royal commissions and other inquiries 'has been a settled feature of Australian public life during the

[1] See E. Campbell and H. P. Lee, *The Australian Judiciary* (Melbourne: Cambridge University Press, 2001), pp. 166–79; F. Wheeler, 'Federal Judges as Holders of Non-judicial Office', in B. Opeskin and F. Wheeler (eds.), *The Australian Federal Judicial System* (Melbourne University Press, 2000), pp. 442–74; G. Brennan, 'Limits on the Use of Judges' (1978) 9 *Federal Law Review* 1; S. D. Connor, 'The Use of Judges in Non-Judicial Roles' (1978) 52 *Australian Law Journal* 482; G. Winterton, 'Judges as Royal Commissioners' (1987) 10 *University of New South Wales Law Journal* 108; R. S. French, 'Executive Toys: Judges and Non-judicial Functions' (2009) 19 *Journal of Judicial Administration* 5.

whole history' of Australia.[2] Judges have been appointed to perform such a role mainly because of their special qualities: 'training and skill to gather facts, identify those which are relevant, assess the honesty of evidence, evaluate competing arguments, act with sensitivity and neutrality in unravelling controversial issues and present an impartial report evidencing legal accuracy and dispassion'.[3] When judges undertake such inquiries, however, or perform other non-judicial functions, there is a danger that they may become embroiled in a political controversy. A fundamental question in Australian constitutional law is, therefore, the extent to which judges are permitted to perform such functions.

The separation of judicial power doctrine

Two features of the Australian constitutional system complicate the issue of the constitutionality of having serving judges perform non-judicial functions: the separation of judicial power at the federal level; and the incorporation of state (sub-federal) courts into the federal judicial system.

Under the Australian (or Commonwealth) Constitution, federal legislative power is vested by Chapter I in the federal or Commonwealth Parliament and the executive power is vested by Chapter II in the Sovereign and is exercisable by the Governor-General as the Sovereign's representative. Chapter III provides that:

> The judicial power of the Commonwealth shall be vested in . . . the High Court of Australia, and in such other federal courts as the Parliament creates, and in such other courts as it invests with federal jurisdiction.[4]

Although the constitution does not expressly recognise the separation of powers, this compartmentalisation of the three broad categories of powers and their vesting in distinct organs of government is regarded as instituting such a separation. As authoritatively stated by the Privy Council, 'the principle of the separation of powers is embodied in the Constitution'.[5]

Because Australia has a parliamentary system of government at both state and federal levels, the separation of legislative and executive power is not a strict one. The separation of federal judicial power is strict, however, in two respects. From soon after federation, the High Court held that the opening words of Chapter III of the Constitution reserve to the specified courts the

[2] *Wilson* v. *Minister for Aboriginal and Torres Strait Islander Affairs* (1996) 189 CLR 1 at 34 *per* Kirby J ('*Wilson*').

[3] *Wilson* (1996) 189 CLR 1 at 36. [4] Section 71.

[5] *Attorney-General for the Commonwealth* v. *R* (1957) 95 CLR 529 at 538.

vesting of federal judicial power – any attempt to vest that power in another body will be unconstitutional.[6] After the Second World War, the High Court went further and held that these words also preclude the vesting in any federal court – the High Court, or any other court created by the Commonwealth Parliament – of any non-judicial power, unless the exercise of that power is ancillary or incidental to the exercise of federal judicial power.[7]

This does not mean, however, that no federal judicial officer may have a non-judicial function conferred upon him or her. This is because, in its exposition of the requirements of the Australian Constitution, the High Court has drawn a distinction between a function *conferred upon a court*, and a function conferred upon a member of the federal judiciary *in his or her personal capacity*, that is, as *persona designata*. Thus, there are two bodies of law that must be understood if we are to understand the ways in which federal judges may undertake non-judicial functions: first, the law that distinguishes judicial from other forms of power; and, second, the law relating to *persona designata*.

State courts, and therefore state judges, are in a slightly different situation. No Australian state constitution mandates a strict separation of judicial from other forms of power, even though there are separate functionaries each entrusted with the exercise of legislative, executive and judicial powers. Thus, as a general rule there is no constitutional obstacle to a state court being vested with the exercise of non-judicial functions. Since the 1996 decision of *Kable* v. *Director of Public Prosecutions (NSW)*,[8] however, an important exception to this general rule has been recognised. This exception arises from the fact that state courts may be vested by the Commonwealth Parliament with the exercise of federal judicial power. The *Kable* principle holds that state courts which are recognised by Chapter III as repositories of federal judicial power cannot be vested (whether by legislation of the state or of the Commonwealth) with powers which are 'repugnant to or incompatible with' their exercise of federal judicial power.

Distinguishing judicial from non-judicial functions

The actual operation of the separation of judicial power doctrine has given rise to much difficulty, particularly in the demarcation between judicial and non-judicial functions. The key indicia, set out in Griffith

[6] *New South Wales* v. *The Commonwealth* (1915) 20 CLR 54.
[7] *R* v. *Kirby ex p. Boilermakers' Society of Australia* (1956) 94 CLR 254 ('*Boilermakers*').
[8] (1996) 189 CLR 51 ('*Kable*').

CJ's 'classic' definition of 'judicial power',[9] are the presence of (1) a dispute, to be resolved, (2) by application of specified legal criteria, (3) to ascertained facts, (4) with the resolution being binding upon the parties.[10] It is accepted, however, that various functions which lack one or more of these characteristics may nevertheless fall within the ambit of judicial power. Examples include the making of guardianship orders and the issuing of administrative directions to trustees, or in contexts of insolvency or the winding up of companies. In these (and similar) cases, there may well be no dispute, nor any adjudication of rights, but rather the creation of new rights.[11] The rationale for nevertheless categorising such functions as judicial is historical: they are part of what was understood, at the time of the drafting of the Constitution, to have 'an acknowledged place in the structure of the judicial system'.[12]

Further complexity arises from judicial recognition of the so-called 'chameleon' doctrine, which states that in certain cases 'A function may take its character from that of the tribunal in which it is reposed.'[13] The chameleon doctrine can be seen as a judicial response to the growth of the administrative role of government over the course of the twentieth century. The doctrine operates, however, only in respect of functions that are in their nature capable of performance either in an administrative or a judicial manner.[14] Some functions, such as industrial arbitration, are inherently administrative and may not be vested in federal courts,[15] while other functions are exclusively judicial in character. Among the latter is 'the adjudgment and punishment of criminal guilt under a law of the Commonwealth'.[16]

[9] *Huddart, Parker & Co Pty Ltd* v. *Moorehead* (1909) 8 CLR 330 at 357.

[10] *Re Judiciary and Navigation Acts* (1921) 29 CLR 257, 265–6 *per* Knox CJ, Gavan Duffy, Powers, Rich and Starke JJ; *Thomas* v. *Mowbray* (2007) 233 CLR 307 at 343–8, 350–5 *per* Gummow and Crennan JJ, 463–9, 472–6, 479 *per* Hayne J ('*Thomas*').

[11] *R* v. *Davison* (1954) 90 CLR 353 at 368 *per* Dixon CJ and McTiernan J.

[12] *R* v. *Davison* (1954) 90 CLR 353 at 382 *per* Kitto J.

[13] *R* v. *Hegarty ex p. City of Salisbury* (1981) 147 CLR 617 at 628 *per* Mason J. See also *Boilermakers'* (1956) 94 CLR 254 at 278 *per* Dixon CJ, McTiernan, Fullagar and Kitto JJ; *R* v. *Quinn ex p. Consolidated Food Corporation* (1977) 138 CLR 1 at 10 *per* Jacobs J; *White* v. *Director of Military Prosecutions* (2007) 231 CLR 570 at 595 *per* Gummow, Hayne and Crennan JJ.

[14] See the discussion in D. Meyerson, 'Using Judges to Manage Risk: The Case of *Thomas* v. *Mowbray*' (2000) 36 *Federal Law Review* 209 at 209–10, 212–15.

[15] *Waterside Workers' Federation of Australia* v. *J. W. Alexander Ltd* (1918) 25 CLR 434 at 463 *per* Isaacs and Rich JJ; *Boilermakers* (1956) 94 CLR 254 at 281 *per* Dixon CJ, McTiernan, Fullagar and Kitto JJ.

[16] *Chu Kheng Lim* v. *The Minister for Immigration, Local Government and Ethnic Affairs* (1992) 176 CLR 1 at 27 *per* Brennan, Deane and Dawson JJ ('*Chu Kheng Lim*').

The requirement that federal courts be vested only with judicial power means also that legislation which confers upon a federal court a function consistent with the exercise of judicial power, but which purports to require the court to perform that function in a manner that is at odds with the character of the court or the nature of judicial power, may be invalid.[17]

These various features of separation doctrine have important implications. Thus, a majority of the High Court held invalid a legislative provision that purported to preclude the courts, regardless of the circumstances, from ordering the release from detention of a particular category of detained non-citizens. The court characterised the provision as 'a direction by the Parliament to the courts as to the manner in which they are to exercise their jurisdiction',[18] and held that legislative provisions which 'purport to direct the courts as to the manner and outcome of the exercise of their jurisdiction' are invalid because 'an impermissible intrusion into the judicial power which Ch III vests exclusively in the courts that it designates'.[19] In a jurisdiction without a federal bill of rights,[20] constitutional limitations arising in this way ensure that a degree of due process is nevertheless constitutionally mandated.[21]

A number of members of the High Court have expressed the view that, with some exceptions, within the Australian constitutional framework detention of a person by governmental authorities is permissible 'only as a consequential step in the adjudication of criminal guilt of that [person] for

[17] *Polyukhovich* v. *The Commonwealth* (1991) 172 CLR 501 at 607 *per* Deane J, 689 *per* Toohey J, 703–4 *per* Gaudron J; *Chu Kheng Lim* (1992) 176 CLR 1 at 27 *per* Brennan, Deane and Dawson JJ; *Thomas* (2007) 233 CLR 307 at 355 *per* Gummow and Crennan JJ.

[18] *Chu Kheng Lim* (1992) 176 CLR 1 at 36 *per* Brennan, Deane and Dawson JJ. Gaudron J agreed with Brennan, Deane and Dawson JJ, at 53. The minority held that the provision was capable of being interpreted otherwise than as such a direction, and hence that it was valid: 11–14 *per* Mason CJ, 50–1 *per* Toohey J, 67–8 *per* McHugh J.

[19] *Chu Kheng Lim* (1992) 176 CLR 1 at 36–7 *per* Brennan, Deane and Dawson JJ. Gaudron J agreed with Brennan, Deane and Dawson JJ, at 53.

[20] A statutory charter of rights comparable in its general terms and operation to the UK Human Rights Act 1998 and the New Zealand Bill of Rights Act 1990 has been adopted in one Australian state – Victoria – and in one self-governing territory – the Australian Capital Territory: Charter of Human Rights and Responsibilities Act 2006 (Vic); Human Rights Act 2004 (ACT).

[21] The classic treatment of this topic is G. Winterton, 'The Separation of Judicial Power as an Implied Bill of Rights', in G. Lindell (ed.), *Future Directions in Australian Constitutional Law: Essays in Honour of Professor Leslie Zines* (Sydney: Federation Press, 1994), pp. 185–208.

past acts'.[22] Given that the adjudication of criminal guilt in Commonwealth matters is an exclusively judicial function, it follows that detention in the federal sphere of government may, as a general rule, be imposed only by a court exercising the judicial power of the Commonwealth in the course of adjudicating and punishing criminal guilt.

There are several exceptions to this general rule, including the power of Parliament to legislate to establish quarantine regimes,[23] and the power 'of arrest and detention in custody, pursuant to executive warrant, of a person accused of a crime to ensure that he or she is available to be dealt with by the courts'.[24] (This power of arrest, however, is 'ordinarily subject to the supervisory jurisdiction of the courts'.[25]) Despite these exceptions, the separation doctrine, in combination with the principle that 'the common law knows neither lettre de cachet nor other executive warrant authorizing ... arrest or detention' without statutory authority,[26] operates to place reasonably strict limits upon the range of detention regimes permissible under Australian law.

Thomas v. *Mowbray*[27] concerned a legislative regime giving federal courts the power, upon an *ex parte* application by the Australian Federal Police (AFP), to issue 'control orders' restricting the liberty of persons in various ways, if (1) the court is satisfied upon the balance of probabilities that making the order would substantially assist in preventing a terrorist act, or that the person subject to the control order has trained with a listed organisation, and (2) the court is satisfied on the balance of probabilities that each element of the control order is reasonably necessary, and reasonably appropriate and adapted, for the purpose of

[22] *Fardon* v. *Attorney-General (Qld)* (2004) 223 CLR 575 at 612 *per* Gummow J ('*Fardon*'). Gummow J presents his formulation of this point as a development of the remark of Brennan, Deane and Dawson JJ that 'the involuntary detention of a citizen in custody by the State ... under our system of government, exists only as an incident of the exclusively judicial function of adjudging and punishing criminal guilt': *Chu Kheng Lim* (1992) 176 CLR 1 at 27. Gummow J uses the word 'citizen' rather than 'person', but makes it clear that, outside the special context of immigration detention, aliens enjoy the same constitutional protection as citizens: *Fardon* (2004) 223 CLR 575 at 611–12. The point was accepted by a majority of the High Court in *Thomas*: (2007) 233 CLR 307 at 330 *per* Gleeson CJ, 356 *per* Gummow and Crennan JJ, 430 *per* Kirby J.

[23] *Chu Kheng Lim* (1992) 176 CLR 1 at 28 *per* Brennan, Deane and Dawson JJ; *Thomas* (2007) 233 CLR 307 at 330 *per* Gleeson CJ.

[24] *Chu Kheng Lim* (1992) 176 CLR 1 at 28 *per* Brennan, Deane and Dawson JJ, 55 *per* Gaudron J; see also *Fardon* (2004) 223 CLR 575 at 613 *per* Gummow J.

[25] *Chu Kheng Lim* (1992) 176 CLR 1 at 28 *per* Brennan, Deane and Dawson JJ.

[26] *Chu Kheng Lim* (1992) 176 CLR 1 at 19 *per* Brennan, Deane and Dawson JJ.

[27] (2007) 233 CLR 307.

protecting the public from a terrorist act.[28] In upholding the constitutionality of the regime, a majority of the High Court distinguished between the constitutionally circumscribed condition of detention in custody, and the lesser restraints on liberty contemplated by the control order regime, such as restrictions on movement and communications, curfews and reporting obligations, and the like.[29] This aspect of the decision in *Thomas* leaves open the questions of where the boundary between detention and lesser burdens on liberty is to be drawn, and of what sorts of powers might permissibly be conferred upon administrative agencies (including judges acting as *persona designata*) to issue orders of a similar nature, and whether such powers, in order to be constitutional, would have to be subject to judicial oversight (as is the case in respect of ordinary executive powers of arrest).[30]

It was also argued that the criteria according to which control orders are issued did not specify, with sufficient precision to amount to an exercise of judicial power, a *legal* (as opposed to political or policy) matter to be resolved by the court. The majority rejected this argument, drawing comparison between the issuing of control orders and such familiar judicial activities as awarding bail upon conditions, issuing apprehended violence orders and binding persons over to keep the peace, all of which restrict liberty by creating new rights and obligations rather than impose such restrictions as the outcome of an adjudication of existing rights.[31] Gummow and Crennan JJ also noted the very broad legal criteria that had been upheld as valid in previous High Court decisions dealing with a range of enactments in such fields as trade

[28] Criminal Code (Cth), s. 104.4. As defined by s. 100.1, 'terrorist act' is a very broad notion encompassing most acts or threats of politically or religiously motivated violence within or outside Australia. Under a regime established by s. 102.1, an organisation may be listed if it has any of a range of direct or indirect connections to an actual or possible terrorist act.

[29] *Thomas* (2007) 233 CLR 307 at 330 *per* Gleeson CJ, 356–7 *per* Gummow and Crennan JJ, 509 *per* Callinan J, concurring with Gummow and Crennan JJ, 526 *per* Heydon J, concurring with the other majority judges. Kirby J expressed the contrary view at 429–33. For criticism of the majority's reasoning, see Meyerson, 'Using Judges to Manage Risk'.

[30] Gleeson CJ appeared to assume that it would be open to the Parliament to vest the executive with the power to issue control orders: *Thomas* (2007) 233 CLR 307 at 329. Hayne J, in dissent, expressly refraining from deciding this point, but expressed doubt that, in a time of 'ostensible peace', such a regime of administrative control orders would be constitutional: at 476. Kirby J agreed, at 429.

[31] *Thomas* (2007) 233 CLR 307 at 326–9 *per* Gleeson CJ, 347–8 *per* Gummow and Crennan JJ, 526 *per* Heydon J, concurring with the other majority judges.

practices and the regulation of trade unions.[32] The decision therefore suggests that broadly conferred discretions typical of modern regulatory enactments will not amount to non-judicial functions, and, hence, cease to be constitutional simply because they are directed not at traditional regulatory aims but at restraining liberty in the manner of a control order. *Thomas* can be seen as a victory for the chameleon doctrine and its underlying rationale, making it clear that the notion of judicial power is considerably broader than it might have appeared to be when Griffith CJ propounded his classic definition of it.

The *persona designata* exception

One purpose of the doctrine of the separation of judicial power is to enable courts to protect their 'reputational capital' from being exploited by the executive or the legislature. The High Court has on a number of occasions invoked the famous passage of the US Supreme Court in *Mistretta* v. *United States*:[33]

> The legitimacy of the Judicial Branch ultimately depends upon its reputation for impartiality and non-partisanship. That reputation may not be borrowed by the political branches to cloak their work in the neutral colours of judicial action.[34]

At first, judicial recognition was given to the concept of *persona designata* as an exception to the separation doctrine.[35] Today, however, mere invocation of the *persona designata* exception is not sufficient to render legitimate the vesting of a non-judicial function in a federal judge. The High Court has adopted an incompatibility test as the criterion of validity of the federal enactment. Even if the non-judicial function is conferred on a judge in a personal capacity, it is necessary to go to the next step and enquire whether the performance of that function is compatible with the performance of judicial functions. It is said that 'When that condition is satisfied, judges not only are, but are seen to be, independent of the other branches of government. The appearance of

[32] *Thomas* (2007) 233 CLR 307 at 345–7, 350–1.

[33] 488 US 361 (1989) ('*Mistretta*'). *Grollo* v. *Palmer* (1995) 184 CLR 348 at 366 *per* Brennan CJ, Deane, Dawson and Toohey J, 377 *per* McHugh J, 392 *per* Gummow J ('*Grollo*'); *Kable* (1996) 189 CLR 51 at 96 *per* Toohey J, 133 *per* Gummow J; *Fardon* (2004) 223 CLR 575 at 615 *per* Gummow J.

[34] *Mistretta* 488 US 361 (1989) at 407.

[35] *Hilton* v. *Wells* (1985) 157 CLR 57 at 68 *per* Gibbs CJ, Wilson and Dawson JJ ('*Hilton*').

independence preserves public confidence in the judicial branch.'[36] Conversely, where an incompatibility arises, the attempt to confer the non-judicial power is rendered invalid, because it fails to conform with the requirements of Chapter III of the Constitution.[37]

A number of commentators have suggested that, in the light of this development, it would make sense to abandon both the *persona designata* exception to the prohibition upon the vesting of federal courts with non-judicial functions, and that prohibition itself, and instead simply to allow federal courts to be vested with non-judicial functions as long as the performance of those functions is compatible with the courts' judicial role.[38] This suggestion has not been taken up by the High Court, however.

The majority of the High Court in *Grollo* v. *Palmer*[39] spelled out the following different ways in which incompatibility between a non-judicial function to be undertaken as *persona designata*, and a judge's performance of his or her judicial role, may arise:

(1) where the performance of non-judicial functions by a judge is 'so permanent and complete a commitment that the further performance of substantial judicial functions by that judge is not practicable';
(2) where the performance of non-judicial functions is 'of such a nature that the capacity of the judge to perform his or her judicial functions with integrity is compromised or impaired'; and
(3) where the performance of non-judicial functions is 'of such a nature that public confidence in the integrity of the judiciary as an institution or in the capacity of the individual judge to perform his or her judicial functions with integrity is diminished'.[40]

Subsequent cases make it clear that 'public confidence' does not refer to an empirical state of affairs, but rather to a normative standard which is

[36] *Wilson* (1996) 189 CLR 1 at 14 *per* Brennan CJ, Dawson, Toohey, McHugh and Gummow JJ. The vesting of the non-judicial function must also be subject to the judge's consent: *Grollo* (1995) 184 CLR 348 at 364–5 *per* Brennan CJ, Deane, Dawson and Toohey JJ.

[37] *Wilson* (1996) 189 CLR 1 at 15–16 *per* Brennan CJ, Dawson, Toohey, McHugh and Gummow JJ.

[38] A. Mason, 'A New Perspective on Separation of Powers' (1996) 82 *Canberra Bulletin of Public Administration* 1 at 5–6; C. Campbell, 'An Examination of the Doctrine of Persona Designata in Australian Law' (2000) 7 *Australian Journal of Administrative Law* 109 at 120; Wheeler, 'Federal Judges as Holders of Non-judicial Office', in Opeskin and Wheeler (eds.), *The Australian Federal Judicial System*, p. 469.

[39] (1995) 184 CLR 348.

[40] *Grollo* (1995) 184 CLR 348 at 365 *per* Brennan CJ, Deane, Dawson and Toohey JJ.

to be determined and applied by the courts themselves.[41] This feature of the incompatibility doctrine reinforces the role of the separation doctrine as a device whereby courts are able to protect their own independence and hence their reputational capital in accordance with their conception of these things.

The third limb of the incompatibility doctrine was applied by the High Court in *Wilson* v. *Minister for Aboriginal and Torres Strait Islander Affairs*.[42] The case arose from a controversial proposal approved by the South Australian government to build a bridge connecting the mainland to Hindmarsh Island in the State of South Australia. The Aboriginal and Torres Islander Heritage Protection Act 1984 (Cth) sought to preserve and protect areas and objects in Australia and Australian waters of particular significance to Indigenous Australians in accordance with their cultural traditions. Following an application in relation to Hindmarsh Island and surrounding areas, the federal Minister for Aboriginal and Torres Strait Islander Affairs appointed a Federal Court judge, Mathews J, to make a report to him under s. 10(1)(c) of the Act. The Act required the reporter to address the nature and extent of the threat to the area of Aboriginal significance and the measures required to preserve and protect the area.

It was accepted by the High Court both that the function of reporting was clearly non-judicial, and that Justice Mathews was appointed to perform the reporting function as an individual, and not as a judge of the Federal Court. However, referring to the third limb of the incompatibility test,[43] a majority of the High Court held that her appointment was invalid. The court explained that to establish constitutional incompatibility the statute or the measures taken pursuant to the statute must be examined in order to determine, first, 'whether the function is an integral part of, or is closely connected with, the functions of the Legislature or the Executive Government'.[44] If the function is not closely connected with the legislature or the executive government, there is no constitutional incompatibility. The second step is to determine 'whether the function is required to be performed independently of any

41 C. Campbell characterises it as 'deemed' public confidence: Campbell, 'An Examination of the Doctrine of Persona Designata in Australian Law', pp. 114, 120.

42 (1996) 189 CLR 1.

43 Wilson (1996) 189 CLR 1 at 16 *per* Brennan CJ, Dawson, Toohey, McHugh and Gummow JJ, 22 *per* Gaudron J.

44 Wilson (1996) 189 CLR 1 at 17 *per* Brennan CJ, Dawson, Toohey, McHugh and Gummow JJ.

instruction, advice or wish of the Legislature or the Executive Government, other than a law or an instrument made under a law'.[45] If the answer is not in the affirmative, it is clear that the separation has been breached. The court then went on:

> If the function is one which must be performed independently of any non-judicial instruction, advice or wish, a further question arises: Is any discretion purportedly possessed by the Ch III judge to be exercised on political grounds – that is, on grounds that are not confined by factors expressly or impliedly prescribed by law? In considering these questions, it will often be relevant to note whether the function to be performed must be performed judicially, that is, without bias and by a procedure that gives each interested person an opportunity to be heard and to deal with any case presented by those with opposing interests. An obligation to observe the requirements of procedural fairness is not necessarily indicative of compatibility with the holding of judicial office under Ch III, for many persons at various levels in the executive branch of government are obliged to observe those requirements. But, conversely, if a judicial manner of performance is not required, it is unlikely that the performance of the function will be performed free of political influence or without the prospect of exercising a political discretion.[46]

The court found that the only power conferred on the minister by s. 10 of the Act was to make a declaration, and that the report was 'no more than a condition precedent to the exercise of the Minister's power to make a declaration'.[47] The reporting function was thus 'an integral part of the process of the Minister's exercise of power',[48] and its performance by a judge placed her 'firmly in the echelons of administration, liable to removal by the Minister before the report is made and shorn of the usual judicial protections, in a position equivalent to that of a ministerial adviser'.[49] The majority judges also noted that the decisions which a reporter has to make, including which of competing Aboriginal and non-Aboriginal interests are to be preferred, are 'political in character'.[50] Although the reporter could choose to act independently of the minister, 'the Act does not require the reporter to disregard ministerial instruction, advice or wish in preparing the report'.[51] The court noted that in the case of a judge who is appointed to conduct a royal commission, the judge delivers a report 'according to the judge's own conscience without regard to the wishes or advice of the

45 Wilson (1996) 189 CLR 1 at 17. 46 Wilson (1996) 189 CLR 1 at 17.
47 Wilson (1996) 189 CLR 1 at 18. 48 Wilson (1996) 189 CLR 1 at 18.
49 Wilson (1996) 189 CLR 1 at 18–19. Footnotes omitted.
50 Wilson (1996) 189 CLR 1 at 19. 51 Wilson (1996) 189 CLR 1 at 19.

Executive Government'.[52] Even then, the majority added a caveat: 'The terms of reference of the particular royal commission and of any enabling legislation will be significant.'[53]

The propriety of judicial participation in royal commissions and similar executive inquiries has been controversial for a long time in Australia. In 1923, the Chief Justice of the Victorian Supreme Court issued a direction that no judge of his court would be available to sit on non-judicial government bodies, referring expressly to the need to retain 'the confidence of the people'.[54] An example of the embroilment in political controversy to which this sort of role has the potential to lead is provided by the 1995 royal commission established by Richard Court, the then Liberal Premier of Western Australia. The commission's purpose was to inquire into the circumstances surrounding the tabling in the Western Australian Legislative Council, in 1992, of a politically contentious petition, and in particular to consider whether members of the then Labor government, including the then premier Dr Carmen Lawrence, had been improperly involved.[55] By 1995, Dr Lawrence was serving as a minister in the Labor government of Prime Minister Paul Keating, and Mr Keating attacked the royal commission in the House of Representatives, describing it as 'a disgraceful exercise ... an abuse of executive government ... [and] one of the low points of Australian public life'.[56] The royal commissioner was Kenneth Marks QC, a retired justice of the Victoria Supreme Court. He was also subject to prime ministerial attack, being described by Mr Keating as 'compliant', a 'hired gun' and a 'hanging judge'.[57] Needless to say, such remarks, and the attendant political controversy, would have been extremely damaging to the public standing of any serving judge and his or her court.

The Marks Royal Commission was politically controversial from its inception,[58] but in some circumstances political controversy may arise where it was not initially foreseen (or foreseeable). This possibility

[52] Wilson (1996) 189 CLR 1 at 17. [53] Wilson (1996) 189 CLR 1 at 17.

[54] See the discussion of the 'Irvine Memorandum' in Winterton, 'Judges as Royal Commissioners', p. 109.

[55] See the account in E. Campbell, 'Royal Commissions, Parliamentary Privilege and Cabinet Confidentiality' (1999) 29 *University of Western Australia Law Review* 239 at 241–3.

[56] The Hon. Paul Keating, Reply to Question Without Notice, *House of Representatives Hansard*, 23 November 2005.

[57] The Hon. Paul Keating, Reply to Question Without Notice, *House of Representatives Hansard*, 23 November 2005.

[58] S. Prasser, 'Royal Commissions in Australia: When Should Governments Appoint Them?' (2006) 65 *Australian Journal of Public Administration* 28 at 34.

highlights the importance of the incompatibility doctrine working in a prophylactic fashion, to protect the standing of the judiciary by preventing that standing being jeopardised by a non-judicial appointment which turns out to have politically controversial dimensions.[59] The majority in *Wilson* indirectly addresses this issue in the following passage:

> Constitutional incompatibility has the effect of limiting legislative and executive power. Where it has that effect, it is discovered on the face of the statute, or on the face of those measures taken pursuant to a statute, that purports or purport to confer a non-judicial function on a Ch III judge. That is not to say that constitutional incompatibility is a matter of mere form. The operation of the statute or of the measures taken pursuant to it is ascertained by looking to the circumstances in which the purported function might be performed.[60]

This suggests that not only the terms of reference of an inquiry, but the circumstances in which it is to be undertaken, will be relevant to the question of constitutionality. And it is easy to see why some commentators have reached the conclusion, as did the Victorian judiciary in 1923, that constitutional propriety precludes serving judges from playing such roles at all.[61]

The reasoning of *Wilson* suggests that a similar conclusion must be reached with respect to many of the other non-judicial offices that have been held by federal judges from time to time in Australia. The decision appears to accept the permissibility of judges serving on administrative tribunals that operate independently of both the legislature and the executive,[62] but offices such as ambassadorships, or directorships of investigative or intelligence agencies, are without doubt closely connected to the executive government, are apt to be performed subject to executive instruction and advice, and in any event bring with them discretions that are to be exercised on political grounds. They therefore fall foul of the third limb of the incompatibility doctrine.[63]

59 See the discussion in Campbell, 'An Examination of the Doctrine of Persona Designata in Australian Law', pp. 113–15.

60 *Wilson* (1996) 189 CLR 1 at 16 *per* Brennan CJ, Dawson, Toohey, McHugh and Gummow JJ.

61 See, e.g., Winterton, 'Judges as Royal Commissioners', pp. 117–18, 120, who argues that whatever benefits government obtains by having judges lead inquiries can be achieved by having retired judges or eminent counsel play that role.

62 *Wilson* (1996) 189 CLR 1 at 17–18 *per* Brennan CJ, Dawson, Toohey, McHugh and Gummow JJ; see also *Hilton* (1985) 157 CLR 57 at 81 *per* Mason and Deane JJ; *Grollo* (1995) 184 CLR 348 at 383 *per* McHugh J.

63 The same conclusion is reached by Wheeler, 'Federal Judges as Holders of Non-judicial Office', in Opeskin and Wheeler (eds.), *The Australian Federal Judicial System*, pp. 470–1.

These consequences of the decision in *Wilson* were criticised by Kirby J, the lone dissenting judge, as a 'significant narrowing of the application of the accepted authority'[64] of the High Court in *Hilton* and *Grollo*. He said that 'If the suggested test is impermissible closeness to the Legislature or the Executive Government and their respective functions', then *Wilson* is incongruous with *Hilton* and *Grollo*.[65] In *Grollo*, the High Court upheld as constitutional the vesting of federal judges with the power to issue warrants authorising the covert interception of telecommunications by law enforcement officers, although such warrants are issued in closed *ex parte* hearings and are not subject to scrutiny or to any practical possibility of challenge.[66] The majority in *Grollo* justified their conclusion that such activity was not incompatible with the performance of judicial functions in the following terms:

> It is an eligible judge's function of deciding independently of the applicant agency whether an interception warrant should issue that separates the eligible judge from the executive function of law enforcement. It is the recognition of that independent role that preserves public confidence in the judiciary as an institution.[67]

McHugh J dissented from the outcome in the *Grollo* case.[68] He expressed concern about the intimate connection that the regime would establish between federal judges and the executive:

> The *persona designata* is given a discretion to approve or disapprove the issue of the warrant, and the grounds to be considered are very general ... The result is that, whenever the issue of the warrant is approved, the *persona designata* becomes open to the criticism that he

64 *Wilson* (1996) 189 CLR 1 at 49.

65 *Wilson* (1996) 189 CLR 1 at 49–50. Some commentators also take the view that the *Grollo* and *Wilson* cases are inconsistent in their applications of the incompatibility doctrine: Wheeler, 'Federal Judges as Holders of Non-judicial Office', in Opeskin and Wheeler (eds.), *The Australian Federal Judicial System*, pp. 469–70; S. Joseph and M. Castan, *Federal Constitutional Law: A Contemporary View*, 3rd edn. (Sydney: Lawbook Co., 2010), p. 205.

66 The relevant legislation is now the Telecommunications (Interception and Access) Act 1979, ss. 6D, 6DB, 46, 46A, 116. Since *Grollo* was decided, the permissible categories of interception have been expanded to include interception of B-party communications, of stored communications, and of services identified by reference to a named user rather than a telecommunications account.

67 *Grollo* (1995) 184 CLR 348 at 367 *per* Brennan CJ, Deane, Dawson and Toohey JJ.

68 Gummow J agreed with the majority, but only because he took a different view from McHugh J on a particular point of statutory construction concerning the secrecy governing the issuing of warrants: *Grollo* (1995) 184 CLR 348 at 395–8.

> or she has preferred the interests of the investigative agency to the privacy and interests of the persons whose communications are to be intercepted – the ordinary citizens whose liberty and interests the separation of powers is designed to protect.[69]

This suggests that McHugh J felt that the last of the *Wilson* requirements was not satisfied, namely, that the activity, being one closely connected to the executive, required the exercise of discretion 'on grounds that are not confined by factors expressly or impliedly prescribed by law'.

The difference between the majority and the minority in *Grollo*, and also in *Wilson*, may be best explained by differing conceptions of what constitutes a 'political' discretion, and that in the view of the majorities in those cases the issuing of warrants authorising criminal investigations is not to be regarded as political in the same way as is reporting to a minister on a controversial matter of public policy. This suggests a parallel to the differing conclusions of the majority and the minority judges in *Thomas* as to whether the control order regime specifies adequate legal criteria to sustain an exercise of judicial, as opposed to non-judicial, power, given that it requires judges, relying to a significant extent on intelligence material presented by the executive, to determine what is necessary to protect the public from a terrorist act.[70]

Commonwealth legislation continues to provide for an increasing variety of covert warrants that may be issued by federal judges. This only increases the importance of the issue decided in *Grollo*. Closely resembling telecommunications interception warrants are warrants authorising criminal investigators to use surveillance devices such as listening and tracking devices.[71] A more coercive investigative regime is established by the Crimes Act 1914 (Cth), under which federal magistrates acting as *persona designata* may, on an application from the AFP, compel a third party to produce a range of documents that are 'relevant to, and will assist, the investigation' of any of a range of offences punishable by two or more years of imprisonment.[72] It is an offence for the third party to fail to comply with, or to disclose the existence or nature of, the notice.[73] The constitutionality of this regime has not been tested, but if

[69] *Grollo* (1995) 184 CLR 348 at 379 *per* McHugh J.

[70] For the relevant dissenting opinions in *Thomas*, see (2007) 233 CLR 307 at 436 *per* Kirby J, 475, 478 *per* Hayne J.

[71] Surveillance Devices Act 2004 (Cth), ss. 12, 14.

[72] Crimes Act 1914 (Cth) Part IAA, Division 4B, Subdivision C. This subdivision was introduced into the Crimes Act by the Anti-Terrorism Act (No. 2) 2005 (Cth).

[73] Crimes Act 1914 (Cth), ss. 3ZQS, 3ZQT.

constitutional it is presumably a more marginal instance of validity than telecommunications interception warrants, given that a notice to produce involves not only a clandestine invasion of privacy, but also the coercive incorporation of a third party into that process.

Even more constitutionally doubtful are two regimes that have been introduced as part of a broader suite of Commonwealth anti-terrorism legislation. The first of these is the regime of preventative detention orders established under the Criminal Code (Cth).[74] A senior member of the AFP may issue such an order upon the application of another member of the AFP, authorising the detention of a person for up to twenty-four hours, if (1) a terrorist act has occurred within the last twenty-eight days, and (2) detaining the person is reasonably necessary in order to preserve evidence of, or relating to, the terrorist act. Alternatively, an order may be issued if the issuing AFP member is satisfied both that detaining the person is reasonably necessary in order to substantially assist in preventing the occurrence of a terrorist act, and that there are reasonable grounds to suspect that the person to be detained either (1) will engage in a terrorist act, or (2) possesses a thing connected with the preparation for, or the engagement of a person in, a terrorist act, or (3) has done an act in preparation for or planning a terrorist act. In each of these latter three cases, reference to a 'terrorist act' is a reference to a terrorist act that is imminent, and that is expected to occur at some time in the next fourteen days.[75] The Criminal Code further vests federal judges, acting as *persona designata*, with the power to extend a preventative detention order that has been issued and executed. The grounds for extension are the same as those on which an order may initially be issued, and the maximum duration of detention is forty-eight hours in total.[76]

While subject to preventative detention, a person is limited to communicating with his or her lawyer, certain public officials, and his or her

[74] Criminal Code 1995 (Cth), Division 105. This division was introduced into the Criminal Code by the Anti-Terrorism Act (No. 2) 2005 (Cth).

[75] Criminal Code 1995 (Cth), ss. 105.4, 105.8. Under Australian law it is an offence to engage in a terrorist act, to possess a thing connected with the preparation for, or the engagement of a person in, a terrorist act while knowing of or being reckless as to that connection, or to do an act in preparation for or planning a terrorist act: Criminal Code 1995 (Cth), ss. 101.1, 101.4, 101.6. However, the threshold for arrest without warrant is *belief* on reasonable grounds that a person has committed or is committing an offence: Crimes Act 1914 (Cth), s. 3W. This is a stricter requirement than *satisfaction that there are reasonable grounds to suspect* that a particular state of affairs obtains.

[76] Criminal Code 1995 (Cth), ss. 105.2, 105.12, 105.14, 105.18.

family – but in the latter case, only to tell them that he or she is 'safe but unable to be contacted for the time being'.[77] A preventative detention order, whether issued by a police officer or a judge, may also prohibit contact with particular family members or lawyers if the AFP member who applies for the order seeks such prohibitions, which may be issued on any of a number of grounds relating to the integrity of ongoing criminal investigations or the prevention of harm or risk.[78]

Independently of the *persona designata* issue, this regime of executive detention is constitutionally suspect, as an attempt to vest a purely judicial function – namely, imprisonment as a response to criminal guilt – in a non-judicial body. The regime has features that appear to be intended to secure its constitutionality by distinguishing it from the paradigm of imprisonment in the course of criminal investigation and punishment. In particular, a person who is being detained under a preventative detention order may not be questioned except for the purposes of confirming that he or she is the person specified in the order, ensuring his or her safety and well-being, or otherwise allowing the questioning police officer to comply with a duty arising under the preventative detention regime. Similarly, identification material such as fingerprints or photographs may be taken from a detained person only for the purposes of confirming his or her identity.[79] Nevertheless, preventative detention is quite different from the other exceptions to the prohibition upon executive detention noted above. Not only is it quite different from detention following arrest upon suspicion of having committed a crime, but there is also little resemblance to regimes of quarantine except perhaps in the most metaphorical of fashions. It is therefore doubtful that the Commonwealth Parliament has the power to enact a detention regime of this sort.

If preventative detention orders are nevertheless constitutional, then it is at least arguable that it is also constitutional to vest federal judges, acting as *persona designata*, with the power to extend such orders. Although these orders are not strictly analogous to telecommunications interception warrants, it seems likely that if the discretion involved in issuing such warrants is not excessively political, then nor is that involved in deciding whether or not to extend a preventative detention order. Nor is the coercive and clandestine character of preventative

[77] Criminal Code1995 (Cth), ss. 105.34, 105.35, 105.36, 105.37, 105.41.

[78] Criminal Code 1995 (Cth), ss. 105.14A, 105.15, 105.16, 105.40.

[79] Criminal Code 1995 (Cth), ss. 105.42, 105.43, 105.44.

detention, given the comparatively short duration of such detention, in any obvious way less compatible with the judicial function than the interference with privacy under a telecommunications interception warrant that may last for up to ninety days.[80]

A countervailing consideration is that a judge becomes involved in the preventative detention regime only once an order has already been issued by a senior member of the AFP and the person taken into custody. The legislative goal seems to be to interpose the judge between executive and detainee as an independent decision-maker, and (consistently with *Grollo*) this is suggestive of compatibility. But the regime creates the obvious possibility of a judge being requested to extend the duration of detention in circumstances where the judge suspects the existing detention to be improper or even unlawful, without giving the judge any power to respond to such circumstances (for example, by revoking the existing order[81]). The possibility of a judge being compromised in this way is compounded by the judge having only a limited power to request further information from the AFP member applying for the extension.[82] This possibility may have the potential to undermine public confidence in the integrity of the federal judiciary. As no preventative detention order has yet been issued, these questions of constitutionality have not been tested in the courts.

The other constitutionally doubtful regime is established by the Australian Security Intelligence Organisation Act 1979 (Cth). Under that Act a federal judge acting as *persona designata* may, at the request of the Director-General of the ASIO, issue a warrant authorising the compulsory questioning of a person by ASIO. Such a warrant may also authorise the detention of that person in custody for up to seven days, in order to enable that person to be questioned.[83] The grounds on which

80 Telecommunications (Interception and Access) Act 1979 (Cth), s. 49.

81 Under the regime, a judge vested with the power to extend a preventative detention order has the power to revoke such extensions upon the application of a member of the AFP: Criminal Code 1995 (Cth), s. 105.17. He or she has no power to revoke an order on his or her own motion, or to revoke an order issued by a senior member of the AFP.

82 Criminal Code 1995 (Cth), s. 105.4(7) limits the judge to requesting information concerning the grounds on which the order is sought, and permits the AFP member to refuse to provide such information. This contrasts with, e.g., s. 44 of the Telecommunications (Interception and Access) Act 1979 (Cth), which permits a judge to require that further information be given in connection with an application for a telecommunications interception warrant.

83 Australian Security Intelligence Organisation Act 1979 (Cth), ss. 34AB, 34E, 34G, 34L, 34S. This regime was introduced into the Act by the Australian Security Intelligence Organisation Legislation Amendment (Terrorism) Act 2003 (Cth).

such a warrant may be issued are that the issuing judge 'is satisfied that there are reasonable grounds for believing that the warrant will substantially assist the collection of intelligence that is important in relation to' any of a range of offences defined by their connection (more or less proximate) to an actual or possible terrorist act.[84] Such a warrant may be sought only with the consent of the Commonwealth Attorney-General, who may grant that consent only if satisfied on reasonable grounds (1) in the same way as the issuing judge and (2) that relying on other methods of collecting the intelligence would be ineffective. In addition, before authorising a request for a warrant that would permit detention, the Attorney-General must be satisfied on reasonable grounds that detention of the subject of the warrant is necessary in order either to compel the person's appearance for questioning, to prevent the person destroying, damaging or altering a record or thing that he or she may be requested to produce in accordance with the warrant, or to prevent that person alerting anyone else involved in a terrorism offence that that offence is being investigated.[85] Once a warrant is issued it is an offence to disclose its existence while it remains in force, and it is an offence to disclose what took place pursuant to the warrant for a further two years.[86] While being questioned or detained under a warrant, it is an offence for a person to speak to anyone but their lawyer or certain public officials.[87]

Like the issuing of telecommunications interception warrants, issuing these warrants is a function closely connected to the executive government. Furthermore, given (1) the broad criteria governing the issue of these warrants, (2) the character of ASIO as an agency quite unlike both state and federal police forces, being governed by more obviously political considerations and being ultimately under the direction of a federal cabinet minister (namely, the Commonwealth Attorney-General)[88] and (3) the direct role played by the Attorney-General in the issuing of a warrant, it seems that this is a function that, in its political character, resembles the reporting function considered in *Wilson*. Therefore, the attempt to vest federal judges with the power to issue ASIO questioning and detention warrants most likely falls foul of the incompatibility doctrine.

The constitutionality of ASIO detention is also doubtful in itself, for much the same reasons as the preventative detention regime. Like that

[84] Australian Security Intelligence Organisation Act 1979 (Cth), ss. 34E, 34G.
[85] Sections 34D, 34F. [86] Section 34ZS. [87] Section 34K. [88] Section 8.

regime, ASIO detention can be distinguished from the paradigm of criminal imprisonment, on the grounds that there is no requirement that the subject of an ASIO detention warrant be the object of criminal suspicion or investigation.[89] But this very feature also establishes a clear distinction between ASIO detention and the ordinary regime of criminal investigation and punishment. Nor is ASIO detention analogous to quarantine. It is therefore doubtful that the Commonwealth Parliament has the power to establish this executive detention regime.[90] No ASIO detention warrant has yet been issued, however, and this question has therefore not been tested in the courts.

The *Kable* principle and state courts

The constitutions of the Australian states do not establish a separation of judicial power comparable to that which obtains at the federal level. Under Chapter III of the Commonwealth Constitution, however, state courts may be vested by the Commonwealth Parliament with the exercise of federal judicial power. It follows from this that 'no State or federal parliament can legislate in a way that might undermine the role of those courts as repositories of federal judicial power'.[91]

This constitutional principle was first stated in *Kable* v. *Director of Public Prosecutions (NSW)*,[92] a case concerning a controversial and *ad hominem* enactment of the New South Wales Parliament. The impugned legislation authorised the Supreme Court of that state to order the detention of Gregory Wayne Kable for a renewable period of up to six months, if satisfied on reasonable grounds and upon the balance of probabilities that he was more likely than not to commit a serious act of violence, and that it was appropriate for the protection of the community generally, or of particular persons, that he be so detained. The

89 Proponents of the regime strongly emphasise this distinction between 'intelligence gathering' and criminal investigation: Parliamentary Joint Committee on ASIO, ASIS and DSD, 'ASIO's Questioning and Detention Powers: Review of the operation, effectiveness and implications of Division 3 of Part III in the Australian Security Intelligence Organisation Act 1979', Canberra, 2005, pp. 24–5.

90 For a fuller discussion of this issue, see G. Carne, 'Detaining Questions or Compromising Constitutionality?: The ASIO Legislation Amendment (Terrorism) Act 2003 (Cth)' (2004) 27 *University of New South Wales Law Journal* 524.

91 *Kable* (1996) 189 CLR 51 at 116 *per* McHugh J.

92 (1996) 189 CLR 51. See H. P. Lee, 'The *Kable* Case: A Guard-Dog that Barked But Once?', in G. Winterton (ed.), *State Constitutional Landmarks* (Sydney: Federation Press, 2006), p. 390.

legislation was a response to popular perceptions of the leniency of his sentence for homicide, and to his sending of threatening letters to his victim's family members while he was in prison.

A majority of the High Court held the legislation to be invalid. McHugh J held that 'the Act and its procedures compromise the institutional impartiality of the Supreme Court' by making it 'an instrument of executive government policy', thereby impairing 'public confidence in the impartial administration of the judicial functions of the Supreme Court'.[93] Gaudron J described the Act as attempting to 'dress up' proceedings under it as 'involving the judicial process. In so doing, the Act makes a mockery of that process'.[94] Gummow J characterised the legislation as 'draw[ing] in the Supreme Court of a State as an essential and determinative integer of a scheme whereby, by its order, an individual is incarcerated in a penal institution otherwise than for breach of the criminal law'.[95] The essence of the *Kable* principle is that a court capable of exercising the judicial power of the Commonwealth, including a state court, must be and must appear to be an independent and impartial tribunal. In reaching this conclusion, three of the four *Kable* majority judges drew upon the *Grollo* incompatibility doctrine, and two emphasised in particular the third limb of that doctrine.[96] Even Gaudron J, who stated that 'The limitation on State legislative power is more closely confined' than the *Grollo* incompatibility doctrine,[97] nevertheless used the necessity to maintain public confidence in the courts, and in particular the criminal process, as a basis for holding the legislation invalid.

Subsequent cases concerned with the application of the *Kable* principle have turned on the question as to whether the legislation whose validity is under challenge unduly subordinates the state court to the imperatives of the executive or the legislature. Of particular recent

[93] *Kable* (1996) 189 CLR 51 at 121, 124. [94] *Kable* (1996) 189 CLR 51 at 108.

[95] *Kable* (1996) 189 CLR 51 at 133. Toohey J, at 99, also stressed that the Act was 'expressed to operate in relation to one person only, the appellant, and has led to his detention without a determination of his guilt for any offence'.

[96] *Kable* (1996) 189 CLR 51 at 96, 98 *per* Toohey J, 116 *per* McHugh J, 132 *per* Gummow J. Gummow J referred in general terms to the importance of maintaining 'the efficacy of the exercise of the judicial power of the Commonwealth' without referring in particular to the need to maintain public confidence, and has subsequently stressed that 'Perception as to the undermining of public confidence is an indicator, but not the touchstone, of invalidity; the touchstone concerns institutional integrity': *Fardon* (2004) 223 CLR 575 at 618.

[97] *Kable* (1996) 189 CLR 51 at 104.

concern have been provisions of state legislation apparently allowing the executive to direct the manner in which a state court is to exercise its powers. Two recent cases – *Gypsy Jokers Motorcycle Club Incorporated* v. *Commissioner of Police*[98] and *K-Generation Pty Ltd* v. *Liquor Licensing Court*[99] – concerned legislation that appeared to give the Commissioner of Police the power to direct a state court to treat certain information as confidential.[100] In each case the High Court upheld the validity of the legislation by interpreting it as in fact reserving to the court a discretion as to whether or not to accept the commissioner's claim for confidentiality, consistent with the principle that legislation 'should be interpreted, so far as its words allow, to keep it within constitutional limits'.[101]

In *International Finance Trust Company Ltd* v. *New South Wales Crime Commission*,[102] however, the High Court applied the *Kable* principle for the second time. The legislation struck down as invalid was s. 10 of the Criminal Assets Recovery Act 1990 (NSW), which permitted the Crime Commission to apply *ex parte* for an order freezing certain assets, and which obliged the court to issue the order if the statutory grounds were made out. In the view of French CJ:

> Procedural fairness or natural justice lies at the heart of the judicial function . . . To require a court, as s. 10 does, not only to receive an *ex parte* application, but also to hear and determine it *ex parte*, if the Executive so desires, is to direct the court as to the manner in which it exercises its jurisdiction and in so doing to deprive the court of an important characteristic of judicial power . . .
>
> It is incompatible with the judicial function of that Court. It deprives the Court of the power to determine whether procedural fairness . . . requires that notice be given to the party affected before an order is made. It deprives the Court of an essential incident of the judicial function. In that way, directing the Court as to the manner of the exercise of its jurisdiction, it distorts the institutional integrity of the Court and affects its capacity as a repository of federal jurisdiction.[103]

The other members of the majority agreed that the legislation was invalid, not simply on the basis that it allowed the executive to mandate an *ex parte* determination, but because of the additional failure of the

98 (2008) 234 CLR 532. 99 (2009) 237 CLR 501 ('*K-Generation*').

100 Respectively, the Corruption and Crime Commission Act 2003 (WA), s. 76(2) and the Liquor Licensing Act 1997 (SA), s. 28A.

101 *K-Generation* (2009) 237 CLR 501 at 519 *per* French CJ. 102 [2009] HCA 49.

103 *International Finance Trust Company Ltd* v. *New South Wales Crime Commission* [2009] HCA 49 at [54]–[56].

legislation to provide a party affected by an *ex parte* order with an adequate opportunity to apply for that order to be dissolved.[104]

A majority of the Full Court of the South Australian Supreme Court also applied the *Kable* principle in the recent case of *Totani* v. *The State of South Australia*,[105] striking down s. 14(1) of the Serious and Organised Crime (Control) Act 2008 (SA), which permits the Police Commissioner to seek the imposition of control orders upon members of 'declared organisations', forbidding those subject to them from associating with specified persons, from entering or being in the vicinity of specified premises and from possessing specified sorts of items. The power to declare organisations is vested by the Act in the Attorney-General of South Australia, who may take into account a wide range of information pertaining to the criminal activity of the organisation and its members.[106] Under the Act, the Attorney-General's declaration is immune to review or challenge.[107]

The court took the view that the control order regime, considered in isolation from the role of the Attorney-General in declaring organisations, does not fall foul of the *Kable* principle.[108] In the view of the majority, however, when the role of the Attorney-General in declaring organisations is taken into account, s. 14(1) can be seen to establish a regime which is unconstitutional because it required the court

> to act on what is, in effect, the certificate of the Attorney-General ... [who] is not subject to or bound by the rules of evidence or any standard of proof ... It is as though the legislation provided for the required elements to be proved on application to the Court, but that the Court was to refer the findings on the major elements to a non-judicial officer, acting without any judicial safeguards, whose decision would be final, not reviewable and binding on the Court. In a very real sense the Court is required to '[act] as an instrument of the Executive'.[109]

The majority rejected a suggested analogy between the Attorney-General's role in the control order regime and the accepted role of the

[104] *International Finance Trust Company Ltd* v. *New South Wales Crime Commission* [2009] HCA 49 at [89], [97] *per* Gummow and Bell JJ, [152]–[160], [165] *per* Heydon J. The minority held that the legislation did not displace the ordinary powers of the Supreme Court of New South Wales to reconsider an order made *ex parte* upon the application of a party adversely affected by that order, and hence that the legislation was not invalidated by the *Kable* principle: at [126]–[134] *per* Hayne, Crennan and Kiefel JJ.

[105] [2009] SASC 301 ('*Totani*'). [106] Section 10. [107] Section 41.

[108] *Totani* [2009] SASC 301 at [84]–[93], [120]–[122], [128]–[143] *per* Bleby J, [216]–[249], [251]–[254], [272]–[275] *per* White J, [277] *per* Kelly J, concurring with Bleby J.

[109] *Totani* [2009] SASC 301 at [155]–[156] *per* Bleby J.

executive in determining prohibited substances for the purposes of drug laws, because the former role 'involves the assessment of and making a judgment about human behaviour and its effects'.[110] The majority did not refer to the principle that the adjudication and punishment of criminal guilt is a strictly judicial function, but their reasoning – that 'it is the integration of the administrative function with the judicial function to an unacceptable degree which compromises the institutional integrity of the Court'[111] – is consistent with that principle. The appeal against the decision of the South Australian Supreme Court was dismissed by a 6–1 majority of the High Court.[112] Importance was placed by the majority of the High Court on the need to protect the 'institutional integrity' of state courts which are receptacles of federal jurisdiction.

Conclusion

The decision of the High Court in *Totani* serves as an illustration of the significance, in Australian law, of the complex and interrelated body of principles governing the relationship between judicial and non-judicial power, and the judicial exercise of non-judicial functions. These principles serve to maintain the independence of the judiciary from the political arms of government, and thereby to ensure the integrity of the judicial system. Furthermore, in the absence of entrenched bills of rights or other express guarantees of due process, the constraints imposed by these principles nevertheless offer some protection for individual liberty against excessive incursions by the legislature and the executive.

Finally, it would be worthwhile to note that the Council of Chief Justices of Australia gave their approval to the publication of the *Guide to Judicial Conduct* to provide 'practical guidance' to members of the Australian judiciary at all levels. Now into its second edition, the *Guide*, in commenting on activities outside the courtroom, states as follows:

> Principle and protocol require that if the executive government is seeking the services of a judge for a non-judicial appointment, the first approach should be to the head of the jurisdiction, seeking the approval of that person for the appointment of a judge from that jurisdiction, and approval to approach the judge in question. The head of jurisdiction will

[110] *Totani* [2009] SASC 301 at [158] *per* Bleby J.
[111] *Totani* [2009] SASC 301 at [157] *per* Bleby J (Kelly J concurring).
[112] *State of South Australia* v. *Totani* [2010] HCA 39.

> consider the propriety of the judge accepting the appointment, with particular reference to the maintenance of the independence of the judiciary and to the needs of the court. The head of jurisdiction will consult with other members of the jurisdiction as may seem appropriate. If there is no objection in principle, the head of jurisdiction will consider whether the judge can be made available, and whether the first approach to the judge in question should be from the head of jurisdiction or from a representative of the executive.[113]

The guide also states that a judge who is approached directly by or on behalf of a member of the executive should, without delay, raise the matter with the head of jurisdiction and should inform the person making the approach that the judge will do so.[114] The *Guide* is not prescriptive, but rigorous observance of this guideline on activities outside the courtroom by all members of the judiciary will minimise the risks of judges being sucked into a vortex of political controversy which may have a damaging impact on the standing of the judiciary.

[113] *Guide to Judicial Conduct*, 2nd edn. (published for the Council of Chief Justices of Australia by the Australasian Institute of Judicial Administration Incorporated, 2007), ch.5.

[114] *Guide to Judicial Conduct*.

21

The impact of extra-judicial service on the Canadian judiciary: the need for reform

PATRICK MONAHAN AND BYRON SHAW

In a 1985 speech to the Canadian Bar Association, Chief Justice Dickson emphasised the importance of an independent and impartial judiciary in maintaining and protecting the rule of law.[1] For Dickson, the rule of law required not only that the judiciary should be the exclusive arbiter of disputes, but that the judges should 'not depart from their proper function of law interpretation and application'[2] and their 'primary task of deciding cases and dispensing justice'.[3] Dickson stressed his increasing concern 'about certain extra-judicial activities which could tend to politicise the role of judges and detract from their impartial and independent status'.[4] He specifically cautioned judges against accepting requests to serve on public inquiries and royal commissions.[5]

Recent experience has demonstrated that Dickson's advice has not always been followed. Canadian governments at both the federal and provincial levels have increasingly looked to sitting judges to occupy non-judicial roles. Sitting judges have not been shy to accept these appointments, particularly to public inquiries. In recent years, inquiries such as Walkerton, Somalia, Gomery, Arar, Cornwall, Goudge, the Computer Leasing Scandal and the Oliphant Inquiry have occupied not only the headlines, but also considerable time and energy of sitting Canadian judges.

The surge in public inquiries provides a unique context to revisit the implications of extra-judicial service on the Canadian judiciary. In our view, the experience with extra-judicial service demonstrates that

[1] The Rt Hon. Brian Dickson, PC, 'The Rule of Law: Judicial Independence and the Separation of Powers', address presented to the Canadian Bar Association, 21 August 1985.
[2] Dickson, 'The Rule of Law', p. 8. [3] Dickson, 'The Rule of Law', p. 22.
[4] Dickson, 'The Rule of Law', p. 22. [5] Dickson, 'The Rule of Law', pp. 22–3.

governments have far too frequently capitalised on the credibility and authority of the judicial office at the expense of public confidence in the judiciary. We argue in favour of greater statutory or ethical constraints on extra-judicial service. In the absence of comprehensive reforms, Canadian judges should pay greater heed to Dickson's caution.

The remainder of this chapter is organised as follows. First, we outline the current constitutional and statutory constraints on extra-judicial service in Canada. Second, we review some of the notable extra-judicial activities that have been undertaken by sitting judges in Canada. Third, we outline the 'case for' as well as the 'case against' extra-judicial service, focusing on the context of public inquiries. Drawing mainly on the Canadian experience with public inquiries, we outline a variety of reasons why judicial independence and impartiality may be undermined by extra-judicial appointments.

In the final part of the chapter, we argue that, given these considerations, the preferable course would be to enact a statutory prohibition on sitting judges serving as commissioners of public inquiries. At the same time, recognising the long tradition of judges serving in this role, we accept that it is unlikely that such a prohibition will be enacted, at least in the short term. We therefore propose reforms to the process whereby judges are appointed to serve on public inquiries, with a view to significantly reducing the use of sitting judges in this role.

Constraints on extra-judicial service

Constitutional constraints

There do not appear to be any significant constitutional constraints on the ability of governments in Canada to appoint sitting members of the judiciary to commissions of inquiry. It is true that the separation of powers is an important constitutional principle, designed to ensure that each branch of government plays its 'proper role' in our constitutional order, 'that no one of them overstep[s] its bounds', and that each branch shows 'proper deference for the legitimate sphere of activity of the other'.[6] At the same time, the separation of powers in Canada is not strict.[7] As Justice Dickson stated in *Re Residential Tenancies Act*,[8] 'our

[6] *New Brunswick Broadcasting Co.* v. *Nova Scotia (Speaker of the House of Assembly)* [1993] 1 SCR 319 at 389 *per* McLachlin J.

[7] *Reference re Secession of Quebec* [1998] 2 SCR 217 at para. 15. [8] [1981] 1 SCR 714.

Constitution does not separate the legislative, executive, and judicial functions and insist that each branch of government exercise only its own function'.[9] A measure of overlap has always been tolerated.

It is generally recognised that in presiding over public inquiries, judges do not sit as part of the judiciary but as part of the executive. In fact, the Supreme Court of Canada has commented favourably on public inquiries that have been chaired by sitting judges. In *Starr* v. *Houlden*,[10] Justice Lamer (perhaps the most ardent advocate of judicial independence and the separation of powers),[11] stated that

> there is no doubt that commissions of inquiry at both the federal and provincial levels have played an important role in the machinery of government . . . [and] . . . in particular [have] served to supplement the activities of mainstream institutions of government.[12]

In a similar vein, Justice Binnie has stated that a statutory provision *requiring* a sitting judge to conduct a public inquiry into malfeasance by municipal officials was an 'important safeguard of the public interest, and should not be diminished by a restrictive or overly technical interpretation of the legislative requirements for its exercise'.[13]

Statutory constraints

Although judges are expected to devote their full time and attention to their judicial duties, the federal Judges Act 1985[14] and provincial statutes explicitly contemplate and approve of certain extra-judicial activities. Section 55 of the Judges Act provides a general prohibition against extra-judicial employment:

> No judge shall, either directly or indirectly, for himself or herself or others, engage in any occupation or business other than his or her judicial duties, but every judge shall devote himself or herself exclusively to those judicial duties.[15]

[9] [1981] 1 SCR 714 at 728. [10] [1990] 1 SCR 1366.

[11] See E. Ratushny and D. Gilbert, 'The Lamer Legacy for Judicial Independence', in A. M. Dodek and D. Jutras (eds.), *The Sacred Fire: The Legacy of Antonio Lamer (Chief Justice of Canada)* (Toronto: Lexis, 2009).

[12] [1990] 1 SCR 1366 at 1410.

[13] *Consortium Developments (Clearwater) Ltd* v. *Sarnia (City)* [1998] 3 SCR 3 at para. 26.

[14] RSC 1985, c. J-1. [15] RSC 1985, s. 55.

This section refers to an 'occupation or business' and would exclude activities that fall short of that description, such as administrative or executive duties performed without pay.[16]

Section 56(1) of the Judges Act explicitly provides that a judge may act as a 'commissioner, arbitrator, adjudicator, referee, conciliator or mediator on any commission or on any inquiry or other proceeding' provided that the judge is appointed or authorised by a statute or a provincial or federal Order-in-Council.[17] Similar statutory provisions exist in most provinces.[18] These sorts of provisions provide legislative authority for the government 'to relieve judges from their normal judicial responsibilities to serve on government commissions, inquiries or similar proceedings' in the name of the public interest.[19]

Section 57 of the Judges Act explicitly contemplates extra-judicial service for the executive branch of government. Section 57 provides that no judge shall receive additional remuneration for acting in a capacity referred to in s. 56(1) 'or as administrator or deputy of the Governor-General or for performing any duty or service, whether judicial or executive, that the judge may be required to perform for or on behalf of the Government of Canada or the government of a province'.[20] This provision reflects the historical practice whereby Chief Justices of each level of court act as deputies where the Governor-General or the Lieutenant Governor-General is unavailable.[21]

Extra-judicial service in Canada

Public inquiries and commissions

As discussed above, extra-judicial service on public inquiries is an established part of the Canadian tradition. There have been over two hundred federal inquiries alone since Confederation in 1867, many of

[16] Thus, a judge cannot be a barrister and solicitor: see *Maurice* v. *Priel* [1989]1 SCR 1023.

[17] Judges Act RSC 1985, s. 56(1).

[18] E.g., see the Courts of Justice Act RSO 1990, c. C 43, s. 46.

[19] *International Brotherhood of Electrical Workers, Local 424* v. *Chemco Electrical Contractors Ltd* (1989) 98 AR 306 at para. 11, CA; *JW Abernethy Management & Consulting Ltd* v. *705589 Alberta Ltd and Trillium Homes Ltd* (2005) 367 AR 38 at para. 19, CA.

[20] Judges Act RSC 1985, s. 57(1).

[21] See A. Dodek, 'Judicial Independence as a Public Policy Instrument' (2009) 5(2) *CLPE Research Paper* 18.

which have been chaired by sitting judges.[22] Below we briefly outline some of the types of inquiries that sitting judges have chaired in the recent past.

Investigative inquiries

Most commentators distinguish between investigative inquiries and policy or advisory commissions. While public inquiries often have both investigative and policy elements, the distinction is widely accepted[23] and useful in practice.

The focus of investigative inquiries is to inquire into specific events and the related conduct of parties involved. The Westray Mine Inquiry provides a good example of an investigative inquiry. In May 1992, an underground explosion at the Westray Coal Mine in Pictou, Nova Scotia trapped and killed twenty-six miners beneath the surface of the mine. The Government of Nova Scotia appointed Justice Peter Richard to inquire into, report findings and make recommendations to the Governor in Council regarding the explosion and its causes. In an appeal to the Supreme Court of Canada on whether the inquiry should be postponed until disposition of penal charges against certain mine employees, Justice Cory commented on the fact-finding nature of investigative inquiries:

> One of the primary functions of public inquiries is fact-finding. They are often convened, in the wake of public shock, horror, disillusionment, or scepticism, in order to uncover 'the truth'.[24]

Policy/advisory commissions

Unlike investigative inquiries, the focus of policy or advisory commissions is to examine broad societal issues and advise governments on how these issues should be addressed through public policy.[25]

One of the most notable examples of judicial service on such a commission is the Royal Commission on Healthcare Services, 1961–4.

[22] Canada, Library and Archives Canada, Index to Federal Royal Commissions, available at: www.collectionscanada.gc.ca/7/6/index-e.html.

[23] See, e.g., D. R. O'Connor and F. Kristanjson, 'Some Observations on Public Inquiries', 10 October 2007, available at: www.ontariocourts.on.ca/coa/en/ps/speeches/publicinquiries.htm; E. Ratushny, *The Conduct of Public Inquiries: Law, Policy and Practice* (Toronto: Irwin Law, 2009), p. 35.

[24] *Phillips* v. *Nova Scotia (Commission of Inquiry into the Westray Mine Tragedy)* [1995] 2 SCR 97 at para. 62.

[25] Ratushny, *The Conduct of Public Inquiries*, p. 50.

The commission is known informally as the Hall Commission, after its chair, Justice Emmett Hall.[26] While Hall was no doubt a competent member of the judiciary, he is most remembered for his extra-judicial service as one of the founding fathers of Canadian Medicare.

Prior to his appointment, Justice Hall served as the Chief Justice of Saskatchewan. Despite his earlier opposition to the appointment of sitting judges to public inquiries,[27] Prime Minister Diefenbaker appointed Hall to chair the Commission on Healthcare Services in 1961. The Hall Commission identified a number of shortcomings in Canada's healthcare system and called for a universal approach to public health insurance based largely on the Saskatchewan model earlier pioneered by Tommy Douglas.[28] In 1966, the Liberal Government under Prime Minister Lester B. Pearson sponsored the enactment of legislation which implemented many of Hall's recommendations and marked the foundation of a comprehensive national healthcare scheme.

Following his appointment to the commission, Hall was appointed to the Supreme Court of Canada in 1962. He served as a judge on the Supreme Court until 1973 where he remained active in extra-judicial service. While sitting as a Supreme Court judge, he co-authored another advisory report on the Ontario public school system with former Ontario high school principal L. A. Dennis. In 1977, some years after retiring from the Supreme Court, Hall was appointed to a second healthcare commission, the Royal Commission on the National Health Service. The report of the Royal Commission,[29] published in 1979, led to the abolition of the 'two-tiered' healthcare system and the enactment of the Canada Health Act 1985.[30]

While the distinction between 'investigative' and policy inquiries is clear as a matter of principle, in practice it is increasingly common for inquiries to combine both fact-finding and policy elements. The Walkerton Inquiry into the contamination of drinking water in Walkerton, Ontario proceeded in two stages and the Honourable Justice Dennis O'Connor released two separate reports. The first report

[26] Although there were six other commissioners, Justice Hall led the commission and had considerable input into the report. See F. Vaughan, 'Mr Justice Emmett Hall as Royal Commissioner' (1978) *University of Western Ontario Law Review* 223.

[27] See J. C. Courtney, 'In Defence of Royal Commissions' (2008) 12(2) *Canadian Public Administration* 198 at 203–4.

[28] *Royal Commission on Health Services* (Ottawa: Queen's Printer, 1964–5).

[29] *Canada's National-Provincial Health Program for the 1980s: A Commitment for Renewal* (Ottawa: Queen's Printer, 1980).

[30] RSC 1985, c. C-6.

examined the events surrounding the contamination of drinking water with E. coli bacteria in Walkerton in May 2000.[31] The second report contained approximately ninety-three broad-based policy recommendations for managing the future safety of drinking water in Ontario.[32] The Walkerton Inquiry, no doubt due to the exceptional talent and compassion displayed by now Ontario Associate Chief Justice O'Connor, is widely recognised as a remarkably successful inquiry that set a 'gold standard' against which all other inquiries are to be measured.[33] Justice O'Connor has also recently completed a successful inquiry into the torture and detainment of Maher Arar in Syria.[34]

Special prosecutors

Following the Second World War, Justice Jackson of the US Supreme Court was temporarily appointed by President Truman as chief prosecutor for the United States at the Nuremburg trials into Nazi war crimes. Justice Jackson's acceptance of such a decidedly non-judicial role is widely recognised in the American literature as one of the reasons for constitutional and ethical constraints on extra-judicial service.[35] At the time of Jackson's appointment, Chief Justice Stone, who had consistently declined extra-judicial service himself, criticised Justice Jackson for his acceptance of the new post. Stone described the Nuremberg trials as a sort of kangaroo court, where the victors acted as prosecutor, judge and

[31] *Report of the Walkerton Inquiry: The Events of May 2000 and Related Issues* (Ontario: Queen's Press, 2002).

[32] *Report of the Walkerton Inquiry: A Strategy for Safe Drinking Water* (Ontario: Queen's Press, 2002).

[33] See, e.g., A. Manson and D. Mullan, 'Lessons from Walkerton', in A. Manson and D. Mullan, (eds.), *Commissions of Inquiry: Praise or Reappraise* (Toronto: Irwin Law, 2003); Dodek, 'Judicial Independence as a Public Policy Instrument', p. 12.

[34] *Commission of Inquiry into the Actions of Canadian Officials in Relation to Maher Arar* (Toronto: Canadian Government Publishing, 2006).

[35] See R. McKay, 'The Judiciary and Nonjudicial Activities' (1970) 35 *Law & Contemporary Problems* 9; P. A. Bell, 'Extrajudicial Activity of Supreme Court Justices' (1969) 22 *Stanford Law Review* 587; S. Slonim, 'Extrajudicial Activities and the Principle of the Separation of Powers' (1975) *Connecticut Bar Journal* 391; W. E. Ackerman, 'Separation of Powers and Judicial Service on Presidential Commissions' (1986) 53 *University of Chicago Law Review* 993; S. Calabresi and J. Larsen, 'One Person, One Office: Separation of Powers or Separation of Personnel?' (1993) 79 *Cornell Law Review* 1045; M. E. Loewenstern, 'The Impartiality Paradox' (2003) 21 *Yale Law & Policy Review* 501. Compare J. J. McLoy, 'Owen Roberts' Extra Curiam Activities' (1955) 104 *University of Pennsylvania Law Review* 350.

jury 'in a Carthagian vengeance' outside 'the processes of the law'.[36] He privately chastised Jackson for unfairly burdening his colleagues with opinion-writing during his absence, distanced himself and his court from the trials and condemned Jackson for undermining the independence of the judiciary by taking on the role.[37]

The Canadian analogue provides a sharp contrast to the American hostility towards extra-judicial service. In 1996, Madam Justice Louise Arbour, then a member of the Ontario Court of Appeal, was appointed Chief Prosecutor of War Crimes before the International Criminal Tribunal for Rwanda and the International Criminal Tribunal for the Former Yugoslavia in the Hague. Immediately prior to this appointment, she had completed a public inquiry into riots at the Kingston Penitentiary for Women.[38]

Upon her appointment as Chief Prosecutor, the federal government amended the prohibition against extra-judicial employment in s. 55 of the Judges Act 1985 to specifically accommodate Justice Arbour's new post. Section 56.1(1) of the Judges Act 1985 provides:

> Notwithstanding section 55, Madam Justice Louise Arbour of the Ontario Court of Appeal is authorised to take a leave from her judicial duties to serve as Prosecutor of the International Tribunal for the Prosecution of Persons Responsible for Serious Violations of International Humanitarian Law Committed in the Territory of the Former Yugoslavia and of the International Tribunal for Rwanda.[39]

In her role as prosecutor, Justice Arbour indicted President Slobodan Milošović for war crimes, marking the first time a head of state had been called to account before an international court. The prosecution was well-publicised and became the subject of a made-for-TV movie. Chief Justice McLachlin, in her retirement address for Justice Arbour, remarked that Justice Arbour arrived in Ottawa 'as a star'. 'She was profiled in every newspaper and magazine you can think of, and even in some you cannot bear to think of.'[40]

36 A. T. Mason, 'Extra-Judicial Work For Judges: The Views of Chief Justice Stone' (1953) 67 *Harvard Law Review* 193 at 210.

37 Mason, 'Extra-Judicial Work For Judges', pp. 213–15.

38 *Commission of Inquiry into Certain Events at the Prison for Women in Kingston* (Ottawa: Public Works and Government Services, 1996).

39 Judges Act RSC 1985, s. 56.1(1).

40 B. McLachlin, 'Remarks by the Right Honourable Beverley McLachlin P.C.', speech given at the retirement ceremony of the Honourable Louise Arbour, 7 June 2004, available at: www.scc-csc.gc.ca/court-cour/ju/spe-dis/bm04-06-07-eng.asp.

Following the indictment of Milošović in 1999, Justice Arbour left her position as war crimes prosecutor and was appointed to the Supreme Court of Canada to replace Justice Peter Cory. In June 2004, Justice Arbour resigned from the Supreme Court to take up an appointment as UN High Commissioner for Human Rights.

Electoral boundaries commissions

Canadian judges have long been involved in electoral boundary commissions. The federal Electoral Boundaries Readjustment Act 1985[41] creates commissions to draw the electoral boundaries for federal elections. Each electoral boundary commission is composed of three members. The chair is selected by the Chief Justice of the province from among the judges of the provincial Court of Appeal or from another level of court within the province. The other two members are selected by the Speaker of the House of Commons.[42]

As Michael Pal and Sujit Choudry observe:

> The mechanisms for appointing members to an electoral boundary commission are potentially controversial ... The chief justice's power of appointment inserts the senior-most members of the judiciary into a process that previously lay at the heart of Parliament's prerogatives. Moreover, judges chair the electoral boundary commissions. Presumably, both features were designed to insulate the process of electoral redistricting from partisanship by shifting important decisions to the judiciary, the most non-partisan and independent branch of government. Further, having a judge serve as chair was likely designed to bring a degree of impartiality to the deliberations of the commissions. However, given the inherently political nature of boundary delimitation, the judiciary has been thrust into a 'political thicket'.[43]

While the direct role of judges in such a partisan political process is perhaps unseemly, it is a historically accepted (or at least tolerated) practice in Canada.

The Order of Canada and provincial orders

Canadian judges also commonly hold positions on advisory councils such as the Order of Canada and provincial orders to recognise

[41] RSC 1985, c. E-3. [42] RSC 1985, ss. 3–6.

[43] M. Pal and S. Choudry, 'Constitutional Boundaries in Canada', in H. MacIvor (ed.), *Election* (Toronto: Emond Montgomery, 2010).

distinguished Canadians.[44] The Order of Canada recognises Canadians for outstanding contributions to communities, to Canada and humanity. The Constitution of the Order is established by Order-in-Council. Pursuant to the Constitution, there are three levels of the Order: members, officers and companions. Qualifications vary for each level, but it is fair to say that the criteria are universally subjective. Recommendations for the Order of Canada are made by a 'duly constituted and independent advisory council' chaired by the Chief Justice of Canada.[45] According to the current chair, Chief Justice McLachlin, her role is limited to administering the meetings, making sure the process runs fairly and not to 'weigh in for, or against, any particular candidate'.[46]

Other extra-judicial service

Numerous federal statutes provide for sitting judges to serve on federally constituted tribunals. The Pension Appeals Board, for example, must consist of a chairman and vice-chairman, each of whom shall be a judge of the Federal Court or the Superior Court of a province.[47] Judicial members of the Competition Tribunal are mandatory, and must be selected from among the judges of the Federal Court.[48] The chairman of the Copyright Board must be either a sitting or retired judge.[49] A judge may be appointed to a review committee under the federal Veterans' Land Act 1970[50] to determine whether a land settlement agreement should be rescinded. Judges may also be appointed to hear references under the Old Age Security Act 1985.[51] Similarly, the Governor in Council may appoint judges to act as assessors to determine compensation and remuneration under various federal statutes.[52]

In most of these cases, the participation of sitting judges is not particularly contentious, as the function performed by the judge is

[44] See Constitution of the Order of Canada, available at: http://archive.gg.ca/honours/nat-ord/oc/oc-con_e.asp.

[45] Constitution of the Order of Canada.

[46] 'Top Judge Rejects Bias Charge', *The Star*, 17 August 2008, available at: www.thestar.com/article/480048. See the discussion in Dodek, 'Judicial Independence as a Public Policy Instrument', p. 29.

[47] Canada Pension Plan Act RSC 1985, c. C-8, s. 83.

[48] Competition Tribunal Act RSC 1985, c. 19 (2nd Supp.), s. 3.

[49] Copyright Act RSC 1985, c. C-42. [50] RSC 1970, c. V-4. [51] CRC, c. 1246.

[52] Emergencies Act RSC 1985, c. 22 (4th Supp.); Employment Insurance Act, SC 1996, c 23; Energy Supplies Emergency Act RSC 1985, c. E-9; Pesticide Residue Compensation Act RSC 1985, c. P-10.

essentially adjudicative in nature and the judge exercises quasi-judicial powers.

The rationale for extra-judicial service

Judges possess the necessary skills

Judges have recognised experience in hearing and evaluating evidence, making findings of fact and drawing inferences and conclusions.[53] The rationale for extra-judicial service, thus, has particular relevance in the case of investigative public inquiries. Although they are not inherently adversarial in nature, in fact-finding inquiries, commissioners are called upon to perform tasks closely related to the judicial function. As Justice Spence once observed:

> it is the essence of [a commissioner's] duty to consider impartially the evidence adduced and the submissions of counsel based thereon. That judges are expected, because of their training and tradition, to be able to make such an impartial survey of evidence and argument is surely the chief reason why they have been so generally appointed as Commissioners. After some sixteen years on the bench, I find such a task natural.[54]

Judges bring an aura of independence

Sitting judges bring an aura of credibility, authority and impartiality due to their institutional independence from the executive and legislative branches of government.[55] As O'Connor and Kristanjson observe in the case of public inquiries:

> The need to hold an inquiry arises because of the need to have an independent, credible assessment of whatever the particular problem happens to be. Judges are seen by the public as having the necessary independence from government and bring with them the credibility of the judicial office.[56]

[53] J. Beatson, 'Should Judges Conduct Public Inquiries' (2004) 37 *Israel Law Review* 238 at 250; G. Winterton, 'Judges as Royal Commissioners' (1987) 10 *University of New South Wales Law Journal* 108 at 112–13.

[54] Courtney, 'In Defence of Royal Commissions', p. 206.

[55] T. Witelson, 'Declaration of Independence: Examining the Independence of Federal Public Inquiries', in Manson and Mullan (eds.), *Commissions of Inquiry*, pp. 350, 349; O'Connor and Kristanjson, 'Some Observations on Public Inquiries'.

[56] O'Connor and Kristanjson, 'Some Observations on Public Inquiries', para. 62.

The impact of extra-judicial service on the judiciary

In our view, there are several negative consequences resulting from sitting judges occupying non-judicial roles. The most significant risk is that taking on extra-judicial duties, particularly in the form of public inquiries, tends to detract from the independence and impartiality of the judiciary. Drawing mainly on recent Canadian experiences with public inquiries, we outline six specific reasons why there is a significant risk that the independence of the judiciary will be undermined.

The judge may be perceived to be affiliated with a political party or a particular political agenda

The risk of perceived partiality is perhaps most acute in the case of policy or advisory commissions. While Justice Hall was widely recognised to have run a 'fair process' during the Commission on Healthcare Services, controversy surrounded both his appointment and the publication of his report, no doubt due largely to the nature of his mandate. Hall was appointed by Conservative Prime Minister John Diefenbaker, with whom he had a very close association. In fact, Hall had run as a Conservative member of Parliament twice in the past.[57] While many of his recommendations were ultimately implemented by a Liberal government, the Minister of Health initially reacted sharply to the report.[58]

The risks of being perceived as aligned with a particular government or policy are not confined to advisory commissions. Even in investigative inquiries, problems can arise from the partisan implications of a judge's findings of fact, particularly where the subject matter of the inquiry is inherently political. For example, the Gomery Commission ended with the unseemly result that a sitting judge was found by a court to have been biased against a former Prime Minister of Canada. One of the factors, although certainly not the only one, was Gomery's appointment of Bernard Roy as lead commission counsel, which raised questions about Gomery's political allegiances and the fairness of the process. Roy, while a respected Queen's Counsel, had formerly served as chief of staff to Prime Minister Mulroney, Chrétien's political rival, and had worked at the same law firm as Mulroney.[59]

[57] Ratushny, *The Conduct of Public Inquiries*, p. 52.

[58] Vaughan, 'Mr Justice Emmett Hall as Royal Commissioner', p. 231.

[59] *Chrétien* v. *Canada (Ex-Commissioner, Commission of Inquiry into the Sponsorship Program and Advertising Activities)* 2008 FC 802 at para. 19.

The judge is and may be perceived to be a temporary and dispensable appendage of the government

In the case of public inquiries in particular, risks to judicial independence arise 'from the fact that it is the government which sets up an inquiry, determines its terms of reference and chooses the person or persons to conduct it'.[60] As the Somalia Inquiry demonstrates, the consequence is that a judge can be a temporary and even dispensable appendage of the executive branch of government.

The Somalia Inquiry was established following media reports that Canadian soldiers had shot and beaten innocent Somalis during the United Nations peace-keeping mission. The federal government established by Order-in-Council a Commission of Inquiry into the Deployment of Canadian Forces to Somalia under Part I of the federal Inquiries Act 1985. Justice Gilles Letourneau of the Federal Court of Appeal was appointed as chair, along with Justice Rutherford of the Ontario Court of Justice and Peter Desbarats, a journalist and former Dean of Journalism at the University of Western Ontario.

The terms of reference for the inquiry were extremely broad, while the time for completing this mandate was unreasonably short, the expectation being that the government would grant extensions as necessary to complete the inquiry.[61] Time limits were extended, but not to the degree requested by the commission or necessary to complete the mandate. Eventually, the Liberal government shut down the inquiry over mounting public concern. An interested party applied to the Federal Court to strike down the government's Order-in-Council terminating the inquiry. His argument was that the government was without jurisdiction in attempting to impose a legal mandate that could not be fulfilled.

The argument was accepted at the trial division in the Federal Court, but was rejected in the Federal Court of Appeal.[62] The Court of Appeal (colleagues of Justice Letourneau) held that there was no principle of public law that would enable a commission of inquiry to acquire, once created, the independence and autonomy necessary to allow it to prevail over the will of the Governor in Council as to its structure and its

[60] Beatson, 'Should Judges Conduct Public Inquiries', p. 262.

[61] See T. Witelson, 'Interview with Mr Justice Gilles Letourneau, Somalia Commission Chair', in Manson and Mullan (eds.), *Commissions of Inquiry*, pp. 316–18, 325.

[62] *Dixon* v. *Canada (Commission of Inquiry into the Deployment of Canadian Forces in Somalia – Létourneau Commission)* (1997) 3 FC 169, CA.

existence.[63] The court held that the trial judge erred in deciding that it was for the commissioners to decide the stage at which the investigation was 'sufficient'.

The wisdom of the Federal Court of Appeal's decision has been debated.[64] However, as Professor Ratushny explains, the decision illustrates the fundamental legal nature of a commission of inquiry: it is simply 'a temporary appendage of the executive branch of government, created and potentially extinguished at its will or whim'.[65] The implication is that governments can capitalise on the independence attached to the judicial office by appointing judges to inquire into a controversial matter of public concern. However, when public support for the inquiry wanes or the political tide changes, they can pull the plug and preclude the original mandate from being fulfilled.

The judge may be forced into an adversarial relationship with the government

Judges derive authority and respect from their institutional independence. When judges confine themselves to the adjudicative role, their decisions are by and large respected. While the merits of judicial decisions may be debated, the rule of law mandates a measure of respect for the supremacy of the judiciary to interpret and apply the law.

The situation is different when judges step off the bench into extra-judicial roles. Judges may find themselves in an adversarial position with the government. In these situations, the temptation to defend the legitimacy of the extra-judicial activity can place judges in a position of open conflict with the government and undermine the principles of impartial and independent adjudication.

The Somalia Inquiry provides a stark example of the confrontation that can arise between commissioners and the government. In their report, the commissioners bitterly described their frustration with the government's decision to shut the inquiry down:

> The unexpected decision to impose a sudden time constraint on an inquiry of this magnitude is without precedent in Canada. There is no question that it has compromised and limited our search for the truth. It

63 *Dixon* v. *Canada* (1997) 3 FC 169 at paras. 12–13.

64 See Witelson, 'Declaration of Independence', in Manson and Mullan (eds.), *Commissions of Inquiry*, pp. 330–4; P. Desbarats, 'Independence of Public Inquiries: *Dixon* v. *Canada*' (1997) 36 *Alberta Law Review* 252.

65 Ratushny, *The Conduct of Public Inquiries*, p. 281.

> will also inhibit and delay corrective action to the very system that allowed the events to occur in the first place.[66]

The commission expressed further frustration with the perceived lack of cooperation from the government, which dragged its heels in producing key documents.[67] For its part, the government blatantly attacked the commission's report. Defence Minister Art Eggleton described the report as a 'blanket condemnation of our military' that was 'unfair and unjust'. The commissioners' 'accusations without proof' were an 'insult'. Eggleton asserted that there was no evidence of a conspiracy or cover-up, that the events in question had occurred years earlier and that 'the time for finger pointing is passed'.[68]

The judge may become an advocate for the extra-judicial assignment

O'Connor and Kristanjson argue that:

> Once a commissioner delivers a report, that should be the end of his or her involvement. This is particularly the case when a sitting judge has served as commissioner. Commissioners should give reasons for their conclusions in the reports and leave it to others to debate questions relating to implementation.[69]

Unfortunately, this sage advice is not always followed in practice. When acting outside the judicial role judges become subjected to criticism, and they are often unable to resist the temptation to rise to their own defence, in the process engaging in advocacy that undermines the appearance of independence and impartiality.

In a speech to McGill Law School in 2006,[70] Justice Gomery observed that:

> Judges are subject to severe limitations as to what they can say publicly, especially about controversial topics like politics and scandals. As a general rule, a judge speaks in public only through the judgments he or

[66] *Dishonoured Legacy: The Lessons of the Somalia Affair*, Executive Summary, available at: www.forces.gc.ca/somalia/somaliae.htm, pp. 2–3.

[67] *Dishonoured Legacy*, p. 5.

[68] Ratushny, *The Conduct of Public Inquiries*, p. 411.

[69] O'Connor and Kristanjson, 'Some Observations on Public Inquiries'. See also A. Cairns, S. Grange, J. and E. C. Harris, 'The Commission and Its Report: Public Education, Advocacy and Lobbying' (1989) 12 *Dalhousie Law Journal* 161 at 163.

[70] Justice J. H. Gomery, 'The Pros and Cons of Commissions of Inquiry', lecture presented to McGill University's Faculty of Law, 15 February 2006, (2006) 51 *McGill Law Journal* 783.

she renders, or, if the judge happens to be acting as an inquiry commissioner, through the reports he or she delivers.[71]

Despite his own admonition, Justice Gomery expressed his indignation of the 'ungrateful' Conservative government who owed 'the fact they are in office' to the work of his commission.[72] After retiring from the bench, he appeared before a parliamentary committee to comment on new legislation proposed by the Conservative government, arguing that it did not go far enough towards adopting his recommendations.[73]

The judge may be exposed to allegations of unfairness and bias and may be subjected to judicial review

The flexibility afforded to judicial commissioners carries a potential for exceeding the boundaries of fairness. Indeed, judicial commissioners are often under the media spotlight and under public pressure to 'root out' a perceived evil.[74] A commissioner can become 'carried away with the general enthusiasm for reform to the point that individual conduct cannot be fairly evaluated'.[75] As the Somalia and Gomery inquiries illustrate, not only may this result in damage to individual reputations,[76] but it may damage the reputation of the judiciary as well. Successful judicial review proceedings may undermine the perception that the judge or the process is fair.[77]

During the course of the Somalia Inquiry, Justice Letorneau intervened in the examination of one of the witnesses before the commission, Brigadier General Beno. Justice Letorneau said that Beno's testimony contradicted an earlier answer he had given. The witness denied the inconsistency and attempted to explain himself. Justice Letorneau quipped back with the following remark: 'I might as well tell you that you won't gain much by fiddling around. It was a clear question and you won't gain much.' A week later, Justice Letourneau took a trip to Calgary

71 Gomery, 'The Pros and Cons of Commissions of Inquiry', p. 785.

72 K. May, 'Gomery: Canada on Road to "One-Man Government"', *Ottawa Citizen*, 12 March 2008.

73 Ratushny, *The Conduct of Public Inquiries*, p. 414.

74 O'Connor and Kristanjson, 'Some Observations on Public Inquiries'.

75 *Canada (Attorney-General)* v. *Canada (Commissioner of the Inquiry on the Blood System)* [1997] 2 FC 36 at para. 32, CA, citing B. Schwartz, 'Public Inquiries', in 1990 Isaac Pitblado Lectures, 'Public Interest v. Private Rights: Striking the Balance in Administrative Law', at pp. 264–65.

76 See B. Schwartz, 'Public Inquiries', in Manson and Mullan (eds.), *Commissions of Inquiry*.

77 Beatson, 'Should Judges Conduct Public Inquiries', p. 263.

to interview soldiers regarding their prospective evidence and spoke to two of Beno's fellow soldiers over breakfast. The soldiers confronted Justice Letorneau about the proceedings and told him that they thought Beno was being treated unfairly. Justice Letourneau apparently replied to the effect that Beno had not given honest answers, that he was trying to deceive and that he didn't want to cooperate with the work of the commission.

The judge at first instance concluded that there was a reasonable apprehension of bias.[78] The decision was then reversed by Justice Letourneau's own colleagues on the Federal Court of Appeal.[79] With respect to the 'fiddling remark', the court held that Justice Letourneau was merely expressing his 'his own honest, although probably mistaken, perception of Beno's evidence'.[80] In regard to the breakfast meeting conversation in Calgary, the court had this to say:

> It must have been a shock for him to hear BGen Meating's and Mr. Mariage's criticisms of his behaviour. It is easy now to say that he should then have remained silent. But it is not abnormal for a person in that situation whose impartiality is openly put in question to try to explain the reasons that motivated his behaviour.[81]

While this may be true at a human level, it is a far from convincing explanation for the court's conclusion that a reasonable and informed member of the public would not have perceived that Justice Letourneau had prejudged Beno's credibility. More importantly, as Professor Ratushny observes, whatever 'the merits of the case, the public optics of [the] process could do little for public confidence in the judiciary'.[82] Justice Letourneau was found to be biased by a subordinate judge and was later exonerated by his own colleagues on the Court of Appeal.

The Gomery Inquiry raised a similar issue regarding the lack of procedural fairness of a public inquiry. Despite Justice Gomery's promises to run a 'scrupulously fair' process, he gave a number of media interviews during the course of the inquiry, which ultimately led Justice

[78] *Beno* v. *Canada (Commission of Inquiry into the Deployment of Canadian Forces in Somalia)* [1997] 1 FC 911.
[79] *Beno* v. *Canada* [1997] 2 FC 527, CA.
[80] *Beno* v. *Canada* [1997] 2 FC 527 at para. 29.
[81] *Beno* v. *Canada* [1997] 2 FC 527 at para. 33.
[82] Ratushny, *The Conduct of Public Inquiries*, p. 155.

Teitelbaum of the Federal Court, Trial Division to conclude that Justice Gomery, a sitting judge, was biased against the former Prime Minister.[83]

Despite his promise at the outset of the proceedings that his spokesperson was 'the only person who will speak on behalf of the Commission', Gomery breached his own rule several times.[84] Justice Gomery also directly insulted Chrétien before he had given evidence with the infamous remark about free golf balls in the sponsorship programme being 'small-town cheap'.[85] In addition, he described Charles Guité, the official in charge of the sponsorship programme, as a 'charming scamp' who had 'got himself promoted just before his retirement' to 'build up his pension'.[86]

Following the release of his report, Justice Gomery authored the foreword of a book published by his Media Relations Director, François Perreault. The book, entitled *Inside Gomery*,[87] was described by Gomery in the foreword as an accurate account of the workings of the inquiry. Portions of it were introduced in Chrétien's application for judicial review.

The *Chrétien* case illustrates the dangers of extra-judicial service, particularly in a politically charged arena. In stepping off of the bench and into the realm of political controversy, Gomery became 'seduced by the media and the limelight to such an extent that the judicial instinct for fairness, objectivity and restraint' were lost.[88] The result tarnished the reputation of Justice Gomery and the judiciary as a whole.

The inquiry chair may be called upon to adjudicate related matters in the future

Upon returning to the bench, judges may be called upon to adjudicate issues related to their extra-judicial service. In the case of policy or advisory commissions chaired by sitting judges, the prospect of subsequent adjudication is readily apparent. Especially with the advent of the Charter of Rights and Freedoms, Canadian judges are increasingly called upon to determine issues of broad social importance and public policy. In *Chaoulli* v. *Quebec (Attorney-General)*,[89] for instance, a majority of

[83] *Chrétien* v. *Canada (Commission of Inquiry into the Sponsorship Program and Advertising Activities, Gomery Commission)* [2009] 2 FCR 417.

[84] *Chrétien* v. Canada [2009] 2 FCR 417 at para. 91.

[85] *Chrétien* v. *Canada* [2009] 2 FCR 417 at para. 93.

[86] *Chrétien* v. *Canada* [2009] 2 FCR 417 at para. 93.

[87] Francois Perrault, *Inside Gomery* (Toronto: Douglas & McIntyre, 2006).

[88] *Chrétien* v. *Canada* [2009] 2 FCR 417 at p. 93.

[89] [2005] 1 SCR 791.

the Supreme Court held that the Quebec Health Insurance Act 1970 and the Quebec Hospital Insurance Act 1961, which prohibited private medical insurance in the face of long wait times, violated the Quebec Charter of Human Rights and Freedoms 1975. Obviously, questions would have been raised about the independence of the judiciary if a member of the court had sat on a commission dealing with the health care system (which would have been the case had such an issue arisen during Justice Hall's time on the court).

Some have argued that the problem of subsequent adjudication is not significant because the judge can be recused.[90] A successful recusal motion may remove the *actual* risk to the impartiality of the court. However, at this stage, the damage to the *appearance* of the independence and impartiality has already been incurred.

Public policy implications

The Canadian experience with extra-judicial service, particularly on public inquiries, demonstrates mixed utility. While sitting judges are an available resource whose impartiality and independence may assist in resolving partisan disputes, this comes at great cost to public confidence in the judiciary. In the light of these considerations, we recommend the following reforms.

Outside public inquiries

Governments should not appoint sitting judges to resolve partisan disputes which have little or no connection to the judicial function. The Electoral Boundaries Readjustment Act 1985, for instance, should be amended so that sitting judges are no longer eligible for appointment on commissions and recommendations for appointment are no longer made by chief justices. Similarly, amendments should be made to the constitution of the Order of Canada and provincial statutes to preclude sitting judges from sitting on advisory councils for honorary orders. These appointments do not draw on judicial skills and carry the potential to thrust judges into inherently partisan disputes, undermining judicial independence in the process.

[90] See Witelson, 'Interview with Mr Justice Gilles Letourneau', in Manson and Mullan (eds.), *Commissions of Inquiry*, p. 374.

Public inquiries

Statutory reform

In our view, given the significant consequences to judicial independence identified above, the ideal result would be to amend the Judges Act 1985 and the provincial and federal inquiries legislation to prohibit sitting judges from serving on public inquiries. While we accept that some notably talented sitting judges have served the public interest well in their capacity as commissioners, there have been several failures. On balance, it is our view that the benefits of extra-judicial service on public inquiries are outweighed by their costs.

It has been observed that the 'case for' extra-judicial service is related to the proximity to the judicial function. The rationale for extra-judicial service on policy or advisory commissions, therefore, is far from compelling. Like advisory councils, honorary orders and boundary commissions, these commissions are by their very nature tasked with making value judgments regarding the merits of legislative and social change. Judges, in their capacity as judges, do not possess the skills necessary to resolve multifaceted partisan controversies. Further, although judges may be able to run a 'fair process', their ultimate conclusions are apt to be interpreted as partisan or politically controversial in one respect or another.

The case for judges chairing investigative inquiries is stronger. Judges are adept at weighing evidence, assessing credibility, fact-finding and coming to reasoned conclusions. Further, the institutional guarantees of independence and impartiality associated with the judicial office transfer a considerable measure of respect and confidence to the inquiry process. As Cory J observed in *Phillips*, the skills, status and high respect for a commissioner – particularly a judicial commissioner – may help to resolve a catharsis and 'restore public confidence not only in the institution or situation investigated but also in the process of government as a whole'.[91]

However, as we have seen, the paradox of independence is real, even where fact-finding forms a critical component of the inquiry. Although the analogy to the judicial function is closer, there are marked differences between acting as a judge and a commissioner of inquiry.

[91] *Phillips* v. *Nova Scotia (Commission of Inquiry into the Westray Mine Tragedy)* [1995] 2 SCR 97 at para. 62.

As we have demonstrated, there are real and demonstrable risks to judicial independence and impartiality as a consequence of extra-judicial service on a public inquiry. The judge may be affiliated with a particular policy or agenda and may become an extra-judicial advocate for his or her recommendations, only to be called upon to adjudicate a related matter in the future. Although the government certainly *capitalises* on the aura of independence, the judicial commissioner serves not as a member of an independent judiciary but as a temporary appendage of the government. Controversy with government may, and often does, ensue, and the inquiry may be curtailed, or even shut down entirely. And the flexibility of the inquiry process, although beneficial for the expeditious resolution of a catharsis, may undermine the perception of fairness on the part of the judge and the judicial process.

Judges are not the only members of society with forensic skills or the status and respect necessary to resolve a worrisome community problem or institutional failure. Retired judges, respected members of the bar and academics have similar skills and instil similar public confidence. In short, there are others who can resolve matters of this kind without damage to judicial independence, impartiality and public confidence in the judiciary.

Ethical reforms

Recognising the established Canadian tradition of appointing sitting judges to chair public inquiries, we acknowledge that, at least in the short term, it is unlikely that the above recommendation will be implemented. If governments continue to seek the appointment of judges to public inquiries, significant reforms to the ethical constraints on extra-judicial service should be put in place.

The Canadian Judicial Council's Position Paper provides a useful starting point for judges and chief justices when faced with a request for an executive or other extra-judicial assignment by the government. The Position Paper requires the consent of the Chief Justice of the relevant court before an appointment of a judge to serve on an inquiry and outlines the various ethical considerations that should be taken into account before the Chief Justice grants consent. These considerations include the impact on the court's workload; whether the subject matter of the inquiry essentially requires advice on public policy or on matters of a partisan nature; whether it involves an investigation into the conduct of agencies of the appointing government; and whether a retired judge or senior lawyer could perform the function equally as well as a judge.

The Position Paper is clearly intended to discourage or at least restrain the appointment of judges to serve on inquiries. In fact, we believe that if weighed carefully, the considerations outlined in the Position Paper would significantly reduce the use of sitting judges on inquiries, particularly in the case of policy or advisory commissions and politically charged investigatory inquiries. The considerations in the Position Paper also provide a measure of institutional independence with respect to time limits and resources and help to ensure that the workload of the courts is not unduly impaired.

Unfortunately, recent experience with the appointment of judges to inquiries demonstrates that the principles outlined in the Position Paper are not being applied consistently. Justice Oliphant's appointment to the inquiry into the business dealings between Karlheinz Schreiber and former Conservative Prime Minister Brian Mulroney is a good example. Justice Oliphant is now embroiled in a scandal that is factually different from the Gomery Inquiry, but no less controversial. Justice Cohen's recent appointment to chair a public inquiry into the decline of the salmon stocks in the Fraser River – although not as political in a strictly partisan sense – will undoubtedly require advice on highly contentious and divisive matters of public policy; indeed, it specifically contemplates policy reform to the Department of Fisheries and Oceans.[92]

Moreover, certain aspects of the Position Paper are themselves problematic. The Protocol contemplates negotiations between the government and the court from which the judge is sought. Such direct involvement carries the potential to undermine the appearance of judicial independence that the Protocol is designed to protect. Insofar as the Protocol contemplates negotiation between the Chief Justice and the appointing government over time limits and provision of inquiry resources, it directly engages the judiciary in the development of government policy and the distribution of resources. The Position Paper also contemplates requests by the Chief Justice for a replacement judge. In our view, such negotiations raise serious concerns regarding the appearance of independence from government.[93] The Position Paper is also problematic in that it provides no means of guaranteeing that government

[92] See Terms of Reference for the Commission of Inquiry into Decline of Sockeye Salmon in the Fraser River, available at: http://pm.gc.ca/en/media.asp?id=2951.

[93] Position of the Canadian Judicial Council on the Appointment of Federally-Appointed Judges to Commissions of Inquiry, available at: www.cjc-ccm.gc.ca/cmslib/general/news_pub_other_PositionCJC_1998_fn.pdf.

assurances will not be subsequently withdrawn. As we have seen, the decision to establish, modify and terminate extra-judicial appointments to public inquiries resides entirely with the government at common law. Further, legislative developments, particularly the recently enacted amendments to the Public Inquiries Act 1990 in Ontario, are giving further and more explicit recognition to the ability of governments to control and direct the inquiry process.[94]

In our view, in the absence of legal prohibitions on extra-judicial conduct, stricter ethical rules should be designed and enforced by the Canadian Judicial Council, the body charged with the oversight of the judiciary. Most importantly, we believe it is inappropriate for a government seeking the appointment of a judge to enter into direct negotiations with the Chief Justice of the relevant court over the terms upon which the judge should be permitted to serve. Governments deal with chief justices on a wide variety of matters on a continuing basis. Given this ongoing relationship, there is the danger that the Chief Justice will face direct or indirect pressure to accept the government's request against his or her better judgement. A preferable system would be for requests to permit judges to serve on inquiries to be directed to a Standing Committee of the Canadian Judicial Council. The Standing Committee would seek the advice and input of the Chief Justice of the relevant court, but it would be for the Standing Committee to make the final determination. Moreover, in the event that a member of the Standing Committee is also a member of the court to which the request has been made, that judge would take not part in the consideration of the request. Insulating the Chief Justice and the other members of the court from direct or indirect pressure would be a significant reform that would reduce the use of sitting judges on public inquiries.

Finally, the considerations or questions outlined in the Position Paper should be replaced with stricter ethical rules, so as to better define the circumstances in which it would be inappropriate to appoint a sitting judge to an inquiry. We offer a few illustrative examples of how better ethical rules could be framed:

- A judge shall not accept a fixed-term appointment to a public inquiry unless the time limit is reasonable having regard to the nature and extent of the mandate.

[94] See Good Government Act SO 2009, c. 33, Schedule 6, Royal Assent 15 December 2009 to come into force on a date to be fixed by proclamation.

- A judge shall not accept an appointment if it would negatively impact on the workload of the court. (Reference could be made to a number of factors including delay, backlog and the proposed or expected time needed to fulfil the extra-judicial role.)
- A judge shall not accept an appointment where there is a significant risk of undermining the independence or impartiality of the judge or the judiciary. In particular, a judge shall refuse an appointment that would require advice or recommendations on matters that are predominantly or essentially political or partisan in nature.
- A judge shall not accept an appointment unless it requires the unique skills, abilities and training of a judge. If legal experience is required, regard should be had as to whether an experienced lawyer, legal academic or retired judge could fulfil the role just as well.
- Where a judge accepts an appointment to a public inquiry, the judge shall never engage in public debate about his or her findings or recommendations.

Development along these lines would help to safeguard the principles of independence and impartiality that are fundamental to public confidence in our judiciary and our constitutional order.

Conclusion

There are relatively few constitutional, statutory and ethical constraints on extra-judicial service in Canada. Many statutory provisions specifically authorise or require sitting judges to carry out non-judicial roles. The constitutional and statutory framework is consistent with historical experience. There is a long history of extra-judicial service in Canada, particularly on commissions of inquiry.

In our view, the case for appointing sitting judges to these types of extra-judicial roles is not particularly compelling and the case against this long-standing Canadian practice is far more persuasive. While some judges have served the public interest in extra-judicial capacities, a number of failures have caused lasting damage to public confidence in the judiciary. We support legislative amendments that would prohibit sitting judges from accepting appointments to public inquiries. In the absence of such a general statutory reform, we believe that significant changes should be made to the current ethical and prudential rules surrounding the appointment of judges to inquiries, with a view to significantly reducing the use of sitting judges in these roles.

22

Judges and the non-judicial function in New Zealand

GEOFFREY PALMER

New Zealand has a population of 4.4 million people and is one of the world's oldest democracies. New Zealand's population is diverse: 78 per cent European ethnicity; 15 per cent Maori, the indigenous people; 6.6 per cent Asian; and 6.5 per cent Pacific peoples. Its British heritage ensured that New Zealand enjoyed strong judicial institutions from the beginning, very much in the tradition of the common law. In 2010 there were almost two hundred permanent judges in the New Zealand judiciary, a quantity that seems generous given the size of the population. But there does exist an elaborate court structure with generous rights of appeal. Furthermore, New Zealand has at present about 11,000 lawyers with current practising certificates, providing one lawyer for approximately every four hundred people. New Zealand has a mature legal system with a strong tradition of the rule of law.

Any analysis of the New Zealand Constitution and the place of the judiciary within it must start with the Constitution Act 1986.[1] This

[1] For discussion on the New Zealand constitution and legal system see G. Palmer and M. Palmer, *Bridled Power – New Zealand's Constitution and Government*, 4th edn. (Melbourne: Oxford University Press, 2004); P. A. Joseph, *Constitutional and Administrative Law in New Zealand*, 3rd edn. (Wellington: Thomson Brookers, 2007); M. S. R. Palmer, 'New Zealand Constitutional Culture' (2007) 22 *New Zealand Universities Law Review* 565; G. Palmer, 'The New Zealand Constitution and the Power of Courts' (2006) 15 *Transnational Law and Contemporary Problems* 551; G. Palmer, 'Muldoon and the Constitution', in M. Clark (ed.), *Muldoon Revisited* (Palmerston North: Dunmore Press, 2004), pp. 167–214; M. S. R. Palmer, 'What is New Zealand's Constitution and Who Interprets It? Constitutional Realism and the Importance of Public Office-holders' (2006) 17 *Public Law Review* 133; M. S. R. Palmer, 'Using Constitutional Realism to Identify the *Complete* Constitution: Lessons from an Unwritten Constitution' (2006) 54 *American Journal of Comparative Law* 587; and M. S. R. Palmer, 'Constitutional Realism about Constitutional Protection: Indigenous Rights under a Judicialized and a Politicized Constitution' (2006) 29 *Dalhousie Law Journal* 1.

ordinary statute is perhaps the most important constitutional law New Zealand has, although it lacks many of the features of constitutions in other countries. The Constitution Act can be amended by an ordinary Act of Parliament. Further, it provides little guidance on the rules and principles under which government will be conducted.

The New Zealand Bill of Rights Act 1990, an important constitutional law, is also an ordinary statute. That statute and the cases decided under it have enhanced the power of the New Zealand judiciary, arming them with what is sometimes called a weak form of judicial review over legislative action. But the power it gives to judges is an enhanced power of interpretation and it carefully preserves the principle of parliamentary supremacy. Other statutes and constitutional conventions provide much of the pith and substance on how government is conducted. Notwithstanding the primacy given to Parliament by these constitutional arrangements, there has been, on occasions, some vigorous debate between the judiciary and ministers as to what is the appropriate role of each.[2]

One unique feature of the New Zealand system of government relates to the Treaty of Waitangi entered into between the crown and Maori, New Zealand's indigenous people, on 6 February 1840. The legal weight the Treaty has within New Zealand's legal system and its importance in constitutional terms remain live issues in New Zealand.[3] The Waitangi Tribunal has jurisdiction to look into Maori grievances under the Treaty and make recommendations to the government. The jurisdiction extends back to 1840.[4] There have been many settlements enacted by the Parliament over the past twenty years to which the Tribunal has often

[2] In 2005 the Chief Justice was reported as saying that the then Prime Minister had 'a profound lack of understanding about judicial independence': F. O'Sullivan, 'Who Rules New Zealand?', *New Zealand Herald*, 25 March 2005, p. B1. In a parliamentary debate on an important occasion, the Deputy Prime Minister, who was also the Attorney-General, drew a direct link between challenges to parliamentary sovereignty, one of which had been mounted by the Chief Justice in a law review article, and judicial activism: Hon. Michael Cullen, 24 May 2004, 617 NZPD 13192. Members of Parliament and even ministers are sometimes quoted criticising judicial decisions or commenting on matters before the courts, although after a report from the Privileges Committee there is a proposal in front of Parliament to change the Standing Orders to allow the Speaker more power to control references to matters awaiting adjudication – Order Paper House of Representatives, Wednesday 16 December 2009, p. 7.

[3] For a complete analysis of the legal and constitutional issues relating to the Treaty of Waitangi in New Zealand see M. S. R. Palmer, *The Treaty of Waitangi in New Zealand's Law and Constitution* (Wellington: Victoria University Press, 2008).

[4] Treaty of Waitangi Act 1975.

contributed as a result of direct negotiation with the crown. Important decisions of the superior courts have also contributed heavily to Treaty of Waitangi jurisprudence.[5]

New Zealand enjoys a system of cabinet government that is highly stable. It has a politically neutral public service, recognises the independence of the judiciary and has a proportional electoral system similar to that in Germany.[6] The country has a remorseless democratic tradition with vigorous public debate.

The first question to address is where the judges fit into this system. The Constitution Act deals with the sovereign, the executive and legislative branches, and the judiciary. The provisions in the Constitution Act are very short and are contained in Part IV of the Act as follows:

> 23. Protection of Judges against removal from Office – A Judge of the High Court shall not be removed from office except by the Sovereign or the Governor-General acting upon an address of the House of Representatives, which address may be moved only on the grounds of that Judge's misbehaviour or of that Judge's incapacity to discharge the functions of that Judge's office.
>
> 24. Salaries of Judges not be reduced – The salary of a Judge of the High Court shall not be reduced during the continuance of the Judge's commission.

Such provisions were not new to New Zealand law in 1986. Similar provisions were included in the Judicature Act 1908 and in earlier statutes including a provision in the New Zealand Constitution Act 1852, an enactment of the Imperial Parliament at Westminster. The principles flowed from the Act of Settlement of 1701 in the United Kingdom. Suffice it to say that the independence of the judiciary was established early in New Zealand and has been constantly maintained.[7]

The salaries of New Zealand judges, their expense allowances and their superannuation are all set by the Remuneration Authority. This body is independent from the executive government. Its determinations have legal effect without the need for the approval or concurrence of any other authority.[8] In the most recent determination effective from

[5] The leading case is *New Zealand Maori Council* v. *Attorney-General* [1987] 1 NZLR 641, CA, but there are many others.

[6] Electoral Act 1993, Part 6.

[7] See G. Palmer, 'Judicial Selection and Accountability: Can the New Zealand System Survive?', in B. D. Gray and R. B. McClintock (eds.), *Courts and Policy: Checking the Balance* (Wellington: Brookers, 1995), pp. 11–90.

[8] Remuneration Authority Act 1977.

October 2009 the Chief Justice receives $NZ437,500 with a yearly principal allowance for general expenses of $7,900. The President of the Court of Appeal receives $410,000, as does a Supreme Court judge. A judge of the High Court receives $366,500, while a District Court judge receives $276,500 with an allowance for general expenses of $4,100.[9] There are other conditions relating to travel expenses, and annual and long service leave, all of which are generous.[10]

One important development in 2004 was the passage of the Judicial Conduct Commissioner and Judicial Conduct Panel Act. This provides a process for dealing with complaints against members of the judiciary. It also provides a process for inquiring into serious cases so that any parliamentary process concerning removal is based on properly tested material before a decision can be made. So far in New Zealand's history no address for removal has been moved.

The most important development for the New Zealand judiciary in recent years has been the ending of appeals to the Judicial Committee of the Privy Council in England. This was accomplished through the Supreme Court Act 2003. While there was some reluctance that this link should end, a demonstration surely of New Zealand's inherent constitutional conservatism, the new court has become well established at the apex of the New Zealand system with little apparent controversy.

There is one provision in the Supreme Court Act of some constitutional interest. Section 3 sets out the purpose of the Act and then provides in subsection (2):[11]

[9] Judicial Salaries and Allowance Determination 2009, SR 2009/419. Conditions relating to leave, long-service leave and travel allowances are dealt with in the case of District Court judges in a handbook known as the 'red book' which was designed to make the entitlements clear and transparent. Its preparation was overseen by the Solicitor-General. Further compilations for the other benches are in the course of preparation.

[10] While comparisons are fraught with difficulties it is interesting to note that the Chief Justice of the US Supreme Court receives US$217,400 (see About.com US Government Info, 'Current US Supreme Court Justices' at: www.usgovinfo.about.com/od/uscourtsystem), the Chief Justice of Australia A$446,580 (Australian Remuneration Tribunal, Determination 2009/17: Judicial and Related Offices – Remuneration and Allowances, 2009) and the top judge in the United Kingdom £236,300 from 1 April 2008 (Review Body on Senior Salaries, *Thirty-First Report on Senior Salaries*, Report No, 68, 2009). Even allowing for exchange rate differences, it is clear that New Zealand judges are comparatively well remunerated.

[11] Subsection (1) of s. 3 of the Supreme Court Act provides as follows:

(1) The purpose of this Act is –
  (a) to establish within New Zealand a new court of final appeal comprising New Zealand judges –

> Nothing in this Act affects New Zealand's continuing commitment to the rule of law and the sovereignty of Parliament.

The time has yet to come for these provisions to receive a judicial interpretation, but the matter will be of interest when it occurs.

The structure of the New Zealand Courts comprises a Supreme Court, Court of Appeal, High Court and District Courts.[12] Within the District Courts are included the Family Courts[13] and the Youth Courts.[14] The Environment Court[15] is separate, but is staffed by District Court judges. There is also a separate Maori Land Court.

New Zealand also has an extensive system of tribunals, numbering more than one hundred, some of which are presided over by District Court judges.[16] Perhaps the most significant tribunals from the point of view of the court structure are the Disputes Tribunal that sit throughout the country in the District Courts. They are presided over by referees and no lawyers may appear. Rulings are enforced through the court system.

The main department of state responsible for serving the courts is the Ministry of Justice. The Minister of Justice and the Minister for Courts are both serviced by the Ministry of Justice. The Attorney-General is responsible for judicial appointments. It was once common for the Attorney-General and Minister of Justice portfolios to be allocated to the same person, but that has not been the case for more than a decade now. The Attorney-General is serviced by the Crown Law Office, which is essentially a large law firm for the crown. It is headed by the Solicitor-General, who is not a Member of Parliament as the Attorney-General is, but a senior public servant often selected from the ranks of senior

(i) to recognise that New Zealand is an independent nation with its own history and traditions; and
(ii) to enable important legal matters, including legal matters relating to the Treaty of Waitangi, to be resolved with an understanding of New Zealand conditions, history, and traditions; and
(iii) to improve access to justice; and

(b) to provide for the court's jurisdiction and related matters; and
(c) to end appeals to the Judicial Committee of the Privy Council from decisions of New Zealand courts; and
(d) to make related amendments to certain enactments relating to courts or judicial proceedings.

12 New Zealand Courts website at: www.courts.govt.nz.
13 Family Courts Act 1980.
14 Child, Young Persons, and their Families Act 1989, Part 4.
15 Resource Management Amendment Act 1996.
16 For a summary of the Tribunal system in New Zealand see Law Commission, *Tribunals in New Zealand* (NZLC, IP6, 2007).

barristers, as was the case with the current Solicitor-General, Dr David Collins QC.

The Attorney-General, as principal law officer of the crown, is the main conduit through which judicial views are funnelled to cabinet. However, in New Zealand there is constant contact between the judges and the policy-makers, including both ministers and public servants, in the small, intimate policy atmosphere of Wellington. Indeed, the extent of extra-judicial influence that the judges exert is to a degree institutionalised, as the following material suggests.

Judicial committees

A further role that judges have in New Zealand is to serve on judicial committees.[17] There are numerous judicial committees in existence to which many judges contribute.

Each judicial bench has internal judicial management and support committees.[18] There are also inter-bench committees relating to areas of mutual interest, which are comprised of judges from different benches. Judges may also serve on external committees that may include Ministry of Justice and other government officials, and non-government members.

Heads of Bench

Central to the system of judicial committees and the role of judges within the system of government in New Zealand is the Heads of Bench, who meet quarterly and hold phone conferences monthly. This forum enables the judiciary to develop positions on matters of principle affecting judicial function, on the basis of which it engages with the executive government. The Heads of Bench receive regular reports from the Ministry of Justice on security, information technology and property, and from the judicial committees on policy issues arising from management and support committees. The Heads of Bench raise policy issues or issues of principle affecting the judiciary as a whole directly with the executive government.

[17] Courts of New Zealand website at: www.courtsofnz.govt.nz.

[18] A diagram representing the judicial committee structure can be found at the Courts of New Zealand website at: www.courtsofnz.govt.nz.

Courts Executive Council

The Heads of Bench also report to the Courts Executive Council. The Council is chaired by the Chief Executive of the Ministry of Justice. The Chief Justice, President of the Court of Appeal, Chief High Court Judge, Chief District Court Judge, Deputy Chief Executive of the Ministry of Justice and the Deputy Secretaries of the Ministry of Justice's Operations, Strategy and Corporate and Policy and Legal sections comprise its membership.

External committees

Judges are involved in the Criminal Practice Committee, a body established in 1988 by then Chief Justice Sir Ronald Davison. Along with judges, legal practitioners, Ministry of Justice policy advisers and representatives of the police, Law Commission, crown law and the New Zealand Law Society meet to discuss matters of importance to the operation of the criminal justice system, which can then be brought to the attention of the executive government.

The Rules Committee, established under the Judicature Act 1908, also includes judges in its membership.[19] This committee is responsible for the procedural rules in the Supreme Court, Court of Appeal, High Court and District Courts. The Rules Committee is highly active and is effectively steered by its judicial membership. Control over the rules cements the power to legislate on substantive matters to some degree. The Rules Committee is an important pivot in the judiciary's policy arsenal. It has the power to make delegated legislation with the approval of cabinet on a number of important issues. For example, it recently determined the rules on access to court records. The committee is extremely active and has recently revised the entire rules of civil procedure for the High Court.

The New Zealand Council for Legal Education is an independent statutory body constituted under the Lawyers and Conveyancers Act

[19] Judicature Act 1908, s. 51B. The Committee is required to have eleven mandatory members: the Chief Justice; Chief High Court judge; two other judges of the High Court appointed by the Chief Justice; the Chief District Court judge; one other District Court judge appointed by the Chief Justice on the recommendation of the Chief District Court judge; the Attorney-General; the Solicitor-General; the Chief Executive of the Ministry of Justice; and two barristers and solicitors nominated by the Council of the New Zealand Law Society and approved by the Chief Justice (s. 51B(1)). In addition, the Chief Justice may appoint any other person to be a member for a special purpose. That person holds office during the pleasure of the Chief Justice (s. 51B(2)).

2006.[20] It prescribes the core curriculum for the Bachelor of Laws degree and monitors these subjects through a moderation system. Since 1997 it has also required a university course in legal ethics. The council defines and prescribes the course of study for the examination and practical legal training of persons wishing to be admitted as barristers and solicitors. It also determines the requirements for those lawyers from overseas who wish to be admitted in New Zealand. The council is chaired by a Supreme Court judge, currently Rt Hon. Sir Andrew Tipping. Two of its members are nominated by the Chief Justice from the High Court bench and one by the Chief District Court judge. At the time of writing a third judge is also serving. He was nominated by the council itself.

Inter-bench committees

The Institute of Judicial Studies has existed since 1998. It is the professional development arm of the New Zealand judiciary. It provides support for judges in the continuing development of their judicial careers and provides a range of courses and continuing education to promote judicial excellence. It is chaired by a judge of the Court of Appeal and contains a majority of judges on its governance board. The institute is funded by the Ministry of Justice.

The inter-bench committees in which judges are involved also includes the Judicial Libraries Management Board, a strategic and advisory body responsible for overseeing and managing the development of information and library services and the Standing Committee on Courthouse Design which allows judges, the Law Society and administrators together to set design standards for courts.

There is also a Media Liaison Committee and the Chief Justice has a full time Judicial Communications Adviser.

Higher Courts management and judicial support committees

The Supreme Court, Court of Appeal and High Court each have management committees, in which some or all of the judges from each bench meet with senior Ministry of Justice officials to discuss issues affecting each court. There is also a Higher Courts Judicial Support Committee, which reviews the support provided by the Ministry of Justice to the

[20] Lawyers and Conveyancers Act 2006, Part 8.

judiciary, such as secretarial services, security, information technology, judge's clerks and building services.

Additionally, a Judicial Research Committee, comprised of judges of the Court of Appeal, High Court and District Courts, considers all requests for judicial participation in various types of research. The committee makes a recommendation to the Chief Justice or relevant Head of Bench regarding each request.

This complex network of committees is administered by the Ministry of Justice, which is also responsible for administering the courts. It provides a structure through which the judges are able to represent their views to members of the executive government on all matters that affect their judicial work. It also provides opportunities for the regular transmission of the policy views of members of the judiciary to the government, often when that policy is in the early stages of formation. Judges are often consulted on draft legislation and do not hesitate to express their views, even forcefully at times.

The use of judges for inquiries

There is a long tradition in New Zealand of setting up inquiries into various public issues. The first was conducted in 1864 for the purpose of recommending the best site for the seat of government on the shores of Cook Strait.[21] The members of the inquiry were Members of Parliament from the Australian colonies. As a result of the inquiry, Wellington was made the capital.

Statutory Commissions of Inquiry were introduced to New Zealand by the Commissioners' Powers Act 1867. The Act was extended in 1872 and replaced in 1903 by the Commissioners Act, a measure that gave more comprehensive powers to commissioners and specified the purposes for which a commission could be established. An amendment in 1905 allowed judges from the Supreme Court (then the first court of competent jurisdiction, now the High Court) who were appointed to a commission to exercise their judicial powers, such as contempt, in the context of the inquiry. This power was extended to former judges in 1995. The Commissions of Inquiry Act 1908 consolidated the 1903 and 1905 Acts. The 1908 Act remains in force at the time of writing, although it is highly likely to be replaced in 2011 by an Inquiries Bill that is at an

[21] *Report of Commission of Inquiry* (1864) AJHR D 2 (Sir Francis Murphy).

advanced stage before the Parliament.[22] The Bill resulted from a Law Commission report.[23]

There has also been an extensive history in New Zealand of using judges to chair royal commissions and commissions of inquiry. This has not occasioned controversy and is not regarded as undermining the independence of the judiciary, although it is known that the practice in the State of Victoria in Australia is different.[24] There is always prior consultation with the Chief Justice, and there have probably been instances where the subject matter of the inquiry was thought, for one reason or another, not to be one suitable for a member of the judiciary to undertake.

Sometimes inquiries are conducted by retired judges, thus reducing the risk of compromising judicial independence compared with the situation of a sitting judge. For example, a royal commission into genetic modification that reported in 2001 was chaired by the former Chief Justice the Rt Hon. Sir Thomas Eichelbaum.[25] The most recent, a royal commission into the reform of local government in the city of Auckland and the surrounding area was chaired by a retired High Court judge, the Hon. Peter Salmon QC.[26]

The distinction between a commission of inquiry and a royal commission in New Zealand is slight – mainly in symbolism and prestige.[27] The legal powers are the same. They differ only in their mode of appointment and title. Both forms are initiated by the executive government and are governed by the same legislation, the Commissions of Inquiry Act. The Law Commission found in reviewing the legislation that while it might be assumed that royal commissions were reserved for the most

[22] Inquiries Bill 2008 (283-2). The Government Administration Select Committee reported to Parliament on this Bill on 20 November 2009.

[23] Law Commission, *The Role of Public Inquiries* (NZLC IP1, 2007); Law Commission, *A New Inquiries Act* (NZLC R102, 2008).

[24] See the 'Irvine Memorandum' reproduced in Hon. Sir M. McInerney QC and G. J. Moloney, 'The Case Against', in G. Fraser (ed.), *Judges as Royal Commissioners and Chairmen of Non-Judicial Tribunals: Two Views presented at the Fourth Annual Seminar of the Australian Institute of Judicial Administration* (Adelaide: Australian Institute of Judicial Administration, 1986), pp. 3, 11.

[25] Rt Hon. Sir T. Eichelbaum, J. Fleming, J. Allan and R. Randerson, *Royal Commission on Genetic Modification* (Wellington, 2001).

[26] Hon. P. Salmon QC, Dame M. Bazley and D. Shand, *Royal Commission into Auckland Governance* (Auckland, 2009).

[27] Rt Hon. Sir I. Richardson, 'Commissions of Inquiry' (1989) 7 *Otago Law Review* 1 at 4.

serious matters of public importance, a survey of the historical record did not bear out that assumption.[28]

Between 1976 and 2010 there have been thirty-four royal commissions or commissions of inquiry conducted in New Zealand, an average of exactly one a year. Sixteen of the inquiries were chaired by retired or serving judges, one of whom came from New South Wales. Despite their comparative frequency, it is clear that commissions of inquiry and royal commissions are much less attractive to cabinets in New Zealand than once they were. Between 1947 and 1980 there was an average of three to four commissions a year, but only ten were established between 1984 and 2009.[29]

The decline in fashion of such inquiries is due to a number of factors. The first is expense. The most expensive inquiry, known as the 'Winebox Inquiry', into the propriety of certain taxation transactions, was conducted by retired Chief Justice Sir Ronald Davison and cost the taxpayer more than $NZ10 million.[30] The Royal Commission on Genetic Modification cost $NZ4.36 million.[31]

Further, it is common for an inquiry to take a long time, a characteristic that is often inconvenient to ministers. Frequently inquiries run over the allotted time and need extensions. The Law Commission found that over thirty years only two commissions reported early and one on time.[32] Where intensely legalistic approaches are adopted with parties cited and extensive cross-examination are permitted time marches on and the costs mount up.

Over the years these tendencies led ministers to search for other avenues where much the same advantages could be achieved but more quickly and cheaply. From the point of view of ministers, there are many mixed motives that go into the setting up of an inquiry. There may be a need to find out what happened, and an independent inquiry will provide ministers with some political cover that they are not manipulating events for their own political purposes. There may be a need for a genuinely independent look at a complex problem on which there are differing points of view or there may be a need to get rid of a political hot potato for a period.

[28] Law Commission, *A New Inquiries Act* (NZLC R102, 2008), p. 45.
[29] Law Commission, *A New Inquiries Act* (NZLC R102, 2008), p. 34.
[30] Law Commission, *A New Inquiries Act* (NZLC R102, 2008), p. 32.
[31] Law Commission, *A New Inquiries Act* (NZLC R102, 2008), p. 32.
[32] Law Commission, *A New Inquiries Act* (NZLC R102, 2008), p. 32.

It has become common to set up what are known as ministerial inquiries. They have no statutory basis. They enjoy no coercive powers. They are the creature of the minister who establishes them, although independent people can be appointed to them and make independent findings. However, they can achieve the same goals as a commission of inquiry in many circumstances, particularly where the matter inquired into lies entirely or mainly within the purview of the executive government. They are often quick and cost-effective. The lack of powers can, in some circumstances, however, be a handicap to arriving at an analysis of what actually happened.[33] In its investigation surrounding public inquiries the Law Commission found that there were at least twenty-eight ministerial inquiries between 1990 and 2008, although complete records are not available. Indeed, of these twenty-eight ministerial inquiries, four were conducted by retired judges and ten by senior lawyers.[34]

So it would appear that neither the lack of coercive powers nor the absence of statutory independence was a deterrent to securing the services of highly qualified people, including retired judges, to conduct ministerial inquiries. Ministerial inquiries have proved to be certainly quicker and cheaper than commissions of inquiry. But the contrast between the formality of the Commissions of Inquiry Act, on the one hand, and the lack of any legal framework, on the other, led the Law Commission to recommend to the government a new structure for public inquiries that would allow more flexibility in procedure and bring all inquiries within the rubric of a new statutory framework. This was done by providing for two categories of inquiry: public inquiries appointed by the Governor-General by Order-in-Council; and government inquiries appointed by the minister. Both will enjoy the same powers.

Clearly, in New Zealand there is a substantial appetite within the executive government for inquiries and an established propensity to involve members of the judiciary in them. This raises the issues of why governments set up such inquiries, what they want to get out of them and how effective they are in producing work of permanent importance.

The motivations of government in setting up inquiries differ greatly depending on the type of inquiry. They are often used to find out the real

[33] See, for instance, N. Ingram QC, *Report to the Prime Minister upon Inquiry into matters relating to Taito Phillip Field* (2006). The findings were inconclusive due to the incapacity of the inquirer to compel evidence. Mr Field, an MP, was later charged with corruption, convicted and jailed ('Ex-minister's Trial a Spectacular Fall from Grace', *New Zealand Herald*, 5 January 2010, available at: www.nzherald.co.nz).

[34] Law Commission, *A New Inquiries Act* (NZLC R102, 2008), pp. 242–3.

facts involved in some event of public importance, such as the cause of disasters like the Abbotsford land slip,[35] the collapse of the Department of Conservation's viewing platform at Cave Creek[36] or the crash of an Air New Zealand DC10 on Mt Erebus in Antarctica with great loss of life.[37] Another type of inquiry, but still principally concerned with fact-finding, involves such matters as whether convictions were correctly arrived at[38] or issues concerning the administration of the Income Tax Act 1976.[39] Even this type of inquiry will be less likely in the future than it has been in the past due to the large number of statutes that have been passed that give powers to inquire into matters in a manner very similar to the Commissions of Inquiry Act 1908.[40] For example, s. 27(4) of the Health and Safety in Employment Act 1992 gives the minister power to appoint an inquiry into the cause of an accident and that inquiry has all the powers of a commission of inquiry. There are a further twelve Acts of Parliament that contain powers to set up one-off inquiries that have powers similar to commissions of inquiry, but do not rely on the 1908 Act as their source.[41]

[35] R. G. Gallen QC, G. S. Beca, Prof J. D. McCraw and T. A. Roberts, *Commission of Inquiry into Abbotsford Landslip Disaster* [1980] IV AJHR H 7.

[36] Judge G. S. Noble, *Commission of Inquiry into the Collapse of a viewing Platform at Cave Creek near Punakaiki on the West Coast* [1995] XL AJHR H 2.

[37] Hon. P. Mahon, *Royal Commission to Inquire into and Report upon the Crash on Mount Erebus Antarctica, of a DC10 Operated by Air New Zealand Limited* [1981] AJHR H 1.

[38] Hon. R. Taylor QC, Rt Hon. J. B. Gordon and Most Reverend A. H. Johnston, *Report of the Royal Commission to Inquire into and Report upon the Circumstances of the Convictions of Arthur Allan Thomas for the Murders of David Harvey Crewe and Jeanette Lenore Crewe* [1980] IV AJHR H 6.

[39] Rt Hon. Sir R. Davison, *Report of the Commission of Inquiry into Certain Matters Relating to Taxation* [1997] LVI AJHR H 3.

[40] Statutory inquiry functions taking powers from Commissions of Inquiry Act 1908 include: Biosecurity Act 1993, Schedule 2; Environment Act 1986, s. 16(2); Fire Service Act 1975, s. 86; Forest and Rural Fires Act 1977, s. 59; Health and Safety in Employment Act 1992, s. 27; Intellectual Disability (Compulsory Care and Rehabilitation) Act 2003, s. 101; Judicial Conduct Commissioner and Judicial Conduct Panel Act 2004, s. 26; Local Government Act 2002, s. 34; Maritime Transport Act 1994, s. 58; Mental Health (Compulsory Assessment and Treatment) Act 1992, s. 95; New Zealand Public Health and Disability Act 2000, s. 71; Police Act 1958, s. 12; Shipping Act 1987, s. 5; State Sector Act 1988, s. 25; Temporary Safeguard Authorities Act 1987, s. 4; Transport Accident Investigation Commission Act 1990.

[41] Inquiry powers conferred by their own statutes include: Children's Commissioner Act 2003, s. 12; Electricity Act 1992, s. 18; Gas Act 1992, s. 19; Hazardous Substances and New Organisms Act 1996, s. 11(1)(e); Health and Disability Commissioner Act 2004, s. 14(1)(e); Human Rights Act 1993, s. 5; Inspector-General of Intelligence and Security Act 1996, s. 11; New Zealand Public Health and Disability Act 2000, s. 7; Ombudsmen Act 1975, s. 13(3); Police Complaints Authority Act 1988, s. 12; Privacy Act 1993, s. 13(1)(m); Public Audit Act 2001, s. 18(1).

The second major category of inquiry concerns policy and legislation. There has been a pronounced tendency in New Zealand to establish a royal commission or commission of inquiry under the chairmanship of a judge or retired judge to report on important matters of high policy. In many instances these reports have led to significant legislative change.

It is not too much to claim that in this way some New Zealand judges have made outstanding contributions to the development of New Zealand public policy. The Rt Hon. Sir Thaddeus McCarthy a President of the Court of Appeal presided over a number of important royal commissions in the 1960s and 1970s including the state services,[42] the racing industry,[43] social security,[44] nuclear power[45] and the Maori Land Court.[46] The Royal Commission on Compensation for Personal Injury in New Zealand of 1967, which was presided over by another judge, the Rt Hon. Sir Owen Woodhouse, who later became the President of the Court of Appeal, recommended the abolition of the tort system for compensating personal injury and its replacement by the accident compensation scheme where there is no inquiry into fault. The scheme was adopted in 1974 and remains a unique feature of the New Zealand legal landscape.[47]

Sir David Beattie, a judge who later became Governor-General, presided in 1978 over the royal commission on the courts that led to a significant restructuring of New Zealand's court system.[48] Another High Court judge, Sir John Wallace, chaired the Royal Commission on the Electoral System that led to the mixed-member proportional representation electoral system being adopted in New Zealand.[49]

[42] Justice T. McCarthy, *Report of the Royal Commission on State Services in New Zealand* [1962] IV AJHR H 41.

[43] Sir T. McCarthy, *Report of the Royal Commission into Horse Racing, Trotting and Dog Racing in New Zealand* [1970] IV AJHR H 51.

[44] Sir T. McCarthy, *Report of the Royal Commission of Inquiry into Social Security in New Zealand* [1972] IV AJHR 1972.

[45] Rt Hon. Sir T. McCarthy, I. Blair, V. Boyd, B. Liley and L. Richardson, *Report of the Royal Commission on Nuclear Power Generation* [1978] VII AJHR H 4.

[46] Sir T. McCarthy, *Report of the Royal Commission on the Maori Land Courts* [1980] IV AJHR H 3.

[47] Hon. O. Woodhouse, H. L. Bockett and G. A. Parsons, *Report of the Royal Commission of Inquiry: Compensation for Personal Injury in New Zealand* (Wellington: Government Printer, 1967). In 1977 the Royal Commission of Inquiry, *Contraception, Sterilisation and Abortion* chaired by Hon. Justice McMullin reported.

[48] Hon. Justice D. Beattie, Professor I. H. Kawharu, R. M. King, J. D. Murray and J. H. Wallace, *Report of the Royal Commission on the Courts* [1978] VII AJHR H 2.

[49] Sir J. Wallace, Sir K. Keith, Professor R. Mulgan, J. Darwin and W. Werata, *Royal Commission on the Electoral System Towards a Better Democracy* [1986] AJHR H3.

Rt Hon. Sir Ivor Richardson, another President of the Court of Appeal, presided over a royal commission that produced a massive report on social policy in 1988, although for a number of complicated political reasons it did not have a great influence on policy development.[50] The report on genetic modification by Sir Thomas Eichelbaum in 2001 has already been referred to. The most recent royal commission report on the governance of Auckland has led to massive change as well.[51]

It is plain from this analysis that policy-makers in New Zealand, both in cabinet and the public service, have found judicially led commissions of inquiry useful in the development of public policy. This leads to the question of why judges would be selected for what is essentially policy work.

The first reason is that judges have prestige. So far the deconstruction of institutions in New Zealand that seems so much a part of the modern political culture has not eaten away at the standing of the judiciary to the degree that it has the political institutions of government. Judges are respected for their impartiality and their political neutrality. That remains the case despite more than twenty years' experience of the superior courts interpreting the New Zealand Bill of Rights Act 1990, a measure that implements a weak form of judicial review of legislative action.

The second reason is that judges are regarded as expert fact-finders and, where that is a feature of the particular inquiry, it is a natural fit with their judicial responsibilities. What is less clear is why judges have been preferred for high-level policy inquiries. The legal profession in New Zealand is not necessarily skilled in matters of government administration and policy. Where the subject matter has a high level of legal content, such as the adequacy of the tort system as a means of compensating personal injury, the structure of the courts or the application of the tax legislation, there is a natural scope for legal expertise. But in the broader realm of social policy, where New Zealand royal commissions have often travelled, the application of judicial method is less straightforward. The nature of the social security system, the electoral system, genetic modification or the structure of the public service are not matters

[50] Rt Hon. Sir I. Richardson, A. Ballin, M. Bruce, L. Cook, M. Durie and R. Noon, *Report of the Royal Commission on Social Policy* [1988] XI–XV AJHR H 2.

[51] Hon. P. Salmon QC, Dame M. Bazley and D. Shand, *Royal Commission into Auckland Governance*; Local Government (Auckland Council) Act 2009; Government (Tamaki Makaurau Reorganisation) Act 2009; Local Government (Auckland Law Reform) Bill (112–1).

in which judges enjoy obvious advantages over other prospective appointees. It must be said that all the commissions reviewed, other than the Mt Erebus Inquiry, had members other than judges on the commission and no doubt they made important contributions. Nevertheless, there is an established tradition of strong leadership being exerted by judges who chair commissions in New Zealand. For example, Sir Owen Woodhouse wrote every word of the 1967 royal commission report himself.

One explanation for the preference for judicial leadership may lie in the need to avoid judicial review. There has been a steady stream of reported decisions involving commissions of inquiry and royal commissions in New Zealand – twenty-three between 1902 and 2000.[52] Having a judge as chair is certainly likely to minimise the risk of successful challenges. That said, however, it must be added that the jurisprudence established in the reported cases in New Zealand is in some respects a difficult one. It has produced some close and highly controversial cases. The standout decision is that of the Privy Council upholding the New Zealand Court of Appeal in *Re Erebus Royal Commission; Air New Zealand Ltd* v. *Mahon* in which the single judicial commissioner was held to have failed to have followed the rules of natural justice.[53] The

[52] *Jellicoe* v. *Haselden* (1902) 22 NZLR 343, SC; *Cock* v. *Attorney-General* (1909) 29 NZLR 405, CA; *In re Waipawa, Waipukurau, and Dannevirke Counties* (1909) 29 NZLR 863, SC; *Hughes* v. *Hanna* (1910) 29 NZLR 16, SC; *Whangarei Co-operative Bacon-Curing and Meat Co.* v. *Whangarei Meat Supply Co.* (1912) 31 NZLR 1223, SC; *In re St Helens Hospital* (1913) 32 NZLR 682, SC; *In re Otara River Bridge* [1916] GLR 38, SC; *Pilkington* v. *Platts and Others* [1925] NZLR 864, SC and CA; *Timberlands Woodpulp Ltd* v. *Attorney-General* [1934] NZLR 271, SC; *King* v. *Frazer* [1945] NZLR 297, SC; *In re Royal Commission on Licensing* [1945] NZLR 665, CA; *In re the Royal Commission to Inquire and Report upon the State Services* [1962] NZLR 96, CA; *Fitzgerald* v. *Commission of Inquiry into Marginal Lands Board* [1980] 2 NZLR 368, HC; *In re Marginal Lands Board Commission of Inquiry into Fitzgerald Loan* [1980] 2 NZLR 395, HC; *Re Royal Commission on Thomas Case* [1982] 1 NZLR 252, CA; *Re Erebus Royal Commission; Air New Zealand Ltd* v. *Mahon (No. 2)* [1981] 1 NZLR 618, CA; *Re Erebus Royal Commission: Air New Zealand Ltd* v. *Mahon* [1983] NZLR 662, PC; *Thompson* v. *Commission of Inquiry into Administration of District Court at Wellington* [1983] NZLR 98, HC; *Badger* v. *Whangarei Refinery Expansion Commission of Inquiry* [1985] 2 NZLR 688, HC; *Fay, Richwhite & Co. Ltd* v. *Davison* [1995] 1 NZLR 517, CA; *Controller and Auditor-General* v. *Sir Ronald Davison*, CA 226/95; *KPMG Peat Marwick* v. *Sir Ronald* Davison, CA 223/95; *Brannigan* v. *Sir Ronald Davison*, CA 231/95, [1996] 2 NZLR 278, CA, [1997] 1 NZLR 140, PC; *Peters* v. *Davison* [1998] NZAR 309, HC, [1999] 2 NZLR 164, CA, [1999] 3 NZLR 744, HC.

[53] *Re Erebus Royal Commission; Air New Zealand Ltd* v. *Mahon (No. 2)* [1981] 1 NZLR 618, CA.

judge subsequently, and probably as a result of the decision, resigned his commission as a judge.

The formulation of policy in a royal commission is not the same as reaching a judicial decision in a court case. The uncritical application of the judicial method is not naturally suited to the development of policy. It is a different intellectual endeavour from the application of law to facts. But it is interesting, based on the New Zealand experience, to reflect upon what judges can do when freed from the restraints of the judicial process, precedent and rules of law. Although judges have a reputation for being conservative, the New Zealand experience suggests that some of them at least can play an important role as generators of important and novel policies. And what is equally important is that the judicial trademark helps those policies to be adopted.[54] In a small society where the talent base tends to be thin the judge as policy-maker is a contribution that deserves to be valued.

The use of judges in other roles

Judges are found in a range of different roles in New Zealand life off the bench. They are not the cloistered and remote figures that tended to be the stereotype of years gone by. They have been used in a variety of public roles. Perhaps the most obvious in recent years has been the number of appointments of judges to the role of Governor-General, the Queen's representative in New Zealand. The serving Governor-General, the Hon. Sir Anand Satyanand, was for many years a District Court judge before being made an ombudsman. His predecessor was Dame Silvia Cartwright, who was at the time of her appointment as Governor-General a serving High Court judge and before that had been the Chief District Court Judge. She had first come to public prominence when she chaired an inquiry under the Health Act 1956 into cervical cancer treatment at the National Women's Hospital, a matter that sparked intense public interest.[55] Her predecessor, Sir Michael Hardie Boyes, was at the time of his appointment a judge of the New Zealand Court of Appeal. Furthermore, the Letters Patent Constituting the Office

[54] For a discussion of these issues in the context of personal injury law see G. Palmer, *Compensation for Incapacity – A Study of Law and Social Change in New Zealand and Australia* (Wellington: Oxford University Press, 1979), pp. 197–213.

[55] S. Cartwright, *Report of the Committee of Inquiry into Allegations Concerning the Treatment of Cervical Cancer at National Women's Hospital and into Other Related Matters* (1988).

of Governor-General of New Zealand provides that the Chief Justice or, if he or she is unavailable, the next most senior judge act as Administrator of the Government where the Governor-General is for any reason unable to perform his or her duties.[56] Administrators have been used increasingly frequently in recent years because Governors-General have often been used to make visits abroad for foreign policy reasons.

The predilection to appoint people with a judicial background to the office of Governor-General appears to have increased with the adoption of the mixed-member proportion electoral system.[57] The first election under that system was held in 1996. It was thought that the new system had the potential to cause hung parliaments, which were never a feature of the first-past-the-post parliaments, and would require intervention from the Queen's representative. This did not in fact turn out to be the case. But in a series of speeches Sir Michael Hardie Boyes laid down clearly what the boundaries of his responsibilities were by expounding the principle that the formation of a government was a political decision and must be arrived at by politicians. In the exposition of these constitutional principles a legal background in the vice-regal representative was a clear advantage.[58]

Serving judges have frequently been appointed as President of the New Zealand Law Commission, although this is not required by the Law Commission Act 1985.[59] The first President was Sir Owen Woodhouse whose background has already been mentioned. He took up the position upon retirement as President of the Court of Appeal. The second President was Sir Kenneth Keith, an academic lawyer who subsequently became a Court of Appeal judge, then a Supreme Court judge when that court was established, and who is currently a judge on the International Court of Justice. He was followed by Hon. Justice Baragwanath, then a High Court judge and now a judge of the Court of Appeal. His successor was Hon. Justice Sir Bruce Robertston, who at the time of writing has just retired as judge of the Court of Appeal. It should be noted that Sir Bruce has served on the Legislation Advisory Committee since its inception in 1986. This committee recommends to cabinet guidelines for the preparation of legislation within the executive branch of government and submits to select committees on occasion where bills do not follow them.

56 Letters Patent Constituting the Office of Governor-General of New Zealand, SR 1983/225, cl. 12.

57 Electoral Act 1993.

58 G. Palmer and M. Palmer, *Bridled Power*, pp. 56–61.

59 For an account of the contribution of the New Zealand Law Commission see G. Palmer (ed.), *Reflections on the New Zealand Law Commission* (Wellington: LexisNexis, 2007).

Judges have an obvious suitability to law reform activities, especially to what is known as lawyers' law. The serving New Zealand judges who have been appointed President of the Law Commission have continued to sit judicially, a matter that may have inhibited them to some extent in their necessary dealings with ministers. One Supreme Court judge, who is also a former law commissioner, Rt Hon. Sir Peter Blanchard, has found the time while a member of the Supreme Court to provide substantial help to the Law Commission on both its Limitation Act 1950 reference, where he chaired the Committee, and the inquiry into the Land Transfer Act 1952.

The Hon. Justice Sir Edward Durie, the first Maori to be appointed to the High Court bench in New Zealand, was later appointed as a Law Commissioner. It should be noted that three District Court judges in all have been appointed as commissioners to the Law Commission.

Another interesting feature of the New Zealand system is the flexibility of roles in which judges can be used. Hon. Justice Lowell Goddard, a serving High Court judge, was appointed as the full-time chair of what is now known as the Independent Police Conduct Authority, an independent statutory body that looks into complaints about police misconduct or neglect of duty.[60] This is a busy and often controversial jurisdiction. Prior to Justice Goddard's appointment, the function had been performed by retired judges.

The Parole Board established by the Parole Act 2002 is presided over by Sir David Carruthers, a District Court judge who was formerly the Chief District Court Judge. The Board uses no fewer than eighteen other former or current High Court and District Court judges in a part-time capacity. There has been a long tradition of using judges on the Parole Board in the various configurations it has had in New Zealand over the years.

Members of the judiciary relatively frequently appear in front of parliamentary select committees. When this practice began in the 1980s the understanding was that no reference could be made to their appearances in the subsequent parliamentary debates. But that seems to have changed in recent years as the appearances of judges can be and are referred to.[61] While their views carry weight with Members of

[60] Independent Police Conduct Authority Act 1988.

[61] D. McGee, *Parliamentary Practice In New Zealand*, 3rd edn. (Wellington: Government Printer, 2005), p. 284 states:

> Whether judges ought or ought not, on constitutional or other grounds, to give evidence to a parliamentary committee on business before the

Parliament they do not necessarily prevail. When the Chief Justice and another judge appeared in front of a select committee to oppose a Bill originally recommended by the Law Commission to codify the law of evidence, their warnings were not heeded.[62]

Judges quite frequently give public talks and lectures at universities and other places on legal topics. These are often published in legal journals. Some of them write or edit important legal texts, which are highly influential. Several of them have joined university councils and even become Chancellor.

Judges are frequently consulted by the Law Commission and by government departments that are developing policy proposals that may impact on the judiciary. Judges often exhibit an appetite to be involved in policy development. They send copies of their decisions showing up defects that may require a legislative remedy to ministers and Members of Parliament. There have been occasions when judges have lobbied Members of Parliament. From time to time judges have conducted quite distinct campaigns of opposition against policy proposals of which they disapproved, such as the Crimes Bill of 1989,[63] or in favour of those that they support, such as the New Zealand Bill of Rights Act 1990. They were involved in moves to abolish appeals to the Privy Council and establish a new Supreme Court. They will also, through such committees as the Rules Committee, advance some policies.[64] The

legislature has been questioned. Judges have occasionally given evidence to select committees, whether at the invitation of a committee or on their own initiative. A committee has devoted an entire report to a briefing it received (partly in public and partly in private) from the Principal Family Court Judge on the work of the court.

A committee is quite likely to agree to hear a submission from the judiciary in private or even in secret and it has been argued that there is a convention that evidence received from members of the judiciary will be treated as private evidence. But there is no requirement that this occur and, in fact, judges have been heard at public hearings of committees. It is in every case a matter for the committee to determine by leave. Where a judge does appear before a committee, it is not out of order to refer to this fact later in debate in the House, nor is there any convention that would prevent such a reference being made.

[62] Evidence Act 2006; Evidence Bill 2005 (256–2) (commentary).

[63] Rt Hon. Sir R. Cooke, 'The Crimes Bill 1989: A Judge's Response' [1989] *New Zealand Law Journal* 235–43.

[64] E.g., compare Law Commission, *Access to Court Records* (NZLC R93, 2006) with the new rules of procedure on access to court records, the Criminal Proceedings (Access to Court Documents) Rules 2009, SR 2009/134.

Principal Youth Court Judge expresses himself frequently and forcefully in the media on policy matters within that arena.[65]

New Zealand has a particularly complex array of tribunals that play an important role in delivering justice. There are more than a hundred bodies established that might in the 'broadest sense be considered as tribunals'.[66] This broader approach included many disparate organisations, including regulatory bodies, standing commissions, occupational regulatory bodies as well as those that are more usually recognised as tribunals in that they decide or resolve some form of question or dispute.

The Law Commission decided that the primary characteristics of a tribunal are that they:[67]

- determine questions affecting people's rights;
- do this by considering facts and evidence and applying standards (generally rules or policies) to the facts;
- exercise defined specialist jurisdiction; and
- are independent of the executive.

Even under that definition the Law Commission identified sixty-five tribunals in New Zealand that satisfied the adjudicative definition. Quite a number of these tribunals are presided over by serving or retired judges. The Disputes Tribunal that deals with small claims in the absence of lawyers is now presided over by a District Court judge. The Liquor Licensing Tribunal, in practice a most important adjudicatory body over all aspects of the liquor industry, is presided over by a retired District Court judge. The Real Estate Agents Disciplinary Tribunal and the Health Act Board of Appeal are presided over by District Court judges.

Land Valuation Tribunals consist of a District Court judge sitting with two expert valuers. The Taxation Review Authority comprise serving or retired District Court judges. The new Immigration and Protection Tribunal is chaired by a District Court judge, as are the Customs Appeal Authorities established under the Customs and Excise Act 1966. The Chief Judge of the Maori Land Court is also chairperson of the Waitangi Tribunal.

[65] For instance, A. Koubaradis, 'Judge: Too-slow System Missing Child Criminals', *New Zealand Herald*, 13 November 2009, available at: www.nzherald.co.nz; 'Youth Judge Wants Core Values Taught in Schools', *The Dominion Post*, 16 April 2008, available at: www.stuff.co.nz.

[66] Law Commission, *Tribunal Reform* (NZLC SP20, 2008), p. 25.

[67] Law Commission, *Tribunal Reform*, p. 26.

Due to the complexity and expense of modern litigation, the delivery of administrative justice by tribunals can only increase in the future in New Zealand, and the role of judges in providing leadership and decision-making in these tribunals will grow with it. At present the unsystematic and higgledy-piggledy character of the structure has resisted attempts to reform it, an effort that cannot be long delayed.[68]

Conclusion

Judges in New Zealand are not particularly inhibited from exerting influence on policy either directly or indirectly by their special situation in society. Nor do they hesitate to publicly express their views on current issues within their areas of expertise. They have historically made a large contribution to important policy developments generated by royal commissions. They participate in an intricate network of committees that allow their voices to be heard by the executive government on a wide range of issues, both those of special concern to the judiciary and matters of policy contained in Bills presented to Parliament. They appear in front of parliamentary select committees. They participate in a wide range of tribunals that have a significant impact on both law and policy. Their independence when it comes to judicial decisions does not seem to be imperilled by this range of activities either in theory or in practice.

Adherence to a more rigorous doctrine of separation of powers would see judicial influence in policy matters reduced. As things have evolved in New Zealand there is little chance of such a development. The interesting point may lie in the fact that it appears that judicial influence over policy issues flows less from judicial decisions in court, although these do influence policy, than from the other sources of influence the judges enjoy as outlined in this chapter. All this goes to show that in a small society it is necessary to make the best use possible of the restricted talent base.

[68] The Law Commission's recommendations in Law Commission, *Tribunal Reform* (NZLC SP20, 2008) have not been adopted and there are currently no plans for these reforms to be carried out in the near future due to cost.

23

Judges and non-judicial functions in South Africa

CORA HOEXTER

The core function of the judiciary in any jurisdiction, it has been suggested, consists in the 'determination of matters in court by the delivery of judgments enforceable by process of law'.[1] Chapter 8 of the South African Constitution affirms this view by associating 'judicial' matters with the business of the courts.[2] Section 165(1) of the Constitution vests the 'judicial authority of the Republic' in 'the courts', and s. 166 indicates that the 'judicial system' consists of the various courts. Tellingly, too, ss. 174 and 175 deal with the appointment of judges and acting judges not in the abstract but as members of particular courts.[3]

Such provisions add colour to the concept of judicial functions, but without necessarily preventing judges from undertaking non-judicial functions in addition to their core activities. South African judges have in fact always performed extraneous functions, and in this country there is a long and notable tradition of depending on judges to chair governmental commissions of inquiry – often, if erroneously, referred to as 'judicial commissions'.

Today South African judges continue to perform a range of ceremonial and administrative functions, and they are still regularly invited to head governmental inquiries. As in so many other areas of life, however, the introduction of constitutional democracy in 1994 has had an effect on the

[1] These words from an address by the Hon. Chief Justice De Jersey of the Queensland Supreme Court were quoted with approval by Swain J in *City of Cape Town* v. *Premier, Western Cape* 2008 (6) SA 345, C, at para. [191]. (The full speech is available at www.samuelgriffiths.org.za, accessed 23 March 2010.) See also *Pretoria Portland Cement Co. Ltd* v. *Competition Commission* 2003 (2) SA 385, SCA, at para. [40] ('*Pretoria Portland Cement*').

[2] Constitution of the Republic of South Africa, 1996 (hereafter 'the Constitution' or 'the 1996 Constitution').

[3] See also the Judges' Remuneration and Conditions of Employment Act 47 of 2001, where 'active service' means service in the courts.

way extra-curial activities are treated. The post-1994 understanding of the separation of powers and the independence of the judiciary has played an important role in this regard. Informed by these constitutional fundamentals, the Constitutional Court of South Africa has developed an incompatibility test for determining on a case-by-case basis whether particular non-judicial activities are permissible. The test was partly inspired by the incompatibility doctrine developed in respect of Australian federal judges in *Grollo* v. *Palmer*[4] and *Wilson* v. *Minister for Aboriginal and Torres Strait Islander and Affairs*,[5] and in formulating it the Constitutional Court drew also on dicta in *Mistretta* v. *United States*.[6]

This chapter begins by examining the performance of non-judicial functions in South Africa during the pre-democratic era. It then focuses on two crucial and closely linked post-1994 developments: first, the emergence of a 'distinctively South African model'[7] of the separation of powers and, concomitantly, of judicial independence; and, second, the Constitutional Court's development of its incompatibility test. That section deals also with a recent example of the application of the test. The final section describes various non-judicial functions performed in South Africa today and briefly considers recent legislative amendments that have implications for the performance of non-judicial functions in future.

The performance of non-judicial functions before 1994

'Over the past approximately 150 years there has never been a time when judges confined themselves to the functions of a judge.'[8] So said Coetzee AJ in the court *a quo* in the *Heath* case, the matter in which the Constitutional Court subsequently gave its seminal decision on the constitutional propriety of non-judicial activity.[9] Coetzee AJ elaborated on his statement by discussing the history of appointing judges to do extra-judicial work in South Africa, and made reference also to criticisms of the practice in Australia, the United Kingdom and the United States.[10]

The South African history is a rich one. In a punctiliously detailed article published in 1980, Professor Ellison Kahn indicates that judges

[4] (1995) 184 CLR 348. [5] (1996) 189 CLR 1 ('*Wilson*'). [6] 488 US 361 (1989).

[7] Ackermann J in *De Lange* v. *Smuts NO* 1998 (3) SA 785, CC, at para. [24].

[8] *South African Association of Personal Injury Lawyers* v. *Heath* 2000 (10) BCLR 1131, T ('*Heath a quo*') at 1154B.

[9] *South African Association of Personal Injury Lawyers* v. *Heath* 2001 (1) SA 883, CC ('*Heath*').

[10] *Heath a quo* 2000 (10) BCLR 1131, T, at 1155.

had since Union in 1910 played a significant role in the delimitation of electoral constituencies – an activity with very obvious political ramifications – and in conducting a great variety of commissions of inquiry.[11] As Kahn sees it,[12] the standing of judges, their integrity and their reputation for impartiality and objectivity was what made them so desirable in such roles. That was certainly the line taken by the white minority government, and it was no doubt true in many instances. What cannot be ignored, however, is that during the apartheid era the government found it expedient to use judges in such extra-judicial roles, either because it could rely on the judge in question to take the pro-executive view or, more broadly, because of the general legitimising effect of having a judge at the helm of any enterprise.[13]

Two illustrations will suffice. In a well-known piece from 1987 Cameron refers to the frequently held suspicion that commissioners were selected to make findings and recommendations to suit the executive, and he identifies a 'flagrant instance' of this in the appointment of the Munnik Commission under the chairmanship of the then Judge President of the Cape.[14] In a study from the same era Suttner explores the broader ideological explanation.[15] He suggests, for instance, that the opening of the first meeting of the South African Indian Council by the Acting Judge President of Natal in 1981 was an attempt to accord legitimacy to a body that was spurned by the Indian population and whose elections had been boycotted by an overwhelming percentage of voters.[16] In relation to so-called judicial inquiries, however, Suttner concedes that sometimes black South Africans – victims of the apartheid order – themselves called for such inquiries; and he concludes that inquiries by a judge may have enjoyed 'marginally greater respect from all sections of the population' than non-judicial ones.[17]

[11] E. Kahn, 'Extra-Judicial Activities of Judges' 1980 *De Jure* 188 at 200ff. See also A. J. Middleton, 'Notes on the Nature and Conduct of Commissions of Inquiry: South Africa' (1986) 19 *Comparative and International Law Quarterly* 252.

[12] Kahn, 'Extra-Judicial Activities of Judges', p. 213.

[13] See L. Boulle, B. Harris and C. Hoexter, *Constitutional and Administrative Law: Basic Principles* (Cape Town: Juta, 1989), p. 207.

[14] E. Cameron, 'Nude Monarchy: The Case of South Africa's Judges' (1987) 3 *South African Journal on Human Rights* 338 at 342, referring to the 1987 Commission of Inquiry into Certain Advertisements.

[15] R. Suttner, 'The Ideological Role of the Judiciary' (1984) 13 *Philosophical Papers* 28 at 40ff.

[16] Suttner, 'The Ideological Role of the Judiciary', p. 42.

[17] Suttner, 'The Ideological Role of the Judiciary', p. 41.

'Judicial inquiries' were certainly in great demand. In the court *a quo* in *Heath*, and relying largely on Kahn as his authority, Coetzee AJ recorded that of the approximately four hundred commissions of inquiry appointed between 1910 and 1980, about ninety had been chaired by a judge.[18] Such inquiries had involved judges in matters ranging from the emoluments of Members of Parliament to security legislation and from civil aviation to secret organisations,[19] and some had been very protracted affairs.[20] A number of commissions had brought notoriety to the judges concerned. One in particular had led to the resignation from the bench of its head and sole member, not to mention the resignation of the then Prime Minister;[21] and a subsequent Commission of Inquiry into Alleged Irregularities in the Former Department of Information had involved its members in litigation to interdict newspapers from publishing details of its report.[22]

As also noted by Coetzee AJ, judges had sometimes been appointed to posts that 'involved them in acrimonious debate concerning public issues' – a prime example being the appointment of Judge Marthinus Steyn as Administrator-General of South West Africa/Namibia, where he was expected to set the scene for free national elections, and where he subsequently became deeply embroiled in the politics of the territory.[23]

The pre-democratic courts seemed for the most part to accept these sorts of activities as a natural and unobjectionable extension of core judicial functions, and (apart from the more cynical views already outlined) criticism of such practices seems to have been scant. However, there was clearly some awareness of the dangers of judicial engagement in extraneous work. Kahn recommended in 1980 that 'in principle' such

18 *Heath a quo* 2000 (10) BCLR 1131, T, at 1153B.

19 *Heath a quo* 2000 (10) BCLR 1131, T, at 1153C–E.

20 *Heath a quo* 2000 (10) BCLR 1131, T, at 1154D–F.

21 In his 1978 inquiry into the evasion of exchange control regulations, Judge Anton Mostert famously incurred the wrath of the government by divulging evidence to the press of wrongdoing in the former Department of Information and by announcing that the commission would in future hear evidence in public. The commission was immediately rescinded and a new one appointed. The 'Information Scandal' ultimately led to the resignation of the then Prime Minister, Mr B. J. Vorster. See further H. G. Rudolph, 'Constitutional and Administrative Law' 1978 *Annual Survey of South African Law* 1 at 23–6 and 1979 *Annual Survey of South African Law* 1 at 14–15 and 17–19.

22 *Erasmus NO* v. *SA Associated Newspapers Ltd* 1979 (3) SA 447, W and *Smalberger* v. *Cape Times Ltd* 1979 (3) SA 457, C.

23 *Heath a quo* 2000 (10) BCLR 1131, T, at 1153E–G. The actions of the Administrator-General included the performance of wide-ranging legislative and executive functions: see the vivid description by Kahn, 'Extra-Judicial Activities of Judges', pp. 189ff.

work should not be undertaken by members of the judiciary, and added that 'the more and the longer they do it, the less they will be considered suitable to do so'.[24] A year later the controversial Rabie Commission into security legislation – whose chair became Chief Justice in 1982 – contributed to general cognisance of the problematic nature of judicial involvement in commissions. Furthermore, more than one pre-1994 court found it necessary to point out that what was popularly referred to as a 'judicial' commission of inquiry was no such thing: the commission could not be equated with a court of law, its chairperson derived no power from his or her judicial office and the matter being inquired into was not *sub judice*.[25]

The courts issued warnings about other non-judicial activities as well. In *Publications Control Board* v. *William Heinemann Ltd* a judge of appeal registered a protest against the performance of administrative work by judges.[26] In *S* v. *Mongale*, in the context of a trap set by a licensing officer who happened also to be a senior magistrate, the court pointed out that 'should magistrates be allowed to investigate crimes themselves, the independence of our courts of justice would soon suffer adverse effects and the independence and impartiality of magistrates would soon be questioned'.[27] And in two cases of illegal immigration in which a repatriation order had been incorporated into the sentence handed down by the magistrate, it was held on review that the magistrate could not combine his functions as judicial officer with his functions as passport control officer.[28]

The post-1994 era

South Africa became a constitutional democracy on 27 April 1994, the date on which the interim Constitution came into operation.[29] A few years later that Constitution gave way to its successor, the 1996 or 'final' Constitution. Today, in this very different constitutional setting, South

[24] Kahn, 'Extra-Judicial Activities of Judges', pp. 215–16, and for a similar view see Boulle, Harris and Hoexter, *Constitutional and Administrative Law*, p. 207.

[25] *Erasmus NO* v. *SA Associated Newspapers Ltd* 1979 (3) SA 447, W, at 456C–F; *S* v. *Sparks NO* 1980 (3) SA 952, T, at 956 and 960.

[26] 1965 (4) SA 137, A, at 156G–H.

[27] 1979 (3) SA 669, B, at 672F–G, as translated by E. Cameron and D. van Zyl Smit, 'The Administration of Justice, Law Reform and Jurisprudence' 1979 *Annual Survey of South African Law* 511 at 514.

[28] *S* v. *Chicaca* 1980 (2) SA 784, T and *S* v. *Noka* 1980 (4) SA 384, T.

[29] Constitution of the Republic of South Africa, Act 200 of 1993 ('interim Constitution').

African judges and magistrates continue to perform a variety of non-judicial functions.[30] As already noted, however, the post-1994 conception of the separation of powers and independence of the judiciary has important implications for the performance by judges of functions that are associated with the other branches.

The separation of powers and judicial independence

The doctrine of separation of powers seeks to divide public power between the branches of state in order to prevent its accumulation in any one branch. Although not explicitly included in the text of the interim Constitution, the doctrine was specifically named in the set of constitutional principles[31] laid down to guide the drafting of the 1996 Constitution by a Constitutional Assembly. Constitutional Principle VI stated: 'There shall be a separation of powers between the legislature, executive and judiciary, with appropriate checks and balances to ensure accountability, responsiveness and openness.'

Though the phrase 'separation of powers' was again absent from the text of the 1996 Constitution, the Constitutional Court pronounced itself satisfied in the *First Certification* case that Constitutional Principle VI had been given effect to by the Constitution as a whole.[32] While the Constitution did not always maintain a rigid separation, particularly in that members of the executive could continue to be members of the legislature at all three levels of government, the court did not read Constitutional Principle VI as requiring a strict model such as that found in the United States or the Netherlands. It concluded that 'the model adopted reflects the historical circumstances of our constitutional development'.[33]

Since then, and notwithstanding the absence of 'bright lines' separating the roles of the three branches,[34] the court has taken various opportunities to pronounce on the distinctive institutional character or pre-eminent domain[35] of each of them; and it has not been slow to prevent intrusions

[30] See 'Non-judicial functions', below. [31] Schedule 4 to the interim Constitution.

[32] *Ex p. Chairperson of the Constitutional Assembly; In re Certification of the Constitution of the Republic of South Africa, 1996* 1996 (4) SA 744, CC ('*First Certification* case') at paras. [106]–[113].

[33] *First Certification* case 1996 (4) SA 744, CC, at para. [112].

[34] *Minister of Health* v. *Treatment Action Campaign (No. 2)* 2002 (5) SA 721, CC, at para. [98].

[35] See S. Seedorf and S. Sibanda, 'Separation of Powers', in S. Woolman *et al.* (eds.), *Constitutional Law of South Africa*, 2nd edn. (Cape Town: Juta, Original Service 2006–8), pp. 12-i, 12–39ff.

into the core functions of any branch. In relation to the judiciary in particular, it has recognised a pre-eminent function in the protection of fundamental freedoms;[36] and it has held that the power to commit a recalcitrant witness to prison was 'within the very heartland of the judicial power' and could not be exercised by an official in the public service.[37] Conversely, it has found that punishment is not the exclusive preserve of the judiciary;[38] and, where a court's award of costs was motivated by the desire to teach municipal councillors a lesson, it described the costs order as 'a dangerous intrusion into the legislative and executive domain'.[39]

Underpinned by the separation of powers, the principle of judicial independence is explicitly upheld in s. 165 of the Constitution. Section 165(2) states that 'the courts are independent and subject only to the Constitution'; s. 165(3) prohibits interference with the functioning of the courts; and s. 165(4) places a duty on all organs of state to help ensure their 'independence, impartiality, dignity, accessibility and effectiveness'. As the Constitutional Court has acknowledged, judicial independence has not only an individual but also an institutional aspect:[40] it is essential that the judiciary should function independently of the legislature and the executive.[41] This applies equally to magistrates, though legislative protection of judicial independence may legitimately vary between higher and lower courts.[42]

In the *Heath* case the Constitutional Court considered the implications of these fundamental principles for non-judicial activity and established a test of incompatibility with judicial office.

Heath *and the incompatibility test*

The *Heath* case arose out of the appointment of the first respondent, a High Court judge, as head of a Special Investigating Unit (SIU), the second respondent. The SIU had been established in 1997 under the

36 *Ferreira* v. *Levin NO* 1996 (1) SA 984, CC, at para. [183].

37 *De Lange* v. *Smuts NO* 1998 (3) SA 785, CC, at para. [61].

38 *S* v. *Dodo* 2001 (3) SA 382, CC, at para. [22].

39 *Swartbooi* v. *Brink (2)* 2003 (5) BCLR 502, CC, at para. [25]. For a detailed survey of the case law in respect of all three branches, see Seedorf and Sibanda, 'Separation of Powers', in Woolman *et al.* (eds.), *Constitutional Law of South Africa*.

40 *De Lange* v. *Smuts NO*, 1998 (3) SA 785, CC, at para [159] in the judgment of O'Regan J, with reference to the judgment of Le Dain J in *Valente* v. *R* (1986) 24 DLR (4th) 161 at 171, SCC; and see also *Van Rooyen* v. *The State* 2002 (5) SA 246, CC, at paras. [19] *et seq.*

41 *First Certification* case 1996 (4) SA 744, CC, at para. [123].

42 *Van Rooyen* v. *The State*, 2002 (5) SA 246, CC, at para. [22]; *Travers* v. *National Director of Public Prosecutions* 2007 (3) SA 242, T, at para. [30].

Special Investigating Units and Special Tribunals Act 74 of 1996, and s. 3(1) of this statute demanded the appointment of a judge or acting judge as head of the SIU. The SIU had extensive powers to investigate allegations of maladministration, corruption or improper conduct connected with the state or involving public money. One might add that the agency seemed to be doing its job very effectively: at the time of the litigation, the court was told, the SIU was engaged in investigations into about one hundred organs of state touching on 221,580 cases and involving approximately R3 billion all told.[43] Nevertheless, the constitutionality of Judge Heath's appointment and of s. 3(1) of the Act (among other provisions) was challenged by the appellant, the South African Association of Personal Injury Lawyers, when it emerged that some of its members were to be investigated for fraud in their handling of claims against the state's Road Accident Fund.

The challenge was unsuccessful in the court *a quo*. For Coetzee AJ, important factors were the 'fixed practice' of appointing judges to head such inquiries and that Judge Heath had been appointed in his personal capacity.[44] Here the judge was mindful perhaps of the *persona designata* doctrine relied on in some jurisdictions which attempts to distinguish between the personal and official capacity of judges. As to the separation of powers, however, Coetzee AJ doubted the relevance of foreign jurisprudence in view of the flexibility of the South African conception of the doctrine; and he was not persuaded that s. 3(1) could properly be set aside on the basis of a principle left unexpressed in the text of the Constitution.[45]

The Constitutional Court took a different view and was quite willing to draw on prominent foreign authority in conveying it, particularly *Mistretta* v. *United States*,[46] *Grollo* v. *Palmer*[47] and *Wilson* v. *Minister for Aboriginal and Torres Strait Islander Affairs*.[48] Interestingly, it did so without referring to the doctrine of *persona designata*, whose artificial and problematic nature inspired the gloss concerning incompatibility in *Grollo* and later in *Wilson*.[49] Giving judgment for the court, Chaskalson P accepted that the South African conception of the separation of powers is not as strict as the American version and is closer to the Australian

43 *Heath* 2001 (1) SA 883, CC, at para. [17].

44 *Heath a quo* 2000 (10) BCLR 1131, T, at 1156A and 1159E–F.

45 *Heath a quo* 2000 (10) BCLR 1131, T, at 1159H–60B.

46 *Mistretta* v. *United States* 488 US 361 (1989).

47 *Grollo* v. *Palmer* (1995) 184 CLR 348. 48 *Wilson* (1996) 189 CLR 1.

49 See D. Meyerson, 'Judicial Independence in Australia and South Africa: Comparative Lessons', *Maquarie Law Working Paper Series* WP 2007–9 (2007) 2.

model.[50] Nevertheless, failure to uphold this constitutionally mandated separation would undermine the role of the courts 'as an independent arbiter of issues involving the division of power between the various spheres of government, and the legality of legislative and executive action'.[51] Certain functions were so far removed from the judicial function or so central to the mission of the other two branches that judges could not be allowed to perform them. In the words of Chaskalson P:

> Ultimately the question is one calling for a judgment to be made as to whether or not the functions that the Judge is expected to perform are incompatible with judicial office and, if they are, whether there are countervailing factors that suggest that the performance of such functions by a Judge will not be harmful to the institution of the Judiciary, or materially breach the line that has to be kept between the Judiciary and the other branches of government in order to maintain the independence of the Judiciary.[52]

The court thought it undesirable to lay down rigid tests, and regarded incompatibility as something best decided on a case-by-case basis.[53] In this regard, it accepted the relevance of various factors gleaned from the foreign authorities and proposed by counsel for the appellant. Relevant considerations included asking whether the performance of the function:

(a) is more usual or appropriate to another branch of government;
(b) is subject to executive control or direction;
(c) requires the judge to exercise a discretion and make decisions on the grounds of policy rather than law;
(d) creates the risk of judicial entanglement in matters of political controversy;
(e) involves the judge in the process of law enforcement;
(f) will occupy the judge to such an extent that he or she is no longer able to perform his or her normal judicial functions.[54]

Applying these factors, the court concluded that the appointment in this instance went beyond what was permissible. The essential functions required of the head of the SIU included intrusive investigations and litigation on behalf of the state in order to recover money, actions that were necessarily partisan[55] and, in this case, inextricably

[50] *Heath* 2001 (1) SA 883, CC, at para. [23]. [51] *Heath* 2001 (1) SA 883, CC, at para. [26].
[52] *Heath* 2001 (1) SA 883, CC, at para. [31]. [53] *Heath* 2001 (1) SA 883, CC, at para. [31].
[54] *Heath* 2001 (1) SA 883, CC, at para. [29], with reference to *Mistretta* v. *United States* 488 US 361 (1989), *Grollo* v. *Palmer* (1995) 184 CLR 348 and *Wilson* (1996) 189 CLR 1.
[55] *Heath* 2001 (1) SA 883, CC, at para. [40].

linked.[56] These activities were close to the 'heartland' of executive power[57] – they were functions usually performed by the police, the National Prosecuting Authority or the State Attorney – and they were inconsistent with judicial functions as ordinarily understood in South Africa.[58] The court took into account, too, the indefinite nature of the appointment. Judge Heath had already been unable to perform his normal judicial duties for more than three years, and he might never return to them.[59]

The court accordingly declared invalid s. 3(1) of the Act and the proclamation in which Judge Heath was appointed to head the SIU.[60] To hold otherwise would undermine the separation of powers and the independence of the judiciary. The danger was that it would open the way for judges to be appointed for indefinite terms to other executive posts. If this happened, the public might come to see the judiciary as 'functionally associated' with the executive, and thus unable independently to control the power of the executive.[61]

The judgment in *Heath* has been criticised both for being too strict and not strict enough. In the first camp, Sarkin takes a pragmatic line in arguing that the judgment retards the war on crime and sends out the message that 'crime does pay'.[62] Currie and De Waal take issue with what they regard as a rigid and formalistic approach to the separation of powers.[63] They find it disappointing that the doctrine was used in *Heath* so as to disqualify a judge from investigating both public and private corruption, particularly since there was no direct allegation before the court of an over-concentration of judicial and executive powers in the head of the SIU.[64] As these authors see it, the problem in *Heath* was purely (and 'merely') one of independence.[65]

[56] *Heath* 2001 (1) SA 883, CC, at paras. [47]–[48] (in response to an argument that the role of the SIU's head as litigator could be separated from that of investigator).

[57] *Heath* 2001 (1) SA 883, CC, at para. [24].

[58] *Heath* 2001 (1) SA 883, CC, at para. [38].

[59] *Heath* 2001 (1) SA 883, CC, at paras. [41]–[43].

[60] *Heath* 2001 (1) SA 883, CC, at para. [46]. The declaration was suspended to allow time for a new head to be appointed.

[61] *Heath* 2001 (1) SA 883, CC, at para. [46].

[62] J. Sarkin, 'Evaluating the Constitutional Court's Decision in *South African Association of Personal Injury Lawyers* v. *Heath & Others* in the Context of Crime and Corruption in South Africa' (2001) 118 *South African Law Journal* 747 at 770.

[63] I. Currie and J. de Waal (contributing eds.), *The New Constitutional and Administrative Law, Vol. I: Constitutional Law* (Cape Town: Juta, 2001), pp. 110–12.

[64] Currie and de Waal (contributing eds.), *The New Constitutional and Administrative Law*, p. 112.

[65] Currie and de Waal (contributing eds.), *The New Constitutional and Administrative Law*, p. 112.

Meyerson, by contrast, is in favour of a blanket rule confining judges to judicial functions, and doubts whether the South African test and its Australian counterpart offer sufficient protection for the institutional integrity of the judiciary.[66] She argues with reference to Australian cases that the test is uncertain and that its results are unpredictable.[67] Furthermore, she sees the case-by-case approach as thoroughly misguided: 'Judged on a case-by-case basis, the benefits of conferring non-judicial functions on judges will be concrete and immediate, whereas the impact on the institutional integrity of the courts will necessarily be remote, speculative and difficult to quantify.'[68] For this reason, the long-term effects of conferring non-judicial functions on judges are likely to be underestimated, and the incompatibility test is likely to lead to 'incremental erosion' of the institutional integrity of the judiciary: an effect which will not become apparent until it is too late.[69]

Meyerson would be heartened by the views expressed by Swain J in *City of Cape Town* v. *Premier, Western Cape*,[70] a case in which the *Heath* test was applied to a commission of inquiry headed by a High Court judge – and a particularly vivid illustration of the pitfalls of such an appointment. The context was a 'political battle'[71] between the Democratic Alliance (DA) and the African National Congress (ANC) for control of the city of Cape Town, and the facts were worthy of a political soap opera. The city council was controlled by a DA-led coalition and its executive mayor was the leader of the DA, but the province was controlled by the ANC. A councillor was suspected of bribing others to cross the floor, thereby seeking to topple the coalition unlawfully. The council had resolved to investigate the councillor concerned and had hired a firm of private investigators to do so. The provincial Premier's response was to establish the Erasmus Commission to investigate the legality of the council's conduct. The

[66] Meyerson, 'Judicial Independence in Australia and South Africa: Comparative Lessons', p. 10. See also D. Meyerson, 'Extra-Judicial Service on the Part of Judges: Constitutional Impediments in Australia and South Africa' (2003) 3 *Oxford University Commonwealth Law Journal* 181.

[67] She points out, for instance, that there were strong dissenting judgments both in *Grollo* v. *Palmer* and in *Wilson*. See Meyerson, 'Judicial Independence in Australia and South Africa: Comparative Lessons', p. 8.

[68] Meyerson, 'Judicial Independence in Australia and South Africa: Comparative Lessons', p. 10.

[69] Meyerson, 'Judicial Independence in Australia and South Africa: Comparative Lessons', p. 10.

[70] 2008 (6) SA 345, C ('*City of Cape Town*'). [71] 2008 (6) SA 345, C, at para. [1].

appointment of the commission[72] and its head was challenged by the council on a number of grounds, including incompatibility.

Swain J (Nicholson J concurring) found that the Premier had established the commission with the ulterior motive of embarrassing his political opponents, and that he had appointed a judge to chair it partly in order to 'cloak his ulterior motive with the neutral colours of the judicial office'.[73] While careful to absolve Judge Erasmus of being a party to such conduct, the court saw the case as a stark illustration of the care to be exercised by any judge in deciding whether to accept an appointment at the behest of a member of the executive.[74] It went on to find that the appointment was incompatible with judicial office. First, the overtly political subject matter of the commission carried a risk of judicial entanglement in political controversy.[75] Second, a judge had been furnished with prosecutorial powers and a member of the executive had been able to 'usurp investigative and prosecutorial powers through his tool, the judge-led commission'.[76] To make matters worse, the judge had apparently been hand-picked by the Premier (rather than being chosen by the Judge President); and the commission had initially conducted its sittings in a courtroom of the Cape High Court. As Swain J noted, in the eyes of the public this served further to blur any distinction between the judge as such and the judge as commissioner.[77]

While in *Heath* the Constitutional Court had countenanced the idea of judges presiding over commissions of inquiry, Swain J was less sanguine:

> With great respect to the views of the Constitutional Court, it seems to me that at this early stage of our fledgling democracy, and with the vital object of preserving public confidence in the independence of the judiciary, active judges should, as a matter of principle, not chair commissions of inquiry. This would eliminate the risk of judges becoming embroiled in disputes such as the present and the need to define in

[72] The Premier in fact appointed two consecutive Erasmus commissions, one in December 2007 and the second in March 2008, and both appointments were challenged together with a decision of the provincial MEC to establish an investigation under s. 106(1)(b) of the Municipal Systems Act 32 of 2000. See *City of Cape Town* 2008 (6) SA 345, C, at paras. [5]–[7].

[73] *City of Cape Town* 2008 (6) SA 345, C, at para. [176], referring to the words of Kirby J in *Wilson* (1996) 189 CLR 1.

[74] *City of Cape Town* 2008 (6) SA 345, C, at para. [177.2].

[75] *City of Cape Town* 2008 (6) SA 345, C, at para. [203].

[76] *City of Cape Town* 2008 (6) SA 345, C, at para. [212].

[77] *City of Cape Town* 2008 (6) SA 345, C, at para. [216].

> what circumstances a judge could 'appropriately' chair a commission of inquiry.[78]

Painful examples such as this instance and the recent case of *Godongwana* v. *Pillay*[79] strengthen the argument for a stricter approach to 'judicial commissions', if not other non-judicial activities. As has often been said, judges do not have a monopoly on qualities such as integrity and the ability to sift facts; and where legal training is thought necessary, senior legal practitioners could be called upon to head governmental inquiries. While the Constitution empowers the President and provincial Premiers to appoint commissions of inquiry, it does not necessarily anticipate the involvement of judges in such inquiries.[80] Furthermore, there are a number of alternatives in the form of constitutionally created organs such as the Public Protector, the Auditor-General and the Human Rights Commission, which have jurisdiction to investigate abuses of various kinds.[81]

Non-judicial functions and activities today and in future

In *Heath* the Constitutional Court recognised that the Constitution itself lays down a number of non-curial functions for the Chief Justice and other judges.[82] It accepted, too, that it is possible for judges to head commissions of inquiry and to issue search warrants without infringing the separation of powers, though 'much may depend on the subject-matter of the commission and the legislation' in question.[83] In practice, South African judges (and magistrates) continue to perform a range of non-judicial functions, many of them envisaged in the Constitution or other legislation; and calls for judicially led inquiries remain frequent.[84]

78 *City of Cape Town* 2008 (6) SA 345, C, at para. [187].

79 [2009] ZAECGHC 29 (18 May 2009). The case concerned a commission appointed by the Premier of the Eastern Cape to inquire into the finances of the provincial administration. The report, which made damaging allegations of financial impropriety and fraud, was set aside by Chetty J because the commission had 'simply ignored' the requirements of procedural fairness (para. [18]). It was also alleged that the Premier had published the report with the ulterior motive of embarrassing her political opponents – a claim which the court found it unnecessary to pursue.

80 Sections 84(2)(f) and 127(2)(e).

81 These and other 'state institutions supporting constitutional democracy' are described in Chapter 9 of the Constitution.

82 *Heath* 2001 (1) SA 883, CC, at para. [32].

83 2001 (1) SA 883, CC, at para. [34].

84 E.g., various acts of xenophobic and other violence that took place in May 2008 resulted in a call for an investigation by 'an independent expert commission, headed by a respected, senior judge': Media Release 'Call for a Commission of Inquiry into 2008 Violence', available at: www.cde.org.za, accessed 11 February 2010.

Some non-judicial activities will, however, be affected by recent amendments to the Judicial Service Commission Act 9 of 1994.

Non-judicial functions and activities today

The Constitution makes provision for judicial representation on the Judicial Service Commission[85] – a state of affairs regarded as unobjectionable in *Heath*.[86] In terms of other constitutional provisions canvassed in that case, the Chief Justice presides over the election of the country's President[87] and designates the judges who preside over the election of provincial Premiers;[88] and he presides over the election of the Speaker of the National Assembly or designates another judge to do so.[89] The Chief Justice determines the timing of elections if a vacancy arises in the office of President[90] or Premier.[91] He also fixes the time of the first sitting of the National Assembly,[92] while judges designated by him perform this function in respect of sittings of provincial legislatures[93] and preside over the election of provincial Speakers.[94]

Judges commonly head organisations such as the Legal Aid Board, the Rules Board and the Inspectorate of Prisons. Seedorf and Sibanda suggest that the functions of these bodies are all 'at least slightly' legislative or executive in nature, but sufficiently close to the heartland of the judicial function to be acceptable.[95] Less officially, judges are in demand as members of the councils of universities, as chairs of such councils and as university Chancellors; and, of course, as speakers at public and private events. It is also common for judges to write books and articles, often but not always of a legal nature.[96]

As regards functions of an administrative nature, the Constitutional Court acknowledged in the *SARFU* case that 'judicial officers may, from time to time, carry out administrative tasks', but warned that the performance of such tasks might sometimes infringe the separation of powers.[97] In

[85] Constitution, s. 178. The Judicial Service Commission is discussed more fully by H. Corder in Chapter 5 of this volume.
[86] *Heath* 2001 (1) SA 883, CC, at para. [32]. [87] Constitution, s. 86(2).
[88] Constitution, s. 128(2). [89] Constitution, s. 52(2). [90] Constitution, s. 86(3).
[91] Constitution, s. 128(3). [92] Constitution, s. 51(1). [93] Constitution, s. 110(1).
[94] Constitution, s. 111(2).
[95] Seedorf and Sibanda, 'Separation of Powers', in Woolman *et al.* (eds.), *Constitutional Law of South Africa*, pp. 12–45.
[96] See I. Currie, Chapter 11, this volume.
[97] *President of the Republic of South Africa* v. *South African Rugby Football Union* 2000 (1) SA 1, CC, at para. [141].

a case concerning the process of replacing death sentences with constitutionally appropriate sentences, the court reiterated that there is no absolute bar to judges performing administrative tasks as long as these are compatible with judicial office.[98] In this case it found, however, that the task of assessing a record to determine an appropriate sentence was 'peculiarly judicial in nature'.[99] While the framework for replacing sentences certainly included administrative elements, the performance of this particular task could not be regarded as 'breach[ing] the line that needs to be maintained between the Judiciary and the other branches of government'.[100]

Perhaps the most common administrative function exercised by judicial officers in South Africa is issuing warrants for search and seizure – though it is not clear whether this amounts to 'administrative action' as narrowly defined in s. 1 of the Promotion of Administrative Justice Act 3 of 2000 (PAJA).[101] Judges are empowered to issue search warrants under a number of statutes, including s. 29 of the National Prosecuting Authority Act 32 of 1998, s. 74 of the Income Tax Act 58 of 1962 and s. 57 of the Value-Added Tax Act 89 of 1991. (In terms of the last two statutes, judges are also required to designate officers to preside at inquiries under those sections.) Another example is the issuing of a letter of request for assistance in a criminal matter. A High Court has regarded this as an administrative function, but, again, without applying the detailed definition of administrative action in the PAJA.[102]

In South Africa, magistrates have always performed a wide range of administrative functions from licensing to the administration of estates, 'moving readily and frequently from the bench to the bureaucracy and back'.[103] The reason is largely historical, for in the pre-democratic era magistrates were civil servants employed by the Department of Justice. In *Van Rooyen* v. *The State* the Constitutional Court struck down a provision enabling the Minister of Justice to assign administrative duties

98 *Sibiya* v. *Director of Public Prosecutions, Johannesburg* 2005 (5) SA 315, CC.

99 *Sibiya* v. *Director of Public Prosecutions, Johannesburg* 2005 (5) SA 315, CC, at para. [39].

100 *Sibiya* v. *Director of Public Prosecutions, Johannesburg* 2005 (5) SA 315, CC, at paras. [38] and [39].

101 In *Pretoria Portland Cement* 2003 (2) SA 385, SCA, para. [41] the Supreme Court of Appeal accepted for argument's sake that a judge acted administratively when issuing a warrant under the Competition Act 89 of 1993. In the court below, however, Roux J had regarded this as a judicial and not an administrative function (2003 (2) SA 381, T, at 384C–D).

102 *Kolbatschenko* v. *King NO* 2001 (4) SA 336, C, at 356A–B.

103 Didcott J in *De Lange* v. *Smuts NO* 1998 (3) SA 785, CC, at para. [124].

to magistrates in addition to those ordinarily vested in them,[104] and it issued a warning:

> Ideally, magistrates should not be required to perform administrative duties unrelated to their functions as judicial officers. To require them to do so may make them answerable to the Executive and, if that happens, the separation of powers that should exist between the Executive and Judiciary would be blurred.[105]

However, the court also accepted that it might be practically necessary at present to confer such duties on magistrates.[106] As commentators have suggested, concerns about disruption tend to reduce the likelihood that the performance of existing administrative functions will be found unconstitutional.[107]

The role given to magistrates in extradition proceedings has also been challenged in court. In the decision whether to issue a warrant of arrest, s. 10(2) of the Extradition Act 67 of 1962 requires a magistrate to accept a certificate from a foreign prosecuting authority as conclusive proof of sufficient evidence to warrant the prosecution of the person concerned. In *Geuking* v. *President of the Republic of South Africa* the Constitutional Court rejected an argument that this provision was inconsistent with judicial independence in that it allowed a foreign prosecutor to dictate the magistrate's decision.[108] The court distinguished between 'ordinary domestic proceedings' and extradition proceedings, which are *sui generis* and do not involve the determination of guilt or innocence; and it reasoned that since the certificate was conclusive only with regard to a question of foreign law, it did not detract from the independence of the judiciary or the separation of powers.[109]

The Judicial Service Commission Amendment Act

The Judicial Service Commission Amendment Act 20 of 2008, which came into force on 1 June 2010, has significant implications for the engagement of judges, and even retired judges, in extra-judicial activities. As a result of it the principal statute, the Judicial Service

[104] *Van Rooyen* v. *The State* 2002 (5) SA 246, CC, at para. [230].
[105] *Van Rooyen* v. *The State* 2002 (5) SA 246, CC, at para. [231].
[106] *Van Rooyen* v. *The State* 2002 (5) SA 246, CC, at para. [234].
[107] I. Currie and J. de Waal, *The Bill of Rights Handbook*, 5th edn. (Cape Town: Juta, 2005), p. 730.
[108] 2003 (3) SA 34, CC. [109] 2003 (3) SA 34, CC, at para. [50].

Commission Act 9 of 1994, now includes a chapter on judicial conduct and accountability. A Judicial Conduct Committee is established to deal with various sorts of complaints against judges – an important piece of reform that resolves uncertainty about the jurisdiction of the Judicial Service Commission over transgressions falling short of impeachable conduct.[110] Section 13 of the principal Act deals with the creation and maintenance of a Register of Judges' Registrable Interests, though the types of interests envisaged and other details remain to be prescribed in regulations. Furthermore, s. 12 envisages a Code of Judicial Conduct which is to be compiled by the Chief Justice in consultation with the Minister of Justice. This will be South Africa's first official code for judges, and will replace the informal 'Guidelines for Judges' which were produced a decade ago by a committee of senior judges.[111]

The thirty-seven provisions of these Guidelines addressed not only judicial but also non-judicial activities in some detail. As to the latter, advice was offered on a wide range of matters including, for instance, the undesirability of accepting gifts that might be perceived as intended to influence a judge; of belonging to a political party or secret organisation; and of commenting on the merits of cases before the courts. In relation to appointments to commissions and the like, Guideline 27 gave the following advice:

> While judges should be available to use their judicial skill and impartiality to further the public interest, they should remain mindful of the separation of powers and the independence of the judiciary when considering a request to perform non-judicial functions for or on behalf of the State. A judge should not accept an appointment that is likely to affect or be seen to affect the independence of the judiciary, or which could undermine the separation of powers.

The new Code of Judicial Conduct is thought likely to repeat many of the Guidelines for Judges.[112] However, in one important respect the amended legislation introduces new stringency. Previously a judge was not permitted, *without the consent of the Minister of Justice*, to hold or perform any other office of profit or receive remuneration other than his

[110] See further H. Corder, Chapter 5, this volume.

[111] See 'Proposals for a Mechanism for Dealing with Complaints Against Judges, and for a Code of Ethics for Judges – A Report of a Committee Chaired by Mr Justice L Harms' (2000) 117 *South African Law Journal* 377 at 406 ('Guidelines').

[112] See, e.g., S. Seedat, 'Setting the Scene', a paper from a Round Table on Judicial Ethics in South Africa held in Cape Town in June 2009, p. 2.

or her salary and any allowances payable to him or her as a judge.[113] In s. 11(1) of the amended Judicial Service Commission Act this prohibition is made almost absolute in respect of a judge performing active service. The only proviso is that a judge may, with the written consent of the Minister of Justice acting in consultation with the Chief Justice, receive royalties for 'legal books written or edited by that judge'.[114]

Remarkably, the legislation goes on to extend the previous prohibition to retired judges. In accordance with the philosophy that a judge is a 'judge for life',[115] those who have been discharged from active service may hold or perform an office of profit only with the written consent of the minister acting after consultation with the Chief Justice.[116] Such consent may be given only if the minister is satisfied that granting it will not have certain deleterious effects – for instance, that it will not adversely affect the administration of justice, undermine the 'judge for life' concept, be in conflict with the vocation of a judge or tarnish the reputation of the judiciary.[117]

It is worth noting that such consent may not be given where it would undermine 'any aspect of the administration of justice, especially the civil justice system'.[118] The apparent purpose of this is to prevent retired judges from acting as arbitrators. As one commentator indicated during the public hearings on the Amendment Bill, there are litigants who 'prefer to have their complex commercial disputes determined by seasoned retired judges or experienced senior counsel rather than recently

[113] Supreme Court Act 59 of 1959, s. 11; Judges' Remuneration and Conditions of Employment Act 47 of 2001, s. 2(6); and see item 25 of the Guidelines, above n. 111, p. 414. The most notorious instance involving the prohibition in recent years is the case of John Hlophe, Judge President of the Western Cape, who accepted regular payments from a company over a period of more than three years and, while receiving such payments, granted the same company permission to sue a fellow judge. In 2007, the Judicial Service Commission decided not to pursue an inquiry into the matter on the basis of insufficient evidence, and in doing so seemed to accept Judge Hlophe's explanation that he had oral permission from a former Minister of Justice, now deceased, to receive the payments. The decision attracted considerable criticism, however. See further H. Corder, Chapter 5, this volume.

[114] The narrow reference to 'legal books' is noteworthy: cf. the commentary on item 25 of the Guidelines, above n. 111, p. 414: 'Royalties and the like are not covered by the general prohibition nor is there any objection to judges writing or editing books or journals.'

[115] This view provided a reason in the last years of apartheid for improving judges' pension benefits, thus making judicial service more attractive financially to senior advocates.

[116] Section 11(2). [117] Section 11(3)(a). [118] Section 11(3)(a)(i).

appointed judges with little or no commercial law experience'[119] – a state of affairs that some attribute to racism.[120] The rather tortuous reasoning behind this particular provision seems to be that a diminished pool of trusted arbitrators will force litigants to rely on the courts. The constitutionality of this measure may be questioned, however, not least because the actions of retired judges must present less of a risk to the independence of the judiciary than those of sitting judges. The effectiveness of the measure is also doubtful. Offering aspirant and recently appointed judges thorough training would seem to be a better and more direct method of upholding the civil justice system.

[119] P. Hoffman SC, 'The Lot of Retired Judges', a submission on behalf of the Centre for Constitutional Rights regarding the Judicial Service Commission Amendment Bill. See the minutes of the Parliamentary Monitoring Group on the Bill, dated 31 March 2008, available at: www.pmg.org.za, accessed 7 February 2010.

[120] For instance (as Hoffman notes in his submission, 'The Lot of Retired Judges'), there was strong criticism of the increasing use of private arbitration in a controversial *Report on Racism in the Cape Provincial Division* prepared by Judge John Hlophe and circulated by him in 2005. The first two recommendations in the report were that 'Permission given to retired judges to sit as Arbitrators should be withdrawn with immediate effect' and that 'Legislative measures should be introduced to control abuse of the Arbitration process'. The report is discussed more fully in D. M. Davis, G. J. Marcus and J. E. Klaaren, 'The Administration of Justice' 2005 *Annual Survey of South African Law* 816 at 817ff.

24

Judges and non-judicial functions in the United Kingdom

ABIMBOLA A. OLOWOFOYEKU

> From Lord Denning on the Profumo scandal to Lord Franks on the Falklands war, from Sir Richard Scott on the sale of arms to Iraq to Sir Anthony Hammond on the Hinduja brothers and the Dome, judicial inquiries have never destroyed governments. The evidence they collect is immensely useful. Eight years before he tore into a Labour government for overthrowing the genocidal Iraqi tyrant, Robin Cook used the facts revealed by the Scott inquiry to tear into the Conservative government for arming the genocidal Iraqi tyrant. But the judges' punches are always pulled. In the case of the Scott report, no minister had to resign because Sir Richard presented a six-volume report that offered no damning conclusion – indeed, it had no conclusions whatsoever.[1]

The United Kingdom constitution has witnessed significant change in recent years. The tremendous pace of change is part of an effort to modernise the constitution, which has had a significant impact on the judiciary. New developments include the 'abolition' of the office of Lord Chancellor (followed by a modification of this office[2]), the establishment of the Judicial Appointments Commission, the opening up of some judicial appointments to public competition and the creation of the new Supreme Court for the United Kingdom.[3] These reforms serve to ensure better separation of powers and to safeguard the independence of the judiciary.

With all these reforms of the judiciary, it is reasonable to expect that some thought would have been given to the kinds of function that judges should not be performing. But this appears not to have happened. The judicial power of the state is now securely in the hands of the judiciary, and the role of the executive in matters such as sentencing is greatly

[1] N. Cohen, 'The Hutton Report – This was the Wrong Inquiry', *New Statesman*, 2 February 2004, available at: www.newstatesman.com/200402020003.htm.

[2] Constitutional Reform Act 2005. [3] Constitutional Reform Act 2005.

reduced. Government ministers no longer sit in any of the UK courts, and the highest court is no longer part of Parliament. With the increasing moves to separate and secure the judicial power from encroachments by the executive and legislature, it is ironic that the judiciary itself is still expected to operate in areas that would fall more readily within the province of the executive. In the United Kingdom, as in much of the Commonwealth, received wisdom suggests that judges are particularly well suited to certain non-judicial official activities. But how appropriate is this received wisdom? This chapter will address some difficult questions raised by serving judges performing non-judicial functions. Special attention will be given to judges conducting or chairing the commissions of inquiry that are often described as 'judicial inquiries' (referred to herein as 'public inquiries'). The term 'public' is employed here not to indicate that the inquiries are held in public, but to signify that they are set up by government ministers, supposedly for the public interest, or on behalf of the public or to inquire into an urgent matter of public concern. The impact of such activities on judicial independence will be examined. Public inquiries serve here as a convenient proxy for the kinds of official duties performed by judges that take them away from their normal judicial roles in the law courts. In this respect, 'public inquiry' is intended to denote those inquiries established by governments to investigate a major public crisis, scandal or disaster.[4]

Public inquiries are an increasingly common feature of modern life in the United Kingdom. They are firmly embedded in the nation's psyche as a desirable response to a major public crisis, disaster or scandal. Many are chaired by serving judges. Although 'no one has a right to a public inquiry' or 'to dictate an inquiry's terms of reference'[5] the frantic soul-searching that follows a crisis, scandal or disaster is almost invariably followed by calls from the press and opposition politicians for a 'judicial inquiry' into the event. While opposition politicians may be cynical in their motives for calling for an inquiry, it is not only politicians and the media that call for inquiries,[6] and these inquiries can serve a therapeutic purpose for society, as Steele thus explains:

[4] There are other kinds of inquiry (e.g., planning inquiries, inquiries by a committee of Privy Councillors and inquiries established to advise the government on some political policy matter). These are not the subject of the current discussion.

[5] Scott Baker J in *Howard* v. *Secretary of State for Health* [2002] EWHC 396 (Admin.) at [68].

[6] See, e.g., the Northern Ireland Human Rights Commission's press release of 14 April 2004, calling for 'international, independent, judicial inquiries to be held into the findings of the Cory Report and others of collusion occurring in the 1980s and 1990s between the security forces and Loyalist paramilitary organisations', available at: www.nihrc.org/

> The types of events which prompt public inquiries are by definition prone to provoking public anxiety. That anxiety can be significantly calmed by the knowledge that action is being taken to ensure that the causes are identified and that the same mistakes will not be repeated. Furthermore, individuals who suffer because of wrongful actions should in principle have a remedy, even if it is merely the publication of a report criticising those at fault. Finally, human progress is predicated upon learning from our mistakes. Unless errors are adequately analysed, lessons will not be learned.[7]

Thus, public inquiries can generally be a good thing. Steele says that the 'goals of scandal-control, blame-attrition and lesson-learning' served by public inquiries are worthwhile, and 'few would argue that major disasters are best left unexamined'.[8] The real question relates to who should undertake the examination. The nature of public inquiries is a significant factor in answering this question. Before examining this, it is important to note that they are not always seen in a positive light. One vocal critic is Cohen, who describes the history of British public inquiries as offering few grounds for optimism, and says that their usual role

> is to provide the illusion of accountability while refusing to lay a finger on the holders of power. America has independent Congressional committees which can tackle the President. Italy and France have investigating magistrates who have subpoena powers to bring criminal charges against a Berlusconi or Chirac. Britain has good chaps with nice manners and life peerages.[9]

Hastings adds that governments 'most commonly convene judicial inquiries to propel difficult issues into the long grass'.[10] These kinds of cynical view are important when considering the role played by judges in public inquiries.

index.php?page=press_news_details&category_id=2&press_id=181&Itemid=65. In September 2004, a Joint Statement from Amnesty International, British Irish Rights Watch, the Committee on the Administration of Justice and Human Rights First called for a public inquiry 'into the 1989 murder of Belfast lawyer Patrick Finucane', available at: www.amnesty.org/en/library/asset/EUR45/022/2004/en/f5983f44-faab-11dd-b6c4-73b1aa157d32/eur450222004en.pdf. The British and Irish Rights Watch also has links on its web pages to resolutions of the US Senate (see: www.birw.org/finucane%20%28House%20of%20Senate%29.html) and House of Representatives (see: www.birw.org/finucane%20%28House%20of%20Rep%29.html) calling for public inquiries into the Finucane case.

7 I. Steele, 'Judging Judicial Inquiries' [2004] *Public Law* 738 at 740.

8 Steele, 'Judging Judicial Inquiries'.

9 N. Cohen, 'A Very British Practice', *The Observer*, 17 August 2003, p. 29.

10 M. Hastings, 'Give us Inquiries into the Banking Crisis and Iraq, not Bloody Sunday', *The Guardian*, 10 November 2008, p. 28.

The nature of public inquiries in the United Kingdom

Public inquiries can be wide-ranging in scope or narrowly focused. They can be established under statute or under prerogative powers. Statutory inquiries may be set up under general inquiries legislation[11] wherein they enjoy wide powers. They may alternatively be set up under specific powers conferred by other statutes, for example, the National Health legislation; or they may be set up under powers incidental to other statutory powers, wherein they might be under significant restrictions as to what they can lawfully do.[12] They can, depending purely on the context and circumstances, be open, that is, held in public, or closed, that is, held in private.[13] The Third Report of the inquiry by the House of Commons Select Committee on Defence[14] explains:

> The history of the British government shows that there are in fact a number of forms of 'inquiry' available, designed, in principle, to fulfil specific functions. Sometimes the wish may be simply to establish the relevant facts, leaving their interpretation, the allocation of 'blame' and recommendations for the future to other agencies such as Ministers, Parliament or the courts. In other circumstances it may be thought desirable that the 'inquiry' itself undertake these broader, perhaps more delicate tasks. A prime purpose of some inquiries may also be to allay public (and Parliamentary) disquiet about some public issue or a 'scandal'.[15]

According to the committee, the relevant minister 'usually establishes the inquiry format, who heads it, its membership, its terms of reference and the form in which the report is to be made. An inquiry headed by a judge or senior lawyer is often called a 'judicial inquiry', although this is simply a descriptive term.[16]

Statutory inquiries

Before the Inquiries Act 2005, the main statutory basis for public inquiries was the Tribunals of Inquiry (Evidence) Act 1921. The House of

[11] Tribunals of Inquiry (Evidence) Act 1921 and Inquiries Act 2005, both discussed in more detail below.

[12] See, e.g., *R* v. *Secretary of State for Health ex p. Wagstaff* [2000] EWHC 634 (Admin.), [2001] 1 WLR 292; *Persey & Others* v. *Secretary of State for Environment, Food and Rural Affairs & Others* [2002] EWHC 371 (Admin.); *Howard* v. *Secretary of State for Health* [2002] EWHC 396 (Admin.); *Crampton* v. *Secretary of State for Health*, CA, unreported, 9 July 1993.

[13] See generally, *Persey & Others* v. *Secretary of State for the Environment, Food, and Rural Affairs & Others* [2002] EWHC 371 (Admin.).

[14] 2004–5, HC 63-I. [15] 2004–5, HC 63-I at [430]. [16] 2004–5, HC 63-I at [431].

Commons Select Committee on Defence noted that, in 2005, only twenty-five inquiries had been established under the 1921 Act, 'the two most recent being the Harold Shipman Tribunal of Inquiry set up in 2001 and the Bloody Sunday Tribunal of Inquiry set up in 1998'.[17] The Committee also referred to the common alternatives to statutory inquiries under the 1921 Act, namely, departmental inquiries set up by ministers, which, even when chaired by judges, do not have statutory powers. Yet they are still described as 'judicial' inquiries, because they are chaired by a judge.[18]

The 1921 Act applied where there had been resolutions by 'both Houses of Parliament that it is expedient that a tribunal be established for inquiring into a definite matter described in the Resolution as of urgent public importance'.[19] When the Act applied, it gave to the inquiry so set up 'all such powers, rights, and privileges as are vested in the High Court, or in Scotland the Court of Session', in respect, *inter alia* of enforcing the attendance of witnesses and examining them on oath, affirmation or otherwise, compelling the production of documents[20] and punishment for contempt.[21] The Act also conferred the same immunities and privileges on witnesses before the inquiry as they would enjoy in civil proceedings before the High Court or Court of Session.[22]

The 1921 Act was augmented by the 'Salmon principles'. These are six principles set out in the 1966 Report of the Royal Commission on Tribunals of Inquiry, chaired by Lord Justice Salmon.[23] These principles served mainly to protect witnesses and parties before statutory inquiries under the 1921 Act, and carried 'strong overtones of ordinary adversarial litigation'.[24] Sir Richard Scott warned that:

> care should be taken lest by an indiscriminate adoption and application of the six 'cardinal principles' the Inquiry's inquisitorial procedures become hampered by an unnecessary involvement of adversarial techniques and of lawyers acting for witnesses and others whose interests may lie in delay and obfuscation.[25]

[17] 2004–5, HC 63-I at [432].

[18] Examples given by the Committee (at [435]) were the Scott Inquiry into Matrix Churchill (1992) and the Hutton Inquiry into the death of Dr David Kelly.

[19] Section 1(1). [20] Section 1(1). [21] Section 1(2).

[22] Section 1(3). [23] Cmnd 3121.

[24] The Scott Report into Arms to Iraq, 1995–96 HC 115 at [K1.4]. L. Blom-Cooper, commenting on the report of the Saville inquiry into the 'Bloody Sunday' shootings has described this as an 'unhelpful infection of legalism brought into tribunals of inquiry', *The Guardian*, 17 June 2010, p. 32.

[25] 1995–96 HC 115 at [K1.5].

The Salmon principles received widespread endorsement, including from senior judges.[26] They afforded judges involved in public inquiries a measure of comfort, helpfully bringing back some semblance of adversarial familiarity to the inquiries' inquisitorial leanings. Despite Sir Richard Scott's backsliding in this regard, the 1921 Act as augmented by Salmon brought statutory inquiries closer to the normalcy of judicial routines. While this may seem to support the argument that judges would, in these circumstances, be appropriate chairs of 1921 Act inquiries, the same cannot be said for non-statutory inquiries, or of those under the Inquiries Act 2005.

The Inquiries Act 2005, which replaced the 1921 Act, empowers a minister to cause an inquiry to be held under the Act where it appears to him or her that 'particular events have caused, or are capable of causing, public concern', or where there is 'public concern that particular events may have occurred'.[27] The minister appoints the members of the inquiry panel[28] and sets out the inquiry's terms of reference.[29] All this must be reported to Parliament or Assembly as the case may be.[30] The minister may subsequently amend the terms of reference[31] after consultation with the inquiry's chair.[32] Where the minister proposes to appoint a judge as a member of an inquiry panel, he or she must first consult with a specified senior judicial officer in relation to the office held by the judge whose appointment is being proposed.[33] A non-statutory inquiry may be converted into an inquiry under the Act.[34] The inquiry's chair is under a duty to act with fairness[35] and is conferred with a number of powers; for example, to manage the procedure,[36] administer oaths and receive evidence on oath,[37] restrict public access[38] and compel the attendance of witnesses.[39] The members of the inquiry panel (as well as assessors, counsel or solicitors to the inquiry) enjoy immunity from suit 'in respect of any act done or omission made in the execution of his duty as such, or

[26] See, e.g., Lord Woolf MR in *R* v. *Lord Saville of Newdigate ex p. B (No. 2)* [2000] 1 WLR 1855 at 1868; Sir Thomas Bingham MR in *Crampton & Others* v. *Secretary of State for Health*, CA, unreported, 9 July 1993.

[27] Section 1(1). In this context, a 'minister' includes ministers of the UK's devolved governments.

[28] Section 4(1). [29] Section 5(1). [30] Section 6. [31] Section 5(3). [32] Section 5(4).

[33] Section 10. The specified person to be consulted may be, e.g., the senior Law Lord, Lord Chief Justice, Lord President of the Court of Session or Lord Chief Justice of Northern Ireland.

[34] Section 15. [35] Section 17(3). [36] Section 17(1).

[37] Section 17(2). [38] Section 19.

[39] Section 21. This is enforceable by the High Court or the Court of Session (s. 36).

any act done or omission made in good faith in the purported execution of his duty as such'.[40]

The Act attempted to address some of the concerns of those opposed to judges conducting public inquiries. The powers of the inquiry are similar to those of a court, and a duty to consult with a specified senior judge is imposed when proposing to appoint a judge as an inquiry's chair. However, the Act does not convert inquiries into judicial proceedings, and this raises a number of issues. The Act has not enjoyed the apparent confidence that was accorded to its predecessor. For example, Amnesty International has recently claimed that the setting up of an inquiry under the 2005 Act 'will effectively extinguish the chances of a genuinely independent and effective investigation'.[41] Finally, the *New Statesman* reported[42] that:

> Lord Saville of Newdigate, chair of the Bloody Sunday inquiry,[43] which has full judicial status, has said that the Inquiries Act 'makes a very serious inroad into the independence of any inquiry; and is likely to damage or destroy public confidence in the inquiry and its findings'. Lord Saville also said that he would not be prepared to serve on the panel of any future inquiry held under the terms of the new legislation.

It is problematic that ministers still have control over the inquiries, and the formal language of the Act does not change the fact that the inquiries are still dealing essentially with highly political controversies.

Are serving judges appropriate for this task?

While judges are considered to be particularly suited to conduct public inquiries, some of the very high profile public inquiries have not been

[40] Section 37.

[41] 'Twenty Years on, Still no Inquiry into Patrick Finucane's Death', 11 February 2009, available at: www.amnesty.org/appeals-for-action/twenty-years-inquiry-patrick-finucanes-death; see also 'UK: The Finucane Case: Judiciary must not take part in Inquiry Sham' (EUR 45/014/ 2005), where Amnesty called upon 'all senior judges in England, Wales and Scotland, as well as on judges in other common law countries, not to serve on an inquiry into Patrick Finucane's case if held under the Inquiries Act 2005'.

[42] M. Bright, 'Shamed', *New Statesman*, 27 February 2006, available at: www.newstatesman.com/200602270004.htm.

[43] On 30 January 1972, British soldiers opened fire with live ammunition during a march in Londonderry, resulting in fourteen civilian deaths and thirteen civilian injuries. After an initial inquiry into this incident, a further inquiry was set up, chaired by Lord Saville, a Lord of Appeal in Ordinary. See generally, B. Hadfield, 'R v. Lord Saville of Newdigate, ex p. Anonymous Soldiers: What is the Purpose of a Tribunal of Inquiry?' [1999] *Public Law* 663.

chaired by judges. For example, the inquiry into the 1982 Falklands War was chaired by Lord Franks, an academic and former diplomat.[44] The 2003–4 Bichard Inquiry into the Soham murders was chaired by Sir Michael Bichard, Rector of the London Institute and a former civil servant. The 2004 Butler Inquiry into, *inter alia*, the accuracy of intelligence about Iraqi weapons of mass destruction was conducted by Lord Butler, a former head of the civil service. Sir Thomas Legg, who chaired the 2009–10 inquiry into the expenses scandal in the House of Commons is a lawyer and former civil servant. And the current inquiry into the Iraq War[45] is being chaired by Sir John Chilcot, a retired civil servant. No one is seriously arguing that these inquiries and other similar high-profile inquiries chaired by non-judges are without credibility simply because they were not chaired by judges.

So why should it be thought that judges are best suited to the task of conducting inquiries? Much has been said about this.[46] Among the reasons commonly proffered are that a judge can ensure that an inquiry is being conducted impartially and efficiently, and that the inquiry is acting judicially. Furthermore, judges enjoy public confidence and have the requisite skill and experience. According to Drewry,[47] it 'is almost a reflex action at times of dire political emergency for judges to be rushed to the scene to extinguish the blaze of concern (often by retrospectively legitimating official actions) and to spread calm and reassurance'. Woodhouse similarly noted:[48]

> A judicial appointment, presumed to be apolitical, acts to reinforce the independence and impartiality of the inquiry and to enhance its credibility and legitimacy. Judges also lend dignity and authority to the proceedings and symbolise the serious nature of the investigation.

In *Persey & Others* v. *Secretary of State for Environment, Food and Rural Affairs & Others*[49] Simon Brown LJ referred to a statement in the

44 This inquiry was conducted in private. 45 See www.iraqinquiry.org.uk.

46 See generally, J. Beatson, 'Should Judges Conduct Public Inquiries?' (2005) 121 *Law Quarterly Review* 221. While not explicitly saying so, the list of attributes expected of a chair of a public inquiry given by Robert Francis QC in his Written Evidence to the House of Commons Select Committee on Public Administration (2004/05 Session (HC 51 I and II), Ev 8, GBI 06 at [8]) is arguably a list describing the attributes of senior judges.

47 G. Drewry, 'Judges and Political Inquiries: Harnessing a Myth?' (1975) *Political Studies* 58.

48 D. Woodhouse, 'Matrix Churchill: A Case Study in Judicial Inquiries' (1995) 48 *Parliamentary Affairs* 24 at 25. See also D. Pannick, 'The High Price to be Paid if Judges Examine our Historical Events', *The Times*, 17 June 2010, p. 81.

49 [2002] EWHC 371 (Admin.) at [26].

guidance note issued by the then Lord Chancellor, Lord Mackay of Clashfern on 16 May 1991, to the effect that:

> The over-riding reason why judicial inquiries are held is the gravity of the incidents, and the belief that both the public anxiety they cause and the interests of the victims can only be satisfied by such an inquiry. In some cases public confidence may be undermined if there is not a perception that an inquiry is full, wide-ranging and independent of Government; for example, in cases where the regulatory functions of the investigatory body are called into question. There will therefore be cases in which public confidence requires there to be an independent judicial figure to hold a public Inquiry.

But there are also problems with judges chairing public inquiries. These have also been well aired.[50] I will summarise the more common ones here. The first problem is that it is a violation of the separation of powers principle. While the reputation of the judiciary and the public confidence in it emerge from the focus on the judicial function, a task such as conducting a public inquiry is not a judicial function. On the contrary, it drags judges into the political arena, and can often be used as a cynical manipulation of the judiciary and its reputation by politicians. According to Jowell,

> there may be inquires which, although not requiring political judgment, are in effect set up in order to achieve a political purpose (e.g. the purpose of sweeping the matter under the carpet for a period of time; or for seeking to demonstrate the government's resolve not to hide anything, etc.). In those circumstances judges are being used to reassure the public and to deflect political criticism.[51]

Judges can be questioned about their conduct of the inquiry, and are fair game for personal attacks in respect of their handling of it.[52] Furthermore, the matter may eventually come to the court for judicial review, and the outcome of such review may leave much to be desired. Hadfield, commenting on the judicial review proceedings on the Saville inquiry notes:[53]

[50] See, e.g., Beatson, 'Should Judges Conduct Public Inquiries?'.

[51] J. Jowell, Written Evidence to the House of Commons Select Committee on Public Administration, 'Government by Inquiry' (2004/05 Session (HC 51 I and II), Ev 39 GBI 17 at [1]).

[52] This is the subject of detailed discussion later in this chapter.

[53] Hadfield, 'R v. Lord Saville of Newdigate, ex p. Anonymous Soldiers: What is the Purpose of a Tribunal of Inquiry?', pp. 677–8.

> Eleven judges have judicially reviewed a Law Lord and two senior Commonwealth judges, albeit not sitting in their judicial capacity, and all but one of the eleven judges have ruled that the Tribunal had acted unlawfully. This is an inevitable corollary of what has been mentioned above (the expansion of judicial review and the use of senior judges to chair, for example, Tribunals of Inquiry) but it is also in some respects unsatisfactory (and no doubt, from the point of view of the general public, perplexing). The establishment of a Tribunal of Inquiry should not be to focus criticism on the judiciary at the expense of the exploration of the serious issues remitted to the Tribunal of Inquiry and the full assessment of responsibility, including in some situations, political responsibility.

Additionally, judges may not be sufficiently trained to handle the issues that arise and so may not avoid pitfalls. Finally, such duties inevitably involve a depletion of judicial resources.[54] According to Beatson, 'only by using retired judges or part time "Recorders" and "Deputy Judges" does the British system cope with the fact that full-time tenured judges are taken away from their primary function'.[55] Jowell provided an apt illustration in 2004:

> Lord Saville's inquiry into the events surrounding the 'Bloody Sunday' killings has been going on for almost a decade. As a result, he has not been able to contribute to the judicial work of the House of Lords but parliament has not been troubled, or the government embarrassed, by having to revisit those grim events.[56]

These can all be subsumed into a single proposition – that, regardless of the factors commending judges for the task, using serving judges to conduct public inquiries impacts negatively on the judiciary and its reputation and independence. In order to substantiate this hypothesis, we will examine a number of areas in which the involvement of judges in public inquiries may compromise the independence of the judiciary.

The impact on judicial independence

Judicial independence connotes a status or relationship between the judiciary and 'others, particularly in the Executive Branch of government, that

[54] See, e.g., *Persey & Others* v. *Secretary of State for Environment, Food and Rural Affairs & Others* [2002] EWHC 371 (Admin.) at [26].

[55] Beatson, 'Should Judges Conduct Public Inquiries?', p. 233.

[56] J. Jowell, 'The Wrong Man for the Job: The Continuing Fallout over the Hutton Report Proves that Judges and Politics don't Mix', *The Guardian*, 3 February 2004, p. 8.

rests on objective conditions or guarantees'.[57] Ministers and all those having responsibilities relating to the judiciary or the administration of justice are obliged to uphold the independence of the judiciary.[58] While judicial independence is an important constitutional principle, it is also largely instrumental. The purpose is not to shield judges from the realities of modern life, but to enable them to dispense justice appropriately. It is well understood that those who have to adjudicate on disputes between their fellows have an onerous task and need protection from those who might come off worse in such a dispute, or those who might want to interfere in its adjudication. Thus, judicial independence is for the benefit of the public, who have a vested interest in the proper functioning of the administration of justice. Anything that impairs the effectiveness and efficiency of the judiciary is contrary to the instrumental purpose of judicial independence.

Appointment

The appointment process is an important marker of independence. It is important that the appointment of judicial officers be insulated from political machinations and executive manipulations. The establishment of the Judicial Appointments Commission serves to secure independence in the process of appointments to the bench. However, as has been seen, the appointment of members of an inquiry panel, and the terms of reference of the inquiry, are entirely a matter for ministers. While the minister is under a statutory duty to consult with a specified senior judge when proposing to appoint a judge to an inquiry panel under the Inquiries Act 2005, there is no such duty in relation to non-statutory inquiries. And, with respect to inquiries under the 2005 Act, there is no indication of what should happen should there be disagreement between the minister and the senior judge who is to be consulted. Furthermore, the minister does not need to explain why he or she has picked a particular judge out of any number of judges who could have been selected. This can give rise to suspicions that the minister has plumbed for a 'safe' judge who can be trusted not to rock the boat. Such suspicions will reflect poorly on the selected judge. That this is not a fanciful proposition will soon become apparent in the discussion below.

[57] Le Dain J in *Valente* v. *R* (1985) 34 DLR (4th) 161 at 170.
[58] Constitutional Reform Act 2005, s. 3.

Immunity

Judges enjoy absolute immunity in respect of their judicial acts only.[59] This is designed to protect their independence. But when they are not acting judicially, they are (as far as civil liability is concerned) acting as private citizens, and are potentially open to liability. As has been seen, immunity is available to judges conducting statutory inquiries. Other kinds of inquiry will depend on the vagaries of the common law principles of judicial immunity. This kind of uncertainty is not something that any serving judge should face.

Resources

An independent judiciary must be adequately resourced, but, of necessity, appointing judges to conduct non-judicial functions involves a raid on judicial resources.[60] The depletion of resources that this entails may last anything from a few weeks to several years,[61] and there is no indication that the senior judiciary can prevent their courts from being raided by the argument that there is no judge to spare. Since no one has ever suggested that the UK judiciary is under-employed, it follows that such resource depletions impact negatively on the performance by the judiciary of its legitimate constitutional functions. The problem is exacerbated where (as seems more likely than not) the judge so appointed is from an appellate court, where the numbers are likely to be fairly restricted. While part-time judges may be appointed to relieve the pressure thereby created, and this might be helpful at the High Court level, that is not the point. There will also be situations where it would be inappropriate; for example, where the judge appointed to conduct the inquiry is from the Court of Appeal or the Supreme Court.

Insulation from political interference

The executive is obliged to obey and comply with judicial decisions. Furthermore, judges are protected from interference and criticism by

[59] See generally, A. A. Olowofoyeku, *Suing Judges* (Oxford University Press, 1993).

[60] D. Pannick, commenting on the Saville inquiry, noted that 'the courts have been deprived of an appellate judge for 12 years', *The Times*, 17 June 2010, p. 81.

[61] The Saville inquiry is a prime example. The inquiry was set up by Tony Blair's government on 29 January 1998 (see www.bloody-sunday-inquiry.org), and published its report on 15 June 2010.

politicians and the other branches of government. As Oliver puts it, 'the bench, unlike other state bodies, is not to be subjected to political forms of accountability'.[62] In particular, there are 'strict parliamentary rules about the criticising of a judge's conduct or of judges generally, which is only permitted on a debate on a substantive motion calling for dismissal'.[63] The press and the public are expected to show restraint in their criticism of individual judges who have delivered judgments in the cases that they have heard. And it is normally inappropriate (apart from in appellate or judicial review proceedings) to investigate the conduct of the trial/case by the judge. All this is necessary in order to protect the independence of both individual judges and the judicial institution itself.

No such restraint is expected or shown in the case of inquiries, and ministers can treat the reports of public inquiries with contempt if they so choose.[64] While some judicial inquiries seem to be held in high esteem, this is not the norm, and such unusual favour appears to be enjoyed mainly by those that find significant fault with something in the state apparatus. Thus, for example, Lord Scarman's inquiry into the 1981 Brixton riots,[65] which reported disturbing social issues and major problems with policing and ethnic minorities (although rejecting the notion that there was institutional racism in the Metropolitan Police Service), was well received,[66] and led to the enactment of the Police and Criminal Evidence Act 1984. His Lordship must have felt slightly embarrassed to be so damned with praise in House of Lords' debates on his report. This, for example, from Lord Elystan-Morgan:

> We wholeheartedly endorse what the noble Lord has said and what indeed has been said by so many, the length and breadth of Britain, by way of tribute to the skill and wisdom of the noble and learned Lord, Lord Scarman. For the way in which he has discharged his massive task, the conscientious incisiveness with which he has analysed the facts, and the clarity with which he has presented the issues, this report must be regarded as a model of its kind.[67]

[62] D. Oliver, *Constitutional Reform in the UK* (Oxford University Press, 2003), p. 333.

[63] Oliver, *Constitutional Reform in the UK*, p. 334.

[64] See generally, Steele, 'Judging Judicial Inquiries', p. 744.

[65] Lord Scarman, *Report on the Brixton Disorders of 10–12 April 1981*, Cmnd. 8427 (1981).

[66] See generally, S. Neal, 'The Scarman Report, the Macpherson Report and the Media: How Newspapers Respond to Race-centred Social Policy Interventions' (2003) 32(1) *Journal of Social Policy* 55, which examines, *inter alia*, some of the media and other reactions to the report.

[67] HL Deb. 4 February 1982, vol. 426 at [1403]. Compare Lord Wigoder (at [1403]) and Lord Hunt (at [1415]). Unfortunately, this great enthusiasm for Lord Scarman's report

Sir William MacPherson's inquiry into the murder of black teenage student Stephen Lawrence[68] by white racists, which found evidence of institutional racism and incompetence in the Metropolitan Police,[69] was also largely well received,[70] although it was not without some academic criticism[71] and political reaction.[72]

Given the complexities of modern society and the competing interests and philosophies of especially the left and the right, the generally positive receptions of Scarman and MacPherson may be seen as the high water-mark of positive responses to judicial inquiries. But many other judges have not been so fortunate. Masterman rightly observed that 'unfortunately for many of the judges who have been involved in such inquiries the collective memory of the episode in many minds seems to be of their unsuitability for the role'.[73] For example, Hastings[74] felt free to describe Lord Saville as a 'weak judge' in respect of his handling of the Bloody Sunday inquiry, and, despite the quite formidable membership of the Saville panel,[75] he had no compunction in describing Lord Saville's

was more a matter of words than deeds on the part of Margaret Thatcher's government (see, e.g., Neal, 'The Scarman Report, the Macpherson Report and the Media', p. 61).

68 Cmnd 4262-I (1999). 69 See particularly, para. 46.1.

70 See generally, N. Rollock, *The Stephen Lawrence Inquiry 10 Years On* (London: The Runnymede Trust, 2009); C. Phillips, 'Facing Inwards and Outwards? Institutional Racism, Race Equality and the Role of Black and Asian Professional Associations' (2005) 5(4) *Criminal Justice* 357; A. Goodman and V. Ruggiero, 'Crime, Punishment, and Ethnic Minorities in England and Wales' (2008) 2(1) *Race/Ethnicity: Multidisciplinary Global Perspectives* 53; the Scottish Executive's endorsement, 'The Stephen Lawrence Inquiry: an Action Plan for Scotland', available at: www.scotland.gov.uk/library2/doc01/sli-01.htm.

71 See, e.g., J. Lea, 'The MacPherson Report and the Question of Institutional Racism' (2000) 39(3) *Howard Journal of Criminal Justice* 219. For a less subtle critique, see N. Dennis, G. Erdos and A. Al-Shahi, *Racist Murder and Pressure Group Politics: The Macpherson Report and the Police* (London: CIVITAS, 2000).

72 E.g., William Hague, the then Tory party leader, is reported to have claimed that the MacPherson report 'led to a collapse in police morale' and helped to brand 'every policeman a racist'. (P. Waugh, 'Hague: Lawrence Report Behind Rise in Muggings', *The Independent*, 14 December 2000, p. 7). See also the details in the interview of Sir William MacPherson by Mary Riddell, *New Statesman*, 21 February 2000, available at: www.newstatesman.com/200002210016.

73 House of Commons Select Committee on Public Administration, '*Government by Inquiry*' (2004/05 Session (HC 51 II)), Written Evidence (Ev 28, GBI 15) at [17].

74 Hastings, 'Give us Inquiries into the Banking Crisis and Iraq, not Bloody Sunday'.

75 As Hadfield noted ('R v. Lord Saville of Newdigate, ex p. Anonymous Soldiers: What is the Purpose of a Tribunal of Inquiry?') 'The Tribunal of Inquiry consist[ed] of a Lord of Appeal in Ordinary, a former judge of the New Zealand Court of Appeal and the present Chief Justice of the Canadian Province of New Brunswick', p. 676.

inquiry as 'The Saville nonsense', thus disparaging not only a Law Lord but also two very senior Commonwealth judges. Cohen felt free to claim that 'Sir Richard offered obscurantism on a Himalayan scale' in respect of the Scott inquiry into arms to Iraq.[76] Cohen was no less critical of Lord Denning's 1963 inquiry into the Profumo scandal. He felt that Lord Denning fell firmly into the category of 'most' judges who 'wouldn't want to lay a finger on the state even if they thought they could get away with it'.[77] According to Cohen,

> Denning's inquiry combined deference and vindictiveness in equal measures. The deference was shown to the Government of the day. The vindictiveness was reserved for Stephen Ward, Keeler's friend and part-time pimp, who was painted as a lascivious monster. Conveniently, he had committed suicide and was in no position to answer back.

There are many other examples of assaults on judges who have conducted public inquiries, but, for the purposes of the present discussion, I will use Lord Hutton as a case study.

Lord Hutton had the misfortune to agree to chair an inquiry[78] into the circumstances surrounding the death of Dr David Kelly, who was apparently the source of BBC reports that the government had 'sexed up' the dossier making the case for the war in Iraq. As is usual when judicial inquiries fail to meet up to the expectations of those who want them to be executioners of governments and ministers,[79] Lord Hutton's Report generated considerable passion. Webster thus described the report:

> He has actually managed to produce a report which, in its manifest unfairness, and its apparent inability to reflect accurately the evidence which was put before him, actually threatens to damage the very government whose interests it seems so cravenly to serve.

[76] See Cohen, 'A Very British Practice'; also his general criticisms of judicial inquiries in 'The Hutton Report – This was the Wrong Inquiry'.

[77] N. Cohen, 'Schooled in Scandal', *The Observer*, 1 February 2004, p. 31.

[78] Full details of the establishment of the inquiry can be found in the Memorandum by Lee Hughes, Secretary to the Inquiry, to House of Commons Select Committee on Public Administration, *Government by Inquiry* (2004/05 Session (HC 51 II)), Written Evidence (Ev 34, GBI 16).

[79] With respect to the Hutton inquiry in particular, Kettle noted that, from the start, 'too many newspapers invested too heavily in a particular preferred outcome on these key points'. The preferred outcome in this case was for the government to be found guilty on the dossier and on the naming of Dr Kelly, and the vindication of the BBC report. See M. Kettle, 'The Threat to the Media is Real. It Comes from Within', *The Guardian*, 3 February 2004, p. 20.

> One of the most significant features of the report is the extraordinary difficulty which Lord Hutton seems to have in facing up to and accurately describing some of the most obvious instances of dishonesty.[80]

Webster proceeded to voice his opinion that, although Lord Hutton may have been trying to be tactful and showing respect for the deceased Dr David Kelly and his family, his own suspicion was that this was a case of a 'particularly dangerous kind of patrician self-deception' on Lord Hutton's part. According to Webster, 'as a faithful public servant himself, Hutton seems to have great difficulty in acknowledging the fact that faithful public servants, among whom David Kelly would once have been numbered, might engage in outright duplicity – might actually lie to parliament itself'. This tirade against Lord Hutton is progressed with the statement that:

> For there is a kind of narcissism of the righteous which, because it makes it very difficult for those who believe they embody truth and justice to acknowledge their own occasional dishonesty, makes its correspondingly difficult for them to accurately perceive the dishonesty of those whom they would normally regard as colleagues, as fellow public servants, or as members of their own patrician class.

Harsh criticism came not only from the media. Gearty was also not pulling any punches, declaring it 'odd' that Lord Hutton had 'managed to find a way to exonerate pretty well everybody else in government, and the oddity of this became self-defeatingly ludicrous when compared with the savagery of his attacks on the media in general, and the BBC in particular'.[81] The Hutton Report, according to him, could, if applied rigorously, 'destroy BBC journalism forever', and then this:

> Imagine a BBC that checks all its output all the time for potentially 'false accusations of fact impugning the integrity of others, including politicians', and refuses to broadcast anything that might conceivably pose such a risk. And there is no reason to stop at the BBC: Lord Hutton's supposed rule must apply generally. So we must also imagine the kind of 'democratic society' we would have if all television, radio and print news organisations followed with Huttonesque rigour what Lord Hutton says is the law.

80 R. Webster, 'Hutton and the Mirror of Dishonesty', 1 February 2004, available at: www.richardwebster.net/print/xhuttonmirror.htm.

81 C. Gearty, 'Hutton Missed the Mark', *The Guardian*, 24 February 2004, available at: www.guardian.co.uk/world/2004/feb/24/law.huttonreport.

Lord Hutton, was, according to Gearty, 'out of his depth', and, in his search for authority to support his stated understanding of the state of the law, apparently compared unfavourably with 'any first-year law student'.

On more than one occasion, Lord Hutton's Northern Irish background was referred to, making him fair game for Northern Ireland's politicians. Sinn Fein's Danny Morrison claimed that Lord Hutton was 'for decades in Northern Ireland . . . a guardian angel of the establishment', and thus described his record:

> Although in the Belfast high court Hutton occasionally acquitted republicans and dismissed the appeals of soldiers, nationalists generally considered him a hanging judge and the guardian angel of soldiers and police officers.[82]

Morrison then proceeded to list a catalogue of cases in which Lord Hutton had allegedly demonstrated these angelic leanings. The conclusion was that one should not be surprised to find Lord Hutton taking on this protective angelic role once again.

Finally, Jenkins claimed that 'The Lord Chancellor, Lord Falconer of Thoroton, assured Mr Blair that Lord Hutton was . . . "safe".'[83] It is not clear where Jenkins obtained this piece of intelligence, but the import is clear. Jenkins also claimed that 'Hutton was not a court of law but a high-risk gamble to conceal Tony Blair's embarrassment over his Iraq intelligence by implicating the BBC in a suicide. The gamble worked.'

Jenkins is correct that the Hutton inquiry was not a court of a law. And therein lies the problem. Had this been a judgment in a court case, however controversial, it is doubtful that the judge would have faced such ferocious personal attacks. These kinds of personal attacks on senior judges arise out of their participation in inquiries on issues that are essentially political in nature.[84] For a judge to have to endure such attacks (to which he or she has no means of responding) is extremely damaging to the judge personally, to the institution that he or she represents and to public confidence in that institution (the judiciary). It thereby poses a significant threat to judicial independence.

[82] D. Morrison, 'My Report on Lord Hutton', *The Guardian*, 3 February 2004, p. 19.

[83] S. Jenkins, 'Triumph of a Paranoid Court over the Media', *The Times*, 30 January 2004, p. 28.

[84] Compare Scott Baker J in *Howard* v. *Secretary of State for Health* [2002] EWHC 396 (Admin.) at [70].

The invidious position of judges asked to conduct public inquiries was well described by Cohen (who, as has been seen above, is no apologist for the judiciary):

> Without statute or precedent to guide him, the judge is meant to deliver a political verdict. A stinging paragraph might bring down the Prime Minister. Yet as the judge sits alone in his study, he wonders whether it is his job to stage a judicial coup d'état. Shouldn't Parliament depose the Prime Minister? Or the electorate? James Dingemans, QC for the Hutton inquiry, said at the end of the hearings that wider questions about the war were raised by the particular circumstances of David Kelly's death. But these were issues for 'other institutions' to investigate.[85]

Judges conducting public inquiries often face the proverbial 'damned if you do, and damned if you don't' scenario. It is wrong for any serving judge to face such a quandary, especially where the thankless task being undertaken does not fall within the judge's role of exercising the judicial power of the state, and does not assist the cause of judicial independence. Involvement in non-judicial functions, such as public inquiries, can seriously compromise a judge. As Masterman has noted, 'it is hard to think of another person or persons whose future career and professional reputation could be as adversely affected by an accusation of partiality than that of a judge'.[86]

Finally, Jowell noted:

> Lord Hutton has now retired as a judge, but his experience shows that political controversies cannot easily be fashioned into judicial disputes. They tend stubbornly to remain in the sphere of politics, where judges are not well equipped to decide, and where they should be reluctant to participate.[87]

Conclusion

The United Kingdom is fond of using serving judges to conduct public inquiries. Government ministers have tremendous control over the process, the selection of the inquiry panel and the inquiry's terms of reference. The judges so tasked work hard to serve the public,[88] making some tremendous

85 Cohen, 'Schooled in Scandal'.

86 R. Masterman, Written Evidence to the House of Commons Select Committee on Public Administration, *Government by Inquiry* (2004/05 Session (HC 51 II, Ev 28, GBI 15)) at [19].

87 Jowell, 'The Wrong Man for the Job'.

88 See Lord Irvine LC, HL Deb. 11 May 2000, cols. 1715–17.

contributions in the process. However, this kind of use of judicial personnel takes judges away from their normal judicial duties, depletes the judiciary's tight human resources, drags judges into the political arena, opens the judiciary to political manipulation and exposes senior judges to uncontrolled personal attacks and insults. In short, it undermines the judiciary, its reputation and its independence. It can be supported only by the doctrine of necessity. But there is no necessity here. Senior police officers and civil servants are, when retired, well able to conduct public inquiries and enjoy the respect and confidence of the public. Should it be thought that legal skills are needed, there is an abundance of senior QCs and legal academics who could equally fit the bill. And should judicial experience be deemed desirable, there is an army of retired senior judges who could be called upon. Therefore, serving judges should be left to serve in the role to which they were appointed and for which they are well qualified – to exercise the judicial power of the state, and to adjudicate on legal disputes. When even non-statutory inquiries, conducted by those who are not judges, have been shown to be effective on many counts,[89] the use of serving judges to conduct public inquiries is even less supportable.

[89] See, e.g., N. Bamforth, 'Political Accountability in Play: the Budd Inquiry and David Blunkett's Resignation' [2005] *Public Law* 229.

25

Judges and non-judicial functions in the United States

JEFFREY M. SHAMAN

In the United States, judicial and extra-judicial behavior is governed primarily by the Code of Judicial Conduct, which originally was set forth in 1972 and which subsequently has been adopted in the federal court system as well as in the court systems of all fifty states. Although there are several different versions of the Code of Judicial Conduct,[1] its widespread adoption provides a certain degree of uniformity from jurisdiction to jurisdiction, and forms the foundation for a national body of law concerning the conduct of judges. Each jurisdiction, however, is free to interpret the Code according to its own understanding of it, which allows for some variation in the application of the Code from one court system to another.

In each of the fifty states, there is a judicial conduct commission, charged with enforcement of the Code of Judicial Conduct and invested with authority to discipline judges for Code violations. The decisions of these commissions may be appealed to a court, usually the highest court in the state. In the federal system, judicial councils in each of the thirteen federal judicial circuits are authorized to enforce the Code of Judicial Conduct and discipline judges for Code violations. Council decisions are reviewable by the Judicial Conference of the United States. In addition, many states have official or unofficial bodies that issue advisory opinions concerning judicial conduct. For federal judges, advisory opinions concerning the Code are available through the Judicial Conference of the United States. The American Bar Association also issues advisory opinions regarding the Code of Judicial Conduct.

The Code of Judicial Conduct sets forth several general principles that pertain to extra-judicial functions. Canon 1 of the Code states that a

[1] The first Code of Judicial Conduct was promulgated in 1972. It was revised in 1990 and again in 2007.

judge shall uphold and promote the independence, integrity, and impartiality of the judiciary, and shall avoid impropriety and the appearance of impropriety.[2] Canon 3 provides that a judge shall conduct his or her personal and extra-judicial activities to minimize the risk of conflict with the obligations of judicial office. The Code also contains more specific rules concerning certain aspects of extra-judicial conduct, some of which will be discussed throughout this chapter.

Appointment to government commissions

Many judges in the United States, including Supreme Court justices, have served on government commissions. In some instances, judges have served on commissions that were the focus of intense public controversy. Five justices of the Supreme Court served on the Electoral Commission that was created to settle the disputed presidential election of 1876.[3] In joining five members of the US Senate and five members of the House of Representatives on the Commission, the justices were expected to provide the Commission with a degree of impartiality and legal expertise lacking in its other members. However, as members of the Commission, each of the five justices voted in favor of the candidate of his own political party, opening the justices to charges of political partisanship. Undoubtedly, the justices' participation on the Electoral Commission tarnished the reputation of the Supreme Court and diminished public confidence in the judiciary.[4]

In the 1960s, Supreme Court Chief Justice Earl Warren served as chairperson of the commission that was formed to investigate the assassination of President John F. Kennedy. In fact, while the official name of the commission was the President's Commission on the Assassination of President John F. Kennedy, it came to be known unofficially as the "Warren Commission." Although Chief Justice Warren's presence on the commission brought with it a high degree of integrity and competence, the commission later was subject to considerable public debate and criticism. Warren himself was criticized for taking time away from

[2] The numbering of the provisions in the Code of Judicial Conduct varies in the three different versions of it. All citations to the Code herein refer to the 2007 Code.

[3] W. H. Rehnquist, *The Centennial Crisis: The Disputed Election of 1876* (New York: Knopf, 2004).

[4] R. McKay, "The Judiciary and Non-Judicial Activities" (1970) 35 *Law & Contemporary Problems* 9 at 25.

his duties as Chief Justice of the Supreme Court, although he seemed to be able to function concurrently in the two posts quite well.[5]

Other judicial appointments to commissions have been less controversial. In the 1890s, Supreme Court Chief Justice Melville Fuller and Associate Justice Daniel Brewer both served on a board arbitrating a border dispute between Venezuela and British Guiana. In the early twentieth century, several Supreme Court justices served on a committee to review and update the Federal Rules of Equity. As an Associate Justice on the Supreme Court, Charles Evans Hughes worked on a commission concerned with setting postal rates. In modern times, judges are frequently appointed to commissions charged with studying or reforming the legal system. Judges have served, for example, on the Commission on Revision of the Federal Court Appellate System, the Federal Courts Study Commission, the National Commission on Judicial Discipline and Removal, and the United States Sentencing Commission.[6] Obviously, judicial service on these commissions, which are concerned directly with the function of courts, is less objectionable than service on other kinds of commissions.

There has been considerable debate in the United States on the question of whether judges should serve on government commissions. There are strong reasons, both for and against, judicial service on government bodies. On the one hand, there are a number of positive aspects to having judges serve on government commissions. Because of their learning and experience, judges bring a unique expertise to their extra-judicial activities that can be extremely valuable to a government commission. In turn, judges may have much to learn from participation on government commissions that will improve their ability as judges. Involvement in the outside world can enrich the judicial temperament and enhance a judge's ability to perform the duties of office.

On the other hand, service on a government commission may cast doubt on a judge's independence or impartiality, thereby diminishing public confidence in the judiciary. Moreover, judges should not allow their extra-judicial activities to interfere with the diligent performance of the duties of judicial office. In fact, the Code of Judicial Conduct states that the duties of judicial office shall take precedence over all of a judge's personal and extra-judicial activities.[7] Clearly, judges should avoid

[5] McKay, "The Judiciary and Non-Judicial Activities."

[6] J. J. Alfini, S. Lubet, J. M. Shaman, and C. G. Geyh, *Judicial Conduct and Ethics*, 4th edn. (Newark, NJ: LexisNexis, 2007), s. 9.03A.

[7] Code of Judicial Conduct, Rule 2.1 (2007).

extra-judicial activities that distract them from the duties of judicial office or that cast doubt upon their independence or ability to decide cases impartially. Where, then, should the line be drawn in regard to allowing judges to serve on government commissions?

The Code of Judicial Conduct attempts to resolve this issue by prohibiting judges from accepting an appointment to a governmental committee, board, or commission, unless it is one that concerns the law, the legal system, or the administration of justice.[8] While not prohibiting judges from serving on commissions concerned with the law, the legal system, or the administration of justice, the Code suggests that a judge should not accept every appointment to such a commission; rather, a judge should assess the appropriateness of each appointment, paying particular attention to his or her time commitments and giving due regard to the requirements of judicial independence and impartiality.[9] Nonetheless, by allowing service on law-related commissions, the Code grants judges latitude to serve on a wide variety of commissions. Indeed, it has been said that there are few governmental bodies whose work bears no meaningful relationship to the "law," the "legal system," or the "administration of justice" broadly defined.[10] Certainly, those terms seem broad enough to have allowed judges to serve on the 1876 Electoral Commission or the President's Commission on the Assassination of President John F. Kennedy. Written in such broad terms, the Code's prescription provides little guidance to judges as to which commission appointments are acceptable and which are not.

A few states have tried to delineate the boundaries of permissible judicial service on government commissions. The Judicial Ethics Advisory Committee of the Arizona Supreme Court has taken the position that a judge may serve on the Governor's Task Force on the Seriously Mentally Ill and may also serve on the Governor's Select Commission on Juvenile Corrections, because both bodies deal with the improvement of the law, the legal system, or the administration of justice.[11] However, in a later opinion the committee concluded that a judge could not serve on an Advisory Council on Spinal and Head Injuries because it was not law-related.[12] The committee's conclusions that the Task Force on the Mentally Ill was law-related, but the Advisory Council on Spinal and

[8] Code of Judicial Conduct, Rule 3.4 (2007).

[9] Code of Judicial Conduct, Rule 3.4, Comment [1] (2007).

[10] Alfini, *et al.*, *Judicial Conduct and Ethics*, s. 9.03A.

[11] Arizona Judicial Ethics Advisory Committee Opinion 90–11 (1990).

[12] Arizona Judicial Ethics Advisory Committee Opinion 94–9 (1994).

Head Injuries was not law-related hardly seem consistent, but the committee offered no explanation as to why it reached different conclusions in those two cases.

In other states, judges have been permitted to serve on an Advisory Committee on the Status of Women,[13] on the ground that it was law-related, but have been precluded from serving on a Mayor's Ethics Committee[14] and an Airport Authority Board[15] because they were not considered to be law-related. These decisions show that the broad prescription in the Code of Judicial Conduct allowing judges to serve on law-related commissions is open to various interpretations that are not always consistent with one another.

As discussed previously, judges should avoid serving on commissions, even if they are law-related, that cast doubt upon their independence or ability to decide cases impartially. Following this principle, a Judicial Ethics Advisory Committee concluded that a judge should not serve on a Domestic Violence Commission because it could give rise to an appearance of favoritism and raise questions concerning the judge's ability to fairly preside over certain cases.[16]

Similar concerns have been evoked about judicial participation on the United States Sentencing Commission, which was created by Congress in 1984 as a permanent independent agency within the judicial branch of government charged with articulating sentencing guidelines for the federal courts. The commission has seven voting members who serve six-year terms, and no more than three of the members at any one time may be federal judges. Over the years, a number of federal judges have served on the commission, along with lawyers and administrators. The Sentencing Commission vividly illustrates the pros and cons of judicial service on government commissions. On one hand, given their training and experience, judges are uniquely qualified to sit on a body responsible for setting sentencing guidelines. On the other hand, service on the commission raises serious doubts about judicial independence and the ability of a judge to decide sentencing matters impartially.

One of the judges appointed to the Sentencing Commission was Stephen Breyer, who served on the commission from 1985 to 1989 while he was a judge on the US Court of Appeals for the First Circuit.

[13] Florida Judicial Ethics Advisory Committee Opinion 2004–05 (2004).

[14] Washington Ethics Advisory Committee Opinion 90–16 (1990).

[15] *In re Complaint against Kelly* 407 NW.2d 182 (Neb. 1987).

[16] Arizona Judicial Ethics Advisory Committee Opinion 97–6 (1997).

In 1994, Breyer was elevated to the US Supreme Court, which in subsequent years accepted a case challenging the constitutionality of the Federal Sentencing Guidelines that had been written by the Sentencing Commission.[17] It was suggested that because of his prior work on the commission, Justice Breyer could not be impartial in the case and therefore should recuse himself from hearing it.[18] Nonetheless, after being advised by an outside source that his former service on the Sentencing Commission did not disqualify him from sitting on the case, Justice Breyer declined to recuse himself.[19] Eventually, the Supreme Court ruled in the case that the Constitution did not permit the guidelines to be enacted as mandatory, but they could be enacted as advisory.[20] While dissenting from the former part of the court's ruling that it was unconstitutional to enact mandatory sentencing guidelines, Justice Breyer cast the decisive vote and wrote the majority opinion in the latter part of the court's 5–4 ruling that the Constitution permitted the guidelines to be enacted on an advisory basis.[21]

This case as well as others demonstrates that judicial service on government commissions remains problematic. While there are strong reasons to allow judges to serve on government commissions, particularly those that concern the law and the administration of justice, judicial service on commissions has the potential to compromise judicial independence and impartiality.

Appearance at public hearings

Because of their learning and experience, judges may have unique insights to offer the other branches of government, especially concerning matters that have to do with the law. Accordingly, the Code of Judicial Conduct allows judges to appear and testify before government bodies or to otherwise consult with government bodies or officials in connection with matters concerning the law, the legal system, or the administration of justice.[22] This sort of testimony can improve the relations between the branches of government, as well as lead to improvements in the law, the

[17] *United States* v. *Booker* 543 US 220 (2005); see also *Blakely* v. *Washington* 542 US 296 (2004).

[18] See M. Freedman, "Judicial Impartiality in the Supreme Court – The Troubling Case of Justice Stephen Breyer" (2005) 30 *Oklahoma City University Law Review* 513 at 529–32.

[19] Freedman, "Judicial Impartiality in the Supreme Court," p. 531.

[20] *United States* v. *Booker* 543 US 220 (2005).

[21] *United States* v. *Booker* 543 US 220 (2005) at 244.

[22] Code of Judicial Conduct, Rule 3.2(C) (2007).

legal system, and the administration of justice. Hence, it is quite common for judges to testify at public hearings conducted by the other branches of government, especially about matters concerning the courts. In testifying before government bodies, however, judges should be careful not to misuse the prestige of office. Because they enjoy considerable influence in society, judges should be cautious when testifying at public hearings about matters beyond their scope of expertise.

By allowing judges to testify before government bodies on any matters concerning the law, the legal system, or the administration of justice, the Code offers judges a good deal of latitude to testify about a wide variety of subjects. As noted previously, there are few governmental bodies whose work bears no meaningful relationship to the "law," the "legal system," or the "administration of justice" broadly defined. Certainly, those terms seem expansive enough to encompass a wide array of topics about which judges may be asked to testify. Therefore, there has been some concern expressed that the Code allows judges too much latitude to testify about such a broad range of subjects. Chief Justice William Rehnquist of the US Supreme Court has suggested that judges should voluntarily limit the occasions on which they testify before public bodies.[23] While noting that individual judges were not prohibited from publicly stating their opinions on matters of policy, he maintained that judges should exercise caution in testifying, because their position as judges may give undue influence to their testimony.[24] The Judicial Ethics Advisory Committee of the State of Washington has taken the position that the scope of permissible judicial testimony before government bodies should be limited to matters that pertain to the judiciary,[25] but no other committee or commission has taken such a restrictive position.

The Code of Judicial Conduct also allows a judge to testify at public hearings or to otherwise consult with government bodies or officials when the judge is acting *pro se* in a matter involving the judge's legal or economic interests, or when the judge is acting in a fiduciary capacity.[26] This provision was added to the Code because it was thought to be unfair to prohibit a judge from appearing before government bodies or consulting with government officials on matters likely to affect the judge as a

[23] Alfini, *et al.*, *Judicial Conduct and Ethics*, s. 9.03A.
[24] Alfini, *et al.*, *Judicial Conduct and Ethics*, s. 9.03A.
[25] See Washington Ethics Advisory Committee Opinion 00–16 (2000).
[26] Code of Judicial Conduct, Rule 3.2(C) (2007).

private citizen.[27] For instance, a judge should be able to appear before a government body or consult with government officials about zoning proposals that might affect the judge's property. In testifying or consulting on a *pro se* basis, however, judges must not refer to their judicial positions and must otherwise exercise caution to avoid using the prestige of office in an improper way.[28]

Teaching and writing

It is a time-honored tradition in the United States that judges engage in teaching and other scholarly activities. From the earliest days of the nation, many judges, including Supreme Court justices, have engaged in teaching, lecturing, and writing, especially about the law. It is widely recognized that these extra-judicial scholarly activities are beneficial to society and help to advance the law and the legal system. The Code of Judicial Conduct acknowledges that judges are uniquely qualified to engage in extra-judicial activities concerning the law, the legal system, and the administration of justice through activities such as speaking, writing, teaching, or participating in scholarly research.[29] The Code also expressly states that a judge may accept compensation in the form of honoraria, stipends, or wages for teaching or lecturing, as long as the compensation is reasonable and commensurate with the task performed.[30]

The ability of judges to teach, lecture, or write about the law or other subjects is protected by the First Amendment of the US Constitution, which guarantees freedom of speech. It is well recognized in the United States that the protection of the First Amendment extends to the speaking and writing activities of judges. In *Republican Party of Minnesota* v. *White*,[31] the nation's highest court ruled that a provision prohibiting candidates for judicial office from announcing their views on disputed or political issues was an unconstitutional violation of the First Amendment guarantee of freedom of speech. Nonetheless, the First Amendment does not afford absolute protection for freedom of speech; speech activities may be restricted if there is a compelling reason to do so.

27 Code of Judicial Conduct, Rule 3.2, Comment [3] (2007).
28 Code of Judicial Conduct, Rule 3.2, Comment [3] (2007).
29 Code of Judicial Conduct, Rule 3, Comment [1] (2007).
30 Code of Judicial Conduct, Rule 3.12, Comment [1] (2007).
31 *Republican Party of Minnesota* v. *White* 536 US 765 (2002).

In some circumstances, there may be more reason to restrict the speech of judges than the speech of ordinary citizens in order to uphold the integrity and impartiality of the judiciary.

Extra-judicial teaching or lecturing rarely, if ever, is improper for a judge, although there are some restrictions upon these activities. As a general matter, a judge should always be mindful that the duties of judicial office take precedence over all extra-judicial activities, including teaching or lecturing.[32] Therefore, a judge should be careful that extra-judicial teaching or lecturing does not interfere with the diligent performance of his or her judicial duties. While teaching or lecturing, a judge should avoid making any comment about a case pending or impending before the judge, as to do so might cast doubt on the judge's ability to decide the case impartially.[33] Moreover, the Code of Judicial Conduct states that a judge should not make any public statement that might reasonably be expected to affect the outcome or impair the fairness of a case pending or impending in *any* court.[34]

Like teaching and lecturing about the law, writing about the law is widely regarded in the United States as a desirable extra-judicial activity that offers considerable benefit to the public. On occasion, however, questions have been raised about certain extra-judicial writing. For example, in one case, *In re Gridley*,[35] a complaint charging judicial misconduct was filed against a trial judge for publishing two letters in a local newspaper and an article in a church newsletter, all of which were highly critical of capital punishment. The complaint asserted that the judge's writing cast doubt on his ability to impartially decide cases involving capital crimes. While remarking that the judge's writing came "close to the dividing line" the state Supreme Court ruled that it did not amount to improper conduct, particularly because the judge had included in his criticism a qualification stating that as a judge he recognized that it was his duty to apply the law of capital punishment despite his personal opposition to it. In reaching this result, the state Supreme Court explained that "There is no doubt that a judge in an appropriate forum may express his protest, dissent, and criticism of the present state of the law . . . as long as he expresses himself in a manner that promotes public confidence in his integrity and impartiality as a judge."[36]

[32] Code of Judicial Conduct, Rule 2.1 (2007).
[33] Code of Judicial Conduct, Rule 2.9 (A) (2007).
[34] Code of Judicial Conduct, Rule 2.10 (2007) (emphasis added).
[35] *In re Gridley* 417 So.2d 950 (Fla. 1982).
[36] *In re Gridley* 417 So.2d 950 (Fla. 1982) at 954.

The *Gridley* case suggests a dilemma concerning the regulation of extra-judicial speech of judges. On one hand, Judge Gridley's letters and article may well have cast doubt on his ability to impartially decide cases involving the death penalty. Had Judge Gridley failed to include a disclaimer in his writings professing his duty to follow the law, there would be even more doubt about his impartiality in death penalty cases. On the other hand, to punish Judge Gridley for his extra-judicial writings comes perilously close to threatening the independence of the judiciary, in that it penalizes a judge for expressing his beliefs concerning the law. Moreover, it severely restricts a judge's freedom of speech, and thereby deprives the public of an invaluable source of expert information and opinion about issues of legal, social, and political importance.

There is a temptation here to say that judges should possess the same right to freedom of speech that other citizens in the United States enjoy, but upon reflection it must be admitted that under the present state of the law this simply is not so. Judges, for instance, may not publicly endorse a candidate for political office, even though other citizens clearly have a right to do so under the First Amendment of the Constitution, which guarantees freedom of speech.[37] However, in order to ensure the independence and impartiality of judges, and to preclude the exercise of undue influence that judges might possess, the Code of Judicial Conduct prohibits judges from publicly endorsing candidates for judicial office.[38] This illustrates that, due to the special position that judges hold in society, there are, in some circumstances, compelling reasons to limit the free speech of judges when it would not be permissible to limit the same sort of speech by an ordinary citizen. Nevertheless, restrictions upon a judge's freedom of speech should not be pushed too far. There is little value in prohibiting judges from speaking when they cannot – and should not – be prohibited from thinking. And there is much to be lost if judges are precluded from participating in matters of public concern.

At times, questions arise concerning extra-judicial speech that is offensive or that manifests prejudice. In *Mississippi Commission on Judicial Performance* v. *Wilkerson*,[39] a judge wrote a letter to the local newspaper, criticizing legislation in other states that granted gay partners the right to sue as spouses. His letter further stated that "in my opinion, gays and lesbians should be put in some type of mental institute

[37] United States Constitution, Amendment I (1791).

[38] Code of Judicial Conduct, Rule 4.1(3) (2007).

[39] *Mississippi Commission on Judicial Performance* v. *Wilkerson* 876 So.2d 1006 (Miss. 2004).

[sic] instead of having a law like this passed for them."[40] At first, the Commission on Judicial Performance, which hears complaints against judges, found that the judge's conduct violated a provision in the Code of Judicial Conduct requiring judges to act at all times in a manner that promotes public confidence in the integrity and impartiality of the judiciary. On appeal, however, the Mississippi Supreme Court rejected the commission's finding, and ruled instead that the judge's speech was protected by the First Amendment. As the court saw it, there was no compelling reason to require judges to conceal their prejudice in order to merely *appear* impartial. On the contrary, dissuading judges from speaking their minds actually undermined the goal of having a court that was truly impartial, because unsuspecting litigants would be unaware of a judge's prejudice and not know they could seek recusal of the judge.

Although the views expressed by the judge in the *Wilkerson* case would be considered by many to be biased and intolerant, there is little to be gained by restricting the judge's right to express his views. As the court explained, it is better to allow the judge to freely reveal his views and thereby expose his prejudice, so that a motion can be made calling for his recusal in cases where he cannot remain impartial. Moreover, judges have a great deal to contribute to society through writing and speaking, and if genuine freedom of speech is to exist, society cannot pick and choose which views will be allowed in the marketplace of ideas. In the long run, there is much more to be gained than lost by granting judges freedom of speech.

The right to freedom of speech for judges was upheld in a case from the State of Washington, *Matter of Staples*,[41] in which a judge was charged with misconduct for circulating petitions, making speeches, organizing a committee, and running advertisements, all on behalf of a campaign to move a county seat. When the case reached the Washington Supreme Court, it ruled that the judge's activities concerned the administration of justice, and therefore were permissible under the Code of Judicial Conduct. The court further noted that the history of the judiciary is replete with instances of judges who have supported a variety of measures regarding the law, and that the restrictions in the Code concerning extra-judicial activities should be construed narrowly in order to avoid a chilling effect on the ability of the very persons who have the best knowledge of the legal system and how it may be improved.

[40] *Mississippi Commission on Judicial Performance* v. *Wilkerson* 876 So.2d 1006 (Miss. 2004) at 1020.

[41] *Matter of Staples* 719 P 2d 558 (Wash. 1986).

It is well recognized in the United States that judges have much to contribute to society through their extra-judicial writing and teaching activities. Writing and teaching by judges is encouraged by the Code of Judicial Conduct and encompassed within the protection of the First Amendment of the US Constitution.

Associational activities

The Code of Judicial Conduct expressly allows judges to participate in the activities of organizations concerned with the law, the legal system, or the administration of justice.[42] The Code further allows judges to participate in activities sponsored by educational, religious, charitable, fraternal, or civic organizations, as long as they are not conducted for profit.[43] Throughout the years, many judges in the United States have belonged to bar associations and actively participated in bar association projects. Traditionally, participation by judges in bar association activities has been regarded as a particularly appropriate and beneficial activity for judges that is directed toward improving the law, the legal system, and the administration of justice. Nonetheless, there are some restrictions upon judicial participation in bar association activities. In participating in bar association activities, judges should be careful to uphold and promote the independence, integrity, and impartiality of the judiciary, and to avoid impropriety or the appearance of impropriety.[44]

A judge should be especially cautious about participating in bar association activities that amount to advocacy concerning legal issues that may come before the judge. If a judge becomes involved with a specialized bar association that advocates for a particular issue or a certain class of litigants, the judge's involvement may give rise to an appearance of favoritism. According to an advisory opinion issued by a judicial ethics board, judges may participate in the American Board of Trial Advocates, because its membership includes a relatively equal number of plaintiffs' and defendants' lawyers.[45] Similarly, another advisory opinion takes the position that judges may belong to the American Academy of Matrimonial Lawyers, because its membership includes both plaintiffs' and defendants' attorneys.[46] In contrast, it may be

[42] Code of Judicial Conduct, Rule 3.7(A) (2007).
[43] Code of Judicial Conduct, Rule 3.7(A) (2007).
[44] Code of Judicial Conduct, Canon One (2007).
[45] Florida Advisory Opinion 95-46 (1995).
[46] West Virginia Advisory Opinion (March 4, 1997).

improper for a judge to belong to an organization whose membership includes only plaintiffs' attorneys or only defendants' attorneys.

American judges also have been advised not to join or participate in the activities of certain civic organizations if doing so might cast doubt on a judge's ability to decide cases impartially. In fact, it has been said that judges should avoid membership even in the most laudable and noncontroversial organizations if the organizations advocate a particular point of view that could raise doubts about a judge's impartiality in cases over which he or she presides. For instance, one judicial ethics board advised a judge against joining a group that counseled victims of domestic violence, because it could cast doubt on the judge's impartiality in cases involving domestic violence.[47] Another judicial ethics board advised a judge against participating in activities sponsored by an organization dedicated to eliminating drunk driving because such participation might raise doubts about the judge's impartiality while presiding over prosecutions of persons who are charged with driving while intoxicated. Along similar lines, another judicial ethics opinion advised a judge not to accept an award from a non-profit organization whose employees regularly testified in proceedings before the judge.[48]

There also are restrictions upon judges' associational activities that apply to membership in social organizations. The Code of Judicial Conduct prohibits a judge from holding membership in any organization that practices invidious discrimination on the basis of race, sex, gender, religion, national origin, ethnicity, or sexual orientation.[49] Commentary to the Code explains that the reason for this prohibition is that a judge's public manifestation of approval of invidious discrimination on any basis gives rise to an appearance of impropriety and diminishes public confidence in the integrity and impartiality of the judiciary.[50] As a result, a judge's membership in an organization that practices invidious discrimination creates the perception that the judge's impartiality is impaired.[51] Commentary to the Code further notes that whether an organization practices invidious discrimination is a complex question that cannot be answered merely from an examination of an organization's membership rolls.[52] Judges are not prohibited from

[47] Florida Judicial Ethics Advisory Committee Opinion 98-8 (1998).
[48] Illinois Judicial Ethics Committee Opinion 01-03 (2001).
[49] Code of Judicial Conduct, Rule 3.6(A) (2007).
[50] Code of Judicial Conduct, Rule 3.6, Comment [1] (2007).
[51] Code of Judicial Conduct, Rule 3.6, Comment [1] (2007).
[52] Code of Judicial Conduct, Rule 3.6, Comment [2] (2007).

belonging to organizations dedicated to the preservation of religious, ethnic, or cultural values of legitimate concern to its members.[53] But where a judge learns that an organization to which he or she belongs engages in invidious discrimination, the judge must immediately resign from that organization.[54]

Certain social contacts may raise problems for judges. In one case, a judge was found to have acted improperly by being a frequent luncheon guest at public restaurants of lawyers and representatives of an insurance company that had matters pending in the judge's court.[55] In the opinion of the court that reviewed the matter, the judge's behavior was inherently wrong, giving rise to an obvious appearance of impropriety, as well as having a subtle corruptive effect, no matter how much the judge may have felt that he was above improper influence.

Judges also may run into trouble for associating with known criminals. In most cases, where judges have been subject to discipline for associating with criminals, they also have engaged in other questionable conduct, such as planning and attending a party when there was gambling, pornography, or prostitution.[56] In one case, however, a judge was disciplined for nothing more than associating with a known felon.[57] In that case, *In re Blackman*,[58] it was found that the judge acted improperly by attending an annual Labor Day picnic that was hosted by a former government official, a long-time friend of the judge, who had been convicted of racketeering charges. The picnic was widely-publicized in the media, which described it as a going-away party for a convicted felon. Upon reviewing the judge's behavior, the state Supreme Court ruled that his attendance at the party could be seen as an expression of sympathy or support for a convicted felon or, at worst, could raise questions about the judge's allegiance to the judicial system. The court concluded that the judge's behavior violated a provision of the Code of Judicial Conduct requiring judges to avoid impropriety and the appearance of impropriety in all their activities.

The court's decision in this case is debatable. In attending the picnic, the judge merely intended to express sympathy for his friend, which hardly seems to be improper. There was no indication from the evidence

[53] Code of Judicial Conduct, Rule 3.6, Comment [2] (2007).
[54] Code of Judicial Conduct, Rule 3.6, Comment [3] (2007).
[55] *In re D'Auria* 334 A.2d 332 (NJ 1975).
[56] See, e.g., *In re Haggerty* 241 So.2d 469 (La. 1970).
[57] *In re Blackman* 591 A.2d 1339 (NJ 1991).
[58] *In re Blackman* 591 A.2d 1339 (NJ 1991).

in the case that the judge intended to condone his friend's criminal behavior or in any way to express disapproval of the judicial system. While the media may have seen fit to ascribe negative meaning to the judge's attendance at the picnic, it seems overly harsh to hold the judge responsible for the media's rendition of his behavior. Nevertheless, the court took the position that the judge should have expected that his attendance at the picnic might be open to criticism by the press and members of the public. The court explained that judges have responsibilities in regard to their personal activities that greatly exceed those of ordinary citizens. Judges, the court said, have a special responsibility because they are the subject of constant public scrutiny and therefore must avoid even the appearance of impropriety so that public confidence in the judiciary is not eroded. Perhaps in recognition that the judge's attendance at the picnic was a lapse of judgment rather than intentional misconduct, the court did no more than reprimand him for misbehavior.

Charitable activities

The Code of Judicial Conduct allows judges in the United States to participate in certain activities sponsored by or on behalf of educational, religious, charitable, fraternal, or civic organizations not conducted for profit.[59] Of course, a judge must limit his or her activities on behalf of charitable or other organizations so that they do not interfere with the performance of judicial duties or cast doubt on the judge's ability to decide cases impartially. In addition, the Code contains several important qualifications upon judicial participation in charitable activities that are examined in the following discussion.

Under the Code, a judge may assist a charitable organization in planning that is related to fund-raising and may participate in the management and investment of a charitable organization's funds, but may not solicit contributions for a charitable organization, except from family members or from other judges over whom the judge does not exercise supervisory or appellate authority.[60] Judicial solicitation of funds (except from family members and other judges) for charitable organizations, although obviously commendable, is nonetheless prohibited in order to prevent misuse of the judicial office. The concern here is that judges should not use the prestige of the judicial office to

[59] Code of Judicial Conduct, Rule 3.7(A) (2007).
[60] Code of Judicial Conduct, Rule 3.7(A)(1), (2).

coerce individuals to make charitable contributions that they would not otherwise make. Another concern is that donors may expect favorable rulings from a judge in return for making donations in response to the judge's solicitation. While actual corruption of a judge through charitable solicitation may be unlikely, it has occurred on at least one occasion;[61] although, certainly, the more common risk is that individuals being solicited by a judge may feel obligated to make contributions or may expect favorable treatment from the judge in return.

In the past, the proscription against solicitation was strictly followed, in some instances even in regard to conduct that did not constitute direct solicitation. In one case, a judge was advised by an ethics committee that he should not appear as Father Christmas at a fund-raising event.[62] In another case, a judge was advised by an ethics committee that he should not participate in a taped interview to be aired on a telethon on behalf of a local boys' club.[63] These examples, and others like them, involved judicial conduct that did not in any way seem coercive or otherwise harmful. Nonetheless, judicial ethics advisory committees tended to give a broad application to the proscription against solicitation that precluded conduct even though it did not amount to direct solicitation and was non-coercive. In recent years, however, a more permissive attitude has been adopted toward charitable activities that do not constitute direct solicitation. Now, a distinction is drawn between actual solicitation of funds, which, of course, is still prohibited, and more general fund-raising activities, which are allowed.[64] New commentary in the latest version of the Code of Judicial Conduct expressly states that judges are permitted to attend fund-raising events sponsored by charitable organizations, and also may perform functions such as ushering or serving food at charitable fund-raising events.[65] According to the commentary, these activities are not considered solicitation and do not amount to coercion or abuse of the prestige of the judicial office.[66] However, the Code states that a judge may not be a speaker or guest of honor at the fund-raising event of a charitable organization unless the organization is law-related.[67]

61 See *In re Murphy* 726 SW.2d 509 (Tenn. 1987).
62 South Dakota Advisory Opinion, 91–4 (1991).
63 Federal Advisory Committee on Judicial Activities, Advisory Opinion No. 32 (March 4, 1974).
64 Alfini, *et al.*, *Judicial Conduct and Ethics*, s. 9.04A.
65 Code of Judicial Conduct, Rule 3.7, Comment [3] (2007).
66 Code of Judicial Conduct, Rule 3.7, Comment [3] (2007).
67 Code of Judicial Conduct, Rule 3.7(A)(4) (2007).

The Code of Judicial Conduct also states that a judge may serve as an officer, director, trustee, or nonlegal advisor of a charitable organization unless it is likely that the organization will be engaged in proceedings that ordinarily come before the judge or is engaged in frequent adversary proceedings in the court of which the judge is a member or is subject to the appellate jurisdiction of a court of which the judge is a member.[68] If a judge is an officer, director, trustee, or nonlegal advisor of a charitable organization, he or she may be identified as such on the organization's letterhead, even if it is used for fund-raising purposes.[69] The letterhead may list the judge's title or judicial office, as long as comparable designations are used for other persons.[70]

Conclusion

In the United States, extra-judicial conduct is mediated through conflicting policy considerations. On the one hand, given their learning and experience, judges bring a unique expertise to their off-the-bench activities that can be of great value. In turn, judges may have much to learn from participating in extra-judicial activities that will improve their ability as judges. Involvement in the outside world can enrich the judicial temperament and enhance a judge's ability to perform the duties of office. On the other hand, extra-judicial activities can take time and attention away from judicial duties and thereby interfere with the proper performance of judicial functions. Extra-judicial activities cast doubt on judicial impartiality or give rise to impropriety or the appearance of impropriety. There are good reasons, then, both to encourage and discourage extra-judicial activities. The Code of Judicial Conduct, adopted throughout the United States, attempts to accommodate these conflicting considerations by allowing some extra-judicial activities while prohibiting others. The line between permissible and impermissible extra-judicial activity is not an easy one to walk, and is redrawn from time to time.

Over the years, judicial service on government boards or commissions has been especially controversial. In recent times, there has been an attempt in the Code of Judicial Conduct to resolve this controversy by prohibiting judges from accepting an appointment to a governmental

[68] Code of Judicial Conduct, Rule 3.7(A)(6) (2007).
[69] Code of Judicial Conduct, Rule 3.7, Comment [4] (2007).
[70] Code of Judicial Conduct, Rule 3.7, Comment [4] (2007).

committee, board, or commission, unless it is one that concerns the law, the legal system, or the administration of justice. Still, that resolution has not proven to be entirely satisfactory, and some judicial appointments to boards or commissions in recent times have been subject to criticism. The Code draws the same line in regard to judges appearing and testifying before government bodies, which has engendered less controversy, although here, too, there are critics who suggest that judges should limit their appearances before public bodies.

Much less controversy exists concerning teaching, lecturing, and writing by judges. These extra-judicial activities have always been accepted in the United States as beneficial to society and the advancement of the law, not to mention as a valuable aspect of freedom of speech. On occasion, a particular article or other writing by a judge is questioned, but these occasions are rare, and extra-judicial teaching, lecturing, and writing remain highly regarded pursuits.

The Code of Judicial Conduct permits judges to participate in the activities of organizations concerned with the law, the legal system, or the administration of justice, and also permits judges to participate in activities sponsored by educational, religious, charitable, fraternal, or civic organizations, as long as they are not conducted for profit. Judges are encouraged to participate in bar association activities, although participation in specialized bar associations should be avoided where it may cast doubt on a judge's impartiality. The Code strictly prohibits judges from holding membership in any organization that practices invidious discrimination on the basis of race, sex, gender, religion, national origin, ethnicity, or sexual orientation. Although there are a number of extra-judicial activities that judges may perform for charitable organizations, judges may not directly solicit money for charities. Judges, though, are permitted to attend fund-raising events for charities and even may help out at these events, as long as they do not directly solicit money.

In sum, American judges are permitted a wide range of extra-judicial activities that concern the law, the legal system, or the administration of justice, as long as they do not demean the judicial office or interfere with judicial functions. Judges are more limited in their extra-judicial activities that are not related to the law, but here, too, there are permissible extra-judicial activities in which judges may participate. Judges have much to contribute to society through their extra-judicial activities, but they also have a special responsibility to uphold the integrity, independence, and impartiality of the judiciary.

PART VI

26

The judiciary: a comparative conspectus

H. P. LEE

Judges in Australia, Canada, New Zealand, South Africa, the United Kingdom and the United States find themselves functioning in an era where it is fashionable to invoke the catch-cry of 'accountability'. Such invocations by critics, politicians and commentators in relation to the judicial arm of government are sometimes made without a proper evaluation of the important contributions an independent and impartial judiciary makes to the maintenance of the rule of law. These six countries operate under a diverse spectrum of constitutional frameworks. South Africa is a unitary state, with a reasonable degree of provincial allocation of power, while the United States is a federal republic. Australia, Canada, New Zealand and the United Kingdom operate under a parliamentary monarchical framework, except that both New Zealand and the United Kingdom are non-federal polities. Despite the diversity in the constitutional frameworks, a common thread runs through these six countries: a shared belief in the fundamental importance of having a judiciary which is both independent and impartial.

In all these countries the judiciary has, from time to time, been affected by controversies which have either engulfed individual judges or the judicial institution as a whole. Judges in contemporary times are experiencing a diminution of the traditional deference accorded to judicial officers and the judiciary as a whole.[1] On many occasions the media has taken an aggressive approach in its reporting of court matters. It is now commonplace for the media, politicians and commentators to attack judges when they disagree with the results of judicial decisions, such as sentences handed down by the courts, particularly in highly

[1] See M. Kirby, *Through the World's Eye* (Sydney: Federation Press, 2000), ch. 13 ('Attacks on Judges: A Universal Phenomenon'). The chapter was based on an earlier version of a paper published in (1998) 72 *Australian Law Journal* 599.

publicised trials, or with decisions which lead to the invalidation of significant legislation. It is quite clear that a traditionally complacent and deferential approach towards the judiciary is giving way to more critical and vocal demands for greater judicial accountability. On the other hand, thoughtful concerns have been raised about the fundamental importance of protecting the independence of the judicial institution and judicial officers.

The contemporary role of the judiciary

The functions of the judiciary are diverse in nature. In countries with a written constitution the notion of the supremacy of parliament inevitably yields to the notion of the supremacy of the constitution, particularly those constitutions operating a federal system of government. The legislative division of law-making powers requires an impartial arbiter to determine disputes over the allocation of powers set out in the constitutional document. The exercise of the power of judicial review over the constitutionality of legislation inevitably thrusts the courts into the spotlight. In South Africa, as Iain Currie points out, this has led to 'a thoroughgoing transformation of the legal parameters of judicial free speech'.[2]

In countries with a constitutionally entrenched bill of rights, the role of the judiciary becomes more pronounced. The courts are entrusted with the role of 'constitutional watch-dog'. They then stand between citizens and the state. The might of the apparatus of a government is kept in check by the courts, and occasions will arise when an impatient government becomes irate with the tempering effect of judicial decisions. The United States, Canada and South Africa have a constitutionally entrenched bill of rights, while New Zealand and the United Kingdom have a statutory bill of rights. Australia stands out with its lack of a federal bill of rights. The fascination of the framers of the Australian Constitution with the US Constitution did not, however, impel them to emulate the United States and embody in the Constitution a bill of rights. Sir Owen Dixon observed:

> The framers of the Australian constitution were not prepared to place fetters upon legislative action, except in as far as it might be necessary for the purpose of distributing between the States and the central government the full content of legislative power. The history of their country had not taught them the need of provisions directed to the control of the legislature itself.[3]

[2] Chapter 11, above.

[3] O. Dixon, 'Two Constitutions Compared', reprinted in *Jesting Pilate* (Sydney: Law Books, 1965), p. 102.

Currently, the political will is lacking to enact a statutory federal bill of rights in Australia, let alone the idea of a constitutionally entrenched bill of rights. Nevertheless, since 1992, the affirmation by the apex court in Australia, the High Court of Australia, of an entrenched concept of representative government has created opportunities for adventurous judges to expand the boundaries of 'implied rights'. Brennan J in the High Court decision of *Nationwide News Pty Ltd* v. *Wills*[4] said:

> Where a representative democracy is constitutionally entrenched, it carries with it those legal incidents which are essential to the effective maintenance of that form of government. Once it is recognised that a representative democracy is constitutionally prescribed, the freedom of discussion which is essential to sustain it is as firmly entrenched in the Constitution as the system of government which the Constitution expressly ordains.[5]

When the courts are called upon to interpret provisions of a bill of rights, or to make a declaration of incompatibility under the UK Human Rights Act 1998, or to consider the application of an implied freedom of 'political communication' in Australia, they face the risk of being drawn into a vortex of political controversy.

There are other areas of judicial activities which commonly attract media interest and attention as judges and courts all over the land carry out a myriad of functions.

The importance of judicial independence

It is necessary for those who shape public opinion to consider why judicial independence is fundamental to a democratic polity. Bradley and Ewing succinctly encapsulate the importance of judicial independence in the following statement: 'If government is to be conducted in accordance with the law, the law must be administered by as independent a judiciary as possible, otherwise there is a danger that the law will serve the ends of government rather than the interests of justice: the two may not always be synonymous.'[6] The clear trend which has emerged is a more pronounced and vigorous evaluation of the functioning of the courts, particularly in the arena of human rights protection. The emergence of that trend has led to expressions of concern over the state of

[4] (1992) 177 CLR 1. [5] (1992) 177 CLR 1 at 48–9.

[6] A. W. Bradley and K. D. Ewing, *Constitutional and Administrative Law*, 14th edn. (Harlow: Pearson Longman, 2007), p. 381.

independence of the judicial institution. In evaluating the importance of judicial independence, there is a need to reconcile the requirement for judicial 'accountability' and the notion of 'judicial independence'.[7] That reconciliation features either explicitly or implicitly in the various authors' excursus on the four major themes of this book.

The appointment, discipline and removal of judges

Subtle and not so subtle pressures bear upon courts which have to perform their judicial role against the backdrop of a constitutionally entrenched or a statutory bill of rights. Judges increasingly find themselves having to make hard choices, given that most fundamental rights are not absolute. Derogations from fundamental rights which are in accord with the maintenance of a free and democratic society repose in judges the task of applying doctrines, such as the 'proportionality' principle and the 'margin of difference' notion. That application can be contentious as that task involves a degree of subjective judgement. Judges are not necessarily on the same wave-length at times, with critics attacking them as 'activist' or 'conservative' judges. Consequently, this has led to calls for changes to the process of appointing judges, especially to the superior courts. Changes to the process of appointing judges have occurred in a number of countries.

Valuable lessons can be learned from a consideration of the reforms which have been effected to the judicial institution in these countries. The Constitutional Reform Act 2005 has made sweeping judicial reforms in the United Kingdom.[8] Key features of those reforms include the establishment of a Judicial Appointments Commission and the appointment of a Judicial Appointments and Conduct Ombudsman.[9] Innovations to the process of appointing judges are also found in Canada, New Zealand, South Africa and the United States. These countries are obvious comparators for lessons to be learned by Australia because of their shared subscription to the rule of law. At the same time, understanding the differences in the political and historical

[7] An exegesis on the constitutional dimensions of judicial independence and its reconciliation with judicial accountability is provided by S. Shetreet, Chapter 1, above.

[8] See Chapter 6 by K. Malleson, above.

[9] In March 2008, the British Government published its plans for constitutional renewal which included proposals to reform the government's role in the judicial appointments process to 'ensure greater transparency and to underline the independence of the judiciary'.

background of some of these countries may dictate the adoption of a different approach in the appointment of judges. Another important issue relates to the appointment of acting judges with concerns that such appointments could impair the independence of the judiciary.

In Australia, there have been calls for the establishment of a special mechanism to deal with complaints against judges. Only one Australian state, New South Wales, to date has a formal body, the New South Wales Judicial Commission, which is entrusted with the responsibility of investigating complaints against judges. The ultimate sanction of removal of a judge is an issue which also generates concern as to the balance between an appropriate mechanism and judicial independence.

Judges and free speech

Judges in all jurisdictions and at all levels have been criticised for, among other things, voicing their concern over problems in the administration of justice, comments made in the course of judging and extra-judicial addresses. They have also been criticised for 'unpopular' decisions and 'light' sentences imposed in the criminal process. Epithets collated by Justice Michael Kirby in relation to the justices of the High Court of Australia following controversial decisions regarding native titles to land include: 'bogus', 'pusillanimous and evasive', a 'pathetic ... self-appointed [group of] Kings and Queens', a body 'packed with feral judges' and 'a professional labour cartel'.[10] Australia is not alone in witnessing such comments.

Determining the parameters of speech about judges and speech by judges is a vexing issue in all jurisdictions. The criticism of judges and courts puts into the spotlight competing public values. A critic of a court might highlight the importance of freedom of speech. The critic might also stress the importance of the judiciary, as a public institution and an arm of government, being held accountable for its actions. Forthright and open criticism may contribute to greater accountability and improvement in the performance of judicial functions. On the other hand, this has to be balanced against the fundamental importance of promoting and maintaining public confidence in the courts; a confidence which might be undermined by unfair or ill-motivated criticism. Courts in liberal democracies rely largely on public confidence to perform their functions and to ensure that their decisions are respected. The

[10] Kirby, *Through the World's Eye*.

acknowledgement by courts of the separation of powers traditionally entails an obligation of judicial reticence which precludes judges from effectively responding to attacks levelled by their critics. However, a convention of judicial reticence is no longer strictly observed.

In the United States a former president of the American Bar Association said: 'the biggest challenge to the profession and the justice system is the continuing attack upon our federal judiciary'.[11] Charles Geyh states that criticism of judges is part of the American political tradition and that 'claims that judges are under attack now to a greater extent than in the past are unsupportable'.[12] In Australia, in 2002, the then federal Attorney-General ignored the established convention of defending the judiciary from unreasonable attack. John Williams observes that this has led to 'a greater self-reliance in terms of dealing with the public'.[13] Grant Hammond concludes in his chapter that personal attacks on judges 'can only realistically be repelled by institutional responses'.[14]

Keith Ewing points out that concerns about judicial independence cannot be one-dimensional. It is necessary for some limits on judicial speech-making to be established. In the Canadian jurisdiction, the famous episode of Justice Berger points to the danger of judges exceeding proper limits.[15] However, Kent Roach in his chapter observes that judges in Canada 'have since the Berger affair been more likely to be removed from the bench for controversial speech made on the bench than for extra-judicial speech'.[16]

Judges, the rule against bias and recusal

It is a fundamental feature of the judicial system that a judge is not only impartial but must be seen to be impartial. When claims of judicial bias are raised the issue of recusal arises. At the same time, it has been pointed out that decisions by judges to disqualify themselves should not be made lightly; otherwise it would lead to a situation where litigants may exploit this avenue in order to choose their own judges. Justice Grant Hammond

[11] N. Lee Cooper, 'On Independence Once and For All: Future of the Justice System Depends on Defense of Federal Judges' (1997) 83 *American Bar Association Journal* 8.

[12] Chapter 13, above. [13] See Chapter 8, above. [14] Chapter 10, above.

[15] See 'Report and Record of the Committee of Investigation into the Conduct of the Hon. Mr Justice Berger and Resolution of the Canadian Judicial Council' (1983) 28 *McGill Law Journal* 378.

[16] Chapter 9, above.

in a scholarly monograph observes that 'the number of high profile recusal cases seems to be on the rise', and adds: 'A number of these cases have, regrettably, tarnished the image of the judiciary.'[17] In the United States, there was much debate over the Scalia/Cheney 'duck-hunting trip'.[18] The controversy over Justice Brent Benjamin of the West Virginia Supreme Court and a US$3 million donation to his judicial election campaign led to a landmark decision by the US Supreme Court.[19] In the United Kingdom, the most obvious example is the disqualification of Lord Hoffmann flowing from his status as an unpaid director and chairman of Amnesty International Charity Ltd, a company controlled by Amnesty International and committed to its purposes.[20] The categories of 'conflict of interest' may vary in prominence in the various jurisdictions. There is a difference of opinion of whether there should be an automatic disqualification if a judge has a direct pecuniary or proprietary interest in the outcome of litigation, otherwise than as a party.[21] The 'purpose of recusal is to underpin [independence and impartiality]',[22] and therefore judges have to be conscious that recusal law is 'vulnerable to manipulation by litigants and their counsel'.[23]

Judges and non-judicial functions

Varying attitudes exist in relation to the propriety of judges agreeing to take on functions which are not essentially judicial in nature, especially the task of chairing a commission of inquiry or a royal commission. The consensus is that judges have the requisite skills which make them ideal to perform such a task. However, there is also a general perception that the acceptance and performance of such a role can pose a danger to the maintenance of public confidence in the judiciary. Instances in which judicial commissioners have been afflicted by controversies can be found in all jurisdictions. Sir Geoffrey Palmer highlights the 'standout' Erebus Royal Commission in which an adverse finding by the Privy Council that the commissioner had failed to comply with the rules of natural justice

[17] G. Hammond, *Judicial Recusal – Principles, Process and Problems* (Oxford: Hart, 2009), p. xi.

[18] See A. A. Olowofoyeku, 'Regulating Supreme Court Recusals' (2006) *Singapore Journal of Legal Studies* 60.

[19] See above, Chapter 19. [20] See *Pinochet* case [2000] 1 AC 119.

[21] See *Ebner* v. *Official Trustee in Bankruptcy* (2000) 205 CLR 337.

[22] S. Sedley, 'Foreword' to Hammond, *Judicial Recusal*, p. ix.

[23] Sedley, 'Foreword' to Hammond, *Judicial Recusal*, p. xi.

led to the commissioner resigning his commission as a judge.[24] Despite this and some other controversial instances, he is of the view that in the context of New Zealand's small society 'where the talent base tends to be thin the judge as policy-maker is a contribution that deserves to be valued'. This view is not shared by countries with a bigger society. The 'Warren Commission' in the United States, the Hutton inquiry in the United Kingdom and the 'Erasmus Commission' in South Africa reinforced the view articulated by Patrick Monahan and Byron Shaw, when evaluating the Canadian situation, that 'the benefits of extra-judicial service on public inquiries are outweighed by their costs'.[25] There is clear merit in the direction issued by Chief Justice Irvine of the Victorian Supreme Court that 'no judge of his court would be available to sit on non-judicial government bodies'.[26] There is hardly any objection to the use of retired judges to perform this role. The following classic pronouncement of the US Supreme Court in *Mistretta* v. *United States*[27] has attracted ringing endorsements by courts in other countries:

> The legitimacy of the Judicial Branch ultimately depends upon its reputation for impartiality and non-partisanship. That reputation may not be borrowed by the political branches to cloak their work in the neutral colours of judicial action.

The courts in Australia and South Africa[28] have invoked this passage and have applied an incompatibility test to determine the validity of the performance by judges of a non-judicial function.

Conclusion

The judiciary plays a pivotal role in promoting the rule of law in a liberal democracy. To carry out that role, it needs to command the confidence of the public. That confidence depends on public trust in the independence and impartiality of the judges and the courts in the administration of the justice system. If confidence in the courts is undermined, great damage might be done to a vital institution. The maintenance of judicial independence has to be reconciled with the growing clamour for 'transparency' and 'accountability'. This reconciliation underpins the four

[24] See above, Chapter 22. [25] See above, Chapter 21. [26] See above, Chapter 20.
[27] (1989) 488 US 361 at 407. [28] See above, Chapter 23.

main themes of this book. It is axiomatic that unprincipled intromission by the non-judicial branches of government into the judicial sphere will only serve to subvert the independence and standing of the courts. When public trust is undermined, disputants may transfer their conflicts from the courts to the streets, and that would spell the death knell of any democracy.

INDEX

For EU product safety concerns, contact us at Calle de José Abascal, 56–1°,
28003 Madrid, Spain or eugpsr@cambridge.org.

www.ingramcontent.com/pod-product-compliance
Lightning Source LLC
LaVergne TN
LVHW011533200926
848484LV00001B/256